The Gnostic Gospels

Adam, Eve, and the Serpent

The Origin of Satan

The Gnostic Gospels

Adam, Eve, and the Serpent

The Origin of Satan

ELAINE PAGELS

Quality Paperback Book Club
New York

The Gnostic Gospels

Grateful acknowledgment is made to the following for permission to reprint previously published material:

Division of Christian Education of the National Council of the Churches of Christ in the U.S.A.: Excerpts from the New Testament. The Scripture quotations in this publication are from the *Revised Standard Version of the Bible*, copyrighted 1946, 1952, © 1971, 1973 by the Division of Christian Education of the National Council of the Churches of Christ in the U.S.A., and used by permission.

Wm. B. Eerdman's Publishing Co.: Excerpts from Tertullian, Iranaeus and Hippolytus. Reprinted from *The Ante Nicene Fathers* by permission of the Wm. B. Eerdman's Publishing Co., Grand Rapids, Michigan.

Harper & Row, Publishers, Inc.: Excerpts from *The Nag Hammadi Library* by James M. Robinson. Copyright © 1977 by E. J. Brill, Leiden, The Netherlands. Reprinted by permission of E. J. Brill and Harper & Row, Publishers, Inc.

Harvard University Press: Excerpts from Clement and Ignatius, in *The Apostolic Fathers*, 1912, The Loeb Classical Library, translated by Kirsopp Lake. Reprinted by permission of Harvard University Press.

Lutterworth Press and The Westminster Press: Excerpts from *New Testament Apocrypha*, Volume I, edited by Wilhelm Schneemelcher and Edgar Hennecke. English translation edited by R. McL. Wilson. Published in the U.S.A. by The Westminster Press, 1963. Copyright © 1959 J. C. B. Mohr (Paul Siebeck), Tübingen. English translation © 1963 Lutterworth Press. Excerpts from *New Testament Apocrypha*, Volume II, edited by Wilhelm Schneemelcher and Edgar Hennecke. English translation edited by R. McL. Wilson. Published in the U.S.A. by The Westminster Press, 1966. Copyright © 1964 J. C. B. Mohr (Paul Siebeck), Tübingen. English translation © 1965 Lutterworth Press. Used by permission.

Oxford University Press: Excerpts from *The Acts of the Christian Martyrs*, translated by Herbert Musurillo. Copyright © Oxford University Press 1972. Reprinted by permission of Oxford University Press.

*To Elizabeth Diggs and Sharon Olds
in loving friendship*

ACKNOWLEDGMENTS

THE WRITING of this book began several years ago with research into the relation between politics and religion in the origins of Christianity. The first four chapters have been published in more technical form in scholarly journals (specific references precede the footnotes of each chapter).

In preparing this volume I have generally chosen to follow the translations offered in *The Nag Hammadi Library*, edited by James M. Robinson, since these are readily available to all readers. In certain cases, however, I have changed the translation for the sake of clarity, consistency or interpretation (for example, I have translated the Coptic transliteration of the Greek term τελείωσις not as "perfection," but as "fulfillment," which seems to me more accurate; in other cases, where the Coptic term πρωμε apparently translates the Greek ἄνθρωπος, I have translated it not as "man" but as "humanity"). In the case of two texts, I have used different translations (see below).

I am especially grateful to those colleagues and friends who have read and criticized the entire manuscript: Peter Berger, John Gager, Dennis Groh, Howard Kee, George MacRae, Wayne Meeks and Morton Smith. For other advice and criticism, specifically of aspects of the introduction, I owe grateful thanks to Marilyn Harran, Marvin Meyer, Birger Pearson, Gilles

Acknowledgments

Quispel, Richard Ogust and James M. Robinson. I am grateful, too, to Bentley Layton for permission to use his translation of the *Treatise on Resurrection*, and to James Brashler for permission to use his translation of the *Apocalypse of Peter*.

Special thanks are due the Rockefeller Foundation, the Lita A. Hazen Foundation and the Guggenheim Foundation for their support, which granted me the time to devote to writing; and to President Jacqueline Mattfeld and Vice President Charles Olton for approving a year's leave from my responsibilities at Barnard College. Especially I wish to thank Lydia Bronte and Lita A. Hazen for their encouragement throughout the whole project.

The present version of the book would have been impossible to produce without the superb editing of Jason Epstein, Vice President and Editorial Director of Random House; the excellent advice of John Brockman; and the conscientious work of Connie Budelis in typing and Barbara Willson in copyediting.

Finally, I wish to thank my husband for his loving encouragement in the process of this work.

CONTENTS

INTRODUCTION

I N December 1945 an Arab peasant made an astonishing
archeological discovery in Upper Egypt. Rumors obscured
the circumstances of this find—perhaps because the discovery
was accidental, and its sale on the black market illegal. For years
even the identity of the discoverer remained unknown. One
rumor held that he was a blood avenger; another, that he had
made the find near the town of Naj 'Hammādī at the Jabal
al-Ṭārif, a mountain honeycombed with more than 150 caves.
Originally natural, some of these caves were cut and painted and
used as grave sites as early as the sixth dynasty, some 4,300 years
ago.

Thirty years later the discoverer himself, Muḥammad 'Alī
al-Sammān, told what happened.[1] Shortly before he and his
brothers avenged their father's murder in a blood feud, they had
saddled their camels and gone out to the Jabal to dig for *sabakh*,
a soft soil they used to fertilize their crops. Digging around a
massive boulder, they hit a red earthenware jar, almost a meter
high. Muḥammad 'Alī hesitated to break the jar, considering that
a *jinn*, or spirit, might live inside. But realizing that it might also
contain gold, he raised his mattock, smashed the jar, and discovered inside thirteen papyrus books, bound in leather. Returning to his home in al-Qaṣr, Muḥammad 'Alī dumped the books

and loose papyrus leaves on the straw piled on the ground next to the oven. Muḥammad's mother, 'Umm-Aḥmad, admits that she burned much of the papyrus in the oven along with the straw she used to kindle the fire.

A few weeks later, as Muḥammad 'Alī tells it, he and his brothers avenged their father's death by murdering Ahmed Ismā'īl. Their mother had warned her sons to keep their mattocks sharp: when they learned that their father's enemy was nearby, the brothers seized the opportunity, "hacked off his limbs . . . ripped out his heart, and devoured it among them, as the ultimate act of blood revenge."[2]

Fearing that the police investigating the murder would search his house and discover the books, Muḥammad 'Alī asked the priest, al-Qummuṣ Bāsīlīyuṣ Abd al-Masīḥ, to keep one or more for him. During the time that Muḥammad 'Alī and his brothers were being interrogated for murder, Rāghib, a local history teacher, had seen one of the books, and suspected that it had value. Having received one from al-Qummus Bāsīlīyūs, Rāghib sent it to a friend in Cairo to find out its worth.

Sold on the black market through antiquities dealers in Cairo, the manuscripts soon attracted the attention of officials of the Egyptian government. Through circumstances of high drama, as we shall see, they bought one and confiscated ten and a half of the thirteen leather-bound books, called codices, and deposited them in the Coptic Museum in Cairo. But a large part of the thirteenth codex, containing five extraordinary texts, was smuggled out of Egypt and offered for sale in America. Word of this codex soon reached Professor Gilles Quispel, distinguished historian of religion at Utrecht, in the Netherlands. Excited by the discovery, Quispel urged the Jung Foundation in Zürich to buy the codex. But discovering, when he succeeded, that some pages were missing, he flew to Egypt in the spring of 1955 to try to find them in the Coptic Museum. Arriving in Cairo, he went at once to the Coptic Museum, borrowed photographs of some of the texts, and hurried back to his hotel to decipher them. Tracing out the first line, Quispel was startled, then incredulous, to read: "These are the secret words which the living Jesus spoke, and which the twin, Judas Thomas, wrote down."³ Quispel knew that his colleague H.-C. Puech, using notes from another French scholar, Jean Doresse, had identified the opening lines with fragments of a Greek *Gospel of Thomas* discovered in the 1890's. But the discovery of the whole text raised new questions: Did Jesus have a twin brother, as this text implies? Could the text be an authentic record of Jesus' sayings? According to its title, it contained the *Gospel According to Thomas*; yet, unlike the gospels of the New Testament, this text identified itself as a *secret* gospel. Quispel also discovered that it contained many sayings known from the New Testament; but these sayings, placed in unfamiliar contexts, suggested other dimensions of meaning. Other passages, Quispel found, differed entirely from any known Christian tradition: the "living Jesus," for example, speaks in sayings as cryptic and compelling as Zen *koans*:

> Jesus said, "If you bring forth what is within you, what you bring forth will save you. If you do not bring forth what is within you, what you do not bring forth will destroy you."⁴

What Quispel held in his hand, the *Gospel of Thomas*, was only one of the fifty-two texts discovered at Nag Hammadi (the usual English transliteration of the town's name). Bound into the same volume with it is the *Gospel of Philip*, which attributes to Jesus acts and sayings quite different from those in the New Testament:

> ... the companion of the [Savior is] Mary Magdalene. [But Christ loved] her more than [all] the disciples, and used to kiss her [often] on her [mouth]. The rest of [the disciples were offended] ... They said to him, "Why do you love her more than all of us?" The Savior answered and said to them, "Why do I not love you as (I love) her?"⁵

Other sayings in this collection criticize common Christian beliefs, such as the virgin birth or the bodily resurrection, as naïve misunderstandings. Bound together with these gospels is the *Apocryphon* (literally, "secret book") *of John*, which opens with an offer to reveal "the mysteries [and the] things hidden in silence" which Jesus taught to his disciple John.[6]

Muḥammad 'Alī later admitted that some of the texts were lost—burned up or thrown away. But what remains is astonishing: some fifty-two texts from the early centuries of the Christian era—including a collection of early Christian gospels, previously unknown. Besides the *Gospel of Thomas* and the *Gospel of Philip*, the find included the *Gospel of Truth* and the *Gospel to the Egyptians*, which identifies itself as "the [sacred book] of the Great Invisible [Spirit]."[7] Another group of texts consists of writings attributed to Jesus' followers, such as the *Secret Book of James*, the *Apocalypse of Paul*, the *Letter of Peter to Philip*, and the *Apocalypse of Peter*.

What Muhammad 'Alī discovered at Nag Hammadi, it soon became clear, were Coptic translations, made about 1,500 years ago, of still more ancient manuscripts. The originals themselves had been written in Greek, the language of the New Testament: as Doresse, Puech, and Quispel had recognized, part of one of them had been discovered by archeologists about fifty years earlier, when they found a few fragments of the original Greek version of the *Gospel of Thomas*.[8]

About the dating of the manuscripts themselves there is little debate. Examination of the datable papyrus used to thicken the leather bindings, and of the Coptic script, place them c. A.D. 350–400.[9] But scholars sharply disagree about the dating of the original texts. Some of them can hardly be later than c. A.D. 120–150, since Irenaeus, the orthodox Bishop of Lyons, writing c. 180, declares that heretics "boast that they possess more gospels than there really are,"[10] and complains that in his time such writings already have won wide circulation—from Gaul through Rome, Greece, and Asia Minor.

Quispel and his collaborators, who first published the *Gospel of Thomas*, suggested the date of c. A.D. 140 for the original.[11] Some reasoned that since these gospels were heretical, they must have been written later than the gospels of the New Testament, which are dated c. 60–110. But recently Professor Helmut Koester of Harvard University has suggested that the collection of sayings in the *Gospel of Thomas*, although compiled c. 140, may include some traditions even *older* than the gospels of the New Testament, "possibly as early as the second half of the first century" (50–100)—as early as, or earlier, than Mark, Matthew, Luke, and John.[12]

Scholars investigating the Nag Hammadi find discovered that some of the texts tell the origin of the human race in terms very different from the usual reading of Genesis: the *Testimony of Truth*, for example, tells the story of the Garden of Eden from the viewpoint of the serpent! Here the serpent, long known to appear in gnostic literature as the principle of divine wisdom, convinces Adam and Eve to partake of knowledge while "the Lord" threatens them with death, trying jealously to prevent them from attaining knowledge, and expelling them from Paradise when they achieve it.[13] Another text, mysteriously entitled the *Thunder, Perfect Mind*, offers an extraordinary poem spoken in the voice of a feminine divine power:

> For I am the first and the last.
> I am the honored one and the scorned one.
> I am the whore and the holy one.
> I am the wife and the virgin. . . .
> I am the barren one,
>   and many are her sons. . . .
> I am the silence that is incomprehensible . . .
> I am the utterance of my name.[14]

These diverse texts range, then, from secret gospels, poems, and quasi-philosophic descriptions of the origin of the universe, to myths, magic, and instructions for mystical practice.

WHY WERE THESE TEXTS BURIED—and why have they remained virtually unknown for nearly 2,000 years? Their suppression as banned documents, and their burial on the cliff at Nag Hammadi, it turns out, were both part of a struggle critical for the formation of early Christianity. The Nag Hammadi texts, and others like them, which circulated at the beginning of the Christian era, were denounced as heresy by orthodox Christians in the middle of the second century. We have long known that many early followers of Christ were condemned by other Christians as heretics, but nearly all we knew about them came from what their opponents wrote attacking them. Bishop Irenaeus, who supervised the church in Lyons, c. 180, wrote five volumes, entitled *The Destruction and Overthrow of Falsely So-called Knowledge*, which begin with his promise to

> set forth the views of those who are now teaching heresy
> ... to show how absurd and inconsistent with the truth are
> their statements ... I do this so that ... you may urge all
> those with whom you are connected to avoid such an abyss
> of madness and of blasphemy against Christ.[15]

He denounces as especially "full of blasphemy" a famous gospel called the *Gospel of Truth*.[16] Is Irenaeus referring to the same *Gospel of Truth* discovered at Nag Hammadi? Quispel and his collaborators, who first published the *Gospel of Truth*, argued that he is; one of their critics maintains that the opening line (which begins "The gospel of truth") is not a title.[17] But Irenaeus does use the same source as at least one of the texts discovered at Nag Hammadi—the *Apocryphon* (Secret Book) *of John*—as ammunition for his own attack on such "heresy." Fifty years later Hippolytus, a teacher in Rome, wrote another massive *Refutation of All Heresies* to "expose and refute the wicked blasphemy of the heretics."[18]

This campaign against heresy involved an involuntary admission of its persuasive power; yet the bishops prevailed. By the time of the Emperor Constantine's conversion, when Christianity became an officially approved religion in the fourth century, Christian bishops, previously victimized by the police, now commanded them. Possession of books denounced as heretical was made a criminal offense. Copies of such books were burned and destroyed. But in Upper Egypt, someone, possibly a monk from a nearby monastery of St. Pachomius,[19] took the banned books and hid them from destruction—in the jar where they remained buried for almost 1,600 years.

But those who wrote and circulated these texts did not regard *themselves* as "heretics." Most of the writings use Christian terminology, unmistakably related to a Jewish heritage. Many claim to offer traditions about Jesus that are secret, hidden from "the many" who constitute what, in the second century, came to be called the "catholic church." These Christians are now called gnostics, from the Greek word *gnosis*, usually translated as "knowledge." For as those who claim to know nothing about ultimate reality are called agnostic (literally, "not-knowing"), the person who does claim to know such things is called gnostic ("knowing"). But *gnosis* is not primarily rational knowledge. The Greek language distinguishes between scientific or reflective knowledge ("He knows mathematics") and knowing through observation or experience ("He knows me"), which is *gnosis*. As the gnostics use the term, we could translate it as "insight," for *gnosis* involves an intuitive process of knowing oneself. And to know oneself, they claimed, is to know human nature and human destiny. According to the gnostic teacher Theodotus, writing in Asia Minor (c. 140–160), the gnostic is one who has come to understand

> who we were, and what we have become; where we were
> . . . whither we are hastening; from what we are being
> released; what birth is, and what is rebirth.[20]

Yet to know oneself, at the deepest level, is simultaneously to know God; this is the secret of *gnosis*. Another gnostic teacher, Monoimus, says:

> Abandon the search for God and the creation and other
> matters of a similar sort. Look for him by taking yourself
> as the starting point. Learn who it is within you who makes
> everything his own and says, "My God, my mind, my

thought, my soul, my body." Learn the sources of sorrow, joy, love, hate . . . If you carefully investigate these matters you will find him *in yourself*.[21]

What Muḥammad 'Alī discovered at Nag Hammadi is, apparently, a library of writings, almost all of them gnostic. Although they claim to offer secret teaching, many of these texts refer to the Scriptures of the Old Testament, and others to the letters of Paul and the New Testament gospels. Many of them include the same *dramatis personae* as the New Testament—Jesus and his disciples. Yet the differences are striking.

Orthodox Jews and Christians insist that a chasm separates humanity from its creator: God is wholly other. But some of the gnostics who wrote these gospels contradict this: self-knowledge is knowledge of God; the self and the divine are identical.

Second, the "living Jesus" of these texts speaks of illusion and enlightenment, not of sin and repentance, like the Jesus of the New Testament. Instead of coming to save us from sin, he comes as a guide who opens access to spiritual understanding. But when the disciple attains enlightenment, Jesus no longer serves as his spiritual master: the two have become equal—even identical.

Third, orthodox Christians believe that Jesus is Lord and Son of God in a unique way: he remains forever distinct from the rest of humanity whom he came to save. Yet the gnostic *Gospel of Thomas* relates that as soon as Thomas recognizes him, Jesus says to Thomas that they have both received their being from the same source:

> Jesus said, "I am not your master. Because you have drunk, you have become drunk from the bubbling stream which I have measured out. . . . He who will drink from my mouth will become as I am: I myself shall become he, and the things that are hidden will be revealed to him."[22]

Does not such teaching—the identity of the divine and human, the concern with illusion and enlightenment, the founder who is presented not as Lord, but as spiritual guide—sound more Eastern than Western? Some scholars have suggested that if the names were changed, the "living Buddha" appropriately could say what the *Gospel of Thomas* attributes to the living Jesus. Could Hindu or Buddhist tradition have influenced gnosticism?

The British scholar of Buddhism, Edward Conze, suggests that it had. He points out that "Buddhists were in contact with the Thomas Christians (that is, Christians who knew and used such writings as the *Gospel of Thomas*) in South India."[23] Trade routes between the Greco-Roman world and the Far East were opening up at the time when gnosticism flourished (A.D. 80–200); for generations, Buddhist missionaries had been proselytizing in Alexandria. We note, too, that Hippolytus, who was a Greek-speaking Christian in Rome (c. 225), knows of the Indian Brahmins—and includes their tradition among the sources of heresy:

> There is . . . among the Indians a heresy of those who philosophize among the Brahmins, who live a self-sufficient life, abstaining from (eating) living creatures and all cooked food . . . They say that God is light, not like the light one sees, nor like the sun nor fire, but to them God is discourse, not that which finds expression in articulate sounds, but that of knowledge (*gnosis*) through which the secret mysteries of nature are perceived by the wise.[24]

Could the title of the *Gospel of Thomas*—named for the disciple who, tradition tells us, went to India—suggest the influence of Indian tradition?

These hints indicate the possibility, yet our evidence is not conclusive. Since parallel traditions may emerge in different cultures at different times, such ideas could have developed in both places independently.[25] What we call Eastern and Western religions, and tend to regard as separate streams, were not clearly differentiated 2,000 years ago. Research on the Nag Hammadi texts is only beginning: we look forward to the work of scholars who can study these traditions comparatively to discover whether they can, in fact, be traced to Indian sources.

Even so, ideas that we associate with Eastern religions emerged in the first century through the gnostic movement in the West, but they were suppressed and condemned by polemicists like Irenaeus. Yet those who called gnosticism heresy were adopting—consciously or not—the viewpoint of that group of Christians who called themselves orthodox Christians. A heretic may be anyone whose outlook someone else dislikes or denounces. According to tradition, a heretic is one who deviates from the true faith. But what defines that "true faith"? Who calls it that, and for what reasons?

We find this problem familiar in our own experience. The term "Christianity," especially since the Reformation, has covered an astonishing range of groups. Those claiming to represent "true Christianity" in the twentieth century can range from a Catholic cardinal in the Vatican to an African Methodist Episcopal preacher initiating revival in Detroit, a Mormon missionary in Thailand, or the member of a village church on the coast of Greece. Yet Catholics, Protestants, and Orthodox agree that such diversity is a recent—and deplorable—development. According to Christian legend, the early church was different. Christians of every persuasion look back to the primitive church to find a simpler, purer form of Christian faith. In the apostles' time, all members of the Christian community shared their money and property; all believed the same teaching, and worshiped together; all revered the authority of the apostles. It was only after that golden age that conflict, then heresy emerged: so says the author of the Acts of the Apostles, who identifies himself as the first historian of Christianity.

But the discoveries at Nag Hammadi have upset this picture. If we admit that some of these fifty-two texts represent early forms of Christian teaching, we may have to recognize that early Christianity is far more diverse than nearly anyone expected before the Nag Hammadi discoveries.[26]

Contemporary Christianity, diverse and complex as we find it, actually may show more unanimity than the Christian churches of the first and second centuries. For nearly all Christians since that time, Catholics, Protestants, or Orthodox, have shared three basic premises. First, they accept the canon of the New Testament; second, they confess the apostolic creed; and third, they affirm specific forms of church institution. But every one of these—the canon of Scripture, the creed, and the institutional structure—emerged in its present form only toward the end of the second century. Before that time, as Irenaeus and others attest, numerous gospels circulated among various Christian groups, ranging from those of the New Testament, Matthew, Mark, Luke, and John, to such writings as the *Gospel of Thomas*, the *Gospel of Philip*, and the *Gospel of Truth*, as well as many other secret teachings, myths, and poems attributed to Jesus or his disciples. Some of these, apparently, were discovered at Nag Hammadi; many others are lost to us. Those who identified themselves as Christians entertained many—and radically differing—religious beliefs and practices. And the communities scattered throughout the known world organized themselves in ways that differed widely from one group to another.

Yet by A.D. 200, the situation had changed. Christianity had become an institution headed by a three-rank hierarchy of bishops, priests, and deacons, who understood themselves to be the guardians of the only "true faith." The majority of churches, among which the church of Rome took a leading role, rejected all other viewpoints as heresy. Deploring the diversity of the earlier movement, Bishop Irenaeus and his followers insisted that there could be only one church, and outside of that church, he declared, "there is no salvation."[27] Members of this church alone are orthodox (literally, "straight-thinking") Christians. And, he claimed, this church must be *catholic*—that is, universal. Whoever challenged that consensus, arguing instead for other forms of Christian teaching, was declared to be a heretic, and expelled. When the orthodox gained military support, sometime after the Emperor Constantine became Christian in the fourth century, the penalty for heresy escalated.

. . .

The efforts of the majority to destroy every trace of heretical "blasphemy" proved so successful that, until the discoveries at Nag Hammadi, nearly all our information concerning alternative forms of early Christianity came from the massive orthodox attacks upon them. Although gnosticism is perhaps the earliest—and most threatening—of the heresies, scholars had known only a handful of original gnostic texts, none published before the nineteenth century. The first emerged in 1769, when a Scottish tourist named James Bruce bought a Coptic manuscript near Thebes (modern Luxor) in Upper Egypt.[28] Published only in 1892, it claims to record conversations of Jesus with his disciples—a group that here includes both men and women. In 1773 a collector found in a London bookshop an ancient text, also in Coptic, that contained a dialogue on "mysteries" between Jesus and his disciples.[29] In 1896 a German Egyptologist, alerted by the previous publications, bought in Cairo a manuscript that, to his amazement, contained the *Gospel of Mary* (Magdalene) and three other texts. Three copies of one of them, the *Apocryphon* (Secret Book) *of John* were also included among the gnostic library discovered at Nag Hammadi fifty years later.[30]

But why is this astonishing discovery at Nag Hammadi only now becoming known for the first time? Why did we not hear news of the Nag Hammadi discovery, as we did about the Dead Sea Scrolls, some twenty-five years ago? Professor Hans Jonas, the eminent authority on gnosticism, wrote in 1962:

> Unlike the Dead Sea finds of the same years, the gnostic find from Nag Hammadi has been beset from the beginning to this day by a persistent curse of political roadblocks, litigations, and, most of all, scholarly jealousies and "firstmanship" (the last factor has grown by now into a veritable *chronique scandaleuse* of contemporary academia).[31]

Access to the texts was deliberately suppressed not only in ancient times but, for very different reasons, in the more than thirty years since the discovery.[32] In the first place, villagers from Upper Egypt and the antiquities dealers who were trying to get rich from the manuscripts hid them to avoid confiscation by government authorities. Their value became clear when the French Egyptologist Jean Doresse saw the first of the recovered manuscripts in 1947 at the Coptic Museum in Cairo. When the museum's director, Togo Mina, asked him to examine it, Doresse identified the manuscript and announced that this discovery would mark an epoch in the study of the origins of Christianity. Fired by his enthusiasm, Mina asked him to look at another manuscript, held by Albert Eid, a Belgian antiquities dealer in Cairo. Following this meeting, Mina went to see Eid to tell him that he would never allow the manuscript to leave Egypt—it must be sold, for a nominal price, to the museum.

But still the majority of the find remained hidden. Bahīj 'Alī, a one-eyed outlaw from al-Qaṣr, had acquired possession of many of the codices in Nag Hammadi and went to Cairo to sell them. Phōcion Tano, an antiquities dealer, bought all that he had, and went to Nag Hammadi to see if he could find more. While Doresse worked in Cairo through the air raids and bombings of 1948 to publish the manuscript of Codex III, the Minister of Public Education negotiated to buy Tano's collection for the museum. Tano worked fast to prevent the government from interfering, by saying that they belonged to a private party, a woman named Dattari, an Italian collector living in Cairo. But on June 10, 1949, Miss Dattari was unsettled to read the following report in Cairo's French newspaper:

> The acquisition of these precious documents by the Egyptian government is in process. According to the specialists consulted, it has to do with one of the most extraordinary discoveries preserved until the present by the ground of Egypt, surpassing in scientific interest such spectacular discoveries as the tomb of Tutankhamen.[33]

When the government nationalized the collection in 1952, government officials claimed the codices, packed in a sealed suitcase. They paid Miss Dattari nothing—although her asking price had been about £100,000. When she retaliated with a lawsuit, she succeeded only in delaying research for three years by gaining a court injunction against it; she lost the case.

But the government failed to confiscate Eid's part of Codex I. In 1949 Albert Eid, worried about government intervention, flew from Cairo to America. By including the manuscript in a large collection of export items, he succeeded in smuggling it out of Egypt. He offered it to buyers for as much as $22,000, but since at least one prospective buyer refused, fearing that the Egyptian government would resent the sale, he returned disappointed to Belgium, where he placed it in a safe-deposit box protected by a secret password.

The Egyptian government indicted Eid for smuggling antiquities, but by the time of his conviction, the antiquities dealer had died. The court imposed a fine of £6,000 on his estate. Meanwhile Eid's widow secretly negotiated to sell the codex, perhaps even to competing bidders. Professor Gilles Quispel, who urged the Jung Foundation in Zürich to buy it, says he did not know that the export and sale were illegal when he made the arrangements. He enjoys telling the dramatic story of his coup:

> On the 10th day of May, 1952, a professor from Utrecht took a train to Brussels. However, due to his absentmindedness, he stepped out of the train in Tilborg, while thinking he was in Roosendaal, and thus missed his connecting train. But when he finally approached the appointed meeting place, a café somewhere in Brussels, two hours too late, he saw the middleman, from Saint Idesbald close by Coxye on the Belgium coast, still waiting at the window and kindly waving to him. The professor then reached out and handed the man a check for 35,000 Frs.S. In return, the man gave the professor about 50 papyri. How does one manage to transfer them over the border without complications? One cannot very easily hide such a package. Thus one must remain honest, and when the customs official asks, "What do you have in that package?" then one just tells the truth: "An old manuscript." And the customs official makes a gesture of

total disinterest and lets one pass. So this is how the Jung Codex was purchased.[34]

Once ownership of the manuscripts was established by 1952 —twelve and a half codices in the Coptic Museum in Cairo, and most of the thirteenth in a safe-deposit box in Zürich—the texts became, for the next twenty years, the focus of intense personal rivalries among the international group of scholars competing for access to them.

Dr. Pahor Labib, who took over directorship of the Coptic Museum in 1952, decided to keep strict control over publication rights. Publishing the definitive first edition of any one of these extraordinary, original texts—let alone the whole collection— would establish a scholar's reputation internationally. The few to whom Dr. Labib did grant access to the manuscripts protected their interests by refusing to allow anyone else to see them. In 1961 the Director General of UNESCO, alerted to the discovery by French scholars, urged publication of the whole find and proposed setting up an international committee to arrange it.[35] The Scandinavian archeologist Torgny Säve-Söderberg wrote to UNESCO, speaking for himself and other scholars, urging UNESCO to intervene, and to prepare a complete edition of photographs of all the manuscripts in order to place the whole of the discovery at the disposal of the many scholars throughout the world who were impatient to see them.

Ten years later, in 1972, the first volume of the photographic edition finally appeared. Nine other volumes followed between 1972 and 1977, thus putting all thirteen codices in the public domain. Since undertaking such a major technical project in Egypt involved many delays, Professor James Robinson, director of the Institute for Antiquity and Christianity, the only American member of the UNESCO committee, had organized an international team to copy and translate most of the material. Robinson and his team privately circulated this material to scholars throughout the world, thus involving many people in the research, effectively breaking the monopoly that had controlled the discovery.

Introduction

I first learned of the Nag Hammadi discoveries in 1965, when I entered the graduate program at Harvard University to study the history of Christianity. I was fascinated to hear of the find, and delighted in 1968 when Professor George MacRae of Harvard received the mimeographed transcriptions from Robinson's team. Because the official publications had not yet appeared, each page was stamped with a warning:

> This material is for private study by assigned individuals only. Neither the text nor its translation may be reproduced or published in any form, in whole or in part.

MacRae and his colleague Professor Helmut Koester encouraged their students to learn Coptic in order to begin research on this extraordinary find. Convinced that the discovery would revolutionize the traditional understanding of the origins of Christianity, I wrote my dissertation at Harvard and Oxford on the controversy between gnostic and orthodox Christianity. After receiving the Ph.D. from Harvard in 1970 and accepting a faculty position at Barnard College, Columbia University, I worked almost exclusively on early Christian gnosticism. After publishing two technical books on this research,[36] I received grants in 1975 (from the American Council of Learned Societies and the American Philosophical Society) so that I could study the manuscripts at the Cairo Museum and attend the First International Conference on Coptic Studies in Cairo. There, like other scholars, I was initiated to the Coptic Museum, amazed to find the library that houses the manuscripts to be a single, small room of the Coptic Museum. Every day, while children played in the library and cleaning women washed the floor around me, I worked at the table, transcribing the papyri. Having seen only black-and-white photographs, I found the originals surprisingly beautiful—each mounted in plexiglass, inscribed in black ink on golden brown leaves. At the First International Conference, held in Cairo while I was there, I delivered a paper on one of the manuscripts (the *Dialogue of the Savior*),[37] and even met one of the middlemen from al-Qaṣr who sold the texts illegally in Cairo.

Having joined the team of scholars, I participated in preparing the first complete edition in English, published in the United States by Harper & Row in 1977. Only with that publication, and with the completion of the photographic edition expected by 1980, have we finally overcome the obstacles to public knowledge caused by what Professor Gérard Garitte of Louvain called "personal rivalries and . . . pretensions to monopolize documents that belong only to science, that is to say, to all."[38]

BY THE TIME I LEARNED of the discovery, however, gnosticism had already had become the focus of a remarkable amount of research. The first to investigate the gnostics were their orthodox contemporaries. Attempting to prove that gnosticism was essentially non-Christian, they traced its origins to Greek philosophy, astrology, mystery religions, magic, and even Indian sources. Often they emphasized—and satirized—the bizarre elements that appear in some forms of gnostic mythology. Tertullian ridiculed the gnostics for creating elaborate cosmologies, with multi-storied heavens like apartment houses, "with room piled on room, and assigned to each god by just as many stairways as there were heresies: The universe has been turned into rooms for rent!"[39] By the end of the nineteenth century, when the few original gnostic sources noted above were discovered, they inspired new research among scholars. The great German historian Adolf von Harnack, basing his research primarily on the church fathers, regarded gnosticism as a Christian heresy. Writing in 1894, Harnack explained that the gnostics, interpreting Christian doctrine in terms of Greek philosophy, became, in one sense, the "first Christian theologians."[40] But in the process, he contended, they distorted the Christian message, and propagated false, hybrid forms of Christian teaching—what he called the "acute Hellenizing of Christianity."[41] The British scholar Arthur Darby Nock agreed: gnosticism, he said, was a kind of "Platonism run wild."[42]

Other historians of religion objected. Far from being a Christian heresy, they said, gnosticism originally was an independent religious movement. In the early twentieth century the New Testament scholar Wilhelm Bousset, who traced gnosticism to ancient Babylonian and Persian sources, declared that

> gnosticism is first of all a pre-Christian movement which had roots in itself. It is therefore to be understood . . . in its own terms, and not as an offshoot or byproduct of the Christian religion.[43]

On this point the philologist Richard Reitzenstein agreed; but Reitzenstein went on to argue that gnosticism derived from ancient Iranian religion and was influenced by Zoroastrian traditions.[44] Others, including Professor M. Friedländer, maintained that gnosticism originated in Judaism: the heretics whom the rabbis attacked in the first and second centuries, said Friedländer, were Jewish gnostics.[45]

In 1934—more than ten years before the Nag Hammadi discoveries—two important new books appeared. Professor Hans Jonas, turning from the question of the historical sources of gnosticism, asked where it originated *existentially*. Jonas suggested that gnosticism emerged in a certain "attitude toward existence." He pointed out that the political apathy and cultural stagnation of the Eastern empire in the first two centuries of this era coincided with the influx of Oriental religion into Hellenistic culture. According to Jonas' analysis, many people at the time felt profoundly alienated from the world in which they lived, and longed for a miraculous salvation as an escape from the constraints of political and social existence. Using the few sources available to him with penetrating insight, Jonas reconstructed a gnostic world view—a philosophy of pessimism about the world combined with an attempt at self-transcendence.[46] A nontechnical version of his book, translated into English, remains, even today, the classic introduction.[47] In an epilogue added to the second edition of this book, Jonas drew a parallel between gnosticism and twentieth-century existentialism, acknowledging his debt to existentialist philosophers, especially to Heidegger, in forming his interpretation of "the gnostic religion."[48]

Another scholar, Walter Bauer, published a very different view of gnosticism in 1934. Bauer recognized that the early Christian movement was itself far more diverse than orthodox sources chose to indicate. So, Bauer wrote,

> perhaps—I repeat, perhaps—certain manifestations of Christian life that the authors of the church renounce as "heresies" originally had not been such at all, but, at least here and there, were the only forms of the new religion; that is, for those regions, they were simply "Christianity." The possibility also exists that their adherents . . . looked down with hatred and scorn on the orthodox, who for them were the false believers.[49]

Bauer's critics, notably the British scholars H. E. W. Turner[50] and C. H. Roberts,[51] have criticized him for oversimplifying the situation and for overlooking evidence that did not fit his theory. Certainly Bauer's suggestion that, in certain Christian groups, those later called "heretics" formed the majority, goes beyond even the gnostics' own claims: they typically characterized themselves as "the few" in relation to "the many" (*hoi polloi*). But Bauer, like Jonas, opened up new ways of thinking about gnosticism.

The discoveries at Nag Hammadi in 1945 initiated, as Doresse had foreseen, a whole new epoch of research. The first and most important task was to preserve, edit, and publish the texts themselves. An international team of scholars, including Professors A. Guillaumont and H.-Ch. Puech from France, G. Quispel from the Netherlands, W. Till from Germany, and Y. 'Abd al Masīḥ from Egypt, collaborated in publishing the *Gospel of Thomas* in 1959.[52] Many of the same scholars worked with Professors M. Malinine of France, R. Kasser of Germany, J. Zandee of the Netherlands, and R. McL. Wilson of Scotland to edit the texts from Codex I. Professor James M. Robinson, secretary of the International Committee for the Nag Hammadi Codices, organized a team of scholars from Europe, Canada, and the United States to edit the facsimile edition of photographs[53] as well as a complete scholarly edition of the whole find in Coptic and English. Robinson sent copies of manuscripts and translations to colleagues in Berlin. There, members of the *Berliner Arbeitskreis für koptisch-gnostische Schriften* (Berlin Working-Group for Coptic-Gnostic Texts), a circle that includes such eminent scholars as Professors H. M. Schenke, K. M. Fischer, and K. W. Tröger, and collaborates with others, including E. Haenchen, W. Schmithals, and K. Rudolf, has prepared editions of the texts in Coptic and German, as well as numerous commentaries, books, and articles.

What could this wealth of new material tell us about gnosticism? The abundance of the texts—and their diversity— made generalization difficult, and consensus even more difficult. Acknowledging this, most scholars now agree that what we call "gnosticism" was a widespread movement that derived its sources from various traditions. A few of the texts describe the multiple heavens, with magic passwords for each one, that the church fathers who had criticized gnosticism led scholars to expect; but many others, surprisingly, contain nothing of the kind. Much of the literature discovered at Nag Hammadi is distinctively Christian; some texts, however, show little or no Christian influence; a few derive primarily from pagan sources (and may not be "gnostic" at all); others make extensive use of Jewish traditions. For this reason, the German scholar C. Colpe has challenged the historians' search for the "origins of gnosticism."[54] This method, Colpe insists, leads to a potentially infinite regress of ever remoter "origins" without contributing much to our understanding of what gnosticism actually is.

Recently several scholars have sought the impetus for the development of gnosticism not in terms of it cultural origins, but in specific events or experiences. Professor R. M. Grant has suggested that gnosticism emerged as a reaction to the shattering of traditional religious views—Jewish and Christian—after the Romans destroyed Jerusalem in A.D. 70.[55] Quispel proposed that gnosticism originated in a potentially universal "experience of the self" projected into religious mythology.[56] Jonas has offered a typological scheme describing gnosticism as a specific kind of philosophical world view.[57] The British scholar E. R. Dodds characterized gnosticism as a movement whose writings derived from mystical experience.[58] Gershom Scholem, the eminent Professor of Jewish Mysticism at the Hebrew University in Jerusalem, agrees with Dodds that gnosticism involves mystical speculation and practice. Tracing esoteric currents in rabbinic circles that were contemporary with the development of gnosticism, Scholem calls them forms of "Jewish gnosticism."[59]

Today, those investigating the Nag Hammadi texts are less concerned about constructing comprehensive theories than analyzing in detail the sources unearthed at Nag Hammadi. There are several different types of research, each investigating primarily those specific groups of texts appropriate to the purposes of the inquiry. One type of research, concerned with the relationship of gnosticism to Hellenistic philosophy, focuses primarily on those Nag Hammadi texts that exemplify this relationship. Contributors to this aspect of research include, for example (besides Hans Jonas), the British scholars A. D. Nock[60] and A. H. Armstrong,[61] and such American scholars as Professors Bentley Layton[62] of Yale University and Harold Attridge of Southern Methodist University.[63] Professor Morton Smith of Columbia University, on the other hand, whose current research concerns the history of magic, investigates the sources that evince magical practice.[64]

A second direction of research investigates gnostic texts from a literary and form-critical point of view. Much of this work was initiated by J. M. Robinson and H. Koester in their book *Trajectories Through Early Christianity*.[65] Others have explored the rich symbolism of gnostic texts. The French scholar M. Tardieu, for example, has analyzed gnostic myths;[66] Professor L. Schottroff has investigated gnostic accounts of the powers of evil.[67] Many of their American colleagues, too, have contributed to the literary analysis of gnostic sources. Professor P. Perkins has investigated both genre[68] and imagery;[69] Professor George MacRae has contributed to our understandings of gnostic metaphors,[70] myth,[71] and literary form;[72] he and others, including Quispel and Professor B. A. Pearson, have shown how certain gnostic myths drew upon material traditional in Judaism.[73]

A third direction of research (which often overlaps with the second) explores the relation of gnosticism to its contemporary religious environment. While Scholem, MacRae, Quispel, Pearson (to name a few) have demonstrated that some gnostic sources refer extensively to Jewish tradition, others are examining the question: What do the gnostic texts tell us about the origins of Christianity? The many scholars who have shared in this research, besides those mentioned above, include Professors R. M. Grant and E. Yamauchi in the United States; R. McL. Wilson in Scotland; G. C. Stead and H. Chadwick in England; W. C. van Unnik in the Netherlands; H.-Ch. Puech and Dr. S. Petrement in France; A. Orbe in Spain; S. Arai in Japan; J. Ménard and F. Wisse in Canada; and, in Germany, besides the members of the Berliner Arbeitskreis, A. Böhlig and Dr. K. Koschorke. Because my own research falls into this category (i.e., gnosticism and early Christianity), I have selected primarily the gnostic Christian sources as the basis for this book. Rather than considering the question of the origins of gnosticism, I intend here to show how gnostic forms of Christianity interact with orthodoxy—and what this tells us about the origins of Christianity itself.

Given the enormous amount of current research in the field, this sketch is necessarily brief and incomplete. Whoever wants to follow the research in detail will find invaluable help in the *Nag Hammadi Bibliography*, published by Professor D. M. Scholer.[74] Kept up to date by regular supplements published in the journal *Novum Testamentum*, Scholer's bibliography currently lists nearly 4,000 books, editions, articles, and reviews published in the last thirty years concerning research on the Nag Hammadi texts.

Yet even the fifty-two writings discovered at Nag Hammadi offer only a glimpse of the complexity of the early Christian movement. We now begin to see that what we call Christianity —and what we identify as Christian tradition—actually represents only a small selection of specific sources, chosen from among dozens of others. Who made that selection, and for what reasons? Why were these other writings excluded and banned as "heresy"? What made them so dangerous? Now, for the first time, we have the opportunity to find out about the earliest Christian heresy; for the first time, the heretics can speak for themselves.

Gnostic Christians undoubtedly expressed ideas that the orthodox abhorred. For example, some of these gnostic texts question whether all suffering, labor, and death derive from human sin, which, in the orthodox version, marred an originally perfect creation. Others speak of the feminine element in the divine, celebrating God as Father *and* Mother. Still others suggest that Christ's resurrection is to be understood symbolically, not literally. A few radical texts even denounce catholic Christians themselves as heretics, who, although they "do not understand mystery . . . boast that the mystery of truth belongs to them alone."[75] Such gnostic ideas fascinated the psychoanalyst C. G. Jung: he thought they expressed "the other side of the mind"—the spontaneous, unconscious thoughts that any orthodoxy requires its adherents to repress.

Yet orthodox Christianity, as the apostolic creed defines it, contains some ideas that many of us today might find even stranger. The creed requires, for example, that Christians confess that God is perfectly good, and still, he created a world that includes pain, injustice, and death; that Jesus of Nazareth was born of a virgin mother; and that, after being executed by order of the Roman procurator, Pontius Pilate, he arose from his grave "on the third day."

Why did the consensus of Christian churches not only accept these astonishing views but establish them as the only true form of Christian doctrine? Traditionally, historians have told us that the orthodox objected to gnostic views for religious and philosophic reasons. Certainly they did; yet investigation of the newly discovered gnostic sources suggests another dimension of the controversy. It suggests that these religious debates—questions of the nature of God, or of Christ—simultaneously bear social and political implications that are crucial to the development of Christianity as an institutional religion. In simplest terms, ideas which bear implications contrary to that development come to be labeled as "heresy"; ideas which implicitly support it become "orthodox."

By investigating the texts from Nag Hammadi, together with sources known for well over a thousand years from orthodox tradition, we can see how politics and religion coincide in the development of Christianity. We can see, for example, the *political* implications of such orthodox doctrines as the bodily resurrection—and how gnostic views of resurrection bear opposite implications. In the process, we can gain a startlingly new perspective on the origins of Christianity.

THE
GNOSTIC
GOSPELS

I

The Controversy over Christ's Resurrection: Historical Event or Symbol?

"JESUS CHRIST ROSE from the grave." With this proclamation, the Christian church began. This may be the fundamental element of Christian faith; certainly it is the most radical. Other religions celebrate cycles of birth and death: Christianity insists that in one unique historical moment, the cycle reversed, and a dead man came back to life! For Jesus' followers this was the turning point in world history, the sign of its coming end. Orthodox Christians since then have confessed in the creed that Jesus of Nazareth, "crucified, dead, and buried," was raised "on the third day."[1] Many today recite that creed without thinking about what they are saying, much less actually believing it. Recently some ministers, theologians, and scholars have challenged the literal view of resurrection. To account for this doctrine, they point out its psychological appeal to our deepest fears and hopes; to explain it, they offer symbolic interpretations.

But much of the early tradition insists literally that a man —Jesus—had come back to life. What makes these Christian accounts so extraordinary is not the claim that his friends had "seen" Jesus after his death—ghost stories, hallucinations, and visions were even more commonplace then than now—but that they saw an actual human being. At first, according to Luke, the disciples themselves, in their astonishment and terror at the appearance of Jesus among them, immediately assumed that they were seeing his ghost. But Jesus challenged them: "Handle me and see, for a spirit does not have flesh and bones, as you see that I have."[2] Since they remained incredulous, he asked for something to eat; as they watched in amazement, he ate a piece of broiled fish. The point is clear: no ghost could do that.

Had they said that Jesus' spirit lived on, surviving bodily decay, their contemporaries might have thought that their stories made sense. Five hundred years before, Socrates' disciples had claimed that their teacher's soul was immortal. But what the Christians said was different, and, in ordinary terms, wholly implausible. The finality of death, which had always been a part of the human experience, was being transformed. Peter contrasts King David, who died and was buried, and whose tomb was well known, with Jesus, who, although killed, rose from the grave, "because it was not possible for him to be held by it"—that is, by death.[3] Luke says that Peter excluded metaphorical interpretation of the event he said he witnessed: "[We] ate and drank with him after he rose from the dead."[4]

Tertullian, a brilliantly talented writer (A.D. c. 190), speaking for the majority, defines the orthodox position: as Christ rose bodily from the grave, so every believer should anticipate the resurrection of the flesh. He leaves no room for doubt. He is not, he says, talking about the immortality of the soul: "The salvation of the soul I believe needs no discussion: for almost all heretics, in whatever way they accept it, at least do not deny it."[5] What is raised is "this flesh, suffused with blood, built up with bones, interwoven with nerves, entwined with veins, (a flesh) which . . . was born, and . . . dies, undoubtedly human."[6] Tertullian expects the idea of Christ's suffering, death, and resurrection to shock his readers; he insists that "it must be believed, because it is absurd!"[7]

Yet some Christians—those he calls heretics—dissent. Without denying the resurrection, they reject the literal interpretation; some find it "extremely revolting, repugnant, and impossible." Gnostic Christians interpret resurrection in various ways. Some say that the person who experiences the resurrection does not meet Jesus raised physically back to life; rather, he encounters Christ on a spiritual level. This may occur in dreams, in ecstatic trance, in visions, or in moments of spiritual illumination. But the orthodox condemn all such interpretations; Tertullian declares that anyone who denies the resurrection *of the flesh* is a heretic, not a Christian.

Why did orthodox tradition adopt the literal view of resurrection? The question becomes even more puzzling when we look at what the New Testament says about it. Some accounts, like the story we noted from Luke, tell how Jesus appears to his disciples in the form they know from his earthly life; he eats with them, and invites them to touch him, to prove that he is "not a ghost." John tells a similar story: Thomas declares that he will not believe that Jesus had actually risen from the grave unless he personally can see and touch him. When Jesus appears, he tells Thomas, "Put your finger here, and see my hands; and put out your hand, and place it in my side; do not be faithless, but believing."[8] But other stories, directly juxtaposed with these, suggest different views of the resurrection. Luke and Mark both relate that Jesus appeared "in another form"[9]—*not* his former earthly form—to two disciples as they walked on the road to Emmaus. Luke says that the disciples, deeply troubled about Jesus' death, talked with the stranger, apparently for several hours. They invited him to dinner; when he sat down with them to bless the bread, suddenly they recognized him as Jesus. At that moment "he vanished out of their sight."[10] John, too, places directly before the story of "doubting Thomas" another of a very different kind: Mary

Magdalene, mourning for Jesus near his grave, sees a man she takes to be the gardener. When he speaks her name, suddenly she recognizes the presence of Jesus—but he orders her *not* to touch him.[11]

So if some of the New Testament stories insist on a literal view of resurrection, others lend themselves to different interpretations. One could suggest that certain people, in moments of great emotional stress, suddenly felt that they experienced Jesus' presence. Paul's experience can be read this way. As he traveled on the Damascus road, intent on arresting Christians, "suddenly a light from heaven flashed about him. And he fell to the ground," hearing the voice of Jesus rebuking him for the intended persecution.[12] One version of this story says, "The men who were traveling with him stood speechless, hearing the voice, but seeing no one";[13] another says the opposite (as Luke tells it, Paul said that "those who were with me saw the light, but did not hear the voice of the one who was speaking to me").[14] Paul himself, of course, later defended the teaching on resurrection as fundamental to Christian faith. But although his discussion often is read as an argument for bodily resurrection, it concludes with the words "I tell you this, brethren: flesh and blood cannot inherit the kingdom of God, nor does the perishable [that is, the mortal body] inherit the imperishable."[15] Paul describes the resurrection as "a mystery,"[16] the transformation from physical to spiritual existence.

If the New Testament accounts could support a range of interpretations, why did orthodox Christians in the second century insist on a literal view of resurrection and reject all others as heretical? I suggest that we cannot answer this question adequately as long as we consider the doctrine only in terms of its religious content. But when we examine its practical effect on the Christian movement, we can see, paradoxically, that the doctrine of bodily resurrection also serves an essential *political* function: it legitimizes the authority of certain men who claim to exercise exclusive leadership over the churches as the successors of the apostle Peter. From the second century, the doctrine has served to validate the apostolic succession of bishops, the basis of papal authority to this day. Gnostic Christians who interpret resurrection in other ways have a lesser claim to authority: when they claim priority over the orthodox, they are denounced as heretics.

Such political and religious authority developed in a most remarkable way. As we have noted, diverse forms of Christianity flourished in the early years of the Christian movement. Hundreds of rival teachers all claimed to teach the "true doctrine of Christ" and denounced one another as frauds. Christians in churches scattered from Asia Minor to Greece, Jerusalem, and Rome split into factions, arguing over church leadership. All claimed to represent "the authentic tradition."

How could Christians resolve such contrary claims? Jesus himself was the only authority they all recognized. Even during his lifetime, among the small group traveling through Palestine with him, no one challenged—and no one matched—the authority of Jesus himself. Independent and assertive a leader as he was, Jesus censured such traits among his followers. Mark relates that when James and John came to him privately to ask for special positions in his administration, he spoke out sharply against their ambition:

> You know that those who are supposed to rule over the Gentiles lord it over them, and their great men exercise authority over them. But it shall not be so among you; but whoever would be great among you must be your servant, and whoever would be first among you must be slave of all.[17]

After Jesus' execution his followers scattered, shaken with grief and terrified for their own lives. Most assumed that their enemies were right—the movement had died with their master. Suddenly, astonishing news electrified the group. Luke says that they heard that "the Lord has risen indeed, and has appeared to Simon [Peter]!"[18] What had he said to Peter? Luke's account suggested to Christians in later generations that he named Peter as his successor, delegating the leadership to him. Matthew says that during his lifetime Jesus already had decided that Peter, the "rock," was to found the future institution.[19] Only John claims to tell what the risen Christ said: he told Peter that he was to take Jesus' place as "shepherd" for the flock.[20]

Whatever the truth of this claim, we can neither verify nor disprove it on historical grounds alone. We have only second-hand testimony from believers who affirm it, and skeptics who deny it. But what we do know as historical fact is that certain disciples—notably, Peter—*claimed* that the resurrection had happened. More important, we know the result: shortly after Jesus' death, Peter took charge of the group as its leader and spokesman. According to John, he had received his authority from the only source the group recognized—from Jesus himself, now speaking from beyond the grave.

What linked the group gathered around Jesus with the world-wide organization that developed within 170 years of his death into a three-rank hierarchy of bishops, priests, and deacons? Christians in later generations maintained that it was the claim that Jesus himself had come back to life! The German scholar Hans von Campenhausen says that because "Peter was the first to whom Jesus appeared after his resurrection,"[21] Peter became the first leader of the Christian community. One can dispute Campenhausen's claim on the basis of New Testament evidence: the gospels of Mark and John both name Mary Magdalene, not Peter, as the first witness of the resurrection.[22] But orthodox churches that trace their origin to Peter developed the tradition —sustained to this day among Catholic and some Protestant churches—that Peter had been the "first witness of the resurrection," and hence the rightful leader of the church. As early as the second century, Christians realized the potential political consequences of having "seen the risen Lord": in Jerusalem, where James, Jesus' brother, successfully rivaled Peter's authority, one tradition maintained that James, not Peter (and certainly not Mary Magdalene) was the "first witness of the resurrection."

New Testament evidence indicates that Jesus appeared to many others besides Peter—Paul says that once he appeared to five hundred people simultaneously. But from the second century, orthodox churches developed the view that only *certain* resurrection appearances actually conferred authority on those who received them. These were Jesus' appearances to Peter and to "the eleven" (the disciples minus Judas Iscariot, who had betrayed Jesus and committed suicide).[23] The orthodox noted the account in Matthew, which tells how the resurrected Jesus announced to "the eleven" that his own authority now has reached cosmic proportions: "All authority, on heaven and on earth, has been given to me." Then he delegated that authority to "the eleven disciples."[24] Luke, too, indicates that although many others had known Jesus, and even had witnessed his resurrection, "the eleven" alone held the position of *official* witnesses—and hence became official leaders of the whole community. Luke relates that Peter, acting as spokesman for the group, proposed that since Judas Iscariot had defected, a twelfth man should now "take the office" that he vacated, restoring the group as "the twelve."[25] But to receive a share in the disciples' authority, Peter declared that he must be

> one of the men who have accompanied us during all the time that the Lord Jesus went in and out among us, beginning from the baptism of John until the day he was taken up from us—*one of these men must become with us a witness to his resurrection.*[26]

Matthias, who met these qualifications, was selected and "enrolled with the eleven apostles."[27]

After forty days, having completed the transfer of power, the resurrected Lord abruptly withdrew his bodily presence from them, and ascended into heaven as they watched in amazement.[28] Luke, who tells the story, sees this as a momentous event. Henceforth, for the duration of the world, no one would ever experience Christ's actual presence as the twelve disciples had during his lifetime—and for forty days after his death. After that time, as Luke tells it, others received only less direct forms of communication with Christ. Luke admits that Stephen saw a vision of Jesus "standing at the right hand of God";[29] that Paul first encountered Jesus in a dramatic vision, and later in a trance[30] (Luke claims to record his words: "When I had returned to Jerusalem and was praying in the temple, I fell into a trance and saw him speaking to me"[31]). Yet Luke's account implies that these incidents cannot compare with the original events attested by the Twelve. In the first place, they occurred to persons *not* included among the Twelve. Second, they occurred only *after* Jesus' bodily ascension to heaven. Third, although visions, dreams, and ecstatic trances manifested traces of Christ's spiritual presence, the experience of the Twelve differed entirely. They alone, having known Jesus throughout his lifetime, could testify to those unique events which they knew firsthand—and to the resurrection of one who was dead to his complete, physical presence with them.[32]

Whatever we think of the historicity of the orthodox account, we can admire its ingenuity. For this theory—that all authority derives from certain apostles' experience of the resurrected Christ, an experience now closed forever—bears enormous implications for the political structure of the community. First, as the German scholar Karl Holl has pointed out, it restricts the circle of leadership to a small band of persons whose members stand in a position of incontestable authority.[33] Second, it suggests that only the apostles had the right to ordain future leaders as their successors.[34] Christians in the second century used Luke's account to set the groundwork for establishing specific, restricted chains of command for all future generations of Christians. Any potential leader of the community would have to derive, or claim to derive, authority from the same apostles. Yet, according to the orthodox view, none can ever claim to equal their authority—much less challenge it. What the apostles experienced and attested their successors cannot verify for themselves; instead, they must only believe, protect, and hand down to future generations the apostles' testimony.[35]

This theory gained extraordinary success: for nearly 2,000 years, orthodox Christians have accepted the view that the apostles alone held definitive religious authority, and that their only legitimate heirs are priests and bishops, who trace their ordination back to that same apostolic succession. Even today the pope traces his—and the primacy he claims over the rest—to Peter himself, "first of the apostles," since he was "first witness of the resurrection."

But the gnostic Christians rejected Luke's theory. Some gnostics called the literal view of resurrection the "faith of fools."[36] The resurrection, they insisted, was not a unique event in the past: instead, it symbolized how Christ's presence could be experienced in the present. What mattered was not literal seeing, but spiritual vision.[37] They pointed out that many who witnessed the events of Jesus' life remained blind to their meaning. The disciples themselves often misunderstood what Jesus said: those who announced that their dead master had come back physically to life mistook a spiritual truth for an actual event.[38] But the true disciple may never have seen the earthly Jesus, having been born at the wrong time, as Paul said of himself.[39] Yet this physical disability may become a spiritual advantage: such persons, like Paul, may encounter Christ first on the level of inner experience.

How is Christ's presence experienced? The author of the *Gospel of Mary*, one of the few gnostic texts discovered before Nag Hammadi, interprets the resurrection appearances as visions received in dreams or in ecstatic trance. This gnostic gospel recalls traditions recorded in Mark and John, that Mary Magdalene was the first to see the risen Christ.[40] John says that Mary saw Jesus on the morning of his resurrection, and that he appeared to the other disciples only later, on the evening of the same day.[41] According to the *Gospel of Mary*, Mary Magdalene, seeing the Lord in a vision, asked him, "How does he who sees the vision see it? [Through] the soul, [or] through the spirit?"[42] He answered that the visionary perceives through the mind. The *Apocalypse of Peter*, discovered at Nag Hammadi, tells how

Peter, deep in trance, saw Christ, who explained that "I am the intellectual spirit, filled with radiant light."[43] Gnostic accounts often mention how the recipients respond to Christ's presence with intense emotions—terror, awe, distress, and joy.

Yet these gnostic writers do not dismiss visions as fantasies or hallucinations. They respect—even revere—such experiences, through which spiritual intuition discloses insight into the nature of reality. One gnostic teacher, whose *Treatise on Resurrection*, a letter to Rheginos, his student, was found at Nag Hammadi, says: "Do not suppose that resurrection is an apparition [*phantasia*; literally, "fantasy"]. It is not an apparition; rather it is something real. Instead," he continues, "one ought to maintain that the world is an apparition, rather than resurrection."[44] Like a Buddhist master, Rheginos' teacher, himself anonymous, goes on to explain that ordinary human existence is spiritual death. But the resurrection is the moment of enlightenment: "It is . . . the revealing of what truly exists . . . and a migration (*metabolē*—change, transition) into newness."[45] Whoever grasps this becomes spiritually alive. This means, he declares, that you can be "resurrected from the dead" right now: "Are you—the real you—mere corruption? . . . Why do you not examine your own self, and see that you have arisen?"[46] A third text from Nag Hammadi, the *Gospel of Philip*, expresses the same view, ridiculing ignorant Christians who take the resurrection literally. "Those who say they will die first and then rise are in error."[47] Instead they must "receive the resurrection while they live." The author says ironically that in one sense, then, of course "it is necessary to rise 'in this flesh,' since everything exists in it!"[48]

What interested these gnostics far more than past events attributed to the "historical Jesus" was the possibility of encountering the risen Christ in the present.[49] The *Gospel of Mary* illustrates the contrast between orthodox and gnostic viewpoints. The account recalls what Mark relates:

> Now when he rose early on the first day of the week, he appeared first to Mary Magdalene . . . She went and told

those who had been with him, as they mourned and wept. But when they heard that he was alive and had been seen by her, they would not believe it.[50]

As the *Gospel of Mary* opens, the disciples are mourning Jesus' death and terrified for their own lives. Then Mary Magdalene stands up to encourage them, recalling Christ's continual presence with them: "Do not weep, and do not grieve, and do not doubt; for his grace will be with you completely, and will protect you."[51] Peter invites Mary to "tell us the words of the Savior which you remember."[52] But to Peter's surprise, Mary does not tell anecdotes from the past; instead, she explains that she has just seen the Lord in a vision received through the mind, and she goes on to tell what he revealed to her. When Mary finishes,

she fell silent, since it was to this point that the Savior had spoken with her. But Andrew answered and said to the brethren, "Say what you will about what she has said. I, at least, do not believe that the Savior has said this. For certainly these teachings are strange ideas!"[53]

Peter agrees with Andrew, ridiculing the idea that Mary actually saw the Lord in her vision. Then, the story continues,

Mary wept and said to Peter, "My brother Peter, what do you think? Do you think that I thought this up myself in my heart? Do you think I am lying about the Savior?" Levi answered and said to Peter, "Peter, you have always been hot-tempered . . . If the Savior made her worthy, who are you to reject her?"[54]

Finally Mary, vindicated, joins the other apostles as they go out to preach. Peter, apparently representing the orthodox position, looks to past events, suspicious of those who "see the Lord" in visions: Mary, representing the gnostic, claims to experience his continuing presence.[55]

These gnostics recognized that their theory, like the orthodox one, bore political implications. It suggests that whoever "sees the Lord" through inner vision can claim that his or her own authority equals, or surpasses, that of the Twelve—and of their successors. Consider the political implications of the *Gospel of Mary*: Peter and Andrew, here representing the leaders of the orthodox group, accuse Mary—the gnostic—of pretending to have seen the Lord in order to justify the strange ideas, fictions, and lies she invents and attributes to divine inspiration. Mary lacks the proper credentials for leadership, from the orthodox viewpoint: she is not one of the "twelve." But as Mary stands up to Peter, so the gnostics who take her as their prototype challenge the authority of those priests and bishops who claim to be Peter's successors.

We know that gnostic teachers challenged the orthodox in precisely this way. While, according to them, the orthodox relied solely on the public, exoteric teaching which Christ and the apostles offered to "the many," gnostic Christians claimed to offer, in addition, their *secret* teaching, known only to the few.[56] The gnostic teacher and poet Valentinus (c. 140) points out that even during his lifetime, Jesus shared with his disciples certain mysteries, which he kept secret from outsiders.[57] According to the New Testament gospel of Mark, Jesus said to his disciples,

> . . . "To you has been given the secret of the kingdom of God, but for those outside everything is in parables; so that they may indeed see but not perceive, and may indeed hear but not understand; lest they should turn again, and be forgiven."[58]

Matthew, too, relates that when Jesus spoke in public, he spoke only in parables; when his disciples asked the reason, he replied, "To you it has been given to know the secrets [*mysteria*; literally, "mysteries"] of the kingdom of heaven, but to them it has not been given."[59] According to the gnostics, some of the disciples, following his instructions, kept secret Jesus' esoteric teaching: this they taught only in private, to certain persons who had proven themselves to be spiritually mature, and who therefore qualified for "initiation into *gnosis*"—that is, into secret knowledge.

Following the crucifixion, they allege that the risen Christ continued to reveal himself to certain disciples, opening to them, through visions, new insights into divine mysteries. Paul, referring to himself obliquely in the third person, says that he was "caught up to the third heaven—whether in the body or out of the body I do not know." There, in an ecstatic trance, he heard "things that cannot be told, which man may not utter."[60] Through his spiritual communication with Christ, Paul says he discovered "hidden mysteries" and "secret wisdom," which, he explains, he shares only with those Christians he considers "mature"[61] but not with everyone. Many contemporary Biblical scholars, themselves orthodox, have followed Rudolph Bultmann, who insists that Paul does not mean what he says in this passage.[62] They argue that Paul does *not* claim to have a secret tradition; such a claim would apparently make Paul sound too "gnostic." Recently Professor Robin Scroggs has taken the opposite view, pointing out that Paul clearly says that he *does* have secret wisdom.[63] Gnostic Christians in ancient times came to the same conclusion. Valentinus, the gnostic poet who traveled from Egypt to teach in Rome (c. 140), even claimed that he himself learned Paul's secret teaching from Theudas, one of Paul's own disciples.

Followers of Valentinus say that only their own gospels and revelations disclose those secret teachings. These writings tell countless stories about the risen Christ—the spiritual being whom Jesus represented—a figure who fascinated them far more than the merely human Jesus, the obscure rabbi from Nazareth. For this reason, gnostic writings often reverse the pattern of the New Testament gospels. Instead of telling the history of Jesus biographically, from birth to death, gnostic accounts begin where the others end—with stories of the spiritual Christ appearing to his disciples. The *Apocryphon of John*, for example, begins as John tells how he went out after the crucifixion in "great grief":

> Immediately . . . the [heavens were opened, and the whole] creation [which is] under heaven shone, and [the world] was shaken. [I was afraid, and I] saw in the light [a child] . . . while I looked he became like an old man. And he [changed his] form again, becoming like a servant . . . I saw . . . a[n image] with multiple forms in the light . . .[64]

As he marveled, the presence spoke:

> "John, Jo[h]n, why do you doubt, and why are you afraid? You are not unfamiliar with this form, are you? . . . Do not be afraid! I am the one who [is with you] always . . . [I have come to teach] you what is [and what was], and what will come to [be] . . ."[65]

The *Letter of Peter to Philip*, also discovered at Nag Hammadi, relates that after Jesus' death, the disciples were praying on the Mount of Olives when

> a great light appeared, so that the mountain shone from the sight of him who had appeared. And a voice called out to them saying "Listen . . . I am Jesus Christ, who is with you forever."[66]

Then, as the disciples ask him about the secrets of the universe, "a voice came out of the light" answering them. The *Wisdom of Jesus Christ* tells a similar story. Here again the disciples are gathered on a mountain after Jesus' death, when "then there appeared to them the Redeemer, not in his original form but in the invisible spirit. But his appearance was the appearance of a great angel of light." Responding to their amazement and terror, he smiles, and offers to teach them the "secrets [*mysteria*; literally, "mysteries"] of the holy plan" of the universe and its destiny.[67]

But the contrast with the orthodox view is striking.[68] Here Jesus does not appear in the ordinary human form the disciples recognize—and certainly not in *bodily* form. Either he appears as a luminous presence speaking out of the light, or he transforms himself into multiple forms. The *Gospel of Philip* takes up the same theme:

Jesus took them all by stealth, for he did not reveal himself in the manner [in which] he was, but in the manner in which [they would] be able to see him. He revealed himself to [them all. He revealed himself] to the great as great . . . (and) to the small as small.[69]

To the immature disciple, Jesus appears as a child; to the mature, as an old man, symbol of wisdom. As the gnostic teacher Theodotus says, "each person recognizes the Lord in his own way, not all alike."[70]

Orthodox leaders, including Irenaeus, accused the gnostics of fraud. Such texts as those discovered at Nag Hammadi—the *Gospel of Thomas*, the *Gospel of Philip*, the *Letter of Peter to Philip*, and the *Apocryphon (Secret Book) of John*—proved, according to Irenaeus, that the heretics were trying to pass off as "apostolic" what they themselves had invented. He declares that the followers of the gnostic teacher Valentinus, being "utterly reckless,"

put forth their own compositions, while boasting that they have more gospels than there really are . . . They really have no gospel which is not full of blasphemy. For what they have published . . . is totally unlike what has been handed down to us from the apostles.[71]

What proves the validity of the four gospels, Irenaeus says, is that they actually *were* written by Jesus' own disciples and their followers, who personally witnessed the events they described. Some contemporary Biblical scholars have challenged this view: few today believe that contemporaries of Jesus actually wrote the New Testament gospels. Although Irenaeus, defending their exclusive legitimacy, insisted that they were written by Jesus' own followers, we know virtually nothing about the persons who wrote the gospels we call Matthew, Mark, Luke, and John. We only know that these writings are attributed to apostles (Matthew and John) or followers of the apostles (Mark and Luke).

Gnostic authors, in the same way, attributed their secret writings to various disciples. Like those who wrote the New

Testament gospels, they may have received some of their material from early traditions. But in other cases, the accusation that the gnostics invented what they wrote contains some truth: certain gnostics openly acknowledged that they derived their *gnosis* from their own experience.

How, for example, could a Christian living in the second century write the *Secret Book of John?* We could imagine the author in the situation he attributes to John at the opening of the book: troubled by doubts, he begins to ponder the meaning of Jesus' mission and destiny. In the process of such internal questioning, answers may occur spontaneously to the mind; changing patterns of images may appear. The person who understands this process not in terms of modern psychology, as the activity of the imagination or unconscious, but in religious terms, could experience these as forms of spiritual communication with Christ. Seeing his own communion with Christ as a continuation of what the disciples enjoyed, the author, when he casts the "dialogue" into literary form, could well give to them the role of the questioners. Few among his contemporaries— except the orthodox, whom he considers "literal-minded"— would accuse him of forgery; rather, the titles of these works indicate that they were written "in the spirit" of John, Mary Magdalene, Philip, or Peter.

Attributing a writing to a specific apostle may also bear a symbolic meaning. The title of the *Gospel of Mary* suggests that its revelation came from a direct, intimate communication with the Savior. The hint of an erotic relationship between him and Mary Magdalene may indicate claims to mystical communion; throughout history, mystics of many traditions have chosen sexual metaphors to describe their experiences. The titles of the *Gospel of Thomas* and the *Book of Thomas the Contender* (attributed to Jesus' "twin brother") may suggest that "you, the reader, are Jesus' twin brother." Whoever comes to understand these books discovers, like Thomas, that Jesus is his "twin," his spiritual "other self." Jesus' words to Thomas, then, are addressed to the reader:

"Since it has been said that you are my twin and true companion, examine yourself so that you may understand who you are . . . I am the knowledge of the truth. So while you accompany me, although you do not understand (it), you already have come to know, and you will be called 'the one who knows himself.' For whoever has not known himself has known nothing, but whoever has known himself has simultaneously achieved knowledge about the depth of all things."[72]

Like circles of artists today, gnostics considered original creative invention to be the mark of anyone who becomes spiritually alive. Each one, like students of a painter or writer, expected to express his own perceptions by revising and transforming what he was taught. Whoever merely repeated his teacher's words was considered immature. Bishop Irenaeus complains that

> every one of them generates something new every day, according to his ability; for no one is considered initiated [or: "mature"] among them unless he develops some enormous fictions![73]

He charges that "they boast that they are the discoverers and inventors of this kind of imaginary fiction," and accuses them of creating new forms of mythological poetry. No doubt he is right: first- and second-century gnostic literature includes some remarkable poems, like the "Round Dance of the Cross"[74] and the "Thunder, Perfect Mind." Most offensive, from his point of view, is that they admit that nothing supports their writings except their own intuition. When challenged, "they either mention mere human feelings, or else refer to the harmony that can be seen in creation":[75]

> They are to be blamed for . . . describing human feelings, and passions, and mental tendencies . . . and ascribing the things that happen to human beings, and *whatever they recognize themselves as experiencing*, to the divine Word.[76]

On this basis, like artists, they express their own insight—their own *gnosis*—by creating new myths, poems, rituals, "dialogues" with Christ, revelations, and accounts of their visions.

Like Baptists, Quakers, and many others, the gnostic is convinced that whoever receives the spirit communicates directly with the divine. One of Valentinus' students, the gnostic teacher Heracleon (c. 160), says that "at first, people believe because of the testimony of others . . ." but then "they come to believe from the truth itself."[77] So his own teacher, Valentinus, claimed to have first learned Paul's secret teaching; then he experienced a vision which became the source of his own *gnosis*:

> He saw a newborn infant, and when he asked who he might be, the child answered, "I am the Logos."[78]

Marcus, another student of Valentinus' (c. 150), who went on to become a teacher himself, tells how he came to his own firsthand knowledge of the truth. He says that a vision

> descended upon him . . . in the form of a woman . . . and expounded to him alone its own nature, and the origin of things, which it had never revealed to anyone, divine or human.[79]

The presence then said to him,

> "I wish to show you Truth herself; for I have brought her down from above, so that you may see her without a veil, and understand her beauty."[80]

And that, Marcus adds, is how "the naked Truth" came to him in a woman's form, disclosing her secrets to him. Marcus expects, in turn, that everyone whom he initiates into *gnosis* will also receive such experiences. In the initiation ritual, after invoking the spirit, he commands the candidate to speak in prophecy,[81] to demonstrate that the person has received direct contact with the divine.

What differentiates these gnostics from those who, throughout the history of Christianity, have claimed to receive special visions and revelations, and who have expressed these in art, poetry, and mystical literature? Christians who stand in orthodox tradition, Catholics and Protestants, expect that the revelations they receive will confirm (in principle, at least) apostolic tradition: this, they agree, sets the boundaries of Christian faith. The apostles' original teaching remains the criterion; whatever deviates is heresy. Bishop Irenaeus declares that the apostles,

> like a rich man (depositing money) in a bank, placed in the church fully everything that belongs to truth: so that everyone, whoever will, can draw from her the water of life.[82]

The orthodox Christian believes "the one and only truth from the apostles, which is handed down by the church." And he accepts no gospels but the four in the New Testament which serve as the canon (literally, "guideline") to measure all future doctrine and practice.

But the gnostic Christians, whom Irenaeus opposed, assumed that they had gone far beyond the apostles' original teaching. Just as many people today assume that the most recent experiments in science or psychology will surpass earlier ones, so the gnostics anticipated that the present and future would yield a continual increase in knowledge. Irenaeus takes this as proof of their arrogance:

> They consider themselves "mature," so that no one can be compared with them in the greatness of their *gnosis*, not even if you mention Peter or Paul or any of the other apostles. . . . They imagine that they themselves have discovered more than the apostles, and that the apostles preached the gospel still under the influence of Jewish opinions, but that they themselves are wiser and more intelligent than the apostles.[83]

And those who consider themselves "wiser than the apostles" also consider themselves "wiser than the priests."[84] For what the gnostics say about the apostles—and, in particular, about the Twelve—expresses their attitude toward the priests and bishops, who claim to stand in the orthodox apostolic succession.

But despite their emphasis on free creativity, some gnostic

teachers—rather inconsistently—claim to have their own, secret sources of "apostolic tradition." Thereby they claim access to different lines of apostolic sucession from that commonly accepted in the churches. The gnostic teacher Ptolemy explains to Flora, a woman he sees as a potential initiate, that "we too have received" apostolic tradition from a sucession of teachers—one that, he says, offers an esoteric supplement to the canonical collection of Jesus' words.[85]

Gnostic authors often attribute their own traditions to persons who stand *outside* the circle of the Twelve—Paul, Mary Magdalene, and James. Some insist that the Twelve—including Peter—had not received *gnosis* when they first witnessed to Christ's resurrection. Another group of gnostics, called Sethians because they identified themselves as sons of Seth, the third child of Adam and Eve, say that the disciples, deluded by "a very great error," imagined that Christ had risen from the dead in bodily form. But the risen Christ appeared to "a few of these disciples, who he recognized were capable of understanding such great mysteries,"[86] and taught them to understand his resurrection in spiritual, not physical, terms. Furthermore, as we have seen, the *Gospel of Mary* depicts Mary Magdalene (never recognized as an apostle by the orthodox) as the one favored with visions and insight that far surpass Peter's. The *Dialogue of the Savior* praises her not only as a visionary, but as the apostle who excels all the rest. She is the "woman who knew the All."[87] Valentinus claims that his apostolic tradition comes from Paul—another outsider to the Twelve, but one of the greatest authorities of the orthodox, and, after Luke, the author most extensively represented in the New Testament.

Other gnostics explain that certain members of the Twelve later received special visions and revelations, and so attained enlightenment. The *Apocalypse of Peter* describes how Peter, deep in trance, experiences the presence of Christ, who opens his eyes to spiritual insight:

> [The Savior] said to me . . . , ". . . put your hands upon (your) eyes . . . and say what you see!" But when I

had done it, I did not see anything. I said, "No one sees (this way)." Again he told me, "Do it again." And there came into me fear with joy, for I saw a new light, greater than the light of day. Then it came down upon the Savior. And I told him about the things which I saw.[88]

The *Secret Book of James* tells how "the twelve disciples were all sitting together and recalling what the Savior had said to each one of them, whether in secret or openly, and [setting it in order] in books."[89] But when Christ appeared, he chose Peter and James, and drew them apart from the rest to tell them what the others were not to know. Either version of this theory bears the same implication: it asserts the superiority of gnostic forms of secret tradition—and hence, of gnostic teachers—over that of the priests and bishops, who can offer only "common" tradition. Further, because earlier traditions, from this point of view, are at best incomplete, and at worst simply false, gnostic Christians continually drew upon their own spiritual experience—their own *gnosis*—to revise and transform them.

But what gnostics celebrated as proof of spiritual maturity, the orthodox denounced as "deviation" from apostolic tradition. Tertullian finds it outrageous that

> every one of them, just as it suits his own temperament, modifies the traditions he has received, just as the one who handed them down modified them, when he shaped them according to his own will.[90]

That they "disagree on specific matters, even from their own founders" meant to Tertullian that they were "unfaithful" to apostolic tradition. Diversity of teaching was the very mark of heresy:

> On what grounds are heretics strangers and enemies to the apostles, if it is not from the difference of their teaching, which each individual of his own mere will has either advanced or received?[91]

Doctrinal conformity defined the orthodox faith. Bishop Irenaeus declares that the catholic church believes these points of doctrine just as if she had only one soul, and one and the same heart, and she proclaims them and teaches them in perfect harmony. . . . For although the languages of the world are different, still the meaning of the tradition is one and the same. For the churches which have been planted in Germany do not believe or hand down anything different, nor do those in Spain, nor those in Gaul, nor those in the east, nor those in Egypt, nor those in Africa, nor those which have been established in the central regions of the world.[92]

What would happen if arguments did arise among such scattered churches? Who should decide which traditions would take priority? Irenaeus considers the question:

But how is it? Suppose a dispute concerning some important question arises among us; should we not have recourse to the most ancient churches, with which the apostles held continual intercourse, and learn from them what is clear and certain in regard to the present question?[93]

Irenaeus prescribes terminating any disagreement

by indicating that tradition, derived from the apostles, of the very great, the very ancient, and universally known church founded and organized at Rome by the two most glorious apostles, Peter and Paul . . . and by indicating the faith . . . which came down to our time by means of the succession of the bishops. For it is necessary that every church should agree with this church, on account of its preeminent authority.[94]

Since no one of later generations can have access to Christ as the apostles did, during his lifetime and at his resurrection, every believer must look to the church at Rome, which they founded, and to the bishops for authority.

Some gnostic Christians counterattacked. The *Apocalypse of Peter*, probably among the latest writings discovered at Nag Hammadi (c. 200–300), tells how dismayed Peter was to hear that many believers "will fall into an erroneous name" and "will be ruled heretically."[95] The risen Christ explains to Peter that those who "name themselves bishop, and also deacon, as if they had received their authority from God," are, in reality, "waterless canals."[96] Although they "do not understand mystery," they "boast that the mystery of truth belongs to them alone."[97] The author accuses them of having misinterpreted the apostles' teaching, and thus having set up an "imitation church" in place of the true Christian "brotherhood."[98] Other gnostics, including the followers of Valentinus, did not challenge the bishop's right to teach the common apostolic tradition. Nor did they oppose, in principle, the leadership of priests and bishops. But for them the church's teaching, and the church officials, could never hold the ultimate authority which orthodox Christians accorded them.[99] All who had received *gnosis*, they say, had gone beyond the church's teaching and had transcended the authority of its hierarchy.

The controversy over resurrection, then, proved critical in shaping the Christian movement into an institutional religion. All Christians agreed in principle that only Christ himself—or God—can be the ultimate source of spiritual authority. But the immediate question, of course, was the practical one: Who, in the present, administers that authority?

Valentinus and his followers answered: Whoever comes into direct, personal contact with the "living One." They argued that only one's own experience offers the ultimate criterion of truth, taking precedence over all secondhand testimony and all tradition—even gnostic tradition! They celebrated every form of creative invention as evidence that a person has become spiritually alive. On this theory, the structure of authority can never be fixed into an institutional framework: it must remain spontaneous, charismatic, and open.

Those who rejected this theory argued that all future generations of Christians must trust the apostles' testimony—even more than their own experience. For, as Tertullian admitted, whoever judges in terms of ordinary historical experience would find the claim that a man physically returned from the grave to be incredible. What can never be proven or verified in the present, Tertullian says, "must be believed, because it is absurd." Since the death of the apostles, believers must accept the word of the priests and bishops, who have claimed, from the second century, to be their only legitimate heirs.

Recognizing the political implications of the doctrine of resurrection does not account for its extraordinary impact on the religious experience of Christians. Whoever doubts that impact has only to recall any of the paintings it evoked from artists as diverse as Della Francesca, Michelangelo, Rembrandt, and Dali, or the music written on the theme by composers from ancient times through Bach, Mozart, Handel, and Mahler.

The conviction that a man who died came back to life is, of course, a paradox. But that paradox may contain the secret of its powerful appeal, for while it contradicts our own historical experience, it speaks the language of human emotions. It addresses itself to that which may be our deepest fear, and expresses our longing to overcome death.

The contemporary theologian Jürgen Moltmann suggests that the orthodox view of resurrection also expressed, in symbolic language, the conviction that human life is inseparable from bodily experience: even if a man comes back to life from the dead, he must come back *physically*.[100] Irenaeus and Tertullian both emphasize that the anticipation of bodily resurrection requires believers to take seriously the ethical implications of their own actions. Certainly it is true that gnostics who ridiculed the idea of bodily resurrection frequently devalued the body, and considered its actions (sexual acts, for example) unimportant to the "spiritual" person. According to the *Gospel of Thomas*, for example, Jesus says,

> "If spirit came into being because of the body, it is a wonder of wonders. Indeed, I am amazed at how this great wealth [the spirit] has made its home in this poverty [the body]."[101]

For the gnostics stood close to the Greek philosophic tradition (and, for that matter, to Hindu and Buddhist tradition) that regards the human spirit as residing "in" a body—as if the actual person were some sort of disembodied being who uses the body as an instrument but does not identify with it. Those who agree with Moltmann may find, then, that the orthodox doctrine of resurrection, far from negating bodily experience, affirmed it as the central fact of human life.

But in terms of the social order, as we have seen, the orthodox teaching on resurrection had a different effect: it legitimized a hierarchy of persons through whose authority all others must approach God. Gnostic teaching, as Irenaeus and Tertullian realized, was potentially subversive of this order: it claimed to offer to every initiate direct access to God of which the priests and bishops themselves might be ignorant.[102]

II

"One God, One Bishop": The Politics of Monotheism

THE CHRISTIAN CREED begins with the words "I believe in one God, Father Almighty, Maker of heaven and earth." Some scholars suggest that this credal statement was originally formulated to exclude followers of the heretic Marcion (c. 140) from orthodox churches. A Christian from Asia Minor, Marcion was struck by what he saw as the contrast between the creator-God of the Old Testament, who demands justice and punishes every violation of his law, and the Father whom Jesus proclaims—the New Testament God of forgiveness and love. Why, he asked, would a God who is "almighty"—all-powerful —create a world that includes suffering, pain, disease—even mosquitoes and scorpions? Marcion concluded that these must be two different Gods. The majority of Christians early condemned this view as dualistic, and identified themselves as orthodox by confessing one God, who is both "Father Almighty" and "Maker of heaven and earth."

When advocates of orthodoxy confronted another challenge —the gnostics—they often attacked them as "Marcionites" and "dualists." Irenaeus states as his major complaint against the gnostics that they, like the Marcionites, say that "there is another God besides the creator." Some of the recently discovered texts confirm his account. According to the *Hypostasis of the Archons*, the creator's vain claim[1] to hold an exclusive monopoly on divine power shows that he

> is blind . . . [because of his] power and his ignorance [and his] arrogance he said . . . , "It is I who am God; there is none [other apart from me]." When he said this, he sinned against [the Entirety]. And a voice came forth from above the realm of absolute power, saying, "You are mistaken, Samael," which means, "god of the blind."[2]

Another text discovered in the same codex at Nag Hammadi, *On the Origin of the World*, tells a variant of the same story:

> . . . he boasted continually, saying to (the angels) . . . "I am God, and no other one exists except me." But when he said these things, he sinned against all of the immortal ones . . . when Faith saw the impiety of the chief ruler, she was angry. . . . she said, "You err, Samael (i.e., "blind god"). An enlightened, immortal humanity [*anthropos*] exists before you!"[3]

A third text bound into the same volume, the *Secret Book of John*, relates how

> in his madness . . . he said, "I am God, and there is no other God beside me," for he is ignorant of . . . the place from which he had come. . . . And when he saw the creation which surrounds him and the multitudes of angels around him which had come forth from him, he said to them, "I am a jealous God, and there is no other God beside me." But by announcing this he indicated to the angels that another God does exist; for if there were no other one, of whom would he be jealous?[4]

When these same sources tell the story of the Garden of Eden, they characterize this God as the jealous master, whose tyranny the serpent (often, in ancient times, a symbol of divine wisdom) taught Adam and Eve to resist:

> . . . God gave [a command] to Adam, "From every [tree] you may eat, [but] from the tree which is in the midst of Paradise do not eat, for on the day that you eat from it you will surely die." But the serpent was wiser than all the animals that were in Paradise, and he persuaded Eve, saying, "On the day when you eat from the tree which is in the midst of Paradise, the eyes of your mind will be opened." And Eve obeyed . . . she ate; she also gave to her husband.[5]

Observing that the serpent's promise came true—their eyes were opened—but that God's threat of immediate death did not, the gnostic author goes on to quote God's words from Genesis 3:22, adding editorial comment:

> . . . "Behold, Adam has become like one of us, knowing evil and good." Then he said, "Let us cast him out of Paradise, lest he take from the tree of life, and live forever." But of what sort is this God? First [he] envied Adam that he should eat from the tree of knowledge. . . . Surely he has shown himself to be a malicious envier.[6]

As the American scholar Birger Pearson points out, the author uses an Aramaic pun to equate the serpent with the Instructor ("serpent," *hewyā*; "to instruct," *ḥawā*).[7] Other gnostic accounts add a four-way pun that includes Eve (Ḥawāh): instead of tempting Adam, she gives life to him and instructs him:

> After the day of rest, Sophia [literally, "wisdom"] sent Zoe [literally, "life"], her daughter, who is called Eve, as an instructor to raise up Adam . . . When Eve saw Adam cast down, she pitied him, and she said, "Adam, live! Rise up upon the earth!" Immediately her word became a deed. For when Adam rose up, immediately he opened his eyes. When he saw her, he said, "You will be called 'the mother of the living,' because you are the one who gave me life."[8]

"One God, One Bishop"

The *Hypostasis of the Archons* describes Eve as the spiritual principle in humanity who raises Adam from his merely material condition:

> And the spirit-endowed Woman came to [Adam] and spoke with him, saying, "Arise, Adam." And when he saw her, he said, "It is you who have given me life; you shall be called "Mother of the living"—for it is she who is my mother. It is she who is the Physician, and the Woman, and She Who Has Given Birth." . . . Then the Female Spiritual Principle came in the Snake, the Instructor, and it taught them, saying, ". . . you shall not die; for it was out of jealousy that he said this to you. Rather, your eyes shall open, and you shall become like gods, recognizing evil and good." . . . And the arrogant Ruler cursed the Woman . . . [and] . . . the Snake.[9]

Some scholars today consider gnosticism synonymous with metaphysical dualism—or even with pluralities of gods. Irenaeus denounced as blasphemy such caricatures of the conviction, fundamental to the Hebrew Scriptures, that "the Lord your God is one God." But Clement of Alexandria, Irenaeus' contemporary, tells us that there was a "monadic *gnosis*"; and the discoveries at Nag Hammadi also disclose that Valentinian gnosticism—the most influential and sophisticated form of gnostic teaching, and by far the most threatening to the church—differs essentially from dualism. The theme of the oneness of God dominates the opening section of the *Tripartite Tractate*, a Valentinian treatise from Nag Hammadi which describes the origin of all being. The author describes God as

> a sole Lord and God . . . For he is unbegotten . . . In the proper sense, then, the only Father and God is the one whom no one else begot. As for the universe (*cosmos*), he is the one who begot and created it.[10]

A Valentinian Exposition speaks of God who is

> [Root] of the All, the [Ineffable One who] dwells in the Monad. [He dwells alone] in silence . . . since, after all, [he was] a Monad, and no one was before him . . .[11]

[3 1]

According to a third Valentinian text, the *Interpretation of Knowledge*, the Savior taught that "Your Father, who is in heaven, is one."[12]

Irenaeus himself tells us that the creed which effectively screened out Marcionites from the church proved useless against the Valentinians. In common with other Christians, they recited the orthodox creed. But Irenaeus explains that although they did "verbally confess one God," they did so with private mental reservations, "saying one thing, and thinking another."[13] While the Marcionites openly blasphemed the creator, the Valentinians, he insists, did so covertly:

> Such persons are, to outward appearances, sheep, for they seem to be like us, from what they say in public, repeating the same words [of confession] that we do; but inwardly they are wolves.[14]

What distressed Irenaeus most was that the majority of Christians did not recognize the followers of Valentinus as heretics. Most could not tell the difference between Valentinian and orthodox teaching; after all, he says, most people cannot differentiate between cut glass and emeralds either! But, he declares, "although their language is similar to ours," their views "not only are very different, but at all points full of blasphemies."[15] The apparent similarity with orthodox teaching only made this heresy more dangerous—like poison disguised as milk. So he wrote the five volumes of his massive *Refutation and Overthrow of Falsely So-called Gnosis* to teach the unwary to discriminate between the truth, which saves believers, and gnostic teaching, which destroys them in "an abyss of madness and blasphemy."[16]

For while the Valentinians publicly confessed faith in one God,[17] in their own private meetings they insisted on discriminating between the popular image of God—as master, king, lord, creator, and judge—and what that image represented—God understood as the ultimate source of all being.[18] Valentinus calls that source "the depth";[19] his followers describe it as an invisible, incomprehensible primal principle.[20] But most Christians, they say, mistake mere images of God for that reality.[21] They point out that the Scriptures sometimes depict God as a mere craftsman, or as an avenging judge, as a king who rules in heaven, or even as a jealous master. But these images, they say, cannot compare with Jesus' teaching that "God is spirit" or the "Father of Truth."[22] Another Valentinian, the author of the *Gospel of Philip*, points out that names can be

> very deceptive, for they divert our thoughts from what is accurate to what is inaccurate. Thus one who hears the word "God" does not perceive what is accurate, but perceives what is inaccurate. So also with "the Father," and "the Son," and "the Holy Spirit," and "life," and "light," and "resurrection," and "the Church," and all the rest—people do not perceive what is accurate, but they perceive what is inaccurate . . .[23]

The Protestant theologian Paul Tillich recently drew a similar distinction between the God we imagine when we hear the term, and the "God beyond God," that is, the "ground of being" that underlies all our concepts and images.

What made their position heretical? Why did Irenaeus find such a modification of monotheism so crucial—in fact, so utterly reprehensible—that he urged his fellow believers to expel the followers of Valentinus from the churches as heretics? He admitted that this question puzzled the gnostics themselves:

> They ask, when they confess the same things and participate in the same worship . . . how is it that we, for no reason, remain aloof from them; and how is it that when they confess the same things, and hold the same doctrines, *we call them heretics!*[24]

I suggest that here again we cannot fully answer this question as long as we consider this debate exclusively in terms of religious and philosophical arguments. But when we investigate how the doctrine of God actually functions in gnostic and orthodox writings, we can see how this religious question also involves social and political issues. Specifically, by the latter part of the second century, when the orthodox insisted upon "one God," they simultaneously validated the system of governance in which the church is ruled by "one bishop." Gnostic modification of monotheism was taken—and perhaps intended—as an attack upon that system. For when gnostic and orthodox Christians discussed the nature of God, they were at the same time debating the issue of *spiritual authority*.

This issue dominates one of the earliest writings we have from the church at Rome—a letter attributed to Clement, called Bishop of Rome (c. 90–100). As spokesman for the Roman church, Clement wrote to the Christian community in Corinth at a time of crisis: certain leaders of the Corinthian church had been divested of power. Clement says that "a few rash and self-willed people" drove them out of office: "those of no reputation [rose up] against those with reputation, the fools against the wise, the young against the old."[25] Using political language, he calls this "a rebellion"[26] and insists that the deposed leaders be restored to their authority: he warns that they must be feared, respected, and obeyed.

On what grounds? Clement argues that God, the God of Israel, alone rules all things:[27] he is the lord and master whom all must obey; he is the judge who lays down the law, punishing rebels and rewarding the obedient. But how is God's rule actually administered? Here Clement's theology becomes practical: God, he says, delegates his "authority of reign" to "rulers and leaders on earth."[28] Who are these designated rulers? Clement answers that they are bishops, priests, and deacons. Whoever refuses to "bow the neck"[29] and obey the church leaders is guilty of insubordination against the divine master himself. Carried away with his argument, Clement warns that whoever disobeys the divinely ordained authorities "receives the death penalty!"[30]

This letter marks a dramatic moment in the history of Christianity. For the first time, we find here an argument for dividing the Christian community between "the clergy" and "the laity." The church is to be organized in terms of a strict order of superiors and subordinates. Even within the clergy, Clement insists on ranking each member, whether bishop, priest, or deacon, "in his own order":[31] each must observe "the rules and commandments" of his position at all times.

Many historians are puzzled by this letter.[32] What, they ask, was the basis for the dispute in Corinth? What *religious* issues were at stake? The letter does not tell us that directly. But this does not mean that the author ignores such issues. I suggest that he makes his own point—his religious point—entirely clear: he intended to establish the Corinthian church on the model of the divine authority. As God reigns in heaven as master, lord, commander, judge, and king, so on earth he delegates his rule to members of the church hierarchy, who serve as generals who command an army of subordinates; kings who rule over "the people"; judges who preside in God's place.

Clement may simply be stating what Roman Christians took for granted[33]—and what Christians outside of Rome, in the early second century, were coming to accept. The chief advocates of this theory, not surprisingly, were the bishops themselves. Only a generation later, another bishop, Ignatius of Antioch in Syria, more than a thousand miles from Rome, passionately defended the same principle. But Ignatius went further than Clement. He defended the three ranks—bishop, priests, and deacons—as a hierarchical order that mirrors the divine hierarchy in heaven. As there is only one God in heaven, Ignatius declares, so there can be only one bishop in the church. "One God, one bishop"— this became the orthodox slogan. Ignatius warns "the laity" to revere, honor, and obey the bishop "as if he were God." For the bishop, standing at the pinnacle of the church hierarchy, presides "in the place of God."[34] Who, then, stands below God? The divine council, Ignatius replies. And as God rules over that council in heaven, so the bishop on earth rules over a council of priests. The heavenly divine council, in turn, stands above the apostles; so, on earth, the priests rule over the deacons—and all three of these rule over "the laity."[35]

Was Ignatius merely attempting to aggrandize his own

position? A cynical observer might suspect him of masking power politics with religious rhetoric. But the distinction between religion and politics, so familiar to us in the twentieth century, was utterly alien to Ignatius' self-understanding. For him, as for his contemporaries, pagan and Christian alike, religious convictions necessarily involved political relationships —and vice versa. Ironically, Ignatius himself shared this view with the Roman officials who condemned him to death, judging his religious convictions as evidence for treason against Rome. For Ignatius, as for Roman pagans, politics and religion formed an inseparable unity. He believed that God became accessible to humanity *through the church*—and specifically, through the bishops, priests, and deacons who administer it: "without these, there is nothing which can be called a church!"[36] For the sake of their eternal salvation he urged people to submit themselves to the bishop and priests. Although Ignatius and Clement depicted the structure of the clergy in different ways,[37] both bishops agreed that this human order mirrors the divine authority in heaven. Their religious views, certainly, bore political implications; yet, at the same time, the practice they urged was based on their beliefs about God.

What would happen if someone challenged their doctrine of God—as the one who stands at the pinnacle of the divine hierarchy and legitimizes the whole structure? We do not have to guess: we can see what happened when Valentinus went from Egypt to Rome (c. 140). Even his enemies spoke of him as a brilliant and eloquent man:[38] his admirers revered him as a poet and spiritual master. One tradition attributes to him the poetic, evocative *Gospel of Truth* that was discovered at Nag Hammadi. Valentinus claims that besides receiving the Christian tradition that all believers hold in common, he has received from Theudas, a disciple of Paul's, initiation into a secret doctrine of God.[39] Paul himself taught this secret wisdom, he says, not to everyone, and not publicly, but only to a select few whom he considered to be spiritually mature.[40] Valentinus offers, in turn, to initiate "those who are mature"[41] into his wisdom, since not everyone is able to comprehend it.

What this secret tradition reveals is that the one whom most Christians naïvely worship as creator, God, and Father is, in reality, only the image of the true God. According to Valentinus, what Clement and Ignatius mistakenly ascribe to God actually applies only to the *creator*.[42] Valentinus, following Plato, uses the Greek term for "creator" (*demiurgos*),[43] suggesting that he is a lesser divine being who serves as the instrument of the higher powers.[44] It is not God, he explains, but the demiurge who reigns as king and lord,[45] who acts as a military commander,[46] who gives the law and judges those who violate it[47]—in short, he is the "God of Israel."

Through the initiation Valentinus offers, the candidate learns to reject the creator's authority and all his demands as foolishness. What gnostics know is that the creator makes false claims to power ("I am God, and there is no other")[48] that derive from his own ignorance. Achieving *gnosis* involves coming to recognize the true source of divine power—namely, "the depth" of all being. Whoever has come to know that source simultaneously comes to know himself and discovers his spiritual origin: he has come to know his true Father and Mother.

Whoever comes to this *gnosis*—this insight—is ready to receive the secret sacrament called the redemption (*apolytrosis*; literally, "release").[49] Before gaining *gnosis*, the candidate worshiped the demiurge, mistaking him for the true God: now, through the sacrament of redemption, the candidate indicates that he has been released from the demiurge's power. In this ritual he addresses the demiurge, declaring his independence, serving notice that he no longer belongs to the demiurge's sphere of authority and judgment,[50] but to what transcends it:

> I am a son from the Father—the Father who is pre-existent. . . . I derive being from Him who is preexistent, and I come again to my own place whence I came forth.[51]

What are the practical—even political—implications of this religious theory? Consider how Valentinus or one of his initiates might respond to Clement's claim that the bishop rules over the community "as God rules in heaven"—as master, king, judge, and lord. Would not an initiate be likely to reply to such a bishop: "You claim to represent God, but, in reality, you represent only the demiurge, whom you blindly serve and obey. I, however, have passed beyond the sphere of his authority—and so, for that matter, beyond yours!"

Irenaeus, as bishop, recognized the danger to clerical authority. The redemption ritual, which dramatically changed the initiate's relation to the demiurge, changed simultaneously his relationship to the bishop. Before, the believer was taught to submit to the bishop "as to God himself," since, he was told, the bishop rules, commands, and judges "in God's place." But now he sees that such restrictions apply only to naïve believers who still fear and serve the demiurge.[52] *Gnosis* offers nothing less than a theological justification for refusing to obey the bishops and priests! The initiate now sees them as the "rulers and powers" who rule on earth in the demiurge's name. The gnostic admits that the bishop, like the demiurge, exercises legitimate authority over most Christians—those who are uninitiated.[53] But the bishop's demands, warnings, and threats, like those of the demiurge himself, can no longer touch the one who has been "redeemed." Irenaeus explains the effect of this ritual:

> They maintain that they have attained to a height beyond every power, and that therefore they are free in every respect to act as they please, having no one to fear in anything. For they claim that because of the *redemption* . . . they cannot be apprehended, or even perceived, by the judge.[54]

The candidate receives from his initiation into *gnosis* an entirely new relation to spiritual authority. Now he knows that the clerical hierarchy derives its authority from the demiurge—not from the Father. When a bishop like Clement commands the believer to "fear God" or to "confess that you have a Lord," or when Irenaeus warns that "God will judge" the sinner, the gnostic may hear all of these as their attempt to reassert the false claims of the demiurge's power, and of his earthly representatives, over the believer. In the demiurge's foolish assertion that "I am God, and there is no other," the gnostic could hear the bishop's claim to exercise exclusive power over the community. In his warning, "I am a jealous God," the gnostic might recognize the bishop's jealousy for those who are beyond his authority. Bishop Irenaeus, in turn, satirizes their tantalizing and seductive style:

> If anyone yields himself to them like a little sheep, and follows out their practice and their *redemption*, such a person becomes so puffed up that . . . he walks with a strutting gait and a supercilious countenance, possessing all the pompous air of a cock![55]

Tertullian traces such arrogance to the example of their teacher Valentinus, who, he says, refused to submit himself to the superior authority of the bishop of Rome. For what reason? Tertullian says that Valentinus wanted to become bishop himself. But when another man was chosen instead, he was filled with envy and frustrated ambition, and cut himself off from the church to found a rival group of his own.[56]

Few historians believe Tertullian's story. In the first place, it follows a typical polemic against heresy which maintains that envy and ambition lead heretics to deviate from the true faith. Second, some twenty years after this alleged incident, followers of Valentinus considered themselves to be fully members of the church, and indignantly resisted orthodox attempts to expel them.[57] This suggests that the orthodox, rather than those they called heretics, initiated the break.

Yet Tertullian's story, even—perhaps especially—if untrue, illustrates what many Christians saw as one of the dangers of heresy: it encourages insubordination to clerical authority. And, apparently, the orthodox were right. Bishop Irenaeus tells us that followers of Valentinus "assemble in unauthorized meetings"[58]—

that is, in meetings that he himself, as bishop, has not authorized. At these meetings they attempted to raise doubts in the minds of their hearers: Does the church's teaching really satisfy them, or not?[59] Have the sacraments which the church dispenses—baptism and the eucharist—given them a complete initiation into Christian faith, or only the first step?[60] Members of the inner circle suggested that what the bishop and priests taught publicly were only *elementary* doctrines. They themselves claimed to offer more—the secret mysteries, the higher teachings.

This controversy occurred at the very time when earlier, diversified forms of church leadership were giving way to a unified hierarchy of church office.[61] For the first time, certain Christian communities were organizing into a strict order of subordinate "ranks" of bishops, priests, deacons, laity. In many churches the bishop was emerging, for the first time, as a "monarch" (literally, "sole ruler"). Increasingly, he claimed the power to act as disciplinarian and judge over those he called "the laity." Could certain gnostic movements represent resistance to this process? Could gnostics stand among the critics who opposed the development of church hierarchy? Evidence from Nag Hammadi suggests that they did. We have noted before how the author of the *Apocalypse of Peter* ridicules the claims of church officials:

> Others . . . outside our number . . . call themselves bishops and also deacons, as if they had received their authority from God. . . . Those people are waterless canals.[62]

The *Tripartite Tractate*, written by a follower of Valentinus, contrasts those who are gnostics, "children of the Father," with those who are uninitiates, offspring of the demiurge.[63] The Father's children, he says, join together as equals, enjoying mutual love, spontaneously helping one another. But the demiurge's offspring—the ordinary Christians—"wanted to command one another, outrivalling one another in their empty ambition"; they are inflated with "lust for power," "each one imagining that he is superior to the others."[64]

If gnostic Christians criticized the development of church hierarchy, how could they themselves form a social organization? If they rejected the principle of rank, insisting that all are equal, how could they even hold a meeting? Irenaeus tells us about the practice of one group that he knows from his own congregation in Lyons—the group led by Marcus, a disciple of Valentinus'.[65] Every member of the group had been initiated: this meant that every one had been "released" from the demiurge's power. For this reason, they dared to meet without the authority of the bishop, whom they regarded as the demiurge's spokesman— Irenaeus himself! Second, every initiate was assumed to have received, through the initiation ritual, the charismatic gift of direct inspiration through the Holy Spirit.[66]

How did members of this circle of "pneumatics" (literally, "those who are spiritual") conduct their meetings? Irenaeus tells us that when they met, all the members first participated in drawing lots.[67] Whoever received a certain lot apparently was designated to take the role of *priest*; another was to offer the sacrament, as *bishop*; another would read the Scriptures for worship, and others would address the group as a *prophet*, offering extemporaneous spiritual instruction. The next time the group met, they would throw lots again so that the persons taking each role changed continually.

This practice effectively created a very different structure of authority. At a time when the orthodox Christians increasingly discriminated between clergy and laity, this group of gnostic Christians demonstrated that, among themselves, they refused to acknowledge such distinctions. Instead of ranking their members into superior and inferior "orders" within a hierarchy, they followed the principle of strict equality. All initiates, men and women alike, participated equally in the drawing; anyone might be selected to serve as *priest, bishop,* or *prophet.* Furthermore, because they cast lots at each meeting, even the distinctions established by lot could never become permanent "ranks." Finally—most important—they intended, through this practice, to remove the element of human choice. A twentieth-century observer might assume that the gnostics left these matters to random chance, but the gnostics saw it differently. They believed that since God directs everything in the universe, the way the lots fell expressed his choice.

Such practices prompted Tertullian to attack "the behavior of the heretics":

> How frivolous, how worldly, how merely *human* it is, without seriousness, without authority, without discipline, as fits their faith! To begin with, it is uncertain who is a catechumen, and who a believer: they all have access equally, they listen equally, they pray equally—even pagans, if any happen to come. . . . They also share the kiss of peace with all who come, for they do not care how differently they treat topics, if they meet together to storm the citadel of the one only truth. . . . *All* of them are arrogant . . . *all* offer you *gnosis!*[68]

The principle of equal access, equal participation, and equal claims to knowledge certainly impressed Tertullian. But he took this as evidence that the heretics "overthrow discipline": proper discipline, in his view, required certain degrees of distinction between community members. Tertullian protests especially the participation of "those women among the heretics" who shared with men positions of authority: "They teach, they engage in discussion; they exorcise; they cure"[69]—he suspects that they might even baptize, which meant that they also acted as bishops!

Tertullian also objected to the fact that

> their ordinations are carelessly administered, capricious, and changeable. At one time they put novices in office; at another, persons bound by secular employment. . . . Nowhere is promotion easier than in the camp of rebels, where even the mere fact of being there is a foremost service. So today one man is bishop and tomorrow another; the person

who is a deacon today, tomorrow is a reader; the one who
is a priest today is a layman tomorrow; for even on the
laity they impose the functions of priesthood![70]

This remarkable passage reveals what distinctions Tertullian
considered essential to church order—distinctions between new-
comers and experienced Christians; between women and men;
between a professional clergy and people occupied with secular
employment; between readers, deacons, priests, and bishops—
and above all, between the clergy and the laity. Valentinian
Christians, on the other hand, followed a practice which insured
the equality of all participants. Their system allowed no hierarchy
to form, and no fixed "orders" of clergy. Since each person's role
changed every day, occasions for envy against prominent persons
were minimized.

How was the bishop who defined his role in traditional
Roman terms, as ruler, teacher, and judge of the church, to
respond to this gnostic critique? Irenaeus saw that he, as bishop,
had been placed in a double-bind situation. Certain members of
his flock had been meeting without his authority in private
sessions; Marcus, a self-appointed leader, whom Irenaeus derides
as an "adept in magical impostures,"[71] had initiated them into
secret sacraments and had encouraged them to ignore the bishop's
moral warnings. Contrary to his orders, he says, they did eat
meat sacrificed to idols; they freely attended pagan festivals, and
they violated his strict warnings concerning sexual abstinence
and monogamy.[72] What Irenaeus found most galling of all was
that, instead of repenting or even openly defying the bishop,
they responded to his protests with diabolically clever *theological*
arguments:

They call [us] "unspiritual," "common," and "ecclesiastic." . . . Because we do not accept their monstrous
allegations, they say that we go on living in the hebdomad
[the lower regions], as if we could not lift our minds to the
things on high, nor understand the things that are above.[73]

Irenaeus was outraged at their claim that they, being spiritual, were released from the ethical restraints that he, as a mere servant of the demiurge, ignorantly sought to foist upon them.[74]

To defend the church against these self-styled theologians, Irenaeus realized that he must forge theological weapons. He believed that if he could demolish the heretical teaching of "another God besides the creator," he could destroy the possibility of ignoring or defying—on allegedly theological grounds—the authority of the "one catholic church" and of its bishop. Like his opponents, Irenaeus took for granted the correlation between the structure of divine authority and human authority in the church. If God is One, then there can be only one true church, and only one representative of the God in the community—the bishop.

Irenaeus declared, therefore, that orthodox Christians must believe above all that God is One—creator, Father, lord, and judge. He warned that it is this one God who established the catholic church, and who "presides with those who exercise moral discipline"[75] within it. Yet he found it difficult to argue theology with the gnostics: they claimed to agree with everything he said, but he knew that secretly they discounted his words as coming from someone unspiritual. So he felt impelled to end his treatise with a solemn call to judgment:

> Let those persons who blaspheme the Creator . . . as
> [do] the Valentinians and all the falsely so-called "gnostics,"
> be recognized as agents of Satan by all who worship God.
> Through their agency Satan even now . . . has been seen to
> speak against God, that God who has prepared eternal fire
> for every kind of apostasy.[76]

But we would be wrong to assume that this struggle involves only members of the laity claiming charismatic inspiration, contending against an organized, spiritless hierarchy of priests and bishops. Irenaeus clearly indicates the opposite. Many whom he censured for propagating gnostic teaching were themselves prominent members of the church hierarchy. In one case Irenaeus wrote to Victor, Bishop of Rome, to warn him that certain gnostic writings were circulating among his congregations.[77] He considered these writings especially dangerous because their author, Florinus, claimed the prestige of being a priest. Yet Irenaeus warns Victor that this priest is also, secretly, a gnostic initiate. Irenaeus warned his own congregations that "those whom many believe to be priests, . . . but who do not place the *fear of God* supreme in their hearts . . . are full of pride at their prominence in the community." Such persons, he explained, are secretly gnostics, who "do evil deeds in secret, saying, 'No one sees us.' "[78] Irenaeus makes clear that he intended to expose those who outwardly acted like orthodox Christians, but who were privately members of gnostic circles.

How could the ordinary Christian tell the difference between true and false priests? Irenaeus declares that those who are orthodox will follow the lines of apostolic succession:

> One must obey the priests who are in the church—that is . . . those who possess the succession from the apostles. For they receive simultaneously with the episcopal succession the sure gift of truth.[79]

The heretics, he explains, depart from common tradition and meet without the bishop's approval:

> One must hold in suspicion others who depart from the primitive succession, and assemble themselves in any place at all. These one must recognize as heretics . . . or as schismatics . . . or as hypocrites. All of these have fallen from the truth.[80]

Irenaeus is pronouncing a solemn episcopal judgment. The gnostics claim to have two sources of tradition, one open, the other secret. Irenaeus ironically agrees with them that there *are* two sources of tradition—but, he declares, as God is one, only one of these derives from God—that is the one the church receives through Christ and his chosen apostles, especially Peter. The other comes from Satan—and goes back to the gnostic teacher Simon Magus (literally, "magician"), Peter's archenemy, who tried to buy the apostle's spiritual power and earned his curse. As Peter heads the true succession, so Simon epitomizes the false, demon-inspired succession of the heretics; he is the "father of all heresies":

> All those who in any way corrupt the truth, and harm the teaching of the church, are the disciples and successors of Simon Magus of Samaria. . . . They put forth, indeed, the name of Jesus Christ as a kind of lure, but in many ways they introduce the impieties of Simon . . . spreading to their hearers the bitter and malignant poison of the great serpent (Satan), the great author of apostasy.[81]

Finally he warns that "some who are considered to be among the orthodox"[82] have much to fear in the coming judgment unless (and this is his main practical point) they now repent, repudiate the teaching of "another God," and submit themselves to the bishop, accepting the "advance discipline"[83] that he will administer to spare them eternal damnation.

Were Irenaeus' religious convictions nothing but political tenets in disguise? Or, conversely, were his politics subordinate to his religious beliefs? Either of these interpretations over-simplifies the situation. Irenaeus' religious convictions and his position—like those of his gnostic opponents—reciprocally in-fluenced one another. If certain gnostics opposed the develop-ment of church hierarchy, we need not reduce gnosticism to a political movement that arose in reaction to that development. Followers of Valentinus shared a religious vision of the nature of God that they found incompatible with the rule of priests and bishops that was emerging in the catholic church—and so they resisted it. Irenaeus' religious convictions, conversely, coin-cided with the structure of the church he defended.

This case is far from unique: we can see throughout the history of Christianity how varying beliefs about the nature of God inevitably bear different political implications. Martin Luther, more than 1,300 years later, felt impelled by his own religious experience and his transformed understanding of God to challenge practices endorsed by his superiors in the Catholic Church, and finally to reject its entire papal and priestly system. George Fox, the radical visionary who founded the Quaker movement, was moved by his encounter with the "inner light" to denounce the whole structure of Puritan authority—legal, governmental, and religious. Paul Tillich proclaimed the doctrine of "God beyond God" as he criticized both Protestant and Catholic churches along with nationalistic and fascist governments.

As the doctrine of Christ's bodily resurrection establishes the initial framework for clerical authority, so the doctrine of the "one God" confirms, for orthodox Christians, the emerging institution of the "one bishop" as monarch ("sole ruler") of the church. We may not be surprised, then, to discover next how the orthodox description of God (as "Father Almighty," for example) serves to define who is included—and who excluded—from participation in the power of priests and bishops.

III

God the Father/
God the Mother

UNLIKE MANY of his contemporaries among the deities of the ancient Near East, the God of Israel shared his power with no female divinity, nor was he the divine Husband or Lover of any.[1] He can scarcely be characterized in any but masculine epithets: king, lord, master, judge, and father.[2] Indeed, the absence of feminine symbolism for God marks Judaism, Christianity, and Islam in striking contrast to the world's other religious traditions, whether in Egypt, Babylonia, Greece, and Rome, or in Africa, India, and North America, which abound in feminine symbolism. Jewish, Christian, and Islamic theologians today are quick to point out that God is not to be considered in sexual terms at all.[3] Yet the actual language they use daily in worship and prayer conveys a different message: who, growing up with Jewish or Christian tradition, has escaped the distinct impression that God is *masculine*? And while Catholics revere Mary as the mother of Jesus, they never identify her as divine in her own right: if she is "mother of God," she is not "God the Mother" on an equal footing with God the Father!

Christianity, of course, added the trinitarian terms to the Jewish description of God. Yet of the three divine "Persons," two—the Father and the Son—are described in masculine terms, and the third—the Spirit—suggests the sexlessness of the Greek neuter term for spirit, *pneuma*. Whoever investigates the early history of Christianity (the field called "patristics"—that is, study of "the fathers of the church") will be prepared for the passage that concludes the *Gospel of Thomas*:

> Simon Peter said to them [the disciples]: "Let Mary leave us, for women are not worthy of Life." Jesus said, "I myself shall lead her, in order to make her male, so that she too may become a living spirit, resembling you males. For every woman who will make herself male will enter the Kingdom of Heaven."[4]

Strange as it sounds, this simply states what religious rhetoric assumes: that the men form the legitimate body of the community, while women are allowed to participate only when they assimilate themselves to men. Other texts discovered at Nag Hammadi demonstrate one striking difference between these "heretical" sources and orthodox ones: gnostic sources continually use sexual symbolism to describe God. One might expect that these texts would show the influence of archaic pagan traditions of the Mother Goddess, but for the most part, their language is specifically Christian, unmistakably related to a Jewish heritage. Yet instead of describing a monistic and masculine God, many of these texts speak of God as a dyad who embraces both masculine and feminine elements.

One group of gnostic sources claims to have received a secret tradition from Jesus through James and through Mary Magdalene. Members of this group prayed to both the divine Father and Mother: "From Thee, Father, and through Thee, Mother, the two immortal names, Parents of the divine being, and thou, dweller in heaven, humanity, of the mighty name . . ."[5] Other texts indicate that their authors had wondered to whom a single, masculine God proposed, "Let us make man [*adam*] in our image, after our likeness" (Genesis 1:26). Since the Genesis account goes on to say that humanity was created "male and female" (1:27), some concluded that the God in whose image we are made must also be both masculine and feminine—both Father and Mother.

How do these texts characterize the divine Mother? I find no simple answer, since the texts themselves are extremely diverse. Yet we may sketch out three primary characterizations. In the first place, several gnostic groups describe the divine Mother as part of an original couple. Valentinus, the teacher and poet, begins with the premise that God is essentially indescribable. But he suggests that the divine can be imagined as a dyad; consisting, in one part, of the Ineffable, the Depth, the Primal Father; and, in the other, of Grace, Silence, the Womb and "Mother of the All."[6] Valentinus reasons that Silence is the appropriate complement of the Father, designating the former as feminine and the latter as masculine because of the grammatical gender of the Greek words. He goes on to describe how Silence receives, as in a womb, the seed of the Ineffable Source; from this she brings forth all the emanations of divine being, ranged in harmonious pairs of masculine and feminine energies.

Followers of Valentinus prayed to her for protection as the Mother, and as "the mystical, eternal Silence."[7] For example, Marcus the magician invokes her as Grace (in Greek, the feminine term *charis*): "May She who is before all things, the incomprehensible and indescribable Grace, fill you within, and increase in you her own knowledge."[8] In his secret celebration of the mass, Marcus teaches that the wine symbolizes her blood. As the cup of wine is offered, he prays that "Grace may flow"[9] into all who drink of it. A prophet and visionary, Marcus calls himself the "*womb* and *recipient* of Silence"[10] (as she is of the Father). The visions he received of the divine being appeared, he reports, in female form.

Another gnostic writing, called the *Great Announcement*, quoted by Hippolytus in his *Refutation of All Heresies*, explains the origin of the universe as follows: From the power of Silence appeared "a great power, the Mind of the Universe, which man-

ages all things, and is a male . . . the other . . . a great Intelligence
. . . is a female which produces all things."[11] Following the
gender of the Greek words for "mind" (*nous*—masculine) and
"intelligence" (*epinoia*—feminine), this author explains that
these powers, joined in union, "are discovered to be duality . . .
This is Mind in Intelligence, and these are separable from one
another, and yet are one, found in a state of duality." This
means, the gnostic teacher explains, that

> there is in everyone [divine power] existing in a latent
> condition . . . This is one power divided above and below;
> generating itself, making itself grow, seeking itself, finding
> itself, being mother of itself, father of itself, sister of itself,
> spouse of itself, daughter of itself, son of itself—mother,
> father, unity, being a source of the entire circle of ex-
> istence.[12]

How did these gnostics intend their meaning to be understood? Different teachers disagreed. Some insisted that the divine
is to be considered masculofeminine—the "great male-female
power." Others claimed that the terms were meant only as
metaphors, since, in reality, the divine is neither male nor
female.[13] A third group suggested that one can describe the
primal Source in either masculine or feminine terms, depending
on which aspect one intends to stress. Proponents of these diverse
views agreed that the divine is to be understood in terms of a
harmonious, dynamic relationship of opposites—a concept that
may be akin to the Eastern view of *yin* and *yang*, but remains
alien to orthodox Judaism and Christianity.

A second characterization of the divine Mother describes her
as Holy Spirit. The *Apocryphon of John* relates how John went
out after the crucifixion with "great grief" and had a mystical
vision of the Trinity. As John was grieving, he says that

> the [heavens were opened and the whole] creation [which
> is] under heaven shone and [the world] trembled. [And I
> was afraid, and I] saw in the light . . . a likeness with
> multiple forms . . . and the likeness had three forms.[14]

To John's question the vision answers: "He said to me, 'John, Jo[h]n, why do you doubt, and why are you afraid? . . . I am the one who [is with you] always. I [am the Father]; I am the Mother; I am the Son.'"[15] This gnostic description of God—as Father, Mother and Son—may startle us at first, but on reflection, we can recognize it as another version of the Trinity. The Greek terminology for the Trinity, which includes the neuter term for spirit (*pneuma*) virtually requires that the third "Person" of the Trinity be asexual. But the author of the *Secret Book* has in mind the Hebrew term for spirit, *ruah*, a feminine word; and so concludes that the feminine "Person" conjoined with the Father and Son must be the Mother. The *Secret Book* goes on to describe the divine Mother:

> . . . (She is) . . . the image of the invisible, virginal, perfect spirit . . . She became the Mother of everything, for she existed before them all, the mother-father [*matropater*] . . .[16]

The *Gospel to the Hebrews* likewise has Jesus speak of "my Mother, the Spirit."[17] In the *Gospel of Thomas*, Jesus contrasts his earthly parents, Mary and Joseph, with his divine Father—the Father of Truth—and his divine Mother, the Holy Spirit. The author interprets a puzzling saying of Jesus' from the New Testament ("Whoever does not hate his father and his mother cannot be my disciple") by adding that "my (earthly) mother [gave me death], but [my] true [Mother] gave me life."[18] So, according to the *Gospel of Philip*, whoever becomes a Christian gains "both father and mother"[19] for the Spirit (*ruah*) is "Mother of many."[20]

A work attributed to the gnostic teacher Simon Magus suggests a mystical meaning for Paradise, the place where human life began:

> Grant Paradise to be the womb; for Scripture teaches us that this is a true assumption when it says, "I am He that formed thee in thy mother's womb" (Isaiah 44:2) . . . Moses . . . using allegory had declared Paradise to be the womb . . . and Eden, the placenta . . .[21]

The river that flows forth from Eden symbolizes the navel, which nourishes the fetus. Simon claims that the Exodus, consequently, signifies the passage out of the womb, and that "the crossing of the Red Sea refers to the blood." Sethian gnostics explain that

> heaven and earth have a shape similar to the womb . . . and if . . . anyone wants to investigate this, let him carefully examine the pregnant womb of any living creature, and he will discover an image of the heavens and the earth.[22]

Evidence for such views, declares Marcus, comes directly from "the cry of the newborn," a spontaneous cry of praise for "the glory of the primal being, in which the powers above are in harmonious embrace."[23]

If some gnostic sources suggest that the Spirit constitutes the maternal element of the Trinity, the *Gospel of Philip* makes an equally radical suggestion about the doctrine that later developed as the virgin birth. Here again, the Spirit is both Mother and Virgin, the counterpart—and consort—of the Heavenly Father: "Is it permitted to utter a mystery? The Father of everything united with the virgin who came down"[24] —that is, with the Holy Spirit descending into the world. But because this process is to be understood symbolically, not literally, the Spirit remains a virgin. The author goes on to explain that as "Adam came into being from two virgins, from the Spirit and from the virgin earth" so "Christ, therefore, was born from a virgin"[25] (that is, from the Spirit). But the author ridicules those literal-minded Christians who mistakenly refer the virgin birth to Mary, Jesus' mother, as though she conceived apart from Joseph: "They do not know what they are saying. When did a woman ever conceive by a woman?"[26] Instead, he argues, virgin birth refers to that mysterious union of the two divine powers, the Father of All and the Holy Spirit.

In addition to the eternal, mystical Silence and the Holy Spirit, certain gnostics suggest a third characterization of the divine Mother: as Wisdom. Here the Greek feminine term for "wisdom," *sophia*, translates a Hebrew feminine term, *hokhmah*. Early interpreters had pondered the meaning of certain Biblical passages—for example, the saying in Proverbs that "God made the world in Wisdom." Could Wisdom be the feminine power in which God's creation was "conceived"? According to one teacher, the double meaning of the term conception—physical and intellectual—suggests this possibility: "The image of thought [*ennoia*] is feminine, since . . . [it] is a power of conception."[27] The *Apocalypse of Adam*, discovered at Nag Hammadi, tells of a feminine power who wanted to conceive by herself:

> . . . from the nine Muses, one separated away. She came to a high mountain and spent time seated there, so that she desired herself alone in order to become androgynous. She fulfilled her desire, and became pregnant from her desire . . .[28]

The poet Valentinus uses this theme to tell a famous myth about Wisdom: Desiring to conceive by herself, apart from her masculine counterpart, she succeeded, and became the "great creative power from whom all things originate," often called Eve, "Mother of all living." But since her desire violated the harmonious union of opposites intrinsic in the nature of created being, what she produced was aborted and defective;[29] from this, says Valentinus, originated the terror and grief that mar human existence.[30] To shape and manage her creation, Wisdom brought forth the demiurge, the creator-God of Israel, as her agent.[31]

Wisdom, then, bears several connotations in gnostic sources. Besides being the "first universal creator,"[32] who brings forth all creatures, she also enlightens human beings and makes them wise. Followers of Valentinus and Marcus therefore prayed to the Mother as the "mystical, eternal Silence" and to "Grace, She who is before all things," and as "incorruptible Wisdom"[33] for insight (*gnosis*). Other gnostics attributed to her the benefits that Adam and Eve received in Paradise. First, she taught them self-awareness; second, she guided them to find food; third, she assisted in the conception of their third and fourth children, who were, according to this account, their third son, Seth, and their

first daughter, Norea.[34] Even more: when the creator became
angry with the human race

> because they did not worship or honor him as Father and
> God, he sent forth a flood upon them, that he might destroy
> them all. But Wisdom opposed him . . . and Noah and his
> family were saved in the ark by means of the sprinkling of
> the light that proceeded from her, and through it the world
> was again filled with humankind.[35]

Another newly discovered text from Nag Hammadi,
Trimorphic Protennoia (literally, the "Triple-formed Primal
Thought"), celebrates the feminine powers of Thought, Intel-
ligence, and Foresight. The text opens as a divine figure speaks:

> [I] am [Protennoia the] Thought that [dwells] in [the
> Light]. . . . [she who exists] before the All . . . I move in
> every creature. . . . I am the Invisible One within the All.[36]

She continues: "I am perception and knowledge, uttering a Voice
by means of Thought. [I] am the real Voice. I cry out in everyone, and they know that a seed dwells within."[37] The second
section, spoken by a second divine figure, opens with the words

> I am the Voice . . . [It is] I [who] speak within every
> creature . . . Now I have come a second time in the likeness
> of a female, and have spoken with them. . . . I have revealed
> myself in the Thought of the likeness of my masculinity.[38]

Later the voice explains:

> I am androgynous. [I am both Mother and] Father,
> since [I copulate] with myself . . . [and with those who
> love] me . . . I am the Womb [that gives shape] to the All
> . . . I am Me[iroth]ea, the glory of the Mother.[39]

Even more remarkable is the gnostic poem called the
Thunder, Perfect Mind. This text contains a revelation spoken
by a feminine power:

> I am the first and the last. I am the honored one and the
> scorned one. I am the whore, and the holy one. I am the

wife and the virgin. I am ⟨the mother⟩ and the daughter.
. . . I am she whose wedding is great, and I have not taken
a husband. . . . I am knowledge, and ignorance. . . . I am
shameless; I am ashamed. I am strength, and I am fear. . . . I
am foolish, and I am wise. . . . I am godless, and I am one
whose God is great.[40]

What does the use of such symbolism imply for the understanding of human nature? One text, having previously described
the divine Source as a "bisexual Power," goes on to say that
"what came into being from that Power—that is, humanity,
being one—is discovered to be two: a male-female being that
bears the female within it."[41] This refers to the story of Eve's
"birth" out of Adam's side (so that Adam, being one, is "discovered to be two," an androgyne who "bears the female within
him"). Yet this reference to the creation story of Genesis 2 (an
account which inverts the biological birth process, and so
attributes to the male the creative function of the female) is
unusual in gnostic sources. More often, gnostic writers refer to
the first creation account in Genesis 1:26–27 ("Then God said,
Let us make man [adam] in our image, after our likeness . . . in
the image of God he created him; male and female he created
them"). Rabbis in Talmudic times knew a Greek version of the
passage that suggested to Rabbi Samuel bar Nachman, influenced
by Plato's myth of androgyny, that

when the Holy one . . . first created mankind, he created
him with two faces, two sets of genitals, four arms and legs,
back to back. Then he split Adam in two, and made two
backs, one on each side.[42]

Some gnostics adopted this idea, teaching that Genesis 1:26–27
narrates an androgynous creation. Marcus (whose prayer to the
Mother is given above) not only concludes from this account
that God is dyadic ("Let us make humanity") but also that
"humanity, which was formed according to the image and likeness of God (Father and Mother) was masculo-feminine."[43] His
contemporary, the gnostic Theodotus (c. 160), explains that the

saying "according to the image of God he made them, male and female he made them," means that "the male and female elements together constitute the finest production of the Mother, Wisdom."[44] Gnostic sources which describe God as a dyad whose nature includes both masculine and feminine elements often give a similar description of human nature.

Yet all the sources cited so far—secret gospels, revelations, mystical teachings—are among those not included in the select list that constitutes the New Testament collection. Every one of the secret texts which gnostic groups revered was omitted from the canonical collection, and branded as heretical by those who called themselves orthodox Christians. By the time the process of sorting the various writings ended—probably as late as the year 200—virtually all the feminine imagery for God had disappeared from orthodox Christian tradition.

What is the reason for this total rejection? The gnostics themselves asked this question of their orthodox opponents and pondered it among themselves. Some concluded that the God of Israel himself initiated the polemics which his followers carried out in his name. For, they argued, this creator was a derivative, merely instrumental power whom the Mother had created to administer the universe, but his own self-conception was far more grandiose. They say that he believed that he had made everything by himself, but that, in reality, he had created the world because Wisdom, his Mother, "infused him with energy" and implanted into him her own ideas. But he was foolish, and acted unconsciously, unaware that the ideas he used came from her; "he was even ignorant of his own Mother."[45] Followers of Valentinus suggested that the Mother Herself had encouraged the God of Israel to think that he was acting autonomously, but, as they explain, "It was because he was foolish and ignorant of his Mother that he said, 'I am God; there is none beside me.' "[46] According to another account, the creator caused his Mother to grieve by creating inferior beings, so she left him alone and withdrew into the upper regions of the heavens. "Since she had departed, he imagined that he was the only being in existence;

and therefore he declared, 'I am a jealous God, and besides me there is no one.' "[47] Others agree in attributing to him this more sinister motive—jealousy. According to the *Secret Book of John*:

> . . . he said . . . , "I am a jealous God, and there is no other God beside me." But by announcing this he indicated to the angels . . . that another God does exist; for if there were no other one, of whom would he be jealous? . . . Then the mother began to be distressed.[48]

Others declared that his Mother refused to tolerate such presumption:

> [The creator], becoming arrogant in spirit, boasted himself over all those things that were below him, and exclaimed, "I am father, and God, and above me there is no one." But his mother, hearing him speak thus, cried out against him, "Do not lie, Ialdabaoth . . ."[49]

Often, in these gnostic texts, the creator is castigated for his arrogance—nearly always by a superior feminine power. According to the *Hypostasis of the Archons*, discovered at Nag Hammadi, both the mother and her daughter objected when

> he became arrogant, saying, "It is I who am God, and there is no other apart from me." . . . And a voice came forth from above the realm of absolute power, saying, "You are wrong, Samael" [which means, "god of the blind"]. And he said, "If any other thing exists before me, let it appear to me!" And immediately, Sophia ("Wisdom") stretched forth her finger, and introduced light into matter, and she followed it down into the region of Chaos. . . . And he again said to his offspring, "It is I who am the God of All." And Life, the daughter of Wisdom, cried out; she said to him, "You are wrong, Saklas!"[50]

The gnostic teacher Justinus describes the Lord's shock, terror, and anxiety "when he discovered that he was not the God of the universe." Gradually his shock gave way to wonder, and finally he came to welcome what Wisdom had taught him. The teacher concludes: "This is the meaning of the saying, 'The fear of the Lord is the beginning of Wisdom.' "[51]

Yet all of these are mythical explanations. Can we find any actual, historical reasons why these gnostic writings were suppressed? This raises a much larger question: By what means, and for what reasons, did certain ideas come to be classified as heretical, and others as orthodox, by the beginning of the third century? We may find one clue to the answer if we ask whether gnostic Christians derive any practical, social consequences from their conception of God—and of humanity—in terms that included the feminine element. Here, clearly, the answer is *yes*.

Bishop Irenaeus notes with dismay that women especially are attracted to heretical groups. "Even in our own district of the Rhône valley," he admits, the gnostic teacher Marcus had attracted "many foolish women" from his own congregation, including the wife of one of Irenaeus' own deacons.[52] Professing himself to be at a loss to account for the attraction that Marcus' group held, he offers only one explanation: that Marcus himself was a diabolically clever seducer, a magician who compounded special aphrodisiacs to "deceive, victimize, and defile" his prey. Whether his accusations have any factual basis no one knows. But when he describes Marcus' techniques of seduction, Irenaeus indicates that he is speaking metaphorically. For, he says, Marcus "addresses them in such seductive words" as his prayers to Grace, "She who is before all things,"[53] and to Wisdom and Silence, the feminine element of the divine being. Second, he says, Marcus seduced women "by telling them to prophesy"[54]— which they were strictly forbidden to do in the orthodox church. When he initiated a woman, Marcus concluded the initiation prayer with the words "Behold, Grace has come upon you; open your mouth, and prophesy."[55] Then, as the bishop indignantly describes it, Marcus' "deluded victim . . . impudently utters some nonsense," and "henceforth considers herself to be a prophet!" Worst of all, from Irenaeus' viewpoint, Marcus invited women to act as priests in celebrating the eucharist with him: he "hands the cups to women"[56] to offer up the eucharistic prayer, and to pronounce the words of consecration.

Tertullian expresses similar outrage at such acts of gnostic Christians:

> These heretical women—how audacious they are! They have no modesty; they are bold enough to teach, to engage in argument, to enact exorcisms, to undertake cures, and, it may be, even to baptize![57]

Tertullian directed another attack against "that viper"[58]—a woman teacher who led a congregation in North Africa. He himself agreed with what he called the "precepts of ecclesiastical discipline concerning women," which specified:

> It is not permitted for a woman to speak in the church, nor is it permitted for her to teach, nor to baptize, nor to offer [the eucharist], nor to claim for herself a share in any *masculine* function—not to mention any priestly office.[59]

One of Tertullian's prime targets, the heretic Marcion, had, in fact, scandalized his orthodox contemporaries by appointing women on an equal basis with men as priests and bishops. The gnostic teacher Marcellina traveled to Rome to represent the Carpocratian group,[60] which claimed to have received secret teaching from Mary, Salome, and Martha. The Montanists, a radical prophetic circle, honored two women, Prisca and Maximilla, as founders of the movement.

Our evidence, then, clearly indicates a correlation between religious theory and social practice.[61] Among such gnostic groups as the Valentinians, women were considered equal to men; some were revered as prophets; others acted as teachers, traveling evangelists, healers, priests, perhaps even bishops. This general observation is not, however, universally applicable. At least three heretical circles that retained a masculine image of God included women who took positions of leadership—the Marcionites, the Montanists, and the Carpocratians. But from the year 200, we have no evidence for women taking prophetic, priestly, and episcopal roles among orthodox churches.

This is an extraordinary development, considering that in its earliest years the Christian movement showed a remarkable openness toward women. Jesus himself violated Jewish convention by talking openly with women, and he included them among his companions. Even the gospel of Luke in the New Testament tells his reply when Martha, his hostess, complains to him that she is doing housework alone while her sister Mary sits listening to him: "Do you not care that my sister has left me to serve alone? Tell her, then, to help me." But instead of supporting her, Jesus chides Martha for taking upon herself so many anxieties, declaring that "one thing is needful: Mary has chosen the good portion, which shall not be taken away from her."[62] Some ten to twenty years after Jesus' death, certain women held positions of leadership in local Christian groups; women acted as prophets, teachers, and evangelists. Professor Wayne Meeks suggests that, at Christian initiation, the person presiding ritually announced that "in Christ . . . there is neither male nor female."[63] Paul quotes this saying, and endorses the work of women he recognizes as deacons and fellow workers; he even greets one, apparently, as an outstanding apostle, senior to himself in the movement.[64]

Yet Paul also expresses ambivalence concerning the practical implications of human equality. Discussing the public activity of women in the churches, he argues from his own—traditionally Jewish—conception of a monistic, masculine God for a divinely ordained hierarchy of social subordination: as God has authority over Christ, he declares, citing Genesis 2–3, so man has authority over woman:

> . . . a man . . . is the image and glory of God; but woman is the glory of man. (For man was not made from woman, but woman from man. Neither was man created for woman, but woman for man.)[65]

While Paul acknowledged women as his equals "in Christ," and allowed for them a wider range of activity than did traditional

Jewish congregations, he could not bring himself to advocate their equality in social and political terms. Such ambivalence opened the way for the statements found in I Corinthians 14, 34 f., whether written by Paul or inserted by someone else: ". . . the women should keep silence in the churches. For they are not permitted to speak, but they should be subordinate . . . it is shameful for a woman to speak in church."

Such contradictory attitudes toward women reflect a time of social transition, as well as the diversity of cultural influences on churches scattered throughout the known world.[66] In Greece and Asia Minor, women participated with men in religious cults, especially the cults of the Great Mother and of the Egyptian goddess Isis.[67] While the leading roles were reserved for men, women took part in the services and professions. Some women took up education, the arts, and professions such as medicine. In Egypt, women had attained, by the first century A.D., a relatively advanced state of emancipation, socially, politically, and legally. In Rome, forms of education had changed, around 200 B.C., to offer to some children from the aristocracy the same curriculum for girls as for boys. Two hundred years later, at the beginning of the Christian era, the archaic, patriarchal forms of Roman marriage were increasingly giving way to a new legal form in which the man and woman bound themselves to each other with voluntary and mutual vows. The French scholar Jérôme Carcopino, in a discussion entitled "Feminism and Demoralization," explains that by the second century A.D., upper-class women often insisted upon "living their own life."[68] Male satirists complained of their aggressiveness in discussions of literature, mathematics, and philosophy, and ridiculed their enthusiasm for writing poems, plays, and music.[69] Under the Empire,

> women were everywhere involved in business, social life, such as theaters, sports events, concerts, parties, travelling—with or without their husbands. They took part in a whole range of athletics, even bore arms and went to battle . . .[70]

and made major inroads into professional life. Women of the Jewish communities, on the other hand, were excluded from actively participating in public worship, in education, and in social and political life outside the family.[71]

Yet despite all of this, and despite the previous public activity of Christian women, the majority of Christian churches in the second century went with the majority of the middle class in opposing the move toward equality, which found its support primarily in rich or what we would call bohemian circles. By the year 200, the majority of Christian communities endorsed as canonical the pseudo-Pauline letter of Timothy, which stresses (and exaggerates) the antifeminist element in Paul's views: "Let a woman learn in silence with all submissiveness. I permit no woman to teach or to have authority over men; she is to keep silent."[72] Orthodox Christians also accepted as Pauline the letters to the Colossians and to the Ephesians, which order that women "be subject in everything to their husbands."[73]

Clement, Bishop of Rome, writes in his letter to the unruly church in Corinth that women are to "remain in the rule of subjection"[74] to their husbands. While in earlier times Christian men and women sat together for worship, in the middle of the second century—precisely at the time of struggle with gnostic Christians—orthodox communities began to adopt the synagogue custom, segregating women from men.[75] By the end of the second century, women's participation in worship was explicitly condemned: groups in which women continued on to leadership were branded as heretical.

What was the reason for these changes? The scholar Johannes Leipoldt suggests that the influx of many Hellenized Jews into the movement may have influenced the church in the direction of Jewish traditions, but, as he admits, "this is only an attempt to explain the situation: *the reality itself is the only certain thing.*"[76] Professor Morton Smith suggests that the change may have resulted from Christianity's move up in social scale from lower to middle class. He observes that in the lower class, where all labor was needed, women had been allowed to perform any services they could (so today, in the Near East, only middle-class women are veiled).

Both orthodox and gnostic texts suggest that this question proved to be explosively controversial. Antagonists on both sides resorted to the polemical technique of writing literature that allegedly derived from apostolic times, professing to give the original apostles' views on the subject. As noted before, the *Gospel of Philip* tells of rivalry between the male disciples and Mary Magdalene, here described as Jesus' most intimate companion, the symbol of divine Wisdom:

> . . . the companion of the [Savior is] Mary Magdalene. [But Christ loved] her more than [all] the disciples and used to kiss her [often] on her [mouth]. The rest of [the disciples were offended by it . . .]. They said to him, "Why do you love her more than all of us?" The Savior answered and said to them, "Why do I not love you as [I love] her?"[77]

The *Dialogue of the Savior* not only includes Mary Magdalene as one of three disciples chosen to receive special teaching but also praises her above the other two, Thomas and Matthew: ". . . she spoke as a woman who knew the All."[78]

Other secret texts use the figure of Mary Magdalene to suggest that women's activity challenged the leaders of the orthodox community, who regarded Peter as their spokesman. The *Gospel of Mary* relates that when the disciples, disheartened and terrified after the crucifixion, asked Mary to encourage them by telling them what the Lord had told her secretly, she agrees, and teaches them until Peter, furious, asks, "Did he really speak privately with a woman, (and) not openly to us? Are we to turn about and all listen to her? Did he prefer her to us?" Distressed at his rage, Mary replies, "My brother Peter, what do you think? Do you think that I thought this up myself in my heart, or that I am lying about the Savior?" Levi breaks in at this point to mediate the dispute: "Peter, you have always been hot-tempered. Now I see you contending against the woman like the adversaries. But if the Savior made her worthy, who are you,

God the Father/God the Mother

indeed, to reject her? Surely the Lord knew her very well. That is why he loved her more than us."[79] Then the others agree to accept Mary's teaching, and, encouraged by her words, go out to preach. Another argument between Peter and Mary occurs in *Pistis Sophia* ("Faith Wisdom"). Peter complains that Mary is dominating the conversation with Jesus and displacing the rightful priority of Peter and his brother apostles. He urges Jesus to silence her and is quickly rebuked. Later, however, Mary admits to Jesus that she hardly dares speak to him freely because, in her words, "Peter makes me hesitate; I am afraid of him, because he hates the female race."[80] Jesus replies that whoever the Spirit inspires is divinely ordained to speak, whether man or woman.

Orthodox Christians retaliated with alleged "apostolic" letters and dialogues that make the opposite point. The most famous examples are, of course, the pseudo-Pauline letters cited above. In I and II Timothy, Colossians, and Ephesians, "Paul" insists that women be subordinate to men. The letter of Titus, in Paul's name, directs the selection of bishops in terms that entirely exclude women from consideration. Literally and figuratively, the bishop is to be a father figure to the congregation. He must be a man whose wife and children are "submissive [to him] in every way"; this proves his ability to keep "God's church"[81] in order, and its members properly subordinated. Before the end of the second century, the *Apostolic Church Order* appeared in orthodox communities. Here the apostles are depicted discussing controversial questions. With Mary and Martha present, John says,

> When the Master blessed the bread and the cup and signed them with the words, "This is my body and blood," he did not offer it to the women who are with us. Martha said, "He did not offer it to Mary, because he saw her laugh." Mary said, "I no longer laugh; he said to us before, as he taught, 'Your weakness is redeemed through strength.' "[82]

But her argument fails; the male disciples agree that, for this reason, no woman shall be allowed to become a priest.

[65]

We can see, then, two very different patterns of sexual attitudes emerging in orthodox and gnostic circles. In simplest form, many gnostic Christians correlate their description of God in both masculine and feminine terms with a complementary description of human nature. Most often they refer to the creation account of Genesis 1, which suggests an equal or androgynous human creation. Gnostic Christians often take the principle of equality between men and women into the social and political structures of their communities. The orthodox pattern is strikingly different: it describes God in exclusively masculine terms, and typically refers to Genesis 2 to describe how Eve was created from Adam, and for his fulfillment. Like the gnostic view, this translates into social practice: by the late second century, the orthodox community came to accept the domination of men over women as the divinely ordained order, not only for social and family life, but also for the Christian churches.

Yet exceptions to these patterns do occur. Gnostics were not unanimous in affirming women—nor were the orthodox unanimous in denigrating them. Certain gnostic texts undeniably speak of the feminine in terms of contempt. The *Book of Thomas the Contender* addresses men with the warning "Woe to you who love intimacy with womankind, and polluted intercourse with it!"[83] The *Paraphrase of Shem*, also from Nag Hammadi, describes the horror of Nature, who "turned her dark vagina and cast from her the power of fire, which was in her from the beginning, through the practice of darkness."[84] According to the *Dialogue of the Savior*, Jesus warns his disciples to "pray in the place where there is no woman," and to "destroy the works of femaleness . . ."[85]

Yet in each of these cases the target is not woman, but the power of sexuality. In the *Dialogue of the Savior*, for example, Mary Magdalene, praised as "the woman who knew the All," stands among the three disciples who receive Jesus' commands: she, along with Judas and Matthew, rejects the "works of femaleness"—that is, apparently, the activities of intercourse and procreation.[86] These sources show that some extremists in the gnostic movement agreed with certain radical feminists who today insist that only those who renounce sexual activity can achieve human equality and spiritual greatness.

Other gnostic sources reflect the assumption that the status of a man is superior to that of a woman. Nor need this surprise us; as language comes from social experience, any of these writers, whether man or woman, Roman, Greek, Egyptian, or Jewish, would have learned this elementary lesson from his or her social experience. Some gnostics, reasoning that as *man* surpasses *woman* in ordinary existence, so the *divine* surpasses the *human*, transform the terms into metaphor. The puzzling saying attributed to Jesus in the *Gospel of Thomas*—that Mary must become male in order to become a "living spirit, resembling you males. For every woman who will make herself male will enter the Kingdom of Heaven"[87]—may be taken symbolically: what is merely human (therefore *female*) must be transformed into what is divine (the "living spirit" the *male*). So, according to other passages in the *Gospel of Thomas*, Salome and Mary become Jesus' disciples when they transcend their human nature, and so "become male."[88] In the *Gospel of Mary*, Mary herself urges the other disciples to "praise his greatness, for he has prepared us, and made us into *men*."[89]

Conversely, we find a striking exception to the orthodox pattern in the writings of one revered father of the church, Clement of Alexandria. Clement, writing in Egypt c. 180, identifies himself as orthodox, although he knows members of gnostic groups and their writings well: some even suggest that he was himself a gnostic initiate. Yet his own works demonstrate how all three elements of what we have called the gnostic pattern could be worked into fully orthodox teaching. First, Clement characterizes God in feminine as well as masculine terms:

> The Word is everything to the child, both father and mother, teacher and nurse . . . The nutriment is the milk of the Father . . . and the Word alone supplies us children with

the milk of love, and only those who suck at this breast are truly happy. For this reason, seeking is called sucking; to those infants who seek the Word, the Father's loving breasts supply milk.[90]

Second, in describing human nature, he insists that

men and women share equally in perfection, and are to receive the same instruction and the same discipline. For the name "humanity" is common to both men and women; and for us "in Christ there is neither male nor female."[91]

As he urges women to participate with men in the community, Clement offers a list—unique in orthodox tradition—of women whose achievements he admires. They range from ancient examples, like Judith, the assassin who destroyed Israel's enemy, to Queen Esther, who rescued her people from genocide, as well as others who took radical political stands. He mentions Arignote the writer, Themisto the Epicurean philosopher, and many other women philosophers, including two who studied with Plato, and one trained by Socrates. Indeed, he cannot contain his praise:

What shall I say? Did not Theano the Pythagorean make such progress in philosophy that when a man, staring at her, said, "Your arm is beautiful," she replied, "Yes, but it is not on public display."[92]

Clement concludes his list with famous women poets and painters.

But Clement's demonstration that even orthodox Christians could affirm the feminine element—and the active participation of women—found little following. His perspective, formed in the cosmopolitan atmosphere of Alexandria and articulated among wealthy and educated members of Egyptian society, may have proved too alien for the majority of Western Christian communities which were scattered from Asia Minor to Greece, Rome, and provincial Africa and Gaul. The majority adopted instead the position of Clement's severe and provincial contemporary, Tertullian:

It is not permitted for a woman to speak in the church,
nor is it permitted for her to teach, nor to baptize, nor to
offer [the eucharist], nor to claim for herself a share in any
masculine function—least of all, in priestly office.[93]

Their consensus, which ruled out Clement's position, has continued to dominate the majority of Christian churches: nearly
2,000 years later, in 1977, Pope Paul VI, Bishop of Rome,
declared that a woman cannot be a priest "because our Lord
was a man"! The Nag Hammadi sources, discovered at a time
of contemporary social crises concerning sexual roles, challenge
us to reinterpret history—and to re-evaluate the present situation.

IV

The Passion of Christ and the Persecution of Christians

THERE IS ONLY one fact on which nearly all accounts about Jesus of Nazareth, whether written by persons hostile or devoted to him, agree: that, by order of the Roman prefect, Pontius Pilate, he was condemned and crucified (c. 30). Tacitus, the aristocratic Roman historian (c. 55–115), knowing virtually nothing about Jesus, mentions only this. Relating the history of the infamous Nero (emperor 54–58), he says that Nero, accused of starting major fires in Rome,

> substituted as culprits and punished with the utmost refinements of cruelty, a class of persons hated for their vices, whom the crowd called Christians. *Christus, the founder of the name, had undergone the death penalty in the reign of Tiberius, by sentence of the procurator Pontius Pilate*, and the pernicious superstition was checked for a moment, only to break out once more, not only in Judea, the home of the disease, but in the capital itself, where everything horrible or shameful in the world gathers and becomes fashionable.[1]

The Jewish historian Josephus mentions Jesus of Nazareth in a list of troubles that disturbed Jewish relations with Rome when Pilate was governor (roughly 26–36). A comment attributed to Josephus reports that "Pilate, having heard him accused by men of the highest standing among us . . . condemned him to be crucified."[2]

Jesus' followers confirm this report. The gospel of Mark, probably the earliest of the New Testament accounts (c. 70–80), tells how Jesus, betrayed by Judas Iscariot at night in the garden of Gethsemane opposite Jerusalem, was arrested by armed men as his disciples fled.[3] Charged with sedition before Pilate, he was condemned to death.[4] Crucified, Jesus lived for several hours before, as Mark tells it, he "uttered a loud cry"[5] and died. The gospels of Luke and John, written perhaps a generation later (c. 90–110), describe his death in more heroic terms: Jesus forgives his torturers, and, with a prayer, yields up his life.[6] Yet all four of the New Testament gospels describe his suffering, death, and hasty burial. The gospels, of course, interpret the circumstances leading to his death to demonstrate his innocence. Mark says that the chief priests and leaders in Jerusalem planned to have Jesus arrested and executed because of his teaching against them.[7] John presents a fuller account, historically plausible. He reports that as Jesus' popularity grew and attracted increasing numbers to his movement, the chief priests gathered the council of the Sanhedrin to discuss the dangers of riot. Some among the uneducated masses already acclaimed Jesus as Messiah[8]—the "anointed king" who they expected would liberate Israel from foreign imperialism and restore the Jewish state. Especially during Passover, when thousands of Jews poured into Jerusalem to celebrate the holiday, this impetus might ignite feelings of Jewish nationalism, already smoldering in the city, into revolt. The council held the responsibility for keeping the peace between the Jewish population and the Roman occupying army—a peace so tenuous that when, only a few years later, a Roman soldier stationed on guard in Jerusalem during Passover expressed his contempt by exposing himself in the Temple courtyard, his act provoked a riot in which 30,000 people are said to have lost their lives. Josephus, who tells this story, adds: "Thus the Feast ended in distress to the whole nation, and bereavement to every household."[9]

John reconstructs the council debate concerning Jesus: "What are we to do? . . . If we let him go on thus," the masses may demonstrate in favor of this alleged new Jewish king, "and the Romans will come and destroy both our holy place and our nation."[10] The chief priest Caiphas argued for the expedience of arresting one man at once, rather than endanger the whole population.[11] Even John had to recognize the political acumen of this reasoning: he wrote his account not long after the Jewish War of 66–70, an insurrection against Rome that ended in the total disaster which, according to John, Caiphas had predicted: the Temple burned to the ground, the city of Jerusalem devastated, the population decimated.

Yet if the sources agree on the basic facts of Jesus' execution, Christians sharply disagree on their interpretation. One gnostic text from Nag Hammadi, the *Apocalypse of Peter*, relates a radically different version of the crucifixion:

> . . . I saw him apparently being seized by them. And I said, "What am I seeing, O Lord? Is it really you whom they take? And are you holding on to me? And are they hammering the feet and hands of another? Who is this one above the cross, who is glad and laughing?" The Savior said to me, "He whom you saw being glad and laughing above the cross is the Living Jesus. But he into whose hands and feet they are driving the nails is his fleshly part, which is the substitute. They put to shame that which remained in his likeness. And look at him, and [look at] me!"[12]

Another of the Nag Hammadi texts, the *Second Treatise of the Great Seth*, relates Christ's teaching that

> it was another . . . who drank the gall and the vinegar; it was not I. They struck me with the reed; it was another, Simon,

who bore the cross on his shoulder. It was another upon
whom they placed the crown of thorns. But I was rejoicing
in the height over . . . their error . . . And I was laughing
at their ignorance.[13]

What does this mean? The *Acts of John*—one of the most
famous gnostic texts, and one of the few discovered before Nag
Hammadi, having somehow survived, in fragmentary form,
repeated denunciations by the orthodox—explains that Jesus was
not a human being at all; instead, he was a spiritual being who
adapted himself to human perception. The *Acts* tells how James
once saw him standing on the shore in the form of a child, but
when he pointed him out to John,

> I [John] said, "Which child?" And he answered me, "The
> one who is beckoning to us." And I said, "This is because
> of the long watch we have kept at sea. You are not seeing
> straight, brother James. Do you not see the man standing
> there who is handsome, fair and cheerful looking?" But he
> said to me, "I do not see that man, my brother."[14]

Going ashore to investigate, they became even more confused.
According to John,

> he appeared to me again as rather bald-⟨headed⟩ but with a
> thick flowing beard, but to James as a young man whose
> beard was just beginning. . . . I tried to see him as he was . . .
> But he sometimes appeared to me as a small man with no
> good looks, and then again as looking up to heaven.[15]

John continues:

> I will tell you another glory, brethren; sometimes when
> I meant to touch him I encountered a material, solid body;
> but at other times again when I felt him, his substance
> was immaterial and incorporeal . . . as if it did not exist at
> all.[16]

John adds that he checked carefully for footprints, but Jesus
never left any—nor did he ever blink his eyes. All of this
demonstrates to John that his nature was spiritual, not human.

The *Acts* goes on to tell how Jesus, anticipating arrest, joined with his disciples in Gethsemane the night before:

> . . . he assembled us all, and said, "Before I am delivered to them, let us sing a hymn to the Father, and so go to meet what lies before (us)." So he told us to form a circle, holding one another's hands, and himself stood in the middle . . .[17]

Instructing the disciples to "Answer Amen to me," he began to intone a mystical chant, which reads, in part,

> "To the Universe belongs the dancer."—"Amen."
> "He who does not dance does not know what happens."—"Amen." . . .
> "Now if you follow my dance, see yourself in Me who am speaking . . .
> You who dance, consider what I do, for yours is
> This passion of Man which I am to suffer. For you could by no means have understood what you suffer
> unless to you as Logos I had been sent by the Father . . .
> Learn how to suffer and you shall be able not to suffer."[18]

John continues:

> After the Lord had danced with us, my beloved, he went out [to suffer]. And we were like men amazed or fast asleep, and we fled this way and that. And so I saw him suffer, and did not wait by his suffering, but fled to the Mount of Olives and wept . . . And when he was hung (upon the Cross) on Friday, at the sixth hour of the day there came a darkness over the whole earth.[19]

At that moment John, sitting in a cave in Gethsemane, suddenly saw a vision of Jesus, who said,

> "John, for the people below . . . I am being crucified and pierced with lances . . . and given vinegar and gall to drink. But to you I am speaking, and listen to what I speak."[20]

Then the vision reveals to John a "cross of light," and explains that "I have suffered none of the things which they will say of me; even that suffering which I showed to you and to the rest in my dance, I will that it be called a mystery."[21] Other gnostics, followers of Valentinus, interpret the meaning of such paradoxes in a different way. According to the *Treatise on Resurrection*, discovered at Nag Hammadi, insofar as Jesus was the "Son of Man," being human, he suffered and died like the rest of humanity.[22] But since he was also "Son of God," the divine spirit within him could not die: in that sense he transcended suffering and death.

Yet orthodox Christians insist that Jesus *was* a human being, and that all "straight-thinking" Christians must take the crucifixion as a historical and literal event. To ensure this they place in the creed, as a central element of faith, the simple statement that "Jesus Christ suffered under Pontius Pilate, was crucified, dead, and buried." Pope Leo the Great (c. 447) condemned such writings as the *Acts of John* as "a hotbed of manifold perversity," which "should not only be forbidden, but entirely destroyed and burned with fire." But because heretical circles continued to copy and hide this text, the second Nicene Council, three hundred years later, had to repeat the judgment, directing that "No one is to copy [this book]: not only so, but we consider that it deserves to be consigned to the fire."

What lies behind this vehemence? Why does faith in the passion and death of Christ become an essential element—some say, *the* essential element—of orthodox Christianity? I am convinced that we cannot answer this question fully until we recognize that controversy over the interpretation of Christ's suffering and death involved, for Christians of the first and second centuries, an urgent practical question: How are believers to respond to persecution, which raises the imminent threat of their *own* suffering and death?

No issue could be more immediate to Jesus' disciples, having themselves experienced the traumatic events of his betrayal and arrest, and having heard accounts of his trial, torture, and final agony. From that time, especially when the most prominent among them, Peter and James, were arrested and executed, every Christian recognized that affiliation with the movement placed him in danger. Both Tacitus and Suetonius, the historian of the imperial court (c. 115), who shared an utter contempt for Christians, mention the group principally as the target of official persecution. In telling the life of Nero, Suetonius reports, in a list of the *good* things the emperor did, that "punishment was inflicted on the Christians, a class of persons given to a new and malificent superstition."[23] Tacitus adds to his remarks on the fire in Rome:

> First, then, those of the sect were arrested who confessed; next, on their disclosures, vast numbers were convicted, not so much on the count of arson, as for hatred of the human race. And ridicule accompanied their end: they were covered with wild beasts' skins and torn to death by dogs; or they were fastened on crosses, and, when daylight failed, were burned to serve as torches by night. Nero had offered his gardens for the spectacle . . .[24]

Tacitus interprets Nero's action in terms of his need for a scapegoat. As yet, the government may have considered the Christians outside Rome—if it considered them at all—too insignificant to initiate systematic action against the movement. But since the time that Augustus ruled as emperor (27 B.C.–A.D. 14), the emperor and the Senate had moved to repress any social dissidents whom they thought potential troublemakers, as they did astrologers, magicians, followers of foreign religious cults, and philosophers.[25] The Christian group bore all the marks of conspiracy. First, they identified themselves as followers of a man accused of magic[26] and executed for that and for treason; second, they were "atheists," who denounced as "demons" the gods who protected the fortunes of the Roman state—even the *genius* (divine spirit) of the emperor himself; third, they belonged to an illegal society. Besides these acts that police could verify, rumor indicated that their secrecy concealed atrocities: their enemies said that they ritually ate human flesh and drank human blood, practices of which magicians were commonly accused.[27] Although at this time no law specifically prohibited conversion to Christianity, any magistrate who heard a person accused of Christianity was required to investigate.[28] Uncertain about how to treat such cases, Pliny, the governor of Bythinia (a province in Asia Minor), wrote (c. 112) to Trajan, the emperor, requesting clarification:

> It is my custom, Lord Emperor, to refer to you all questions whereof I am in doubt. Who can better guide me . . . ? I have never participated in investigations of Christians; hence I do not know what is the crime usually punished or investigated, or what allowances are made . . . Meanwhile, this is the course I have taken with those who were accused before me as Christians. I asked them whether they were Christians, and I asked them a second and third time with threats of punishment. If they kept to it, I ordered them taken off for execution, for *I had no doubt that whatever it was they admitted, in any case they deserve to be punished for obstinacy and unbending pertinacity* . . . *As for those who said they neither were nor ever had been Christians, I thought it right to let them go*, when they recited a prayer to the gods at my dictation, and made supplication with incense and wine to your statue, which I had ordered to be brought into court for the purpose, and moreover, cursed Christ—things which (so it is said) those who are really Christians cannot be made to do.[29]

Trajan replied with approval for Pliny's handling of the matter:

> You have adopted the proper course, my dear Secundus, in your examination of the cases of those who were accused before you as Christians, for indeed, nothing can be laid down as a general rule involving something like a set form of procedure. *They are not to be sought out; but if they are accused and convicted, they must be punished*—but on the condition that whoever denies that he is a Christian, and makes the fact plain by his action, that is, by worshipping our gods, shall obtain pardon on his repentance, however suspicious his past conduct may be.[30]

But Trajan advised Pliny against accepting anonymous accusations, "since they are a bad example, and unworthy of our time." Pliny and Trajan agreed that anyone who would refuse such a gesture of loyalty must have serious crimes to hide, especially since the penalty for refusing was immediate execution.

Justin, a philosopher who had converted to Christianity (c. 150–155 A.D.), boldly wrote to the Emperor Antoninus Pius and to his son, the future emperor, Marcus Aurelius, whom he addressed as a colleague in philosophy and "a lover of learning,"[31] protesting the injustice Christians endured in imperial courts. Justin relates a recent case in Rome: a woman who had participated with her husband and their servants in various forms of sexual activity, fueled by wine, then converted to Christianity through the influence of her teacher Ptolemy, and subsequently refused to take part in such activities. Her friends persuaded her not to divorce, hoping for some reconciliation. But when she learned that, on a trip to Alexandria in Egypt, her husband had acted more flagrantly than ever, she sued for divorce and left him. Her outraged husband immediately brought a legal accusation against her, "affirming that she was a Christian." When she won a plea to delay her trial, her husband attacked her teacher in Christianity. Judge Urbicus, hearing the accusation, asked Ptolemy only one question: Was he a Christian? When he acknowledged that he was, Urbicus immediately sentenced him to death. Hearing this order, a man in the courtroom named Lucias challenged the judge:

> "What is the good of this judgment? Why have you punished this man, not as an adulterer, nor fornicator, nor thief, nor robber, nor convicted of any crime at all, but one who has only confessed that he is called by the name of Christian? This judgment of yours, Urbicus, does not become the Emperor Pius, nor the philosopher, the son of Caesar [Marcus Aurelius], nor the sacred Senate."[32]

Urbicus replied only, "You also seem to be one." And when Lucias said "Indeed I am," Urbicus condemned him—and a second protester in the audience—to follow Ptolemy to death.

Recounting this story, Justin points out that anyone can use the charge of Christianity to settle any personal grudge against a Christian: "I, too, therefore, expect to be plotted against and crucified"[33]—perhaps, he adds, by one of his professional rivals, the Cynic philosopher named Crescens. And Justin was right: apparently it was Crescens whose accusation led to his own arrest, trial, and condemnation in A.D. 165. Rusticus, a personal friend of Marcus Aurelius (who, by that time, had succeeded his father as emperor), conducted the trial. Rusticus ordered Justin's execution along with that of a whole group of his students, whose crime was learning Christian philosophy from him. The record of their trial shows that Rusticus asked Justin,

> "Where do you meet?" . . . "Wherever it is each one's preference or opportunity," said Justin. "In any case, do you suppose we can all meet in the same place? Not so; for the Christians' God is not circumscribed by place; invisible, he fills the heavens and the earth, and is worshipped and glorified by believers everywhere."
>
> Rusticus the prefect said, "Tell me, where do you meet? Where do you gather together your disciples?"
>
> Justin said, "I have been living above the baths of a certain Martinus, son of Timiotinus, and for the entire period of my stay at Rome (and this is my second) I have known no other meeting place but there. Anyone who wished could come to my abode and I would impart to him the words of truth."
>
> The prefect Rusticus said, "You do admit, then, that you are a Christian?" "Yes, I am," said Justin.[34]

Then Rusticus interrogated Cariton, the woman named Charito, Euelpistis, a slave in the imperial court, Hierax, Liberian, and Paeon—all of them Justin's students. All declared themselves Christians. The account proceeds:

> "Well, then," said the prefect Rusticus, "let us come to the point at issue, a necessary and pressing business. Agree to offer sacrifice to the gods."

"No one of sound mind," said Justin, "turns from piety to impiety."

The prefect Rusticus said, "If you do not obey, you will be punished without mercy."[35]

When they replied, "Do what you will; we are Christians, and we do not offer sacrifice to idols," Rusticus pronounced sentence: "Let those who have refused to sacrifice to the gods and to yield to the emperor's edict be led away to be scourged and beheaded in accordance with the laws."[36]

Given this danger, what was a Christian to do? Once arrested and accused, should one confess to being a Christian, only to receive an order of execution: immediate beheading if one was fortunate enough to be a Roman citizen, like Justin and his companions, or, for noncitizens, extended torture as a spectacle in the public sports arena? Or should one deny it and make the token gesture of loyalty—intending afterwards to atone for the lie?

Charged with the unpleasant duty of ordering executions for noncompliance, Roman officials often tried to persuade the accused to save their own lives. According to contemporary accounts (c. 165), after the aged and revered Bishop Polycarp of Smyrna, in Asia Minor, was arrested by the police,

> the governor tried to persuade him to recant, saying, "Have respect for your age," *and other similar things that they usually say*; "Swear by the *genius* of the emperor. Recant. Say, 'Away with the atheists!' " Polycarp, with a sober expression, looked at all the mob of lawless pagans who were in the stadium . . . and said, "Away with the atheists!" The governor persisted and said, "Swear and I will let you go. Curse Christ!" But Polycarp answered, "For eighty-six years I have been his servant, and he has done me no wrong . . . If you delude yourself into thinking that I will swear by the emperor's *genius*, as you say, and if you pretend not to know who I am, listen and I will tell you plainly: I am a Christian."[37]

Polycarp was burned alive in the public arena.

An account from North Africa (c. 180) describes how the proconsul Saturninus, confronted by nine men and three women arraigned as Christians, worked to spare their lives, saying,

> "If you return to your senses, you can obtain pardon of our lord the emperor . . . We too are a religious people, and our religion is a simple one: We swear by the *genius* of our lord the emperor and offer prayers for his health—as you ought to do too."[38]

Meeting their determined resistance, Saturninus asked, "You wish no time for reconsideration?" Speratus, one of the accused, replied, "In so just a matter, there is no need for consideration." In spite of this, the proconsul ordered a thirty-day reprieve with the words "Think it over." But thirty days later, after interrogating the accused, Saturninus was forced to give the order:

> Whereas Speratus, Narzalus, Cittinus, Donata, Vestia, Secunda, and the others have confessed that they have been living in accordance with the rites of the Christians, and whereas, though they have been given the opportunity to return to the Roman usage, they have persevered in their obstinacy, they are hereby condemned to be executed by the sword.[39]

Speratus said, "We thank God!" Narzalus said, "Today we are martyrs in heaven. Thanks be to God!"

Such behavior provoked the scorn of the Stoic Emperor Marcus Aurelius, who despised the Christians as morbid and misguided exhibitionists. Many today might agree with his judgment, or else dismiss the martyrs as neurotic masochists. Yet for Jews and Christians of the first and second centuries, the term bore a different connotation: *martus* simply means, in Greek, "witness." In the Roman Empire, as in many countries throughout the world today, members of certain religious groups fell under government suspicion as organizations that fostered criminal or treasonous activities. Those who, like Justin, dared to protest publicly the unjust treatment Christians received in court made themselves likely targets of police action. For those caught in such a situation then, as now, the choice was often simple: either to speak out, risking arrest, torture, the formality of a futile trial, and exile or death—or to keep silent and remain safe. Their fellow believers revered those who spoke out as "confessors" and regarded only those who actually endured through death as "witnesses" (*martyres*).

But not all Christians spoke out. Many, at the moment of decision, made the opposite choice. Some considered martyrdom foolish, wasteful of human life, and so, contrary to God's will. They argued that "Christ, having died for us, was killed so that we might not be killed."[40] As past events become matters of religious conviction only when they serve to interpret present experience, here the interpretation of Christ's death became the focus for controversy over the practical question of martyrdom.

The orthodox who expressed the greatest concern to refute "heretical" gnostic views of Christ's passion were, without exception, persons who knew from firsthand experience the dangers to which Christians were exposed—and who insisted on the necessity of accepting martyrdom. When that great opponent of heresy, Ignatius, Bishop of Antioch, was arrested and tried, he is said to have accepted the death sentence with joyful exultation as his opportunity to "imitate the passion of my God!"[41] Condemned to be sent from Syria to Rome to be killed by wild beasts in the public amphitheater, Ignatius, chained and heavily guarded, wrote to the Christians in Rome, pleading with them not to interfere in his behalf:

> I am writing to all the churches, and I give injunction to everyone, that I am dying willingly for God's sake, if you do not prevent it. I plead with you not to be an "unseasonable kindness" to me. Allow me to be eaten by the beasts, through whom I can attain to God. I am God's wheat, and I am ground by the teeth of wild beasts, so that I may become pure bread of Christ . . . Do me this favor . . . Let there come upon me fire, and the cross, and struggle with wild beasts, cutting and tearing apart, racking of bones,

mangling of limbs, crushing of my whole body . . . may I
but attain to Jesus Christ![42]

What does Christ's passion mean to him? Ignatius says that
"Jesus Christ . . . was truly persecuted under Pontius Pilate, was
truly crucified, and died."[43] He vehemently opposes gnostic
Christians, whom he calls "atheists" for suggesting that since
Christ was a spiritual being, he only *appeared* to suffer and die:

> But if, as some say . . . his suffering was only an appear-
> ance, then *why am I a prisoner, and why do I long to fight
> with the wild beasts? In that case, I am dying in vain.*[44]

Ignatius complains that those who qualify his view of Christ's
suffering "are not moved by my own personal sufferings; for
they think the same things about me!"[45] His gnostic opponents,
challenging his understanding of Christ's passion, directly call
into question the value of his voluntary martyrdom.

Justin, whom tradition calls "the martyr," declares that
before his own conversion, when he was still a Platonist
philosopher, he personally witnessed Christians enduring public
torture and execution. Their courage, he says, convinced him
of their divine inspiration.[46] Protesting the world-wide persecution of Christians, he mentions those persecuted in Palestine
(c. 135):

> It is clear that no one can terrify or subdue us who
> believe in Jesus Christ, throughout the whole world. For it
> is clear that though beheaded, and crucified, and thrown to
> the wild beasts, in chains, in fire, and all other kinds of
> torture, we do not give up our confession; but the more
> such things happen, the more do others, in larger numbers,
> become believers.[47]

Consistent with his personal convictions concerning martyrdom
and his courageous acceptance of his own death sentence is
Justin's view that "Jesus Christ, our teacher, who was born for
this purpose, was crucified under Pontius Pilate and died, and

rose again."[48] Justin concludes his second *Apology* ("Defense" for the Christians) saying that he has written it for the sole purpose of refuting "wicked and deceitful" gnostic ideas. He attacks those who, he says, are "called Christians," but whom he considers heretics—followers of Simon, Marcion, and Valentinus.[49] "We do not know," he says darkly—combining admission with insinuation—whether they actually indulge in promiscuity or cannibalism, but, he adds, "we do know" one of their crimes: unlike the orthodox, "they are neither persecuted nor put to death" as martyrs.

Irenaeus, the great opponent of the Valentinians, was, like his predecessors, a man whose life was marked by persecution. He mentions many who were martyred in Rome, and he knew from personal experience the loss of his beloved teacher Polycarp, caught in mob violence, condemned, and burned alive among his enemies. Only twelve years later, in the summer of 177, Irenaeus witnessed growing hostility to Christians in his own city, Lyons. First they were prohibited from entering public places—the markets and the baths. Then, when the provincial governor was out of the city,

> the mob broke loose. Christians were hounded and attacked openly. They were treated as public enemies, assaulted, beaten, and stoned. Finally they were dragged into the Forum . . . were accused, and, after confessing to being Christians, they were flung in prison.[50]

An influential friend, Vettius Epagathus, who tried to intervene at their trial, was shouted down: "The prefect merely asked him if he too was a Christian. When he admitted, in the clearest voice, that he was,"[51] the prefect sentenced him to death along with the others. Their servants, tortured to extract information, finally "confessed" that, as the Romans suspected, their Christian employers committed sexual atrocities and cannibalism. An eyewitness account reports that this evidence turned the population against them: "These stories got around, and all the people raged against us, so that even those whose attitude had been moderate before because of their friendship with us now became greatly angry and gnashed their teeth against us."[52]

Every day new victims—the most outspoken members of the churches in Lyons or the neighboring town of Vienne, twenty miles down the Rhône River, were arrested and brutally tortured in prison as they awaited the day set for the mass execution, August 1. This was a holiday to celebrate the greatness of Rome and the emperor. Such occasions required the governor to display his patriotism by sponsoring lavish public entertainment for the whole population of the city. These obligations burdened provincial officials with enormous expenses for hiring professional gladiators, boxers, wrestling teams, and swordsmen. But the year before, the emperor and the Senate had passed a new law to offset the cost of gladitorial shows. Now the governor could legally substitute condemned criminals who were noncitizens, offering the spectacle of their torture and execution instead of athletic exhibitions—at the cost of six aurei per head, one-tenth the cost of hiring a fifth-class gladiator, with proportionate savings for the higher grades. This consideration no doubt added incentive to the official zeal against Christians, who could provide, as they did in Lyons, the least expensive holiday entertainment.

The story of one of the confessors in Lyons, the slave woman Blandina, illustrates what happened:

> All of us were in terror; and Blandina's earthly mistress, who was herself among the martyrs in the conflict, was in agony lest because of her bodily weakness she would not be able to make a bold confessor of her faith. Yet Blandina was filled with such power that even those who were taking turns to torture her in every way from dawn to dusk were weary and exhausted. They themselves admitted that they were beaten, that there was nothing further they could do to her, and they were surprised that she was still breathing, for her entire body was broken and torn.

[85]

On the day set for the gladitorial games, Blandina, along with three of her companions, Maturus, Sanctus, and Attalus, were led into the amphitheater:

> Blandina was hung on a post and exposed as bait for the wild animals that were let loose on her. She seemed to hang there in the form of a cross, and by her fervent prayer she aroused intense enthusiasm in those who were undergoing their ordeal . . . But none of the animals had touched her, and so she was taken down from the post and brought back to the jail to be preserved for another ordeal . . . tiny, weak, and insignificant as she was, she would give inspiration to her brothers . . . Finally, on the last day of the gladitorial games, they brought back Blandina again, this time with a boy of fifteen named Ponticus. Every day they had been brought in to watch the torture of the others, while attempts were made to force them to swear by the pagan idols. And because they persevered and condemned their persecutors, the crowd grew angry with them, so that . . . they subjected them to every atrocity and led them through every torture in turn.

After having run through the gauntlet of whips, having been mauled by animals, and forced into an iron seat placed over a fire to scorch his flesh, Ponticus died. Blandina, having survived the same tortures,

> was at last tossed into a net and exposed to a bull. After being tossed a good deal by the animal, she no longer perceived what was happening . . . Thus she too was offered in sacrifice, while the pagans themselves admitted that no woman had ever suffered so much in their experience.[53]

Although Irenaeus himself somehow managed to escape arrest, his association with those in prison compelled him to bring an account of their terrible suffering to Christians in Rome. When he returned to Gaul, he found the community in mourning: nearly fifty Christians had died in the two-month ordeal. He himself was persuaded to take over the leadership of the community, succeeding the ninety-year-old Bishop Pothinus, who had died of torture and exposure in prison.

In spite of all this, Irenaeus expresses no hostility against his fellow townsmen—but plenty against the gnostic "heretics." Like Justin, he attacks them as "false brethren" who

> have reached such a pitch of audacity that *they even pour contempt upon the martyrs, and vituperate those who are killed on account of confessing the Lord*, and *who . . . thereby strive to follow in the footsteps of the Lord's passion*, themselves bearing witness to the one who suffered.[54]

This declaration concludes his detailed attack on the Valentinian interpretation of Christ's passion. Condemning as blasphemy their claim that only Christ's *human* nature experiences suffering, while his divine nature transcends it, Irenaeus insists that

> *the same being who was seized and experienced suffering, and shed his blood for us, was both Christ and the Son of God* . . . and he became the Savior of those who would be delivered over to death for their confession of him, and lose their lives.[55]

Indeed, he adds, "if any one supposes that there were two natures in Christ," the one who suffered was certainly superior to the one who escaped suffering, sustaining neither injury nor insult." In the day of judgment, he warns, when the martyrs "attain to glory, then all who have cast a slur upon their martyrdom shall be confounded by Christ."[56]

Tertullian, another fierce opponent of heresy, describes how the sight of Christians tortured and dying initiated his own conversion: he saw a condemned Christian, dressed up by Roman guards to look like the god Attis, torn apart alive in the arena; another, dressed as Hercules, was burned alive. He admits that he, too, once enjoyed "the ludicrous cruelties of the noonday exhibition,"[57] watching another man, dressed as the god Mercury, testing the bodies of the tortured with a red-hot iron, and one dressed as Pluto, god of the dead, dragging corpses out of the arena. After his own conversion Tertullian, like Irenaeus, connected the teaching of Christ's passion and death with his own enthusiasm for martyrdom: "You must take up your cross and bear it after your Master . . . The sole key to unlock Paradise is your own life's blood."[58] Tertullian traces the rise of heresy directly to the outbreak of persecution. This, he says, impelled terrified believers to look for theological means to justify their cowardice:

> This among Christians is a time of persecution. *When, therefore, the faith is greatly agitated and the church on fire . . . then the gnostics break out; then the Valentinians creep forth; then all the opponents of martyrdom bubble up* . . . for they know that many Christians are simple and inexperienced and weak, and . . . they perceive that they will never be applauded more than when fear has opened the entries of the soul, especially when some terrorism has already arrayed with a crown the faith of martyrs.[59]

To what he considers "heretical" arguments against martyrdom Tertullian replies:

> Now we are in the midst of an intense heat, the very dogstar of persecution . . . the fire and the sword have tried some Christians, and the beasts have tried others; others are in prison, longing for martyrdoms which they have tasted already, having been beaten by clubs and tortured . . . We ourselves, having been appointed for pursuit, are like hares being hemmed in from a distance—*and the heretics go about as usual!*[60]

This situation, he explains, inspired him to attack as heretics those "who oppose martyrdom, representing salvation to be destruction," and who call encouragement to martyrdom foolish and cruel.

Hippolytus, the learned Greek teacher in Rome, also had witnessed the terror of the persecution under the Emperor Severus in the year 202. Hippolytus' zeal for martyrdom, like Tertullian's, was matched by his hatred of heresy. He concludes his massive *Refutation of All Heresies* insisting that only orthodox doctrine concerning Christ's incarnation and passion enables the believer to endure persecution:

> *If he were not of the same nature with ourselves, he would command in vain that we should imitate the teacher* . . . He did not protest against his passion, but became obedient unto death . . . now in all these acts *he offered up, as the first fruits, his own humanity, in order that you, when you are in tribulation, may not be discouraged, but, confessing yourself to be one like the redeemer,* may dwell in expectation of receiving what the Father has granted to the Son.[61]

In his mid-seventies, Hippolytus himself fulfilled his own exhortation: arrested on the order of the Emperor Maximin in 235, he was deported to Sardinia, where he died.

What pattern, then, do we observe? The opponents of heresy in the second century—Ignatius, Polycarp, Justin, Irenaeus, Tertullian, Hippolytus—are unanimous both in proclaiming Christ's passion and death and in affirming martyrdom. Also, they all accuse the heretics of false teaching about Christ's suffering and of "opposing martyrdom." Irenaeus declares:

> *The church in every place, because of the love which she cherishes toward God, sends forth, throughout all time, a multitude of martyrs to the Father; while all others not only have nothing of this kind to point to among themselves, but even maintain that bearing witness (martyrium) is not at all necessary* . . . with the exception, perhaps, of one or two among them . . . who have occasionally, along with our martyrs, borne the reproach of the name . . . For the church alone sustains with purity the reproach of those who suffer persecution for righteousness' sake, and endure all sorts of punishments, and are put to death because of the love which they bear toward God, and their confession of his Son.[62]

Irenaeus here denies to gnostics who die for the faith even the name of martyrs: at best they are only "a sort of retinue" granted to the *true* martyrs, who are orthodox Christians.

Although Irenaeus undoubtedly exaggerated the infrequency of martyrdom among the heretics, martyrdom did occur rarely among gnostic Christians. The reason was not simply cowardice, as the orthodox charged, but also the differences of opinion among them. What attitudes did gnostics take toward martyrdom, and on what grounds? Evidence from Nag Hammadi shows that their views were astonishingly diverse. Some advocated it; others repudiated it on principle. Followers of Valentinus took a mediating position between these extremes. But one thing is clear: in every case, the attitude toward martyrdom corresponds to the interpretation of Christ's suffering and death.

Some groups of gnostics, like the orthodox, insisted that Christ really suffered and died. It is claimed that several texts discovered at Nag Hammadi, including the *Secret Book of James*, the *Second Apocalypse of James*, and the *Apocalypse of Peter*, were written by disciples known to have undergone martyrdom —James, the brother of Jesus, and Peter. The author of the *Secret Book of James*, probably a Christian living in the second century who was anxious about the prospect of persecution, places himself in the situation of James and Peter. As they anticipate undergoing torture and death, he reports, they receive a vision of the risen Lord, who interprets the ordeals they face in terms of his own:

> . . . If you are oppressed by Satan and persecuted, and you do his [the Father's] will, I [say] that he will love you and make you equal with me . . . *Do you not know that you have yet to be abused and to be accused unjustly; and have yet to be shut up in prison, and condemned unlawfully, and crucified ⟨without⟩ reason, and buried ⟨shamefully⟩, as I ⟨was⟩ myself?* . . . Truly I say to you, none will be saved unless they believe in my cross. But those who have believed in my cross, theirs is the kingdom of God. . . . Truly I say to you, none of those who fear death will be saved; for *the kingdom of death belongs to those who put themselves to death.*[63]

This gnostic author not only insists that Christ really suffered and died, but even encourages believers to choose suffering and death. Like Ignatius, this gnostic teacher believes that one becomes identified with Christ through suffering: "Make yourselves like the Son of the Holy Spirit!"[64]

The same concern with persecution, and a similar analogy between the believer's experience and the Savior's passion, dominates the *Second Apocalypse of James*. The Savior, "who lived [without] blasphemy, died by means of [blasphemy]."[65] As he dies he says, "I am surely dying, but I shall be found in life."[66] The *Apocalypse* climaxes with the brutal scene of James's own torture and death by stoning:

> . . . the priests . . . found him standing beside the columns of the temple, beside the mighty corner stone. And they decided to throw him down from the height, and they cast him down. And . . . they seized him and [struck] him as they dragged him on the ground. They stretched him out, and placed a stone on his abdomen. They all placed their feet on him, saying, "You have erred!" Again they raised him up, since he was alive, and made him dig a hole. They made him stand in it. After having covered him up to his abdomen, they stoned him.[67]

As he dies he offers a prayer intended to strengthen other Christians who face martyrdom. Like Jesus, James is "surely dying," but "shall be found in life."

But while some gnostics affirmed the reality of Christ's passion and expressed enthusiasm for martyrdom, others denied that reality and attacked such enthusiasm. The *Testimony of Truth* declares that enthusiasts for martyrdom do not know "who Christ is":

> The foolish—thinking in their heart that if they confess, "We are Christians," in word only [but] not with power, while giving themselves over to ignorance, to a human death, not knowing where they are going, nor who Christ is, thinking that they will live, when they are (really) in

error—hasten toward the principalities and authorities. They fall into their clutches because of the ignorance that is in them.[68]

The author ridicules the popular view that martyrdom ensures salvation: if it were that simple, he says, *everyone* would confess Christ and be saved! Those who live under such illusions

> are [empty] martyrs, since they bear witness only [to] themselves. . . . When they are "perfected" with a (martyr's) death, this is what they are thinking: "If we deliver ourselves over to death for the sake of the Name, we shall be saved." These matters are not settled in this way. . . . They do not have the Word which gives [life].[69]

This gnostic author attacks specific views of martyrdom familiar from orthodox sources. First, he attacks the conviction that the martyr's death offers forgiveness of sins, a view expressed, for example, in the orthodox account of Polycarp's martyrdom: "Through suffering of one hour they purchase for themselves eternal life."[70] Tertullian, too, declares that he himself desires to suffer "that he may obtain from God complete forgiveness, by giving in exchange his blood."[71] Second, this author ridicules orthodox teachers who, like Ignatius and Tertullian, see martyrdom as an offering to God and who have the idea that God desires "human sacrifice": such a belief makes God into a cannibal. Third, he attacks those who believe that martyrdom ensures their resurrection. Rusticus, the Roman judge, asked Justin, only moments before ordering his execution, "Listen, you who are considered educated . . . do you suppose you will ascend to heaven?" Justin answered, "I do not *suppose* it, but I know it certainly and am fully persuaded of it."[72] But the *Testimony of Truth* declares that such Christians are only "destroying themselves"—they were deluded into thinking that Christ shared their own mortality, when in reality he, being filled with divine power, was alien to suffering and to death:

> The Son of Man [came] forth from imperishability, [being] alien to defilement. . . . he went down to Hades

and performed mighty works. He raised the dead therein
. . . and he also destroyed their works from among men, so
that the lame, the blind, the paralytic, and the dumb, (and)
the demon-possessed were granted healing. . . . For this
reason he [destroyed] his flesh from [the cross] which he
[bore].[73]

The *Apocalypse of Peter* discloses how Peter, noted for his
misunderstanding, becomes enlightened and discovers the true
secret of Jesus' passion. The author of this book, like the author
of the *Secret Book of James*, apparently was a gnostic Christian
concerned with the threat of persecution. As the *Apocalypse*
opens, "Peter" fears that he and his Lord face the same danger:
". . . I saw the priests and the people running up to us with
stones as if they would kill us; and I was afraid we were going
to die."[74] But Peter falls into an ecstatic trance and receives a
vision of the Lord, who warns him that many who "accept our
teaching in the beginning"[75] will fall into error. These "false
believers" (described, of course, from the gnostic viewpoint)
represent orthodox Christians. All who fall under their influence
"shall become their prisoners, since they are without perception."[76]

What the gnostic author dislikes most about these Christians
is that they coerce innocent fellow believers "to the executioner"
—apparently the forces of the Roman state—under the illusion
that if they "hold fast to the name of a dead man," confessing
the crucified Christ, "they will become pure."[77] The author says,

". . . These are the ones who oppress their brothers,
saying to them, 'Through this [martyrdom] our God shows
mercy, since salvation comes to us from this.' They do not
know the punishment of those who are gladdened by those
who have done this deed to the little ones who have been
sought out and imprisoned."[78]

The author rejects orthodox propaganda for martyrdom—that
it earns salvation—and expresses horror at their exclamations of
joy over acts of violence done to the "little ones." In this way

the catholic community will "set forth a harsh fate";[79] many believers "will be ground to pieces among them."[80]

Yet while the *Apocalypse of Peter* rejects the orthodox view of martyrdom, it does not reject martyrdom altogether: "others of those who suffer" (that is, those who have attained *gnosis*) acquire a new understanding of the meaning of their own suffering; they understand that it "will perfect the wisdom of the brotherhood that really exists."[81] In place of the teaching that enslaves believers—the orthodox teaching of the crucified Christ—the Savior gives Peter the new vision of his passion that we noted before:

> . . . He whom you saw being glad and laughing above the cross, he is the Living Jesus. But he into whose hands and feet they are driving the nails is his fleshly part, which is the substitute. They put to shame that which remained in his likeness. And look at him, and (look at) me!"[82]

Through this vision, Peter learns to face suffering. Initially, he feared that he and the Lord "would die"; now he understands that only the body, "the fleshly counterpart," the "substitute," can die. The Lord explains that the "primal part," the intelligent spirit, is released to join "the perfect light with my holy spirit."[83]

Gnostic sources written by Valentinus and his followers are more complex than either those which simply affirm Christ's passion or those which claim that, apart from his mortal body, Christ remained utterly impervious to suffering. Several major Valentinian texts discovered at Nag Hammadi clearly acknowledge Jesus' passion and death. The *Gospel of Truth*, which Quispel attributes to Valentinus or a follower of his, tells how Jesus, "nailed to a tree," was "slain."[84] Extending the common Christian metaphor, the author envisions Jesus on the cross as fruit on a tree, a new "fruit of the tree of knowledge" that yields life, not death:

> . . . nailed to a tree; he became a fruit of the knowledge [*gnosis*] of the Father, which did not, however, become destructive because it ⟨was⟩ eaten, but gave to those who

ate it cause to become glad in the discovery. For he discovered them in himself, and they discovered him in themselves . . .[85]

Contrary to orthodox sources, which interpret Christ's death as a sacrifice redeeming humanity from guilt and sin, this gnostic gospel sees the crucifixion as the occasion for discovering the divine self within. Yet with this different interpretation, the *Gospel of Truth* gives a moving account of Jesus' death:

> . . . the merciful one, the faithful one, Jesus, was patient in accepting sufferings . . . since he knows that his death is life for many. . . . He was nailed to a tree . . . He draws himself down to death though eternal life clothes him. Having stripped himself of the perishable rags, he put on imperishability . . .[86]

Another remarkable Valentinian text, the *Tripartite Tractate*, introduces the Savior as "the one who will be begotten and who will suffer."[87] Moved by compassion for humanity, he willingly became

> what they were. So, for their sake, he became manifest in an involuntary suffering. . . . Not only did he take upon himself the death of those whom he intended to save, but also he accepted their smallness . . . He let himself be conceived and born as an infant in body and soul.[88]

Yet the Savior's nature is a paradox. The *Tripartite Tractate* explains that the one who is born and who suffers is the Savior foreseen by the Hebrew prophets; what they did not envision is "that which he was before, and what he is eternally, an unbegotten, impassible Word, who came into being in flesh."[89] Similarly, the *Gospel of Truth*, having described Jesus' human death, goes on to say that

> the Word of the Father goes forth into the all . . . purifying it, bringing it back into the Father, into the Mother, Jesus of the infiniteness of gentleness.[90]

A third Valentinian text, the *Interpretation of the Gnosis*, articulates the same paradox. On the one hand the Savior becomes vulnerable to suffering and death; on the other, he is the Word, full of divine power. The Savior explains: "I became very small, so that through my humility I might take you up to the great height, whence you had fallen."[91]

None of these sources denies that Jesus actually suffered and died; all assume it. Yet all are concerned to show how, in his incarnation, Christ transcended human nature so that he could prevail over death by divine power.[92] The Valentinians thereby initiate discussion of the problem that became central to Christian theology some two hundred years later—the question of how Christ could be simultaneously human and divine. For this, Adolf von Harnack, historian of Christianity, calls them the "first Christian theologians."

What does this mean for the question of martyrdom? Irenaeus accuses the Valentinians of "pouring contempt" on the martyrs and "casting a slur upon their martyrdom." What is their position? Heracleon, the distinguished gnostic teacher, himself a student of Valentinus', directly discusses martyrdom as he comments on Jesus' saying:

> ". . . every one who acknowledges me before men, the Son of Man also will acknowledge before the angels of God; but he who denies me before men will be denied before the angels of God. . . . And when they bring you before . . . the rulers and the authorities, do not be anxious how or what you are to answer . . ."[93]

Heracleon considers the question, What does it mean to "confess Christ"? He explains that people confess Christ in different ways. Some confess Christ in their faith and in their everyday conduct. However, most people consider only the second type of confession—making a verbal confession ("I am a Christian") before a magistrate. The latter, he says, is what "the many" (orthodox Christians) consider to be the *only* confession. But, Heracleon points out, "even hypocrites can make this confession." What is required universally of all Christians, he says, is the first type of confession; the second is required of some, but not of all. Disciples like Matthew, Philip, and Thomas never "confessed" before the magistrates; still, he declares, they confessed Christ in the superior way, "in faith and conduct throughout their whole lives."[94]

In naming these specific disciples, who often typify gnostic initiates (as in the *Gospel of Philip* and the *Gospel of Thomas*), Heracleon implies that they are superior to such martyr-apostles as Peter, whom the Valentinians consider typical of "the many" —that is, of merely *orthodox* Christians. Is he saying that martyrdom is fine for ordinary Christians, but not necessary for gnostics? Is he offering a rationale for gnostics to avoid martyrdom?

If that is what he means, he avoids stating it directly: his comments remain ambiguous. For he goes on to say that although confessing Christ "in faith and conduct" is more universal, this leads naturally to making an open confession at a trial, "if necessity and reason dictate." What makes such confession "necessary" and "rational"? Simply that a Christian accused before a judge cannot *deny* Christ: in that case, Heracleon admits, verbal confession is the necessary and rational alternative to denial.

Yet Heracleon articulates a wholly different attitude toward martyrdom from his orthodox contemporaries. He expresses none of their enthusiasm for martyrdom, none of their praise for the "glorious victory" earned through death. Above all, he never suggests that the believers' suffering imitates Christ's. For if only the *human* element in Christ experienced the passion, this suggests that the believer, too, suffers only on a human level while the divine spirit within transcends suffering and death. Apparently the Valentinians considered the martyr's "blood witness" to be second best to the superior, *gnostic* witness to Christ—a view that could well have provoked Irenaeus' anger that these gnostics "show contempt" for the martyrs and devalue what he considers the "ultimate sacrifice."

Although Irenaeus acknowledges that the gnostics are attempting to raise the level of theological understanding, he declares that "they cannot accomplish a reformation effective enough to compensate for the harm they are doing."[95] From his viewpoint, any argument that Christians could use to avoid martyrdom undermines the solidarity of the whole Christian community. Rather than identifying with those held in prison, facing torture or execution, gnostic Christians might withdraw support from those they consider overzealous and unenlightened fanatics. Such actions serve, Irenaeus says, to "cut in pieces the great and glorious body of Christ [the church] and . . . destroy it."[96] Preserving unity demands that all Christians confess Christ "persecuted under Pontius Pilate, crucified, dead, and buried," implicitly affirming the necessity of the "blood witness" that imitates his passion.

Why did the orthodox view of martyrdom—and of Christ's death as its model—prevail? I suggest that persecution gave impetus to the formation of the organized church structure that developed by the end of the second century. To place the question in a contemporary context, consider what recourse remains to dissidents facing a massive and powerful political system: they attempt to publicize cases of violence and injustice to arouse world-wide public support. The torture and execution of a small group of persons known only to their relatives and friends soon fall into oblivion, but the cases of dissidents who are scientists, writers, Jews, or Christian missionaries may arouse the concern of an international community of those who identify with the victims by professional or religious affiliation.

There is, of course, a major difference between ancient and modern tactics. Today the purpose of such publicity is to generate pressure and gain the release of those who are tortured or imprisoned. The apologists, like Justin, did address the Roman authorities, protesting the unjust treatment of Christians and calling on them to end it. But Christians wrote the stories of the martyrs for a different purpose, and for a different audience. They wrote exclusively to other Christian churches, not in hope of ending persecution, but to warn them of their common danger, to encourage them to emulate the martyrs' "glorious victory," and to consolidate the communities internally and in relation to one another. So, in the second and third centuries, when Roman violence menaced Christian groups in remote provinces of the Empire, these events were communicated to Christians throughout the known world. Ignatius, condemned to execution in the Roman arena, occupied himself on his final journey writing letters to many provincial churches, telling them of his own situation and urging them to support the catholic ("universal") church organized around the bishops. He warned them above all to avoid heretics who deviate from the bishops' authority and from the orthodox doctrines of Christ's passion, death, and resurrection. His letters to the Christians in Rome, whom he had never met, testify to the efficacy of such communication: Ignatius was confident that they would intervene to prevent his execution if he allowed them to do so. Later, when some fifty Christians in Lyons and Vienne were arrested in June 177, they immediately wrote to "our brothers in Asia and Phyrgia who have the same faith," describing their suffering, and sent Irenaeus to inform the well-established church in Rome.

Pressed by their common danger, members of scattered Christian groups throughout the world increasingly exchanged letters and traveled from one church to another. Accounts of the martyrs, often taken from records of their trials and from eyewitnesses, circulated among the churches in Asia, Africa, Rome, Greece, Gaul, and Egypt. By such communication, members of the diversified earlier churches became aware of regional differences as obstacles to their claim to participate in one catholic church. As noted earlier, Irenaeus insisted that all churches throughout the world must agree on all vital points of doctrine, but even he was shocked when Victor, Bishop of Rome, attempted to move the regional churches toward greater uniformity. In 190, Victor demanded that Christians in Asia Minor abandon their traditional practice of celebrating Easter on Passover, and conform instead to Roman custom—or else give up their claim to be "catholic Christians." At the same time, the Roman church was compiling the definitive list of books eventually accepted by all Christian churches. Increasingly stratified orders of institutional hierarchy consolidated the communities internally and regularized communication with what Irenaeus called "the catholic church dispersed throughout the whole world, even to the ends of the earth"—a network of groups becoming increasingly uniform in doctrine, ritual, canon, and political structure.

Among outsiders, reports of brutality toward Christians aroused mixed emotions. Even the arrogant Tacitus, describing how Nero had Christians mocked and tortured to death, is moved to add:

> Even for criminals who deserve extreme and exemplary punishment, there arose a feeling of compassion; for it was not, as it seemed, for the public good, but to glut one man's cruelty, that they were being destroyed.[97]

Among the townspeople of Lyons, after the slaughter in the arena, some wanted to mutilate the corpses; others ridiculed the martyrs as fools, while others, "seeming to extend a measure of compassion," pondered what inspired their courage: "What advantage has their religion brought them, which they preferred to their own life?"[98] No doubt the persecutions terrified many into avoiding contact with Christians, but Justin and Tertullian both say that the sight of martyrs aroused the wonder and admiration that impelled them to investigate the movement, and then to join it. And both attest that this happened to many others. (As Justin remarked: "The more such things happen, the more do others, in larger numbers, become believers.")[99] Tertullian writes in defiance to Scapula, the proconsul of Carthage:

> Your cruelty is our glory . . . All who witness the noble patience of [the martyrs], are struck with misgivings, are inflamed with desire to examine the situation . . . and as soon as they come to know the truth, they immediately enroll themselves as its disciples.[100]

He boasts to the Roman prosecutor that "the oftener we are mown down by you, the more we grow in numbers: the blood of the Christians is seed!"[101] Those who followed the orthodox consensus in doctrine and church politics also belonged to the church that—confessing the crucified Christ—became conspicuous for its martyrs. Groups of gnostic Christians, on the other hand, were scattered and lost—those who resisted doctrinal conformity, questioned the value of the "blood witness," and often opposed submission to episcopal authority.

Finally, in its portrait of Christ's life and his passion, orthodox teaching offered a means of interpreting fundamental elements of human experience. Rejecting the gnostic view that Jesus was a spiritual being, the orthodox insisted that he, like the rest of humanity, was born, lived in a family, became hungry and tired, ate and drank wine, suffered and died. They even went so far as to insist that he rose *bodily* from the dead. Here again, as we have seen, orthodox tradition implicitly affirms bodily experience as the central fact of human life. What one does physically—one eats and drinks, engages in sexual life or avoids it, saves one's life or gives it up—all are vital elements in one's *religious* development. But those gnostics who regarded the essential part of every person as the "inner spirit" dismissed such physical experience, pleasurable or painful, as a distraction from spiritual reality—indeed, as an illusion. No wonder, then, that far more people identified with the orthodox portrait than with the "bodiless spirit" of gnostic tradition. Not only the martyrs, but all Christians who have suffered for 2,000 years, who have feared and faced death, have found their experience validated in the story of the *human* Jesus.

V

Whose Church Is the "True Church"?

FOR NEARLY 2,000 years, Christian tradition has preserved and revered orthodox writings that denounce the gnostics, while suppressing—and virtually destroying—the gnostic writings themselves. Now, for the first time, certain texts discovered at Nag Hammadi reveal the other side of the coin: how gnostics denounced the orthodox.[1] The *Second Treatise of the Great Seth* polemicizes against orthodox Christianity, contrasting it with the "true church" of the gnostics. Speaking for those he calls the sons of light, the author says:

> . . . we were hated and persecuted, not only by those who are ignorant [pagans], but also by those who think they are advancing the name of Christ, since they were unknowingly empty, not knowing who they are, like dumb animals.[2]

The Savior explains that such persons made an imitation of the true church, "having proclaimed a doctrine of a dead man and lies, so as to resemble the freedom and purity of the perfect church (*ekklesia*)."[3] Such teaching, he charges, reconciles its adherents to fear and slavery, encouraging them to subject themselves to the earthly representatives of the world creator, who, in his "empty glory," declares, "I am God, and there is no other beside me."[4] Such persons persecute those who have achieved liberation through *gnosis*, attempting to lead them astray from "the truth of their freedom."[5]

The *Apocalypse of Peter* describes, as noted before, catholic Christians as those who have fallen "into an erroneous name and into the hand of an evil, cunning man, with a teaching in a multiplicity of forms,"[6] allowing themselves to be ruled heretically. For, the author adds, they

> blaspheme the truth and proclaim evil teaching. And they will say evil things against each other. . . . many others . . . who oppose the truth and are the messengers of error . . . set up their error . . . against these pure thoughts of mine . . .[7]

The author takes each of the characteristics of the catholic church as evidence that this is only an imitation church, a counterfeit, a "sisterhood" that mimics the true Christian brotherhood. Such Christians, in their blind arrogance, claim exclusive legitimacy: "Some who do not understand mystery speak of things which they do not understand, but they will boast that the mystery of the truth belongs to them alone."[8] Their obedience to bishops and deacons indicates that they "bow to the judgment of the leaders."[9] They oppress their brethren, and slander those who attain *gnosis*.

The *Testimony of Truth* attacks ecclesiastical Christians as those who say "we are Christians," but "who [do not know who] Christ is."[10] But this same author goes on to attack other gnostics as well, including the followers of Valentinus, Basilides, and Simon, as brethren who are still immature. Another of the Nag Hammadi texts, the *Authoritative Teaching*, intends to demolish all teaching, especially orthodox teaching, that the author considers *un*authoritative. Like Irenaeus—but diametrically opposed —he says of "those who contend with us, being adversaries,"[11] that they are "dealers in bodies,"[12] senseless, ignorant, worse than pagans, because they have no excuse for their error.

The bitterness of these attacks on the "imitation church" probably indicates a late stage of the controversy. By the year 200, the battle lines had been drawn: both orthodox and gnostic Christians claimed to represent the true church and accused one another of being outsiders, false brethren, and hypocrites.

How was a believer to tell true Christians from false ones? Orthodox and gnostic Christians offered different answers, as each group attempted to define the church in ways that excluded the other. Gnostic Christians, claiming to represent only "the few," pointed to qualitative criteria. In protest against the majority, they insisted that baptism did not make a Christian: according to the *Gospel of Philip*, many people "go down into the water and come up without having received anything,"[13] and still they claimed to be Christians. Nor did profession of the creed, or even martyrdom, count as evidence: "anyone can do these things." Above all, they refused to identify the church with the actual, visible community that, they warned, often only imitated it. Instead, quoting a saying of Jesus ("By their fruits you shall know them") they required evidence of spiritual maturity to demonstrate that a person belonged to the true church.

But orthodox Christians, by the late second century, had begun to establish objective criteria for church membership. Whoever confessed the creed, accepted the ritual of baptism, participated in worship, and obeyed the clergy was accepted as a fellow Christian. Seeking to unify the diverse churches scattered throughout the world into a single network, the bishops eliminated qualitative criteria for church membership. Evaluating each candidate on the basis of spiritual maturity, insight, or personal holiness, as the gnostics did, would require a far more complex administration. Further, it would tend to exclude many who much needed what the church could give. To become truly *catholic*—universal—the church rejected all forms of elitism, attempting to include as many as possible within its embrace. In the process, its leaders created a clear and simple framework, consisting of doctrine, ritual, and political structure, that has proven to be an amazingly effective system of organization.

So the orthodox Ignatius, Bishop of Antioch, defines the church in terms of the bishop, who represents that system:

> Let no one do anything pertaining to the church without the bishop. Let that be considered a valid eucharist which is celebrated by the bishop, or by the person whom he appoints . . . Wherever the bishop offers [the eucharist], let the congregation be present, just as, wherever Jesus Christ is, there is the catholic church.[14]

Lest any "heretic" suggest that Christ may be present even when the bishop is absent, Ignatius sets him straight:

> It is not legitimate either to baptize or to hold an *agapē* [cult meal] without the bishop . . . To join with the bishop is to join the church; to separate oneself from the bishop is to separate oneself not only from the church, but from God himself.[15]

Apart from the church hierarchy, he insists, "there is nothing that can be called a church."[16]

Irenaeus, Bishop of Lyons, agrees with Ignatius that the only true church is that which "preserves the same form of ecclesiastical constitution":

> True *gnosis* is that which consists in the doctrine of the apostles, and the ancient constitution [*systema*] of the church throughout the whole world, and the character of the body of Christ according to the successions of bishops, by which they have handed down that which exists everywhere.[17]

Only this system, Irenaeus says, stands upon the "pillar and ground" of those apostolic writings to which he attributes absolute authority—above all, the gospels of the New Testament. All others are false and unreliable, unapostolic, and probably composed by heretics. The catholic church alone offers a "very complete system of doctrine,"[18] proclaiming, as we have seen, one God, creator and father of Christ, who became incarnate, suffered, died, and rose bodily from the dead. Outside of this church there is no salvation: "she is the entrance to life; all others are thieves and robbers."[19] As spokesman for the church of God, Irenaeus insists that those he calls heretics stand outside the church. All who reject his version of Christian truth are "false persons, evil seducers, and hypocrites" who "speak to the multitude about those in the church, whom they call *catholic*, or *ecclesiastical*."[20] Irenaeus says he longs to "convert them to the church of God"[21]—since he considers them apostates, worse than pagans.

Gnostic Christians, on the contrary, assert that what distinguishes the false from the true church is not its relationship to the clergy, but the level of understanding of its members, and the quality of their relationship with one another. The *Apocalypse of Peter* declares that "those who are from the life . . . having been enlightened,"[22] discriminate for themselves between what is true and false. Belonging to "the remnant . . . summoned to knowledge [*gnosis*],"[23] they neither attempt to dominate others nor do they subject themselves to the bishops and deacons, those "waterless canals." Instead they participate in "the wisdom of the brotherhood that really exists . . . the spiritual fellowship with those united in communion."[24]

The *Second Treatise of the Great Seth* similarly declares that what characterizes the true church is the union its members enjoy with God and with one another, "united in the friendship of friends forever, who neither know any hostility, nor evil, but who are united by my *gnosis* . . . (in) friendship with one another."[25] Theirs is the intimacy of marriage, a "spiritual wedding," since they live "in fatherhood and motherhood and rational brotherhood and wisdom"[26] as those who love each other as "fellow spirits."[27]

Such ethereal visions of the "heavenly church" contrast sharply with the down-to-earth portrait of the church that orthodox sources offer. Why do gnostic authors abandon concreteness and describe the church in fantastic and imaginative terms? Some scholars say that this proves that they understood little, and cared less, about social relationships. Carl Andresen, in his recent, massive study of the early Christian church, calls them "religious solipsists" who concerned themselves only with their own individual spiritual development, indifferent to the community responsibilities of a church.[28] But the sources cited above show that these gnostics defined the church *precisely* in terms of the quality of interrelationships among its members.

Orthodox writers described the church in concrete terms because they accept the status quo; that is, they affirmed that the actual community of those gathered for worship *was* "the church." Gnostic Christians dissented. Confronted with those in the churches whom they considered ignorant, arrogant, or self-interested, they refused to agree that the whole community of believers, without further qualification, constituted "the church." Dividing from the majority over such issues as the value of martyrdom, they intended to discriminate between the mass of believers and those who truly had *gnosis*, between what they called the imitation, or the counterfeit, and the true church.

Consider, for example, how specific disputes with other Christians drove even Hippolytus and Tertullian, those two fervent opponents of heresy, to redefine the church for themselves. Hippolytus shared his teacher Irenaeus' view of the church as the sole bearer of truth. Like Irenaeus, Hippolytus defined that truth as what the apostolic succession of bishops guaranteed on the basis of the canon and church doctrine. But when a deacon named Callistus was elected bishop of his church in Rome, Hippolytus protested vehemently. He publicized a scandalous story, slandering Callistus' integrity:

> Callistus was a slave of Carpophorus, a Christian employed in the imperial palace. To Callistus, as being of the faith, Carpophorus entrusted no inconsiderable amount of money, and directed him to bring in profit from banking. He took the money and started business in what is called Fish Market Ward. As time passed, not a few deposits were

entrusted to him by widows and brethren . . . Callistus, however, embezzled the lot, and became financially embarrassed.[29]

When Carpophorus heard of this, he demanded an accounting, but, Hippolytus says, Callistus absconded and fled: "finding a vessel in the port ready for a voyage, he went on board, intending to sail wherever she happened to be bound for."[30] When his master pursued him onto the ship, Callistus knew he was trapped, and, in desperation, jumped overboard. Rescued against his will by the sailors as the crowd on the shore shouted encouragement, Callistus was handed over to Carpophorus, returned to Rome, and placed in penal servitude. Apparently Hippolytus was trying to explain how Callistus came to be tortured and imprisoned, since many revered him as a martyr; Hippolytus maintained instead that he was a criminal. Hippolytus also objected to Callistus' views on the Trinity, and found Callistus' policy of extending forgiveness of sins to cover sexual transgressions shockingly "lax." And he denounced Callistus, the former slave, for allowing believers to regularize liaisons with their own slaves by recognizing them as valid marriages.

But Hippolytus found himself in the minority. The majority of Roman Christians respected Callistus as a teacher and martyr, endorsed his policies, and elected him bishop. Now that Callistus headed the Roman church, Hippolytus decided to break away from it. In the process, he turned against the bishop the same polemical techniques that Irenaeus had taught him to use against the gnostics. As Irenaeus singled out certain groups of Christians as heretics, and named them according to their teachers (as "Valentinians," "Simonians," etc.), so Hippolytus accused Callistus of teaching heresy and characterized his following as "the Callistians"—as if they were a sect separate from "the church," which Hippolytus himself claimed to represent.

How could Hippolytus justify his claim to represent the church, when he and his few adherents were attacking the great majority of Roman Christians and their bishop? Hippolytus explained that the majority of "self-professed Christians" were incapable of living up to the standard of the *true* church, which consisted of "the community of those who live in holiness." Like his gnostic opponents, having refused to identify the church through its official hierarchy, he characterized it instead in terms of the spiritual qualities of its members.

Tertullian presented an even more dramatic case. As long as he identified himself as a "catholic Christian," Tertullian defined the church as Irenaeus had. Writing his *Preemptive Objection against Heretics*, Tertullian proclaimed that his church alone bore the apostolic rule of faith, revered the canon of Scriptures, and bore through its ecclesiastical hierarchy the sanction of apostolic succession. Like Irenaeus, Tertullian indicted the heretics for violating each of these boundaries. He complains that they refused simply to accept and believe the rule of faith as others did: instead, they challenged others to raise theological questions, when they themselves claimed no answers,

> being ready to say, and sincerely, of certain points of their belief, "This is not so," and "I take this in a different sense," and "I do not admit that."[31]

Tertullian warns that such questioning leads to heresy: "This rule . . . was taught by Christ, and raises among ourselves no other questions than those which the heresies introduce and which make men heretics!"[32] He also charges that the heretics did not restrict themselves to the Scriptures of the New Testament: either they added other writings or they challenged the orthodox interpretation of key texts.[33] Further, as noted already, he condemns the heretics for being "a camp of rebels" who refused to submit to the authority of the bishop. Arguing for a strict order of obedience and submission, he concludes that "evidence of a stricter discipline existing among us is an additional proof of truth."[34]

So speaks Tertullian the catholic. But at the end of his life, when his own intense fervor impelled him to break with the orthodox community, he rejected and branded it as the church of mere "psychic" Christians. He joined instead the Montanist movement, whose adherents called it the "new prophecy," claiming to be inspired by the Holy Spirit. At this time Tertullian began to distinguish sharply between the empirical church and another, spiritual vision of the church. Now he no longer identified the church in terms of its ecclesiastical organization, but only with the spirit that sanctified individual members. He scorns the catholic community as "the church of a number of bishops":

> For the church itself, properly and principally, is spirit, in which there is the trinity of one divinity, Father, Son, and Holy Spirit. . . . The church congregates where the Lord plans it—a spiritual church for spiritual people—*not* the church of a number of bishops![35]

What impelled dissidents from catholic Christianity to maintain or develop such visionary descriptions of the church? Were their visions "up in the air" because they were interested in theoretical speculation? On the contrary, their motives were sometimes traditional and polemical, but also sometimes political. They were convinced that the "visible church"—the actual network of catholic communities—either had been wrong from the beginning or had gone wrong. The true church, by contrast, was "invisible": only its members perceived who belonged to it and who did not. Dissidents intended their idea of an invisible church to oppose the claims of those who said they represented the universal church. Martin Luther made the same move 1,300 years later. When his devotion to the Catholic Church changed to criticism, then rejection, he began to insist, with other protestant reformers, that the true church was "invisible"—that is, not identical with Catholicism.

The gnostic author of the *Testimony of Truth* would have agreed with Luther and gone much further. He rejects as fallacious all the marks of ecclesiastical Christianity. Obedience to the clerical hierarchy requires believers to submit themselves to "blind guides" whose authority comes from the malevolent creator. Conformity to the rule of faith attempts to limit all Christians to an inferior ideology: "They say, '[Even if] an [angel] comes from heaven, and preaches to you beyond what we preach to you, let him be accursed!' "[36] Faith in the sacraments shows naïve and magical thinking: catholic Christians practice baptism as an initiation rite which guarantees them "a hope of salvation,"[37] believing that only those who receive baptism are "headed for life."[38]

Against such "lies" the gnostic declares that "this, therefore, is the *true* testimony: when man knows himself, and God who is over the truth, he will be saved."[39] Only those who come to recognize that they have been living in ignorance, and learn to release themselves by discovering who they are, experience enlightenment as a new life, as "the resurrection." Physical rituals like baptism become irrelevant, for "the baptism of truth is something else; it is by renunciation of [the] world that it is found."[40]

Against those who claimed exclusive access to truth, those who followed law and authority, and who placed their faith in ritual, this author sets his own vision: "Whoever is able to renounce them [money and sexual intercourse] shows [that] he is [from] the generation of the [Son of Man], and that he has power to accuse [them]."[41] Like Hippolytus and Tertullian, but more radical than either, this teacher praises sexual abstinence and economic renunciation as the marks of the true Christian.

The *Authoritative Teaching,* another text discovered at Nag Hammadi, also offers vehement attack on catholic Christianity. The author tells the story of the soul, who originally came from heaven, from the "fullness of being,"[42] but when she "was cast into the body"[43] she experienced sensual desire, passions, hatred, and envy. Clearly the allegory refers to the individual soul's struggle against passions and sin; yet the language of the account suggests a wider, social referent as well. It relates the struggle of those who are spiritual, akin to the soul (with whom the author identifies), against those who are essentially alien to her. The author explains that some who were called "our brothers," who claimed to be Christians, actually were outsiders. Although "the word has been preached"[44] to them, and they heard "the call"[45] and performed acts of worship, these self-professed Christians were "worse than . . . the pagans,"[46] who had an excuse for their ignorance.

On what counts does the gnostic accuse these believers? First, that they "do not seek after God."[47] The gnostic understands Christ's message not as offering a set of answers, but as encouragement to engage in a process of searching: "seek and inquire about the ways you should go, since there is nothing else as good as this."[48] The rational soul longs to

> see with her mind, and perceive her kinsmen, and learn about her root . . . in order that she might receive what is hers . . .[49]

What is the result? The author declares that she attains fulfillment:

> . . . the rational soul who wearied herself in seeking— she learned about God. She labored with inquiring, enduring distress in the body, wearing out her feet after the evangelists, learning about the Inscrutable One. . . . She came to rest in him who is at rest. She reclined in the bride-chamber. She ate of the banquet for which she had hungered. . . . She found what she had sought.[50]

Those who are gnostics follow her path. But non-gnostic Christians "do not seek":

> . . . these—the ones who are ignorant—do not seek after God. . . . they do not inquire about God . . . the senseless man hears the call, but he is ignorant of the place to which he has been called. And he did not ask, during the preaching, "Where is the temple into which I should go and worship?"[51]

Those who merely believe the preaching they hear, without asking questions, and who accept the worship set before them, not only remain ignorant themselves, but "if they find someone else who asks about his salvation,"[52] they act immediately to censor and silence him.

Second, these "enemies" assert that they themselves are the soul's "shepherd":

> . . . They did not realize that she has an invisible, spiritual body; they think "We are her shepherd, who feeds her." But they did not realize that she knows another way which is hidden from them. This her true shepherd taught her in *gnosis*.[53]

Using the common term for bishop (*poimen*, "shepherd"), the author refers, apparently, to members of the clergy: they did not know that the gnostic Christian had direct access to Christ himself, the soul's true shepherd, and did not need their guidance. Nor did these would-be shepherds realize that the true church was not the visible one (the community over which they preside), but that "she has an invisible, spiritual body"[54]—that is, she included only those who were spiritual. Only Christ, and they themselves, knew who they were. Furthermore, these "outsiders" indulged themselves in drinking wine, in sexual activity, and they worked at ordinary business, like pagans. To justify their conduct, they oppressed and slandered those who had attained *gnosis*, and who practiced total renunciation. The gnostic declares:

> . . . we take no interest in them when they [malign] us. And we ignore them when they curse us. When they cast shame in our face, we look at them, and do not speak. For they work at their business, but we go around in hunger and thirst . . .[55]

These "enemies," I submit, were following the kind of advice that orthodox leaders like Irenaeus, Tertullian, and Hippolytus prescribed for dealing with heretics. In the first place, they refused to question the rule of faith and common doctrine. Tertullian warns that "the heretics and the philosophers" both ask the same questions, and urges believers to dismiss them all:

> Away with all attempts to produce a mixed Christianity of Stoic, Platonic, or dialectic composition! We want no curious disputation after possessing Christ Jesus, no inquiring after enjoying the gospel! With our faith, we desire no further belief.[56]

He complains that heretics welcome anyone to join with them, "for they do not care how differently they treat topics," so long as they meet together to approach "the city of the one sole truth."[57] Yet their metaphor indicates that the gnostics were neither relativists nor skeptics. Like the orthodox, they sought the "one sole truth." But gnostics tended to regard all doctrines, speculations, and myths—their own as well as others'—only as approaches to truth. The orthodox, by contrast, were coming to identify their own doctrine as itself the truth—the sole legitimate form of Christian faith. Tertullian admits that the heretics claimed to follow Jesus' counsel ("Seek, and you shall find; knock, and it shall be opened to you").[58] But this means, he says, that Christ taught "one definite thing"—what the rule of faith contains. Once having found and believed this, the Christian has nothing further to seek:

> Away with the person who is seeking where he never finds; for he seeks where nothing can be found. Away with him who is always knocking; because it will never be opened to him, for he knocks where there is no one to open. Away with the one who is always asking, because he will never be heard, for he asks of one who does not hear.[59]

Irenaeus agrees: "According to this course of procedure, one would be always inquiring, but never finding, because he has rejected the very method of discovery."[60] The only safe and accurate course, he says, is to accept in faith what the church teaches, recognizing the limits of human understanding.

As we have seen, these "enemies" of the gnostics followed the church fathers' advice in asserting the claims of the clergy over gnostic Christians. Also, they treated "unrepentant" gnostics as outsiders to Christian faith; and finally, they affirmed the value of ordinary employment and family life over the demands of radical asceticism.

While catholic Christians and radical gnostics took opposite stands, each claiming to represent the church, and each denouncing the others as heretics, the Valentinians took a mediating position. Resisting the orthodox attempt to label them as outsiders, they identified themselves as fully members of the church. But the Valentinians engaged in vehement debate among themselves over the opposite question—the status of *catholic* Christians. So serious was their disagreement over this question that the crisis finally split the followers of Valentinus into two different factions.

Were catholic Christians included in the church, the "body of Christ"? The Eastern branch of Valentinians said *no*. They maintained that Christ's body, the church, was "purely spiritual," consisting only of those who were spiritual, who had received *gnosis*. Theodotus, the great teacher of the Eastern school, defined the church as "the chosen race,"[61] those "chosen before the foundation of the world."[62] Their salvation was certain, predestined—and exclusive. Like Tertullian in his later years, Theodotus taught that only those who received direct spiritual inspiration belonged to the "spiritual church."[63]

But Ptolemy and Heracleon, the leading teachers of the Western school of Valentinians, disagreed. Against Theodotus, they claimed that "Christ's body," the church, consisted of two distinct elements, one spiritual, the other unspiritual. This meant, they explained, that *both* gnostic and non-gnostic Christians stood within the same church. Citing Jesus' saying that "many are called, but few are chosen," they explained that Christians who lacked *gnosis*—by far the majority—were the many who were called. They themselves, as gnostic Christians, belonged to the few who were chosen. Heracleon taught that God had given them spiritual understanding for the sake of the rest—so that they would be able to teach "the many" and bring them to *gnosis*.[64]

The gnostic teacher Ptolemy agreed: Christ combined

within the church both spiritual and unspiritual Christians so that eventually all may become spiritual.[65] Meanwhile, both belonged to one church; both were baptized; both shared in the celebration of the mass; both made the same confession. What differentiated them was the level of their understanding. Uninitiated Christians mistakenly worshiped the creator, as if he were God; they believed in Christ as the one who would save them from sin, and who they believed had risen bodily from the dead: they accepted him by faith, but without understanding the mystery of his nature—or their own. But those who had gone on to receive *gnosis* had come to recognize Christ as the one sent from the Father of Truth, whose coming revealed to them that their own nature was identical with his—and with God's.

To illustrate their relationship, Heracleon offers a symbolic interpretation of the church as a temple: those who were ordinary Christians, not yet gnostics, worshiped like the Levites, in the temple courtyard, shut out from the mystery. Only those who had *gnosis* might enter within the "holy of holies," which signified the place "where those who are spiritual worship God." Yet one temple—the church—embraced both places of worship.[66]

The Valentinian author of the *Interpretation of the Knowledge* agrees with this view. He explains that although Jesus came into the world and died for the sake of the "church of mortals,"[67] now this church, the "place of faith," was split and divided into factions.[68] Some members had received spiritual gifts—power to heal, prophecy, above all, *gnosis*; others had not.

This gnostic teacher expresses concern that this situation often caused hostility and misunderstanding. Those who were spiritually advanced tended to withdraw from those they considered "ignorant" Christians, and hesitated to share their insights with them. Those who lacked spiritual inspiration envied those who spoke out in public at the worship service and who spoke in prophecy, taught, and healed others.[69]

The author addresses the whole community as he attempts to reconcile both gnostic and non-gnostic Christians with one another. Drawing upon a traditional metaphor, he reminds them that all believers are members of the church, the "body of Christ." First he recalls Paul's words:

> For just as the body is one and has many members, and all the members of the body, though many, are one body, so it is with Christ. . . . The eye cannot say to the hand, "I have no need of you," nor again the head to the feet, "I have no need of you."[70]

Then he goes on to preach to those who feel inferior, lacking spiritual powers, who are not yet gnostic initiates:

> . . . Do not accuse your Head [Christ] because it has not made you as an eye, but a finger; and do not be jealous of what has been made an eye or a hand or a foot, but be thankful that you are not outside the body.[71]

To those who are spiritual, who have *gnosis*, and who have received "gifts," he says:

> . . . Does someone have a prophetic gift? Share it without hesitation. Do not approach your brother with jealousy . . . How do you know [that someone] is ignorant? . . . [You] are ignorant when you [hate them] and are jealous of them.[72]

Like Paul, he urges all members to love one another, to work and suffer together, mature and immature Christians alike, gnostics and ordinary believers, and so "to share in the (true) harmony."[73] According to the Western school of Valentinian gnostics, then, "the church" included the community of catholic Christians, but was not limited to it. Most Christians, they claimed, did not even perceive the most important element of the church, the spiritual element, which consisted of all who had *gnosis*.

From the bishop's viewpoint, of course, the gnostic position was outrageous. These heretics challenged his right to define what he considered to be his own church; they had the audacity to debate whether or not catholic Christians participated; and they claimed that their own group formed the essential nucleus, the "spiritual church." Rejecting such religious elitism, orthodox leaders attempted instead to construct a *universal* church. Desiring to open that church to everyone, they welcomed members from every social class, every racial or cultural origin, whether educated or illiterate—everyone, that is, who would submit to their system of organization. The bishops drew the line against those who challenged any of the three elements of this system: doctrine, ritual, and clerical hierarchy—and the gnostics challenged them all. Only by suppressing gnosticism did orthodox leaders establish that system of organization which united all believers into a single institutional structure. They allowed no other distinction between first- and second-class members than that between the clergy and the laity, nor did they tolerate any who claimed exemption from doctrinal conformity, from ritual participation, and from obedience to the discipline that priests and bishops administered. Gnostic churches, which rejected that system for more subjective forms of religious affiliation, survived, as churches, for only a few hundred years.

VI

Gnosis: Self=Knowledge as Knowledge of God

> ... Thomas said to him, "Lord, we do not know where
> you are going; how can we know the way?" Jesus said to
> him, "I am the way, the truth, and the life; no one comes
> to the Father, but by me."[1]

THE GOSPEL OF JOHN, which contains this saying, is a
remarkable book that many gnostic Christians claimed for
themselves and used as a primary source for gnostic
teaching.[2] Yet the emerging church, despite some orthodox
opposition, included John within the New Testament. What
makes John acceptably "orthodox"? Why did the church accept
John while rejecting such writings as the *Gospel of Thomas* or
the *Dialogue of the Savior*? In considering this question, remember that anyone who drives through the United States is
likely to see billboards proclaiming this saying from John—
billboards signed by any of the local churches. Their purpose is
clear: by indicating that one finds God only through Jesus, the
saying, in its contemporary context, implies that one finds Jesus
only through the church. Similarly, in the first centuries of this
era, Christians concerned to strengthen the institutional church
could find support in John.

Gnostic sources offer a different religious perspective. According to the *Dialogue of the Savior*, for example, when the disciples asked Jesus the same question ("What is the place to which we shall go?") he answered, "the place which you can reach, stand there!"[3] The *Gospel of Thomas* relates that when the disciples asked Jesus where they should go, he said only, "There is light within a man of light, and it lights up the whole world. If he does not shine, he is darkness."[4] Far from legitimizing any institution, both sayings direct one instead to oneself—to one's inner capacity to find one's own direction, to the "light within."

The contrast sketched above is, of course, somewhat simplistic. Followers of Valentinus themselves demonstrated—convincingly—that many sayings and stories in John could lend themselves to such interpretation. But Christians like Irenaeus apparently decided that, on balance, the gospel of John (especially, perhaps, when placed in sequence after Matthew, Mark, and Luke) could serve the needs of the emerging institution.

As the church organized politically, it could sustain within itself many contradictory ideas and practices as long as the disputed elements supported its basic institutional structure. In the third and fourth centuries, for example, hundreds of catholic Christians adopted ascetic forms of self-discipline, seeking religious insight through solitude, visions, and ecstatic experience. (The terms "monk" and "monastic" come from the Greek word *monachos*, meaning "solitary," or "single one," which the *Gospel of Thomas* frequently uses to describe the gnostic.) Rather than exclude the monastic movement, the church moved, in the fourth century, to bring the monks into line with episcopal authority. The scholar Frederik Wisse has suggested that the monks who lived at the monastery of St. Pachomius, within sight of the cliff where the texts were found, may have included the Nag Hammadi texts within their devotional library.[5] But in 367, when Athanasius, the powerful Archbishop of Alexandria, sent an order to purge all "apocryphal books" with "heretical" tendencies, one (or several) of the monks may have hidden the precious manuscripts in the jar and buried it on the cliff of the Jabal al-Ṭārif, where Muḥammad ʿAlī found it 1,600 years later.

Furthermore, as the church, disparate as it was internally, increasingly became a political unity between 150 and 400, its leaders tended to treat their opponents—an even more diverse range of groups—as if they, too, constituted an *opposite* political unity. When Irenaeus denounced the heretics as "gnostics,"[6] he referred less to any specific doctrinal agreement among them (indeed, he often castigated them for the variety of their beliefs) than to the fact that they all resisted accepting the authority of the clergy, the creed, and the New Testament canon.

What—if anything—did the various groups that Irenaeus called "gnostic" have in common? Or, to put the question another way, what do the diverse texts discovered at Nag Hammadi have in common? No simple answer could cover all the different groups that the orthodox attack, or all the different texts in the Nag Hammadi collection. But I suggest that the trouble with gnosticism, from the orthodox viewpoint, was not only that gnostics often disagreed with the majority on such specific issues as those we have explored so far—the organization of authority, the participation of women, martyrdom: the orthodox recognized that those they called "gnostics" shared a fundamental religious perspective that remained antithetical to the claims of the institutional church.

For orthodox Christians insisted that humanity needs a way beyond its own power—a divinely given way—to approach God. And this, they declared, the catholic church offered to those who would be lost without it: "Outside the church there is no salvation." Their conviction was based on the premise that God created humanity. As Irenaeus says, "In this respect God differs from humanity; God makes, but humanity is made."[7] One is the originating agent, the other the passive recipient; one is "truly perfect in all things,"[8] omnipotent, infinite, the other an imperfect and finite creature. The philosopher Justin Martyr says that when he recognized the great difference between the human mind and God, he abandoned Plato and became a

Christian philosopher. He relates that before his conversion an old man challenged his basic assumption, asking, "What affinity, then, is there between us and God? Is the soul also divine and immortal, and a part of that very regal mind?" Speaking as a disciple of Plato, Justin answered without hesitation, "Certainly."[9] But when the old man's further questions led him to doubt that certainty, he says he realized that the human mind could not find God within itself and needed instead to be enlightened by divine revelation—by means of the Scriptures and the faith proclaimed in the church.

But some gnostic Christians went so far as to claim that humanity created God—and so, from its own inner potential, discovered for itself the revelation of truth. This conviction may underlie the ironic comment in the *Gospel of Philip*:

> . . . God created humanity; [but now human beings] create God. That is the way it is in the world—human beings make gods, and worship their creation. It would be appropriate for the gods to worship human beings![10]

The gnostic Valentinus taught that humanity itself manifests the divine life and divine revelation. The church, he says, consists of that portion of humanity that recognizes and celebrates its divine origin.[11] But Valentinus did not use the term in its contemporary sense, to refer to the human race taken collectively. Instead, he and his followers thought of *Anthropos* (here translated "humanity") as the underlying nature of that collective entity, the archetype, or spiritual essence, of human being. In this sense, some of Valentinus' followers, "those . . . considered more skillful"[12] than the rest, agreed with the teacher Colorbasus, who said that when God revealed himself, He revealed himself in the form of *Anthropos*. Still others, Irenaeus reports, maintained that

> the primal father of the whole, the primal beginning, and the primal incomprehensible, is called *Anthropos* . . . and that this is the great and abstruse mystery, namely, that the

power which is above all others, and contains all others in
its embrace, is called *Anthropos*.[13]

For this reason, these gnostics explained, the Savior called himself "Son of Man" (that is, Son of *Anthropos*).[14] The Sethian
gnostics, who called the creator Ialdabaoth (a name apparently
derived from mystical Judaism but which here indicates his
inferior status), said that for this reason, when the creator,

> Ialdabaoth, becoming arrogant in spirit, boasted himself over
> all those who were below him, and explained, "I am father,
> and God, and above me there is no one," his mother, hear-
> ing him speak thus, cried out against him: "Do not lie,
> Ialdabaoth; for the father of all, the primal *Anthropos*, is
> above you; and so is *Anthropos*, the son of *Anthropos*.[15]

In the words of another Valentinian, since human beings created
the whole language of religious expression, so, in effect, humanity
created the divine world: ". . . and this [*Anthropos*] is really he
who is God over all."

Many gnostics, then, would have agreed in principle with
Ludwig Feuerbach, the nineteenth-century psychologist, that
"theology is really anthropology" (the term derives, of course,
from *anthropos*, and means "study of humanity"). For gnostics,
exploring the *psyche* became explicitly what it is for many people
today implicitly—a religious quest. Some who seek their own
interior direction, like the radical gnostics, reject religious institutions as a hindrance to their progress. Others, like the
Valentinians, willingly participate in them, although they regard
the church more as an instrument of their own self-discovery
than as the necessary "ark of salvation."

Besides defining God in opposite ways, gnostic and orthodox
Christians diagnosed the human condition very differently. The
orthodox followed traditional Jewish teaching that what separates humanity from God, besides the essential dissimilarity, is
human sin. The New Testament term for sin, *hamartia*, comes
from the sport of archery; literally, it means "missing the mark."

New Testament sources teach that we suffer distress, mental and physical, because we fail to achieve the moral goal toward which we aim: "all have sinned, and fall short of the glory of God."[16] So, according to the gospel of Mark, when Jesus came to reconcile God and humanity, he announced: "The time is fulfilled, and the kingdom of God is at hand; repent, and believe in the gospel."[17] Mark announces that Jesus alone could offer healing and forgiveness of sins; only those who receive his message in faith experience deliverance. The gospel of John expresses the desperate situation of humanity apart from the Savior:

> For God sent the Son into the world . . . that the world might be saved through him. He who believes in him is not condemned; he who does not believe is condemned already, because he has not believed in the name of the only Son of God.[18]

Many gnostics, on the contrary, insisted that ignorance, not sin, is what involves a person in suffering. The gnostic movement shared certain affinities with contemporary methods of exploring the self through psychotherapeutic techniques. Both gnosticism and psychotherapy value, above all, knowledge—the self-knowledge which is insight. They agree that, lacking this, a person experiences the sense of being driven by impulses he does not understand. Valentinus expressed this in a myth. He tells how the world originated when Wisdom, the Mother of all beings, brought it forth out of her own suffering. The four elements that Greek philosophers said constituted the world—earth, air, fire, and water—are concrete forms of her experiences:

> Thus the earth arose from her confusion, water from her terror; air from the consolidation of her grief; while fire . . . was inherent in all these elements . . . as ignorance lay concealed in these three sufferings.[19]

Thus the world was born out of suffering. (The Greek word *pathos*, here translated "suffering," also connotes being the passive recipient, not the initiator, of one's experience.) Valentinus or one of his followers tells a different version of the myth in the *Gospel of Truth*:

> . . . Ignorance . . . brought about anguish and terror. And the anguish grew solid like a fog, so that no one was able to see. For this reason error is powerful . . .[20]

Most people live, then, in oblivion—or, in contemporary terms, in unconsciousness. Remaining unaware of their own selves, they have "no root."[21] The *Gospel of Truth* describes such existence as a nightmare. Those who live in it experience "terror and confusion and instability and doubt and division," being caught in "many illusions."[22] So, according to the passage scholars call the "nightmare parable," they lived

> as if they were sunk in sleep and found themselves in disturbing dreams. Either (there is) a place to which they are fleeing, or, without strength, they come (from) having chased after others, or they are involved in striking blows, or they are receiving blows themselves, or they have fallen from high places, or they take off into the air though they do not even have wings. Again, sometimes (it is as) if people were murdering them, though there is no one even pursuing them, or they themselves are killing their neighbors, for they have been stained with their blood. When those who are going through all these things wake up, they see nothing, they who were in the midst of these disturbances, for they are nothing. Such is the way of those who have cast ignorance aside as sleep, leaving [its works] behind like a dream in the night. . . . This is the way everyone has acted, as though asleep at the time when he was ignorant. And this is the way he has come to knowledge, as if he had awakened.[23]

Whoever remains ignorant, a "creature of oblivion,"[24] cannot experience fulfillment. Gnostics said that such a person "dwells in deficiency" (the opposite of fulfillment). For deficiency consists of ignorance:

> . . . As with someone's ignorance, when he comes to have knowledge, his ignorance vanishes by itself; as the

darkness vanishes when light appears, so also the deficiency vanishes in the fulfillment.[25]

Self-ignorance is also a form of self-destruction. According to the *Dialogue of the Savior*, whoever does not understand the elements of the universe, and of himself, is bound for annihilation:

> . . . If one does not [understand] how the fire came to be, he will burn in it, because he does not know his root. If one does not first understand the water, he does not know anything. . . . If one does not understand how the wind that blows came to be, he will run with it. If one does not understand how the body that he wears came to be, he will perish with it. . . . Whoever does not understand how he came will not understand how he will go . . .[26]

How—or where—is one to seek self-knowledge? Many gnostics share with psychotherapy a second major premise: both agree—against orthodox Christianity—that the psyche bears *within itself* the potential for liberation or destruction. Few psychiatrists would disagree with the saying attributed to Jesus in the *Gospel of Thomas*:

> "If you bring forth what is within you, what you bring forth will save you. If you do not bring forth what is within you, what you do not bring forth will destroy you."[27]

Such insight comes gradually, through effort: "Recognize what is before your eyes, and what is hidden will be revealed to you."[28]

Such gnostics acknowledged that pursuing *gnosis* engages each person in a solitary, difficult process, as one struggles against internal resistance. They characterized this resistance to *gnosis* as the desire to sleep or to be drunk—that is, to remain unconscious. So Jesus (who elsewhere says "I am the knowledge of the truth")[29] declares that when he came into the world

> I found them all drunk; I found none of them thirsty. And my soul became afflicted for the sons of men, because they are blind in their hearts and do not have sight; for empty they came into this world, and empty they seek to leave this world. But for the moment they are drunk.[30]

The teacher Silvanus, whose *Teachings*[31] were discovered at Nag Hammadi, encourages his followers to resist unconsciousness:

> . . . end the sleep which weighs heavy upon you. Depart from the oblivion which fills you with darkness . . . Why do you pursue the darkness, though the light is available for you? . . . Wisdom calls you, yet you desire foolishness. . . . a foolish man . . . goes the ways of the desire of every passion. He swims in the desires of life and has foundered. . . . he is like a ship which the wind tosses to and fro, and like a loose horse which has no rider. For this (one) needed the rider, which is reason. . . . before everything else . . . know yourself . . .[32]

The *Gospel of Thomas* also warns that self-discovery involves inner turmoil:

> Jesus said, "Let him who seeks continue seeking until he finds. When he finds, he will become troubled. When he becomes troubled, he will be astonished, and he will rule over all things."[33]

What is the source of the "light" discovered within? Like Freud, who professed to follow the "light of reason," most gnostic sources agreed that "the lamp of the body is the mind"[34] (a saying which the *Dialogue of the Savior* attributes to Jesus). Silvanus, the teacher, says:

> . . . Bring in your guide and your teacher. The mind is the guide, but reason is the teacher. . . . Live according to your mind . . . Acquire strength, for the mind is strong . . . Enlighten your mind . . . Light the lamp within you.[35]

To do this, Silvanus continues,

> Knock on yourself as upon a door and walk upon yourself as on a straight road. For if you walk on the road, it is impossible for you to go astray. . . . Open the door for yourself that you may know what is . . . Whatever you will open for yourself, you will open.[36]

The *Gospel of Truth* expresses the same thought:

> ... If one has knowledge, he receives what is his own, and draws it to himself ... Whoever is to have knowledge in this way knows where he comes from, and where he is going.[37]

The *Gospel of Truth* also expresses this in metaphor: each person must receive "his own name"—not, of course, one's ordinary name, but one's true identity. Those who are "the sons of interior knowledge"[38] gain the power to speak their own names. The gnostic teacher addresses them:

> ... Say, then, from the heart that you are the perfect day, and in you dwells the light that does not fail. ... For you are the understanding that is drawn forth. ... Be concerned with yourselves; do not be concerned with other things which you have rejected from yourselves.[39]

So, according to the *Gospel of Thomas*, Jesus ridiculed those who thought of the "Kingdom of God" in literal terms, as if it were a specific place: "If those who lead you say to you, 'Look, the Kingdom is in the sky,' then the birds will arrive there before you. If they say to you, 'It is in the sea,' " then, he says, the fish will arrive before you. Instead, it is a state of self-discovery:

> "... Rather, the Kingdom is inside of you, and it is outside of you. When you come to know yourselves, then you will be known, and you will realize that you are the sons of the living Father. But if you will not know yourselves, then you dwell in poverty, and it is you who *are* that poverty."[40]

But the disciples, mistaking that "Kingdom" for a future event, persisted in their questioning:

> His disciples said to him, "When will . . . the new world come?" He said to them, "What you look forward to has already come, but you do not recognize it." ... His disciples said to him, "When will the Kingdom come?"

⟨Jesus said,⟩ "It will not come by waiting for it. It will not be a matter of saying 'Here it is' or 'There it is.' Rather, the Kingdom of the Father is spread out upon the earth, and men do not see it."[41]

That "Kingdom," then, symbolizes a state of transformed consciousness:

Jesus saw infants being suckled. He said to his disciples, "These infants being suckled are like those who enter the Kingdom." They said to him, "Shall we, then, as children, enter the Kingdom?" Jesus said to them, "When you make the two one, and when you make the inside like the outside and the outside like the inside, and the above like the below, and when you make the male and the female one and the same . . . then you will enter [the Kingdom]."[42]

Yet what the "living Jesus" of Thomas rejects as naïve—the idea that the Kingdom of God is an actual event expected in history—is the notion of the Kingdom that the synoptic gospels of the New Testament most often attribute to Jesus as his teaching. According to Matthew, Luke, and Mark, Jesus proclaimed the coming Kingdom of God, when captives shall gain their freedom, when the diseased shall recover, the oppressed shall be released, and harmony shall prevail over the whole world. Mark says that the disciples expected the Kingdom to come as a cataclysmic event in their own lifetime, since Jesus had said that some of them would live to see "the kingdom of God come with power."[43] Before his arrest, Mark says, Jesus warned that although "the end is not yet,"[44] they must expect it at any time. All three gospels insist that the Kingdom will come in the near future (though they also contain many passages indicating that it is here already). Luke makes Jesus say explicitly "the kingdom of God is within you."[45] Some gnostic Christians, extending that type of interpretation, expected human liberation to occur not through actual events in history, but through internal transformation.

For similar reasons, gnostic Christians criticized orthodox

views of Jesus that identified him as one external to the disciples, and superior to them. For, according to Mark, when the disciples came to recognize who Jesus was, they thought of him as their appointed King:

> And Jesus went on with his disciples to the villages of Caesarea Philippi; and on the way he asked his disciples, "Who do men say that I am?" And they told him, "John the Baptist; and others say, Elijah; and others one of the prophets." And he asked them, "But who do you say that I am?" Peter answered him, "You are the Christ."[46]

Matthew adds to this that Jesus blessed Peter for the accuracy of his recognition, and declared immediately that the church shall be founded upon Peter, and upon his recognition of Jesus as the Messiah. One of the earliest of all Christian confessions states simply, "Jesus is Lord!" But *Thomas* tells the story differently:

> Jesus said to his disciples, "Compare me to someone and tell me whom I am like." Simon Peter said to him, "You are like a righteous angel." Matthew said to him, "You are like a wise philosopher." Thomas said to him, "Master, my mouth is wholly incapable of saying whom you are like." Jesus said, "I am not your master. Because you have drunk, you have become drunk from the bubbling stream which I have measured out."[48]

Here Jesus does not deny his role as Messiah or as teacher, at least in relation to Peter and Matthew. But here they—and their answers—represent an inferior level of understanding. Thomas, who recognizes that he cannot assign any specific role to Jesus, transcends, at this moment of recognition, the relation of student to master. He becomes himself like the "living Jesus," who declares, "Whoever will drink from my mouth will become as I am, and I myself will become that person, and the things that are hidden will be revealed to him."[49]

Gnostic sources often do depict Jesus answering questions, taking the role of teacher, revealer, and spiritual master. But here, too, the gnostic model stands close to the psychotherapeutic one. Both acknowledge the need for guidance, but only as a provisional measure. The purpose of accepting authority is to learn to outgrow it. When one becomes mature, one no longer needs any external authority. The one who formerly took the place of a disciple comes to recognize himself as Jesus' "twin brother." Who, then, is Jesus the teacher? *Thomas the Contender* identifies him simply as "the knowledge of the truth."[50] According to the *Gospel of Thomas*, Jesus refused to validate the experience that the disciples must discover for themselves:

> They said to him, "Tell us who you are so that we may believe in you." He said to them, "You read the face of the sky and of the earth, but you have not recognized the one who is before you, and you do not know how to read this moment."[51]

And when, in frustration, they asked him, "Who are you, that you should say these things to us?" Jesus, instead of answering, criticized their question: "You do not realize who I am from what I say to you."[52] We noted already that, according to *Thomas*, when the disciples asked Jesus to show them where he was so that they might reach that place as well, he refused, directing them instead to themselves, to discover the resources hidden within. The same theme occurs in the *Dialogue of the Savior*. As Jesus talks with his three chosen disciples, Matthew asks him to show him the "place of life," which is, he says, the "pure light." Jesus answers, "Every one [of you] who has known himself has seen it."[53] Here again, he deflects the question, pointing the disciple instead toward his own self-discovery. When the disciples, expecting him to reveal secrets to them, ask Jesus, "Who is the one who seeks, [and who is the one who] reveals?"[54] he answers that the one who seeks the truth—the disciple—is also the one who reveals it. Since Matthew persists in asking him questions, Jesus says that he does not know the answer himself, "nor have I heard about it, except from you."[55]

The disciple who comes to know himself can discover, then, what even Jesus cannot teach. The *Testimony of Truth* says that the gnostic becomes a "disciple of his [own] mind,"[56] discovering that his own mind "is the father of the truth."[57] He learns what he needs to know by himself in meditative silence. Consequently, he considers himself equal to everyone, maintaining his own independence of anyone else's authority: "And he is patient with everyone; he makes himself equal to everyone, and he also separates himself from them."[58] Silvanus, too, regards "your mind" as "a guiding principle." Whoever follows the direction of his own mind need not accept anyone else's advice:

> Have a great number of friends, but not counselors.
> ... But if you do acquire [a friend], do not entrust yourself
> to him. Entrust yourself to God alone as father and as
> friend.[59]

Finally, those gnostics who conceived of *gnosis* as a subjective, immediate experience, concerned themselves above all with the internal significance of events. Here again they diverged from orthodox tradition, which maintained that human destiny depends upon the events of "salvation history"—the history of Israel, especially the prophets' predictions of Christ and then his actual coming, his life, and his death and resurrection. All of the New Testament gospels, whatever their differences, concern themselves with Jesus as a historical person. And all of them rely on the prophets' predictions to prove the validity of the Christian message. Matthew, for example, continually repeats the refrain, "This was done to fulfill what was spoken by the prophets."[60] Justin, too, attempting to persuade the emperor of the truth of Christianity, points as proof toward the fulfillment of prophecy: "And this indeed you can see for yourselves, and be convinced of by fact."[61] But according to the *Gospel of Thomas*, Jesus dismisses as irrelevant the prophets' predictions:

> His disciples said to him, "Twenty-four prophets spoke
> in Israel, and all of them spoke in you." He said to them,
> "You have ignored the one living in your presence, and
> have spoken (only) of the dead."[62]

Such gnostic Christians saw actual events as secondary to their perceived meaning.

For this reason, this type of gnosticism shares with psychotherapy a fascination with the nonliteral significance of language, as both attempt to understand the internal quality of experience. The psychoanalyst C. C. Jung has interpreted Valentinus' creation myth as a description of the psychological processes. Valentinus tells how all things originate from "the depth," the "abyss"[63]—in psychoanalytic terms, from the unconscious. From that "depth" emerge Mind and Truth, and from them, in turn, the Word (Logos) and Life. And it was the word that brought humanity into being. Jung read this as a mythical account of the origin of human consciousness.

A psychoanalyst might find significance as well in the continuation of this myth, as Valentinus tells how Wisdom, youngest daughter of the primal Couple, was seized by a passion to know the Father which she interpreted as love. Her attempts to know him would have led her to self-destruction had she not encountered a power called The Limit, "a power which supports all things and preserves them,"[64] which freed her of emotional turmoil and restored her to her original place.

A follower of Valentinus, the author of the *Gospel of Philip*, explores the relationship of experiential truth to verbal description. He says that "truth brought names into existence in the world because it is not possible to teach it without names."[65] But truth must be clothed in symbols: "Truth did not come into the world naked, but it came in types and images. One will not receive truth in any other way."[66] This gnostic teacher criticizes those who mistake religious language for a literal language, professing faith in God, in Christ, in the resurrection or the church, as if these were all "things" external to themselves. For, he explains, in ordinary speech, each word refers to a specific, external phenomenon; a person "sees the sun without being a sun, and he sees the sky and the earth and everything else, but he is not these things."[67] Religious language, on the other hand, is a language of internal transformation; whoever perceives divine reality "becomes what he sees":

> . . . You saw the spirit, you became spirit. You saw Christ, you became Christ. You saw [the Father, you] shall become Father. . . . you see yourself, and what you see you shall [become].[68]

Whoever achieves *gnosis* becomes "no longer a Christian, but a Christ."[69]

We can see, then, that such gnosticism was more than a protest movement against orthodox Christianity. Gnosticism also included a religious perspective that implicitly opposed the development of the kind of institution that became the early catholic church. Those who expected to "become Christ" themselves were not likely to recognize the institutional structures of the church—its bishop, priest, creed, canon, or ritual—as bearing ultimate authority.

This religious perspective differentiates gnosticism not only from orthodoxy, but also, for all the similarities, from psychotherapy, for most members of the psychotherapeutic profession follow Freud in refusing to attribute real existence to the figments of imagination. They do not regard their attempt to discover what is within the psyche as equivalent to discovering the secrets of the universe. But many gnostics, like many artists, search for interior self-knowledge as the key to understanding universal truths—"who we are, where we came from, where we go." According to the *Book of Thomas the Contender*, "whoever has not known himself has known nothing, but he who has known himself has at the same time already achieved knowledge about the depths of all things."[70]

This conviction—that whoever explores human experience simultaneously discovers divine reality—is one of the elements that marks gnosticism as a distinctly religious movement. Simon Magus, Hippolytus reports, claimed that each human being is a dwelling place, "and that in him dwells an infinite power . . . the root of the universe."[71] But since that infinite power exists in two modes, one actual, the other potential, so this infinite power "exists in a latent condition in everyone," but "potentially, not actually."[72]

How is one to realize that potential? Many of the gnostic sources cited so far contain only aphorisms directing the disciple to search for knowledge, but refraining from telling anyone how to search. Discovering that for oneself is, apparently, the first step toward self-knowledge. Thus, in the *Gospel of Thomas*, the disciples ask Jesus to tell them what to do:

> His disciples questioned him and said to him, "Do you want us to fast? How shall we pray? Shall we give alms? What diet shall we observe?" Jesus said, "Do not tell lies, and do not do what you hate . . ."[73]

His ironic answer turns them back to themselves: who but oneself can judge when one is lying or what one hates? Such cryptic answers earned sharp criticism from Plotinus, the neo-Platonic philosopher who attacked the gnostics when their teaching was attracting some of his own students away from philosophy. Plotinus complained that the gnostics had no program for teaching: "They say only, 'Look to God!,' but they do not tell anyone *where* or *how* to look."[74]

Yet several of the sources discovered at Nag Hammadi do describe techniques of spiritual discipline. *Zostrianos*, the longest text in the Nag Hammadi library, tells how one spiritual master attained enlightenment, implicitly setting out a program for others to follow. Zostrianos relates that, first, he had to remove from himself physical desires, probably by ascetic practices. Second, he had to reduce "chaos in mind,"[75] stilling his mind with meditation. Then, he says, "after I set myself straight, I saw the perfect child"[76]—a vision of the divine presence. Later, he says, "I was pondering these matters in order to understand them. . . . I did not cease seeking a place of rest worthy of my spirit . . ."[77] But then, becoming "deeply troubled," discouraged with his progress, he went out into the desert, half anticipating being killed by wild animals. There, Zostrianos relates, he first received a vision of "the messenger of the knowledge of the eternal Light,"[78] and went on to experience many other visions, which he relates in order to encourage others: "Why are you hesitating? Seek when you are sought; when you are invited, listen. . . . Look at the Light. Flee the darkness. Do not be led astray to your destruction."[79]

Other gnostic sources offer more specific directions. The *Discourse on the Eighth and the Ninth* discloses an "order of tradition" that guides the ascent to higher knowledge. Written in dialogue form, the *Discourse* opens as the student reminds his spiritual master of a promise:

> "[O my father], yesterday you promised me [that you would bring] my mind into [the] eighth and afterwards you would bring me into the ninth. You said that this is the order of the tradition."[80]

His teacher assents: "O my son, indeed this is the order. But the promise was according to human nature."[81] He explains that the disciple himself must bring forth the understanding he seeks: "I set forth the action for you. But the understanding dwells in you. In me, (it is) as if the power were pregnant."[82] The disciple is astonished; is the power, then, actually within him? The master suggests that they both must pray that the disciple may come to the higher levels, the "eighth and the ninth." Already he has progressed through the first seven levels of understanding, impelled by moral effort and dedication. But the disciple admits that, so far, he has no firsthand experience of divine knowledge: "O my father, I understand nothing but the beauty which came to me in books."[83]

Now that he is ready to go beyond vicarious knowledge, the two join in prayer "to the perfect, invisible God to whom one speaks in silence."[84] The prayer moves into a chant of sacred words and vowels: "Zoxathazo a ōō ēē ōōō ēēē ōōōō ēē ōōōōōōōōōōōō ōōōōōō uuuuuu ōōōōōōōōōōōō ōōō Zozazoth."[85] After intoning the chant, the teacher prays, "Lord . . . acknowledge the spirit that is in us."[86] Then he enters into an ecstatic state:

> ". . . I see! I see indescribable depths. How shall I tell
> you, O my son? . . . How [shall I describe] the universe?
> I [am mind and] I see another mind, the one that [moves]
> the soul! I see the one that moves me from pure forgetful-
> ness. You give me power! I see myself! I want to speak!
> Fear restrains me. I have found the beginning of the power
> that is above all powers, the one that has no beginning. . . .
> I have said, O my son, that I am Mind. I have seen! Language
> is not able to reveal this. For the entire eighth, O my son,
> and the souls that are in it, and the angels, sing a hymn in
> silence. And I, Mind, understand."[87]

Watching, the disciple himself is filled with ecstasy: "I rejoice, O my father, because I see you smiling. And the universe rejoices." Seeing his teacher as himself embodying the divine, the disciple pleads with him, "Let not my soul be deprived of the great divine vision. For everything is possible for you as master of the universe." The master tells him to sing in silence, and to "ask what you want in silence":

> When he had finished praising he shouted, "Father
> Trismegistus! What shall I say? We have received this light.
> And I myself see the same vision in you. I see the eighth
> and the souls that are in it and the angels singing a hymn
> to the ninth and its powers. . . . I pray to the end of the
> universe and the beginning of the beginning, to the object
> of man's quest, the immortal discovery . . . I am the instru-
> ment of thy spirit. Mind is thy plectrum. And thy counsel
> plucks me. I see myself! I have received power from thee.
> For thy love has reached us."[88]

The *Discourse* closes as the master instructs the student to write his experiences in a book (presumably the *Discourse* itself) to guide others who will "advance by stages, and enter into the way of immortality. . . . into the understanding of the eighth that reveals the ninth."[89]

. . .

Another extraordinary text, called *Allogenes*, which means "the stranger" (literally, "one from another race"), referring to the spiritually mature person who becomes a "stranger" to the world, also describes the stages of attaining *gnosis*. Here Messos, the initiate, at the first stage, learns of "the power that is within you." Allogenes explains to him his own process of spiritual development:

> . . . [I was] very disturbed, and [I] turned to myself. . . . [Having] seen the light that [surrounded] me and the good that was within me, I became divine.[90]

Then, Allogenes continues, he received a vision of a feminine power, Youel, "she who belongs to all the glories,"[91] who told him:

> . . . "Since your instruction has become complete, and you have known the good that is within you, hear concerning the Triple Power those things that you will guard in great silence and great mystery . . ."[92]

That power, paradoxically, is silent, although it utters sound: zza zza zza.[93] This, like the chant in the *Discourse*, suggests a meditative technique that includes intoning sound.

Having first discovered "the good . . . within me," Allogenes advanced to the second stage—to know oneself.

> [And then I] prayed that [the revelation] might occur to me. . . . I did not despair . . . I prepared myself therein, and I took counsel with myself for a hundred years. And I rejoiced exceedingly, since I was in a great light and a blessed path . . .[94]

Following this, Allogenes says, he had an experience out of the body, and saw "holy powers" that offered him specific instruction:

> . . . "O Allo[g]enes, behold your blessedness . . . in silence, wherein you know yourself as you are, and, seeking yourself, ascend to the Vitality that you will see moving. And if it is impossible for you to stand, fear nothing; but

if you wish to stand, ascend to the Existence, and you will find it standing and stilling itself . . . And when you receive a revelation . . . and you become afraid in that place, withdraw back because of the energies. And when you have become perfect in that place, still yourself."[95]

Is this speech of the "holy powers" to be recited in some dramatic performance enacted by members of the gnostic sect for the initiate in the course of ritual instruction? The text does not say, although the candidate goes on to describe his response:

Now I was listening to these things as those present spoke them. There was a stillness of silence within me, and I heard the blessedness whereby I knew myself as ⟨I am⟩.[96]

Following the instruction, the initiate says he was filled with "revelation . . . I received power . . . I knew the One who exists in me, and the Triple Power, and the revelation of his uncontainableness."[97] Ecstatic with this discovery, Allogenes desires to go further: "I was seeking the ineffable and Unknown God."[98] But at this point the "powers" tell Allogenes to cease in his futile attempt.

Contrary to many other gnostic sources, *Allogenes* teaches that, first, one can come to know "the good that is within," and second, to know oneself and "the one who exists within," but one cannot attain knowledge of the Unknown God. Any attempt to do so, to grasp the incomprehensible, hinders "the effortlessness which is within you." Instead, the initiate must content himself to hear about God "in accordance with the capacity provided by a primary revelation."[99] One's own experience and knowledge, then, essential for spiritual development, provides the basis for receiving understanding about God in *negative* form. *Gnosis* involves recognizing, finally, the limits of human knowledge:

". . . (Whoever) sees (God) as he is in every respect, or would say that he is something like *gnosis*, has sinned against him . . . because he did not know God."[100]

The powers instructed him "not [to] seek anything more, but go . . . It is not fitting to spend more time seeking."[101] Allogenes says he wrote this down for "the sake of those who will be worthy."[102] The detailed exposition of the initiate's experience, including sections of prayers, chants, instruction, punctuated by his retreat into meditation, suggest that the text records actual techniques of initiation for attaining that self-knowledge which is knowledge of divine power within.

But much of gnostic teaching on spiritual discipline remained, on principle, unwritten. For anyone can read what is written down—even those who are not "mature." Gnostic teachers usually reserved their secret instruction, sharing it only verbally, to ensure each candidate's suitability to receive it. Such instruction required each teacher to take responsibility for highly select, individualized attention to each candidate. And it required the candidate, in turn, to devote energy and time—often years—to the process. Tertullian sarcastically compares Valentinian initiation to that of the Eleusinian mysteries, which

> first beset all access to their group with tormenting conditions; and they require a long initiation before they enroll their members, even instruction for five years for their adept students, so that they may educate their opinions by this suspension of full knowledge, and, apparently, raise the value of their mysteries in proportion to the longing for them which they have created. Then follows the duty of silence . . .[103]

Obviously, such a program of discipline, like the higher levels of Buddhist teaching, would appeal only to a few. Although major themes of gnostic teaching, such as the discovery of the divine within, appealed to so many that they constituted a major threat to catholic doctrine, the religious perspectives and methods of gnosticism did not lend themselves to mass religion. In this respect, it was no match for the highly effective system of organization of the catholic church, which expressed a unified religious perspective based on the New Testament canon, offered a creed requiring the initiate to confess only the simplest essentials of faith, and celebrated rituals as simple and profound as baptism and the eucharist. The same basic framework of doctrine, ritual, and organization sustains nearly all Christian churches today, whether Roman Catholic, Orthodox, or Protestant. Without these elements, one can scarcely imagine how the Christian faith could have survived and attracted so many millions of adherents all over the world, throughout twenty centuries. For ideas alone do not make a religion powerful, although it cannot succeed without them; equally important are social and political structures that identify and unite people into a common affiliation.

CONCLUSION

I T IS THE WINNERS who write history—their way. No wonder, then, that the viewpoint of the successful majority has dominated all traditional accounts of the origin of Christianity. Ecclesiastical Christians first defined the terms (naming themselves "orthodox" and their opponents "heretics"); then they proceeded to demonstrate—at least to their own satisfaction —that their triumph was historically inevitable, or, in religious terms, "guided by the Holy Spirit."

But the discoveries at Nag Hammadi reopen fundamental questions. They suggest that Christianity might have developed in very different directions—or that Christianity as we know it might not have survived at all. Had Christianity remained multiform, it might well have disappeared from history, along with dozens of rival religious cults of antiquity. I believe that we owe the survival of Christian tradition to the organizational and theological structure that the emerging church developed. Anyone as powerfully attracted to Christianity as I am will regard that as a major achievement. We need not be surprised, then, that the religious ideas enshrined in the creed (from "I believe in one God," who is "Father Almighty," and Christ's incarnation, death, and bodily resurrection "on the third day," to faith in the "holy, catholic, and apostolic church") coincide with social and political issues in the formation of orthodox Christianity.

Furthermore, since historians themselves tend to be intellectuals, it is, again, no surprise that most have interpreted the controversy between orthodox and gnostic Christians in terms of the "history of ideas," as if ideas, themselves assumed to be the essential mainspring of human action, battled (presumably in some disembodied state) for supremacy. So Tertullian, himself a highly intelligent man, fond of abstract thought, complained that "heretics and philosophers" concerned themselves with the same questions. The "questions that make people heretics"[1] are, he says, the following: Where does humanity come from, and how? Where does evil come from, and why? Tertullian insists (at least before his own violent break with the church) that the catholic church prevailed because it offered "truer" answers to these questions.

Yet the majority of Christians, gnostic and orthodox, like religious people of every tradition, concerned themselves with ideas primarily as expressions or symbols of religious experience. Such experience remains the source and testing ground of all religious ideas (as, for example, a man and a woman are likely to experience differently the idea that God is masculine). Gnosticism and orthodoxy, then, articulated very different kinds of human experience; I suspect that they appealed to different types of persons.

For when gnostic Christians inquired about the origin of evil they did not interpret the term, as we do, primarily in terms of moral evil. The Greek term *kakía* (like the English term "ill-ness") originally meant "what is bad"—what one desires to avoid, such as physical pain, sickness, suffering, misfortune, every kind of harm. When followers of Valentinus asked about the source of *kakía*, they referred especially to emotional harm—

fear, confusion, grief. According to the *Gospel of Truth*, the process of self-discovery begins as a person experiences the "anguish and terror"[2] of the human condition, as if lost in a fog or haunted in sleep by terrifying nightmares. Valentinus' myth of humanity's origin, as we have seen, describes the anticipation of death and destruction as the experiential beginning of the gnostic's search. "They say that all materiality was formed from three experiences [or: sufferings]: terror, pain, and confusion [*aporia*; literally, "roadlessness," not knowing where to go]."[3]

Since such experiences, especially the fear of death and dissolution, are located, in the first place, in the body, the gnostic tended to mistrust the body, regarding it as the saboteur that inevitably engaged him in suffering. Nor did the gnostic trust the blind forces that prevail in the universe; after all, these are the forces that constitute the body. What can bring release? Gnostics came to the conviction that the only way out of suffering was to realize the truth about humanity's place and destiny in the universe. Convinced that the only answers were to be found within, the gnostic engaged on an intensely private interior journey.

Whoever comes to experience his own nature—human nature—as itself the "source of all things," the primary reality, will receive enlightenment. Realizing the essential Self, the divine within, the gnostic laughed in joy at being released from external constraints to celebrate his identification with the divine being:

> The gospel of truth is a joy for those who have received from the Father of truth the grace of knowing him . . . For he discovered them in himself, and they discovered him in themselves, the incomprehensible, inconceivable one, the Father, the perfect one, the one who made all things.[4]

In the process, gnostics celebrated—their opponents said they overwhelmingly exaggerated—the greatness of human nature. Humanity itself, in its primordial being, was disclosed to be the "God over all." The philosopher Plotinus, who agreed with his master, Plato, that the universe was divinely created and that nonhuman intelligences, including the stars, share in immortal soul,[5] castigated the gnostics for "thinking very well of themselves, and very ill of the universe."[6]

Although, as the great British scholar Arthur Darby Nock has stated, gnosticism "involves no recoil from society, but a desire to concentrate on inner well being,"[7] the gnostic pursued an essentially solitary path. According to the *Gospel of Thomas*, Jesus praises this solitude: "Blessed are the solitary and the chosen, for you will find the Kingdom. For you are from it, and to it you will return."[8]

This solitude derives from the gnostics' insistence on the primacy of immediate experience. No one else can tell another which way to go, what to do, how to act. The gnostic could not accept on faith what others said, except as a provisional measure, until one found one's own path, "for," as the gnostic teacher Heracleon says, "people at first are led to believe in the Savior through others," but when they become mature "they no longer rely on mere human testimony," but discover instead their own immediate relationship with "the truth itself."[9] Whoever follows secondhand testimony—even testimony of the apostles and the Scriptures—could earn the rebuke Jesus delivered to his disciples when they quoted the prophets to him: "You have ignored the one living in your presence and have spoken (only) of the dead."[10] Only on the basis of immediate experience could one create the poems, vision accounts, myths, and hymns that gnostics prized as proof that one actually has attained *gnosis*.

Compared with that achievement, all others fall away. If "the many"—unenlightened people—believed that they would find fulfillment in family life, sexual relationships, business, politics, ordinary employment or leisure, the gnostic rejected this belief as illusion. Some radicals rejected all transactions involving sexuality or money: they claimed that whoever rejects sexual intercourse and Mammon "shows [that] he is [from] the generation of the [Son of Man]."[11] Others, like the Valentinians, married, raised children, worked at ordinary employment, but like devout Buddhists, regarded all these as secondary to the solitary, interior path of *gnosis*.

Orthodox Christianity, on the other hand, articulated a different kind of experience. Orthodox Christians were concerned—far more than gnostics—with their relationships with other people. If gnostics insisted that humanity's original experience of evil involved internal emotional distress, the orthodox dissented. Recalling the story of Adam and Eve, they explained that humanity discovered evil in human violation of the natural order, itself essentially "good." The orthodox interpreted evil (*kakía*) primarily in terms of violence against others (thus giving the moral connotation of the term). They revised the Mosaic code, which prohibits physical violation of others—murder, stealing, adultery—in terms of Jesus' prohibition against even mental and emotional violence—anger, lust, hatred.

Agreeing that human suffering derives from human fault, orthodox Christians affirmed the natural order. Earth's plains, deserts, seas, mountains, stars, and trees form an appropriate home for humanity. As part of that "good" creation, the orthodox recognized the processes of human biology: they tended to trust and affirm sexuality (at least in marriage), procreation, and human development. The orthodox Christian saw Christ not as one who leads souls out of this world into enlightenment, but as "fullness of God" come down into human experience—into *bodily* experience—to sacralize it. Irenaeus declares that Christ

> did not despise or evade any condition of humanity, nor set aside for himself the law which he had appointed for the human race, but sanctified every age . . . He therefore passes through every age, becoming an infant for infants, thus sanctifying infants; a child for children, thus sanctifying those who are at this age . . . a youth for youths . . . and . . . because he was an old man for old people . . . sanctifying at the same time the aged also . . . then, at last, he came onto death itself.[12]

To maintain the consistency of his theory, Irenaeus revised the common tradition that Jesus died in his thirties: lest old age be left unsanctified by Christ's participation, Irenaeus argued that Jesus was more than fifty years old when he died.[13]

But it is not only the story of Christ that makes ordinary life sacred. The orthodox church gradually developed rituals to sanction major events of biological existence: the sharing of food, in the eucharist; sexuality, in marriage; childbirth, in baptism; sickness, in anointment; and death, in funerals. The social arrangements that these events celebrated, in communities, in the family, and in social life, all bore, for the orthodox believer, vitally important ethical responsibilities. The believer heard church leaders constantly warning against incurring sin in the most practical affairs of life: cheating in business, lying to a spouse, tyrannizing children or slaves, ignoring the poor. Even their pagan critics noticed that Christians appealed to the destitute by alleviating two of their major anxieties: Christians provided food for the poor, and they buried the dead.

While the gnostic saw himself as "one out of a thousand, two out of ten thousand,"[14] the orthodox experienced himself as one member of the common human family, and as one member of a universal church. According to Professor Helmut Koester, "the test of orthodoxy is whether it is able to build a *church* rather than a club or school or a sect, or merely a series of concerned religious individuals."[15] Origen, the most brilliant theologian of the third century, expressed, although he was himself brought under suspicion of heresy, the orthodox viewpoint when he declared that God would not have offered a way of salvation accessible only to an intellectual or spiritual elite. What the church teaches, he agreed, must be simple, unanimous, accessible to all. Irenaeus declares that

> as the sun, that creature of God, is one and the same throughout the whole world, so also the preaching of the truth shines everywhere, and enlightens all people who are willing . . . Nor will any one of the rulers in the churches,

however highly gifted he may be in matters of eloquence,
teach doctrines different from these.[16]

Irenaeus encouraged his community to enjoy the security of
believing that their faith rested upon absolute authority: the
canonically approved Scriptures, the creed, church ritual, and
the clerical hierarchy.

If we go back to the earliest known sources of Christian
tradition—the sayings of Jesus (although scholars disagree on
the question of *which* sayings are genuinely authentic), we can
see how both gnostic and orthodox forms of Christianity could
emerge as variant interpretations of the teaching and significance
of Christ. Those attracted to solitude would note that even the
New Testament gospel of Luke includes Jesus' saying that
whoever "does not hate his own father and mother and wife and
children and brothers and sisters, yes, and even his own life, he
cannot be my disciple."[17] He demanded that those who followed
him must give up everything—family, home, children, ordinary
work, wealth—to join him. And he himself, as prototype, was
a homeless man who rejected his own family, avoided marriage
and family life, a mysterious wanderer who insisted on truth at
all costs, even the cost of his own life. Mark relates that Jesus
concealed his teaching from the masses, and entrusted it only to
the few he considered worthy to receive it.[18]

Yet the New Testament gospels also offer accounts that
lend themselves to a very different interpretation. Jesus blessed
marriage and declared it inviolable;[19] he welcomed the children
who surrounded him;[20] he responded with compassion to the
most common forms of human suffering,[21] such as fever, blindness, paralysis, and mental illness, and wept[22] when he realized
that his people had rejected him. William Blake, noting such
different portraits of Jesus in the New Testament, sided with the
one the gnostics preferred against "the vision of Christ that all
men see":

The vision of Christ that thou dost see
Is my vision's deepest enemy . . .

Thine is the friend of all Mankind,
Mine speaks in parables to the blind:
Thine loves the same world that mine hates,
Thy Heaven doors are my Hell gates ...
Both read the Bible day and night
But thou read'st black where I read white ...
Seeing this False Christ, In fury and passion
I made my Voice heard all over the Nation.[23]

Nietzsche, who detested what he knew as Christianity, nevertheless wrote: "There was only one Christian, and he died on the cross."[24] Dostoevsky, in *The Brothers Karamazov*, attributes to Ivan a vision of the Christ rejected by the church, the Christ who "desired man's free love, that he should follow Thee freely,"[25] choosing the truth of one's own conscience over material well-being, social approval, and religious certainty. Like the author of the *Second Treatise of the Great Seth*, Ivan denounced the orthodox church for seducing people away from "the truth of their freedom."[26]

We can see, then, how conflicts arose in the formation of Christianity between those restless, inquiring people who marked out a solitary path of self-discovery and the institutional framework that gave to the great majority of people religious sanction and ethical direction for their daily lives. Adapting for its own purposes the model of Roman political and military organization, and gaining, in the fourth century, imperial support, orthodox Christianity grew increasingly stable and enduring. Gnostic Christianity proved no match for the orthodox faith, either in terms of orthodoxy's wide popular appeal, what Nock called its "perfect because unconscious correspondence to the needs and aspirations of ordinary humanity,"[27] or in terms of its effective organization. Both have ensured its survival through time. But the process of establishing orthodoxy ruled out every other option. To the impoverishment of Christian tradition, gnosticism, which offered alternatives to what became the main thrust of Christian orthodoxy, was forced outside.

The concerns of gnostic Christians survived only as a suppressed current, like a river driven underground. Such currents resurfaced throughout the Middle Ages in various forms of heresy; then, with the Reformation, Christian tradition again took on new and diverse forms. Mystics like Jacob Boehme, himself accused of heresy, and radical visionaries like George Fox, themselves unfamiliar, in all probability, with gnostic tradition, nevertheless articulated analogous interpretations of religious experience. But the great majority of the movements that emerged from the Reformation—Baptist, Pentecostal, Methodist, Episcopal, Congregational, Presbyterian, Quaker—remained within the basic framework of orthodoxy established in the second century. All regarded the New Testament writings alone as authoritative; most accepted the orthodox creed and retained the Christian sacraments, even when they altered their form and interpretation.

Now that the Nag Hammadi discoveries give us a new perspective on this process, we can understand why certain creative persons throughout the ages, from Valentinus and Heracleon to Blake, Rembrandt, Dostoevsky, Tolstoy, and Nietzsche, found themselves at the edges of orthodoxy. All were fascinated by the figure of Christ—his birth, life, teachings, death, and resurrection: all returned constantly to Christian symbols to express their own experience. And yet they found themselves in revolt against orthodox institutions. An increasing number of people today share their experience. They cannot rest solely on the authority of the Scriptures, the apostles, the church—at least not without inquiring how that authority constituted itself, and what, if anything, gives it legitimacy. All the old questions—the original questions, sharply debated at the beginning of Christianity—are being reopened: How is one to understand the resurrection? What about women's participation in priestly and episcopal office? Who was Christ, and how does he relate to the believer? What are the similarities between Christianity and other world religions?

That I have devoted so much of this discussion to gnosticism does not mean, as the casual reader might assume, that I advocate going back to gnosticism—much less that I "side with it" against orthodox Christianity. As a historian, of course, I find the discoveries at Nag Hammadi enormously exciting, since the evidence they offer opens a new perspective for understanding what fascinates me most—the history of Christianity. But the task of the historian, as I understand it, is not to advocate any side, but to explore the evidence—in this instance, to attempt to discover how Christianity originated. Furthermore, as a person concerned with religious questions, I find that rediscovering the controversies that occupied early Christianity sharpens our awareness of the major issue in the whole debate, then and now: What is the source of religious authority? For the Christian, the question takes more specific form: What is the relation between the authority of one's own experience and that claimed for the Scriptures, the ritual, and the clergy?

When Muḥammed 'Alī smashed that jar filled with papyrus on the cliff near Nag Hammadi and was disappointed not to find gold, he could not have imagined the implications of his accidental find. Had they been discovered 1,000 years earlier, the gnostic texts almost certainly would have been burned for their heresy. But they remained hidden until the twentieth century, when our own cultural experience has given us a new perspective on the issues they raise. Today we read them with different eyes, not merely as "madness and blasphemy" but as Christians in the first centuries experienced them—a powerful alternative to what we know as orthodox Christian tradition. Only now are we beginning to consider the questions with which they confront us.

NOTES

INTRODUCTION

1. J. M. Robinson, Introduction, in *The Nag Hammadi Library* (New York, 1977), 21–22. Hereafter cited as NHL.

2. *Ibid.*, 22.

3. *Gospel of Thomas* 32.10–11, in NHL 118.

4. *Ibid.*, 45.29–33, in NHL 126.

5. *Gospel of Philip* 63.32–64.5, in NHL 138.

6. *Apocryphon of John* 1.2–3, in NHL 99.

7. *Gospel of the Egyptians* 40.12–13, in NHL 195.

8. See discussion by W. Schneemelcher in E. Hennecke, W. Schneemelcher, *New Testament Apocrypha* (transl. from *Neutestamentliche Apocryphen*), (Philadelphia, 1963), I, 97–113. Hereafter cited as NT APOCRYPHA. J. A. Fitzmyer, "The Oxyrhynchus Logoi of Jesus and the Coptic Gospel According to Thomas," in *Essays on the Semitic Background of the New Testament* (Missoula, 1974), 355–433.

9. Robinson, Introduction, in NHL 13–18.

10. Irenaeus, *Libros Quinque Adversus Haereses* 3.11.9. Hereafter cited as AH.

11. M. Malanine, H.-Ch. Puech, G. Quispel, W. Till, R. McL. Wilson, *Evangelium Veritatis* (Zürich and Stuttgart, 1961), Introduction.

12. H. Koester, Introduction to the *Gospel of Thomas*, NHL 117.

13. *Testimony of Truth* 45:23–48:18, in NHL 411–412.

14. *Thunder, Perfect Mind* 13:16–14:15, in NHL 271–272.

15. Irenaeus, AH *Praefatio*.

16. Irenaeus, AH 3.11.9.

17. H. M. Schenke, *Die Herkunft des sogennanten Evangelium Veritatis* (Berlin, 1958; Göttingen, 1959).

Notes

18. Hippolytus, *Refutationis Omnium Haeresium* 1. Hereafter cited as REF.

19. See F. Wisse, "Gnosticism and Early Monasticism in Egypt," in *Gnosis: Festschrift für Hans Jonas* (Göttingen, 1978), 431–440.

20. Theodotus, cited in Clemens Alexandrinus, *Excerpta ex Theodoto* 78.2. Hereafter cited as EXCERPTA.

21. Hippolytus, REF 8.15.1–2. Emphasis added.

22. *Gospel of Thomas* 35.4–7 and 50.28–30, conflated, in NHL 119 and 129.

23. E. Conze, "Buddhism and Gnosis," in *Le Origini dello Gnosticismo: Colloquio di Messina 13–18 Aprile 1966* (Leiden, 1967), 665.

24. Hippolytus, REF 1.24.

25. Conze, "Buddhism and Gnosis," 665–666.

26. One scholar who, even before the Nag Hammadi find, *did* suspect such diversity is W. Bauer, whose book, *Rechtgläubigkeit und Ketzerei im ältesten Christentum*, first appeared in 1934. It was translated and published in English as *Orthodoxy and Heresy in Earliest Christianity* (Philadelphia, 1971).

27. See, for example, Bauer, *Orthodoxy and Heresy*, 111–240.

28. See discussion by H.-Ch. Puech, in NT APOCRYPHA 259 f.

29. *Ibid.*, 250 f.

30. *Ibid.*, 244.

31. H. Jonas, *Journal of Religion* (1961) 262, cited in J. M. Robinson, "The Jung Codex: The Rise and Fall of a Monopoly," in *Religious Studies Review* 3.1 (January 1977), 29.

32. For a more complete account of the events briefly sketched here, see Robinson, "The Jung Codex," 17–30.

33. *La bourse égyptienne* (June 10, 1949), cited in Robinson, "The Jung Codex," 20.

34. G. Quispel, *Jung—een mens voor deze tijd* (Rotterdam, 1975), 85.

35. Robinson, "The Jung Codex," 24 f.

36. E. Pagels, *The Johannine Gospel in Gnostic Exegesis* (Nashville, 1973); *The Gnostic Paul: Gnostic Exegesis of the Pauline Letters* (Philadelphia, 1975).

37. E. Pagels, with H. Koester, "Report on the Dialogue of the Savior" (CG III.5), in R. McL. Wilson, *Nag Hammadi and Gnosis* (Leiden, 1978), 66–74.

38. G. Garitte, *Le Muséon* (1960), 214, cited in Robinson, "The Jung Codex," 29.

39. Tertullian, *Adversus Valentinianos* 7.

40. A. von Harnack, *History of Dogma*, trans. from 3rd German ed. (New York, 1961), I.4, 228.

41. *Ibid.*, 229.

42. A. D. Nock, *Early Gentile Christianity and Its Hellenistic Background*, 2nd ed. (New York, 1964), xvi.

Notes

43. W. Bousset, *Kyrios Christos* (1st ed., Göttingen, 1913; 2nd ed., 1921; English trans., 1970), 245.

44. R. Reitzenstein, *Poimandres: Studien zur griechisch-ägyptischen und frühchristlichen Literatur* (Leipzig, 1904; repr. Darmstadt, 1966), 81. See also *Das iranische Erlösungmysterium* (Leipzig, 1921).

45. M. Friedländer, *Der vorchristliche jüdische Gnosticismus* (Göttingen, 1898; 2nd ed., 1972).

46. H. Jonas, *Gnosis und spätantiker Geist, I: Die mythologische Gnosis* (Göttingen, 1st ed., 1934; 2nd ed., 1964).

47. H. Jonas, *The Gnostic Religion* (Boston, 1st ed., 1958; 2nd ed., 1963).

48. *Ibid.*, 320–340.

49. W. Bauer, *Orthodoxy and Heresy in Earliest Christianity* (trans. from 2nd ed., Philadelphia, 1971), xxii.

50. H. E. W. Turner, *The Pattern of Christian Truth: A Study in the Relations Between Orthodoxy and Heresy in the Early Church* (London, 1954).

51. C. H. Roberts, *Manuscript, Society, and Belief in Early Christian Egypt* (London, 1979).

52. A. Guillaumont, H.-Ch. Puech, G. Quispel, W. Till, Y. 'Abd al Masīḥ, *The Gospel According to Thomas: Coptic Text Established and Translated* (Leiden/New York, 1959).

53. *The Facsimile Edition of the Nag Hammadi Codices*, Codices I–XIII (Leiden, 1972). For discussion, see J. M. Robinson, "The Facsimile Edition of the Nag Hammadi Codices," in *Occasional Papers of the Institute for Antiquity and Christianity*, 4 (Claremont, 1972).

54. C. Colpe, *Die religionsgeschichtliche Schule: Darstellung und Kritik ihres Bildes von gnostischen Erlosermythus* (Göttingen, 1961).

55. R. M. Grant, *Gnosticism and Early Christianity*, 2nd ed. (New York, 1966), 27 ff.

56. G. Quispel, *Gnosis als Weltreligion* (Leiden, 1951).

57. H. Jonas, "Delimitation of the gnostic phenomenon—typological and historical," in *Le Origini dello Gnosticismo* (Leiden, 1967), 90–108.

58. E. R. Dodds, *Pagan and Christian in an Age of Anxiety* (Cambridge, 1965), 69–101.

59. G. G. Scholem, *Jewish Gnosticism, Merkabah Mysticism, and Talmudic Tradition* (New York, 1st ed., 1960; 2nd ed., 1965).

60. A. D. Nock, *Essays on Religion and the Ancient World*, ed. Z. Stewart (Cambridge, 1972), II, "Gnosticism," 940 ff.

61. Cf. A. H. Armstrong, "Gnosis and Greek Philosophy," in *Gnosis: Festschrift für Hans Jonas* (Göttingen, 1978), 87–124.

62. B. Layton, *Treatise on Resurrection: Editing, Translation, Commentary* (Missoula, 1979); "Vision and Revision: A Gnostic View of Resurrection," in *Proceedings: Quebec Colloquium on the Texts of Nag Hammadi* (Quebec, 1979).

Notes

63. See, for example, H. Attridge, "Exegetical Problems in the Tripartite Tractate," prepared for the SBL meetings in New Orleans, 1978, and his edition of Codex I from Nag Hammadi, to be published in *Nag Hammadi Studies* (Leiden, 1980).

64. M. Smith, *Clement of Alexandria and a Secret Gospel of Mark* (Cambridge, 1973); *Jesus the Magician* (San Francisco, 1978).

65. J. M. Robinson, H. Koester, *Trajectories Through Early Christianity* (Philadelphia, 1971): see especially Robinson, "*Logoi Sophon*: On the Gattung of Q," 71-113; Koester, "One Jesus and Four Primitive Gospels," 158-204.

66. M. Tardieu, *Trois mythes gnostiques: Adam, Eros et les animaux dans un écrit de Nag Hammadi* (Paris, 1974).

67. L. Schottroff, *Der Glaubende und die feindliche Welt* (Neukirchener, 1970).

68. P. Perkins, *The Gnostic Dialogue* (New York, 1979).

69. P. Perkins, "Deceiving the Deity: Self-Transcendence and the Numinous in Gnosticism," in *Proceedings of the Tenth Annual Institute for Philosophy and Religion* (Boston, 1981).

70. G. MacRae, "Sleep and Awakening in Gnostic Texts," in *Le Origini dello Gnosticismo*, 496-510.

71. G. MacRae, "The Jewish Background of the Gnostic Sophia Myth," *Novum Testamentum* 12 (1970), 97 ff.

72. For a recent example, see G. MacRae, "Nag Hammadi and the New Testament," in *Gnosis: Festschrift für Hans Jonas*, 144-157.

73. See, for example, B. A. Pearson, "Jewish Haggadic Traditions in the *Testimony of Truth* from Nag Hammadi (CGIX, 3)," in *Ex Orbe Religionum: Studia Geo Widengren* (Leiden, 1972), 457-470; "Biblical Exegesis in Gnostic Literature," in *Armenian and Biblical Studies*, ed. M. E. Stone (Jerusalem, 1975), 70-80; "The Figure of Melchizedek," in *Proceedings of the XIIth International Congress of the International Association for the History of Religions* (Leiden, 1975), 200-208.

74. D. M. Scholer, *Nag Hammadi Bibliography* (Leiden, 1971).

75. *Apocalypse of Peter* 76.27-30, in NHL 342. In quotations from this text, I am following the translations of J. Brashler, *The Coptic Apocalypse of Peter: A Genre Analysis and Interpretation* (Claremont, 1977).

CHAPTER ONE

For a more technical discussion of this topic, scholars are advised to consult E. Pagels, "Visions, Appearances, and Apostolic Authority: Gnostic and Orthodox Traditions," in *Gnosis: Festschrift für Hans Jonas*, ed. B. Aland (Göttingen, 1978), 415-430.

Notes

1. K. Stendahl, *Immortality and Resurrection* (New York, 1968).
2. Luke 24:36–43.
3. Acts 2:22–36.
4. *Ibid.*, 10:40–41.
5. Tertullian, *De Resurrectione Carnis* 2.
6. Tertullian, *De Carne Christi* 5.
7. *Ibid.*
8. John 20:27.
9. Mark 16:12; Luke 24:13–32.
10. Luke 24:31.
11. John 20:11–17.
12. Acts 9:3–4.
13. *Ibid.*, 9:7.
14. *Ibid.*, 22:9.
15. I. Corinthians 15:50.
16. *Ibid.*, 15:51–53.
17. Mark 10:42–44.
18. Luke 24:34.
19. Matthew 16:13–19.
20. John 21:15–19.
21. H. von Campenhausen, *Ecclesiastical Authority and Spiritual Power* (London, 1969), trans. by J. A. Baker (original title: *Kirchliches Amt und geistliche Vollmacht*, Tübingen, 1953), 17 (see discussion in Ch. 1).
22. Mark 16:9; John 20:11–17.
23. Matthew 28:16–20; Luke 24:36–49; John 20:19–23.
24. Matthew 28:18.
25. Acts 1:15–20.
26. *Ibid.*, 1:22. Emphasis added.
27. *Ibid.*, 1:26.
28. *Ibid.*, 1:6–11.
29. *Ibid.*, 7:56.
30. Acts 9:1–6.
31. *Ibid.*, 22:17–18; cf. also Acts 18:9–10.
32. See J. Lindblom, *Gesichte und Offenbarungen: Vorstellungen von göttlichen Weisungen und übernatürlichen Erscheinungen im ältesten Christentum* (Lund, 1968), 32–113.
33. See K. Holl, *Der Kirchenbegriff des Paulus in seinem Verhältnis zu dem der Urgemeinde*, in *Gesammelte Aufsätze zur Kirchengeschichte* (Tübingen, 1921), II, 50–51.
34. G. Blum, *Tradition und Sukzession: Studium zum Normbegriff des Apostolischen von Paulus bis Irenaeus* (Berlin, 1963), 48.
35. Campenhausen, *Ecclesiastical Authority and Spiritual Power*, 14–24. For discussion, see E. Pagels, "Visions, Appearances, and Apostolic Authority," 415–430.

36. Origen, *Commentarium in I Corinthians*, in *Journal of Theological Studies* 10 (1909), 46–47.

37. Tertullian, *De Resurrectione Carnis*, 19–27.

38. Irenaeus, AH 1.30.13.

39. I Corinthians 15:8.

40. Mark 16:9.

41. John 20:11–19.

42. *Gospel of Mary* 10.17–21, in NHL 472.

43. *Apocalypse of Peter* 83.8–10, in NHL 344. For discussion of Peter in gnostic traditions, see P. Perkins, "Peter in Gnostic Revelations," in *Proceedings of SBL: 1974 Seminar Papers II* (Washington, 1974), 1–13.

44. *Treatise on Resurrection* 48.10–16, in NHL 52–53. See M. L. Peel, *The Epistle to Rheginos; A Valentinian Letter on the Resurrection: Introduction, Translation, Analysis, and Exposition* (London/Philadelphia 1969); B. Layton, *The Gnostic Treatise on Resurrection from Nag Hammadi. Edited, with Translation and Commentary* (Missoula, 1979). The translation I cite follows that of Layton, as noted in the Acknowledgments.

45. *Treatise on Resurrection* 48.34–38, in NHL 53.

46. *Ibid.*, 47.18–49.24, in NHL 53.

47. *Gospel of Philip* 73.1–3, in NHL 144.

48. *Ibid.*, 57.19–20, in NHL 135.

49. Cf. H. Koester, "One Jesus and Four Primitive Gospels," in J. M. Robinson and H. Koester, *Trajectories through Early Christianity* (Philadelphia, 1971), 158–204, and Robinson, "The Johannine Trajectory," *ibid.*, 232–268.

50. Mark 16:9–20.

51. *Gospel of Mary* 9.14–18, in NHL 472.

52. *Ibid.*, 10.4–5, in NHL 472.

53. *Ibid.*, 17.8–15, in NHL 473.

54. *Ibid.*, 18.1–12, in NHL 473.

55. The author of the *Gospel of Mary* may have noted that neither Mark nor John specifies that the resurrected Jesus appeared *physically* to Mary. Mark's account, which adds that Jesus later appeared "in another form," could be taken to suggest that he was a disembodied presence who took on various forms in order to become visible. John's account relates that Jesus warned Mary not to touch him—in contrast to the stories that say he insisted on the disciples' touching him to prove that he was "not a ghost."

56. Irenaeus, AH 3.2.1–3.3.1. See also M. Smith, *Clement of Alexandria and a Secret Gospel of Mark* (Cambridge, 1973), 197–278.

57. *Ibid.*, 3.4.1–2.

58. Mark 4:11.

59. Matthew 13:11.

60. II Corinthians 12:2–4.

Notes

61. I Corinthians 2:6.

62. R. Bultmann, *Theology of the New Testament*, trans. by K. Grobel (London, 1965), I, 327; U. Wilckens, *Weisheit und Torheit* (Tübingen, 1959), 44 f., 214–224.

63. R. Scroggs, "Paul: Σόφος and πνευμάτικος," *New Testament Studies* 14, 33–55. See also E. Pagels, *The Gnostic Paul* (Philadelphia, 1975), 1–10; 55–58; 157–164.

64. *Apocryphon of John* 1.30–2.7, in NHL 99.

65. *Ibid.*, 2.9–18, in NHL 99.

66. *Letter of Peter to Philip* 134.10–18, in NHL 395. For analysis, see M. Meyer, *The Letter of Peter to Philip NHL VIII, 2: Text, Translation, and Commentary* (Claremont, 1979).

67. *Sophia Jesu Christi* 91.8–13, in NHL 207–208.

68. For discussion, see H.-C. Puech, "Gnostic Gospels and Related Documents," in *New Testament Apocrypha* I. 231–362.

69. *Gospel of Philip* 57.28–35, in NHL 135.

70. Clemens Alexandrinus, EXCERPTA 23.4.

71. Irenaeus, AH 3.11.9.

72. *Book of Thomas the Contender* 138.7–18, in NHL 189.

73. Irenaeus, AH 1.18.1.

74. *Acts of John* 94–96, in *New Testament Apocrypha* II. 227–232. For brief discussion, see E. Pagels, "To the Universe Belongs the Dancer," in *Parabola* IV.2 (1979), 7–9.

75. Irenaeus, AH 2.15.3.

76. *Ibid.*, 2.13.3–10. Emphasis added.

77. Heracleon, Frag. 39, in Origen, *Commentarium in Johannes.* Hereafter cited as COMM. JO.

78. Hippolytus, REF 6.42.

79. Irenaeus, AH 1.14.1.

80. *Ibid.*, 1.14.3.

81. *Ibid.*, 1.13.3–4.

82. *Ibid.*, 3.4.1.

83. *Ibid.*, 1.13.6.

84. *Ibid.*, 3.2.2.

85. Ptolemy, *Epistula ad Floram* 7.9; for discussion, see Campenhausen, *Ecclesiastical Authority and Spiritual Power*, 158–161.

86. Irenaeus, AH 1.30.13.

87. *Dialogue of the Savior* 139.12–13, in NHL 235.

88. *Apocalypse of Peter* 72.10–28, in NHL 340–341.

89. *Apocryphon of James* 2.8–15, in NHL 30.

90. Tertullian, *De Praescriptione Haereticorum* 42. Hereafter cited as DE PRAESCR.

91. *Ibid.*, 37.

92. Irenaeus, AH 1.10.2.

93. *Ibid.*, 3.4.1.

Notes

94. *Ibid.*, 3.3.2.

95. *Apocalypse of Peter* 74.16–21, in NHL 341. Cf. Brashler, *The Coptic Apocalypse of Peter*; Perkins, "Peter in Gnostic Revelations."

96. *Apocalypse of Peter* 79.24–30, in NHL 343.

97. *Ibid.*, 76.27–34, in NHL 342.

98. *Ibid.*, 78.31–79.10, in NHL 343.

99. For discussion, see E. Pagels, "The Demiurge and his Archons: A Gnostic View of the Bishop and Presbyters?" in *Harvard Theological Review* 69.3–4 (1976), 301–324.

100. Tertullian, *De Carne Christi* 5.

101. *Gospel of Thomas*, 38.33–39.2, in NHL 121.

102. Cf. E. Leach, *Melchisedek and the Emperor: Icons of Subversion and Orthodoxy*, in *Proceedings of the Royal Anthropological Institute of Great Britain and Ireland for 1972* (London, 1973), 1 ff.

CHAPTER TWO

For a more technical discussion of this subject, see E. Pagels, "The Demiurge and his Archons: A Gnostic View of the Bishop and Presbyters?" in *Harvard Theological Review* 69.3–4 (1976), 301–324.

1. Cf. N. A. Dahl, "The Gnostic Response: The Ignorant Creator," documentation prepared for the Nag Hammadi Section of the Society of Biblical Literature Annual Meeting, 1976.

2. *Hypostasis of the Archons* 86.27–94.26, in NHL 153–158. Note that the citation is conflated from two separate variants of the story in 86.27–87.4 and 94.19–26; a third occurs in the same text at 94.34–95.13. Cf. B. Layton, "The Hypostasis of the Archons," *Harvard Theological Review* 67 (1974), 351 ff.

3. *On the Origin of the World* 103.9–20, in NHL 165. For analysis of the texts, see F. L. Fallon, *The Sabaoth Accounts in "The Nature of the Archons" (CG 11,4) and "On the Origin of the World" (CG 11,5): An Analysis* (Cambridge, 1974).

4. *Apocryphon of John* 11.18–13.13, in NHL 105–106.

5. *Testimony of Truth* 45.24–46.11, in NHL 411.

6. *Ibid.*, 47.7–30, in NHL 412.

7. See excellent discussion by B. A. Pearson, "Jewish Haggadic Traditions in the Testimony of Truth from Nag Hammadi, CG IX, 3," in *Ex Orbe Religionum: Studia Geo Widengren oblata* (Leiden, 1972), 458–470.

8. *On the Origin of the World* 115.31–116.8, in NHL 172.

9. *Hypostasis of the Archons* 89.11–91.1, in NHL 154–155.

10. *Tripartite Tractate* 51.24–52.6, in NHL 55.

11. *A Valentinian Exposition* 22.19–23, in NHL 436.

12. *Interpretation of Knowledge* 9.29, in NHL 430.
13. Irenaeus, AH 4.33.3.
14. *Ibid.*, 3.16.6.
15. *Ibid.*, 3.16.8.
16. *Ibid., Praefatio* 2.
17. *Ibid.*, 4.33.3; 3.16.8.
18. For discussion and references, see Pagels, "The Demiurge and his Archons."
19. Irenaeus, AH 1.11.1.
20. *Ibid.*, 1.1.1; cf. *Tripartite Tractate* 51.1 ff., in NHL 55 ff.
21. Heracleon, Frag. 22, in Origen, COMM. JO. 13.19.
22. *Ibid.*, Frag. 24, in Origen, COMM. JO. 13.25.
23. *Gospel of Philip* 53.24–34, in NHL 132–133.
24. Irenaeus, AH 3.15.2. Emphasis added.
25. Clemens Romanus, *I Clement* 3.3.
26. *Ibid.*, 1.1.
27. *Ibid.*, 14.19–20; 60.
28. *Ibid.*, 60.4–61.2; 63.1–2.
29. *Ibid.*, 63.1.
30. *Ibid.*, 41.3.
31. *Ibid.*, 41.1.
32. See, for example, Campenhausen, *Ecclesiastical Authority and Spiritual Power*, 86–87: "Dogmatic issues are nowhere mentioned. We can no longer discern the background and the real point of the quarrel."
33. So says H. Beyschlag, *Clemens Romanus und der Frühkatholizismus* (Tübingen, 1966), 339–353.
34. Ignatius, *Magnesians* 6.1; *Trallians* 3.1; *Ephesians* 5.3.
35. *Magnesians* 6.1–7.2; *Trallians* 3.1; *Smyrneans* 8.1–2. For citations and discussion, see Pagels, "The Demiurge and his Archons," 306–307.
36. *Trallians* 3.1; *Smyrneans* 8.2.
37. See, for example, Campenhausen, *Ecclesiastical Authority and Spiritual Power*, 84–106.
38. Tertullian, *Adversus Valentinianos* 4.
39. Clemens Alexandrinus, *Stromata* 7.7.
40. Irenaeus, AH 3.2.1–3.1.
41. *Ibid., Praefatio* 2; 3.15.1–2.
42. Clemens Alexandrinus, *Stromata* 4.89.6–90.1.
43. Cf. Plato, *Timaeus* 41. For discussion, see G. Quispel, "The Origins of the Gnostic Demiurge," in *Kyriakon: Festschrift Johannes Quasten* (Münster, 1970), 252–271.
44. Heracleon, Frag. 40, in Origen, COMM. JO. 13.60.
45. *Lord*: Irenaeus, AH 4.1–5.
46. *commander: Ibid.*, 1.7.4.
47. *judge*: Heracleon, Frag. 48, in Origen, COMM. JO. 20.38.
48. Irenaeus, AH 3.12.6–12.

49. *Ibid.*, 1.21.1–4.
50. *Ibid.*, 1.13.6.
51. *Ibid.*, 1.21.5.
52. *Ibid.*, 3.15.2.
53. *Ibid.*, 1.7.4.
54. *Ibid.*, 1.13.6.
55. *Ibid.*, 3.15.2.
56. Tertullian, *Adversus Valentinianos* 4.
57. Irenaeus, AH 3.15.2.
58. *Ibid.*, 3.3.2.
59. *Ibid.*, 3.15.2.
60. *Ibid.*, 1.21.1–2.
61. For a detailed discussion of this process, see Campenhausen, *Ecclesiastical Authority and Spiritual Power*, 76 ff.
62. *Apocalypse of Peter* 79.22–30, in NHL 343.
63. *Tripartite Tractate* 69.7–10, in NHL 64; 70.21–29, in NHL 65; 72.16–19, in NHL 66.
64. *Ibid.*, 79.20–32, in NHL 69.
65. Irenaeus, AH 1.13.1–6.
66. *Ibid.*, 1.13.3
67. *Ibid.*, 1.13.4; for technical discussion of the lot (*kleros*), see Pagels, "The Demiurge and his Archons," 316–318.

Irenaeus tries to deny this: AH 1.13.4.

Such use of lots had precedent both in ancient Israel, where God was thought to express His choice through the casting of lots, and also among the apostles themselves, who selected by lot the twelfth apostle to replace Judas Iscariot (Acts 1:17–20). Apparently the followers of Valentinus intended to follow their example.

68. Tertullian, DE PRAESCR. 41. Emphasis added.
69. *Ibid.*, 41.
70. *Ibid.*, 41.
71. Irenaeus, AH 1.13.1.
72. *Ibid.*, 1.6.2–3.
73. *Ibid.*, Quotation conflated from 3.15.2 and 2.16.4.
74. *Ibid.*, 3.15.2.
75. *Ibid.*, 3.25.1.
76. *Ibid.*, 5.26.1.
77. Irenaeus, *Ad Florinum*, in Eusebius, *Historia ecclesiae* 5.20.4–8.
78. Irenaeus, AH 4.26.3. Emphasis added.
79. *Ibid.*, 4.26.2.
80. *Ibid.*, 4.26.2.
81. *Ibid.*, 1.27.4.
82. *Ibid.*, 5.31.1.
83. *Ibid.*, 5.35.2.

Notes

CHAPTER THREE

1. Where the God of Israel is characterized as husband and lover in the Old Testament, his spouse is described as the community of Israel (e.g., Isaiah 50:1; 54:1–8; Jeremiah 2:2–3; 20–25; 3:1–20; Hosea 1–4, 14) or as the land of Israel (Isaiah 62:1–5).

2. One may note several exceptions to this rule: Deuteronomy 32:11; Hosea 11:1; Isaiah 66:12 ff.; Numbers 11:12.

3. Formerly, as Professor Morton Smith reminds me, theologians often used the masculinity of God to justify, by analogy, the roles of men as rulers of their societies and households (he cites, for example, Milton's *Paradise Lost* IV.296 ff., 635 ff.).

4. *Gospel of Thomas* 51.19–26, in NHL 130.

5. Hippolytus, REF 5.6.

6. Irenaeus, AH 1.11.1.

7. *Ibid.*, 1.13.6.

8. *Ibid.*, 1.13.2.

9. *Ibid.*, 1.13.2.

10. *Ibid.*, 1.14.1.

11. Hippolytus, REF 6. 18.

12. *Ibid.*, 6.17.

13. Irenaeus, AH 1.11.5; Hippolytus, REF 6.29.

14. *Apocryphon of John* 1.31–2.9, in NHL 99.

15. *Ibid.*, 2.9–14, in NHL 99.

16. *Ibid.*, 4.34–5.7, in NHL 101.

17. *Gospel to the Hebrews*, cited in Origen, COMM. JO. 2.12.

18. *Gospel of Thomas* 49.32–50.1, in NHL 128–129.

19. *Gospel of Philip* 52.24, in NHL 132.

20. *Ibid.*, 59.35–60.1, in NHL 136.

21. Hippolytus, REF 6.14.

22. *Ibid.*, 5.19.

23. Irenaeus, AH 1.14.7–8.

24. *Gospel of Philip* 71.3–5, in NHL 143.

25. *Ibid.*, 71.16–19, in NHL 143.

26. *Ibid.*, 55.25–26, in NHL 134.

27. Hippolytus, REF 6.38.

28. *Apocalypse of Adam* 81.2–9, in NHL 262. See note #42 for references.

29. Irenaeus, AH 1.2.2–3.

30. *Ibid.*, 1.4.1.–1.5.4.

31. *Ibid.*, 1.5.1–3. For discussion of the figure of Sophia, see the excellent articles of G. C. Stead, "The Valentinian Myth of Sophia," in *Journal of Theological Studies* 20 (1969), 75–104; and G. W. MacRae,

"The Jewish Background of the Gnostic Sophia Myth," in *Novum Testamentum* 12.

32. Clemens Alexandrinus, EXCERPTA 47.1.
33. Irenaeus, AH 1.13.1–6.
34. *Ibid.*, 1.30.9.
35. *Ibid.*, 1.30.10.
36. *Trimorphic Protennoia* 35.1–24, in NHL 461–462.
37. *Ibid.*, 36.12–16, in NHL 462.
38. *Ibid.*, 42.4–26, in NHL 465–466.
39. *Ibid.*, 45.2–10, in NHL 467.
40. *Thunder, Perfect Mind* 13.16–16.25, in NHL 271–274.
41. Hippolytus, REF 6.18.
42. *Genesis Rabba* 8.1, cited in an excellent discussion of androgyny by W. A. Meeks, "The Image of the Androgyne: Some Uses of a Symbol in Earliest Christianity," in *History of Religions* 13.3 (February 1974), 165–208. For a discussion of androgyny in gnostic sources, see Pagels, "The Gnostic Vision," in *Parabola* 3.4 (November 1978), 6–9.
43. Irenaeus, AH 1.18.2.
44. Clemens Alexandrinus, EXERPTA 21.1.
45. Hippolytus, REF 6.33.
46. Irenaeus, AH 1.5.4; Hippolytus, REF 6.33.
47. *Ibid.*, 1.29.4.
48. *Apocryphon of John* 13.8–14, in NHL 106.
49. Irenaeus, AH 1.30.6.

Note the collection of passages cited by N. A. Dahl in "The Gnostic Response: The Ignorant Creator," prepared for the Nag Hammadi Section of the Society of Biblical Literature Annual Meeting, 1976.

50. *Hypostasis of the Archons* 94.21–95.7, in NHL 158.
51. Hippolytus, REF 6.32.
52. Irenaeus, AH 1.13.5.
53. *Ibid.*, 1.13.3.
54. *Ibid.*, 1.13.4.
55. *Ibid.*, 1.13.3.
56. Hippolytus, REF 6.35; Irenaeus, AH 1.13.1–2.
57. Tertullian, DE PRAESCR. 41.
58. Tertullian, *De Baptismo* 1.
59. Tertullian, *De Virginibus Velandis* 9. Emphasis added.
60. Irenaeus, AH 1.25.6.
61. This general observation is not, however, universally applicable. At least two circles where women acted on an equal basis with men—the Marcionites and the Montanists—retained a traditional doctrine of God. I know of no evidence to suggest that they included feminine imagery in their theological formulations. For discussion and references, see J. Leipoldt, *Die Frau in der antiken Welt und im Urchristentum* (Leipzig,

1955), 187 ff.; E. S. Fiorenza, "Word, Spirit, and Power: Women in Early Christian Communities," in *Women of Spirit*, ed. R. Reuther and E. McLaughlin (New York, 1979), 39 ff.

62. Luke 10:38-42.

Cf. Romans 16:1-2; Colossians 4:15; Acts 2:25; 21:9; Romans 16:6; 16:12; Philippians 4:2-3.

63. See W. Meeks, "The Image of the Androgyne," 180 f. Most scholars agree with Meeks that in Galatians 3:28, Paul quotes a saying that itself belongs to pre-Pauline tradition.

64. Romans 16:7.

This was first pointed out to me by Cyril C. Richardson, and confirmed by recent research of B. Brooten, "Junia . . . Outstanding Among the Apostles," in *Women Priests*, ed. L. and A. Swidler (New York, 1977), 141-144.

65. I Corinthians 11:7-9.

For discussion of I Corinthians 11:7-9, see R. Scroggs, "Paul and the Eschatological Woman," in *Journal of the American Academy of Religion* 40 (1972), 283-303, and the critique by Pagels, "Paul and Women: A Response to Recent Discussion," in *Journal of the American Academy of Religion* 42 (1974), 538-549. Also see references in Fiorenza, "Word, Spirit, and Power," 62, n. 24 and 25.

66. See Leipoldt, *Die Frau*; also C. Schneider, *Kulturgeschichte des Hellenismus* (Munich, 1967), I, 78 ff.; S. A. Pomeroy, *Goddesses, Whores, Wives, and Slaves* (New York, 1975).

67. Cf. C. Vatin, *Recherches sur le mariage et la condition de la femme mariée à l'époque hellénistique* (Paris, 1970).

68. J. Carcopino, *Daily Life in Ancient Rome*, trans. by E. O. Lorimer (New Haven, 1951), 95-100.

69. *Ibid.*, 90-95.

70. L. Swidler, "Greco-Roman Feminism and the Reception of the Gospel," in *Traditio—Krisis—Renovatio*, ed. B. Jaspert (Marburg, 1976), 41-55; see also J. Balsdon, *Roman Women, Their History and Habits* (London, 1962); L. Friedländer, *Roman Life and Manners Under the Early Empire* (Oxford, 1928); B. Förtsch, *Die politische Rolle der Frau in der römischen Republik* (Stuttgart, 1935). On women in Christian communities, see Fiorenza, "Word, Spirit, and Power"; R. Gryson, *The Ministry of Women in the Early Church* (Minnesota, 1976); K. Thraede, "Frau," *Reallexikon für Antike und Christentum* VIII (Stuttgart, 1973), 197-269.

71. Leipoldt, *Die Frau*, 72 ff.; R. H. Kennet, *Ancient Hebrew Social Life and Custom* (London, 1933); G. F. Moore, *Judaism in the First Centuries of the Christian Era* (Cambridge, 1932).

72. I Timothy 2:11-12.

73. Ephesians 5:24; Colossians 3:18.

74. *1 Clement* 1.3.

75. Leipoldt, *Die Frau*, 192; *Hippolytus of Rome*, 43.1, ed. Paul de Lagarder (*Aegyptiaca*, 1883), 253.

76. Leipoldt, *Die Frau*, 193. Emphasis added.

77. *Gospel of Philip* 63.32–64.5, in NHL 138.

78. *Dialogue of the Savior* 139.12–13, in NHL 235.

79. *Gospel of Mary* 17.18–18.15, in NHL 473.

80. *Pistis Sophia* 36.71.

81. I Timothy 3:1–7; Titus 1:5–9.

82. *Apostolic Tradition* 18.3.

83. *Book of Thomas the Contender* 144.8–10, in NHL 193.

84. *Paraphrase of Shem* 27.2–6; in NHL 320.

85. *Dialogue of the Savior* 144.16–20, in NHL 237.

86. *Ibid.*, 139.12–13, in NHL 235.

87. *Gospel of Thomas* 51.23–26, in NHL 130.

88. *Ibid.*, 37.20–35, in NHL 121; 43.25–35, in NHL 124–125.

89. *Gospel of Mary* 9.20, in NHL 472. Emphasis added.

90. Clemens Alexandrinus, *Paidagogos* 1.6.

91. *Ibid.*, 1.4.

92. *Ibid.*, 1.19.

93. Tertullian, DE VIRG. VEL. 9.

CHAPTER FOUR

For a more technical discussion of this topic, see E. Pagels, "Gnostic and Orthodox Views of Christ's Passion: Paradigms for the Christian's Response to Persecution?" in *The Rediscovery of Gnosticism*, ed. B. Layton (Leiden, 1979), I.

1. Tacitus, *Annals* 15.44.2–8. Emphasis added.

2. Josephus, *Antiquities of the Jews* 18.63.

3. Mark 14:43–50.

4. *Ibid.*, 15:1–15.

5. *Ibid.*, 15:37.

6. Luke 23:34–46; John 19:17–30.

7. Mark 15:10.

8. John 11:45–53.

9. Josephus, *The Jewish War* 2.223–233.

10. John 11:47–48.

11. *Ibid.*, 11:49–50.

12. *Apocalypse of Peter* 81.4–24, in NHL 344. Note, again, use of translation by J. Brashler, *The Coptic Apocalypse of Peter*.

13. *Second Treatise of the Great Seth* 56.6–19 in NHL 332.

14. *Acts of John* 88, in NT APOCRYPHA II, 225.

15. *Ibid.*, 89, in NT APOCRYPHA II, 225.
16. *Ibid.*, 93, in NT APOCRYPHA II, 227.
17. *Ibid.*, 94, in NT APOCRYPHA II, 227.
18. *Ibid.*, 95.16–96.42, in NT APOCRYPHA II, 229–231. For discussion, see E. Pagels, "To the Universe Belongs the Dancer," in *Parabola* IV.2 (1979), 7–9.
19. *Ibid.*, 97, in NT APOCRYPHA II, 232.
20. *Ibid.*, 97, in NT APOCRYPHA II, 232.
21. *Ibid.*, 101, in NT APOCRYPHA II, 234.
22. *Treatise on Resurrection* 44.13–45.29, in NHL 51; for discussion, see Pagels, "Gnostic and Orthodox Views of Christ's Passion," also K. F. Tröger, *Die Passion Jesu Christi in der Gnosis nach den Schriften von Nag Hammadi* (Berlin, 1978).
23. Suetonius, *Life of Nero* 6.16.
24. Tacitus, *Annals* 15.44–2–8.
25. See the discussion by R. MacMullen, *Enemies of the Roman Order: Treason, Unrest, and Alienation in the Empire* (Cambridge, 1966).
26. M. Smith, *Jesus the Magician* (San Francisco, 1978).
27. *Ibid.*; especially 81–139.
28. For a fuller discussion, see W. H. C. Frend, *Martyrdom and Persecution in the Early Church* (Oxford, 1965; New York, 1967); Frend, "The Gnostic Sects and the Roman Empire," in *Journal of Ecclesiastical History*, Vol. V (1954), 25–37.
29. Pliny, *Epistles* 10.96. Emphasis added.
30. *Ibid.*, 10.97. Emphasis added.
31. Justin Martyr, I *Apology* 1.
32. Justin, II *Apology* 2.
33. *Ibid.*, *Apology* 3.
34. "The Martyrdom of Saints Justin, Chariton, Charito, Euelpistis, Hierax, Paeon, Liberian, and Their Community," Recension A, 3, in *The Acts of the Christian Martyrs*, ed. H. Mursurillo (Oxford, 1972), 47–53. Hereafter cited as CHRISTIAN MARTYRS.
35. *Ibid.*, Recension B, 5, in CHRISTIAN MARTYRS, 53.
36. *Loc. cit.*
37. "Martyrdom of Saint Polycarp" 9–10, in CHRISTIAN MARTYRS, 9–11. Emphasis added.
38. "Acts of the Scillitan Martyrs" 1–3, in CHRISTIAN MARTYRS, 86–87.
39. *Ibid.*, 14, in CHRISTIAN MARTYRS, 88–89.
40. Tertullian contemptuously cites their arguments in *Scorpiace* 1.
41. Ignatius, *Romans* 6.3.
42. *Ibid.*, 4.1–5.3.
43. Ignatius, *Trallians* 9.1.
44. *Ibid.*, 10.1. Emphasis added.
45. Ignatius, *Smyrneans* 5.1–2.
46. Justin, II *Apology* 12.

47. Justin, *Dialogue with Trypho* 110.4.
48. Justin, I *Apology* 13.
49. Justin, II *Apology* 15.
50. Frend, *Martyrdom and Persecution in the Early Church*, 5–5.
51. "Martyrs of Lyons" 9, in CHRISTIAN MARTYRS, 64–65.
52. *Ibid.*, 15, in CHRISTIAN MARTYRS, 66–67.
53. *Ibid.*, 18–56, in CHRISTIAN MARTYRS, 67–81.
54. Irenaeus, AH 3.18.5.
55. *Ibid.*, 3.16.9–3.18.4. Emphasis added.
56. *Ibid.*, 3.18.5. Emphasis added.
57. Tertullian, *Apology* 15.
58. Tertullian, *De Anima* 55.
59. Tertullian, *Scorpiace* 1. Emphasis added.
60. *Ibid.*, 1, 5, 7. Emphasis added.
61. Hippolytus, REF 10.33. Emphasis added.
62. Irenaeus, AH 4.33.9. Emphasis added.
63. *Apocryphon of James* 4.37–6.18, in NHL 31–32. Emphasis added. On the figure of James, see S. K. Brown, *James: A Religio-Historical Study of the Relations between Jewish, Gnostic, and Catholic Christianity in the Early Period through an Investigation of the Traditions about James the Lord's Brother* (Providence, 1972).
64. *Apocryphon of James*, 6.19–20, in NHL 32.
65. *2 Apocalypse of James* 47.24–25, in NHL 250.
66. *Ibid.*, 48.8–9, in NHL 250.
67. *Ibid.*, 61.9–62.12, in NHL 254–255.
68. *Testimony of Truth* 31.22–32.8, in NHL 407.
69. *Ibid.*, 33.25–34.26, in NHL 408.
70. "Martyrdom of Polycarp" 2, in CHRISTIAN MARTYRS, 4–5.
71. Tertullian, *Apology* 50.
72. "Martyrdom of Saint Justin" (Recension C) 4, in CHRISTIAN MARTYRS, 58–59.
73. *Testimony of Truth* 30.18–20; 32.22–33.11, in NHL 408.
74. *Apocalypse of Peter* 72.5–9, in NHL 340.
75. *Ibid.*, 73.23–24, in NHL 341.
76. *Ibid.*, 74.1–3, in NHL 341.
77. *Ibid.*, 74.5–15, in NHL 341.
78. *Ibid.*, 79.11–21, in NHL 343.
79. *Ibid.*, 78.1–2, in NHL 342.
80. *Ibid.*, 80.5–6, in NHL 343.
81. *Ibid.*, 78.31–79.2, in NHL 343.
82. *Ibid.*, 81.15–24, in NHL 344.
83. *Ibid.*, 83.12–15, in NHL 344.
84. *Gospel of Truth* 18.24–20.6, in NHL 38–39.
85. *Ibid.*, 18.24–31, in NHL 38.
86. *Ibid.*, 20.10–32, in NHL 39.

Notes

87. *Tripartite Tractate* 113.32–34, in NHL 86–87.

88. *Ibid.*, 114.33–115.11, in NHL 87.

89. *Ibid.*, 113.35–38, in NHL 87.

90. *Gospel of Truth* 23.33–24.9, in NHL 41.

91. *Interpretation of the Knowledge* 10.27–30, in NHL 430.

92. Irenaeus, AH 3.18.5.

93. Luke 12:8–12.

94. Clemens Alexandrinus, *Stromata* 4.71 ff.

95. *Ibid.*, 4.33.7.

96. *Loc. cit.*

97. Tacitus, *Annals* 15.44.2–8.

98. "Martyrs of Lyons" 57–60, in CHRISTIAN MARTYRS, 80–81.

99. Justin, *Dialogue with Trypho* 110.

100. Tertullian, *Ad Scapulam* 5.

101. Tertullian, *Apology* 50.

CHAPTER FIVE

1. For excellent discussions of gnostic polemic against orthodox Christianity, see K. Koschorke, *Die Polemik der Gnostiker gegen das kirchliche Christentum* (Leiden, 1978); P. Perkins, "The Gnostic Revelation: Dialogue as Religious Polemic," in W. Haase, *Aufstieg und Niedergang der römischer Welt* II.22 (Berlin/New York, 1980); also P. Perkins, *The Gnostic Dialogue* (New York, 1980).

2. *Second Treatise of the Great Seth* 59.22–29, in NHL 333–334. For analysis, see J. A. Gibbons, *A Commentary on "The Second Logos of the Great Seth"* (New Haven, 1972).

3. *Ibid.*, 60.21–25, in NHL 334.

4. *Ibid.*, 53.27–33, in NHL 331.

5. *Ibid.*, 61.20, in NHL 334.

6. *Apocalypse of Peter* 74.16–22, in NHL 341.

7. *Ibid.*, 74.24–77.28, in NHL 341–342.

8. *Ibid.*, 76.27–34, in NHL 342.

9. *Ibid.*, 79.28–29, in NHL 343.

10. *Testimony of Truth* 31.24–32.2, in NHL 407.

11. *Authoritative Teaching* 26.20–21, in NHL 280.

12. *Ibid.*, 32.18–19, in NHL 282.

13. *Gospel of Philip* 64.23–24, in NHL 139.

14. Ignatius, *Smyrneans* 8.1–2.

15. *Ibid.*, 8.2.

16. *Trallians* 3.1.

17. Irenaeus, AH 4.33.8.

18. *Loc. cit.*

Notes

19. *Ibid.*, 3.4.1.
20. *Ibid.*, 3.15.2.
21. *Ibid.*, 5, *Praefatio*.
22. *Apocalypse of Peter* 70.24–71.4, in NHL 340.
23. *Ibid.*, 71.20–21, in NHL 340.
24. *Ibid.*, 79.1–4, in NHL 343.
25. *Second Treatise of the Great Seth* 67.32–68.9, in NHL 337.
26. *Ibid.*, 67.2–5, in NHL 336.
27. *Ibid.*, 70.9, in NHL 338.
28. C. Andresen, *Die Kirche der alten Christenheit* (Stuttgart, 1971), 100 ff.; see also Jonas, *Gnosis und spätantiker Geist* (Göttingen, 1964), "Solipcismus und Brüderethik," I.171–172.
29. Hippolytus, REF 9.7.
30. *Ibid.*, 9.12.
31. Tertullian, *Adversus Valentinianos* 4.
32. Tertullian, DE PRAESCR. 13.
33. *Ibid.*, 38.
34. *Ibid.*, 44.
35. Tertullian, *De Pudicitia* 21.
36. *Testimony of Truth* 73.18–22, in NHL 415.
37. *Ibid.*, 69.9–10, in NHL 414.
38. *Ibid.*, 69.18, in NHL 414.
39. *Ibid.*, 44.30–45.4, in NHL 411. Emphasis added.
40. *Ibid.*, 69.22–24, in NHL 414.
41. *Ibid.*, 68.8–12, in NHL 414.
42. *Authoritative Teaching* 22.19 (*passim*), in NHL 278 ff.
43. *Ibid.*, 23.13–14, in NHL 279.
44. *Ibid.*, 34.19, in NHL 283.
45. *Ibid.*, 34.4, in NHL 282.
46. *Ibid.*, 34.12–13, in NHL 282.
47. *Ibid.*, 33.4–5, in NHL 282.
48. *Ibid.*, 34.20–23, in NHL 283.
49. *Ibid.*, 22.28–34, in NHL 278.
50. *Ibid.*, 34.32–35.16, in NHL 283.
51. *Ibid.*, 33.4–34.9, in NHL 282.
52. *Ibid.*, 33.16–17, in NHL 282.
53. *Ibid.*, 32.30–33.3, in NHL 282.
54. *Ibid.*, 32.30–32, in NHL 282.
55. *Ibid.*, 27.6–15, in NHL 280.
56. Tertullian, DE PRAESCR. 7.
57. *Ibid.*, 41.
58. *Ibid.*, 8–11.
59. *Ibid.*, 11.
60. Irenaeus, AH 2.27.2.
61. Clemens Alexandrinus, EXCERPTA 4.1.

Notes

62. *Ibid.*, 41.2.
63. *Ibid.*, 24.1–2
64. Heracleon, Frag. 37–38, in Origen, COMM. JO. 13.51–13.53.
65. Irenaeus, AH 1.8.3–4.
66. Heracleon, Frag. 13, in Origen, COMM. JO. 10.33. For discussion, see E. Pagels, *The Johannine Gospel in Gnostic Exegesis* (Nashville, 1973), 66–74.
67. *Interpretation of Knowledge* 5.33, in NHL 429.
68. *Ibid.*, 6.33–38, in NHL 429.
69. For discussion, see Koschorke, *op. cit.*, 69–71; Koschorke, "Eine neugefundene gnostische Gemeindeordnung," in *Zeitschrift für Theologie und Kirche* 76.1 (February 1979), 30–60; J. Turner and E. Pagels, introduction to *Interpretation of Knowledge* (CG XI, 1) in *Nag Hammadi Studies* (Leiden, 1980).
70. I Corinthians 12:14–21.
71. *Interpretation of Knowledge* 18.28–34, in NHL 433.
72. *Ibid.*, 15.35–17.27, in NHL 432–433.
73. *Ibid.*, 18.24–25, in NHL 433.

CHAPTER SIX

1. John 14:5–6.
2. Irenaeus, AH 3.11.7. For discussion, see E. Pagels, *The Johannine Gospel in Gnostic Exegesis* (Nashville, 1973).
3. *Dialogue of the Savior* 142.16–19, in NHL 237.
4. *Gospel of Thomas* 38.4–10, in NHL 121.
5. F. Wisse, "Gnosticism and Early Monasticism in Egypt," in *Gnosis: Festschrift für Hans Jonas* (Göttingen, 1978), 431–440.
6. B. Layton, ed., *The Rediscovery of Gnosticism* (forthcoming).
7. Irenaeus, AH 4.11.2.
8. *Ibid.*, 4.11.2.
9. Justin Martyr, *Dialogue with Trypho* 4.
10. *Gospel of Philip* 71.35–72.4, in NHL 143.
11. Irenaeus, AH 1.11.1.
12. *Ibid.*, 1.12.3.
13. *Ibid.*, 1.12.3.
14. *Ibid.*, 1.12.4.
15. *Ibid.*, 1.30.6.
16. Romans 3:23.
17. Mark 1:15.
18. John 3:17–19.
19. Irenaeus, AH 1.5.4.

20. *Gospel of Truth* 17.10–16, in NHL 38.

21. *Ibid.*, 28.16–17, in NHL 42.

22. *Ibid.*, 29.2–6, in NHL 43.

23. *Ibid.*, 29.8–30.12, in NHL 43.

24. *Ibid.*, 21.35–36, in NHL 40.

25. *Ibid.*, 24.32–25.3, in NHL 41.

26. *Dialogue of the Savior* 134.1–22, in NHL 234.

27. *Gospel of Thomas* 45.30–33, in NHL 126.

28. *Ibid.*, 33.11–13, in NHL 118.

29. *Book of Thomas the Contender* 138.13, in NHL 189.

30. *Gospel of Thomas* 38.23–29, in NHL 121. For a discussion of these metaphors, see H. Jonas, *The Gnostic Religion* (Boston, 1963), 48–96, and G. MacRae, "Sleep and Awakening in Gnostic Texts," in *Le Origini dello Gnosticismo*, 496–507.

31. Professors M. L. Peel and J. Zandee have stated that the *Teachings of Silvanus* is clearly "non-Gnostic" (NHL 346). Nevertheless, what Peel and Zandee describe as characteristic of gnostic teaching (dualistic theology, docetic Christology, the doctrine that "only some persons are saved 'by nature'") does not, as they apparently assume, characterize such teaching as that of Valentinus (which undisputably *is* gnostic). The *Teachings of Silvanus* certainly is unique among the Nag Hammadi find in that most of its elements do not contradict orthodox doctrine. Whether or not it is itself a gnostic document, I suggest that what warrants its inclusion with gnostic writings is its premise that divine reason (and, apparently, divine nature) is discovered *within* oneself.

32. *Teachings of Silvanus* 88.24–92.12, in NHL 349–350.

33. *Gospel of Thomas* 32.14–19, in NHL 118.

34. *Dialogue of the Savior* 125.18–19, in NHL 231.

35. *Teachings of Silvanus* 85.24–106.14, in NHL 347–356.

36. *Ibid.*, 106.30–117.20, in NHL 356–361.

37. *Gospel of Truth* 21.11–22.15, in NHL 40.

38. *Ibid.*, 32.38–39, in NHL 44.

39. *Ibid.*, 32.31–33.14, in NHL 44.

40. *Gospel of Thomas* 32.19–33.5, in NHL 118. Emphasis added.

41. *Ibid.*, 42.7–51.18, in NHL 123–130.

42. *Ibid.*, 37.20–35, in NHL 121.

43. Mark 9:1; cf. Mark 14:62.

44. *Ibid.*, 13:5–7.

45. Luke 17:21.

46. Mark 8:27–29.

47. Matthew 16:17–18.

48. *Gospel of Thomas* 34.30–35.7, in NHL 119.

49. *Ibid.*, 50.28–30, in NHL 129.

50. *Book of Thomas the Contender* 138.13, in NHL 189.

51. *Gospel of Thomas* 48.20–25, in NHL 128.

52. *Ibid.*, 40.20–23, in NHL 122.

53. *Dialogue of the Savior* 132.15–16, in NHL 233.

54. *Ibid.*, 126.5–8, in NHL 231.

55. *Ibid.*, 140.3–4, in NHL 236.

56. *Testimony of Truth* 44.2, in NHL 410–411.

57. *Ibid.*, 43.26, in NHL 410.

58. *Ibid.*, 44.13–16, in NHL 411.

59. *Teachings of Silvanus* 97.18–98.10, in NHL 352.

60. Matthew 2:15, *passim*.

61. Justin, I *Apology* 31.

62. *Gospel of Thomas* 42.13–18, in NHL 124.

63. Irenaeus, AH 1.11.1.

64. *Ibid.*, 1.2.2.

65. *Gospel of Philip* 54.13–15, in NHL 133.

66. *Ibid.*, 67.9–12, in NHL 140.

67. *Ibid.*, 61.24–26, in NHL 137.

68. *Ibid.*, 61.29–35, in NHL 137.

69. *Ibid.*, 67.26–27, in NHL 140.

70. *Book of Thomas the Contender* 138.16–18, in NHL 189.

71. Hippolytus, REF 6.9.

72. *Ibid.*, 6.17.

73. *Gospel of Thomas* 33.14–19, in NHL 118.

74. Plotinus, "Against the Gnostics," *Enneads* 2.9.

75. *Zostrianos* 1.12, in NHL 369.

76. *Ibid.*, 2.8–9, in NHL 369.

77. *Ibid.*, 3.14–21, in NHL 370.

78. *Ibid.*, 3.29–30, in NHL 370.

79. *Ibid.*, 131.16–132.5, in NHL 393.

80. *Discourse on the Eighth and the Ninth* 52.1–7, in NHL 292.

81. *Ibid.*, 53.7–10, in NHL 293.

82. *Ibid.*, 52.15–18, in NHL 293.

83. *Ibid.*, 54.23–25, in NHL 293.

84. *Ibid.*, 56.10–12, in NHL 294.

85. *Ibid.*, 56.17–22, in NHL 294.

86. *Ibid.*, 57.3–11, in NHL 294.

87. *Ibid.*, 57.31–58.22, in NHL 295.

88. *Ibid.*, 58.31–61.2, in NHL 295–296.

89. *Ibid.*, 63.9–14, in NHL 297.

90. *Allogenes* 52.8–12, in NHL 446.

91. *Ibid.*, 50.19, in NHL 445.

92. *Ibid.*, 52.15–21, in NHL 446.

93. *Ibid.*, 53.36–37, in NHL 447.

94. *Ibid.*, 55.31–57.34, in NHL 447–448.

95. *Ibid.*, 59.9–37, in NHL 449.

96. *Ibid.*, 60.13–18, in NHL 449.

97. *Ibid.*, 60.37–61.8, in NHL 449.
98. *Ibid.*, 61.14–16, in NHL 449–450.
99. *Ibid.*, 61.29–31, in NHL 450.
100. *Ibid.*, 64.16–23, in NHL 451.
101. *Ibid.*, 67.23–35, in NHL 451–452.
102. *Ibid.*, 68.18–19.
103. Tertullian, *Adversus Valentinianos* 1.

CONCLUSION

1. Tertullian, DE PRAESCR. 13.
2. *Gospel of Truth* 17.10–11, in NHL 38.
3. Irenaeus, AH 1.5.4.
4. *Gospel of Truth* 16.1–18.34, in NHL 37–38.
5. Plotinus, "Against the Gnostics," *Enneads* 2.9.
6. A. D. Nock, "Gnosticism," in *Arthur Darby Nock: Essays on Religion and the Ancient World*, ed. Z. Stewart (Cambridge, 1972), Vol. 2, 943.
7. Nock, "Gnosticism," 942.
8. *Gospel of Thomas* 41.27–30, in NHL 123.
9. Heracleon, Frag. 39, in Origen, COMM. JO. 13.53.
10. *Gospel of Thomas* 42.16–18, in NHL 124.
11. *Testimony of Truth* 68.8–12, in NHL 414.
12. Irenaeus, AH 2.22.4.
13. *Ibid.*, 2.22.5–6.
14. *Gospel of Thomas* 38.1–3, in NHL 121.
15. H. Koester, "The Structure of Early Christian Beliefs," in *Trajectories Through Early Christianity* (Philadelphia, 1971), 231.
16. Irenaeus, AH 1.10.2.
17. Luke 14:26.
18. Mark 4:10–12, *par.*
19. Matthew 19:4–6, *par.*
20. *Ibid.*, 19:13–15, *par.*
21. Mark 1:41, 3:3–5, *par.*
22. Luke 19:41–44.
23. W. Blake, "The Everlasting Gospel," 2a and g.
24. F. Nietzsche, *The Antichrist*.
25. F. Dostoevsky, "The Grand Inquisitor," in *The Brothers Karamazov*.
26. *Second Treatise of the Great Seth* 61.20, in NHL 334.
27. A. D. Nock, "The Study of the History of Religion," in *Arthur Darby Nock*, Vol. 1, 339.

INDEX

Adam, Eve, and the Serpent

Grateful acknowledgment is made to the following for permission
to reprint previously published material:

Harvard Theological Review Excerpts from "Christian Apologists and the
'Fall of the Angels': An Attack on Roman Imperial Power?" by Elaine
Pagels, which appeared in *Harvard Theological Review* 78, 3–4 (1985),
pp. 301–325, and "The Politics of Paradise: Augustine's Exegesis of
Genesis 1–3 Versus That of John Chrysostom," by Elaine Pagels, which
appeared in *Harvard Theological Review* 78, 1–2 (1985), pp 67–95.
Copyright © 1985 by the President and Fellows of Harvard College.
Reprinted by permission.

Hendrickson Publishers, Inc.: Excerpts from "Exegesis and Exposition
of the Genesis Creation Accounts in Selected Texts from Nag Hammadi," by Elaine Pagels, in *Nag Hammadi, Gnosticism, and Early Christianity,* edited by C. Hedrick and R. Hodgson, pp. 257–286 Used by
permission of Hendrickson Publishers, Inc., Peabody, Mass.

T&T Clark Ltd : Excerpts by Elaine Pagels from *The New Testament and
Gnosis: Essays in Honour of R McL Wilson,* edited by A.H.B. Logan and
A.J.M. Wedderburn (Edinburgh, Scotland, 1983), pp. 146–175.

National Council of the Churches of Christ in the U S.A.· Scripture
quotations are from the Revised Standard Version Bible. Copyright
1946, 1952, © 1971 by the Division of Christian Education of the
National Council of the Churches of Christ in the U S.A. Used by
permission.

To our beloved son, Mark,
who for six and a half years
graced our lives with his presence

October 26, 1980–April 10, 1987

ACKNOWLEDGMENTS

THIS BOOK is based upon research originally presented, for the most part, in scholarly publications (cited at the beginning of each chapter's footnotes), and revised to make it more generally accessible. During the eight years of research and writing, I have consulted with many scholars and friends. I am especially grateful to those who read the entire manuscript and helped me with corrections, criticism, and encouragement: Thomas Boslooper, Peter Brown, Elizabeth Clark, Linda Hess, Martha Himmelfarb, Bentley Layton, Wayne Meeks, William Meninger, O.C.S.O., Alan Segal, S. David Sperling, and Robert Wilken; and to those who offered comments and criticism on portions of the work as it was in progress, especially Harry Attridge, Glen Bowersock, Bernadette Brooten, Mary Douglas, Theodor H. Gaster, John Gager, Marilyn Harran, Dennis MacDonald, Birger Pearson, Gilles Quispel, Morton Smith, and Lewis Spitz. Helmut Koester, formerly my thesis adviser, remains for me, as for many others, a respected and loved mentor and friend. I owe special thanks, too, to those friends and fellow writers who not only shared to some extent in the process of the work, but also read the manuscript and helped me with their criticism: Lydia Bronte, Elizabeth Diggs, Nick Herbert, Ralph Hiesey, my brother, Emily McCulley, Richard Ogust, and Sharon Olds.

Soon after I had begun the research for this book, the John D. and Catherine T. MacArthur Foundation astonished me with the award of a MacArthur Prize Fellowship, which gave me the most welcome and unexpected gift of all—time for research and writing. For this, and for the continuing work of the foundation on behalf of other recipients, I will always be grateful. Ellen Futter, president of Barnard College, and Charles Olton, then dean of the faculty, graciously arranged the first year of leave from full-time teaching and chairing the Department of Religion, so that I could devote the time to this research. I wish to thank my present colleagues in the Department of Religion at Princeton University, both for conversations that have contributed much to the process, and for their considerable grace during the years of research and writing, and also to thank the students, both graduate and undergraduate, who have struggled through these texts with me.

There are certain people without whose participation I cannot imagine having written this book. I have enjoyed working with Jason Epstein as editor, and deeply appreciate the insight, wit, and passion for clarity he has brought to this process, along with his enthusiastic support. My colleague Tom Boslooper has participated in the entire process of research and the preparation of the manuscript with an equanimity, generosity, and wisdom that always amaze me. John Brockman and Katinka Matson have seen the project through from the beginning, and have contributed in innumerable ways with sage advice and encouragement. I am very grateful to William T. Golden, who has lent me the use of an office for research and writing, which has proven to be a haven from the noises of New York: much of this book was written there. I wish to thank Richard Lim, too, for his prompt and increasingly expert assistance in finding research materials, and Dotty Holliger and Carol Shookhoff for their conscientious typing of parts of the manuscript.

Finally, I am grateful to those many friends whose presence and personal support in ways known to each of them have helped see me through these years, and mention in particular my parents, Louise and William M. Hiesey; Edith Davis; Jean Da Silva; Lita A. Hazen and Joseph H. Hazen; Betsy Herbert; Rev. Jane Henderson and Rev. Hugh Hildesley; Lucy and Robert Mann, Barbara Munsell, Richard Olney, and Katy Smith.

My most personal thanks I owe to my husband, Heinz Pagels, not only for reading the manuscript and offering excellent criticism while he was working on his own most recent book, but much more, of course, for his constant and loving presence during these years that included the lifetime and the death of our son, Mark, and the arrival of our daughter, Sarah.

THE BOOK OF GENESIS

CHAPTERS 1–3
(Revised Standard Version)

IN THE BEGINNING God created the heavens and the earth. ²The earth was without form and void, and darkness was upon the face of the deep; and the Spirit of God was moving over the face of the waters.

3 And God said, "Let there be light"; and there was light. ⁴And God saw that the light was good; and God separated the light from the darkness. ⁵God called the light Day, and the darkness he called Night. And there was evening and there was morning, one day.

6 And God said, "Let there be a firmament in the midst of the waters, and let it separate the waters from the waters." ⁷And God made the firmament and separated the waters which were under the firmament from the waters which were above the firmament. And it was so. ⁸And God called the firmament Heaven. And there was evening and there was morning, a second day.

9 And God said, "Let the waters under the heavens be gathered together into one place, and let the dry land appear." And it was so. ¹⁰God called the dry land Earth, and the waters that were gathered together he called Seas. And God saw that it was good. ¹¹And

God said, "Let the earth put forth vegetation, plants yielding seed, and fruit trees bearing fruit in which is their seed, each according to its kind, upon the earth." And it was so. ¹²The earth brought forth vegetation, plants yielding seed according to their own kinds, and trees bearing fruit in which is their seed, each according to its kind. And God saw that it was good. ¹³And there was evening and there was morning, a third day.

14 And God said, "Let there be lights in the firmament of the heavens to separate the day from the night; and let them be for signs and for seasons and for days and years, ¹⁵and let them be lights in the firmament of the heavens to give light upon the earth." And it was so. ¹⁶And God made the two great lights, the greater light to rule the day, and the lesser light to rule the night; he made the stars also. ¹⁷And God set them in the firmament of the heavens to give light upon the earth, ¹⁸to rule over the day and over the night, and to separate the light from the darkness. And God saw that it was good. ¹⁹And there was evening and there was morning, a fourth day.

20 And God said, "Let the waters bring forth swarms of living creatures,

and let birds fly above the earth across the firmament of the heavens." 21So God created the great sea monsters and every living creature that moves, with which the waters swarm, according to their kinds, and every winged bird according to its kind. And God saw that it was good. 22And God blessed them, saying, "Be fruitful and multiply and fill the waters in the seas, and let birds multiply on the earth." 23And there was evening and there was morning, a fifth day.

24 And God said, "Let the earth bring forth living creatures according to their kinds: cattle and creeping things and beasts of the earth according to their kinds." And it was so. 25And God made the beasts of the earth according to their kinds and the cattle according to their kinds, and everything that creeps upon the ground according to its kind. And God saw that it was good.

26 Then God said, "Let us make man in our image, after our likeness; and let them have dominion over the fish of the sea, and over the birds of the air, and over the cattle, and over all the earth, and over every creeping thing that creeps upon the earth." 27So God created man in his own image, in the image of God he created him; male and female he created them. 28And God blessed them, and God said to them, "Be fruitful and multiply, and fill the earth and subdue it; and have dominion over the fish of the sea and over the birds of the air and over every living thing that moves upon the earth." 29And God said, "Behold, I have given you every plant yielding seed which is upon the face of all the earth, and every tree with seed in its fruit; you shall have them for food. 30And to every beast of the earth,

and to every bird of the air, and to everything that creeps on the earth, everything that has the breath of life, I have given every green plant for food." And it was so. 31And God saw everything that he had made, and behold, it was very good. And there was evening and there was morning, a sixth day.

2 Thus the heavens and the earth were finished, and all the host of them. 2And on the seventh day God finished his work which he had done, and he rested on the seventh day from all his work which he had done. 3So God blessed the seventh day and hallowed it, because on it God rested from all his work which he had done in creation.

4 These are the generations of the heavens and the earth when they were created.

In the day that the Lord God made the earth and the heavens, 5when no plant of the field was yet in the earth and no herb of the field had yet sprung up—for the Lord God had not caused it to rain upon the earth, and there was no man to till the ground; 6but a mist went up from the earth and watered the whole face of the ground— 7then the Lord God formed man of dust from the ground, and breathed into his nostrils the breath of life; and man became a living being. 8And the Lord God planted a garden in Eden, in the east; and there he put the man whom he had formed. 9And out of the ground the Lord God made to grow every tree that is pleasant to the sight and good for food, the tree of life also in the midst of the garden, and the tree of the knowledge of good and evil.

10 A river flowed out of Eden to water the garden, and there it divided

and became four rivers. ¹¹The name of the first is Pishon; it is the one which flows around the whole land of Hav'- ilah, where there is gold; ¹²and the gold of that land is good; bdellium and onyx stone are there. ¹³The name of the second river is Gihon; it is the one which flows around the whole land of Cush. ¹⁴And the name of the third river is Tigris, which flows east of Assyria. And the fourth river is the Euphra'tes.

15 The Lord God took the man and put him in the garden of Eden to till it and keep it. ¹⁶And the Lord God commanded the man, saying, "You may freely eat of every tree of the garden; ¹⁷but of the tree of the knowledge of good and evil you shall not eat, for in the day that you eat of it you shall die."

18 Then the Lord God said, "It is not good that the man should be alone; I will make him a helper fit for him." ¹⁹So out of the ground the Lord God formed every beast of the field and every bird of the air, and brought them to the man to see what he would call them; and whatever the man called every living creature, that was its name. ²⁰The man gave names to all cattle, and to the birds of the air, and to every beast of the field; but for the man there was not found a helper fit for him. ²¹So the Lord God caused a deep sleep to fall upon the man, and while he slept took one of his ribs and closed up its place with flesh; ²²and the rib which the Lord God had taken from the man he made into a woman and brought her to the man. ²³Then the man said,

"This at last is bone of my bones
   and flesh of my flesh;
she shall be called Woman,
   because she was taken out of
      Man."

²⁴Therefore a man leaves his father and his mother and cleaves to his wife, and they become one flesh. ²⁵And the man and his wife were both naked, and were not ashamed.

3 Now the serpent was more subtle than any other wild creature that the Lord God had made. He said to the woman, "Did God say, 'You shall not eat of any tree of the garden'?" ²And the woman said to the serpent, "We may eat of the fruit of the trees of the garden; ³but God said, 'You shall not eat of the fruit of the tree which is in the midst of the garden, neither shall you touch it, lest you die.'" ⁴But the serpent said to the woman, "You will not die. ⁵For God knows that when you eat of it your eyes will be opened, and you will be like God, knowing good and evil." ⁶So when the woman saw that the tree was good for food, and that it was a delight to the eyes, and that the tree was to be desired to make one wise, she took of its fruit and ate; and she also gave some to her husband, and he ate. ⁷Then the eyes of both were opened, and they knew that they were naked; and they sewed fig leaves together and made themselves aprons.

8 And they heard the sound of the Lord God walking in the garden in the cool of the day, and the man and his wife hid themselves from the presence of the Lord God among the trees of the garden. ⁹But the Lord God called to the man, and said to him, "Where are you?" ¹⁰And he said, "I heard the sound of thee in the garden, and I was afraid, because I was naked; and I hid myself." ¹¹He said, "Who told you that you were naked? Have you eaten of the tree of which I commanded you not to eat?" ¹²The man said, "The woman

whom thou gavest to be with me, she gave me fruit of the tree, and I ate." ¹³Then the Lord God said to the woman, "What is this that you have done?" The woman said, "The serpent beguiled me, and I ate." ¹⁴The Lord God said to the serpent,

"Because you have done this,
    cursed are you above all cattle,
    and above all wild animals;
upon your belly you shall go,
    and dust you shall eat
    all the days of your life.
¹⁵I will put enmity between you
        and the woman,
        and between your seed and her
        seed;
    he shall bruise your head,
        and you shall bruise his heel."

¹⁶To the woman he said,

"I will greatly multiply your pain
        in childbearing;
    in pain you shall bring forth
        children,
yet your desire shall be for your
        husband,
    and he shall rule over you."

¹⁷And to Adam he said,

"Because you have listened to the
        voice of your wife,
    and have eaten of the tree
of which I commanded you,

'You shall not eat of it,'
cursed is the ground because of you;
    in toil you shall eat of it all the
        days of your life;
¹⁸thorns and thistles it shall bring
        forth to you;
    and you shall eat the plants of
        the field.
¹⁹In the sweat of your face
    you shall eat bread
till you return to the ground,
    for out of it you were taken;
you are dust,
    and to dust you shall return."

20 The man called his wife's name Eve, because she was the mother of all living. ²¹And the Lord God made for Adam and for his wife garments of skins, and clothed them.

22 Then the Lord God said, "Behold, the man has become like one of us, knowing good and evil; and now, lest he put forth his hand and take also of the tree of life, and eat, and live for ever"— ²³therefore the Lord God sent him forth from the garden of Eden, to till the ground from which he was taken. ²⁴He drove out the man; and at the east of the garden of Eden he placed the cherubim, and a flaming sword which turned every way, to guard the way to the tree of life.

CONTENTS

INTRODUCTION

BRUPT CHANGES in social attitudes have recently become commonplace, especially with respect to sexuality, including marriage, divorce, homosexuality, abortion, contraception, and gender. Whether we welcome these changes or not, they have altered the way we think of other people and ourselves, how we act, and how we respond to the actions of others. For Christians, in particular, such changes may seem to challenge not only traditional values but the very structure of human nature.

But how did these traditional patterns of gender and sexual relationship arise in the first place—patterns so obvious and "natural" to those who have accepted them that nature itself seemed to have ordained them? Reflecting on this question, I soon began to see that the sexual attitudes we associate with Christian tradition evolved in western culture at a specific time—during the first four centuries of the common era, when the Christian movement, which had begun as a defiant sect, eventually transformed itself into the religion of the Roman Empire. I saw, too, that these attitudes had not previously existed in their eventual Christian form; and that they represented a departure from both pagan practices and Jewish tradition. Many Christians of the first four centuries took pride in their sexual restraint; they eschewed polygamy and often divorce as well, which Jewish tradition allowed; and they repudiated extramarital sexual practices commonly accepted among their pagan contemporaries, practices including prostitution and homosexuality.

Certain Christian moralists of this period insisted that sexual intercourse should not be pursued for pleasure, even among those monogamously married, but should be reserved solely for procreation. Not all these attitudes were original with the Christians, who borrowed much from Jewish and philosophical, particularly Stoic, tradition; but the Christian movement emphasized and institutionalized such views, which soon became inseparable from Christian faith.

Heroic Christians went even further and embraced celibacy "for the sake of the Kingdom of Heaven," behavior which, they said, Jesus and Paul had exemplified, and which they had urged upon those capable of the "angelic life." By the beginning of the fifth century, Augustine had actually declared that spontaneous sexual desire is the proof of—and penalty for—universal original sin, an idea that would have baffled most of his Christian predecessors, to say nothing of his pagan and Jewish contemporaries.

Many pagan contemporaries of the early Christians in the Graeco-Roman society of the first four centuries pursued sexual practices that superficially may look familiar to some people in the twentieth century. The Romans, for example, legalized and taxed prostitution, both male and female; and some of them easily tolerated divorce, as well as homosexual and bisexual relationships, especially during adolescence or, in the case of married men, as a diversion from family obligations. Yet when we investigate Roman practices more closely, we find ourselves upon more unfamiliar ground; we may be dismayed to see, for example, that exposing and abandoning infants was widely and openly practiced during the first and second centuries of the common era, as was the routine sexual use and abuse of slaves. To the extent that we recoil from such practices, we reveal, whether or not we explicitly identify ourselves with religious tradition, that we too are affected by the transformation of sexual values that Christian tradition introduced into western culture.

From the first century, when the Christian movement appeared as a new and "deadly superstition" (in the words of the Roman historian Tacitus), through two centuries of persecution, during which its members were subject to arrest, torture, and execution, the movement continued to grow. Then in 313 occurred an event of incalculable significance—the conversion to Christianity of the emperor Constantine; and from that time, with only a two-year interruption during the brief reign of the neopagan emperor Julian, called the Apostate, Christianity increasingly became the official religion of the empire. Accompanying the spread of Christianity—although, as classical historians remind us, not limited to it—was a revolution in sexual attitudes and practices.

Yet when we explore Jewish and Christian writers from the first centuries of the common era, we find that they seldom talk directly about sexual behavior, and they seldom write treatises on such topics as marriage, divorce, and gender. Instead they often talk about Adam, Eve, and the serpent—the story of creation—and when they do, they tell us what they think about sexual matters. From about 200 B.C.E. (before the common era), the story of creation became, for certain Jews, and later for Christians, a primary means for revealing and defending basic attitudes and values. Our spiritual ancestors argued and speculated over how God had commanded the first man and woman to "be fruitful and multiply, and fill the earth," and how he instituted the first marriage; how Adam, after he found among the animals no "helper fit for him" (Genesis 2:20), met Eve, with well-known and disastrous consequences. Such interpretations of the first three chapters of Genesis, as we can see, engaged intensely practical concerns and articulated deeply felt attitudes.

As I investigated these Jewish and Christian sources, I found myself fascinated with the story of Adam, Eve, and the serpent, written down by members of Hebrew tribes about three thousand years ago, and probably told for generations before that. I had always assumed that this archaic story wields an extraordinary influence upon western culture, but as my work progressed I was surprised to discover how complex and extensive its effect has been.

The anthropologist Clifford Geertz defines culture as

> an historically transmitted pattern of meaning embodied in symbols; a system of inherited conceptions expressed in symbolic form, by means of which men communicate, perpetuate, and develop their knowledge about and attitudes toward life.[1]

If any of us could come to our own culture as a foreign anthropologist and observe traditional Christian attitudes toward sexuality and gender, and how we view "human nature" in relation to politics, philosophy, and psychology, we might well be astonished at attitudes that we take for granted. Augustine, one of the greatest teachers of western Christianity, derived many of these attitudes from the story of Adam and Eve: that sexual desire is sinful; that infants are infected from the moment of conception with the disease of original sin; and that Adam's sin corrupted the whole of nature itself. Even those who think of Genesis only as literature, and those who are not Christian, live in a culture indelibly shaped by such interpretations as these.

But the Genesis accounts of creation introduced into Graeco-Roman culture many values other than sexual ones—for example, the intrinsic worth of every human being, made in God's image (Genesis 1:26). Often these other values would prove immensely influential. Although the early Christians thought of this conviction of human worth in moral—not social or political—terms, Christians living more than fifteen hundred years later would invoke this idea to help transform the laws, ethics, and political institutions of the West. In 1776 the authors of the Declaration of Independence invoked the biblical account of creation to declare that "we hold these truths to be self-evident, that all men are created equal . . ."—an idea so familiar that we may have difficulty seeing that it is empirically unprovable; Aristotle, among others, would have considered it absurd. As we shall see, the idea of human moral equality flourished among converts to Christianity, many of whom, especially slaves and women, were anything but equal under Roman law.

Some Christians today, of course, invoke Genesis against the theory of evolution, criticizing the claims of scientific objectivity and the relative values they associate with "secular humanism"; many insist that the creation story validates their own social and sexual attitudes. Liberal critics accuse such interpreters of literalism; and it is true that such believers often insist that they understand perfectly well what "the Bible says," without considering that what *they* assume it means may differ entirely from what others—even their Christian predecessors—have taken it to mean. Yet such evangelical Christians intuitively understand one thing that their critics often miss: that the biblical creation story, like the creation stories of other cultures, communicates social and religious values and presents them as if they were universally valid. Many people who have—intellectually, at least—discarded the creation story as a mere folk tale nevertheless find themselves engaged with its moral implications concerning procreation, animals, work, marriage, and the human striving to "subdue" the earth and "have dominion" over all its creatures (Genesis 1:28).

This book explores, among other things, how these Christian interpretations of Genesis emerged in the first four centuries, and how Christians invoked the story of Adam and Eve to justify and establish their beliefs; how they saw their own situations, their sufferings, and their hopes mirrored in the story of the creation and the fall. I have not, by any means, written a history of early Christianity; instead, I am interested in a process of intellectual history—how these ideas of sexuality and moral equality, among others, came about; and I am interested in the hermeneutical process—how Christians read the story of Adam and Eve, and often projected themselves into it, as a way of reflecting upon such matters as sexuality, human freedom, and human nature.

As I began to explore these questions, both substantive and hermeneutical, I soon discovered that Jews and Christians in various times and places have read the creation story—and its practical implications—quite differently, sometimes even antithetically. What Christians see, or claim to see, in Genesis 1–3 changed as the church itself changed from a dissident Jewish sect to a popular movement persecuted by the Roman government, and changed further as this movement increasingly gained members throughout Roman society, until finally even the Roman emperor himself converted to the new faith and Christianity became the official religion of the Roman Empire.

During recent decades, several distinguished scholars, including Professors Robert M. Grant, Georges de Ste. Croix, Ramsay MacMullen, Wayne Meeks, and Paul Veyne, have pointed out that Christians were in many ways similar to their pagan neighbors.[2] Their works document, among other things, social, political, economic, and cultural parallels that I have not reviewed here. Instead I focus upon ways in which Christians *differed* from pagans, or claimed to differ—what made them, in other words, specifically Christian within the pagan world; I am interested, in Tertullian's words, in the "peculiarities of the Christian society."[3]

In each chapter I take up a theme that Christians attempted to understand or justify by means of the creation story. Jewish teachers of Jesus' time and earlier, as I show in Chapter 1, often invoked the story of Adam and Eve to defend Jewish sexual practices ranging from abhorrence of public nakedness (for God clothed Adam and Eve in Paradise) to marital practices designed to facilitate reproduction (for hadn't God said, "Be fruitful and multiply, and fill the earth"?). These Jewish teachers noted that Genesis contains not one but two distinct accounts of creation, of which the first begins with the opening chapter of Genesis and tells how God created the world in six days, crowning his achievement by creating *adam*—that is, humanity—in his image (Genesis 1:26). But this account ends with Genesis 2:3; and the following verse, Genesis 2:4, begins a different narrative. This second story tells how the Lord made a man out of earth, and, after making all the animals and finding none of them a suitable companion for Adam, he put Adam to sleep, brought woman out of his side, and presented her to Adam as his wife. The woman then persuaded her husband to disobey divine law and earned with him their expulsion from Paradise.

Most biblical scholars today agree that the two creation accounts, originally separate, were later joined to make up the first three chapters of Genesis. The story of Adam and Eve (Genesis 2:4f), told in the language of folklore, is considered the older of the two accounts, dating to 1000–900 B.C.E.; the account now placed first (Genesis 1:1–2:3) dates to postexilic theologians (c. 400 B.C.E.). Jewish teachers in antiquity, like many Christians after them, turned to theological ingenuity rather than historical or literary analysis to account for contradictions in the texts.

According to New Testament accounts, Jesus himself mentioned the story of Adam and Eve only once; and, like many other Jewish teachers, Jesus used Genesis to make a moral point—specifically, to answer a practical question put to him by the Pharisees, the interpreters of Jewish law, about the legitimate grounds for divorce. Jesus' reply—that what God has joined together, let no one put asunder—shocked his questioners, for instead of answering the question he had been asked about the *grounds* for divorce, he simply ruled out divorce altogether. Since procreation was assumed by many Jews to be the purpose of marriage, and since Jewish tradition had taken divorce for granted as a male prerogative—and sometimes as a necessity, in cases of a wife's infertility—Jesus' answer to the Pharisees broke with Jewish teaching. When even his own followers objected ("If such is the case of a man with his wife, it is not expedient to marry"), Jesus must have startled them even more than he had the Pharisees by suggesting that celibacy "for the sake of the Kingdom of Heaven" may, in fact, be preferable to marriage (Matthew 19:10–12). For generations—even millennia—ever since, Christians have been trying to work out the practical implications of such sayings, and those of Paul, Jesus' zealous disciple.

Paul himself, some twenty years after Jesus' death, urged an even more austere discipline upon his followers than Jesus had preached. Although Paul acknowledged that marriage was not sin (1 Corinthians 7:3), he encouraged those who were able to renounce it to do so. Paul invoked the creation account to urge Christians to avoid prostitution (1 Corinthians 6:15–20), and later to argue that women must veil their heads in church, apparently to acknowledge their subordination to men as a kind of divine order given in nature ("For man was not made from woman, but woman from man. Neither was man created for woman, but woman for man," 1 Corinthians 11:3–16). In the generations following Paul, Christians fiercely debated what the apostle meant. Some insisted that only those who "undo the sin of Adam and Eve" by practicing celibacy—even within marriage—can truly practice the gospel. Others, who were to predominate within the majority of churches, rejected such austerity and composed, in Paul's name, other letters, later incorporated into the New Testament as if Paul himself had written them, which used the story of Adam and Eve to support traditional marriage and to prove that women, being naturally gullible, are unfit for any role but raising children and keeping house (see, for example, 1 Timothy 2:11–15); thus the story of Eden was made to reinforce the patriarchal structure of community life.

But the majority of Christians, as I also show in Chapter 1, rejected the claim made by radical Christians that the sin of Adam and Eve was sexual—that the forbidden "fruit of the tree of knowledge" conveyed, above all, *carnal* knowledge. On the contrary, said Clement of Alexandria (c. 180 C.E.), conscious participation in procreation is "cooperation with God in the work of creation." Adam's sin was not sexual indulgence but disobedience; thus Clement agreed with most of his Jewish and Christian contemporaries that the real theme of the story of Adam and Eve is moral freedom and moral responsibility. Its point is to show that we are responsible for the choices we freely make—good or evil—just as Adam was.

In Chapter 2 I show how Christians also began to apply the creation account to their own precarious political situation, in which they were constantly subject to persecution by the Roman authorities. About one hundred years after Jesus' death, when many Christians lived in fear of a similar fate—arrest, torture, and execution—for refusing ordinary allegiance to the emperor and the gods, the Christian philosopher Justin invoked Genesis to argue that humankind owes allegiance only to the God who created all humanity—the God of Israel, now the God of the Christians—and not to the gods of Rome, whom Justin denounced as demons. Justin turned Genesis 6, which tells of the fall of the angels, into an indictment of the Roman emperors and their gods; for these dignitaries were, Justin said, none other than the demon offspring of the fallen angels.

About twenty years after Justin had been beheaded for refusing to worship the Roman gods, Clement of Alexandria took the statement that God had created humanity in his image as evidence of human equality—and as an indictment of the imperial cult. From such beginnings, in open defiance of the totalitarian Roman state, and often met with brutal violence, Christians forged the basis for what would become, centuries later, the western ideas of freedom and of the infinite value of each human life.

Clement realized, too, that certain inquiring and restless Christians saw in the Genesis story not only sexual and political implications but disturbing philosophical and religious ones as well. How could an all-powerful God have created the world "good" when we find in it so much suffering? Whence came the serpent? Why did God begrudge Adam and Eve the knowledge that even he admitted would make them "like one of us" (Genesis 3:22)? Such questions, and the underlying one, *unde malum* ("Whence is evil?"), were, the Christian writer Tertullian said, "the questions that make people heretics."

In Chapter 3 I explore how some of these followers of Jesus, often called gnostics, read the story of Adam and Eve in ways that dismayed and outraged orthodox Christians. For gnostic Christians declared that the story, taken literally, made no sense; thus they themselves set out to read it symbolically, often allegorically. The most radical gnostics turned the story upside down and told it, in effect, from the serpent's point of view: some said he was "wiser" than all the other animals and so tried desperately to persuade Adam and Eve to partake of the tree of knowledge, defying their jealous and hostile creator; this wise serpent, some dared say, was a manifestation of Christ himself! Other gnostics read the story of Adam and Eve as an allegory of religious experience, as relating the discovery of the authentic spiritual self (Eve) hidden within the soul (Adam). The gnostic author of the *Interpretation of the Soul* saw Eve as representing the alienated soul seeking spiritual union; the author of *Thunder: Perfect Mind* saw her as the divine energy underlying all existence, human and divine. Gnostic Christians, who disagreed with one another on almost everything else, agreed that this naïve story hid profound truths about human nature, and they vied with one another to come up with ingenious and imaginative interpretations of its deeper meaning.

Leaders of the church who called themselves orthodox (literally, "straight-thinking") Christians denounced such interpretations and accused gnostics of projecting their own bizarre fantasies upon the text. Above all, they said, gnostic Christians deny the primary reality of the Genesis account—namely, that it depicts humanity created morally free and entrusted with free will. Gnostic Christians, who denied that the human will has the power to prevent error and suffering, also denied, in effect, that baptism fully delivers us from sin and suffering and restores our moral freedom, and for this reason, among others, the gnostics were expelled by the leaders of the church and consigned to oblivion.

As the Christian movement increasingly gained converts throughout Roman society during the third and fourth centuries, some of the most ardent Christians insisted that to realize the greatest freedom one must "renounce the world" and choose poverty and celibacy. For certain Christians, celibacy was a way of rejecting Roman social life. In Genesis 1–3, where Jews—and many Christians, for that matter—traditionally saw God's endorsement of marriage and procreation, ascetic Christians saw the opposite: Adam and Eve were virgins in Paradise and should have remained so; as Gregory of Nyssa explained, God could have arranged for the human race to "multiply" in completely nonsexual ways, as angels do. But when one Roman monk, Jovinian, although himself celibate, tried to prove from the Scriptures that celibate Christians were no holier than their married sisters and brothers, Jerome, Ambrose, and Augustine, three future saints of the church, attacked him, while Pope Siricius of Rome denounced and excommunicated Jovinian for his "heresy." In Chapter 4 I explore what motivated men—and especially women—to embrace that ascetic life; and what kinds of freedom its advocates did indeed find in choosing celibacy.

From these explorations I came to see that for nearly the first four hundred years of our era, Christians regarded *freedom* as the primary message of Genesis 1–3—freedom in its many forms, including free will, freedom from demonic powers, freedom from social and sexual obligations, freedom from tyrannical government and from fate; and self-mastery as the source of such freedom. With Augustine, as I show in Chapter 5, this message changed. In the late fourth century, Augustine was living in an entirely different Christian world—one that Justin and his contemporaries could hardly have imagined—for Christianity was no longer a dissident sect. The Christian movement, having been oppressed and persecuted by Rome for some three hundred years, over several generations, with Constantine's conversion in 313, came into imperial favor and, throughout the later fourth century, consolidated its new position as the official religion of the empire. Christian bishops, once targets for arrest, torture, and execution, now received tax exemptions, gifts from the imperial treasury, prestige, and even influence at court; their churches gained new wealth, power, and prominence. Some

Christians, who once defiantly proclaimed their freedom against their persecutors, now found that their old rhetoric—and even their traditional understanding of human nature and its relation to social and political order—no longer applied to this new circumstance, which made them allies of the emperor. In a world in which Christians not only were free to follow their faith but were officially encouraged to do so, Augustine came to read the story of Adam and Eve very differently than had the majority of his Jewish and Christian predecessors. What they had read for centuries as a story of human freedom became, in his hands, a story of human bondage. Most Jews and Christians had agreed that God gave humankind in creation the gift of moral freedom, and that Adam's misuse of it brought death upon his progeny. But Augustine went further: Adam's sin not only caused our mortality but cost us our moral freedom, irreversibly corrupted our experience of sexuality (which Augustine tended to identify with original sin), and made us incapable of genuine political freedom. Furthermore, Augustine read back into Paul's letters his own teaching of the moral impotence of the human will,[4] along with his sexualized interpretation of sin.

Augustine's theory of original sin not only proved politically expedient, since it persuaded many of his contemporaries that human beings universally need external government—which meant, in their case, both a Christian state and an imperially supported church—but also offered an analysis of human nature that became, for better and worse, the heritage of all subsequent generations of western Christians and the major influence on their psychological and political thinking. Even today, many people, Catholics and Protestants alike, regard the story of Adam and Eve as virtually synonymous with original sin. During Augustine's own lifetime, as we shall see, various Christians objected to his radical theory, and others bitterly contested it; but within the next few generations, Christians who held to more traditional views of human freedom were themselves condemned as heretics.

Augustine spent the last twelve years of his life battling for his interpretation of Genesis against a young Christian bishop, Julian of Eclanum, who attacked and criticized his theory of original sin not only as an abrupt departure from orthodox Christian thought but as Manichaean heresy, the very heresy that Augustine had once admired and later attacked. When Julian challenged Augustine to define what is "nature"—human nature and nature in general—Augustine replied that mortality and sexual desire are not "natural";

both, he insists, entered into human experience only to punish Adam's sin. Chapter 6 considers this debate on the nature of nature and suggests ways in which Augustine's views—antinatural and even preposterous as they will appear to many readers—nevertheless became deeply rooted in our cultural attitudes toward suffering and death.

One of my colleagues, misunderstanding the viewpoint presented here and in my previous book, *The Gnostic Gospels,* has objected that religious ideas cannot be reduced to practical (or, in his words, political) agendas. On this I wholeheartedly agree with him. I am not saying that religious ideas are nothing but a cover for political motives, as if, for example, Christians in the fourth century first chose to join forces with the Roman state and then adopted the doctrine of original sin to justify their new political direction. Instead, I intend to show that religious insights and moral choices, in actual experience, coincide with practical ones. Scholars and theologians may separate them theoretically, but at the cost of distorting our understanding: in our actual experience—as in that of Christians in the first four centuries—moral choices often are political choices. An act of religious affirmation is always, in some sense, a practical and consequential act.

Some readers may ask, "Are you saying, then, that biblical interpretation is nothing but projection? Is *exegesis* (what one reads out of the text) merely *eisegesis* (reading into the text)?" Certainly not; but anyone concerned with the history of hermeneutics confronts the question of interpretation, a question biblical interpreters share with lawyers who debate the meaning of the Constitution, with psychiatrists as they reflect upon their interpretation of case histories, and with anthropologists and historians who ponder their data. What I am thinking of is what the anthropologist Foucault calls "the politics of truth"—that is, that what each of us perceives and acts upon as true has much to do with our situation, social, political, cultural, religious, or philosophical.

Those who are unfamiliar with biblical interpretation or cynical about it may assume that the controversies and diverging interpretations described here merely confirm what they have suspected all along: that biblical interpretation is no more than ideology under a different name. Yet those who seriously confront the Bible will realize that genuine interpretation has always required that the reader actively and imaginatively engage the texts. Through the process of interpretation, the reader's living experience comes to be woven into ancient texts, so that what was "dead letter" again comes to life.

What I intend to show in this book is how certain ideas—in particular, ideas concerning sexuality, moral freedom, and human value—took their definitive form during the first four centuries as interpretations of the Genesis creation stories, and how they have continued to affect our culture and everyone in it, Christian or not, ever since.

ADAM, EVE,
AND THE
SERPENT

"THE KINGDOM OF GOD IS AT HAND"

J ESUS AND HIS FOLLOWERS lived at a time when the situation of
the Jews was particularly turbulent and potentially explosive.
The rural communities of what has come to be called the Holy
Land, where Jews had practiced traditional ways of life for centuries,
increasingly confronted an encroaching pagan culture that baffled
and repelled them, not so much in their insulated villages, but from
what they heard of city life in such places as Jerusalem.[1] Centuries
of domination by foreign empires had, by the time of Jesus, brought
once isolated Jewish communities into direct, often unwilling, contact with their pagan neighbors—Babylonians, Romans, Asians,
Egyptians, Greeks, Africans, and Persians. Many Jews, especially the
richer and more worldly ones, struggled with questions of whether,
or to what extent, they should act "like the nations." Should Jews
seek foreign citizenship, with its great economic and political advantages? Should they hire pagan slaves to teach their children Greek
and Latin, and risk encouraging them to exercise naked in the public
baths? Should they strive to enter the lively and cosmopolitan world
of pagan culture and social life, abandoning ancient customs like
circumcision and kosher laws that their pagan neighbors considered
barbaric?

In Jesus' time, these urban Jewish communities were uneasily
divided between those who accommodated pagan culture and accepted its political domination and those who resisted both pagan
culture and politics. Once allies of the Romans, the Jews were now
their subjects, and Judea had become a Roman province ruled by the
puppet Jewish dynasty of Herod the Great for their pagan masters.

Even those who resisted pagan culture had been deeply affected by it; yet they held to the customs that distinguished and separated them from their pagan neighbors. Many Jews, especially poorer ones, and those who lived in the rural villages where John and Jesus preached, detested the court of the Herods, with its luxurious entertainments and extravagant palaces, which the Herods sometimes named for the emperors but financed with heavy taxes, extortion, and bribes extracted from their fellow Jews. What angered these rural people especially was the way the Herods, neglecting Jewish tradition, courted and copied the Romans.[2] Prince Herod Antipas, grandson of Herod the Great, had gone to Rome to be tutored by the same philosophers who tutored the prince Claudius, future emperor of Rome. The Jewish historian Josephus says that not long before Jesus' birth, two thousand Jews had been crucified in his native Galilee for rebelling against Rome, leaving a forest of crosses littered with rotting corpses as a warning to others.[3] Jesus himself, charged with treason against Rome, would one day suffer the same penalty. Especially among the poor, the pious, and the rural Jews, antipagan feeling ran deep; and it was among such people that Jesus found his following.

Many Jews distrusted, too, their own religious leaders who served at the Jerusalem Temple, especially the powerful and wealthy men who surrounded the high priest, for their open collusion with the Roman occupiers. Members of Jewish communities responded to this situation in a variety of ways. The most popular sect, the Pharisees, bitterly criticized these leaders for having subverted the Temple,[4] while some devout people went further and withdrew in protest from ordinary Jewish life. The Essenes, for example, during the first century B.C.E., abandoned Jerusalem, denounced the Temple worship as polluted, and formed a "pure" community in desert caves overlooking the Dead Sea. There they renounced private property to live in a monastic community; they observed the rules prescribed for holy war; and they avoided sexual contact and impure food, thoughts, and practices as they awaited the battle of Armageddon. They warned that on that day of judgment God himself would annihilate the hypocrites and evildoers and vindicate the Essenes as the righteous.

Jesus' predecessor John the Baptist, a passionate reformer who may have lived for some years with the Essenes, publicly harangued Herod Antipas, then tetrarch of Galilee, for having married his brother's ex-wife; at the instigation of Herod's wife—she was the mother of Salome—John was imprisoned and beheaded.[5] There were many people who agreed with John that the times called for radical reform. No longer was it enough merely to follow traditional Jewish patterns or to stay within the boundaries of the law. John demanded much more; he demanded, in fact, that people return not just to the letter but to the moral spirit of the law.[6] Yet for all of John's claim to speak for authentic Jewish tradition, there remained a more difficult question: Which elements of the Jewish tradition were essential and true, and which were antiquated relics of an archaic past? Which should one follow, and which discard?

Jesus of Nazareth was baptized by John and then, according to the Gospel of Mark, was driven by the spirit into the wilderness (Mark 1:12). He returned from his solitude fired with the conviction that the Kingdom of God was at hand. Like the Essenes, Jesus declared that the crisis of the times required radical sacrifice. Going from village to village near his birthplace in Galilee, Jesus warned that the coming day of judgment was about to turn the social and political world upside down. Then "many that are first will be last, and the last first" (Matthew 19:30); and the coming kingdom would be given to those who were now "despised and rejected." Jesus declared in his famous Sermon:

> *"Blessed are you poor, for yours is the kingdom of God.*
> *Blessed are you that hunger now, for you shall be satisfied.*
> *Blessed are you that weep now, for you shall laugh. . . .*
> *But woe to you that are rich, for you have received your consolation.*
> *Woe to you that are full now, for you shall hunger.*
> *Woe to you that laugh now, for you shall mourn and weep."*
> (LUKE 6:20–25)

Jesus disregarded—and, his accusers claimed, dismissed—strict kosher and Sabbath observance and attacked the legal casuistry that enabled people to evade responsibility for those in need. As biblical scholars generally acknowledge, the gospels of the New Testament are neither histories nor biographies in our sense of these terms; we have no independent sources with which to compare their accounts. But as they recount his life and message, Jesus demanded sacrifice and transformation, extraordinary measures to prepare for the coming new age. His message could hardly have been more radical, then or now:

> *"Give to everyone who begs from you; and of him who takes your goods, do not ask them again.*
>
> *"But love your enemies and do good, and lend, expecting nothing in return."*

(LUKE 6:30; 35)

As for the Ten Commandments:

> *"You have heard that it was said to the men of old, '*You shall not kill, and whoever kills shall be liable to judgment.' *But I say to you that everyone who is angry with his brother shall be liable to judgment; whoever insults his brother shall be liable to the council; and whoever says, 'You fool' shall be liable to the hell of fire.*
>
> *"You have heard that it was said, '*You shall not commit adultery.' *But I say to you that every one who looks at a woman lustfully has already committed adultery with her in his heart."*

(MATTHEW 5:21–22; 27–28)

Jesus attacked Israel's religious leaders with irony and anger:

> *"The scribes and Pharisees sit in Moses' seat: so practice and observe whatever they tell you, but not what they do; for they preach, but do not practice.*
>
> *"Woe to you, scribes and Pharisees, hypocrites! For you tithe mint and dill and cumin, and have neglected the weightier matters of the law, justice and mercy and faith. . . . You blind guides, straining out a gnat and swallowing a camel!*
>
> *"You serpents; you brood of vipers; how are you to escape being sentenced to hell?"*

(MATTHEW 23:2; 23–24; 33)

Jesus' passionate and powerful presence aroused enormous response, especially when he preached among the crowds of pilgrims gathered in Jerusalem to celebrate Passover. As the Jewish and Roman authorities well knew, tensions were high during the religious holidays when Jewish worshipers found themselves face to face with the Roman soldiers. Jesus' near contemporary the Jewish historian Josephus, himself a governor of Galilee, tells of a Roman soldier on guard near the Temple who contemptuously exposed himself before just such a crowd, an outrage that incited a riot in which twenty thousand died.[7] When Jesus dared enter the Temple courtyard before a certain Passover, brandishing a whip, throwing down the tables of those changing foreign money, and quoting the words of the prophet Jeremiah to attack the Temple leaders for turning God's

◆ 6 ◆

house into a "den of robbers," the Gospel of Mark says, "he would not allow any one to carry anything through the temple" (Mark 11:16). But soon afterward the authorities took action to prevent this firebrand village preacher from fanning the religious and nationalistic passions already smoldering among the restless crowds. The Jewish Council, eager to keep the peace, and hoping to avoid recriminations from their Roman masters, collaborated with the Roman procurator to have Jesus arrested, tried, and hastily executed on charges of having threatened to tear down the Temple single-handed, and having conspired to rise against Rome and make himself king of the Jews (Mark 14:58–15:26).

Jesus himself, according to the New Testament, saw himself very differently, not as a revolutionary but as a man seized by the spirit that inspired Isaiah and Jeremiah—the spirit of God—as a prophet sent to warn humankind of the approaching Kingdom of God and to offer purification to those who would listen.[8] Repeatedly, according to the New Testament accounts, Jesus chose to risk death rather than allow himself to be silenced.

Leaving aside, for the moment, the religious meaning of Jesus' message, one could say from a strictly historical perspective that Jesus foresaw events accurately: in many ways the world in which he and his Jewish contemporaries lived *would* soon come to an end, less than forty years after his death, with the catastrophic Jewish war against Rome. In 66 C.E., the religious and patriotic feeling that the Jewish Council feared Jesus might ignite finally caught fire. Outbreaks of violence against the Roman occupation exploded into a civil war that finally engulfed the whole province that the Romans called Judea. Josephus, born in 37 C.E., a few years after Jesus' death, participated in that war, and described its horrifying devastation, as Titus's clanking Roman forces marched upon Jerusalem. The streets streamed with blood; the inner city was ground to rubble, and the Temple itself burned to a heap of ruins. Titus, the Roman conqueror and future emperor, annihilated Jerusalem politically as well, reestablishing in its place the colony the Romans called Aelia Capitolina, sacred to the gods of Rome.

The "new age" that followed the Roman victory challenged and split Jewish communities from Judea to Rome and throughout the world. Some Jews simply gave up and followed pagan customs, but the majority gradually came to adopt the forms in which the party of the Pharisees salvaged and recast their ancient traditions. According to Professor Jacob Neusner, the Pharisees hoped to reunite the

Jewish communities by providing a common code of law; thus they gave birth to the rabbinic movement.[9] These rabbis, or teachers, replaced the priests and the animal sacrifices that they had offered in the destroyed Jerusalem Temple—that Temple having been for many Jews the central focus of Jewish life—with the "sacrifices" of prayer, Torah study, and worship in synagogues scattered throughout the world wherever Jews lived. And the rabbis themselves, as "teachers of the law," came to replace the hereditary caste of Jewish priests who had for generations officiated in that Temple.[10]

But the radical sectarians who called themselves followers of Jesus of Nazareth went further. Having refused to fight in the Jewish war against Rome, they had already alienated themselves from the Jewish communities; now they broke with their fellow Jews and proclaimed that they themselves were the "new Israel," even the "true Israel," of this shattering new age. Some Jews who joined this Christian movement, especially those influenced by Paul's teaching, abandoned, within one or two generations of Jesus' death, the characteristic practices that had distinguished them as Jews. Many gave up circumcision, kosher laws, and Sabbath observance, claiming, in Paul's words, to be "Jews inwardly," circumcised "in the heart" (Romans 2:28–29) and not in the flesh. All converts to this new movement, whether they had once been Jews or pagans, tended to distinguish their "new Israel" from the rest of the world by insisting upon strict, even extreme, moral practices. The most controversial aspect of this new moral austerity was the sexual attitudes and practices of its adherents.[11]

This is a book not about Jesus' message but about practical elements of his message, especially as he and his followers read these elements back into the story of creation. According to the New Testament, Jesus himself mentioned the story of Adam and Eve only once, in answer to a question about the legitimate grounds for divorce. To judge by New Testament reports of his few comments concerning marriage, divorce, and celibacy, such concerns seem almost incidental to Jesus' message. But after his death, as the movement he inspired grew to include Greeks, Asians, Africans, Romans, and Egyptians, as well as Palestinian Jews, his followers struggled with questions of how to translate his spiritual teaching into the practical terms of everyday living. Should Christians marry or not? Should the roles of men and women in the community differ, and, if so, how? Should converts avoid sexual activity outside of marriage—or even within it? What about prostitution, abortion, and the sexual use of slaves? These questions, too, bore wider implications: How are Christians to understand human nature? Are slaves, for example, essentially any different from free persons?

Such questions did not, of course, originate with Christians. Jewish teachers debated such topics, and as the French scholar Paul Veyne, among others, has shown, certain pagan philosophers advocated sexual restraint similar to that adopted by Christians.[12] But the Christian movement popularized these changing attitudes with momentous consequences, especially after the fourth century, when the Roman emperor Constantine declared his own allegiance to Christ and granted Christianity not only legal but privileged status within the empire. It was from that time that Christian attitudes began to transform the consciousness, to say nothing of the moral and legal systems, that continue to form western society.

This book will explore the attitudes that Jesus and his followers took toward marriage, family, procreation, and celibacy, and thus toward "human nature" in general, and the controversies these attitudes sparked as they were variously interpreted among Christians for generations—or for millennia, depending on how one counts. It will also show how men and women who converted to Christianity often adopted attitudes toward sexuality that their families and friends considered bizarre. Moreover, I shall further speculate on how we have come to take for granted the set of attitudes about sexuality and human nature arising from "Judeo-Christian culture," attitudes that many people today take to be normal and obvious but that were, in the context of early Christian times, anything but normal and, from the anthropologically informed perspective of our own contemporaries, anything but obvious.

JESUS AND HIS FOLLOWERS, at the beginning of what came to be called the Christian Era, took up startlingly different attitudes toward divorce, procreation, and family from those that had prevailed for centuries among most of their fellow Jews. So powerful were these challenges to convention that they precipitated, or at least accompanied, the birth of a new religious movement. Despite Jesus' radical message—or perhaps because of it—the movement quickly spread throughout the Roman world and within three centuries came to dominate it.

As the Christian movement emerged within the Roman Empire, it challenged pagan converts, too, to change their attitudes and behavior. Many pagans who had been brought up to regard marriage essentially as a social and economic arrangement, homosexual relationships as an expected element of male education, prostitution, both male and female, as both ordinary and legal, and divorce, abortion, contraception, and exposure of unwanted infants as matters of practical expedience, embraced, to the astonishment of their families, the Christian message, which opposed these practices.

Certain scholars, prominently including Paul Veyne, as we have noted, have recently downplayed these differences and have pointed out that philosophical moralists such as Musonius Rufus and Plutarch advocated similar moral practices. Veyne concludes that "we must not argue in stereotypes, and imagine a conflict between pagan and Christian morality."[13] Yet as the philosopher and convert Athenagoras (c. 160 C.E.) points out in his defense of the Christians, addressed to their persecutors, the emperors, what philosophers advocate may have little or nothing to do with what actually motivates people to change, as conversion has done to many Christians.[14] Indeed, such converts as Justin, Athenagoras, Clement, and Tertullian all describe specific ways in which conversion changed their own lives and those of many other, often uneducated, believers, in matters involving sex, business, magic, money, paying taxes, and racial hatred.[15] Justin and Tertullian both relate cases in which the moral transformation accompanying a believer's conversion aroused pagan relatives to outrage and even led to legal accusations and disinheritance. Of course these Christians were writing in defense of their faith; we need not accept all their rhetoric as fact to acknowledge that they and many others certainly *did* "imagine a conflict between pagan and Christian morality" and tried to act accordingly.

Their own accounts suggest that such converts changed their attitudes toward the self, toward nature, and toward God, as well as their sense of social and political obligation, in ways that often placed them in diametric opposition to pagan culture. For the most dedicated Christians, conversion transformed both consciousness and behavior; and such converts, gathered in the increasingly popular Christian movement, would profoundly affect the consciousness of all subsequent generations as well.[16]

Other Jewish teachers of Jesus' time, and for generations before, had pronounced certain pagan sexual practices abominable. Among conscientious Jews, only the worship of pagan gods aroused more outrage than pagan sexual behavior. Generations of Jewish teachers had warned that pagans thought nothing of pederasty, promiscuity, and incest. Yet the clash with outside cultures challenged Jewish customs in turn. Many pagans found such practices as circumcision to be peculiar, antiquated, and no less barbaric than Jews found the sexual habits of pagans. Babylonians and Romans, themselves monogamous, criticized the ancient Jewish custom of polygamous marriage, practiced by such venerable patriarchs as Abraham, David, and Solomon, as well as by the wealthy few who could afford it, even in Jesus' time and later.[17] The Jewish historian Josephus, himself apparently polygamous, tried to justify to his Roman readers the ten wives of King Herod the Great (and possibly his own bigamy as well)[18] by explaining that "among us it is the custom to have many wives simultaneously."[19] Those familiar with Roman law could also question traditional Jewish divorce law, which granted to the husband (but not to the wife) the often easy right of divorce.

For centuries—indeed, for over a millennium—Jews had taught that the purpose of marriage, and therefore of sexuality, was procreation. Jewish communities had inherited their sexual customs from nomadic ancestors whose very survival depended upon reproduction, both among their herds of animals and among themselves. According to the story of Abraham told in Genesis 22, the great blessing promised through God's covenant with Israel was progeny innumerable as the sands of the sea and the stars in the sky (verse 17). To ensure the stability and survival of the nation, Jewish teachers apparently assumed that sexual activity should be committed to the primary purpose of procreation. Prostitution, homosexuality, abortion, and infanticide, practices both legal and tolerated among certain of their pagan neighbors, contradicted Jewish custom and law.

Both polygamy and divorce, on the other hand, increased opportunities for reproduction—not for women, but for the men who wrote the laws and benefited from them. Jewish law even went so far as to require that a man bound for ten years in a childless marriage should either divorce his wife and marry another, or else keep his barren wife and take a second to produce his children.[20] Jewish custom banned as "abominations" sexual acts not conducive to procreation, and the impurity laws even prohibited marital intercourse except at times most likely to result in conception.

Generations before Jesus, Jews, like so many other peoples, had begun to invoke their creation accounts, specifically in Genesis, to prove that such tribal customs as these were not barbaric or peculiar, as their pagan critics charged, but were part of the very structure of the universe itself. In their arguments from Scripture, Jewish teachers often avoided speaking directly about sexual practices but engaged in heated discussions about Adam, Eve, and the serpent, and in this metaphorical way revealed what they thought about human sexuality—and about human nature in general. The *Book of Jubilees*, for example, written about 150 years before Jesus' birth by a Palestinian Jew, retells the story of Adam and Eve to prove, among other things, that Jewish customs concerning childbirth and nakedness were not arbitrary or trivial but actually built into human nature from the beginning. As this author tells it, Adam entered Eden during the first week of creation, but Eve entered the garden only during the second week; this explains why a woman who gives birth to a male child remains ritually impure for only *one* week, while she who bears a female remains impure for two weeks.[21] The author goes on to recall that God made leather garments for Adam and Eve, and clothed them before expelling them from Paradise (Genesis 3:21); this shows that Jews must "cover their shame, and not go naked, as the Gentiles do," in public places like the baths and the gymnasia.[22] Throughout subsequent generations, what Jews and Christians read into the creation accounts of Genesis came, for better and worse, to shape what later came to be called Judeo-Christian tradition.

By the time Jesus preached, his Jewish contemporaries had no difficulty defending their ancestral emphasis upon procreation by showing from Genesis 1 that as soon as God created all living creatures, culminating with the first man and woman, he commanded them to "be fruitful and multiply, and fill the earth" (Genesis 1:28). Whatever disagreements existed between various groups of Jews (the Pharisees, for example, apparently approved of sexual pleasure within the bonds of marriage, while the Essenes practiced sexual restraint), Jewish teachers agreed that this primary and sacred obligation to procreate took precedence even over marital obligations—thus a barren marriage could be invalidated—and dictated its structure. They pointed out from Genesis that God first commanded man and woman to procreate, and only afterward, to help them do so, he brought Eve to Adam and joined them in the first marriage:

> *Then the man said,*
> *"This at last is bone of my bones*
> *and flesh of my flesh;*
> *she shall be called Woman,*
> *because she was taken out of Man."*

> *Therefore a man leaves his father and his mother and cleaves to his*
> *wife, and they become one flesh.*
>
> (GENESIS 2:23–24)

For centuries Jewish teachers built from this passage the basic laws of marital behavior. Certain rabbis actually turned these lines from Genesis into a code of sexual conduct. Rabbi Eliezer (c. 90 C.E.) took the words "Therefore a man leaves his father and his mother" to mean not only that a man must not marry his mother, but that he must also refuse to marry "her who is related to his father or to his mother" within the degrees of kinship prohibited as incest. Rabbi Akiba (c. 135 C.E.) took the next phrase, "and cleaves to his wife," to mean, in his words, "But not to his neighbor's wife, nor to a male, nor to an animal"—thus disposing of adultery, homosexuality, and bestiality. Rabbi Issi (c. 145 C.E.) among others, took the phrase "and they become one flesh" to mean, in his words, that the man "shall cleave to the place where both form one flesh," prohibiting through this euphemistic phrase what the rabbis called "unnatural intercourse"—sexual acts or positions that might inhibit conception.[23] Other Jewish teachers agreed that the purpose of marriage is to "increase and multiply"; that one must accept whatever facilitates procreation, including divorce and polygamy; and that one must reject whatever hinders procreation—even a marriage itself, in the case of an infertile wife.

Jesus radically challenged this consensus. Like other Jewish teachers, Jesus, when he speaks about marriage, goes back to the Genesis account of the first marriage; but he reads the same passage very differently than others did. Asked by conservative teachers of the law, the so-called Pharisees, about the legitimate grounds for divorce, Jesus answered that there were none:[24]

> *"Have you not read that he who made them from the beginning made them*
> *male and female and said, 'For this reason a man shall leave his father*
> *and mother and be joined to his wife, and the two shall become one'? So*
> *they are no longer two but one. What therefore God has joined together,*
> *let no man put asunder."*
>
> (MATTHEW 19:4–6)

This answer shocked his Jewish listeners and, as Matthew tells it, pleased no one. Among Jesus' Jewish contemporaries no one questioned the legitimacy of divorce. The only question was what constituted adequate grounds; and it was this question of grounds, not the legitimacy of divorce as such, that split religious schools into opposing factions. The teacher Shammai, for one, took the conservative position: the only offense serious enough to justify divorce was the wife's infidelity. Shammai's opponent Hillel, famous for his liberal judgments, argued instead that a man may divorce his wife for any reason he chooses, "even if she burn his soup!" The well-known teacher Akiba, who agreed with Hillel, added emphatically, "and even if he finds a younger woman more beautiful than she." But however various teachers disputed the grounds for divorce, no one went so far as Jesus did and prohibited it altogether. Those among his audience familiar with Jewish law demanded to know how he dared question divorce, a right—and, in some cases, an obligation—provided in Mosaic law as essential to procreation. Jesus admitted that divorce is technically legal, but he rejected the practice nevertheless. "Moses allowed you to divorce your wives, but from the beginning [i.e., from the time of creation] it was not so" (Matthew 19:8). Moses took it upon himself, Jesus says, to change what God had created and to permit divorce as a concession to "your hardness of heart."

When his own followers, offended by such vehemence, complained, "If such is the case . . . it is not expedient to marry," Jesus must have astonished them even more by agreeing that, yes, it *is* better not to marry, and praising "those who have made themselves eunuchs for the sake of the Kingdom of Heaven" (Matthew 19:12). Luke says that Jesus even praised barren women: "Blessed are . . . the wombs that never bore, and the breasts that never gave suck" (Luke 23:29), implying that the time was coming when the people who did *not* have children would be the lucky ones. Luke probably saw this as Jesus' prophecy of the coming war against Rome (66–70 C.E.); but later readers often took it as referring to the Kingdom of God. In another passage, Luke has Jesus link marriage with death, and celibacy with eternal life:

> *And Jesus said to them, "The sons of this age marry and are given in marriage; but those who are accounted worthy to attain to that age and to the resurrection from the dead neither marry nor are given in marriage, for they cannot die any more, because they are equal to angels and are sons of God, being sons of the resurrection."*
>
> (LUKE 20:34–36)

Such statements must have horrified Jewish traditionalists, for barren women, whom Jesus blessed, had traditionally been seen as accursed, and eunuchs, whom Jesus praised, were despised by rabbinic teachers for their sexual incapacity. Unmarried himself, Jesus praised the very persons most pitied and shunned in Jewish communities for their sexual incompleteness—those who were single and childless; for Jesus' radical message of the impending Kingdom of God left his followers no time to fulfill the ordinary obligations of everyday life. First-century Christians saw themselves participating at the birth of a revolutionary movement that they expected would culminate in the total social transformation that Jesus promised in the "age to come."

To prepare themselves for these events, Jesus commanded his followers to forget ordinary concerns about food and clothing, "sell your possessions, and give alms" (Luke 12:33), divest themselves of all property, and abandon family obligations, whether to parents, spouses, or children, for such obligations would interfere with their dedication to the apocalyptic hopes Jesus announced; the disciple must become wholly free to serve God. According to Luke, Jesus even went so far as to say, "If any one comes to me and does not hate his own father and mother and wife and children and brothers and sisters, yes, and even his own life, he cannot be my disciple" (Luke 14:26). The coming new age demands new—and total—allegiance, no longer to family and nation but to the kingdom itself. Thus Jesus urges his followers to break their merely natural relationships in favor of spiritual ones. Acknowledging that such teaching divides and disrupts family relationships, Jesus boldly declares:

> *"I came to cast fire upon the earth; and would that it were already kindled! . . . Do you think that I have come to give peace to the earth? No, I tell you, but rather division; for henceforth in one house there will be five divided, three against two and two against three; they will be divided, father against son and son against father, mother against daughter and daughter against her mother, mother-in-law against her daughter-in-law and daughter-in-law against her mother-in-law."*
>
> (LUKE 12:49–53)

Mark tells how Jesus rejected his own mother and brothers in favor of the family of his followers. When his mother and brothers came to speak with him and stood outside the crowded room where he was preaching, he refused to go to them, saying,

> *"Who are my mother and my brothers?" And looking around on those who sat about him, he said, "Here are my mother and my brothers! Whoever does the will of God is my brother, and sister, and mother."*
>
> (MARK 3:33–35)

Thus Jesus dismisses the family obligations considered most sacred in Jewish community life, including those to one's parents, siblings, spouse, and children. By subordinating the obligation to procreate, rejecting divorce, and implicitly sanctioning monogamous relationships, Jesus reverses traditional priorities, declaring, in effect, that other obligations, including marital ones, are now more important than procreation. Even more startling, Jesus endorses—and exemplifies—a new possibility and one he says is even better: rejecting both marriage and procreation in favor of voluntary celibacy, for the sake of following him into the new age.

Twenty years later, Jesus' zealous disciple Paul will go even further. Paul, born in the cosmopolitan Asian city of Tarsus, brought up in the strictly observant tradition of the Pharisees, was suddenly converted from bitter hostility toward Christians to become one of their leaders. While we know little of him as a person, we know from his letters, now preserved in the New Testament, that Paul was a man of intense convictions. Paul accepts Jesus' judgment that marriage is indissoluble and, like Jesus, not only subordinates but actually ignores the command to procreate. But he often speaks of marriage in negative terms, as a sop for those too weak to do what is best: renounce sexual activity altogether. Paul admits that marriage is "not sin" yet argues that it makes both partners slaves to each other's sexual needs and desires, no longer free to devote their energies "to the Lord" (1 Corinthians 7:1–35).[25] Paul sees not only marriage but even the most casual sexual encounter as a form of bondage. Shockingly, he takes the passage from Genesis traditionally used to describe the institution of marriage and applies it instead to an encounter with a prostitute: "Do you not know that he who joins himself to a prostitute becomes one body with her? For, as it is written, 'The two shall become one' " (Genesis 2:24). Paul then contrasts such sexual union with the believer's spiritual union with Christ: "But he who is united to the Lord becomes one spirit with him" (1 Corinthians 6:16–17).

Neither Jesus nor Paul, of course, invented religious celibacy. But those few Jews among their contemporaries who practiced it— some of the Essenes who lived in caves overlooking the Dead Sea, as well as Essene groups in other places, and the Therapeutae, a monastic group of men and women in Egypt—were widely considered extremists. Paul, however, declares, on the contrary, that he wishes that everyone were voluntarily celibate, for the sake of the kingdom, like himself (1 Corinthians 7:7–8). Single people, spared the anxieties and obligations that plague married people, are not only freer but, Paul says, happier. He concedes, however, that "if they cannot contain themselves, let them marry. For it is better to marry than to be aflame with passion" (1 Corinthians 7:9). Yet Paul encourages even those who are married to live as if they, too, were unmarried: "Let those who have wives live as though they had none" (1 Corinthians 7:29b).

George Bernard Shaw was wrong when he accused Paul of inventing religious celibacy, which Shaw called "this monstrous imposition upon Jesus"; and Shaw was also wrong to attribute Paul's celibacy to his "terror of sex and terror of life."[26] For Jesus and Paul, as for the Essenes, such drastic measures were not a reflection of sexual revulsion but a necessity to prepare for the end of the world, and to free oneself for the "age to come." Paul, like Jesus, encouraged celibacy not because he loathed the flesh (which in my opinion he did not) but out of his urgent concern for the practical work of proclaiming the gospel. Paul himself insisted that he did not want to place constraints upon believers, but instead, in view of "the present distress," wanted to free them from external anxieties:

> *I mean, brethren, the appointed time has grown very short. . . . I say this for your own benefit, not to lay any restraint upon you, but to promote good order and to secure your undivided devotion to the Lord.*
>
> (1 CORINTHIANS 7:29, 35)

Paul had established groups of followers among Jews and Gentiles from the Greek seaport cities of Corinth and Thessalonica to the Asian coastal cities of Galatia and Ephesus, and he jealously watched over each of these groups to keep them pure while awaiting the kingdom. He told his converts in Corinth that he saw the Christian church as Christ's "bride," and himself as a father or marriage broker anxious to preserve a young girl's virginity for her future husband:

> *I feel a divine jealousy for you, for I betrothed you to Christ to present you as a pure bride to her one husband. But I am afraid that as the serpent deceived Eve by his cunning, your thoughts will be led astray from a sincere and pure devotion to Christ.*
>
> (2 CORINTHIANS 11:2–3)

Here Paul speaks of protecting the church's virginity as a metaphor for maintaining his pure and original teaching; but certain Christians in following generations took his words literally, as an injunction to celibacy.[27]

Although Paul intended his first letter to the Christians at Corinth, and especially its seventh chapter, to settle community disputes over marital issues, the result was that he raised more questions than he answered. Some Christians took Jesus and Paul at what they believed to be their word and preached the gospel message as liberation from all worldly concerns, especially from care for family and children, which preoccupied the majority of their contemporaries. Some of Paul's converts in Corinth, both women and men, enthusiastically embraced celibacy. Although Paul specifically had advised married Christians against unilaterally refusing marital relations (1 Corinthians 7:2–5), some married Christians, prohibited by Jesus' command from divorce, chose to take Paul's advice ("Let those who have wives live as though they had none," 1 Corinthians 7:29) as if Paul had, in fact, urged sexual abstinence *within* marriage.

Within about a century of Paul's death, ascetic versions of Jesus' message were spreading rapidly, especially in the cities of Asia Minor where Paul himself once preached. What prompted this enthusiasm for renunciation is unclear, but it expressed itself in such widely popular narratives as the story of Thecla, the lovely young virgin who renounced a lucrative marriage which her mother had arranged for her, cut off her hair and dressed in men's clothes, and ran off to join the movement that Jesus and Paul had initiated. According to the *Acts of Paul and Thecla,* she was determined, in fact, to do what she believed the gospel required of her—to become, like Paul himself, a celibate evangelist, and reject her wealthy fiancé, Thamyris, who would have supported not only Thecla but her aging and impoverished mother. When Paul came to preach "the word of the virgin life"[28] in her home city of Iconium, in Asia Minor, Thecla's mother forbade her to leave the house to hear him. So Thecla sat at the window, straining to hear what Paul was saying to the crowds of young people and women pressing around him:

> "Blessed are the pure in heart, for they shall see God [Cf. Matthew 5:8]. Blessed are they who have kept the flesh pure, for they shall become a temple of God [Cf. 2 Corinthians 6:16]. Blessed are the continent, for to them God will speak. Blessed are they who have wives as if they had none, for they shall inherit God [Cf. 1 Corinthians 7:29]. Blessed are the bodies of the virgins, for they shall be well pleasing to God, and shall not lose the reward of their purity [Cf. Matthew 10:42]."[29]

Her mother, alarmed when for three days Thecla refused to leave her place even to eat or sleep, told her daughter's fiancé about the "strange man who teaches deceptive and subtle words. . . . Thamyris, this man is disturbing the city of the Iconians, and your Thecla too; for all the women and young people go in to him. 'You must,' he says, 'fear one single God only, and live in chastity.' And my daughter, too, like a spider at the window, bound by his words, is dominated by a new desire and a fearful passion; for the girl hangs upon the things he says, and is taken captive. But you go and speak to her, for she is engaged to you."[30]

But Thecla vehemently rejected Thamyris's loving pleas, as she had her mother's orders; and he, grieving and furious, immediately arranged to have Paul arrested for encouraging people to defy traditional customs and even the laws. Hearing of Paul's arrest, Thecla stole out of the house secretly at night to go to the prison, bribing the warden with her bracelets and the guard with a silver mirror to let her enter Paul's cell to talk with him privately.

The next day, when the governor, at Paul's hearing, demanded to know why Thecla refused to marry her legal fiancé, she "stood there looking steadily at Paul" and refused to answer. Her mother, enraged that Thecla would jeopardize her own future as well as her family's, burst into a violent tirade:

"Burn the lawless one! Burn her that is no bride in the middle of the amphitheater, so that all the women who have been taught by this man may be struck with terror!"[31]

The governor, shaken by Thecla's defiance and her mother's rage, ordered Paul to be beaten and driven out of town. Thecla he condemned to be burned alive for violating the laws of the city and so threatening the social order. Brought naked into the amphitheater for execution, Thecla was stretched out on a pile of wood, and the kindling lighted, but suddenly a raincloud overshadowed the amphitheater and burst. Escaping in the confusion, Thecla went searching for Paul. But a Syrian nobleman, aroused by this young woman traveling alone in Antioch, tried to rape her. To protect herself from such attacks, Thecla cut off her hair and dressed herself as a man. Thecla's story celebrates her as someone who resisted family pressure, social ostracism, rape, torture, and even execution to "follow the word of the virgin life as it was spoken by Paul." Even the apostle himself, the story says, at first would not take her seriously, refusing to baptize her or to accept her as a fellow evangelist. So she, in desperation, baptized herself, and persisted in pursuing Paul until he reluctantly granted her his blessing. Having achieved her vocation,

Thecla became a famous teacher and holy woman, revered for centuries throughout the eastern churches as a beloved saint.

Although many legends grew up around Thecla,[32] and some scholars regard her story as fiction, she may well have been an actual person.[33] Whether or not she in fact heard Paul himself preach, she—and thousands like her—welcomed such radical versions of the gospel. Following Jesus' advice, these young disciples broke with their families and refused to marry, declaring themselves now members of "God's family." Their vows of celibacy served many converts as a declaration of independence from the crushing pressures of tradition and of their families, who ordinarily arranged marriages at puberty and so determined the course of their children's lives. As early as the second century of the Christian Era, and for many generations thereafter, Christian celibates may have invoked Thecla's example to justify the right of Christian women to baptize and to preach. Even two hundred years later, Christian women who chose the way of asceticism, whether living in solitude at home or in monastic communities founded and often financed by wealthy women, called themselves "new Theclas."[34]

The enormous popularity of Thecla's story suggests how the Christian movement might have appealed to young people, to Thecla's adolescent peers. Yet other popular stories—themselves probably legends—tell how the radical message seized some of their older, married sisters and brothers and irrevocably changed their lives too. According to another widely told Christian story, the *Acts of Thomas,* the lovely Mygdonia, wife of an aristocrat in India, having heard that the Christian apostle Thomas was about to arrive in her city, was filled with curiosity and immediately set out to hear him. But as her elegant litter, carried by slaves, approached and parted the crowd surrounding Thomas, the apostle pointedly ignored Mygdonia and, turning instead to her slaves, addressed to them these vehement words:

> "This blessing and warning are *for you* who are 'heavy laden.' For although you are human beings, those who have authority over you think that you are not human beings, as they are. . . . They do not know that all people are alike before God, whether slave or free."

Mygdonia, shocked and chagrined by these words, sprang from her litter and threw herself on the ground before Thomas, acknowledging that "we act, indeed, like irrational animals," and asked him to pray for her and teach her the gospel.[35]

Thomas consented, and Mygdonia discovered through his words a sense of inner freedom and spiritual dignity she had never before experienced. Thomas persuaded her, too, that to follow the gospel she must devote herself to celibacy, even within her marriage: "This sordid communion with your husband will mean nothing if you are deprived of true communion."[36] Convinced by Thomas's words, Mygdonia turned away from her husband's anxious and loving pleas and then rejected his "shameless" sexual overtures. At first pleading headaches, she finally struck him on the face and ran naked from the bedroom, ripping down the bedroom curtains to cover herself as she escaped to sleep with her childhood nurse. Although her husband grieved, suffered, and raged, he finally yielded, and, receiving baptism himself, agreed to live with her henceforth in celibate marriage.

Such popular stories about the apostles graphically describe how some early Christian preachers, attempting to persuade men and women to "undo the sin of Adam and Eve" by choosing celibacy, disrupted the traditional order of family, village, and city, encouraging believers to reject ordinary family life for the sake of Christ.[37]

But many other Christians sharply protested. Such radical asceticism was not, they argued, the primary meaning of Jesus' gospel, and they simply ignored the more radical implications of what Jesus and Paul taught. One anonymous Christian living a generation after Paul wrote to a pagan friend that far from rejecting marriage and procreation, "Christians marry, like everyone else; they beget children; but they do not destroy fetuses."[38] His contemporary, the Christian teacher Barnabas, a convert from Judaism, assumes that Christians who follow the "way of light" act like pious Jews, abstaining only from sexual practices that violate marriage or frustrate its fulfillment in legitimate procreation.[39] Clement of Alexandria, a liberal, urbane, and sophisticated Christian teacher living in Egypt more than a hundred years after Paul (c. 180 C.E.), denounced celibates and beggars

> who say that they are "imitating the Lord" who never married, nor had any possessions in the world, and who boast that they understand the gospel better than anyone else.[40]

For Clement, such extremists are arrogant, foolish and wrong.[41]

But how could such Christians as Barnabas or Clement, who

sought a more moderate message, deal with certain well-known sayings of Jesus—for example, his categorical rejection of divorce, or his statement that "if anyone does not hate his own father and mother and wife and children and brothers and sisters, yes, and even his own life, he cannot be my disciple" (Luke 14:26)? The impact of such sayings might have limited the Christian movement to only the most zealous converts. Within two generations of Jesus' death, however, some of his followers dared to change the wording of such extreme sayings and insert modifying phrases. The author of the Gospel of Matthew, for example, finding Jesus' prohibition of divorce impossibly severe, added a phrase that apparently allowed divorce in the case of the wife's infidelity: Μὴ ἐπί πορνείᾳ, "for immorality," a crucial exception that placed Jesus on the side of teacher Shammai. So according to Matthew, Jesus says, "Whoever divorces his wife, *except for immorality,* and marries another, is guilty of adultery" (Matthew 19:9). And Matthew softens what, according to Luke, Jesus had said about hating one's family: Matthew rephrases the statement so that Jesus says, "Whoever *loves* father or mother *more than* me is not worthy of me; and whoever *loves* son or daughter *more than* me is not worthy of me" (Matthew 10:37).

The author of Matthew not only apparently changes words and injects phrases but goes further, deliberately juxtaposing Jesus' more radical sayings with more moderate sayings on the same theme. According to Matthew, for example, Jesus concludes his ringing rejection of divorce—"What God has joined together, let no man put asunder"—with Matthew's modification *allowing* for divorce— "Whoever divorces his wife, except for immorality, and marries another, is guilty of adultery" (Matthew 19:9). Only a few verses later, Matthew juxtaposes Jesus' promise of great rewards to "every one that has left houses or brothers or sisters or father or mother or children or lands for my name's sake" (19:29), with Jesus' reaffirmation of the traditional commandment "Honor your father and mother" (19:19). Thus Matthew, obviously aware of such discrepancies, and perhaps embarrassed by them, implicitly discriminates between two types of saying—and two levels of discipleship. Matthew gives the reader the impression that Jesus' message and the movement he inspired need not place extreme demands upon every believer, but only upon would-be spiritual heroes—those who want to follow Jesus' command to "be perfect" (Matthew 5:48). But followers of Jesus who want to stay home with their spouses and children and continue to support their aging parents can, according to Matthew, remain committed to family life and still find their place within the Christian community.

Certain followers of Paul, concerned to make Paul's message equally accessible, and finding some statements in his first letter to the Corinthians, for example, too extreme, decided that he could not have meant what he said there, much less what enthusiastically ascetic Christians took him to mean. Thus some of Paul's followers proceeded to compose, in Paul's name, letters of their own designed to correct what they believed were dangerous misinterpretations of Paul's teaching. Several of these anonymous admirers of Paul, a generation or two after his death, forged letters, filling them with personal details of Paul's life and greetings to his friends, hoping to make them appear authentic. Many people—then and now—have assumed that these letters are genuine, and five of them were in fact incorporated into the New Testament as "letters of Paul." Even today, scholars dispute which are authentic and which are not. Most scholars, however, agree that Paul actually wrote only eight of the thirteen "Pauline" letters now included in the New Testament collection: Romans, 1 and 2 Corinthians, Galatians, Philippians, 1 Thessalonians, and Philemon. Virtually all scholars agree that Paul himself did not write 1 or 2 Timothy or Titus—letters written in a style different from Paul's and reflecting situations and viewpoints very different from those in Paul's own letters. About the authorship of Ephesians, Colossians, and 2 Thessalonians, debate continues; but the majority of scholars include these, too, among the "deutero-Pauline"—literally, secondarily Pauline—letters.[42]

Although the deutero-Pauline letters differ from one another in many ways, on *practical* matters they all agree. All reject Paul's most radically ascetic views to present instead a "domesticated Paul"[43]—a version of Paul who, far from urging celibacy upon his fellow Christians, endorses only a stricter version of traditional Jewish attitudes toward marriage and family. Just as Matthew juxtaposed Jesus' more radical sayings with modified versions of them, so the New Testament collection juxtaposes Paul's authentic letters with the deutero-Paulines, offering a version of Paul that softens him from a radical preacher into a patron saint of domestic life.

The anonymous author of 1 Timothy, for example, makes "Paul" attack as demon-inspired those "liars . . . who forbid marriage and enjoin abstinence from foods which God created" (1 Timothy 4:1–3), taking aim, presumably, at the preachers of asceticism, who depict Paul as one of themselves, indeed as their model.[44]

Denouncing the characterizations of Paul that appear in such works as the *Acts of Paul and Thecla*, the author of 2 Timothy almost goes so far as to take sides with Thecla's mother, warning people to avoid those who

> *make their way into households and capture weak women, burdened with sins and swayed by various impulses, who will listen to anybody and can never arrive at a knowledge of the truth.*
>
> (2 TIMOTHY 3:6–7)

The conservative Paul of Timothy directly contradicts the advice Paul gives in 1 Corinthians, where he urges virgins and widows to remain unmarried. According to 1 Timothy, Paul, concerned that the presence of unmarried women among the Christians may arouse suspicions and scandalous gossip, declares, "I would have the younger widows marry, bear children, rule their households, and give the enemy no occasion to revile us" (1 Timothy 5:14). Dismissing ascetic discipline as mere "bodily training" (1 Timothy 4:8), worth little for developing piety, this "Paul" warns his readers to "have nothing to do with godless and silly myths" (1 Timothy 4:7). As Dennis MacDonald persuasively shows, the author of 1 Timothy is denouncing, in all probability, such stories as those of Thecla and Mygdonia, which circulated for generations, perhaps especially among women storytellers. (See notes 33 and 34, above.) Challenging those who, like Thecla herself, claim that women have the right to teach and baptize, the author of 1 Timothy recalls Eve's sin and commands that women must

> *learn in silence with all submissiveness. I permit no woman to teach or to have authority over men; she is to keep silent. For Adam was formed first, then Eve; and Adam was not deceived, but the woman was deceived and became a transgressor. Yet woman will be saved through bearing children, if she continues in faith and love and holiness, with modesty.*
>
> (1 TIMOTHY 2:11–15)

Read this way—as it still is read by the majority of Christian churches—the story of Eve both proves woman's natural weakness and gullibility and defines her present role. Chastened by reminders of Eve's sin, deprived of all authority, women must silently submit to their husbands, grateful that they too may be saved, provided they adhere to their traditional domestic roles.[45] The "Paul" of 1 Timothy goes so far as to judge even men's leadership abilities on the basis of their domestic roles as family patriarchs:

Now a bishop must be above reproach, the husband of one wife. . . . He must manage his own household well, keeping his children submissive and respectful . . . for if a man does not know how to manage his own household, how can he care for God's church?

(1 TIMOTHY 3:2–5)

Thus, whereas the authentic Paul declares in his letter to the Corinthians, "I wish that all were as I myself am," voluntarily celibate, the "Paul" of 1 Timothy urges marriage and family upon men and women alike.

The Letter to the Hebrews expresses a positive reverence for marriage—and specifically for sexually active marriage: "Marriage is honorable unto all, and the marriage bed is not polluted" (Hebrews 13:4). The deutero-Pauline letter to the Ephesians calls ascetic Christians foolish, insisting that "no man ever hates his own flesh, but nourishes and cherishes it" (Ephesians 5:29). The author of Ephesians goes so far as to attribute to Paul a vision of Adam and Eve—and, consequently, of marriage itself—as symbolizing the "great mystery . . . of Christ and the church" (Ephesians 5:32). "Paul's" Christian vision of marriage confirms, this author claims, the traditional patriarchal pattern of marriage,

for the husband is the head of the wife, as Christ is the head of the church. . . . As the church is subject to Christ, so let the wives also be subject in everything to their husbands.

(EPHESIANS 5:23–24)

Taking his cue from Paul's saying that "the head of every man is Christ, the head of a woman is her husband" (1 Corinthians 11:3), the author of Ephesians explains that since the man, like Christ, is the head, and the woman his body, "so husbands should love their wives as their own bodies," and wives, in turn, should submit to the higher judgment of their husbands, as their "heads" (Ephesians 5:28–33).

Within thirty to fifty years of Paul's death, then, partisans of the ascetic Jesus—and of the ascetic Paul—were contending against those who advocated a much more moderate Jesus and a much more conservative Paul. Like relatives in a large family battling over the inheritance, both ascetic and nonascetic Christians laid claim to the legacies of Jesus and Paul, both sides insisting that they alone were the true heirs.

Many Christians—perhaps the majority—were more concerned to accommodate themselves to ordinary social and marital structures than to challenge them. By the end of the second century, as the majority of churches accepted as canonical the list of gospels and letters now formed into the collection we call the New Testament, the moderates could claim victory and so dominate all future Christian churches. Writers now revered as the fathers of the church seized upon the tamed and domesticated version of Paul to be found in the deutero-Paulines as a primary weapon against the ascetic extremists. Clement of Alexandria, writing more than a hundred years after Paul's death, himself far less militant and far more sympathetic toward conventional social and family life than the apostle, spoke for the majority when he argued that the ascetics had exaggerated and misunderstood Paul's teaching.[46] Clement resolved to win back for the majority the disputed territory of the gospels and Paul's letters.

Taking on his opponents' arguments point for point, Clement began by saying that although Jesus never married, he did not intend for his human followers, in this respect at least, to follow his example:

> the reason that Jesus did not marry was that, in the first place, he was already engaged, so to speak, to the church; and, in the second place, he was not an ordinary man.[47]

Ascetically inclined Christians had argued that Jesus' words prove that he advocated celibacy: why else, they asked, would he have praised women whose "wombs never bore," or men who "made themselves eunuchs for the sake of the Kingdom of Heaven"? Clement admits that such sayings are puzzling, but he avoids the issue that they raise by refusing to take them literally. He maintains that Jesus could not have meant by "eunuch" what most readers assume (a celibate man). Instead, "what Jesus meant," Clement clumsily argues, "is that a married man who has divorced his wife because of her infidelity should not *remarry.*"[48]

What about Paul, who remained, as he boasted, voluntarily celibate; or Peter, who, according to Luke 18:28, left his home to follow Jesus? Paul himself tells us, Clement could argue, that Peter, like "other apostles and the brothers of the Lord," traveled with his wife at church expense (1 Corinthians 9:5)! Then, in a passage that surely would have surprised Paul, Clement argues that Paul too was married: "The only reason he did not take [his wife] with him is that it would have been an inconvenience for his ministry."[49]

When Clement attacks ascetic interpretations of Paul's message, he finds in the deutero-Pauline letters all the ammunition he needs. For example, "to those who slander marriage," he replies by quoting the antiascetic Paul of 1 Timothy.[50] But when he confronts the authentic letters, Clement finds his task much harder. Insisting, however, that the same man wrote both groups of letters, Clement skillfully interweaves passages from the authentic and the deutero-Pauline letters. Thus Clement, and the majority of Christians ever since, can claim that Paul endorses *both* marriage and celibacy:

> In general, all the letters of the apostle teach self-control and continence, and contain numerous instructions about marriage, begetting children, and domestic life, but they nowhere exclude self-controlled marriage.[51]

Clement rejects, above all, the claim that Adam and Eve's sin was to engage in sexual intercourse—a view common among such Christian teachers as Tatian the Syrian, who taught that the fruit of the tree of knowledge conveyed *carnal* knowledge. Tatian had pointed out that after Adam and Eve ate the forbidden fruit, they became sexually aware: "Then the eyes of both were opened, and they knew that they were naked" (Genesis 3:7). Other interpreters agreed that the accuracy of this interpretation is proved in Genesis 4:1, where the Hebrew verb "to know" *('yada)* connotes sexual intercourse: "And Adam *knew* his wife, and she conceived, and bore a son." Tatian blamed Adam for inventing marriage, believing that for this sin God expelled Adam and his partner in crime from Paradise.[52] The distinguished ascetic Julius Cassianus instead blamed Satan, not Adam, for inventing sexual intercourse. According to Cassianus, Satan "borrowed this practice from the irrational animals, and persuaded Adam to have sexual union with Eve."[53] But Clement denounces all such views. Sexual intercourse, he declares, was not sinful, but part of God's original—and "good"—creation: "Nature led [Adam and Eve], like the irrational animals, to procreate";[54] "and," Clement might well have added, "when I say *nature,* I mean *God."* Clement says that those who engage in procreation are not sinning but "cooperating with God in his work of creation."[55] Thus Clement confirms the traditional Jewish conviction, expressed in the deutero-Pauline letters, that legitimate procreation is a good work, blessed by God from the day of human creation.

If engaging in sexual intercourse was *not* the sin of Adam and Eve, what *was* that first and fatal transgression? Such fathers of the church as Clement and Irenaeus insist that the first sin was disobeying God's command. Yet even Clement and his contemporary Bishop Irenaeus of Lyons, although eager to exempt sexual desire from primary blame for the fall, admit that, as they imagined it, "man's first disobedience" and the fall did, in fact, take sexual form. Clement carefully explains that the disobedience of Adam and Eve involved not what they did, but how they did it. As Clement imagines the scene, Adam and Eve, like impatient adolescents, rushed into sexual union before they had received their Father's blessing. Irenaeus explains that Adam and Eve were, in fact, underage:

> For having been created just a short time before, they had no understanding of procreation of children. It was necessary that first they should come to adult age, and then "multiply" from that time onwards.[56]

Clement blames Adam, who, he says, "desired the fruit of marriage before the proper time, and so fell into sin. . . . they were impelled to do it more quickly than was proper because they were still young, and had been seduced by deceit."[57] Irenaeus adds that Adam's guilty response shows that he was well aware that sexual desire had incited him to sin, for he covered himself and Eve with scratchy fig leaves, "while there were many other leaves which would have irritated his body much less."[58] Thus Adam punished the very organs that had led them into sin.

The attitudes that Clement and Irenaeus helped to shape more than one hundred years after Paul's death set the standard of Christian behavior for centuries—indeed, for nearly two thousand years. What would prevail in Christian tradition was not only the stark sayings of the gospels attributed to Jesus and the encouragements to celibacy that Paul urges upon believers in 1 Corinthians, but versions of these austere teachings modified to suit the purposes of the churches of the first and second centuries. Clement and his colleagues established, too, a durable double standard that endorses marriage, but only as second best to celibacy. Clement and his fellow Christians constructed elaborate arguments, drawn primarily from the Hebrew Bible and the deutero-Pauline letters, to show that marriage, for Christians as well as for Jews, is a positive act, involving "cooperation with God's work of creation." Yet Clement can revere it as such only by going back to the consensus Jesus challenged. Clement, influenced, no doubt, by Stoic philosophers who agreed with him in principle, insisted that marriage finds its sole legitimate purpose—and sexual intercourse its only rationale—in procreation.[59] Thus even Clement, certainly the most liberal of the fathers of the church, and one who, more emphatically than any other, affirms God's blessing upon marriage and procreation, expresses deep ambivalence toward sexuality—an ambivalence that has resounded throughout Christian history for two millennia.

Clement believes that Jesus meant both to confirm and to transform traditional patterns of marriage; that he did not challenge the patriarchal structure of marriage (which for Clement expresses the natural superiority of men, as well as God's punishment upon Eve); but that Jesus did intend to eradicate such pagan sexual practices as incest, adultery, "unnatural intercourse," homosexuality, abortion, and infanticide, as well as the Hebrew practices of polygamy and divorce.

Marriage, now monogamous and indissoluble, as God originally intended it, may become, for believers, a "sacred image." But to experience it as such, the believer must be purged of the sexual passion that led Adam and Eve into sin. The married Christian must not only subordinate desire to reason but strive to annihilate desire entirely:

> Our ideal is not to experience desire at all. . . . We should do nothing from desire. Our will is to be directed only toward what is necessary. For we are children not of desire but of will. A man who marries for the sake of begetting children must practice continence so that it is not desire he feels for his wife . . . that he may beget children with a chaste and controlled will.[60]

To accomplish this, as one might imagine, is not easy. "The gospel," as Clement reads it, not only restricts sexuality to marriage but, even within marriage, limits it to specific acts intended for procreation. To engage in marital intercourse for any other reason is to "do injury to nature."[61] Clement excludes not only such counterproductive practices as oral and anal intercourse but also intercourse with a menstruating, pregnant, barren, or menopausal wife, and, for that matter, with one's wife "in the morning," "in the daytime," or "after dinner." Clement warns, indeed, that

> not even at night, although in darkness, is it fitting to carry on immodestly or indecently, but with modesty, so that whatever happens, happens in the light of reason . . . for even that union which is legitimate is still dangerous, except in so far as it is engaged in procreation of children.[62]

Even at best, however, Christian marriage remains inferior to chastity. "Chaste marriage," in which both partners devote themselves to celibacy, is better than a sexually active one. To the dedicated Christian,

> his wife, after conception, is as a sister, and is judged as if of the same father; who only recalls her husband when she looks at the children; as one destined to become a sister in reality after putting off the flesh, which separates and limits the knowledge of those who are spiritual by the specific characteristics of the sexes.[63]

Only spouses who are celibate and thereby recover, so to speak, their virginity transcend the whole structure of bodily existence and recover the spiritual equality Adam and Eve lost through the fall,

> for souls, by themselves, are equal. Souls are "neither male nor female," when "they no longer marry nor are given in marriage" [cf. Luke 20:35].[64]

Such, Clement says, was the marriage of the blessed apostles, and

> such their perfect control over their feelings even in the closest human relationships. So, too, the apostle says, "Let him who marries be as if he were not married" [cf. 1 Corinthians 7:29], requiring that marriage should not be enslaved to passion. . . . thus the soul acquires a mental disposition corresponding to the gospel in every relation of life.[65]

Like Clement, the majority of Christians for the past two thousand years have chosen to maintain simultaneously Jesus' most extreme—even shocking—sayings, such as those prohibiting divorce and encouraging renunciation, together with others that modify their severity. By the end of the second century, Christians, as we have seen, had also incorporated within the New Testament a similar double image of Paul and his message. The churches that collected Paul's letters during the second century generally included, first of all, the authentic letters, which express Paul's own complex and often ambivalent attitudes, ranging from his preference for celibacy to his admission that "the weak" are better off married than promiscuous.[66] But the majority of Christians chose the domesticated Paul over the ascetic one and tolerated contradictory statements attributed to the apostle (just as Matthew attributes contradictory statements to Jesus himself). In this way, Christians could attract into the movement those who were married—and even divorced—as well as those eager for celibacy. Clement, like most of his contemporaries, chose to subordinate Jesus' calls for radical renunciation and to endorse instead procreation within marriage—as Jesus and Paul did not—not only as the normal, but even as the sanctified, course of Christian life. But Clement and his fellows did not renounce the ascetic ideal entirely. Instead, they used the diversity of New Testament sources to establish an extraordinary view of marriage and celibacy; for Clement's views on marriage virtually ensure that anyone who takes them seriously will judge himself or herself to be deficient by their standard. And Clement goes on to invite to the "angelic life" those eager few who shun the dangerous shoals of married life. For continence and virginity are, he assumes, better still—certainly safer, and far holier.

As the Christian movement, in Clement's time and later, became more complex, gathering hundreds of thousands of converts from Rome and Greece, from Africa and Asia, and throughout the regions of Spain and Gaul, the message of Jesus and Paul, intended originally for a largely Hebrew constituency, had to be refracted through that increasingly diverse movement. Jesus' radical call to repent and purify oneself to prepare for the Kingdom of God remained, for many, the primary point of reference. Simultaneously, however, Christians developed multiple images of Jesus and Paul and multiple interpretations of their message to suit a variety of mundane and spiritual purposes.

What made such an austere message, in its many versions, attractive to so many people? How did Christianity succeed in becoming the religion of the Roman Empire? In the next chapters we take up these questions and see how, within its practical severity, many saw a new vision of human nature—one that had power to validate and transform the lives of the multitudes who heard it.

CHRISTIANS AGAINST THE ROMAN ORDER

I N THE PREVIOUS CHAPTER I attempted to show how Christianity sprang up as a movement that challenged converts to break all that bound them to their families, to their cities, to the nation—all, in short, that conscientious people, whether Jews, Greeks, Asians, Africans, or Romans, held most sacred—where these commitments conflicted with the Christian commitment to their "brothers and sisters in Christ," fellow members of the sect that called itself God's family.

By the end of the second century, the Christian movement had spread through all parts of the empire, so that the North African convert Tertullian, writing in Carthage around 200 C.E., said that

> the outcry is that the state is filled with Christians—that they are in the fields; in the cities; in the islands; [pagans] lament, as for some kind of catastrophe, that people of both sexes, every age and status, even those of high rank, are passing over to the profession of the Christian faith.[1]

In an open letter addressed to "rulers of the Roman Empire," Tertullian acknowledges that pagan critics detest the movement: "You think that a Christian is a man of every crime, an enemy of the gods, of the emperor, of the law, of good morals, of all nature."[2] In a sense such critics were right; for Christians did threaten the social and ethical system of the ancient world in ways that eventually would alter the structure of the empire itself. Going into the marketplaces, the shops of cobblers and carpenters, and the kitchens of great houses, Christians offered to working people and to slaves, as well as to anyone else who would listen,[3] a message that, as some preached it, seemed to threaten the hierarchical structure of Roman society. Yet other Christians, as we have seen, did everything they could to accommodate to that hierarchical structure and to avoid offending their pagan neighbors.[4] But what made Christians especially dangerous to the Roman order was their refusal to pay what Romans regarded as ordinary respect to their Roman rulers; and this brought some of them into direct and total opposition to the temporal as well as the divine authorities—to the emperors and to their divine patrons, the gods.[5]

A widely popular true story of the time tells of a mistress and her personal slave who were convicted as Christians after they refused to revere the emperor's image. Together they were thrown to wild animals and slaughtered in the public amphitheater in Carthage in a spectacle celebrating the emperor's birthday. The aristocratic protagonist, Vibia Perpetua, fluent in both Greek and Latin, wrote about her experiences from the time of her arrest until the evening of her execution. Perpetua, twenty-two years old, recently married, and nursing her infant son, was arrested along with her friends Saturus and Saturninus and her personal slave Felicitas and the slave Revocatus. Perpetua and her companions were thrown into a stifling and crowded African jail. After her arrest, Perpetua's father, "out of love for me," she wrote, "was trying to persuade me to change my decision."[6] Refusing his pleas to give up the name Christian, Perpetua rejected her familial name instead, although she says she grieved to see her father, mother, and brothers "suffering out of compassion for me."[7] At first, she wrote, "I was tortured with worry for my baby there," but after she gained permission for him to stay with her in prison, "at once I recovered my health, relieved as I was of my worry and anxiety for the child."[8]

Perpetua's father, anticipating that the Christians were about to be given a hearing, returned to the prison "worn with worry" to plead with Perpetua to offer sacrifice for the welfare of the emperors, kissing her hands as he spoke:

> "Daughter . . . have pity on your father, if I deserve to be called your father, if I have loved you more than all your brothers; do not abandon me. . . . Think of your brothers; think of your mother and your aunt; think of your child, who will not be able to live once you are gone. . . . Give up your pride! You will destroy all of us. None of us will ever be able to speak freely again if anything happens to you."[9]

But Perpetua refused and, she said, "he left me in great sorrow." Then, she continued,

> one day while we were eating breakfast we were suddenly hurried off for a hearing. We arrived at the forum, and straightaway the story went about the neighborhood near the forum and a huge crowd gathered. We walked up to the prisoner's dock. All the others when questioned admitted their guilt. Then, when it came my turn, my father appeared with my son, dragged me from the step, and said: "Perform the sacrifice—have pity on your baby!"
>
> Hilarianus the governor, who had received his judicial powers as the successor of the late proconsul Minucius Timinianus, said to me: "Have pity on your father's grey head; have pity on your infant son. Offer the sacrifice for the welfare of the emperors."
>
> "I will not," I retorted.
>
> "Are you a Christian?" said Hilarianus. And I said: "Yes, I am."
>
> When my father persisted in trying to dissuade me, Hilarianus ordered him to be thrown to the ground and beaten with a rod. I felt sorry for my father, just as if I myself had been beaten. I felt sorry for his pathetic old age.
>
> Then Hilarianus passed sentence on all of us: we were condemned to the beasts, and we returned to prison in high spirits.[10]

Even before she was sentenced, Perpetua knew that she was going to die, for she had dreamed that she was climbing a bronze ladder of tremendous height, bristling with daggers, swords, and spikes, reaching all the way to the heavens. On the day before her execution, Perpetua wrote down another vision: She dreamed that she was led to the amphitheater, where enormous crowds waited to see her fight with a ferocious Egyptian athlete. "My clothes were stripped off, and suddenly I was a man." She fought and wrestled until she got him into a headlock and so won the fight. "Then I awoke; I realized that it was not with wild animals that I would fight, but with the devil; but I knew that I would win the victory." Perpetua concludes her journal with the words "So much for what I did until the evening of the contest. About what happened at the contest itself, let whoever write about it who will."[11]

Perpetua's slave Felicitas was pregnant when she was arrested and was in her eighth month as the execution date approached: "Felicitas was very distressed that her martyrdom would be postponed because of her pregnancy; for it is against the law for pregnant women to be executed." She feared she would have to survive her Christian companions and alone endure a later execution along with criminals.

Two days before the execution the Christians prayed for her

> in one torrent of common grief, and immediately after their prayer the labor pains came upon her. She suffered a good deal in her labor because of the natural difficulty of an eight-month delivery.[12]

One of the Christian women took the infant daughter to raise as her own, leaving Felicitas free to join her companions. As Perpetua had hoped, a fellow Christian continued the story, telling two anecdotes about her imperious response to the harsh treatment to which the Christians were subjected in prison. Perpetua dared speak directly to the tribune in charge, protesting, "We are to fight on the emperor's birthday. Would it not be to your credit if we were brought forth on that day in a healthier condition?"[13] The officer, visibly disturbed, ordered improvements in the prisoners' treatment and granted increased visiting privileges for their families and friends. When the day arrived, Perpetua and Felicitas, together with their Christian brothers Revocatus, Saturninus, and Saturus, were led out of the prison to the gates of the amphitheater. The officer in charge, following the common practice, ordered the men to dress in robes of priests of the god Saturn, and the women to dress in the costumes of priestesses of the goddess Ceres, as if they were offering their deaths in sacrifice to the gods. Perpetua adamantly refused, saying,

> "We came to this of our own free will, so that our liberty should not be violated. We agreed to pledge our lives in order to do no such thing [as sacrifice to the gods]. And you agreed with us to do this."[14]

Again her plea prevailed, and the officer yielded. But just as Perpetua and Felicitas were to enter the arena, they were forcibly stripped naked and placed in nets, so that

> even the crowd was horrified when they saw that one was a delicate young girl, and the other woman fresh from childbirth, with milk still dripping from her breasts. And so they were brought back again and dressed in loose tunics.[15]

A mad heifer was set loose after them; Perpetua was gored and thrown to the ground. She got up and, seeing Felicitas crushed and fallen, went over to her and lifted her up, and the two stood side by side. Then, after undergoing further ordeals and seeing Saturus endure agonizing torture, Perpetua and Felicitas, along with the others, were called to the center of the arena to be slaughtered. A witness records that Perpetua "screamed as she was struck on the bone; then she took the trembling hand of the young gladiator, and guided it to her throat."[16]

Some spectators at such martyrdoms shook their heads and said, "What good was their religion to them, which they preferred even over their own lives?"[17] But others, including Tertullian himself, were sufficiently shaken by such sights to join this movement, knowing that they risked their lives by doing so.

JUSTIN THE PHILOSOPHER, born c. 110 C.E. into an affluent family in the city of Flavia Neopolis in Samaria, and having gone to Rome to practice philosophy, says that he, like Tertullian, was astonished and moved "when I saw Christians . . . fearless of death."[18] Justin had heard rumors that Christians secretly indulged in cannibalism and promiscuity; but the superhuman courage they displayed in the amphitheater as they endured torture and execution convinced him that they were possessed by an extraordinary power.

Justin began to ask himself who are these emperors—and who are these gods—in whose names government agents committed such atrocities? He knew, of course, the conventional answers—the emperors are men blessed by the gods, the powers of the universe, and divinely charged to rule over humankind—for as Justin admits, he too once worshiped the same gods as everyone else. But he was shocked by the Christians' ordeals and moved by his own subsequent conversion to see both the emperors and the gods with different eyes:

> We—who out of every race of people, used to worship Bacchus the son of Semele, and Apollo the son of Latone, who in their love affairs with human beings did such things as are shameful to mention, and Persephone and Venus, who were driven insane by love of Adonis, and whose mysteries, too, you celebrate—*we have now, through Jesus Christ, learned to despise these gods, although we be threatened with death for it.* We have dedicated ourselves to the unbegotten, impassible God, of whom we are persuaded that he was never goaded by lust for Antiope, and for Ganymede . . . we

pity those who believe such things, and we know that those who invented them are demons.[19]

Justin found among the Christians what he had vainly sought for years in philosophy. He tells us little about his background but much about his passionate longing to understand the questions that obsessed him: What is true? What makes a person happy? How can one find God? Having set out as a young man upon a philosophic search, Justin says, "First I surrendered myself to a certain Stoic." But when he complained that this teacher taught nothing about God and the Stoic replied that he did not bother with such questions, considering them irrelevant, Justin left him and joined the students of a Peripatetic philosopher with a reputation for keen intellect. After he had listened several days to this new teacher, Justin says, "he required me to settle the [tuition] fee."[20] Indignant at this request, Justin decided that since the man asked for money, "he was no philosopher at all," and abruptly departed. Finally, Justin says, he investigated Platonic philosophy, and

> then I spent as much time as possible with one who had recently arrived in our city—a wise man, holding a high position among the Platonists—and I progressed, and made the greatest improvements daily.[21]

From his Platonist teacher, Justin learned to discriminate between the appearances created by mere sense impressions and the reality that Plato says only a mind purified and disciplined by philosophy can perceive. But one day, when an older Christian philosopher whom Justin came to revere as a second Socrates challenged his Platonist assumptions, Justin admitted that his own experience of philosophic searching forced him to a conclusion that he had long resisted: that the human mind by itself cannot grasp ultimate truth. Instead, Justin came to believe, one must receive illumination through the spirit of God descending from above—the same spirit that had possessed the Christian martyrs in the amphitheater.

Once converted, and believing himself illuminated by the spirit in his baptismal initiation, Justin opened his apartment above the Baths of Timothy in Rome to philosophically minded seekers of Christian truth. But arbitrary arrests and executions of Christians, even though they occurred sporadically, reminded him that professing his newfound faith placed him in danger of being accused, arrested, and put to the test—either to make a token sacrifice to the

Roman gods or to be sentenced to torture and execution.[22] After he had described the trial and condemnation of three of his fellow Christians, Justin declared, "I, too, therefore, expect to be plotted against and crucified." Yet he decided to ignore the danger to himself, and he boldly addressed an open letter of protest directly to the emperors[23]—to Marcus Aurelius, his son Commodus, and his imperial father, Antoninus Pius. Justin initially addresses the emperors as fellow philosophers, and assures them that Christians intend to be loyal, even the best, citizens. He speaks so persuasively that the eminent historian Robert Grant has cited Justin as exemplifying "Christian devotion to the monarchy."[24] In all probability, Justin received no answer to his petition, so he addressed a second to the Senate, protesting a recent and typical case. Justin told the story of an aristocratic lady who, having converted to Christianity, refused to participate any longer with her husband in drunken sexual parties involving their household slaves. Although she wanted a divorce, her friends persuaded her to wait, hoping for a reconciliation. But when she learned that her husband, on a trip to Alexandria, had behaved worse than ever, she sued him for divorce and left. Her enraged husband accused Ptolemy, her teacher in Christianity, who was then arrested, imprisoned, and brought to trial before the judge Urbicus, who asked him only one question: "Are you a Christian?" Ptolemy said yes, whereupon Urbicus pronounced the mandatory death sentence. But as Ptolemy was being marched out to die, Lucius, one of the courtroom spectators, cried in protest:

> "What is the ground for this judgment? Why have you punished this man, not as an adulterer, nor a fornicator, nor murderer, nor thief, nor robber, nor convicted by any crime at all but who has only confessed that he is called by the name 'Christian'? This judgment of yours, Urbicus, does not become the Emperor Pius, nor the philosopher, Caesar's son Marcus Aurelius, nor the sacred Senate."[25]

Urbicus answered that Lucius himself sounded suspiciously like a Christian; when Lucius admitted as much, the prefect ordered that he and another protestor in the audience follow Ptolemy to execution. As soldiers led the condemned men from the courtroom, Lucius loudly thanked God for delivering him and his companions "from such wicked rulers" and releasing them instead to the "Father and King of the Universe."

What kinds of emperors, then, are these, Justin asked himself—

and what kinds of gods—whose laws support sexual promiscuity and private vengeance and sanction the slaughter of innocent people? Justin knew, of course, that the story he told, like the story of Perpetua and Felicitas, would raise very different questions in the minds of pagan readers. What kinds of people are these Christians, pagan critics would ask, who refuse to worship the gods and who, from the viewpoint of Roman traditionalists, are *atheists*? And why do these Christians refuse to perform ordinary token acts of loyalty, choosing to die rather than sacrifice to the emperor's divine spirit?

Justin answered that Christians had discovered a terrible secret: the powers behind the Roman magistrates—and, in particular, behind the emperors themselves—are not gods, nor are they mere appearances, as the Platonists said, but demons, active evil forces bent upon corrupting and destroying human beings, determined to blind people to the truth that there is only one God, creator of all, who made all humankind alike. Although Justin did not explicitly derive from Genesis an egalitarian view of humanity, certain other Christians did. Twenty years after Justin was beheaded by the Roman authorities, Clement of Alexandria declared that, since God made every human being "in his image,"

> I would ask you, does it not seem to you monstrous that you—human beings who are God's own handiwork—should be subjected to another master, and, even worse, serve a tyrant instead of God, the true king?[26]

Deriding the imperial cult, Clement declared that since Christ's coming, divinity now "pervades all humankind equally . . . deifying humanity,"[27] the slave equally with the master, Felicitas equally with her owner and "sister in Christ" Perpetua. Clement agreed with Justin that the worship of the emperor's *genius* (that is, his divine spirit)[28] is a lie perpetrated by demons.

Thus Christians threatened to replace the Roman pantheon of gods and goddesses, those Olympian aristocrats, with One God, creator of all humankind alike. Even worse, they threatened to replace the image of the emperor as the manifestation of divine power on earth with Jesus, a condemned criminal, whom the pagan satirist Lucian derisively called "a crucified sophist"[29]—an illiterate barbarian executed by the Romans for treason against the state! When Perpetua, Felicitas, and their companions refused to venerate the image of the emperor Geta, they did so in the name of Jesus. They insisted that although he had been defeated by the powers of Rome,

Jesus ultimately proved victorious not only over Rome but over death itself, for he was enthroned triumphant "at the right hand of God," where the martyrs confidently expected to join him after following him to their deaths in the arena.

Pagan skeptics might ridicule the Roman gods as naïve and foolish illusions; but for Justin and many of his fellow Christians these gods were real and dangerous adversaries. Justin, for example, agreed with his fellow philosopher and adversary the devout pagan emperor Marcus Aurelius that the gods embodied elemental forces at work in the universe. Marcus, however, identified himself with these powers, which he also called *providence, necessity,* and *nature,* and revered them as his divine patrons and protectors. While camped with soldiers on a military expedition, the philosopher-emperor, alone in his tent at night, wrote moral injunctions to himself:

> Providence is the source from which all things flow; and allied with it is Necessity, and the welfare of the universe. You yourself are a part of that universe. . . . Think of your procrastination, how the gods have repeatedly granted you further periods of grace. . . . It is time now to realize the nature of the universe in which you belong, and of that controlling Power whose offspring you are. . . . Hour by hour resolve fully, like a Roman and a man, to do what comes to hand with correct and natural dignity, and with humanity, independence, and justice. . . . the gods will ask nothing more.[30]

The French scholar Jean Beaujeu recently has shown that such convictions about the emperors' divinely sanctioned role had become basic to Roman political life and to Marcus himself, as well as his imperial family, his predecessors, sons, and successors. Especially since the time of Marcus Aurelius's adoptive grandfather, the great military emperor Hadrian, who rose to power from a relatively obscure Spanish family, the emperors increasingly represented themselves as the gods' agents on earth. These emperors vigorously promoted the massive imperial propaganda they had inherited from their predecessors, publicizing on coins, on stone monuments, in public entertainments from horse races and sports events to religious festivals, their claim that the gods had appointed them and their dynasty to rule over the whole human race, and over the whole known world.[31] Hadrian ordered that he himself be portrayed as a god in statues and on coins, most often represented in the form of Jupiter, "greatest of gods." Marcus Aurelius's imperial father, Antoninus, had earned from the Senate his honorific title "the Pious" for successfully lobbying to pass a decree in the Senate declaring Hadrian to be a god after his death. During his lifetime, Hadrian had scandalized conservative senators by insisting upon deifying his dead lover, Antinous, after the boy had drowned in the Nile under suspicious circumstances. When Marcus Aurelius admonished himself in his private *Meditations* to remember that he was only mortal, he was trying to keep in perspective his public role as the "greatest and most manifest of all the gods."[32]

Such propaganda involved more than personal grandiosity, and certainly more than the insane egotism that had driven the "mad emperors" Caligula and Nero one hundred years earlier to demand that their subjects worship them as incarnate gods. Belief that the emperors embodied divine powers reflected the way traditionally minded Romans already perceived the gods. For traditional religion in the Roman Empire had always held that the elemental forces of the universe—what we call natural forces—are, in fact, divine forces. The sun's energy, thunder and lightning, as well as the internal forces of passion, manifested themselves respectively in the forms of the gods Apollo, Jupiter, and Venus. Social and political experiences of power, too, could be interpreted as manifestations of those same elemental forces. Yet the much-debated question of whether educated pagans "believed in" the gods or the emperor's divinity is anachronistic, as the classicist Simon Price has pointed out.[33] Many educated pagans, like many of the empire's provincial subjects, participated in sacrifice to the gods or the emperor's *genius* as a way of demonstrating their proper relationship to the "powers that be," both human and divine. No intelligent person, the sophisticated pagan might have explained, actually *worshiped* images of the gods, or *worshiped* living emperors; instead, the gods' images—and the images of the emperors themselves—provided an accessible focus for revering the cosmic forces they represented.[34]

Yet Justin and his Christian contemporaries, far from expressing the "enlightened" or skeptical attitudes that later historians have projected upon them, usually regarded pagan practices with the utmost seriousness and recoiled from them in disgust. Justin agreed with pious pagans that the gods and emperors reflected elemental forces in the universe, but there agreement ended. For the gods that Marcus Aurelius revered as his divine patrons Justin detested as demons—evil forces manipulating the law to enforce the inequities that Christians protested and the injustices that they, among many others, suffered.

Following his conversion, Justin had been shocked to learn that the gods that he, too, once had worshiped were actually mere pretenders to divine power. Writing his open letter to the emperors, he unmasked the gods' secret identity: the patron gods of Rome were none other than the fallen angels, who, according to Genesis 6, were cast out of heaven at the beginning of time. For Justin, like many Jews and many of his fellow Christians, tended to interpret the difficulties of human life less in terms of the fall of Adam and Eve (Genesis 2–3) than in terms of the fall of the angels (Genesis 6:1–6). According to Genesis 6, the great and famous men of ancient times—those called giants—were the result of a hybrid union between God's angels and human women:

> *The sons of God [angels] saw that the daughters of men were fair; and they took to wife such of them as they chose. . . . There were giants on the earth in those days, . . . when the sons of God came in to the daughters of men, and they bore children to them, the mighty men of renown.*
>
> (GENESIS 6:2–4)

Justin explained that after some of the angels whom God had entrusted to administer the universe betrayed their trust by seducing women and corrupting boys (so Justin amplified the story of Genesis 6), they "begot children, who are called demons."[35] When God discovered the corruption of his administration, he expelled them from heaven. But then these exiled angels tried to compensate for their lost power by joining with their offspring, the demons, to enslave the human race. Drawing upon the supernatural powers that even disgraced angels still retain, they awed and terrified people into worshiping them instead of God. Thus, Justin said:

> The truth shall be told; since of old these evil demons, effecting apparitions of themselves, both polluted women and corrupted boys, and showed such terrifying visions to people that those who did not use their reason . . . were struck by terror; and being carried away by fear, and not knowing that these were demons, they called them gods.[36]

The majority of humankind fell under their power, and only an exceptional few, like Socrates and Jesus, escaped demonically induced mental slavery. This invisible network of supernatural energies proceeded, then, to promote the fortunes of their henchmen. "Taking as their ally the desire for evil in everyone," Justin explained, the demons became the patrons of powerful and ruthless men, and "instituted private and public rites in honor of those who are most powerful."[37]

Justin saw the result at every turn—above all in the vast panoply of imperial propaganda, which claimed for the Roman emperors and their governors, magistrates, and armies the power and protection of the gods. The injustice that dominated the law courts indisputably proved, according to Justin, that they were controlled by demons, who manipulated the judges to destroy anyone, from Socrates and Jesus to the present-day Christians, who opposed the demons or threatened to expose them:

> And when Socrates attempted by true reason and investigation to . . . deliver men from the demons, then the demons themselves, using men as their instruments, brought upon him death for being an "atheist"; and in our case, too, they do the same things.[38]

What happened in Urbicus's courtroom, where the judge protected the interests of a ruthless and immoral man while condemning a Christian teacher and his defenders to torture and death, revealed, Justin believed, this same demonic inversion of justice. As the historian Peter Brown says:

> For Justin and his contemporaries, the story of the mating of the angels with the daughters of men and its dire consequences for the peace of society was not a distant myth; it was a map on which they plotted the disruptions and tensions around them.[39]

What clinched the gods' identity as fallen angels was their arrogance, brutality, and licentiousness. Wherever Justin turned in Rome, he, like everyone else, encountered images of the gods; and what once he had admired as splendid, beautiful, or awesome he now saw as the leering masks of corruption and wickedness. Statues of Jupiter, often identified with the emperors, stood not only in temples but also in the public squares and government buildings and dominated the Roman amphitheater. In other cities, other gods shared the place of honor, as Saturn and Ceres did in the amphitheater at Carthage, presiding over the slaughter of Perpetua and her companions. Within these arenas, on religious holidays, actors and gladiators paraded images of the gods; often they dressed as Hercules or Attis while fighting each other to the death. Condemned criminals were forced into costume to die as if in sacrifice to the gods, as Perpetua narrowly escaped doing; her contemporary, the North African Christian Tertullian, saw in the same amphitheater men dressed as Mercury and Pluto, the gods of the dead, poking at the bodies of the dying with red-hot irons, as if the same gods who once delighted in the violence of the Trojan War now presided over the everyday brutality of slaughter for public entertainment. Images of Apollo, Mercury, Hercules, and Venus adorned the public baths, while Apollo and the Roman Dionysus, Bacchus, presided over the theaters, where actors often played out the stories of the gods on stage. Among the most popular were amorous adventures, such as those of Apollo and Daphne; Venus's affair with Mars; Zeus, whom the Romans called Jupiter, appearing in multiple forms to his human lovers—to Danae in a shower of gold, to Leda in the form of a swan, to Europa in the form of a bull, or to the boy Ganymede, whom Zeus, as an older lover, abducted and raped. Justin's student in Christianity, Tatian, charged that even the solemn festivals of religious drama offered public demonstrations of promiscuity: "Your sons and daughters see [the gods] giving lessons in adultery on stage."[40] The Christian philosopher Athenagoras said that stories such as those celebrating Zeus's rape of the boy Ganymede not only lent false glamor to those who seduce young boys but also encouraged merchants who set up "marketplaces for immorality, and establish infamous resorts for the young for every kind of corrupt pleasure."[41]

Besides the many well-known public statues, many people, as the Christian teacher Clement of Alexandria said accusingly,

> depict in their houses the unnatural passions of the demons.
> . . . they decorate their bedroom with paintings hung there,
> regarding licentiousness as religion; and lying in bed, in the midst
> of their embraces, they see Aphrodite locked in the embrace of
> her lover. . . . Such are the theologies of arrogance [*hybris*]; such
> are the instructions of your gods, who commit immorality with
> you.[42]

Clement's account is amply corroborated by the frescoes discovered at Pompeii and the annals of the court historian Suetonius, who noted, for example, that the emperor Tiberius kept in his bedroom a painting of Juno performing fellatio on Jupiter.[43]

Clement's attack upon Jupiter thinly veiled his contempt for some of the rulers themselves:

Is Jupiter, then, the good, the prophetic, the patron of hospitality, the protector of supplicants, the avenger of wrongs? No: he is instead unjust, the violator of right and law, the impious, the inhuman, the violent, the seducer, the adulterer, the incestuous . . . so given to sexual pleasures as to lust after everyone, and to indulge his lust upon everyone.[44]

Clement also attacked the cult that the emperor Hadrian had established in Clement's native city of Alexandria to honor his dead lover, the boy Antinous:

Another new deity was added to the number with great religious pomp in Egypt, and nearby Greece as well, by the King of the Romans, who deified Antinous, whom he loved as Jupiter loved Ganymede, and whose beauty was extremely rare; for lust is not easy to restrain, being devoid of fear, as it now is; and people observe the "Sacred Nights of Antinous," the shameful nature of which the lover who spent them with him knew. Why count him among the gods—a boy honored because of impurity? . . . And why should you expand upon his beauty? Beauty damaged by corruption is horrible. . . . Now the grave of the prostituted boy is the temple of Antinous![45]

Such things happen, Clement concluded, when people worship as gods "those who themselves are only human—and often the worst of humankind!"

When Justin wrote his open letter to Hadrian's son and grandsons, some of the most distinguished emperors in Roman history, he initially addressed them respectfully, as we have seen, as "fellow philosophers and lovers of learning." But as soon as he brought up the treatment of Christians, Justin showed that he saw even Antoninus Pius and Marcus Aurelius as men dedicated to perpetuating the "violence and tyranny" of a system that treated Christians as capital criminals for refusing to worship demons. Justin darkly hinted that these emperors, too, for all their personal virtues and public rhetoric, were actually no better than a band of criminals—"robbers in a desert"[46]—who rule by force, not justice. Justin warned Antoninus, Marcus, and Commodus to "be on your guard, lest the demons whom we have been attacking deceive you, and distract you from reading and understanding what we say," for, Justin told the rulers of the world, "these demons strive to keep you as their slaves!"[47]

Had Marcus Aurelius and his colleagues bothered to listen to such diatribes, they might well have perceived at once how subversive the Christian message actually was. By publicizing his address to the emperors, Justin had launched an open attack upon the official propaganda that portrayed them as universal rulers by divine right. Where outsiders would have seen the all-powerful emperors disposing of a handful of dissidents accused as Christians, Justin depicted puppet-tyrants, enslaved to demons, contending against people allied with the one invincible and true God. Though they claimed to be exemplary citizens, some Christians covertly attacked the whole basis of Roman imperial power and preached instead, in the name of Jesus Christ, a radical message that was spreading rapidly throughout the cities of the empire.

Some Roman officials, dumbfounded by this Christian defiance, agreed with Marcus Aurelius's private assessment: what motivates the Christians is not courage but a perverse desire for notoriety. Other officials burst out angrily, as if suspecting that they were being manipulated by suicidal fanatics: "If you want to die, go kill yourselves, and do not bother us."[48] Pagans might well suspect their motives. If Christians believe that demons rule the world, if they thank God for their death sentences, why do they not kill themselves and be done with it? Why do they claim, on the contrary, to be good, even exemplary, citizens of a regime they profess to despise? Why does Justin, for all his defiance, insist that Christians, "more readily than any other people,"[49] pay their full share of all taxes, and that "we, more than any other people, are your helpers and allies in preserving peace"?[50]

Justin explains to the emperors that, in each of these cases, Christians intend to obey God, not the human government. As for suicide, he says:

> I will tell you why we do not do so, and yet why, when interrogated, we fearlessly confess. We have been taught that God did not make the world aimlessly, but for the sake of the human race. . . . If then we killed ourselves, we would be acting in opposition to the will of God. But when we are interrogated, we make no denial, because . . . we consider it impious not to speak the truth in all things, which we know pleases God.[51]

Christians pay their taxes, Justin continues, in obedience to Christ's own command ("Render unto Caesar . . . ").[52] As for their civic behavior, Christians serve One who demands complete righteousness, whose judgment no secret act or thought escapes.[53] God commands his people, too, to render obedience—although strictly limited and secularized obedience—to the human authorities. Justin and his fellow Christians had inherited the capacity to make this distinction from the experience of Jews living for centuries under foreign imperialism. Irenaeus borrows a rabbinic image to interpret Paul's saying that the "powers that be are ordained of God":

> Earthly rule has been appointed by God for the benefit of nations, so that, under the fear of human rule, men may not devour one another like fishes, but, by means of the establishment of laws, may restrain an excess of wickedness among the nations.[54]

Finally, Justin and his Christian contemporaries, having found themselves, like the Jews, often the target of public violence, had come to appreciate the government's role in preserving public order. So Athenagoras informs the emperors Marcus Aurelius and Commodus that Christians, like the Jews,

> pray for your government, that you may . . . receive the kingdom, son from father, and that your empire may receive increase and additions, and all people become subject to your rule, since . . . this is for our advantage, too, that we may lead peaceful and tranquil lives.[55]

Yet Justin, Irenaeus, and Athenagoras, each writing in full awareness of the imminent dangers of persecution, acknowledge that, if some human rulers may serve the purposes of God, others serve those of Satan. Athenagoras explains that

> because the demonic movements and functions proceeding from Satan . . . sometimes move men in one way and sometimes in another, as individuals and as nations, separately and collectively, some have thought that this universe is constituted without any definite order.[56]

Christians believe, nevertheless, that even at their worst, demonically inspired rulers, "in spite of their disobedience, cannot transgress the order prescribed for them." God retains ultimate power over his universe and holds in his hands the final vindication of his servants and the coming destruction of his enemies. Meanwhile, like Socrates, who, freed from demonic deception, "tried to deliver people from the demons,"[57] Christians maintain the truth of their freedom by repudiating pagan worship. So, Justin says, "you consecrate the images of your emperors when they die, and you call them gods; but we do not honor such deities as human beings have made and placed in shrines."[58]

Justin admitted that he wrote in fear of his life, hoping desperately to change government policy, to convince the Roman authorities that Christians did not intend to be subversive; he himself, like the great majority of Christians, preferred to live quietly, and Christians did so wherever possible. In many cities Christian life continued uninterrupted, often for generations; yet many more than were persecuted must have nevertheless shared Justin's apprehension. What sounded like arrogant defiance was the response of people forced against their will to make the terrible choice between pagan sacrifice and death—between denying Christ or bearing witness to their faith in him to the end of their lives: the term *martyr,* in Greek, means "witness."

Some Roman officials, for their part, may have realized that such Christian attacks upon the Roman gods—and thus upon the emperors—could undermine the state's absolute claim upon its citizens and subjects; and that these inflammatory views, accompanied by passionate religious fervor, could catch fire among the disaffected and the restless, especially among subject nations and slaves. Thus Rome showed no toleration for these dangerous Christians.

One day Justin himself, as he had anticipated and feared, stood in court, arrested and charged with being a Christian. His judge, Rusticus, urban prefect of Rome, was Marcus Aurelius's personal friend and longtime advisor, who had inspired the young emperor, Marcus says, "with the idea of a state based upon equality and freedom of speech, and of a monarchy which values above all the liberty of the subject."[59] Justin probably knew that his judge's very name evoked the political philosophy with which Justin himself identified; for Rusticus proudly claimed to be descended from a famous Stoic philosopher who had defied the tyranny of the self-styled "lord and god," the emperor Domitian, and had paid for his courage with his execution.

Yet Rusticus acknowledged no affinity with Justin—much less the affinity Justin dared claim between himself and Socrates—and saw in this itinerant philosopher only a stubborn dissident who refused to obey Rusticus's simple command: "Obey the gods and submit to the emperors."[60] Both men—the judge and the accused—took for granted the implied connection between religious sacrifice and political submission. But Rusticus saw both as the minimum obligations of any citizen, while Justin and his companions saw such acts as betrayal of Christ, their true King.

After his interrogation, Rusticus repeated his demand: "Let us come to the point at issue—a necessary and urgent matter. Agree together to offer sacrifice to the gods."

Justin said, "No one of sound mind turns from piety to sacrilege."

The prefect said, "If you do not obey, you will be punished without mercy."

Justin and his companions replied, "Do what you will: we are Christians, and will not sacrifice to idols."

The prefect Rusticus then passed judgment, saying, "Those who have refused to sacrifice to the gods and yield to the emperor's edict are to be taken away to be beaten and beheaded, in accordance with the laws."[61]

Later generations of readers, whose perceptions were shaped by long-established Christian ideas that Justin and the other martyrs were simply following their religious convictions and were not offering a political challenge, have often missed seeing how genuinely radical Justin's stand actually was—as Rusticus, clearly, did not. Justin himself had argued that the state's policy of executing Christians was based upon a mistake. Christians were, in reality, the best of citizens, who willingly obeyed the laws and paid their full taxes.[62] This much was true; yet Justin also knew that Christians, himself included, refused to do the one thing that the magistrates actually *did* command them to do—to make token sacrifices to the gods or to the emperor's *genius.*

For Rusticus, Justin's refusal to perform such a routine token of loyalty belied the claims of these Christians to good citizenship. For most Romans, political and social obligations *were* religious obligations—the center of all that they held sacred. Only the Jews, of all the nations under Roman rule, had won the right to separate their political obligations from religious ones, to obey Roman law as subjects of the emperor but to worship their own God. The Roman historian Tacitus, a member of the senatorial aristocracy, wrote in his *Histories:* "Among the Jews, all things are profane that we hold sacred; on the other hand, they regard as permissible what seems to us immoral. . . . Proselytes to Jewry adopt the same practices, and the very first lesson they learn is to despise the gods, and shed all feelings of patriotism."[63] The Romans considered the Jews "atheists"—people who refused to worship the gods—but they were, so to speak, *licensed* atheists. Even Tacitus admitted that "whatever their origin, [the Jews'] observances are sanctioned by their antiquity,"[64] and the Romans respected tradition.

Christians, however, had no such excuse. Having broken with their fellow Jews to follow what Tacitus called a new and "deadly superstition,"[65] and having refused worship to the pagan gods, they set out, in effect, to secularize—and so radically to diminish—the power of social and political obligations. Thirty years after Justin and his companions were beaten and beheaded, the rebellious North African convert Tertullian, who had chosen baptism after he saw Christians die in the arena, boasted to his Roman rulers that executions only accelerated Christian conversion: "The more we are mown down by you, the more we multiply: the blood of Christians is seed!"[66]

Certain Christians, like followers of the Cynic philosopher Diogenes, dared denounce all the values of their society—all its political and religious "currency"—as counterfeit. They attacked the pretensions of the emperors as demonic lies and sought to expose their bronze and gilded images as a set of empty masks, or, worse, as masks for the human lust for power, inspired by evil spirits.

Cynical pagans might actually have agreed; the bolder among them dared even to say so, at least in private. Yet only a handful of proud philosophers and senators were willing to risk their lives to defy imperial power. But the boldest Christians not only defied pagan society to the death but also set out to create in its place a new social order—what Tertullian called "the Christian society"—based upon a new religious ideology and a new vision of human nature. The emperors rule by force and violence; but among the Christians, Tertullian said, "everything is voluntary." Instead of extracting taxes to pay for the emperors' luxuries, building projects, and wars, Christians voluntarily contributed

> to support the destitute, and to pay for their burial expenses; to supply the needs of boys and girls lacking money and power, and of old people confined to the home. . . . we do not hesitate to share our earthly goods with one another.[67]

People in need, especially old people, abandoned children, and widows, welcomed Christian generosity and flocked to the movement, where, Tertullian boasted, "we hold everything in common but our spouses," exactly reversing the practice in outside society, where, he said sardonically, most people voluntarily share nothing else![68]

As the religious basis of this new society, Christians were to look to one another and to themselves—not to pagan images, and certainly not to the imperial cult—to find "God manifest on earth." Clement, a neo-Platonist, urged Christians to turn away from "statues sculpted in human form . . . mere copies of bodies,"[69] to look within, to find there, within the moral consciousness of the human mind, an invisible image of the one invisible God. Since God created everyone "in his image," Clement added,

> both slave and free must equally philosophize, whether male or female in sex . . . for the individual whose life is framed as ours is may philosophize without education, whether barbarian, Greek, slave, whether an old man, or a boy, or a woman. For moral self-restraint is common to all human beings who have chosen it. And we admit that the same nature exists in every race, and the same virtue.[70]

Marcus Aurelius himself, a Stoic philosopher, might have agreed with this statement, at least in principle. But discussing such well-worn philosophic questions as universal human brotherhood in conversation with one's peers at the baths or at the dinner table was one thing. To allow people who openly despised the gods and flouted imperial authority to preach such things in public was something else. For public consumption, Marcus Aurelius no doubt preferred the official propaganda concerning imperial power to any form of moral egalitarianism, whether Stoic or Christian. For the Christian message could prove powerfully explosive in a society that ranked each person within a social hierarchy according to class, family, wealth, education, sex, and status—above all, the status that distinguished free persons from slaves. Within the capital city of Rome, three quarters of the population either were slaves—persons legally classified as property—or were descended from slaves. Besides being subjected to their owners' abuses, fits of violence, and sexual desires, slaves were denied such elementary rights as legitimate marriage, let alone legal recourse for their grievances. Clement attacked the widespread Roman custom of exposing abandoned infants on garbage dumps, or raising them for sale: "I pity the children owned by slave dealers, who are dressed up for shame,"[71] says Clement, and trained in sexual specialties, to be sold to gratify their owner's sexual tastes. Justin, in his *Defense of the Christians*, complained that "not only the females, but also the males" were commonly raised "like herds of oxen, goats, or sheep," as a profitable crop of child prostitutes. "And you," Justin accused the emperors, "receive profit from these, and duty and taxes from those whom you ought to exterminate from your realm!"[72] Many Christians were themselves slave owners and took slavery for granted as unthinkingly as their pagan neighbors. But others went among the hovels of the poor and into slave quarters, offering help and money and preaching to the poor, the illiterate, slaves, women, and foreigners—the good news that class, education, sex, and status made no difference, that every human being is essentially equal to any other "before God," including the emperor himself, for all humankind was created in the image of the one God.

The great majority of Christians of the first few centuries did not advocate—and probably did not imagine—that such moral equality could be implemented in society. Most assumed, no doubt, that they could realize such moral equality only in the coming Kingdom of God. Yet even such limited claims to moral equality aroused anger among educated and thoughtful pagans, as the African Christian Minucius Felix, writing a dialogue between pagans and Christians, articulates through his pagan character:

> "Everyone must be outraged—or, rather grieved—that certain people, uneducated, illiterate, and ignorant, dare to claim certainty concerning nature itself, and the divine being."[73]

But Minucius's Christian character challenged "my [pagan] brother, who expressed rage, grief, and indignation that illiterate, poor, and unskilled people" dared discuss subjects that baffled their betters:

> "Let him know that all people are begotten alike, with a capacity and ability for reasoning and emotion, without preference to age, sex, or social status. Nor do they gain wisdom by fortune, but have it implanted in them by nature . . . for intelligence is not given to wealth, nor is it acquired by study but is begotten with the very formation of the mind."[74]

Clement, too, scolded those "who have not recognized the autonomy of the human soul, which cannot be treated as a slave." And though he knew that such words might incite rebellion, he encouraged such behavior: "We [Christians] know that children, women, and slaves have often, against their fathers' or masters' or husbands' will, reached the highest pitch of excellence."[75] What Clement meant by that "highest pitch of excellence" was doing what Perpetua had done—rejecting allegiance to one's family, nation, and to the gods, in order to declare one's allegiance to God alone, anticipating the "glory" of public execution as a martyr. Minucius Felix, answering pagans who charged that Christians refused to offer sacrifices out of foolish and superstitious fear, declares that "our refusal is not an admission of fear, but an assertion of our true *liberty!*"[76]

Such defiant Christians as Justin and Perpetua understood liberty very differently than did their Roman masters. Marcus Aurelius and Rusticus, standing at the apex of Roman society, proudly claimed to rule in a way that "honors above everything else the liberty of the subject." To Marcus and his friends "liberty" meant living under the rule of a "good emperor"—that is, an emperor whom the Senate, consisting of wealthy and powerful men, approved. From his own point of view, Marcus and his colleagues admirably provided for such liberty; and men who have identified with their reign, from Plutarch through Gibbon, have agreed. In Gibbon's words:

> If a man were called to fix the period in the history of the world during which the condition of the human race was most happy and prosperous, he could, without hesitation, name that which elapsed from the death of Domitian to the accession of Commodus (i.e., the reigns of the emperors Nerva, Trajan, Hadrian, Antoninus Pius, and Marcus Aurelius). *The vast extent of the Roman Empire was governed by absolute power,* under the guidance of virtue and wisdom. *The forms of the civil administration were carefully preserved by Nerva, Trajan, Hadrian, and the Antonines, who delighted in the image of liberty* . . . the labors of these monarchs were overpaid by the immense reward that inseparably waited on their success; by the honest pride of virtue, and by the exquisite delight of beholding the general happiness of which they were the authors.[77]

Yet there were many—often at the opposite end of the social and political scale—who dissented. As the classicist Mason Hammond points out, it was under the reign of these "good emperors," famous for their caution and humanity, that the policy of persecuting Christians first became widespread.[78] Simultaneously the Roman provinces were racked with the revolt of the Jews under Trajan and Hadrian, and revolts of the Egyptians under Antoninus Pius and

Marcus Aurelius.[79] How many of those suffering the pressures of imperial power, the historian Naphtali Lewis asks, "would have recognized Gibbon's words as a description of the world in which they lived?"[80]

G. de Ste. Croix, in his massive Marxist history of social class in ancient times, indicts Christians for failing to criticize the dominant ideology of the Roman Empire. The Christians failed, he argues, because their ideas were molded by "irresistible social pressures"[81] (which he does not enumerate) and because of what he calls their "complete indifference, as Christians, to the institutions of the world in which they lived."[82] Yet Christian apologists certainly *did* attack not only the pagan gods and the imperial cult,[83] as we have seen, but also the traditional construction of the origins of the Roman Empire. They offered in its place a damning and, in effect, "demythologizing" view of Roman history. Tertullian, for example, challenges "the groundless assertion of those who maintain that, as a reward for their unique devotion to religion, the Romans have been raised to such heights of power as to become masters of the world."[84] Is "the progress of the empire," then, as Roman patriotic myth contends, "the reward the gods have paid to the Romans for their devotion"? On the contrary, says Tertullian, "if I am not mistaken, kingdoms and empires are acquired by wars, and expanded by victories. Moreover, you cannot have wars and victories without taking—and often destroying—cities."[85] In their wars of conquest, he continues, the Romans have destroyed and despoiled temples indiscriminately with houses and palaces. The Romans succeeded, he concludes, by subordinating their purported piety to their obsession for conquest.

Minucius Felix, too, challenged those who said the Romans "deserved their power" because of their consummate piety; he argued instead that the empire originated from a defensive pact formed by criminals and murderers: "Did not [the Romans] in their origin, when gathered together and fortified by crime, grow by the terror of their own ferocity?" First they started wars, drove their neighbors from their lands, and destroyed nearby cities through military force. Capturing, raping, and enslaving their victims, they increased their power: "The Romans were not so great because they were religious, but because they were sacrilegious with impunity."[86]

It was from this perspective on imperial power that Christians took their very different view of liberty from that of their Roman masters. They sided with a tradition of dissident philosophers who mocked the senatorial aristocracy's version of liberty as being, in effect, slavery. True liberty, such dissidents argued, involves freedom of speech—that is, the freedom to stand up to unjust rulers.[87] Conservative senators, of course, regarded this philosophic version of liberty as mere license—an invitation to anarchy. So long as they remained a persecuted, illegal minority, Christians insisted that only Christian baptism—certainly not the Roman government—conveyed liberty. For baptism liberated the convert simultaneously from sin, from enslavement to the pagan gods, and from the power of their human agents, who could only execute—and thus set free—Christian martyrs. Minucius Felix drew a rhetorical and vivid picture of a Christian who underwent torture for his faith, but maintained his liberty:

> "How beautiful is the spectacle to God when a Christian does battle with pain, when he is drawn up against threats, and punishment, and torture; when, mocking the noise of death, he treads underfoot the horror of the executioner; when *he raises up his liberty against kings and princes,* and yields to God alone . . . when, triumphant and victorious, he tramples upon the very man who has passed sentence upon him!"[88]

Out of such agony as Perpetua, Justin, and others endured, and that of Jewish martyrs before them,[89] was eventually born a new vision of the basis of social and political order—an order no longer founded upon the divine claims of the ruler or the state, but upon qualities that Christians believed were inherent within every man, and, some dared insist, within every woman as well, through our common creation "in God's image." The Christians of Justin's time, as we have seen, would not have imagined their vision as the basis for a political agenda. Yet sixteen hundred years later, in a totally different social and political context, American revolutionaries would invoke the same creation story against the British king's claim to divine right, declaring:

> We hold these truths to be self-evident; that all men are created equal, that they are endowed by their Creator with certain unalienable Rights . . .

In Justin's world—and some might argue even in our own—such alleged "truths" were anything but self-evident. Aristotle had deduced from observation what seemed to him far more obvious: that human beings are essentially unequal, some born to rule, and others to be slaves. But the Christian movement popularized the Hebrew creation story that implicitly asserted the intrinsic value of every human being; and throughout the Roman Empire, despite the Christians' criminal status and the consequent dangers that threatened them, the movement flourished. Tertullian even made the unprecedented claim that every human being has a right to religious liberty:

> It should be considered absurd for one person to compel another to honor the gods, when he should voluntarily, and in the awareness of his own need, seek their favor *in the liberty which is his right.* [90]

In centuries to come, others would infuse into the creation story even bolder moral visions and insist, for example, that human creation "in the image of God" not only conveys "unalienable rights" but also extends to people of every race, to slaves, to women, and, some would argue, to defective infants, or even to the unborn.

The legacy of such convictions would remain, for centuries and even millennia to come, an untried dream. When Perpetua and Justin, along with their Christian contemporaries, acted out their vision of liberty by refusing to sacrifice to the gods and the emperors, they marked themselves as targets for arrest, torture, and execution. So long as Christians remained members of a suspect society, subject to death, the boldest among them maintained that, since demons controlled the government and inspired its agents, the believer could gain freedom at their hands only in death.

III

GNOSTIC
IMPROVISATIONS
ON GENESIS

A S CHRISTIANITY SPREAD throughout the empire and took
root, its leaders began to develop various strategies of
community organization. They developed, too, ways of discriminating between those they accepted as orthodox ("straight-
thinking") Christians and those they rejected as deviants, including,
among the latter, many known as "gnostic" Christians.[1] Since to
profess Christianity was still suspect and potentially dangerous
throughout the Roman Empire, many Christian churches owed their
coherence and their survival to the astuteness and courage of their
leaders, the bishops. When Ignatius, bishop of Antioch in Syria, was
arrested (c. 110 C.E.) and sent by ship to Rome for trial and execution, chained, as he said, to "ten leopards, I mean a band of soldiers,"[2] he spent his final journey writing letters to the churches
surrounding his home church in Antioch and to the Christians in
Rome, his final destination. Ignatius urged these and all other Christians to stand together under persecution and to maintain unanimous
loyalty to the clergy, which he envisioned as a threefold hierarchy
of bishop, priests, and deacons who ruled each church "in God's
place,"[3] and who maintained communication among Christians scattered throughout the world.[4]

Such crises as a bishop's arrest and execution emphasized how
much the threatened Christian groups needed strong leaders; Ignatius knew that he was appealing to a still emerging and fragile
institutional system. What concerned Ignatius especially was that this

system had not yet won the allegiance of all who counted themselves among the believers. Nor was there as yet, among Christian groups scattered throughout the Roman world, a single central organization. Christians in different provinces—and even in neighboring communities—demonstrated great diversity, from the wandering ascetics of Asia Minor[5] to the settled "house churches" that were becoming established in Asian and Greek cities.[6] Converts from Judaism, for example, whether they lived in Judea or Greece, Asia or Egypt, tended to borrow the structure of the synagogues, where a leader presided over a group of "elders," or in the Greek, *presbyteroi,* later translated as "priests." Other converts, originally Gentiles, developed a different administrative system adapted from large households, consisting of a group of servants, called in Greek *diakones,* which became the English term "deacons," headed by an "overseer," called in Greek *episcopos,* our word for "bishop." Within the next three centuries these bishops came to assume responsibility for specific areas, or dioceses, a pattern modeled on the organization of the Roman army.

But persecution, which, however intense, remained sporadic, was not the only reason that the majority of Christians came to accept an increasingly institutionalized structure to oversee each group internally and instruct and discipline its members. By the second century many Christians wanted to incorporate Jesus' moral fervor into everyday life by turning his Sermon on the Mount into a set of rules, an ethical system that set Christians apart from their pagan environment, and sometimes placed them in direct opposition to it; this ethical imperative became still another reason for the increasingly institutionalized church.

What distinguished Christians from everyone else, according to both pagan and Christian contemporaries, was their moral rigor, which impressed even pagans hostile to the movement. The famous Galen, for example, personal physician to the emperor Marcus Aurelius and the imperial family, admired Christian courage and "abstinence from the use of the sexual organs."[7] When the Christian philosopher Justin wrote to the same emperors to defend his fellow Christians, he boasted that they were people who had completely changed their attitudes and behavior in matters of sex, money, and racial relations:

> We, who used to take pleasure in immorality, now embrace chastity alone; we, who valued above everything else the acquisition

of wealth and possessions, now bring what we have into common ownership, and share with those in need; we, who hated and destroyed one another, refusing to live with those of a different race, now live intimately with them.[8]

The practices Justin praised—sexual self-restraint, sharing one's goods with the destitute, and living with people of all races—appealed especially, as we have seen, to those people most vulnerable to sexual abuse, financial exploitation, poverty, and racial hatred—that is, to freedmen, noncitizens, and slaves, to the despised and rejected within the Roman world. Despite the suspicion of certain Roman officials toward Christians, the movement, strengthened by its developing institutional structures, grew.

But as the churches became more institutionalized, some Christians resisted that process. For while certain bishops, including, for example, Irenaeus of Lyons, attempted to formulate community morals and to enforce discipline by teaching, penalizing, or expelling those who, for whatever reason, dissented, some, no doubt, resented these intrusions upon their behavior. Others, although they accepted the ethical basis of Christian teaching, regarded conformity, whether in doctrine or discipline, as something that only beginners needed to take seriously. Some ardent Christians wanted to recover the sense of spiritual transformation that they found in Jesus' message. For these Christians conversion meant more than accepting baptism and following a new set of moral rules derived from Jesus' teaching. Becoming a Christian meant discovering one's spiritual nature—discovering, as one teacher put it,

who we are, and what we have become; where we were . . . whither we are hastening; from what we are being released; what birth is, and what is rebirth.[9]

Many Christians striving for a higher level of spiritual consciousness had no quarrel with what the bishops taught; they agreed that moral guidance concerning good works and sexual restraint was not only welcome but essential, for most people. But some Christians objected to being told what to think and how to behave. Although they agreed that the first step toward becoming a Christian was to accept the faith and receive baptism from the bishop, these Christians wanted to go further. They yearned to become spiritually "mature,"[10] to go beyond such elementary instruction toward higher levels of understanding. And this higher awareness they called *gnosis,* which means "knowledge," or "insight."[11] To achieve gnosis, these Christians said, they no longer needed the bishop or the clergy.

When Irenaeus, bishop at Lyons (c. 180 C.E.), discovered among his own congregation a large group of such Christians who sought to exempt themselves from his authority and set out to know God directly through gnosis, or immediate experience, he recognized—and even grudgingly respected—their spiritual purpose.[12] As bishop, however, he soon came into conflict with their determination to follow Christ in their own way. He decided that they were divisive and arrogant upstarts who threatened to undermine church unity and discipline, for they "disturb the faith of many by alluring them under a pretense of superior knowledge."[13] Above all, as we shall see, Irenaeus was concerned that gnostic teaching threatened the message of freedom that he and many others considered central to the gospel. Irenaeus read some of the writings of these gnostic Christians and engaged in conversation with several of them. He then composed a five-volume polemic against them, which he called "The Refutation and Overthrow of Falsely So-Called Knowledge (*Gnosis*)." The term "gnostics," now often used descriptively for such dissident spiritual seekers, may have been their own term, or it may have originated as a derisive name for those Christians whom Irenaeus regarded as self-appointed "know-it-alls."[14]

These so-called gnostics, then, did not share a single ideology or belong to a specific group; not all, in fact, were Christians. Those who did identify themselves as Christians included a wide variety of people who chose to follow their faith in their own way. Many gnostic Christians were members of Christian congregations, including both lay people and members of the clergy, who wanted no more than to supplement the teaching and worship common to all Christians with deeper insights derived from their own spiritual experience. Many gnostics also followed certain spiritual teachers who promised to initiate them into deeper mysteries of the faith.

Irenaeus directed his polemic primarily at the group of gnostic Christians whom members of his own congregation found most attractive and powerful—a group the bishop considered especially dangerous and divisive. These were followers of a spiritual master called Valentinus, who some forty years before Irenaeus wrote, and while Justin was still teaching in Rome, had joined the Christian group there as a newcomer (c. 140–160 C.E.). Before coming to Rome, Valentinus had already established himself among Christians of the Egyptian city of Alexandria as a poet, visionary, and spiritual teacher; and in Rome, where his abilities were widely recognized, he was considered a likely candidate for bishop. Even Tertullian, who would bitterly denounce Valentinus's followers a generation later, admitted that their teacher had been "a capable man, both in intelligence and eloquence."[15]

Valentinus urged Christians to go beyond the elementary steps of faith, baptism, and moral reform to spiritual illumination. His followers claimed, moreover, to have received from him access to secret teachings of Paul, the "deeper mysteries" that Paul reserved from his public teaching and taught only to a few chosen disciples in secret.[16] Other gnostics claimed to know the secret teaching of Jesus himself—teaching only hinted at, they said, in the New Testament gospels but revealed more fully in such secret writings as the *Gospel of Thomas,* the *Gospel of Mary Magdalene,* and the *Dialogue of the Savior.*[17]

Such writings, suppressed and lost for nearly sixteen hundred years, remained, until recently, virtually unknown. But in December of 1945, two years before the Dead Sea Scrolls were discovered in desert caves in Israel, copies of these very writings and many others were discovered unexpectedly in the Egyptian desert near the town of Nag Hammadi in Upper Egypt. This extraordinary find disclosed, in fact, more than fifty texts that date back to the first centuries of the Christian Era, including a collection of early Christian "gospels" and other writings attributed to Jesus and his disciples. While the original language of these texts was Greek (the language of the New Testament), the copies discovered in Egypt had been translated from Greek into Coptic, the common language of Egypt in the third and fourth centuries. Whether these writings—or which of them—contain authentic teaching of Jesus and his disciples we do not know, any more than we know with certainty which sayings or teachings in the New Testament are authentic. What the discovery certainly *does* offer, however, is extraordinary insights into the early Christian movement. For the first time, we can read firsthand works later condemned and destroyed by the bishops as heretical. Now for the first time the "heretics" can speak to us in their own words. For church leaders of the second century, including Ignatius, Justin, Irenaeus, Tertullian, and Clement, had attacked the gnostic Christians, condemned their teachings, and attempted to drive them out of the churches.

A century and a half later, when the emperor Constantine abruptly changed Roman policy from one of persecuting Christians to protecting and favoring them with massive gifts of money, tax exemptions, and enormous prestige, the bishops, now in political favor, sometimes used these new resources to promote unanimity; thus in 381, the Christian emperor Theodosius made "heresy" a crime against the state.

The texts discovered in a jar near Nag Hammadi show us more clearly than we had ever known that some of these so-called gnostic Christians sought divine illumination through a process of spiritual self-discovery.[18] The Christian bishops who called themselves orthodox might no doubt claim that they, too, sought spiritual illumination; but their methods differed considerably. Justin the philosopher followed a common Christian tradition when he called the ritual of baptism itself "illumination" and explained that "since at our birth we were born without our knowledge or choice, by our parents' union, and were raised with bad habits and false education," so converts had been born first as "children of necessity and ignorance." But Christians, through baptism, were born again as "children of choice and knowledge."[19] Justin sought to increase his own understanding of the faith—and that of his students—through moral action and philosophic discourse. Followers of Valentinus, on the other hand, tended to regard baptism as only the elementary initiation ritual, and one that, for many people, lacked real spiritual content.[20] Instead of following a philosophic path, like Justin, Valentinus looked within himself to dreams and visions to deepen his gnosis. He traced his own spiritual process, in fact, to a vision in which a newborn infant appeared to him and said, "I am the Logos."[21] Like Justin, Valentinus sought spiritual illumination in the Scriptures; but where Justin wrestled with their moral, philosophical, and historical dimensions, Valentinus claimed to explicate their "deeper meaning" through secret traditions known only to initiates like himself.[22] My first two books, written before *The Gnostic Gospels,* attempt to show how Valentinian Christians interpreted the New Testament Gospel of John and the letters of Paul.[23]

When gnostic and orthodox Christians disagreed, each reached back to the Scriptures that they revered in common, and each claimed the Scriptures' support. But gnostic and orthodox Christians read the same Scriptures in radically different ways; to borrow the words of the nineteenth-century poet William Blake, "Both read the Bible day and night; but you read black where I read white!"

The majority of orthodox Christians in the first and second centuries, like most Jews and Christians ever since, read the Scriptures as Justin did, primarily as practical guides to moral living. They read the Genesis story, in particular, as *history with a moral:* that is, they regarded Adam and Eve as actual historical persons, the venerable ancestors of our race; and from the story of their disobedience, orthodox interpreters drew practical lessons in moral behavior. Tertullian, for example, took Genesis 3 as an opportunity to warn his "sisters in Christ" that even the best of them were, in effect, Eve's co-conspirators:

> You are the devil's gateway. . . . you are she who persuaded him whom the devil did not dare attack. . . . *Do you not know that every one of you is an Eve? The sentence of God on your sex lives on in this age; the guilt, of necessity, lives on too.* [24]

In other contexts, Tertullian can derive from the story different moral lessons: for example, to warn against gluttony, because "eating led to Adam's fall,"[25] or to urge believers to marry only once, since God made for Adam "only one wife."[26] Orthodox Christians who disagree with one another over the interpretation of Genesis disagree primarily on the question of *which* moral to draw from it: for example, where Clement sees God's blessing on marriage and procreation in Paradise,[27] the fourth-century Christian ascetic Jerome will insist, as we shall see, that Adam and Eve were originally meant to be virgins, and were joined in marriage only after they sinned and were expelled in disgrace "from the Paradise of virginity."[28]

Gnostic Christians, on the other hand, castigated the orthodox for making the mistake of reading the Scriptures—and especially Genesis—literally, and thereby missing its "deeper meaning." Read literally, they said, the story of creation made no sense. Are we to believe that Adam and Eve actually heard God's footsteps rustling in the garden of Eden, as the text suggests, when it says that Adam and Eve hid themselves, for "they heard the sound of the Lord God walking in the garden in the cool of the day" (Genesis 3:8)? Or did God lie when he warned Adam and Eve, "You shall not eat of the fruit of the tree of the knowledge of good and evil, for on the day you eat of it you shall surely die" (Genesis 2:17), though they went on to live for hundreds of years? To whom was God speaking when he said, "Let *us* make man in *our* image" (Genesis 1:26)? And why did God try to keep from Adam and Eve the knowledge that he admits could make them "like one of us" (Genesis 3:22)?

Certain gnostic Christians suggested that such absurdities show that the story was never meant to be taken literally but should be understood as spiritual allegory—not so much *history with a moral* as *myth with meaning*. These gnostics took each line of the Scriptures as an enigma, a riddle pointing to deeper meaning. Read this way, the text became a shimmering surface of symbols, inviting the spiritually adventurous to explore its hidden depths, to draw upon their own inner experience—what artists call the creative imagination—to interpret the story. Irenaeus describes various gnostic interpretations of the creation story and then complains that "while they claim such things as these concerning the creation, every one of them generates something new every day, according to his ability; for, among them, no one is considered mature [or "initiated"] who does not develop some enormous fictions."[29] Consequently, gnostic Christians neither sought nor found any consensus concerning what the story meant but regarded Genesis 1–3 rather like a fugal melody upon which they continually improvised new variations, all of which, Bishop Irenaeus said, were "full of blasphemy."[30]

Gnostic Christians did not invent this technique of allegorical interpretation; on the contrary, pagan and Jewish teachers had used such methods for many generations to interpret venerated but puzzlingly archaic texts. Certain Stoic philosophers, for example, had suggested that the Homeric poems, the *Iliad* and the *Odyssey,* which formed the basis of Greek education, should not be read simply *literally* as accounts of ancient battles or of the gods' conflicts and amours. Such allegorists claimed that whoever looked beyond their obvious meaning and read them symbolically could find hidden in them the deeper truths of natural philosophy. Certain Jewish teachers, too, prominently including Jesus' contemporary the wealthy and educated Philo of Alexandria, applied allegorical exegesis to the Scriptures to discover the deeper meaning that they believed lay "beneath the surface."

Philo interprets the Genesis creation accounts in various ways. Sometimes he reads it as history with a moral, and he warns people against disobeying God, and warns men, in particular, against women, whose creation from Adam's side ended the first man's lofty and solitary communion with God and was, for Philo, "the beginning of all evils." But Philo also can interpret the story allegorically, as myth with meaning—that is, as a story containing profound truths hidden in symbols. In his ingenious *Allegorical Interpretation,* Philo takes Adam and Eve as representing two elements within human nature: he says that Adam represents the *mind* (*nous*), the nobler, masculine, and rational element, which is "made in God's image";[31] and Eve represents the body or *sensation (aisthesis),* the lower, feminine element, source of all passion.[32] (The scholar Richard Baer shows, too, that Philo's view of men and women follows a similar—and predictable—pattern.[33])

Gnostic interpreters, equally fascinated with the story of Adam and Eve, found in the Garden of Eden a wild flowering of interpretations. Yet many of these gnostic interpretations, however diverse they appear, share a common—and entirely *unorthodox*—premise. For orthodox interpreters, both Jewish and Christian, tend to emphasize the distinction between the infinite God and his finite creatures —a distinction expressed, for example, by the twentieth-century Jewish theologian Martin Buber's description of God as "wholly other," which means, above all, other than human. Even the mystics of Jewish and Christian tradition who seek to find their identity in God often are careful to acknowledge the abyss that separates them from their divine Source. When the Dominican monk Meister Eckhart (c. 1260–1328 C.E.), for example, failed to do so and preached instead that "our whole perfection and blessing depends upon our stepping across the estate of creaturehood, and on getting at last to the Cause that has no cause"[34]—that is, attaining "God [who] lies hidden in the soul's core"[35]—his boldness so outraged the archbishop of Cologne that he succeeded in obtaining a papal bull condemning Eckhart's writings as heresy. And when the Jewish theologian Martin Buber sought to explore the sources of religious experience, he characterized the Jewish devotee's relationship to God as "I *and* Thou"; but no orthodox Jew, any more than an orthodox Christian, could say, with the Hindu devotee, "I *am* Thou."[36]

But gnostic interpreters share with the Hindu and with Eckhart that very conviction—that the divine being is hidden deep within human nature, as well as outside it, and, although often unperceived, is a spiritual potential latent in the human psyche. According to Ptolemy, a follower of Valentinus, the story of Adam and Eve shows that humanity "fell" into ordinary consciousness and lost contact with its divine origin.[37] Another follower of Valentinus, the author of the *Gospel of Philip,* says that human beings fell into the error of projecting divinity onto beings external to themselves, and so created religion:

> In the beginning, God created humanity. But now humanity creates God. This is the way it is in the world—human beings

invent gods and worship their creation. It would be more fitting for the gods to worship human beings![38]

Some gnostics adopted a pattern of interpretation similar to Philo's but changed the content. Instead of characterizing human psychodynamics, as Philo had, in terms of an interaction between *mind* and *sensation,* gnostics pictured it in terms of the interaction of *soul* and *spirit*—that is, between the *psyche* (ordinary consciousness, understood to include both mind and sensation) and the *spirit,* the potential for a higher, spiritual consciousness. Many gnostics read the story of Adam and Eve, consequently, as an account of what takes place within a person who is engaged in the process of spiritual self-discovery. The gnostic text called *Interpretation of the Soul,* for example, tells how the soul, represented as Eve, became alienated from her spiritual nature, and so long as she denied that spiritual nature and distanced herself from it, she fell into self-destruction and suffering. But when she became willing to be reconciled and reunited with her spiritual nature, she once again became whole; the gnostic author explains that this process of spiritual self-integration is the hidden meaning of the marriage of Adam and Eve: "This marriage has brought them back together again, and the soul has been joined to her true love, her real master,"[39] that is, to her spiritual self. Many other gnostic texts reverse the symbolism; the majority of the known gnostic texts depict Adam (not Eve) as representing the psyche, while Eve represents the higher principle, the spiritual self. Gnostic authors loved to tell, with many variations, the story of Eve, that elusive spiritual intelligence: how she first emerged within Adam and awakened him, the soul, to awareness of its spiritual nature; how she encountered resistance, was misunderstood, attacked, and mistaken for what she was not; and how she finally joined with Adam "in marriage," so to speak, and so came to live in harmonious union with the soul.[40] According to the gnostic text called *Reality of the Rulers,* when Adam first recognized Eve, he saw in her not a mere marital partner but a spiritual power:

> And when he saw her, he said, "It is you who have given me life: you shall be called Mother of the Living [Eve]; for it is she who is my Mother. It is she who is the Physician, and the Woman, and She Who Has Given Birth."[41]

The *Reality of the Rulers* went so far as to say that when Adam was warned by the creator to disregard her voice, he lost contact with the spirit, until she reappeared to him in the form of the serpent:

Then the Female Spiritual Principle came [in] the Snake, the Instructor; and it taught [them], saying, "What did he [say to] you [pl.]? Was it, 'From every tree in the Garden shall you [sing.] eat; yet—from [the tree] of recognizing evil and good do not eat'?"

The carnal Woman said, "Not only did he say 'Do not eat,' but even 'Do not touch it; for the day you [pl.] eat from it, with death you [pl.] are going to die.' "

And the Snake, the Instructor, said, "With death you [pl.] shall not die; for it was out of jealousy that he said this to you [pl.]. Rather your [pl.] eyes shall open and you [pl.] shall come to be like gods, recognizing evil and good." And the Female Instructing Principle was taken away from the Snake, and she left it behind merely a thing of the earth.[42]

An extraordinary gnostic poem called *Thunder: Perfect Mind* depicts the spirit, manifested variously as Wisdom and as Eve, speaking as follows:

> I am the first and the last.
> I am the honored one and the scorned one.
> I am the whore and the holy one.
> I am the wife and the virgin.
> I am the bride and the bridegroom,
>   and it is my husband who begot me.
> I am knowledge and ignorance. . . .
> I am foolish and I am wise. . . .
> I am the one whom they call life [Eve]
>   and you have called Death. . . . [43]

The *Secret Book of John* suggests that Adam's experience as he awakened to Eve's presence prefigures that of the gnostic who, sunk into a state of oblivion, suddenly awakens to the presence of the spirit hidden deep within. The *Secret Book* concludes as Eve, the "perfect primal intelligence," calls out to Adam—to the psyche (and so, in effect, to you and me, the readers)—to wake up, recognize her, and so receive spiritual illumination:

I entered into the midst of their prison, which is the prison of the body. And I said, "Whoever hears, let him arise from the deep sleep." And he wept and shed bitter tears. Bitter tears he wiped from himself, and he said, "Who is it who calls my name, and whence has this hope come to me while I am in the chains of this prison?" And I said, "I am the intelligence [*pronoia*] of the pure life; I am the thinking of the virginal spirit. . . . Arise and remember . . . and follow your root, which is I . . . and beware of the deep sleep."[44]

Gnostic Christians who projected such "bizarre inventions" onto Genesis ignored matters of practical morality—or so Bishop Irenaeus charged, and at first glance one must agree. For while their contemporary Christians were drawing moral injunctions from Genesis, certain gnostic Christians seemed to be merely improvising myths on the story of Paradise. Some gnostics dared go further: instead of blaming the human desire for knowledge as the root of all sin, they did the opposite and sought redemption through gnosis. And whereas the orthodox often blamed Eve for the fall and pointed to women's submission as appropriate punishment, gnostics often depicted Eve—or the feminine spiritual power she represented—as the source of spiritual awakening.[45]

Yet many gnostic Christians struggled with the same urgent ethical questions that preoccupied their orthodox contemporaries: Should Christians avoid marriage or embrace it? Are Christians, like Jews, commanded to "be fruitful and multiply"? What kind of relationship is possible, or desirable, between Christian men and women?

When gnostic Christians asked themselves these questions, however, they often approached them differently than did their orthodox contemporaries. Instead of formulating a set of community rules, some gnostic Christians sought instead to discover and articulate— precisely through the "bizarre inventions" of gnostic myth—the internal sources of desire and action. What fascinated them was psychodynamics, or, as they might have put it, pneumato-psychodynamics: the interaction between the *pneuma,* the spiritual element of our nature, and the *psyche,* that is, the emotional and mental impulses. The Valentinian author of the *Gospel of Philip,* speaking in mythic language, said, for example, that death began when "the woman separated . . . from the man"[46]—that is, when Eve (the spirit) became separated from Adam (the psyche). Only when one's psyche, or ordinary consciousness, becomes integrated with one's spiritual nature—when Adam, reunited with Eve, "becomes complete again"[47]—can one achieve internal harmony and wholeness. According to this Valentinian author, only the person who has "remarried" the psyche with the spirit becomes capable of withstanding physical and emotional impulses that, unchecked, could drive him or her toward self-destruction and evil. Irenaeus was wrong, then, to suggest that gnostic Christians ignored moral issues. But they sometimes engaged them in a way that encouraged each person to explore his or her own internal experience, believing that each one could discover the spirit within. Commenting on their method, Irenaeus said sarcastically that "they imagine that, by means of their obscure interpretations, each of them has discovered a god of his own!"[48] But what especially bothered Irenaeus was that gnostic Christians engaged moral issues in ways that made them seem indifferent—or worse, insubordinate—to the community ethics that the bishops sought to impose upon all believers alike.

Meanwhile certain radical gnostics, far from criticizing the bishops for being too severe, criticized them instead for being too lenient. One such gnostic Christian, the author of the *Testimony of Truth,* sided with the ascetics and railed against both orthodox and gnostics alike who endorsed marriage and procreation and who worshiped the God who had created such impurities. This radical teacher dared to tell the story of Paradise from the serpent's point of view, and depicted the serpent as a teacher of divine wisdom who desperately tried to get Adam and Eve to open their eyes to their creator's true—and despicable—nature:

> For the serpent was *wiser* than any of the animals that were in Paradise. . . . But the creator cursed the serpent, and called him devil. And he said, "Behold, Adam has become like one of us, knowing evil and good."[49]

Then he said, "Let us cast him out of Paradise lest he take from the tree of life and live forever" (Genesis 3:22). Who is this God, who calls evil "good" and good "evil"?

> What kind of God is this? First, he envied Adam that he should eat from the tree of knowledge. . . . And secondly he said, "Adam, where are you?" And God does not have foreknowledge, since he did not know this from the beginning. And afterwards, he said, "Let us cast him [out] of this place lest he eat of the tree of life and live forever." Surely he has shown himself to be a malicious envier. And what kind of God is this? Great is the blindness of those who read, and they did not know it.[50]

What church leader would not have bridled at a critic who turned the Genesis account upside down, and who blasted all Christians who married or conducted ordinary business for being igno-rant, false, and foolish? The same gnostic author attacked the martyrs themselves as "empty martyrs, who witness only to themselves,"[51] and castigated their leaders as "blind guides,"[52] who were at best immature and at worst liars.

Church leaders like Irenaeus who confronted the followers of Valentinus must have found them almost as maddening as the more radical gnostics, but for different reasons. Valentinian Christians agreed with the bishop that practicing good works and sexual re-straint was good for those they called "the many" but claimed these were optional for spiritual Christians like themselves.[53] Irenaeus complained that these gnostic positions were hard to pin down; they were as wildly inconsistent as their interpretations of the Scriptures. Irenaeus admitted that some Valentinians lived exemplary lives as celibates, but others, he said, only pretended piety to cover their secret licentiousness.[54] On the other hand, Clement of Alexandria praised the Valentinians he knew in Egypt because they, unlike most other "heretics," *approved* of marriage.[55]

Where *did* the Valentinian gnostics stand, then, on the questions that divided their Christian contemporaries—whether, for example, Christians should marry or remain celibate? One certainly would have expected to find a clear answer in their writings; for marriage (or, as the *Gospel of Philip* calls it, "the mystery of marriage") figured as a primary theme of their whole theology. Valentinian rituals ap-parently culminated in the sacrament they called the "bridecham-ber."[56] Yet astonishingly, in spite of all this, their writings on such practical questions as their attitude toward marriage remain so am-biguous that various scholars have convincingly argued opposite cases. The prominent Dutch scholar Gilles Quispel insists that the Valentinians virtually *required* marriage of gnostic Christians, and that they celebrated marriage—between gnostics, at any rate—as a sacrament, embodying the divine harmonies of masculine and femi-nine energies in the divine being.[57] The younger American scholar Michael Williams argues, on the contrary, that Valentinian Chris-tians, like medieval Catholic mystics, used sexual imagery only to contrast actual marriage, which they considered to be "polluted," with heavenly marriage to Christ.[58]

The remarkable collection of sayings we know as the *Gospel of Philip* may offer us clues to sort out such contradictions, for its author challenged the way that most people set up moral questions in the first place. Christians then, as now, ordinarily assumed that certain acts are good and others bad; but they furiously debated *which* acts—marriage or celibacy, for example—belong to which category. The gnostic author of the *Gospel of Philip* rejects this whole way of thinking. As this author sees it, no act in itself—and specifically neither celibacy nor marriage—is necessarily good or bad. Instead the moral significance of any act depends upon the situation, intentions, and level of consciousness of the participants. This author characterizes such terms as "good" and "bad," like other pairs of opposites, as merely mental categories that necessarily imply one another:

> Light and darkness, life and death, right and left, are brothers of one another. They are inseparable. Because of this, the "good" are not good, nor the "evil" evil, nor is "life" life, nor is "death" death.[59]

For "the names given to things in the world are very deceptive,"[60] especially when one mistakes the names for reality. The author traces this deception directly back to the Garden of Eden, where Adam and Eve first sought to gain knowledge through such deceptive categories, by partaking of the *"tree of the knowledge of good and evil."* Then the law, based on the same categories, continued the same process of deception:

> The law was the tree. . . . For when [the law] said, "Eat this, do not eat that," it became the beginning of death.[61]

Leaders of the church who confronted such Valentinians among their congregations must have recognized themselves—and their "simpleminded" moralism—as the target of such criticisms; but they were not the only targets, for these gnostic Christians would have been equally critical of the advocates of asceticism. The *Gospel of Philip* suggests that those who say that celibacy is good err as much as those who pronounce marriage good—and those who call either bad err equally. It may be no accident, then, that not one of the extant Valentinian texts unequivocally endorses marriage over celibacy, or the opposite. The author of *Philip* implies instead that what each person should do depends upon each person's intention and level of consciousness. The same author compares the gnostic teacher to a householder who is responsible for the care of children, slaves, cattle, dogs, and pigs:

> [being] a sensible person, he knew what each one should eat.
> . . . Compare the disciple of God; if he is a sensible man, he understands what discipleship is all about. . . . He will not be

misled by the physical appearance of anyone, but will look at the condition of each one's soul, and so speak to each one.[62]

Yet the author of *Philip* warns that gnostic Christians are not to think of themselves as exempt from sin:

> Those who think that sinning does not apply to them are called "free" by the world. Knowledge of the truth makes such people arrogant. . . . It even gives them a sense of superiority over everyone else.[63]

The author goes on to quote and interpret Paul's letter to the Corinthians, saying,

> "Love builds up" [1 Corinthians 8:1b] . . . in fact, one who is really free through knowledge is a servant for the sake of love to those who have not yet been able to attain to the freedom of *gnosis.*[64]

But how was the gnostic Christian to deal with the actual experience of evil—and, in particular, evil found within himself or herself? Orthodox Christians often attempted to prescribe rules for the whole community, but the author of *Philip* suggests that one can deal with evil only in oneself:

> As for ourselves, *let each one of us dig down after the root of evil which is within one, and let one pluck it out of one's heart from the root. It will be plucked out,* if we recognize it. But if we are ignorant of it, it takes root in us and produces its fruit in our heart; it masters us. . . . it is powerful because we have not recognized it.[65]

The author advises, then, that each person practice self-examination and look for such potential sources of evil as envy, lust, anger, in his or her own intentions, words, and acts. What transforms one spiritually, according to the *Gospel of Philip,* is continual self-awareness and acknowledging the evil within oneself wherever one finds it.[66] This suggests that Valentinian Christians indeed may have rejected the bishops' commands, ignored community regulations, and followed their inner guidance, insisting that moral acts are essentially private matters that every person, or at least every mature person, must deal with independently.

Such independence, as we have seen, threatened church unity and discipline. Bishop Irenaeus charged that Valentinian Christians were concerned only for their own spiritual advantage, indifferent to the church as an institution. He accused them of "having no respect for others" (does he mean for the bishops in particular?) and for "thinking that they are better than any one else."[67]

But what bothered Irenaeus even more than the gnostics' rejection of moral absolutism or their violation of church discipline was that gnostic readings of Genesis threatened the message of freedom that had made Christianity so powerfully compelling to so many converts. This debate over Genesis revealed a major disagreement among second-century Christians, a disagreement whose outcome would shape church doctrine ever after.

As we have seen, the majority of Christian converts of the first four centuries regarded the proclamation of moral freedom, grounded in Genesis 1–3, as effectively synonymous with "the gospel." As Justin interpreted Jesus' message, it celebrated not only Christian freedom from domination by sexual passion, and from such passions as greed and hatred, but also from external domination by the Roman state. Clement of Alexandria praised Christian freedom to choose even death rather than yield to the oppressive weight of Roman social custom. Bishop Methodius, writing years later in Asia Minor, envisioned the whole of human history, ever since Eden, as a progressive evolution of human freedom, which culminates in the greatest freedom of all—the life of voluntary renunciation.[68] Gregory of Nyssa spoke for the whole tradition when he said, "The soul directly reveals its royal and excellent quality in that . . . it is governed and ruled autonomously by its own will."[69]

Most orthodox Christians agreed with many of their Jewish contemporaries that Adam's fatal misuse of this freedom was so momentous that his transgression brought pain, labor, and death into an originally perfect world. Yet Justin, Irenaeus, Tertullian, and Clement also agreed that Adam's transgression did not encroach upon our own individual freedom: even now, they said, every person is free to choose good or evil, just as Adam was.

These same church leaders unanimously denounced the gnostics for denying what the orthodox considered to be humanity's essential, God-given attribute, free will. For Irenaeus, the story of Adam and Eve proclaimed "the ancient law of human liberty."[70] Most other Christians also agreed with their Jewish contemporaries that the point of the creation story was that God bestowed upon every person the gift of moral freedom. Certain Christians, from Paul through Augustine, may have noted what this implied socially: that slavery is not a natural condition, as Aristotle had taught, but an artificial and sinful human invention.[71] (Yet neither Paul nor Augustine advocated abolishing slavery; instead, both, like the Stoic philosophers, urged slaves to use their moral freedom to overcome the hardships of servitude.)[72] For Clement of Alexandria, moral freedom is our glory; that we are made in the image of God really means that we have what he calls *autexousia*, a term often translated as "free will," but, more accurately, "the power to constitute one's own being."[73]

But gnostic Christians qualified—and some denied—this optimistic message of freedom. Certain radical gnostics ridiculed the orthodox claim that human beings have free will or, for that matter, any power to constitute their own destiny. The *Reality of the Rulers* depicted Adam, prototype of humanity, as a kind of victim, morally and physically crippled from the start. Betrayed and deceived by the forces of evil, created as a by-product of their desires and jealousies, Adam was helplessly caught within a battle of spiritual forces and could only hope that the powers above would defeat his tormentors and release their human prisoner from his cosmic confinement.

Valentinus and his followers did not go so far as to deny that human beings have free will; but they believed its role to be far more limited than orthodox Christians imagined. Human beings—or some of them, at least—may have moral freedom, they said, but human free will—even Adam's—was never so great as to bring suffering upon humanity, or to allow us to evade it altogether.[74] On the contrary, suffering is built into the structure of the universe itself. Followers of Valentinus expressed this conviction in a *precreation* myth that hinted that something else besides human sin—events far more primordial and powerful—already had cast a shadow of suffering over human existence. This was the story of Wisdom, whose "fall" occurred long before Adam's and long before he was created. As Ptolemy's disciples told the story, before the beginning of time there existed in the primal aeon only the primordial Source of all being, what they called the abyss, the depth, or primal origin, progenitor of all that was to come into being. After existing for immeasurable ages in a state of profound rest, this Source wanted other beings to know and love him; and so he brought forth from himself "the beginning of all things"[75] and projected this into his only companion, the primordial Silence, like sperm into a womb. The Silence conceived, so to speak, and brought forth a pair of emanations of divine being, the primordial Mind together with his counterpart, Truth—the first masculine, the second feminine, according to the gender of their Greek names. This pair, structured as a dynamic relationship between masculine and feminine energies, then brought forth a second pair, Logos and Life; and they, in turn, brought forth Humanity and the Church. Each pair of complementary divine energies brought forth others until the divine being reached its "fullness." Last of all, the youngest of these pairs consisted of What-has-been-willed together with his feminine counterpart, Wisdom (Sophia). In this way the Valentinians expressed their conviction that it is wisdom to live in harmony with "what [the Father] has willed."

But Wisdom belied her name and acted foolishly. Because she longed to know the Father, she rejected her place in the scheme of things, severed her relationship with What-has-been-willed, and plunged herself into a desperate search to understand the nature of her divine Source. As Irenaeus told her story,

> when she could not achieve her purpose, both because of the enormous depth and the incomprehensible nature of the Father, she stretched herself forward, and was in danger of being absorbed into His sweetness and dissolved into His absolute essence, until she encountered the Power that sustains and preserves all things, called "the Limit" . . . the power by whom, they say, she was restored and supported. Then, having with great difficulty been brought back to herself, she became convinced that the Father is incomprehensible.[76]

Then the Father, wanting to spare others from suffering as Wisdom had, sent a sixteenth pair of masculine and feminine energies, Christ and the Holy Spirit, to reveal to the other aeons that although none but the primal Mind could possibly comprehend God, all other beings, too, come from him, "in whom we live and move and have our being," and are to rejoice and celebrate together in this paradoxical knowledge.

When Wisdom was restored to her place within the divine being, she left her sufferings behind her. Followers of Ptolemy said that these sufferings—the fear, confusion, grief, and ignorance she suffered in her search for God—had to be excluded from the divine being. Yet Wisdom joined herself with Christ to recover the residual spiritual energy left in these experiences. Together, she and Christ set out to transform those sufferings: they turned her fear into water, her grief into air, her confusion into earth, and her ignorance into fire. Then they used these elements of suffering to create the present universe.[77]

The orthodox insisted that Adam and Eve inherited a perfect

world and brought upon it, through their misuse of free will, all the harms known to humankind. But the Valentinians believed that human beings, though they undoubtedly received a measure of freedom to make moral choices, are not free—nor ever were—to avoid suffering, from which the very universe itself was made. The orthodox church offered "good news" of human power and freedom; but the Valentinians, more like Buddhists, saw acceptance of suffering as the first prerequisite for spiritual understanding.

We may infer from the sophistication of many of their writings that Valentinian Christians tended to be people of education and privilege. If so, they may have been able to take their personal freedom for granted, as many people in the Roman Empire could not. And we may also infer that they knew from experience the limits of human freedom. For their myths suggest that even those who are gifted with freedom—moral and intellectual, of course, as well as social or political—must remain acutely aware of the limits of freedom and of the ways in which even the freest of human beings remain dependent upon what is beyond human power. The gnostics' vision was a dark one, pervaded by suffering; yet it was, nevertheless, a religious vision, in which ultimately everything depended upon what they called the will of the Father, that mysterious Source, the "abyss,"[78] who, according to the *Gospel of Truth,* "discovered ['his own'] in himself, and they discovered him in themselves, the incomprehensible, inconceivable one, the Father, the perfect one, the one who made the all."[79]

But orthodox Christians of the second and third centuries, from Justin and Irenaeus through Tertullian, Clement, and the brilliant teacher Origen, stood unanimously against the gnostics in proclaiming the Christian gospel as a message of freedom—moral freedom, freedom of the will, expressed in Adam's original freedom to choose a life free of pain and suffering. In the name of that moral freedom, Justin and Origen, among many others, chose to endure torture and death. Still others, in the name of that freedom, renounced all that the majority of their contemporaries believed made life worthwhile—home, family, wealth, and public reputation. So long as Christianity remained a persecuted movement, the majority of Christian preachers proclaimed the plain and powerful message of freedom that appealed to so many people within the Roman world—perhaps especially to those who had never experienced freedom in their everyday lives.

Finally, in the name of that freedom, as the Valentinians must have noted with irony, the orthodox suppressed gnostic teaching, and rejected their subtle reflections on the scope and limits of human choice. For as the churches, scattered throughout the world, became increasingly institutionalized, their leaders attempted to strengthen them against the pressures of persecution by joining them into a common doctrine and discipline. Irenaeus boasted that each group, however vulnerable on its own, belonged to a movement that was *universal,* or, in the Greek term, "catholic."[80] To the bishops, non-conformists and dissidents, even when they seemed to be sincere Christians intent on striking out on their own spiritual paths, were dangerous to the movement. The bishops may have been right; as Tertullian said, gnostic Christians agreed only to disagree. While certain groups demanded celibacy of all members, others may have encouraged people to decide these matters privately. Furthermore, some gnostics ridiculed those who died as martyrs, while others advocated martyrdom; a third group, like the Valentinians, urged people to accept martyrdom only if their sole alternative was to deny their faith in Christ. Equally divisive were the gnostic Christians who revered Eve, or the divine spirit they took her to represent, and accorded to their women members respect and participation increasingly denied to women in the institutionalized churches of the second and third centuries.[81]

Above all, their opponents charged that these dissident Christians challenged what the majority regarded as the fundamental theme of the Christian gospel: that human beings, created by God and endowed with moral freedom, received in baptism the power to live transformed lives, the power to overcome evil and death. Let us turn next to see how some of the boldest of these orthodox Christians actually put the "angelic life" into practice.

IV

THE "PARADISE OF VIRGINITY" REGAINED

FOR MANY CHRISTIANS of the first four centuries and ever since, the greatest freedom demanded the greatest renunciation—above all, celibacy. This identification of freedom with celibacy involved a paradox, then as now, for celibacy (to say nothing of fasting and other forms of renunciation) is an extreme form of self-restraint. Yet as Christians saw it, celibacy involved rejection of "the world" of ordinary society and its multitudinous entanglements and was thereby a way to gain control over one's own life.

Advocates of renunciation insisted that the solitary Christian could achieve freedom unknown even to the emperor; and Marcus Aurelius, that most reflective of emperors, might well have agreed. As a young man, he longed for the freedom to devote himself to philosophic study and contemplation, but he reluctantly assumed the burdens of his imperial destiny. He accepted a marriage, arranged by his family, in which nine of the twelve or thirteen children his wife bore him died in infancy or childhood; he assumed the major responsibility for political decisions and for judging legal cases and precedents; and he served as commander in chief of the armies through decades of war and rebellions that racked the empire from Egypt and Africa to the provinces of Gaul and Germany. At times when other men might expect a few hours of leisure, Marcus's imperial presence was required at the theater or sports arena, where his subjects ridiculed him for surreptitiously bringing documents to read during the performances. Although Marcus well understood the irony that made the "master of the world" the slave of all his constituents, he consciously strove to suppress any temptation to ignore his obligations, which he regarded as his sacred duty. As he wrote in his private journal:

> In what I do, I am to do it with reference to the service of mankind; in what befalls me, I am to accept it with reference to the gods. . . . My own nature is a rational and civic [or "political," Greek, πολιτικήν] one; I have a city, and I have a country; as Marcus I have Rome, and as a human being I have the universe; and, consequently, what benefits these communities is the only good for me.[1]

Marcus admonished himself:

> When it is hard to shake off sleep, remind yourself that to be going about the duties you owe society is to be obeying the laws of human nature and your own constitution. . . . As a unit yourself, you help to complete the social whole; similarly, therefore, your every action should help to complete the life of society.[2]

More than two hundred years later the Christian convert Augustine, then a brilliantly successful young orator, was walking through the streets of Milan one night, dreading the speech he had to give the following day in praise of the emperor. In the midst of these anxieties he noticed a drunken beggar. Why, Augustine asked himself, did this beggar seem so happy, when he himself was so miserable? Augustine later described his overwhelming relief when at last he gave up his career, his ambition, the woman who had lived with him and borne him a son, as well as his impending marriage to a wealthy heiress, for the freedom of celibacy and renunciation. His pagan contemporaries regarded such renunciation not only as social suicide but as the worst impiety and dishonor. But Augustine came to believe that it meant no more than "dying to the world"—destroying the false self, constructed according to worldly custom and tradition, in order to "raise his own life above the world."[3]

Ascetically inclined Christians even projected their idealized celibacy back into Paradise, as we shall see, and turned the story of the first marriage into a story of two virgins whose sin and consequent sexual awakening ended in their expulsion from the "Paradise of virginity" into marriage and all its attendant sufferings, from labor pains to social domination and death.[4]

The renowned teacher and bishop Gregory of Nyssa (c. 331–

395 C.E.) declared, "Marriage, then, is the last stage of our separation from the life that was led in Paradise; marriage therefore . . . is the first thing to be left behind; it is the first station, as it were, for our departure to Christ."[5]

Even today, an adolescent who takes time to think before plunging into ordinary adult society—into marriage, and the double obligations of family and career—may hesitate, for such obligations usually cost nothing less than one's life, the expense of virtually all one's energy attempting to fulfill obligations to family and society, especially if one also wants to be recognized and celebrated within one's community. It is in this sense that Christian renunciation, of which celibacy is the paradigm, offered freedom—freedom, in particular, from entanglement in Roman society.

In classical Greek and Roman society, a young man or woman who hesitated or refused to marry the person chosen by his or her family would be considered insubordinate or possibly even insane. Many parents expected their daughters to marry at about the age of puberty or soon after; in aristocratic circles, advantageous marriages sometimes were arranged when the children were as young as six or seven. Through marriage, as the historian Peter Brown says, "a girl was conscripted as a fully productive member by her society, as was her spouse."[6] Young men were expected to marry between the ages of seventeen and twenty-five and then to place themselves at the service of their communities, according to their family tradition and station.

Most Roman citizens would probably have agreed with Aristotle that "a human being is a political animal" (πολιτικήν ζώων), that the measure of one's worth was what one contributed to the "common good" or to the business of the state (πολίτευμα), as defined by men of influence and power. Thus was social and political recognition bestowed. Anyone who chose to withdraw and to go a solitary way risked extreme ostracism: in Greek, the term "idiot" literally referred to a person concerned solely with personal or private matters (ἴδιος, "one's own") instead of the public and social life of the larger community.

Jesus' message attacked such assumptions. "What profit is it for a man if he gains the whole world, but loses his own soul?" Jesus asks in Matthew.[7] Jesus himself, as we have seen, belonged to the tradition of Jewish people who for many centuries had lived as groups of outsiders, often noncitizens, within the pagan empires of the Persians, Babylonians, Egyptians, Greeks, and Romans. These outsiders apparently rejected the view that human value depends upon one's contribution to the state and originated instead the idea that developed much later in the West as the "absolute value of the individual." The idea that each individual has intrinsic, God-given value and is of infinite worth quite apart from any social contribution—an idea most pagans would have rejected as absurd—persists today as the ethical basis of western law and politics. Our secularized western idea of democratic society owes much to that early Christian vision of a new society—a society no longer formed by the natural bonds of family, tribe, or nation but by the voluntary choice of its members.[8] From the classical point of view, however, those Christians who "renounced the world"—who rejected family, tribe, and nation—effectively declared themselves "idiots."

Even apart from renunciation of the world, the strict ethical attitudes of Christians had enormously raised the stakes involved in sexual activity. The casual sexual behavior that many pagans took for granted—homosexual encounters among mentors and friends at the baths, or the sexual use of slaves and prostitutes—were rejected by most Christians, who simultaneously rejected homosexuality, contraception, abortion, and infanticide. For most Christians, therefore, sexual activity risked conception and so involved both partners, potentially, at least, in the economic and social obligations of family life. The example of Jesus and his followers encouraged them instead to take the subversive path *away* from such obligations—toward freedom.

A famous Egyptian Christian named Anthony chose such freedom, and generations of ascetically inclined Christians loved to tell his story. Anthony was the son of affluent Christian parents who lived in a small town in Egypt around the year 260. When Anthony was about eighteen, his parents died and left him responsible for a large household. He had to care for his young sister, supervise the slaves, and manage three hundred acres of fertile and beautiful farmland. Some six months after his parents' death, Anthony was pondering his future when in church one day he heard the words Jesus spoke to a rich young man: "Go, sell what you have, and give to the poor, and you shall have treasure in heaven; come and follow me."[9] Anthony's biographer tells us that he immediately left the church and gave to the villagers the property he had received as his inheritance, "so that he and his sister would not be encumbered with it."[10] He sold all their possessions, gave most of the money to the poor, and kept only a little in reserve to provide for his sister; soon afterward, he placed her in a home with some ascetic Christian women and left the village, "watching over himself and patiently disciplining himself."[11]

Instead of marrying and entering into the lifelong obligations of a wealthy landowner in his hometown, Anthony took Jesus' words as permission—indeed, as encouragement—to shrug off these onerous responsibilities. Intense, solitary, and self-involved, Anthony was not seeking an easy escape from difficulty. Instead, he abruptly abandoned a traditional and respectable life to make his own way to self-discovery—and the discovery of God. Anthony devoted himself to *ascesis*—which literally means "exercise"—in order to "attend to his soul,"[12] but first he had to battle a residual desire for human company and approval. His biographer tells us that at first the devil tormented Anthony with "memories of his property; anxiety for his sister; intimacy with his relatives; desire for money and for power; and the manifold enjoyment of food and the other pleasures of life," and finally with vivid sexual fantasies.[13]

What Anthony wanted to learn was what human life was or could be apart from ordinary social expectations. He did not reject all human society but sought out the society of an aristocracy quite different from the local Egyptian landholders—experts, or so he believed, in the practice of divine wisdom. Though he rejected family, marriage, and kinship, he willingly subjected himself to those whose self-mastery he admired, and sought to become one of them: "he noticed the courtesy of one; another's constancy in prayer; one's humility; another's kindness," and, above all, "their devotion to Christ, and their love for one another."[14]

Anthony was to become famous among Christians as a spiritual pioneer, one who set out to discover what happens beyond the boundaries of civilization when one ventures alone into the harsh desert. Anthony—and others like him—sought the shape of his own soul, hoping to accept the terrors and ecstasies of direct and unremitting encounters with himself and, having mastered himself, to discover his relationship to the Infinite God.

The number of those who chose such *ascesis,* or spiritual "exercise," was not large, compared with the number of believers who increasingly crowded the churches in the third century, but their role is significant; for these hermits lived out the ideal of which many other Christians only dreamed. The classical scholar Ramsay MacMullen estimates that during the century following Constantine's conversion the number of Christians grew from about five million to thirty million,[15] while the monks in Egypt came to number about thirty thousand.[16] These ascetics were called what Mother Teresa in Calcutta still calls them, "athletes" for God, and were revered as many people today revere certain athletes, men and women who discipline themselves to achieve what their thousands of admirers only dream of doing. Anthony and other ascetics spoke of their struggle for self-control in athletic terms, as an attempt to control the body and mind and to maintain both in seemingly effortless mastery. Many Christians who engaged in their own limited ascetic practices on certain days, and many more who may never have made the effort to control their diet and to strengthen themselves as "athletes" did, nevertheless, admire those who achieved such discipline.

Gregory of Nyssa, a married Christian from a wealthy family in Asia Minor, wrote with passionate regret that he wished he had dared "raise his own life above the world,"[17] to live for himself and for God alone, despite the expectations of family and friends and the pressures of social and political obligations. For, as he wrote, no doubt from his own experience,

> he whose life is contained in himself either escapes [sufferings] altogether, or can bear them easily, having a collected mind which is not distracted from itself; while he who shares himself with wife and child often has not a moment to give even to regretting his own condition, because anxiety for those he loves fills his heart.[18]

Gregory also understood how people suffer through their natural desire for children:

> There is pain always, whether children are born, or can never be expected; whether they live or die. One person has many children, but not enough means to support them; another feels the lack of an heir to the great fortune he has worked for. . . . one man loses by death a beloved son; another has a reprobate son alive; both equally pitiable, although one mourns over the death, the other over the life, of his son. Nor will I do more than mention how sadly and disastrously family jealousies and arguments, arising from real or imagined causes, end.[19]

Gregory describes how people pursue wealth, distinctions, public office, and power over others, making themselves "slaves of futility," all chasing illusions. But one who chooses to liberate himself from the chains of ordinary life "in a sense exiles himself entirely from human life by abstaining from marriage."[20] As a man bound by his multiple obligations, Gregory writes longingly of the freedom to be antisocial, to choose, as more valuable than anything else, his own, single life before God. Many people then—and many now, no doubt—may have considered the desire for the ascetic life to be selfish. But Gregory saw in that life the potential for becoming what God originally intended human beings to be: beings made "in God's image," radiant with his love and light; "the work and the excellence [of monks] is to contemplate the Father of all purity, and to beautify the lineaments of their own characters from the Source of all beauty."[21]

Gregory adds, "Let no one think that, in saying this, we deprecate marriage. We are well aware that it is not a stranger to God's blessing"; but, he continues, urging people to marry is entirely unnecessary, since "the common instincts of humanity plead sufficiently on its behalf," while virginity "thwarts these natural impulses."[22] Thus Christians repudiated what Marcus Aurelius regarded as the highest virtue, for, as we have seen, Marcus saw his religious destiny given in his familial, social, and political situation, and in the duties his imperial role placed upon him. Stoic philosophy encouraged him to embrace and even to love his fate, submit to its demands, and patiently endure its frustrations, whereas Christians sought the opposite—to free themselves from the bonds of tradition and custom, from what pious pagans called destiny.

An anonymous Christian, probably a near contemporary of the emperor Marcus, wrote a fictionalized biography of Clement, an aristocratic Roman convert who denied that destiny ruled his life, who rejected his family's demands and expectations, and who repudiated paganism, along with his own Greek education, to devote himself to God's truth alone. But like everyone else who had chosen that path, Clement found that the obstacles—the physical and emotional instincts that clamored for gratification—were within himself. Only those who dared deny these interior as well as exterior demands could claim chastity as their way to freedom.

For Clement, the "good news" of Christianity meant autonomy: that a Christian could actually defy destiny by mastering bodily impulses. Forces conjured by such names as Aphrodite and Eros, who overpowered their multiple human lovers, must now yield themselves, like beasts before a lion tamer, to the rational will. As Clement saw it, ascetic Christians were no longer at the mercy of uncontrollable forces—neither the powers of destiny, or fate, that Stoics revered, nor the passions that arose from within. Christian conversion promised an enormous gain in self-control for those "athletes" of asceticism.[23]

Clement knew, of course, that self-control was the practical gospel of Platonic and Stoic philosophers. But Plato considered self-control the rarest of all accomplishments, attained by Socrates alone, whereas Christians announced that this virtue was within reach of every convert, although not every convert could achieve perfect celibacy. The Christian teacher Origen called the teaching of pagan philosophers fine meals prepared for sophisticated palates, but "we [Christians] cook for the masses." Yet while Christian teachers popularized such philosophic attitudes, they also threw out much of what these philosophers taught.

Methodius, a celibate Asian Christian who served Christian churches in Asia and Greece as bishop and died a martyr (c. 260), wrote a famous polemic against the "great lie" of Greek philosophy and education—namely, the conviction that destiny, fate, and necessity are actual, external forces in the universe that control human affairs, and that sexual desire, like destiny, is beyond human control.

Methodius's polemic was a deliberate parody of Plato's *Symposium,* in which Plato praised the power of Eros—sexual desire—as one of the great cosmic forces. As Methodius saw it, Plato's *Symposium* epitomized false philosophic education. Where Plato showed in his *Symposium* a group of men fighting hangovers from the night before by praising the glories of erotic—and especially homoerotic—love, Methodius presents his *anti*-erotic *Symposium of the Ten Virgins* through the dramatis personae of ten women ascetics who compete with one another in praising virginity! Thecla, that famous ascetic, is the star debater, whose speech in praise of virginity wins the laurel crown.

The first speaker in Methodius's dialogue, Marcella, describes the whole course of human history as a progression toward freedom. Although marriage and procreation were necessary "in the beginning" to multiply the human race, they now represent only a crude and archaic relic of human origins, a kind of dinosaur age preceding the evolution of the true human being, the celibate.[24]

But the second speaker, Theophila, objects to Marcella and articulates instead the viewpoint of the many Christians who favor marriage and procreation and claim for both God's blessings. In the beginning, Theophila says, the Creator made man and woman; but "at the present time . . . humanity must cooperate in forming the image of God, so long as the world exists . . . for it is said, 'Increase and multiply' (Genesis 1:28)."[25] Theophila chides those who reject marriage: "We must not be offended at the ordinance of the Creator from which, indeed, we ourselves have our existence."

When Theophila finishes, Thaelia replies: If Christians were meant to take Genesis literally, Paul would not have spoken of Adam's union with Eve as a "great mystery" which signifies "Christ and the Church" (Ephesians 5:32). Without accusing Theophila directly, she charges that

> people who are undisciplined because of the uncontrolled impulses of sensuality in them dare to force the Scriptures beyond their true meaning, and so twist the sayings "Increase and multiply" [Genesis 1:28] and "Therefore a man shall leave his father and mother" [Genesis 2:24] into a defense of their own incontinence. . . .

As Thaelia sees it, such Christians use these passages to gratify themselves sexually, while pretending that their concern is with procreation. She admits that Paul did not *require* celibacy, but says he certainly preferred it for any who were capable of achieving this "means of restoring humanity to Paradise."[26]

Finally Thecla is introduced by her sister in virginity Arete (whose name in Greek means "virtue") as one "who yields to none in universal philosophy, having been taught by Paul in evangelical and apostolical doctrines."[27] Thecla sides with Thaelia and goes on to denounce the great lie of philosophical education: "The greatest of all evils is to say that this life is governed by inevitable necessities of fate."[28] Thecla herself stands as living evidence against those who say that one must "accept one's destiny"—whether that destiny arises from one's anatomy, or from the familial and social circumstances of one's birth. In praising human freedom, Thecla declares that only those who live in chastity actually achieve mastery of themselves and of their destinies. She addresses her sisters as women warriors who "struggle and wrestle, according to our teacher Paul. For she who has overcome the devil, having undergone the seven great struggles of chastity, comes to possess seven crowns." Whoever wins this battle receives "a masculine . . . and voluntary mind, one free from necessity, in order to choose, like masters, the things which please us, not being enslaved to fate nor fortune."[29]

Arete judges that Thecla's is the best speech in praise of virginity and awards her the crown for her defense of virginity as freedom. Thecla then stands in the place of honor and leads the others in a hymn to welcome Christ, their heavenly bridegroom; her sisters respond, in chorus, "I keep myself pure for Thee, O Bridegroom; and holding a lighted torch, I go to meet thee."[30]

This fanciful dialogue of virgins nevertheless reflects the actual activities of Christian women dedicated to asceticism who gathered throughout Asia Minor, as this group did, in households and gardens provided by wealthy members, to devote themselves to spiritual disciplines and to prayer. Because such women often did reject what their pagan neighbors and relatives regarded as their destiny and their fortune, Methodius believed they exemplified what Christian life really meant—the realization of human freedom.

For women, as several women historians recently have demonstrated, celibacy sometimes offered immediate rewards on earth, as well as eventual rewards in heaven. We have seen how Thecla's own story celebrated a young woman's achievement of autonomy as a "holy woman," an ascetic, evangelist, and healer; during the third and fourth centuries, an increasing number of Christian women resolved to follow her example and become "new Theclas."[31]

One of these was Melania the Younger, heiress to an enormous fortune from her noble Roman family. According to her biographer, Melania "had from her earliest youth yearned for Christ, and longed for bodily chastity." Her parents, however, "very forcibly united her in marriage with her blessed husband, Pinian, who was from a consular family, when she was fourteen years old and her spouse was about seventeen."[32] Melania first pleaded with Pinian to live with her in celibate marriage and then offered to give him all her wealth and property if he would agree to "leave [her] body free." But Pinian insisted that they first have two children to ensure the family succession; after that, "both of us together shall renounce the world."[33] First they had a daughter, whom they vowed to virginity; then, a son, who died in infancy. It grieved Pinian to see Melania "exceedingly troubled, and . . . giving up on life,"[34] and he hastily promised her that they would spend the rest of their lives in chastity. Not long afterward, when their young daughter also died, Pinian and Melania, after six years of marriage, when she was twenty and he was twenty-four, put on the rough clothes of peasants, gave up their ordinary social obligations, and fulfilled Christ's commands. They offered hospitality to strangers, gave money to the poor and destitute, visited the prisons and the mines to inquire which prisoners were held there for debt, and provided money for their release.

It was rumored that Melania and Pinian were now ready to go

further—in Jesus' words, to "sell all that you have, and give to the poor" (Matthew 19:21). At this, the slaves on their Roman estate rebelled, for they did not want to be sold, probably separately, on the open slave market, but preferred to be sold together to Pinian's brother. Melania's biographer says that she and Pinian suspected the brother of inciting the uprising because "he wanted to take all their property for himself; and in fact all their relatives schemed for their possessions, wanting to make themselves richer from them."[35] Pinian's father, they suspected, intended to give their possessions to his other children.

Although Melania and Pinian wanted to "renounce the world," they were intensely concerned to protect their rights to dispose of their riches themselves for the religious purposes they chose. Melania went to Serena, mother-in-law of the emperor Honorius, to ask for protection against their relatives' greed. Soon afterward, the emperor Honorius decreed that their possessions should be sold by government agents, and that the proceeds should go to Melania and Pinian. Thus, the young couple left Rome for the Holy Land with great anticipation: "they looked forward to scattering on the earth what they believed could store up pure treasures in heaven."[36] When they traveled to Africa, Augustine and his fellow bishops persuaded them to found and endow monasteries there. Later they visited the monks in Egypt and Jerusalem, where Melania constructed a monastery for ninety women. She lived there austerely, giving shelter to former prostitutes, studying the Scriptures and the church fathers, and struggling to establish her monastic community. She chose another woman to direct the monastery while she herself tended to the physical needs of her sisters, especially those who were sick. When Pinian died, Melania settled on the Mount of Olives in a tiny cell, where she prayed and meditated. There she constructed a chapel, a shrine to the martyrs, and another monastery for men in honor of her late husband.

Melania and Pinian, like many others before and since, saw renunciation as a higher alternative to family obligations—obligations all the heavier because they were, in worldly terms, so privileged. As the historian Elizabeth Clark so ably has shown, "renouncing the world" sometimes brought wealthy and aristocratic women like Melania practical benefits often denied to them in secular society. They could retain control of their own wealth, travel freely throughout the world as "holy pilgrims," devote themselves to intellectual and spiritual pursuits, and found institutions which they could personally direct.[37]

Virtually all Christians agreed that ascetics, especially celibates, were closer to the kingdom than married people; for hadn't Jesus praised those who "made themselves eunuchs for the sake of the kingdom of heaven" (Matthew 19:12) and called them "equal to angels" (Luke 20:36); and hadn't Paul described the celibate's dedication to Christ as a kind of spiritual marriage (1 Corinthians 6:17)? Enthusiasm for the ascetic life had spread quickly in Syria and in Asia Minor, the source of such radical Christian literature as the *Acts of Paul and Thecla;* and also in Egypt, where stories of Anthony and others attracted thousands of young Christians eager to test their strength in the wild and solitary deserts.

But not everyone accepted asceticism as a superior virtue. In Rome, when Melania and Pinian "renounced the world" (c. 390), the ascetic movement was explosively controversial, especially in rich and aristocratic circles. Even Christian parents like Melania's father protested when their children succumbed to the preaching of such enthusiasts of asceticism as Jerome, then secretary to Damasus, bishop of Rome. In his youth Jerome had lived with the hermits in the Syrian desert; and even after he had returned to civilized life, he loved to think of himself as an expert on asceticism. Later, he looked back on his experiences living in a cave and recalled

> how often, when I was living in the desolate, lonely desert, parched by the burning sun, how often I imagined myself among the pleasures of Rome! I used to sit alone, because my heart was filled with bitterness; my limbs stuck inside an ugly sackcloth, my skin black as an Ethiopian's. . . . Day after day I cried and sighed, and when, against my will, I fell asleep, my bare bones clashed against the ground. I say nothing about my eating and drinking. Even when sick, solitaries drink only cold water, and a cooked meal is considered excessive. And yet he who, in fear of hell, had banished himself to this prison, found himself again and again surrounded by dancing girls! My face grew pale with hunger, yet in my cold body the passions of my inner being continued to glow. This human being was more dead than alive; only his burning lust continued to boil.[38]

After two years, Jerome left the desert for Antioch, and later he went to Constantinople and Rome. It was there that the former monk became papal secretary and later spokesman for Damasus, the first pope to live with the princely panoply of ceremonial that has characterized the Vatican in post-Constantinian times.

Yet as the Christian movement gained in numbers and influence during the third and fourth centuries and finally became not only legal but imperially patronized, the situation of Christian bishops changed radically. No longer targets of arrest, torture, and execution, now they received tax exemptions, donations in gold, great prestige, and, in some cases, even influence at the imperial court. Now that becoming a Christian was no longer the heroic choice it had been for Christians like Perpetua, some of the most intense believers in the age of Constantine longed for the ascetic life as proof of devotion, a kind of self-inflicted martyrdom. As we have seen, many regarded ascetic Christians as celebrities, living examples of "God's athletes."

Moving among the most powerful Christians in Rome, Jerome adopted the role of spiritual advisor and devoted himself especially to a circle of aristocratic women, including Paula, a widow of enormous wealth. To her daughter Eustochium, Jerome wrote one of his most famous letters, urging her to embrace Christ alone:

> Always allow the privacy of your own room to protect you: always let the Bridegroom play with you within. Do you pray? You speak to the Bridegroom. Do you read? He speaks to you. When sleep overtakes you, he will come from behind and put his hand through the hole of the door, and your heart shall be moved for him.[39]

Jerome encouraged Eustochium to acknowledge her superiority, as virgin, over all married women, including her own married sister, Blaesilla: "Learn from me a holy arrogance: know that you are better than they are!"[40]

But the twenty-year-old Blaesilla, some months after her wedding, suddenly found herself a widow and, in her grief, ripe for religious conversion. For thirty days she suffered a high fever, and yet she obeyed Jerome's program of radical austerity. She slept on the ground, refused food, and devoted herself to penitential prayer. Her friends and relatives, shocked by the change in her, criticized or ridiculed her extreme practices—and her teacher. When she wasted away and died two months later, many people were openly bitter. Jerome reproached Paula in these words:

> When you were carried fainting out of the funeral procession, whispers such as these were audible in the crowd: "Isn't this what

we often have said? She weeps for her daughter, killed by fasting. She wanted her to marry again so that she might have grandchildren. How long must we refrain from driving these detestable monks out of Rome? Why don't we stone them or throw them into the Tiber river? They have misled this wretched lady; it is clear that she is not a nun by choice."[41]

But Jerome's critics vehemently blamed him for Blaesilla's death. His reputation as spiritual director was badly shaken. Still worse, his patron, Pope Damasus, had died several weeks before. Jerome hastily left Rome for the Holy Land, where Blaesilla's mother and sister, still devoted to their mentor, later joined him.

About five years later, a friend traveling from Rome brought to Jerome's monastic cell in Bethlehem a copy of a writing that challenged the supremacy of asceticism over married life. Its author, Jovinian, himself a celibate Christian monk, argued that celibacy in itself is no holier than marriage and accused certain fanatical Christians of having invented—and then having attributed to Jesus and Paul—this "novel dogma against nature."[42]

Jerome saw Jovinian as a serious threat and set out "to crush with evangelical and apostolical vigor the Epicurus of Christianity."[43] Yet Jerome also knew that Jovinian had once shared his enthusiasm for the ascetic movement. Barefoot and unshaven, Jovinian had dressed in a rough coat and grimy tunic, refused to eat meat or drink wine, and strictly avoided any contact with women. But after some years of these austerities, Jovinian underwent a change of heart and questioned whether they were spiritually beneficial. Although he remained sexually abstinent, he soon challenged certain premises of Christian asceticism on religious, and specifically on scriptural, grounds. Jerome tells us that Jovinian began from the "primary commands of God" concerning procreation (Genesis 1:28) and marriage (Genesis 2:24), and then, lest anyone object that these occur only in the Old Testament, Jovinian

> answers that it has been confirmed by the Lord in the gospel; "What God has joined together, let no one put asunder," and he adds immediately, "Be fruitful and multiply, and fill the earth" (Matthew 19:6; Genesis 1:28).[44]

Thus Jovinian rejected the common belief that celibate persons are holier than those who marry and declared that "virgins, widows, and married women, who have once gone through Christian baptism, if they are equal in other respects, are of equal merit."[45] Furthermore, abstinence from food or meat or wine does not make a person holier than one who enjoys them with gratitude toward their Creator. Jovinian concluded that all Christians who remain faithful to their baptismal vows can expect the same heavenly reward: heaven is not arranged in first-class, second-class, and third-class compartments, according to the degree of renunciation one has practiced in this life.

Such proposals brought upon their author a storm of abuse. Led by three future saints of the church—Jerome, Ambrose, and their younger contemporary Augustine—Pope Siricius, bishop of Rome, condemned what he called Jovinian's *scriptura horrifica* and, to protect innocent believers from what he called this "dangerous heresy," excommunicated him.

Jovinian vigorously protested his excommunication and wrote commentaries to prove that the Scriptures were on his side. Besides referring to God's original blessing on procreation and marriage, Jovinian named all the biblical figures, from the patriarchs to the apostles, who married and had children, and he added that Jesus joined in celebrating the marriage at Cana, where he turned water into wine.

When he turned to Paul to defend marriage, Jovinian, like Clement, two centuries before, found in the deutero-Pauline letters the support he needed:

> listen to the words of Paul: "I desire, therefore, that younger widows marry and bear children" [1 Timothy 5:14], and "marriage is honorable unto all, and the marriage bed undefiled" [Hebrews 13:4].[46]

When Jovinian *did* refer to Paul's authentic letters, he instinctively followed selective techniques of exegesis that certain Protestants later perfected. He ignored those passages that express Paul's religious preferences for celibacy (including much of 1 Corinthians 7), and seized instead upon those in which Paul offered merely pragmatic reasons for sexual abstinence, such as the statement that "concerning virgins I have no command from the Lord, but I give my opinions. . . . I think that it is good, 'because of the present distress,' for a person to remain as he is" (1 Corinthians 7:25–26). "Here," Jerome said, "our opponent goes utterly wild with excitement: This is his strongest battering ram with which he shakes the walls of virginity."[47]

According to Jovinian, where Paul *did* advise celibacy, he recommended it only on practical grounds, not moral ones. Jovinian himself endorsed and lived by such advice. He maintained his own celibacy, but warned others who made the same choice, "Do not be proud; you and your married sisters are equally members of the same church."[48]

When Jerome read Jovinian's treatise, he said, he heard "the hissing of the old serpent; by counsel such as this, the dragon drove man from Paradise."[49] What bothered Jerome especially was that Jovinian, despite his excommunication, was supported by some of the leading Christians of Rome—the same Christians for whom Jerome, the champion of asceticism, was now *persona non grata.* Jerome acknowledged that even though everyone praised celibacy, not everyone took it seriously, even as a qualification for the priesthood:

> That married men are elected to the priesthood, I do not deny; the number of virgins is not so great as that of the priests that are needed. Does it follow that because all the strongest men are chosen for the army, weaker ones should not be taken as well? ... How is it, then, you will say, that frequently, when priests are ordained, a virgin is passed over, and a married man taken? Perhaps because he lacks other qualities in keeping with virginity.[50]

Jerome adds that many factors flaw elections:

> Sometimes the judgment of the commoner people is at fault; ... often it happens that married people, who form the larger portion of the people, in approving married candidates, in effect approve themselves; and it does not occur to them that the mere fact that they prefer a married person to a virgin proves their inferiority to virgins.

Jerome dared point out that even bishops

> choose from the ranks of the clergy not the best, but the cleverest, men ... or, as though they were handing out positions in an earthly service, they give them to their kinsmen or relatives; or they listen to the dictates of money. And, worse than all, they promote the clergy who smear them with flattery.[51]

When Jerome set out to refute Jovinian, he went through many of the scriptural passages cited by Jovinian and claimed that they supported opposite conclusions. Jerome was famous—and still is—for his knowledge of the Scriptures, and he undoubtedly knew that Genesis 2 describes the institution of marriage *before* the fall; but he tendentiously switched the order of verses in order to make it appear that marriage *followed* sin, and so fell under God's curse:

> As for Adam and Eve, we must maintain that before the fall they were virgins in Paradise; but after they sinned, and were cast out of Paradise, they were immediately married. *Then* we have the passage, "For this cause a man shall leave his father and mother, and cleave to his wife, and they shall become one flesh."[52]

Jerome declares that Jesus himself remained "a virgin in the flesh and a monogamist in the spirit," faithful to his only bride, the church, and adds that "although I know that crowds of matrons will be furious at me, . . . I will say what the apostle [Paul] has taught me. . . . indeed in view of the purity of the body of Christ, all sexual intercourse is unclean."[53] In such passages Jerome expresses a loathing for the flesh, the revulsion of a man ashamed of his own past sexual conduct, as he himself admitted. Other advocates of celibacy, however, from Clement to such married Christians as Tertullian in his early years[54] and Gregory of Nyssa, express no such revulsion. Indeed, much of the evidence we have surveyed suggests that loathing for the flesh was not, as some have tried to argue, the basis for advocating celibacy, although, in cases like Jerome's, such responses no doubt intensified the inclination toward celibacy.

Then Jerome finally turns to Paul:

> I will therefore do battle with the whole army of enemies. In the front rank I will set up the apostle Paul, and, since he is the bravest of generals, I will arm him with his own weapons, that is, with his own statements.[55]

Jovinian had invoked the deutero-Pauline letters, but Jerome draws primarily from what scholars regard as Paul's genuine letters, and emphasizes 1 Corinthians 7, infusing Paul's words with vehement hyperbole:

> If "it is good for a man not to touch a woman," it is bad to touch one. . . . [Paul allows marriage only] "because of fornication," as if one were to say, "it is good to eat the finest wheat flower," and yet to prevent a starving man from devouring excrement, I may allow him to also eat barley. . . . the reason why he says "it is better to marry" is that it is worse to burn. . . . It is as though he said, "it is better to have one eye than to be totally blind; it is better to stand on one foot and support the body with a cane than to crawl upon broken legs."[56]

Finally, Jerome accused Jovinian of secret and uncontrollable lust, and simultaneously ridiculed his fellow monk for remaining irreproachably celibate: "to prove that virginity and marriage are equal, he himself should marry; or, if he does not marry, it is useless for him to bandy words with us, when his acts are on our side."[57] That many prominent Roman Christians welcomed Jovinian's teachings proved no more than that Jovinian was pandering to a popular audience of self-indulgent Christians by giving them "scriptural authority to console their incontinence." Jerome, foreshadowing the Puritanism of a later time, caricatured Jovinian as

> our modern Epicurus, wantoning in his garden with his favorites of both sexes. Whenever I see a dandy, or a man who is no stranger to a hairdresser, with his hair nicely done and his cheeks all aglow, he belongs to your herd, or, rather, grunts in concert with your swine. To our flock belong the sad, the pale, the poorly dressed. . . . You have in your army . . . the full-bellied, the well-dressed, the luxurious . . . who defend you tooth and nail. Aristocrats make way for you; the wealthy print kisses on your face.[58]

When Jerome's books *Against Jovinian* arrived in Rome, they set off an uproar. Even those who agreed that virginity surpassed marriage were embarrassed by Jerome's vehemence. Jerome's influential friend Pammachius tried to withdraw his books from consideration but failed, for they were too sensational to suppress. Jerome, writing to thank Pammachius for his efforts, admitted that he never imagined that

> those on my own side would lay traps for me. I praise virginity to the skies, not because I myself possess it, but because, not possessing it, I admire it all the more.

His quarrel with Jovinian concerned one basic issue:

> He puts marriage on a level with virginity, while I make it inferior; he declares that there is little or no difference between the two states; I claim that there is a great deal. Finally . . . he has dared to place marriage on an equal level with perpetual chastity.[59]

To many twentieth-century readers, Jovinian's argument may sound like mere common sense against Jerome's fanaticism. Yet such Christian leaders and future saints as Siricius, bishop of Rome, Ambrose, bishop of Milan, Jerome himself, and Augustine condemned

Jovinian and placed his name on their growing list of heretics. Most Christians—all but the most radical, who rejected marriage altogether—acknowledged that Christians who honorably fulfilled their marital vows thereby pleased God; even Paul urged those who could not refrain from marriage to marry "in the Lord." But to claim that marriage is as meritorious as repudiating marriage "for the sake of the kingdom of heaven" implied Christian sanction for traditional pagan values, as if honoring family and social obligations—the ancient pagan ethical ideal in Christian dress—were morally equivalent to renunciation. Those Christians who proclaimed freedom from social and political entanglements defied those who valued human life according to its social contribution, and in the process, as we have seen, envisioned a new society based on free and voluntary choice. The majority of Christians married but continued nonetheless to assert the primacy of renunciation. In their resistance to conventional definitions of human worth based upon social contribution, I suggest, we can see the source of the later western idea of the absolute value of the individual—the value of every human being, including the destitute, the sick, and the newborn—quite apart from any contribution, real or potential, to the "common good."[60]

Those who actually chose renunciation often found, no doubt, the freedom they sought: we have seen how women who "renounced the world"—whether wealthy and aristocratic, like Melania, or women without means, like Thecla—thereby claimed the opportunity to travel, to devote themselves to intellectual and spiritual pursuits, to found institutions, and to direct them.

Yet the men who wrote most of the literature in praise of virginity undoubtedly also found, in chastity and renunciation, the rewards of liberty they sought—freedom from the oppressive weight of imperial rule, of custom, tradition, "destiny," or fate, and from the internal tyranny of the passions. The appeal of that ascetic life is by no means confined to the past: the twentieth-century writer Thomas Merton, who, following his conversion, entered a Cistercian monastery, no doubt was speaking of his own resolve as well as that of the early desert fathers when he said:

> What the fathers sought most of all was their own true self, in Christ. And in order to do this, they had to reject completely the false, formal self, fabricated under social compulsion "in the world."[61]

For the fourth-century theologian Augustine, who was to become the greatest teacher of the future Christian church, the climax of his conversion was his decision, inspired by the story of Anthony, to give up a Christian marriage that would have ensured him wealth and social status, along with a brilliantly promising career, to embrace the ascetic life. Augustine would eventually transform traditional Christian teaching on freedom, on sexuality, and on sin and redemption for all future generations of Christians. Where earlier generations of Jews and Christians had once found in Genesis 1–3 the affirmation of human freedom to choose good or evil, Augustine, living after the age of Constantine, found in the same text a story of human bondage. Yet as Augustine grew older, he argued that even the most saintly ascetic was not, in himself, capable of self-mastery; that all humankind was fallen; and that the human will was incorrigibly corrupt. This cataclysmic transformation in Christian thought from an ideology of moral freedom to one of universal corruption coincided, as we shall presently see, with the evolution of the Christian movement from a persecuted sect to the religion of the emperor himself.

V

THE POLITICS OF
PARADISE

RE HUMAN BEINGS CAPABLE OF governing themselves?
Defiant Christians hounded as criminals by the Roman government emphatically answered *yes*. But in the fourth and fifth
centuries, after the emperors themselves became patrons of Christianity, the majority of Christians gradually came to say *no*. Early
Christian spokesmen, like Jews before them and the American colo-
nists long after, had claimed to find in the biblical creation account
divine sanction for declaring their independence from governments
they considered corrupt and arbitrary. The Hebrew creation account
of Genesis 1, unlike its Babylonian counterpart, claims that God gave
the power of earthly rule to *adam*—not to the king or emperor but
simply to "mankind" (and some even thought this might include
women).[1] Most Christian apologists in the first three centuries would
have agreed with Gregory of Nyssa, who followed rabbinic tradition
by explaining that after God created the world "as a royal dwelling
place for the future king,"[2] he made humanity "as a being fit to
exercise royal rule" by creating it "the living image of the universal
King."[3] Consequently, Gregory concludes, "the soul immediately
shows its royal and exalted character, far removed as it is from the
lowliness of private station, in that it owns no master, and is self-
governed, ruled autocratically by its own will."[4] Besides dominion
over the earth and animals, this gift of sovereignty conveys the
quality of moral freedom:

> Preeminent among all is the fact that we are free from any neces-
> sity, and not in bondage to any power, but have decision in our
> own power as we please; for virtue is a voluntary thing, subject

to no dominion. Whatever is the result of compulsion and force cannot be virtue.[5]

Many Christian converts of the first three centuries—centuries in which civil authorities treated the church as a subversive sect—regarded the proclamation of αὐτεξουσία—the moral freedom to rule oneself—as virtually synonymous with "the gospel."

Yet with Augustine, in the late fourth and early fifth centuries, this message changed. The work of his later years, in which he radically broke with many of his predecessors, and even with his own earlier convictions, effectively transformed much of the teaching of the Christian faith. Instead of the freedom of the will and humanity's original royal dignity, Augustine emphasizes humanity's enslavement to sin. Humanity is sick, suffering, and helpless, irreparably damaged by the fall,[6] for that "original sin," Augustine insists, involved nothing else than Adam's prideful attempt to establish his own autonomous self-government.[7] Astonishingly, Augustine's radical views prevailed, eclipsing for future generations of western Christians the consensus of more than three centuries of Christian tradition.

As he matured, Augustine repudiated the Manichaean version of Christian doctrine he had embraced as an enthusiastic young seeker, a doctrine that categorically denied the goodness of creation and the freedom of the will. Augustine, the chastened convert, now claimed to accept Catholic orthodoxy, and affirmed both. But, as he grasped for ways to understand his own tumultuous experience, Augustine concluded that the qualities of that original state of creation no longer applied—at least not directly—to human experience in the present. Humanity, once given the unflawed glory of creation and the freedom of the will, actually enjoyed these only in those brief primordial moments in Paradise. Ever since the fall, they have been apprehended only in moments of inspired imagination, and even then but partially. For all practical purposes they are wholly lost.

Given the intense inner conflicts involving his passionate nature and the struggle to control sexual impulses he reveals in his *Confessions,* Augustine's decision to abandon his predecessors' emphasis on free will need not surprise us. Much more surprising, in fact, is the result. Why did the majority of Latin Christians, instead of repudiating Augustine's idiosyncratic views as marginal—or rejecting them as heretical—eventually embrace them? Why did his teaching on "original sin" become the center of western Christian tradition, displacing, or at least wholly recasting, all previous views of creation and free will?

The political and social situation of Christians in the early centuries had changed radically by Augustine's time. Traditional declarations of human freedom, forged by martyrs defying the emperor as anti-Christ incarnate, no longer fit the situation of Christians who now found themselves, under Constantine and his Christian successors, the emperor's "brothers and sisters in Christ." But Augustine's theory conformed to this new situation and interpreted the new arrangement of state, church, and believer in ways that, many agreed, made religious sense of the new political realities.

Both Augustine and his Christian opponents recognized the political dimensions of the controversy, yet none of them discussed government in what we would consider strictly political terms. Instead, since everyone agreed that the story of Adam and Eve offered a basic paradigm for ordering human society, argument over the role of government most often took the form of conflicting interpretations of that story. Let us consider, then, how Augustine and his predecessors—taking as their representative John Chrysostom—read, in opposite ways, the politics of Paradise.

Both John Chrysostom and Augustine, born around the year 354,[8] had grown up in an empire nominally Christian. During the forty years since Constantine's conversion to Christianity in 313, Christian emperors not only had reversed the orders of persecution but had poured magnanimous benefits upon the Christian churches. John was a young priest in Antioch when a public riot against the emperor's taxation policies had broken out, and angry crowds had smashed the statues of the emperor and his family. Rumors of the emperor's rage and his planned retribution preceded his return to Antioch. Yet John, so famous for his riveting speeches that he was later nicknamed *chrysostom,* "golden mouth," in this time of public crisis boldly declared to the crowds that the right of government belongs not to the emperor alone but to the human race as a whole: "In the beginning, God honored our race with sovereignty." For, John asked rhetorically, what else does it mean that God made us "in his image"? "The image of government [νῆς ἀρχῆς] is what is meant; and as there is no one in the heavens superior to God, so there is no one on earth superior to humankind."[9]

John's listeners, concerned with the immediate political crisis, might have wondered at first what he meant in specific political terms. Would the priest go on to say that the emperor embodied *in himself* the sovereignty God bestowed upon Adam? Did the emperor now represent God's rule to the rest of humankind, as some Christians previously had argued? John answered no to such questions. Instead he agreed with Gregory of Nyssa, who declared that since "any particular man is limited . . . the entire plentitude of humanity was included" in God's good gift of his own royal image:

> For the image is not in part of our nature, *nor is the divine gift in any single person . . . but this power extends equally to the whole race;* and a sign of this is that the mind is implanted alike in all; for all have the power of understanding and reflecting. . . . *they equally bear within themselves the divine image.* [10]

John wrote:

> For of governments, some are natural [φυσικαί], and others artificial [χειροτονηταί]: natural, such as the rule of the lion over the quadrupeds, or the eagle over the birds; artificial, as of an emperor over us; for he does not reign over his fellow slaves by any natural authority. Therefore it happens that emperors often lose their sovereignty. [11]

As John saw it, imperial rule epitomizes the social consequences of sin. Like his persecuted Christian predecessors, John ridiculed imperial propaganda that claimed that the state rests upon concord, justice, and liberty. On the contrary, he said, the state relies upon force and compulsion, often using these to violate justice and to suppress liberty. But because the majority of humankind followed Adam's example in sinning, government, however corrupt, has become indispensable and, for this reason, even divinely endorsed:

> [God] himself has armed magistrates with power. . . . God provides for our safety through them. . . . If you were to abolish the public court system, you would abolish all order from our life. . . . If you deprive the city of its rulers, we would have to live a life less rational than that of the animals, biting and devouring one another. . . . For what crossbeams are in houses, rulers are in cities, and just as, if you were to take away the former, the walls, being separated, would fall in upon one another, so, if you were to deprive the world of magistrates and the fear that comes from them, houses, cities, and nations would fall upon one another in unrestrained confusion, there being no one to repress, or repel, or persuade them to be peaceful through the fear of punishment. [12]

John believes that because of human sin, fear and coercion have infected the whole structure of human relationships, from family to city and nation. Everywhere he sees the disastrous results: "Now we are subjected to one another by force and compulsion, and every day we are in conflict with one another."[13]

While granting that the imperial system preserves social order, he charges that it tolerates—or, worse, even enforces—injustice, immorality, and inequality. Roman laws, John says, are, "for the most part, corrupt, useless, and ridiculous." They expose to torture or execution the man who steals clothes or money, but they ignore worse crimes: "Who would be considered wiser, by most people, than the persons considered worthy to legislate for the cities and nations? But yet to these wise men sexual immorality is unworthy of punishment; at least, none of the pagan laws . . . bring men to trial for this reason."[14] Chrysostom explains specifically what kind of case he has in mind: "If a married man has intercourse with a female slave, it seems to be nothing to pagan laws, nor to people in general."[15] Most people, he admits, would laugh at anyone who tried to bring such a case to court, and the judge would dismiss it. The same is true for a married man involved with an unmarried woman or with a prostitute. Roman law protects only the man's rights in such cases, but, Chrysostom declares, "we are punished, though not by the Roman laws, yet by God."[16]

Roman laws, John continues, allow dealers to enslave children and to train them in sexual specialties for sale as prostitutes. And pagan tradition praises the legislators as "common benefactors of the city" for instituting public entertainment that features, in the theaters, prostitutes and prostituted children and, in the sports arena, contests between men and wild animals:

> Those places, too, being full of all senseless excitement, train the people to acquire a merciless and savage and inhuman kind of temperament, and give them practice in seeing people torn in pieces, and blood flowing, and the viciousness of wild beasts upsetting everything. Now all these our wise lawgivers introduced from the beginning—so many plagues—and our cities applaud and admire them.[17]

So much for the masses; but what about the few who, chastened by the example of Adam's sin, and recovered from sin through baptism, exercise appropriate restraint over themselves? Such persons, Chrysostom declares, remain exempt from the punishment that falls upon the corrupt majority—exempt, in fact, from the constraints of human government as a whole: "For those who live in a state of piety require no correction on the part of the magistrates, for 'the law was not made for a righteous man.' But the more numerous, if they had no fear of these hanging over them, would fill the cities with innumerable evils."[18]

The tyranny of external government sharply contrasts with the liberty enjoyed by those capable of autonomous self-rule—above all, by those who, through Christian baptism, have recovered the capacity for self-government.[19] Chrysostom, like the apologists, identifies the former with the Roman Empire and the latter with the emerging new society that constitutes the Christian church: "There, everything is done through fear and constraint; here, through free choice and liberty."[20] The use of force, the driving energy of imperial society, is utterly alien to church government:

> Christians, more than all people, are not allowed to correct by force the faults of those who sin. Secular judges, indeed, when they have captured wrongdoers under the law, demonstrate that their authority is great by preventing them, even against their own will, from following their own desires; but in our case the wrongdoer must be corrected not by force, but by persuasion.[21]

What prevents church leaders from exercising the same authority as imperial magistrates, he explains, has nothing to do with lack of power, much less inferior status. On the contrary, he says, a priest's authority far *surpasses* the emperor's. What restrains a priest from attempting to use such authority, however, is religious principle:

> For neither has the authority of this kind to restrain sinners been given to us by law, *nor, if it had been given, should we have any place to exercise our power,* since God rewards those who abstain from evil out of their own choice, and not out of necessity. . . . If a person wanders away from the right path, great effort, perseverance, and patience are required; for he cannot be dragged back by force, nor restrained by fear, but must be led back by persuasion to the truth from which he originally swerved.[22]

The Christian leader, refraining not only from the use of force but even from the subtler pressures of fear and coercion, must evoke each member's voluntary participation. Failing that, he must respect, however misguided he considers it to be, each member's freedom of choice and action:

We do not have "authority over your faith," beloved, nor do we command these things as your lords and masters. We are appointed for the teaching of the word, not for power, nor for absolute authority. We hold the place of counsellors to advise you. The counsellor speaks his own opinions, not forcing his listener, but *leaving him full master of his own choice in what is said.* He is blameworthy only in this respect, if he fails to say the things that present themselves.[23]

Church government, unlike Roman government, remains wholly voluntary and, although hierarchically structured, is essentially egalitarian, reflecting, in effect, the original harmony of Paradise.

Yet Chrysostom remains uncomfortably aware that the actual churches he knows in Antioch and Constantinople fall far short of such celestial harmony. Having inherited his vision of the church from such heroic predecessors as Justin, Athenagoras, Clement, and Origen, Chrysostom, measuring the church of his own day against theirs, alternatively grieves and lashes out in anger:

Plagues, teeming with untold mischiefs, have come upon the churches. The primary offices have become marketable. Hence innumerable evils are arising, and there is no one to redress, no one to reprove them. Indeed, the disorder has taken on a kind of method and consistency of its own.[24]

Excessive wealth, enormous power, and luxury, Chrysostom charges, are destroying the integrity of the churches. Clerics, infected by the disease of "lust for authority," are fighting for candidates on the basis of family prominence, wealth, or partisanship. Others support the candidacy of their friends, relatives, or flatterers, "but no one will look to the man who is really qualified." They ignore, Chrysostom says, the only valid qualification, "excellence of character."[25] Pagans rightly ridicule the whole business: " 'Do you see,' they say, 'how all matters among the Christians are full of vainglory? And there is ambition among them, and hypocrisy. Strip them,' they say, 'of their numbers, and they are nothing.' "[26]

Could the vision forged by the embattled Christians of earlier times, who saw the church as an island of purity in an ocean of corruption, fit the circumstances of a state religion, a church that had come into imperial favor, wealth, and power? Chrysostom saw his church as still contending against powerful rivals.[27] He did not consider the possibility that his vision of the church, sanctioned by nearly four centuries of tradition, might no longer fit the situation of his fellow Christians at the beginning of the fifth century. Now that the world had invaded the church and the church the world, new questions had arisen: How, for example, were Christians to envision the new role of a Christian emperor and the legitimacy of his rule, not only over unruly pagans, but over Christians themselves (notably including the increasing flood of nominal converts)? And how were Christians to account for the unsettling new prominence of the churches, in which becoming a bishop now guaranteed a man tax exemptions, vastly increased income, social power, and possibly even influence at court?

The traditional Christian answers to the question of power no longer applied by the later fourth century, when not only Constantine but several others, including Theodosius the Great, had ruled as Christian emperors. Augustine's opposite interpretation of the politics of Paradise—and, in particular, his insistence that the whole human race, including the redeemed, remains wholly incapable of self-government—offered Christians radically new ways to interpret this unprecedented situation.

Whereas Chrysostom proclaims human freedom, Augustine reads from the same Genesis story the opposite—human bondage. As for αὐτεξουσία, the power to rule oneself, Augustine cannot acknowledge it as a reality, or even a genuine good, in his own experience, let alone for all humanity. And Augustine begins his reflections on government, characteristically, with introspection.

Recalling in the *Confessions* his own experience, Augustine instinctively identifies the question of self-government with rational control over sexual impulses. Describing his struggle to be chaste, Augustine recalls how, "in the sixteenth year of the age of my flesh . . . the madness of raging lust exercised its supreme dominion over me."[28] Augustine was powerless, a captive and victim. Through sexual desire, he says, "my invisible enemy trod me down and seduced me."[29] Of his sexual involvements he admits, "I drew my shackles along with me, terrified to have them knocked off."[30] Acknowledging that his friend was "amazed at my enslavement," Augustine reflects that "what made me a slave to it was the habit [*consuetudo*] of satisfying an insatiable lust."[31]

Had Augustine confessed as much to a spiritual advisor such as John Chrysostom, he would have been urged to undo the chains that bound him to bad habits and to recover and strengthen, like unused muscles, his own neglected capacity for moral choice. But Augustine in his *Confessions* came directly to challenge such assumptions. Free will is only an illusion—an illusion that Augustine himself once shared: "As for continence, I imagined it to be in the liberty of our own power, which I, for my part, felt I did not have."[32] As he grew older, Augustine changed his mind. Instead of indicting his own lack of faith in the power of free will, Augustine came to lash out at those who falsely assume that they *do* possess such power: "What man is there, who, being aware of his own weakness, dares so much as to attribute his chastity and innocence to his own virtue?"[33] The aging Augustine then takes his own experience as paradigmatic for all human experience—indeed, for Adam's: "Being a captive," he says, "I feigned a show of counterfeit liberty,"[34] as, he says, Adam had done, bringing upon himself and his progeny an avalanche of sin and punishment.

No wonder, then, that the Manichaean theory of human origins, which had "explained" the sense of helplessness he experienced, had at first attracted Augustine. He identified, too, with the way the Manichaeans interpreted the tendency to sin not simply as human weakness but (as the rabbis had taught of the "evil impulse," *yetṣer hara'*) as an internal energy actively resisting God's will. When he abandoned Manichaean theology, Augustine admitted he was at a loss to understand the Christian teaching on free will. Later he would claim, of course, that in denying the power of the will he was only repeating what Paul had said long before ("I do not do what I will, but I do the very thing I hate. . . . I can will what is right, but I cannot do it"; see Romans 7:15–25). Many Christians ever since—including that famous Augustinian monk Martin Luther—would find Augustine's interpretation of Paul's words persuasive. Yet such recent scholarly studies as the work of Peter Gorday confirm an impression that Augustine effectively *invented* this interpretation of Paul's words, by daring to apply them to the baptized Christian.[35] Augustine's Christian predecessors, including John Chrysostom and Origen, had assumed that Paul's statements about the will's incapacity applied only to those who lacked the grace of Christian baptism. Augustine himself acknowledged this and worked hard, he says, to understand the Catholic teaching (in his words) "that free will is the cause of our doing evil. . . . But I was not able to understand it clearly." Once he began to recognize the power of his own will, he says, "I knew that I had a will . . . and when I did either will or nill anything, I was more sure of it, that I and no other did will or nill; and here was the cause of my sin, as I came to perceive."[36] Yet far from relinquishing entirely the role of victim, Augustine says, "But what I did *against* my will, that I seemed to suffer rather than do. That I considered not to be my fault, but my punishment."[37]

Through the agonizing process of his conversion Augustine claims to have discovered that he was bound by conflict within his own will:

> I was bound, not with another man's chains, but with my own iron will. The enemy held my will, and, indeed, made a chain of it for me, and constrained me. Because of a perverse will, desire was made; and when I was enslaved to desire [*libido*] it became habit; and habit not restrained became necessity. By which links . . . a very hard bondage had me enthralled.[38]

Augustine came to see his own will, then, divided and consequently impotent: "Myself I willed it, and myself I nilled it: it was I myself. I neither willed entirely, nor nilled entirely. Therefore I was in conflict with myself, and . . . was distracted by my own self."[39] How did he account for such conflict? Augustine insists that, since he suffered much of this "against my own will, . . . I was not, therefore, the cause of it, but the 'sin that dwells in me': from the punishment of that *more voluntary sin, because I was a son of Adam.*"[40]

In his earlier writings, as Edward Cranz points out, Augustine expresses views on human freedom and self-government that virtually echo those of his predecessors, such as Chrysostom.[41] But in the fourteenth chapter of *The City of God* Augustine seems intent on proving that, even if Adam once had free will, he himself had never received it. Even in his account of Adam's case Augustine betrays his own ambivalence or, indeed, outright hostility toward the possibility of human freedom. What earlier apologists had celebrated as God's greatest gift to humankind—free will, liberty, autonomy, self-government—Augustine characterizes in surprisingly negative terms. Adam had received freedom as his birthright, but nonetheless, as Augustine tells it, the first man "conceived a desire for freedom,"[42] and his desire became, in Augustine's eyes, the root of sin, betraying nothing less than contempt for God. The desire to master one's will, far from expressing what Origen, Clement, and Chrysostom consider the true nature of rational beings, becomes for Augustine the great and fatal temptation: "The fruit of the tree of knowledge of good and evil is personal control over one's own will" (*proprium voluntatis arbitrium*).[43] Augustine cannot resist reading that desire for self-government as total, obstinate perversity: "The soul, then, delighting in its own freedom *to do wickedness,* and scorning to serve God

. . . willfully deserted its higher master."[44] Seduced by this desire for autonomy, Adam entered into a "life of cruel and wretched slavery instead of the freedom for which he had conceived a desire."[45]

Uncomfortably aware of a contradiction in his argument, Augustine explains that obedience, not autonomy, should have been Adam's true glory, "since man has been naturally so created that it is advantageous for him to be submissive, but disastrous for him to follow his own will, and not the will of his creator."[46] Admitting that "it does, indeed, seem something of a paradox,"[47] Augustine resorts to paradoxical language to describe how God "sought to impress upon this creature, for whom free slavery [*libera servitus*] was expedient, that he was the Lord."[48] Augustine insists, however, that whatever the constraints upon Adam's freedom, the first man was more free than any of his progeny, for only the story of Adam's misuse of free will can account for the contradictions he discovered within himself, his own will caught in perpetual conflict, "much of which I suffered against my own will, rather than did by my will."[49]

Augustine knows that most of his Christian contemporaries would find this claim incredible, if not heretical. John Chrysostom, indeed, warns the fainthearted not to blame Adam for their own transgressions. Answering one who asks, "What am I to do? Must I die because of him?," he replies, "It is not because of him; for you yourself have not remained without sin. Even though it is not the same sin, you have, at any rate, committed others."[50] That Adam's sin brought suffering and death upon humankind most Christians, like their Jewish predecessors and contemporaries, would have taken for granted. But most Jews and Christians would also have agreed that Adam left each of his offspring free to make his or her own choice of good or evil. The whole point of the story of Adam, most Christians assumed, was to warn everyone who heard it not to misuse that divinely given capacity for free choice.

But Augustine, intending to prove the opposite point, laboriously attempts to show that Adam, far from being the single individual Chrysostom envisioned, was instead a corporate personality. Pointing out that Adam's genesis from earth differs essentially from that of any of his progeny born through childbirth, Augustine declares:

> The entire human race that was to pass through woman into offspring was contained in the first man when that married couple received the divine sentence condemning them to punishment,

and *humanity produced what humanity became, not what it was when created, but when, having sinned, it was punished.* [51]

The punishment itself, Augustine continues, "effected in their original nature a change for the worse." Augustine derived the nature of that change from an idiosyncratic interpretation of Romans 5:12.

The Greek text reads, "Through one man [or "because of one man," δι' ἑνὸς ἀνθρώπου] sin entered the world, and through sin, death; and thus death came upon all men, *in that* [ἔφ' ᾧ] all sinned." John Chrysostom, like most Christians, took this to mean that Adam's sin brought death into the world, and death came upon all because *"all* sinned." But Augustine read the passage in Latin, and so either ignored or was unaware of the connotations of the Greek original; thus he misread the last phrase as referring to Adam. Augustine insisted that it meant that "death came upon all men, *in whom* all sinned"—that the sin of that "one man," Adam, brought upon humanity not only universal death, but also universal, and inevitable, sin. Augustine uses the passage to deny that human beings have free moral choice, which Jews and Christians had traditionally regarded as the birthright of humanity made "in God's image." Augustine declares, on the contrary, that the whole human race inherited from Adam a nature irreversibly damaged by sin. "For we all were in that one man, since all of us were that one man who fell into sin through the woman who was made from him." [52]

How can one imagine that millions of individuals not yet born were "in Adam" or, in any sense, "were" Adam? Anticipating objections that would reduce his argument to absurdity, Augustine declares triumphantly that, although "we did not yet have individually created and apportioned forms in which to live as individuals," what did exist already was the "nature of the semen from which we were to be propagated." [53] That semen itself, Augustine argues, already "shackled by the bond of death," transmits the damage incurred by sin. [54] Hence, Augustine concludes, every human being ever conceived through semen already is born contaminated with sin. Through this astonishing argument, [55] Augustine intends to prove that every human being is in bondage not only from birth but indeed from the moment of conception. And since he takes Adam as a corporate personality, Augustine applies his account of Adam's experience, disrupted by the first sin, to every one of his offspring (except, of course, to Christ, conceived, Augustine ingeniously argued, without semen).

When he describes the onset of original sin in Adam, Augustine chooses political language—and specifically the language of sexual politics.[56] He describes his experience of passion in political metaphors—as "rebellion" against the mind's governance. For in the beginning, when there was only one man in the world, Adam discovered within himself the first government—the rule of the rational soul, the "better part of a human being," over the body, the "inferior part." Augustine, influenced, no doubt, by his study of Platonic philosophy, characterizes their respective roles in political terms: the soul by divine right is to subjugate every member of its "lower servant," the body, to the ruling power of its will. Within Adam as within Eve both soul and body originally obeyed the authority of rational will: "Although they bore an animal body, yet they felt in it no disobedience moving against themselves. . . . Each received the body as a servant . . . and the body obeyed God . . . in an appropriate servitude, without resistance."[57]

But the primal couple soon experienced within themselves not only the first government on earth but also the first revolution. Adam's assertion of his own autonomy was, Augustine insists, tantamount to rebellion against God's rule. Augustine appreciates the aptness with which the punishment for this uprising fits the crime: "The punishment for disobedience was nothing other than disobedience. For human misery consists in nothing other than man's disobedience to himself."[58] Augustine stresses, however, that the penalty for sin involves more than bodily impulses rebelling against the mind. Instead, the "flesh" that wars against the "law of the mind" includes, he says, the "whole of one's natural being."[59] The commonest experiences of frustration—mental agitation, bodily pain, aging, suffering, and death—continually prove to us our incapacity to implement the rule of our will, for who would undergo any of these, Augustine asks, if our nature "in every way and every part obeyed our will?"[60]

But what epitomizes our rebellion against God, above all, is the "rebellion in the flesh"—a spontaneous uprising, so to speak, in the "disobedient members":

> After Adam and Eve disobeyed . . . they felt for the first time a
> movement of disobedience in their flesh, as punishment in kind
> for their own disobedience to God. . . . The soul, which had taken
> a perverse delight in its own liberty and disdained to serve God,
> was now deprived of its original mastery over the body.[61]

Specifically, Augustine concludes, "the sexual desire [*libido*] of our disobedient members arose in those first human beings as a result of the sin of disobedience . . . and because a shameless movement [*impudens motus*] resisted the rule of their will, they covered their shameful members."[62] At first, the Adam and Eve whom God had created enjoyed mental mastery over the procreative process: the sexual members, like the other parts of the body, enacted the work of procreation by a deliberate act of will, "like a handshake." Ever since Eden, however, spontaneous sexual desire is, Augustine contends, the clearest evidence of the effect of original sin: this, above all, manifests passion's triumph. What impresses Augustine most is that such arousal functions independently of the will's rightful rule: "Because of this, these members are rightly called *pudenda* [parts of shame] because they excite themselves just as they like, in opposition to the mind which is their master, as if they were their own masters."[63] Sexual excitement differs from other forms of passion, Augustine contends, since in the case of anger and the rest, it is not the impulse that moves any part of the body but the will, which remains in control and consents to the movement. An angry man makes a decision whether or not to strike; but a sexually aroused man may find that erection occurs with alarming autonomy. Augustine considers this irrefutable evidence that lust *(libido),* having wrested the sexual organs from the control of the will, now has "brought them so completely under its rule that they are incapable of acting if this one emotion [*libido*] is lacking."[64] So disjoined is will from desire that even a man who wills to be sexually aroused may find that *libido* deserts him.

> At times, the urge intrudes uninvited; at other times, it deserts the panting lover, and, although desire blazes in the mind, the body is frigid. In this strange way, desire refuses service, not only to the will to procreate, but also to the desire for wantonness; and though for the most part, it solidly opposes the mind's command, at other times it is divided against itself, and, having aroused the mind, it fails to arouse the body.[65]

The experience of arousal apart from any action taken, Augustine insists, itself is sin: "Such disobedience of the flesh as this, which lies in the very excitement, even when it is not allowed to take effect, did not exist in the first man and woman."[66] Augustine admits, however, that

> the trouble with the hypothesis of a passionless procreation controlled by the will, as I am here suggesting it, is that it has never

been verified in experience, not even in the experience of those who could have proved that it was possible. In fact, they sinned too soon, and brought upon themselves exile from Eden.[67]

But Augustine believes that each person *can* verify from experience the radical leap to which his own inner turmoil impelled him—the leap that identifies sexual desire itself as evidence of, and penalty for, original sin. That each of us experiences desire spontaneously *apart* from will means, Augustine assumes, that we experience it *against* our will. Hence, he continues, sexual desire naturally involves shame: "A man by his very nature is ashamed of sexual desire."[68] What proves the truth of such assertions, Augustine believes, is the universal practice of covering the genitals and of shielding the act of intercourse from public view.[69]

One might, of course, ask the obvious question: Is it not possible to experience desire *in accordance with the will* (as, for example, when engaging in intercourse for the purpose of procreation)? Chrysostom would say yes; but Augustine's very definition of sexual desire excludes that possibility. Having entered into human experience through an act of rebellion against the will, desire can never cooperate with will to form, so to speak, a coalition government. For Augustine, "lust is an usurper, defying the power of the will, and tyrannizing the human sexual organs."[70]

Augustine believes that by defining spontaneous sexual desire as the proof and penalty of original sin he has succeeded in implicating the whole human race, except, of course, for Christ. Christ alone of all humankind, Augustine explains, was born without *libido*—being born, he believes, without the intervention of semen that transmits its effects. But the rest of humankind issues from a procreative process that, ever since Adam, has sprung wildly out of control, marring the whole of human nature.

What, then, can remedy human misery? How can anyone achieve internal balance, much less establish social and political harmony between man and woman, man and man? Augustine's whole theology of the fall depends upon his radical claim that no human power can effect such restoration. Knowing, however, that many philosophically minded people (including philosophically educated Christians from Justin Martyr through Chrysostom) stand against him and would invoke against his argument the evidence of all who successfully practice self-control—pagan philosophers and Christian ascetics alike—Augustine seizes the offensive. There are, he admits, a few people who restrain their passions through self-control, leading temperate, just, and holy lives. But while others honor such people for their achievement, Augustine accuses them, in effect, of neurosis: "This is by no means a healthy state due to nature [*sanitas ex natura*], but an illness due to guilt [*languor ex culpa*]."[71] For not only the "common mass of men, but even the most godly and righteous," he insists, are ravaged by sin and dominated by passion. The Stoic attempt to achieve *apatheia*—mastery of passion—he dismisses as leading its practitioners into arrogance and isolation from the rest of humanity, "not tranquility."[72] Thus ridiculing such efforts to reassert the power of the will, Augustine concludes that the "rebellion in our members, . . . that proof and penalty of man's rebellion against God," is not only universal but also ineradicable. Part of our nature stands in permanent revolt against the "law of the mind"—even among the philosophers, even among the baptized and the saints. And since, he insists, everyone, even the most advanced ascetic, confronts the same continual insurrection within, Augustine concludes that humankind has wholly lost its original capacity for self-government.

Augustine draws so drastic a picture of the effects of Adam's sin that he embraces human government, even when tyrannical, as the indispensable defense against the forces sin has unleashed in human nature. His analysis of internal conflict, indeed, leads directly into his view of social conflict in general. The war within us drives us into war with one another—and no one, pagan or Christian, remains exempt. So, he explains, "while a good man is progressing to perfection, one part of him can be at war with another of his parts; hence, two good men can be at war with one another."

In the beginning, Augustine agrees with Chrysostom, politics began at home:

> The union of male and female is the seed-bed, so to speak, from which the city must grow. . . . Since, then, a man's home [*hominis domus*] ought to be the beginning or elementary constituent of the city, and every beginning serves some end of its own, and every part serves the integrity of the whole of which it is a part, it follows clearly enough that domestic peace serves civic peace, that is, that the ordered agreement of command and obedience among those who live together in a household serves the ordered agreement of command and obedience among citizens.[73]

Recognizing that Adam and Eve originally were created to live together in a harmonious order of authority and obedience, superiority and subordination, like soul and body, "we must conclude," says Augustine, "that a husband is meant to rule over his wife as the spirit rules the flesh." But once each member of the primal couple had experienced that first internal revolt in which the bodily passions arose against the soul, they experienced analogous disruption in their relationship with one another. Although originally created equal with man in regard to her rational soul, woman's formation from Adam's rib established her as the "weaker part of the human couple."[74] Being closely connected with bodily passion, woman, although created to be man's helper, became his temptress and led him into disaster.[75] The Genesis account describes the result: God himself reinforced the husband's authority over his wife, placing divine sanction upon the social, legal, and economic machinery of male domination.

Apart from the relationship between the sexes, however, Augustine again agrees with Chrysostom that "God did not want a rational being, made in his image, to have dominion over any except irrational creatures; not man over men, but man over the beasts."[76] Unlike man's dominion over woman, man's dominion over other men violates their original equality; hence, "such a condition as slavery could only have arisen as a result of sin."[77] Augustine diverges sharply from Chrysostom, however, when he traces how sin, transmitted from the primal parents through sexual reproduction, infected their offspring, so that now "everyone, arising as he does from a condemned stock, is from the first necessarily evil and carnal through Adam."[78] So Cain, when another form of carnal desire, envy, overcame his rational judgment, murdered his brother, exemplifying the lust for power that now dominates and distorts the whole structure of human relationships.

Those who share Augustine's vision of the disastrous results of sin must, he believes, accept as well the rule of one man over others—master over slave, ruler over subjects—as the inescapable necessity of our universal fallen nature:

> Such, as men are now, is the order of peace. Some are in subjection to others and, while humility helps those who serve, pride harms those in power. But as men once were, when their nature was as God created it, no man was a slave either to man or to sin. However, *slavery is now penal in character, and planned by that law which commands the preservation of the natural order and forbids its disturbance.*[79]

Human nature, Augustine explains, instinctively desires social harmony: "By the very laws of his nature man is, so to speak, forced into social relationships and peace [*societatem pacemque*] with other men, so far as possible."[80] Yet sin distorts this universal impulse, turning it instead into the enforced order that constitutes "earthly peace."

Certain scholars have emphasized—quite rightly—how carefully Augustine qualifies his affirmation of secular government. The Dutch scholar Henrik Berkhof, writing during the Second World War, takes Augustine as representing what he calls the "theocratic" view, which subordinates the interests of the state to those of the church. Wilhelm Kamlah, writing in Germany after the war, declares that Augustine's theory deprives the state of any claim to ultimate religious value, regarding it, in effect, as a "necessary evil."[81] R. Markus points out that as Augustine matured, he decisively rejected the classical belief—earlier shared even by Christians who were enamored of the "Christian empire"—that the state and its power served humanity's ultimate good. Augustine expresses no illusions, certainly, about the rulers' motives for enforcing peace. Even a solitary criminal, he says, "demands peace in his own home, and, if need be, gets it by sheer brutality. He knows that the price of peace is to have everyone subject to some one head—in this case, to himself."[82] Should such a man gain power over a larger society, Augustine continues, he would rule through the same brutal impulse:

> Thus it is that all men want peace in their own society, and they all want it on their own terms. When they go to war, what they want is to make, if they can, their enemies their own, and to impose on them the victor's will, and call it a peace. . . . Sinful man hates the equality of all men under God, and, as though he were God, loves to impose his own sovereignty upon his fellow men.[83]

Such pragmatic and negative assessments of the function of government are not, of course, original with Augustine. As we have seen, Justin Martyr, addressing the emperors Antoninus Pius, Marcus Aurelius, and Lucius Verus two and a half centuries earlier, had borrowed an image from philosophical tradition[84] to say that those who rule by brute force "have just as much power as robbers in a desert."[85] Marcus Aurelius used the same image in his own *Meditations*[86]—as, indeed, does Augustine in another famous passage:

"Without justice, what then are kingdoms but great robberies? For what are robberies themselves but little kingdoms?"[87] No more original is Augustine's insistence that political authority is not natural to man but a result of his sinful condition.[88] Justin's younger colleague Irenaeus had described how

> God imposed upon humankind the fear of men since they did not acknowledge the fear of God, so that, being subject to human authority and kept under restraints by their laws, they might attain to some degree of justice. . . . Earthly rule, therefore, has been appointed by God, and not by the devil, for the benefit of nations . . . so that, under fear of human rule, people may not devour one another like fishes.[89]

Irenaeus was drawing in turn upon much older tradition—using, in fact, a rabbinic image to interpret Paul's warning to Christians about the positive uses of governmental coercion (Romans 13:1–6).

Yet Augustine's predecessors Justin and Irenaeus had affirmed the necessity of coercive government only for "those outside." Both, like Chrysostom, clearly discriminate between the coercive government necessary for outsiders and the internal rule of the church. Baptized Christians, Justin and Irenaeus agree, essentially have recovered from the damage inflicted by sin. Baptism transforms converts from their former state as "children of necessity and ignorance . . . to become children of choice and knowledge," washed clean of sin, illuminated, and, Justin says, "by our deeds, too, found to be good citizens and keepers of the commandments."[90]

Augustine agreed with his predecessors in delineating two distinct modes of relationship—one motivated by impulses of domination and submission, the other by mutually affirming love. But what sets Augustine's mature position apart from that of his predecessors is his refusal simply to identify the first with the state and the second with the church. As he redefines them, the "city of man" and the "city of God" cut across both categories. Even baptized Christians are not exempt from either the war of conflicting impulses or the need for external government.

Augustine insists, on the contrary, that all government remains only a superstructure imposed upon the internal rebellion that sin has instigated within everyone, pagan and Christian alike. Consequently he believes the situation of the baptized Christian is far more complex than Chrysostom imagined. The Christian, like the unbeliever, has to contend against the enemy within that holds power over his will; hence he, too, needs the help of external discipline. So even in his domestic life, Augustine says, although the Christian longs for heaven,

> where there will be no further need for giving orders to other human beings, . . . meanwhile, in case anyone in the household breaks its peace by disobedience, he is disciplined by words or whipping or other kinds of punishment lawful and licit in human society, and for his own good, to readjust to the peace he has abandoned.[91]

If Christians cannot even be trusted to govern themselves, how are they to approach church government? Later in his life Augustine came to endorse, for the church as well as the state, the whole arsenal of secular government that Chrysostom had repudiated—commands, threats, coercion, penalties, and even physical force. Whereas Chrysostom had defined his own role as that of advisor, not ruler, Augustine, like Ignatius of Antioch, sees the bishop as ruling "in God's place." One of Augustine's favorite images for church leaders, as for their model, Christ, is that of the physician, ministering to those who have been baptized but, like himself, are still sick, each one infected with the same ineradicable disease contracted through original sin.[92] Augustine tends, consequently, to discount the patients' opinions. It is the physician's responsibility not only to administer to sick and suffering humanity the life-giving medication of the sacraments, but also to carry out, when necessary, disciplinary procedures as a kind of surgery.

This vision of the church, advocated by others, such as Augustine's close friend and fellow bishop Alypius, corresponds in a sense to Augustine's own experience. In his *Confessions* he admits how desperately lost, sick, and helpless he felt, believing his will to be morally paralyzed, as he awaited the revelation of grace mediated through the church to penetrate him from without and effect his healing.[93] But other Christians surely would not have recognized their own experiences in his account. The British monk Pelagius, for one, sharply objected, criticizing Augustine's *Confessions* for popularizing a kind of pious self-indulgence. How, then, did Augustine's idiosyncratic views on the effects of original sin—and hence on the politics of the church and state—come to be accepted in the fifth and sixth centuries, first by the leadership of the Catholic church and then by the majority of its members? The question is, of course, wildly ambitious; but let us attempt to sketch out the beginning of an answer.

Let us consider first how the conflicting views of Chrysostom and Augustine might sound to their contemporaries. By the beginning of the fifth century Catholic Christians lived as subjects of an empire they could no longer consider alien, much less wholly evil. Having repudiated the patronage of the traditional gods some two generations earlier, the emperors now sometimes used military force to help stamp out pagan worship. Furthermore, the two sons of Theodosius the Great, reigning since his death in 395 as emperors of East and West, continued their father's policy of withdrawing patronage from Arian Christians and placing themselves wholly in alliance with the Catholic bishops and clergy. An earlier generation of Christian bishops, including Eusebius of Caesarea, deeply impressed by the events they had witnessed and convinced that they lived at a turning point in history, had hailed Constantine and his successors as God's chosen rulers. Augustine, like most of his fellow Christians, once had shared that conviction. But after two generations the Christian empire and its rulers, if no longer alien, remained in many respects all too human. By the beginning of the fifth century few who dealt with the government firsthand—certainly not Chrysostom and finally not Augustine either—would have identified it with God's reign on earth.[94]

The mature Augustine offers a theology of politics far more complex and compelling than any of its rivals. Chrysostom claimed that imperial rule is unnecessary for believers, but Augustine insists that God has placed everyone, whether pagan or priest, equally in subjection to external government. Yet Augustine's reasoning diverges sharply from the naïve endorsement of Constantine's court theologian, Eusebius. Augustine's dark vision of a human nature ravaged by original sin and overrun by lust for power rules out uncritical adulation and qualifies his endorsement of imperial rule.[95] That same dark vision impels him to reject Chrysostom's more optimistic premise that imperial power is necessary for pagans, but, in effect, superfluous in the lives of pious citizens. Augustine, on the contrary, places secular government at the center of human society, indispensable for the best as well as the worst among its members. For a Christian, civic obligations rank second, certainly, to one's obligation to God (or, as this usually meant in practice, to the church). Yet apart from direct conflict of interest, even the bishop must render appropriate obedience to secular authority.[96] Augustine acknowledges the emperor's rule, however limited (or even however brutal), to be, nevertheless, as permanent and ineradicable—in this world, at least—as the effects of original sin. More effectively than either Eusebius on the one hand or Chrysostom on the other, Augustine's theory enabled his contemporaries to come to terms both with the fact of Christian empire and with its intractably human nature.

For if the fifth-century state no longer looked so evil as it once had, the church, in turn, no longer looked so holy. Chrysostom, holding to his by now essentially sectarian theory, deplored what had happened to the church since imperial favor first shone upon Christians: first, the massive influx of nominal converts; and second, the way that a shower of imperial privileges had radically changed the dynamics—and raised the stakes—of ecclesiastical politics. But what Chrysostom could only denounce, Augustine could interpret. Challenging the traditional model of the church and the assumption on which it rested—free will—Augustine's theory of original sin could make theologically intelligible not only the state's imperfections but the church's imperfections as well.

Secondly, while changing the way Catholic Christians understood the psychological and religious meaning of freedom (*libertas*), Augustine's theory bore the potential for changing as well their understanding of, and relationship to, political liberty. Throughout the Roman republic men of wealth and power tended to agree that *libertas* meant living under the rule of a "good governor," that is, an emperor of whom the senate approved.[97]

We have seen, however, that certain Christians, among others, despised the patricians' version of *liberty*, regarding it as a euphemism for *slavery*—that is, for political subjugation induced by the totalitarian rule of the later Caesars. For some people, *liberty* meant freedom from superior authority and freedom from constraint—including, for example, freedom of speech.

We have seen, too, how Christians, so long as they remained a persecuted, illegal, and minority sect, sided with the latter position. We recall how Minucius Felix, writing c. 200 C.E., rhetorically described the Christian who, undergoing torture for his faith, maintains his *libertas:*

> "How beautiful is the spectacle to God when a Christian does battle with pain, when he is brought up against threats, and punishment, and torture; when, mocking the noise of death, he treads underfoot the horror of the executioner; when *he raises up his liberty against kings and princes,* and yields to God alone . . . when, triumphant and victorious, he tramples on the very one who has passed sentence upon him."[98]

Repudiating the charge that Christians were afraid for superstitious reasons to offer pagan sacrifice, Minucius Felix had declared that "it is not a confession of fear, but an assertion of our true liberty."[99] Tertullian, Minucius's contemporary, when he challenged imperial authority in the name of that "liberty which is [the individual's] right,"[100] had assumed that the term meant freedom from superior authority.[101]

Augustine, on the contrary, having denied that human beings possess any capacity whatever for free will, accepts a definition of liberty far more agreeable to the powerful and influential men with whom he himself wholeheartedly identifies. As Augustine tells it, it is the *serpent* who tempts Adam with the seductive lure of liberty. The forbidden fruit symbolizes, he explains, "personal control over one's own will."[102] Not, Augustine adds, "that it is evil in itself, but it is placed in the garden to teach him the primary virtue"—obedience. So, as we noted above, Augustine concludes that humanity never was really meant to be, in any sense, truly free. God allowed us to sin in order to prove to us from our own experience that "our true good is free slavery"[103]—slavery to God in the first place and, in the second, to his agent, the emperor. Idiosyncratic as it sounds, Augustine's paradox finds a parallel in the political rhetoric of his contemporaries. Claudian, pagan court poet and propagandist in the service of Stilicho and of Honorius, the Christian emperor of the West, challenges those who call the emperor's rule slavery (*servitium*): "Never is liberty more appreciated than under a good king!"[104] During the following centuries a similar view was incorporated into the imperial Catholic mass, which directs the priest to pray that, "the enemies of peace being overthrown, Roman liberty may serve Thee in security" (*secura tibi serviat Romana libertas*).[105]

Finally, anyone observing the contrast between the careers of the two bishops might well conclude that Augustine's version of the politics of Paradise proved effective in dealing with the politics of the fifth-century Roman Empire, whereas Chrysostom's version failed. Both Augustine, born in Tagaste, North Africa, in 354, and John Chrysostom, born in Antioch either the same year or a few years earlier,[106] grew up in a world ruled for more than a generation by Christian emperors—a succession interrupted only by Julian's abrupt two-year reversion to imperial patronage of paganism. But Augustine's responses to the new constellation of imperial power were very different from Chrysostom's.

Chrysostom lost his father at a young age, was raised with his sister by his Christian mother, was baptized at the age of eighteen, and became a monk. In one of his first publications, *Comparison Between a King and a Monk,* written at a time when the world, the imperial court, and the church were mingling in unprecedented ways, Chrysostom passionately defended sacred against secular power—a theme that would preoccupy him throughout his lifetime. Some twelve years later, as we noted earlier, after the people of Antioch had rioted and smashed the imperial statues in protest against the emperor, John Chrysostom addressed an audience waiting in terror of imperial reprisals, and dared proclaim, not, as Augustine might have, that even the Christian is subject to the emperor, but that the emperor himself needs the priest and is subject to the priest's superior authority: "He is himself a ruler, and a ruler of greater dignity than the other; for the sacred laws place under his hands even the royal head."[107] When the bishop intervened with the emperor to settle the crisis, John said that those events proved to unbelievers "that the Christians are the saviors of the city; that they are its guardians, its patrons, and its teachers. . . . Let all unbelievers learn that the fear of Christ is a bridle to every kind of authority."[108]

In 397 Chrysostom received an unexpected summons to Constantinople, the eastern capital of the empire. Hurrying there in secret, he was surprised to find himself appointed bishop of Constantinople, a position near the pinnacle of ecclesiastical power. By canon law of 391, the bishop of Constantinople ranked second only to the bishop of Rome; but often a man in that position, as chief spiritual advisor to the emperor, to the imperial family, and to the whole court, surpassed all others in actual influence. Eutropius, the brilliant and powerful eunuch who controlled much of court politics for the emperor Arcadius, his ineffectual young charge, had arranged for the appointment. Eutropius probably guessed that the pious and eloquent Chrysostom had neither the taste nor the talent for court politics. Eutropius was right; Chrysostom was so impolitic, so concerned with his responsibilities as moral advisor to the powerful, advocate for the destitute and oppressed, and austere guardian of clerical discipline, that within three years he had offended virtually everyone who had once welcomed his appointment. His acts of social conscience turned powerful people among the court and clergy against him. And his attempt to build a hospital for lepers directly outside the city walls set off a "war" of protest that ended with his expulsion from office.[109] One historian concludes that Chrysostom "proudly disdained the favor of the court, on which the high position of his episcopate alone rested, by his foolish idealism."[110] Another wonders whether he deserves to be revered as a saint and martyr or condemned "comme un idéaliste dépourvu de finesse diplomatique, un zélote sans tact, ou un fanatique incapable de nuances et victime de son emportement."[111] John's admirers attributed the bishop's actions to his deep religious convictions and to his uncompromising moral consciousness. Yet even they could see how those very qualities had led to accusations of "hardness and rudeness," and of arrogance intolerable in a man in his position, and so played into the hands of his enemies.

After six years in office Chrysostom learned that his enemies had prevailed over his former supporters: deposed from episcopal office, perhaps narrowly escaping death, he began under heavy guard the arduous journey into exile. Ill and alone, defended and consoled by a few loyal friends, he lived only three years longer. But Chrysostom's convictions never swerved: secular and spiritual powers are antithetical and mutually exclusive. From exile he wrote to his close woman friend and supporter, the deaconess Pentadia, words that no doubt express his reflections upon his own sufferings, as well as upon hers:

> I rejoice . . . and find the greatest consolation, in my solitude, in the fact that you have been so manly and steadfast, and that you have not allowed yourself to do wrong. . . . Be glad, therefore, and rejoice over your victory. For they have done everything they could against you. You, who knew only the church and your monastic cell, they have dragged out into the public eye, from there to the court, and from court to prison. They have brought false witnesses, have slandered, murdered, shed streams of blood . . . and left nothing undone to terrify you, and to obtain from you a lie. . . . But you have brought them all to shame.[112]

Now consider Augustine. Born into a nonpatrician family, Augustine tells us that his pagan father, Patricus, a man habitually unfaithful to Augustine's mother, not only failed to "root out the brambles of lust" from his son but expressed pleasure in his adolescent son's sexual appetite. (Perhaps Augustine had his hot-tempered father somehow in mind when he complained that "traditional education taught me that Jupiter punishes the wicked with his thunderbolts, and yet commits adultery himself!") His Christian mother, Monica, patiently endured her husband's infidelities, Augustine says, but "most earnestly implored me not to commit fornication." As a young man he would have been embarrassed to take such "woman-ish" advice; much later, looking back, he came to believe that God had spoken to him through his mother, and that "when I disregarded her, I disregarded [God]." Augustine sought a secular career with intense ambition and plunged into the life of the city—theatrical performances, dinner parties, rhetorical competition, many friend-ships. After various earlier sexual relationships he lived for years with a lower-class woman who engaged his passions and bore him a son, but then he abandoned her for the sake of a socially advan-tageous marriage his mother arranged for him. Yet once he had become a successful rhetor, Augustine found himself divided. Al-though attracted to philosophical and religious contemplation, he was unwilling to give up marriage and career. Then, at the age of thirty-two, spurred by stories of the desert solitaries, he renounced the world and was baptized. Three years later, having "given up all hope in this world," Augustine went to Hippo to set up the commu-nal monastic life he intended to enter. Later he protested to his congregation that he had had no intention whatever of seeking church office and expressed ambivalence about his successful ec-clesiastical career: "I was grabbed, I was made a priest . . . and, from there, I became your bishop."[113]

The church that Augustine chose to join, as Peter Brown points out, "was not the old church of Cyprian"—not, that is, the select community of the holy, willing to risk persecution and death or, lacking the opportunity for martyrdom, eager to leave the world;

> it was the new, expanding church of Ambrose, rising above the Roman world like "a moon waxing in its brightness." It was a confident, international body, established in the respect of Chris-tian emperors, sought out by noblemen and intellectuals, capable of bringing to the masses of the known civilized world the eso-teric truths of the philosophy of Plato, a church set no longer to defy society but to master it.[114]

As Augustine understood their task, having learned it from Am-brose, church leaders participate in the divinely ordained work of government: "You teach kings to rule for the benefit of their people; and it is you who warn the people to be subservient to their kings."[115] At the time of Augustine's baptism, the Catholic church was in the process of consolidating its identification with imperial rule. Armed with support from the emperor Honorius, the leaders of the western church, intent on preventing a rival group of Christians from returning to favor, committed themselves to the policy of implementing imperial authority and so, in the process, asserting and consolidating the primacy of Catholicism over all its Christian rivals.

Augustine's position as bishop of a provincial North African city can scarcely be compared with Chrysostom's far more prominent position three years later in the capital city of the eastern empire. Still, in accepting the episcopate, Augustine, too, became a public figure and ruler of a community. When his authority was challenged by the rival church of Donatists, Augustine came to appreciate—and manipulate—the advantages of his alliance with the repressive power of the state. His opponents were Christians who had refused to acknowledge the episcopacy of Caecilian, elected bishop of Carthage in 311, on the grounds that Caecilian had allowed Roman government authorities to confiscate and destroy his church's copies of the Scriptures during the Great Persecution of 303–304. Called Donatists after one of their leaders, Donatus of Casae Nigrae, these Christians identified with the "church of the martyrs." Donatist Christians denounced the "unholy alliance" between Catholic Christians and the Roman state. Echoing Chrysostom's principle, they insisted that the church must employ only spiritual sanctions and not force.

Yet Augustine abandoned the policy of toleration practiced by the previous bishop of Carthage and pursued the attack on the Donatists. Like Chrysostom, he praised the church's use of persuasion, not force; yet he himself, after beginning with polemics and propaganda, turned increasingly to force. First came laws denying civil rights to non-Catholic Christians; then the imposition of penalties, fines, eviction from public office; and finally, denial of free discussion, exile of Donatist bishops, and the use of physical coercion. According to Catholic historians, the Donatist cause became increasingly identified with active resistance to authority, including outbreaks of violence.[116] Despite his earlier misgivings, Augustine came to find military force "indispensable" in suppressing the Donatists and "wrote the only full justification, in the history of the early church, of the right of the state to suppress non-Catholics."[117] He came to realize, he explained, that fear and coercion, which Chrysostom had considered necessary only to govern outsiders, were necessary within the church as well; many Christians as well as pagans, he noted regretfully, respond only to fear.[118]

After Augustine had spent more than thirty years battling the Donatists, he was dismayed to confront Christians he called the Pelagians who, despite many differences, as we shall see in Chapter 6, shared with the Donatists both a sectarian view of the church and an insistence on free will. When his own party was outvoted in the Christian synods, Augustine unhesitatingly allied himself with imperial officials against the clergy who defended Pelagius. In 416 Innocent, bishop of Rome, received from African synods two condemnations of Pelagian ideas, together with a long personal letter from Augustine and his closest associates as well as an open letter from Augustine challenging Pelagius. The documents went beyond a condemnation of Pelagius and his followers. They went on to warn, in Peter Brown's words, that

> the ultimate consequence of [Pelagian] ideas . . . cut at the roots of episcopal authority. . . . The documents claimed that by appeasing the Pelagians the Catholic church would *lose the vast authority it had begun to wield as the only force that could "liberate" men from themselves.* [119]

Pelagius's supporters would make the counterclaim (and with reason) that they were following ancient tradition concerning the church and human nature—tradition most recently championed by John Chrysostom himself. But the declarations of the African synods, engineered primarily by Augustine and his associates, signaled a major turning point in the history of western Christianity. They offered to the bishop of Rome and to his imperial patrons a clear demonstration of the political efficacy of Augustine's doctrine of the fall. By insisting that humanity, ravaged by sin, now lies helplessly in need of outside intervention, Augustine's theory could not only validate secular power but justify as well the imposition of church authority—by force, if necessary—as essential for human salvation.

Augustine, having outlived by twenty-seven years his exiled and disgraced colleague, achieved, unlike John Chrysostom, a position of extraordinary power and influence in the Roman world, until his death on 28 August 430. Augustine's ideas certainly did not win immediate or universal acceptance. Throughout the following century, until the Council of Orange in 529, Augustine's views were ardently debated. Even in the centuries following that council, which endorsed Augustine's views, many theologians held—or were accused of holding—"semi-Pelagian" views. Yet far beyond his lifetime, even for a millennium and a half, the influence of Augustine's teaching throughout western Christendom has surpassed that of any other church father. There are many reasons for this, but I suggest, as primary among them, the following: It is Augustine's theology of the fall that made the uneasy alliance between the Catholic churches and imperial power palatable—not only justifiable but necessary—for the majority of Catholic Christians. Augustine's doctrine, of course, was not, either for him or for the majority of his followers, a matter of mere expedience. Serious believers concerned primarily with the deeper questions of theology, as well as those concerned with political advantage, could find in Augustine's theological legacy ways of making sense out of a situation in which church and state had become inextricably interdependent.

The eventual triumph of Augustine's theology required, however, the capitulation of all who held to the classical proclamation concerning human freedom, once so widely regarded as the heart of the Christian gospel. By the beginning of the fifth century those who still held to such archaic traditions—notably including those the Catholics called Donatists and Pelagians—came to be condemned as heretics. Augustine's theory of Adam's fall, once espoused in simpler forms only by marginal groups of Christians, now moved, together with the imperially supported Catholic church that proclaimed it, into the center of western history.

VI

THE NATURE
OF NATURE

W E HAVE SEEN HOW Christian perspectives on freedom
and the power of the will changed as the situation of
Christians changed from that of persecuted sectarians to
that of the emperor's coreligionists. In this chapter I wish to point
out another element of Augustine's theology that accompanied this
enormous transformation: the holistic view of nature that came to
dominate Christian thought, and whose first principle is that human
beings wield—or once did, through Adam—great power over nature (an apparent paradox, given Augustine's conviction that human
beings, whose common ancestor had the power to transform nature,
now are powerless to evade the consequences of that transformation).

For millennia, Jews and Christians have attempted to explain the
mystery of human suffering as moral judgment—the price of Adam
and Eve's sin. The creation story of Genesis, addressing the question
Why do we suffer and why do we die?, makes the empirically absurd
claim that death does not constitute the natural end of all lives but
intruded upon our species solely because Adam and Eve made the
wrong choice. According to Genesis, God said to the woman,

> "I will greatly multiply your pain in childbearing; in pain you
> shall bring forth children, yet your desire shall be for your hus-
> band, and he shall rule over you." And to Adam he said, "Be-
> cause you have listened to the voice of your wife, and have eaten
> of the tree of which I commanded you, 'You shall not eat of it,'
> cursed is the ground because of you; in toil you shall eat of it all
> the days of your life; thorns and thistles it shall bring forth to you;
> . . . In the sweat of your face you shall eat bread till you return

to the ground, for out of it you were taken; you are dust, and to
dust you shall return."

(GENESIS 3:16–19)

Thus pain, oppression, labor, and death are punishments that we (or
our ultimate ancestors) *brought upon ourselves.* "In the beginning" the
willful choice of the first man and woman changed the nature of
nature itself, and all humankind thereafter suffered and died.

Perhaps part of the power of this archaic story, from which
Christians have inferred a moral system, lies in its blatant contradiction of everyday experience, its attribution of supernatural power to
certain human beings. What Adam's supernatural power once effected, Paul declares, only Christ's supernatural power can undo:
*"For as by a man came death, by a man has come also the resurrection of
the dead.* For as in Adam all die, so also in Christ shall all be made
alive" (1 Corinthians 15:21–22). The gospels claim that Jesus' mer-
est word could not only still a thunderstorm and heal diseases but call
the dead back to life. In the Sermon on the Mount Jesus himself
demanded that his followers control their own natures by taking
moral responsibility for their acts, and mastering such instinctual
responses as anger and sexual desire (Matthew 5:21–22, 27–28).

Zealous Christians of the first few centuries, as we have seen,
tested the extreme limits of human virtue (Latin *virtus,* literally
"strength") by demonstrating their power over their own sexuality.
Many early Christians also believed that they could triumph even
over death, not only in the future resurrection but here and now, if
they could break the power of natural impulses—above all, sexual
desire.[1] According to the Gospel of Luke Jesus himself had said:

> *"The children of this age marry, and are given in marriage; but those
> who are accounted worthy of the age to come and the resurrection from
> the dead neither marry nor are given in marriage, nor can they die any
> more; for they are equal to the angels in heaven, and, being children of
> God, are children of the resurrection."*

(LUKE 20:34–36)

Inspired by such words, many Christians pursued that unnatural—or,
as they would say, supernatural—life.

Yet stories of heroic ascetics, including the story of Jerome's
protégée the young widow Blaesilla, who died in her attempted
asceticism, raised obvious questions among Christians, as well as
among their critics. What is the extent—and what are the limits—of
human choice? What can we control, and what is beyond us? Can we

◆ 128 ◆

actually govern sexual desire, suffering, and death, or do these conditions belong to the structure of nature? Are they "acts of God" and thus beyond our power—or is this power a matter of degree? Is death, in particular, *natural*? Or is it *unnatural,* an enemy, as Paul said (1 Corinthians 15:26), intruding on human life because of Adam's sin?

During the formative period of Christian tradition, as we have seen, many thoughtful Christians struggled to understand not only the nature of the universe but human nature in particular. During the fourth and fifth centuries, certain Christians—including Pelagius, a devout Catholic ascetic from Britain—influenced by Greek science and philosophy, argued in his later teaching that human desires and human will, in themselves, have no effect on natural events—that humanity neither brought death upon itself nor could it, by an act of will, overcome death: death was in the nature of things, despite the clear statement to the contrary in Genesis. But Pelagius's contemporary Augustine vehemently rejected this view of nature, and the majority of Christians for more than a thousand years thereafter followed his example.

During his later years, as we have seen, Augustine argued against those who agreed with John Chrysostom,[2] and then against followers of Pelagius, both of whom insisted that Christians, through their baptism, are free to make moral choices; that, although our will cannot affect the course of nature, it can—and must—effect our moral decisions. By 417, the city of Rome was so divided between the supporters and the opponents of Pelagius that partisans of both sides had actually rioted in the streets. Two years earlier, two councils of bishops in Palestine had declared Pelagius orthodox; but two opposing councils of African bishops, led by Augustine and his colleagues, condemned him and persuaded Pope Innocent, bishop of Rome, to take their side. When Innocent died, his successor, Pope Zosimus, at first declared Pelagius's teaching orthodox; but after receiving vehement protests from Augustine and other African bishops, he reversed himself and excommunicated Pelagius.[3]

By this time, too, Christian bishops had learned to use for their own purposes not only ecclesiastical censure but also imperial power.[4] During the battle against Pelagius and his advocates, many of them influential Romans,[5] Augustine and his colleagues openly courted the emperor's support. Augustine's friend and fellow African bishop Alypius brought eighty Numidian stallions as bribes to the imperial court and successfully lobbied there against Pelagius.

The result gratified Augustine: in April 418, not only did the pope excommunicate Pelagius, but the emperor Honorius condemned the newly declared heretic and ordered him fined, expelled from office, and exiled along with his intransigent supporters.

The exiled Pelagius died soon afterward; but the most energetic of his followers refused to yield. Julian of Eclanum, an articulate and intellectual young Italian bishop, took up Pelagius's views and extended them. Julian even dared challenge the powerful Augustine, the most famous theologian of his day, and engaged the aging bishop in a battle that obsessed Augustine during the last twelve years of his life.

Augustine, summoning all his eloquence and fury, argued for a view of nature utterly antithetical to scientific naturalism. It was human choice—Adam's sin—that brought mortality and sexual desire upon the human race and, in the process, deprived Adam's progeny of the freedom to choose not to sin. Augustine amplified his argument in the six volumes of his *Opus Imperfectum Contra Julianum* ("Unfinished Work Against Julian"). Although Augustine is perhaps the greatest teacher of the church, this last work of his has so far remained untranslated into English.

Augustine's views prevailed, but the question is why? Why did the eloquent, passionate, and politically able Augustine finally succeed, after more than a decade of struggle, in having Pelagius's powerful supporters and friends, many of whom were monks, priests, bishops, and lay Christian persons, condemned as heretics, exiled, and deposed? How did Augustine persuade the majority of Christians that sexual desire and death are essentially "unnatural" experiences, the result of human sin?[6]

Certainly neither Pelagius nor Augustine set out to be "scientific" in anything like our sense of the word; neither, I suspect, would have regarded the term as a compliment. Instead, both began their reflections upon the natural universe with a common religious perspective, beginning with Genesis 1–4, from which each drew very different conclusions.

Pelagius, who shared the common Christian conviction that nature was good, as God created it, and that humankind was morally free, made in God's image, was dismayed when he first read Augustine's *Confessions.* For years Pelagius had respected Augustine's work, especially *On Free Will,* the treatise praising human freedom that Augustine had written as a young man. But when Augustine wrote his *Confessions* in his mature years, he declared that he had overestimated the power of human freedom. Now, he said, he realized that human beings are not free, as Adam was, to resist sin. We have no power to choose not to sin, and we cannot even control our sexual impulses. What is worse, "fleshly desire"—*concupiscentia carnis*—involves far more than its surface manifestations, which are only a symptom of deeper impulses that baffle, confound, and defeat our best attempts to control them.[7] Yet since everyone is conceived, as Augustine argued, through sexual desire, and since sexual desire is transmitted to everyone through the very semen involved in conception, he concludes, as we have seen, that all humankind is tainted with sin "from the mother's womb."

Augustine's theory, as we have also seen, was a radical departure from previous Christian doctrine, and many Christians found it pernicious. Many traditional Christians believed that this theory of "original sin"—the idea that Adam's sin is directly transmitted to his progeny—repudiated the twin foundations of the Christian faith: the goodness of God's creation; and the freedom of the human will. Most Christians agreed, at any rate, that even if before baptism we are stained by sin—Adam's sin and our own—baptism cleanses the believer from *all* sin, so that, in the words of the Egyptian teacher Didymus the Blind, "now we are found once more such as we were when we were first made: sinless and masters of ourselves."[8] In their argument with Augustine, Pelagius and his followers could claim the support of the revered fathers of the church, from Justin, Irenaeus, Tertullian, and Clement of Alexandria in the second century through John Chrysostom in the fourth.

According to his biographer Georges de Plinval, Pelagius himself had once agreed with the majority of his Jewish and Christian contemporaries—and with Augustine himself, for that matter—that death came upon the human race to punish Adam's sin. Yet as Augustine developed his view into a theory of human depravity, Pelagius's followers came to argue the opposite.[9] Universal mortality cannot be the result of Adam's punishment, since God, being just, would not have punished anyone but Adam for what Adam alone had done; certainly he would not condemn the whole human race for one man's transgression. Mortality, therefore, must belong to the structure of nature: mortality, which human beings share with every other species, is not, nor ever was, within the power of any human being to choose or reject.

Julian of Eclanum, the son of one of Augustine's fellow bishops, and himself the bishop of a provincial town in southern Italy, saw the controversy between Pelagius and Augustine engage Christians from Rome to Africa.[10] Julian, who once shared the nearly universal admiration for Augustine's learning and teaching, became convinced that on the question of nature, the aging bishop was simply wrong. He charged, too, that Pelagius's opponents had engineered his condemnation through personal influence at court, bribery, and false accusations. He himself intended to defend Pelagius's views through the serious theological debate he believed they deserved. Thus Julian championed and extended the ideas earlier expressed by John Chrysostom and other Christian teachers in order to reduce to absurdity Augustine's idea of original sin.

Augustine's enormous error, Julian believed, was to regard the present state of nature as punishment. For Augustine went further than those Jews and Christians who agreed that Adam's sin brought death upon the human race: he insisted that Adam's sin *also* brought upon us universal moral corruption. Julian replied to this that "natural sin" does not exist":[11] no physically transmitted, hereditary condition infects human nature, much less nature in general. To understand the human condition, Julian says, we must begin by distinguishing what is *natural* from what is *voluntary.*[12] Which conditions belong to the structure of nature, and so to "acts of God" beyond our power, and which depend upon human choice? What is natural, and therefore beyond our will, and what is voluntary?

Such questions led both Julian and Augustine back to Genesis, and each claimed its authority. Julian insisted that neither death nor sexual desire troubled Adam and Eve in Paradise, for both death and desire were, "from the beginning," natural:

> God made bodies, distinguished the sexes, made genitalia, bestowed affection through which bodies would be joined, gave power to the semen, and operates in the secret nature of the semen—and God made nothing evil.[13]

What about death? Doesn't Genesis teach that death is punishment for sin? Certainly, Julian responds, but not *physical* death. He insists that the death one suffers as punishment for Adam's sin is different from the universal mortality natural to all living species. Although the Genesis account says that God warned Adam that "on the day" of his transgression, "you shall surely die," Adam did not die *physically.* Instead, Julian says, Adam began to die morally and spiritually from the day he chose to sin. Adam's progeny confronts the same choice that Adam faced. For God gives to every human being what he gave to Adam—the power to choose one's own moral destiny, the power to choose the spiritual way of life or spiritual self-destruction. As for original sin, "the *merit of one single person is not such that it could change the structure of the universe itself.*"[14]

But Augustine insists that through an act of will Adam and Eve *did* change the structure of the universe; that their single, willful act permanently corrupted human nature as well as nature in general. Augustine's position is paradoxical in that he attributes virtually unlimited power to the human will but confines that power to an irretrievable past—to a lost paradise. According to Augustine, human power alone reduced us to our present state, one in which we have wholly lost that power. In our present state of moral corruption, what we need *spiritually* is divine grace, and what we need *practically* is external authority and guidance from both church and state.

Augustine, in his debate with Julian, contrasts actual human experience with an imaginative reconstruction of our lost Paradise—human life as he believes it "ought to be," a condition in which women experience painless childbearing and enjoy marriage without oppression or coercion.[15] But now Eve is under punishment, for God had said to her, "I will greatly multiply your pains in childbearing; in pain you shall bring forth children, yet your desire shall be for your husband, and he shall rule over you" (Genesis 3:16). As a result, Augustine says, women suffer the nausea, illness, and pains of pregnancy as well as the painful contractions of parturition that accompany normal labor. Many women experience the greater agonies of miscarriage, or "tortures inflicted by doctors, or the shock and loss of giving birth to an infant stillborn or moribund."[16] According to Augustine, these sufferings are not *natural,* but prove that nature itself, as we now experience it, is diseased:

> *Nature, which the first human being harmed, is miserable.* . . . What passed to women was not the burden of Eve's fertility, but of her transgression. Now fertility operates under this burden, having fallen away from God's blessing.[17]

As woman's fertility brings involuntary suffering, so also does sexual desire: the blight of male domination has fallen upon the whole structure of sexual relationships.[18] In their dealings with men, as in the pains they suffer with their children, women experience the consequences of the fall. Augustine catalogues these sufferings like a man who has felt and witnessed them: some babies, he says, are born blind, deaf, deformed, or without the use of their limbs; and others are born into such other forms of human suffering as demonic insanity or chronic and fatal disease. Even the fortunate ones, the children born normal and healthy, Augustine says, evince the terrifying vulnerability that pervades nature: every infant is born ignorant, wholly subject to passions and sensations, bereft of reason or articulate speech, entirely helpless.[19]

As Eve's sin brought suffering upon women, Adam's sin brought suffering upon men, according to Genesis 3:17–19:

> Cursed is the ground because of you; in toil you shall eat of it all the days of your life; thorns and thistles it shall bring forth to you; and you shall eat the plants of the field. In the sweat of your face you shall eat bread till you return to the ground, for out of it you were taken; you are dust, and to dust you shall return.

As God had first created it, the earth was free of thorns and thistles, bringing forth a marvelous abundance of food, according to Augustine. Then Adam sinned, and "all nature was changed for the worse";[20] thorns and thistles suddenly sprang up from the once fertile land. God had placed man in Eden "to till it and to cultivate it," and before he sinned, Adam worked "not only without laboring, but, indeed, with pleasure for the soul."[21] But now, Augustine says, every man experiences pain, frustration, and hardship in his labor, as every woman does in hers: the miseries of human nature now beset both sexes "from infancy to the grave."[22]

Worst of all is what awaits us at the end—"the last enemy, death." In the beginning, God granted "the power to live, not any necessity of dying."[23] Death was in no sense *natural* but arose only after Adam chose to sin, bringing upon himself and all his progeny this dreadful agony, along with "the innumerable forms of illness that bring people to death."[24] Adam's single arbitrary act of will rendered all subsequent acts of human will inoperative. Humankind, once harmonious, perfect, and free, now, through Adam's choice, is ravaged by mortality and desire, while all suffering, from crop failure, miscarriage, fever, and insanity to paralysis and cancer, is evidence of the moral and spiritual deterioration that Eve and Adam introduced. Ever since Augustine, the hereditary transmission of original sin has been the official doctrine of the Catholic church.

Augustine thus denies the existence of nature *per se*—of nature as natural scientists have taught us to perceive it—for he cannot think of the natural world except as a reflection of human desire and will. Where there is suffering, there must have been evil and guilt, for,

Augustine insists, God would not allow suffering where there was no prior fault. How, Augustine challenges Julian, could a just and all-powerful God allow infants to suffer

> the evils that nearly all infants suffer in this transitory life, if nothing calling for punishment were contracted from parents? Without a glance you bypass those evils which . . . all of us see them suffer. You say, "Human nature, at the beginning of life, is adorned with the gift of innocence." We agree, in regard to personal sins, but not about original sin. . . . You must explain why such great innocence is sometimes born blind or deaf. If nothing deserving punishment passes from parents to infants, who could bear to see the image of God sometimes born retarded, since this afflicts the soul itself? Consider the plain facts; consider why some infants suffer from a demon.[25]

In reply, Julian cites the New Testament Gospel of John, in which Jesus is asked whether a certain man was born blind because he had sinned or because his parents had sinned. Jesus answers, "Neither, but so that the glory of God might be revealed in him" (John 9:3), and proceeds to heal the man, restoring his sight. For Augustine, this story is irrelevant; what Jesus says about one man he healed cannot apply to people in general:

> These words cannot be applied to the innumerable infants born with such a wide variety of physical and mental handicaps. For many, indeed, are never healed, but die, disabled by their disabilities . . . even in infancy. Some infants retain the disabilities with which they were born, while others are afflicted with even more.[26]

Suffering *proves* that sin is transmitted from parents to children: "If there were no sin, then infants, bound by no evil, would suffer nothing harmful in body or soul under the great power of the just God."[27] To say that infants are innocent but suffer nonetheless, Augustine believes, is to abandon faith in divine justice. Augustine taunts Julian, "You see your whole heresy shipwrecked upon the misery of infants!"[28]

For Augustine, natural and moral evils collapse into one another. But Julian objects that "what is natural cannot be called evil," to which Augustine answers, "To say nothing of many other natural defects that afflict the body, we could regard natural deafness as an evil."[29] Such a perception of evil necessarily implicates everyone, for such infirmities as deafness are part of everyone's experience. What we now call *nature* we have come to know only in a state of chronic disease.

Julian predictably opposes this view and says that Augustine, like the Manichaeans, "defends natural evil . . . against the truth of the Catholic faith."[30] Christian faith, as Julian sees it, rests upon what he calls the five praises: the praise of creation; the praise of marriage; the praise of the law; the praise of the saints; the praise of the will. He rejects Augustine's equation of suffering with evil and guilt, and insists that nature is good—although, he admits, its "good" includes physical suffering.

Julian answers Augustine's reading of Genesis 3 point for point, claiming to have

> explained these things from the sound testimonies of the Scriptures, so that nothing remains of all Augustine's arguments and propositions that has not been refuted. . . . I proved that many things in his invention are false, many foolish, and many are sacrilegious.[31]

As for Augustine's claim that Eve's punishment has fallen upon all women, "This indeed is insane that the pains of parturition came into being because of sin."[32] Labor pains, which form part of "the condition of the sexes," have nothing to do with sin.[33] Innocent animals, including cattle, sheep, and cats, experience similar contractions to expel foetuses from the womb. If labor pains indicate sin, why do baptized women, released from sin, experience them as other women do? Furthermore, Julian continues, the severity of labor pains varies considerably. Arguing that extreme pain in childbirth cannot be regarded simply as a universal "given," Julian observes that

> certain barbarian women and nomads, accustomed to endure physical exertion, give birth in the course of their travels with such facility that, without stopping, they go out to gather food for their young, and continue on their way, transferring the burden of their womb to their shoulders; and, in general, village women do not require physicians for childbirth. . . . in fact, where luxury and softness increase, more women die in childbirth.[34]

But why does God say to Eve, "I will greatly multiply your pain in childbearing; in pain you shall bring forth children; yet your desire shall be for your husband, and he shall rule over you" (Genesis 3:16)? Julian insists that the passage means exactly what it says. The painful contractions that women, like animals, suffer are a natural part of the birth process *(naturaliter instituta).* [35] But the suffering involved in that natural process was increased and amplified in Eve's case to punish her disobedience. Man's rule over woman, Julian adds, forms part of the order of nature, "an institution of nature, not a punishment for sin."[36] Both Julian and Chrysostom concede, however, that male domination, like labor pain, while originating in God's "good" creation, may become, through sin, both painful and oppressive.

What about the man? Julian recalls the language of Genesis 3:17–19, emphasizing the words that refer to Adam's *experience* of nature:

> Cursed is the ground *in your works;* in sorrow *you shall eat from it all the days of your life;* thorns and thistles it shall bring forth *for you,* and you shall eat the produce of the field, in the sweat of your face you shall eat bread, until you return to the earth, for you were taken from it; for you are earth, and you shall return to earth.

Although the passage gives no hint that thorns, thistles, and sweat already existed on earth before sin, Julian asks, did these, then, as Augustine claims, spring up only after Adam's transgression, to punish Adam and his progeny?

Even before sin, Julian points out, Adam's task was to cultivate the garden (Genesis 2:15), as Eve's work was to bear children (Genesis 1:28). As contractions already formed a natural part of a woman's labor, Julian says, so sweating, exertion, and physical pain formed part of the man's. "Sweat is a natural help in physical exertion,"[37] not an innovation introduced to punish sin. Furthermore, Julian continues, just as in the case of women, the extent to which a man suffers in his work varies according to his physical condition, social position, and cultural situation. Not all men sweat in the fields; the rich do not labor, and not all who work sweat: "Some work with hard labor; others, with responsibilities." Some accomplish their work by thinking and writing, or engage in philosophy and learning; others choose, as their only "exercise" *(askesis)*, an ascetic vocation.

What actually changed, then, after sin? For Julian the Genesis passage does not indicate a universal and permanent change in nature, or even in human nature, nor does the passage intend to express objective fact. Would God curse and blight the innocent earth because of human sin? Are we to believe Augustine that thornbushes and thistles—species previously nonexistent—suddenly sprang up on earth to torment us? No, Julian argues; instead, the passage expresses the subjective experience of one who sins. Calling the earth " 'cursed in [Adam's] works' expresses the viewpoint of a person who is spiritually dying," the emptiness of one who, having "failed to cultivate his own possibilities," projects onto the world his own sense of loss. Such a person foolishly sees the earth itself—indeed, all of nature—as cursed and afflicted. Yet, Julian adds—perhaps referring to the pessimistic Augustine himself—"this lie cannot injure nature, nor the earth, in this curse, but only his own person, and his own will."

The person who is spiritually dying, then, experiences nature as resistant, hostile, the source of nearly intolerable frustrations and disasters. So Cain and Abel, who shared the same human nature but differed in their exercise of will, experienced nature in entirely different ways. Abel successfully cultivated the fields and praised God for his abundant harvest. He experienced no evil at the hands of nature herself, but only at his brother's hands: "That first death clearly showed that it was not a bad thing to die, for the righteous one was the first one to die." But when Cain, on the contrary, chose to sin, polluting the ground with his brother's blood, his own act set him into an antagonistic relationship with the earth, "as if by a curse from the earth, as it is written: 'cursed are you from the earth' " (Genesis 4:11).[38]

For Julian, such sufferings are more than merely a projection onto the world of one's own anger, grief, and terror. Cain's story suggests to Julian that sin actually has the power to transform the experience of the sinner. One who first chooses to sin, and then becomes enmeshed in sin, actually experiences life as unremitting misery. As Julian sees it, Augustine is just such a person: one whose view of "vitiated nature" reflects back to him his own obstinate sinfulness. Such a person would see bodily death, too, as Augustine characterizes it, as the final and worst affliction of all, as a kind of punishment. To this Augustine angrily replies, How *else* could anyone envision our "last enemy"?

Julian answers that the sentence concerning death ("until you return to the earth from which you came; for you are earth, and you shall return to earth") shows God's mercy, not his wrath: "Through the promise of an end to suffering he consoles humankind." Everyone, "through the natural senses," remains vulnerable to pain, but God promises that every suffering known to humankind "is moderated by the specific span of time, as though God were to say, 'Truly, you shall not suffer this forever,' but only 'until you return to earth:' "

> Our mortality is not the result of sin, but of nature! Why does Genesis not say, "because you sinned and transgressed my precepts"? This should have been said, if bodily dissolution were connected with a crime. But recall, what does it say? "because you are earth." Surely this is the reason why one returns to earth, "because you were taken out of it." If this, then, is the reason God gives, that one was from earth, I think it can be assumed that one cannot blame sin. Without doubt it is not because of sin, but because of our mortal nature . . . that the body dissolves back into the elements.[39]

That death forms a natural and necessary condition of human existence Christ himself confirms; for, Julian says, he teaches that God created and blessed human fertility, even before sin, to "replenish the earth" that was to be depleted by mortality.

Physical death merely offers us the necessary transition to eternal life, "so that in the corruptible bodies of the holy ones, eternal glory shall prevail, 'for this corruptible must put on incorruption, and this mortal must put on immortality' " (1 Corinthians 15:53). Julian continues to quote Saint Paul:

> "Death, where is your victory? Grave, where is your sting? The sting of death is sin . . ." That is, you, eternal death, who bear the sting of sin, wounding those who have abandoned justice, if you were not armed with this sting—that is, voluntary sin—you would not harm anyone![40]

Those who allow themselves to be wounded by sin and who live, consequently, in guilt, anger, terror, and despair, may experience, through their own fault, with unspeakable agony, the "sting of death." Yet, Julian adds,

> you see this sin and this sting shattered by people of faith, who resist sin through God, "who gives us the victory." Such persons pass from corruptible life on earth to eternal life with God.

Julian says that "God created fully innocent natures, capable of virtue according to their will,"[41] not only in Paradise, but now as well. Human nature—mortal, sexual, and vulnerable as it is—participates in the wholeness and goodness of the original creation.

Augustine, when he looks at nature, sees the opposite. For

Augustine, the truth of his own experience (and so, he believes, of everyone's) involves, above all, human helplessness. Three primary experiences—infancy, sexuality, and mortality—offer, he believes, irrefutable evidence of such helplessness. Julian, however, answers that "human nature in infants is whole and sound, and, in adults, capable of choosing [good or evil]."

But since Augustine believes that suffering comes from prior guilt, he rejects the moral innocence of infants and insists upon their helplessness, their incapacity to survive by themselves, much less to speak or reason. For Augustine finds the rage, weeping, and jealousy of which infants are capable proof of original sin, and he recalls his own infancy for confirmation. Augustine chides these "foolish new heretics," and especially their spokesman Julian ("O abominable and damnable voice!"), for saying that, even apart from sin, the natural human condition includes not only mortality but all its accompanying forms of disease and deformity. "Behold, then," Augustine mocks, "the Paradise of the Pelagians":

> Let us place there, then, men and women dedicated to chastity, struggling against sexual desire; pregnant women, nauseated, pale, unable to tolerate nourishment; others in labor, pouring forth immature foetuses in miscarriage; others, groaning and screaming in labor; and those that are born, all wailing, or laughing at one moment, then talking and babbling, later brought into school, that they might be taught to read, under the threat of whips, crying like girls because of an ingenious variety of punishments; and above all, innumerable diseases; incursions of demons, and attacks with various blows, some by which they are tormented, others by which they are consumed; and those, indeed, those who are healthy, are nurtured through difficult times of suffering through their parents' solicitude, for there are bereavements and mourning everywhere. . . .
>
> But the task is a long one, to relate how many evils abound in this life.[42]

In his later life, Augustine had only contempt for those who regarded sexual desire as a natural energy which every person may express or sublimate—who held that one's sexual impulses, in other words, are subject to one's will. For Augustine, these assumptions were facile and contrary to his own experience. What he believed instead was that we are helpless to control sexual desire; that "this diabolical excitement of the genitals"[43] arises in everyone, hideously out of control. Even in marriage he finds "boundless sloughs of lust and damnable craving."[44] If not for the restraints imposed by Christian marriage, "people would have intercourse indiscriminately, like dogs." Julian calls sexual desire "vital fire"; but Augustine admonishes us:

> Behold the "vital fire" *which does not obey the soul's decision, but, for the most part, rises up against the soul's desire* in disorderly and ugly movements.[45]

Julian believes that Augustine confuses sexual excess with desire itself; we must, he says, choose how we express that desire. Augustine replies in anger:

> Who can control this when its appetite is aroused? No one! In the very movement of this appetite, then, it has no "mode" that responds to the decisions of the will. . . . What married man *chooses* that the appetite be aroused, except when needed? What honest celibate *chooses* that the appetite *ever* be aroused? Yet what he wishes he cannot accomplish. . . . In the very movement of the appetite, *it has no mode corresponding to the decision of the will.*[46]

Bitterly, Augustine adds:

> You say, "In the married, it is exercised honestly; in the chaste, it is restrained by virtue." *Is this your experience of it?* . . . Indeed, since it is very pleasant, let the married effusively and impulsively seek each other whenever it titillates. . . . Let the union of bodies be legitimate wherever this, your *"natural good,"* spontaneously arises![47]

Julian was evidently restrained in sexual matters, and probably had little experience of the passions Augustine describes. Yet Augustine's question came from the heart, for the celibate Augustine was, by his own admission, insatiable, a man who never married and whose experience of sexual pleasure was illicit and guilt-provoking. Augustine assumes that frustrated desire is universal, infinite, and all-consuming. Julian, who had once—and probably briefly—been married to the daughter of a bishop, in a ceremony celebrated by a family friend as renewing the innocence of Adam and Eve, obviously wrote from a different kind of experience. For Julian, sexual desire is innocent, divinely blessed, and, once satisfied, entirely finite. Sexual desire, as Julian sees it, offers us the opportunity to exercise our capacity for moral choice.

Augustine concludes that not only are we helpless in infancy, and defenseless against sexual passion, but we are equally helpless in the face of death. We die; *therefore* we must be guilty of sin. For if we are not all sinners, then God is unjust to let us all die alike, even infants prematurely born, who have had no opportunity to sin.

If we are helpless before physical death, we are also helpless before spiritual death. This is a paradox; for spiritual death, Augustine says, comes from choosing evil; but even in our "free will" we are incapable of avoiding evil. *We choose evil involuntarily,* even "against our better judgment." Even when we want to do good, we cannot. "Is one driven, then," Julian asks, "by a captive will?" Yes, replies Augustine. "If a person is aware of the 'law of the [bodily] members,' and cries out with Paul, 'I cannot do what is good,' should you not say that the person is driven to evil by a captive will?"[48] So, Augustine concludes, physical death and spiritual death collapse into one: both rule over a lost humankind.

But according to Julian, here, too, Augustine confuses physiology with morality. Death is not a punishment for sin but a natural process, like sexual arousal and labor pains, natural, necessary, and universal for all living species. Such processes have nothing to do with human choice—and nothing to do with sin:

> Whatever is *natural* is shown not to be *voluntary.* If [death] is *natural,* it is not *voluntary.* If *voluntary,* it is not *natural.* These two, by definition, are opposites, like necessity and will. . . . The two cannot exist simultaneously; they cancel each other out.[49]

Although we are helpless before physical death, Julian says, *spiritual* death is a matter of choice. Here we are not mere animals but can exercise the free choice that God bestowed upon humankind in creation. Our free will engages us in the sphere of the *voluntary*—and the multiple possibilities available to individual choice: "Naturalia ergo necessaria sunt; possibilita autem voluntaria" ("Natural things, therefore, are necessary; possible things are voluntary").[50]

Although death is necessary and universal, each of us has the means—indeed, the responsibility—to choose the response we take to our mortal condition. Rather than resisting death as a mortal enemy, Julian says, the sinner may welcome death or even seek it as a relief from the sufferings induced by sin, while the saint may receive death as a spiritual victory. No one, saint or sinner, escapes suffering, which remains unavoidable in nature. Yet each of us holds in our hands our spiritual destiny, which depends upon the choices we make.

For more than twelve years Augustine and Julian debated, shouting back and forth their respective views, until Augustine died. After considerable controversy, the church of the fifth century accepted his view of the matter and rejected Julian's, having concluded that Augustine, the future saint, read Scripture more accurately than the heretic Julian. Recently, however, several scholars have pointed out that Augustine often interprets scriptural passages by ignoring fine points—or even grammar—in the texts. Augustine attempts to rest his case concerning original sin, for example, upon the evidence of one prepositional phrase in Romans 5:12, insisting that Paul said that death came upon all humanity because of Adam, *"in whom* all sinned." But Augustine misreads and mistranslates this phrase (which others translate "in that [i.e., because] all sinned") and then proceeds to defend his errors *ad infinitum,* presumably because his own version makes intuitive sense of his own experience.[51]

When Julian accused him of having invented this view of original sin, Augustine indignantly replied that he was only repeating what Paul had said before him. Had not the "great apostle" confessed that even he was incapable of doing what he willed?

> *I do not do what I will, but I do the very thing I hate. . . . So then it is no longer I that do it, but sin which dwells in me. For I know that nothing good dwells in me, that is, in my flesh. I can will what is good, but I cannot do it.*
>
> (ROMANS 7:15–18)

Augustine's argument has persuaded the majority of western Catholic and Protestant theologians to agree with him; and many western Christians have taken his interpretation of this passage for granted. But, as Peter Gorday has shown,[52] when we actually compare Augustine's interpretation with those of theologians as diverse as Origen, John Chrysostom, and Pelagius, we can see that Augustine found in Romans 7 what others had not seen there—a sexualized interpretation of sin and a revulsion from "the flesh" based on his own idiosyncratic belief that we contract the disease of sin through the process of conception. Other theologians assumed that Paul used these words to dramatize the situation of one who, still unbaptized and unredeemed, lacks hope; for Paul goes on to praise God for his own freedom, found in Christ:

> *Thanks be to God, through Jesus Christ our Lord. . . . For the law of the spirit of life in Christ Jesus has set me free.*
>
> (ROMANS 7:25; 8:2)

Augustine alone applied the despairing expressions of the previous passage to the baptized Christian; other readers assumed that the triumphant and joyful note of the rest of the chapter expressed Paul's experience of his life in Christ.

Julian often attends more carefully than Augustine to the wording and context, but he, too, reads his own experience—experience very different from Augustine's—into the biblical texts. The controversy between Augustine and Julian, as the German scholar Bruckner says, comes down to a clash between "two different worldviews." Bruckner happens to side with Augustine, claiming that "the strength of Augustine's view must be in his 'deeper experience of life' " (which depths Bruckner does not elaborate).[53] Augustine's argument may be arbitrary, but Bruckner contends that his *"deeper religious experience* . . . more adequately interprets the contents of the Holy Scriptures than the *superficial rationalism* of Julian."[54] The British scholar John Ferguson disagrees and sides instead with his fellow Briton Pelagius. What Bruckner takes as evidence of Augustine's "deeper religious experience" Ferguson sees as his stubborn refusal to acknowledge the data of ordinary experience:

> There is another side to our experience, of equal validity, and that
> is our knowledge of our own free will. It is there that Augustine
> lapses alike from logic and from common human experience.[55]

And so, after 1600 years, the argument goes on.

If Julian's argument looks simple—merely common sense—that simplicity is deceptive. In fact, it presupposes a Copernican revolution in religious perspective. That we suffer and die does not mean that we participate in guilt—neither Adam's guilt nor our own. That we suffer and die shows only that we are, by nature (and indeed, Julian would add, by divine intent), mortal beings, simply one living species among others. Arguing against the penal interpretation of death, Julian says, "If you say it is a matter of *will,* it does not belong to *nature;* if it is a matter of nature, it has nothing to do with *guilt.* "[56]

Like Copernicus's revolution, Julian's threatens to dislodge humanity, psychologically and spiritually, from the center of the universe, reducing it to one natural species among others. He rejects Augustine's primary assumption that Adam's sin transformed nature. To claim that a single human will ever possessed such power reflects a presumption of supernatural human importance. When Augustine claims that a single act of Adam's will "changed the structure of the universe itself," he denies that we confront in our mortality a natural order beyond human power.[57] For Augustine insists that we became susceptible to death solely through an act of will: "Death comes to us by *will*, not by *necessity*."[58]

Why did Catholic Christianity adopt Augustine's paradoxical—some would say preposterous—views? Some historians suggest that such beliefs validate the church's authority, for if the human condition is a disease, Catholic Christianity, acting as the Good Physician, offers the spiritual medication and the discipline that alone can cure it. No doubt Augustine's views did serve the interests of the emerging imperial church and the Christian state, as I have tried to show in the preceding chapter.

For what Augustine says, in simplest terms, is this: human beings cannot be trusted to govern themselves, because our very nature—indeed, *all* of nature—has become corrupt as the result of Adam's sin. In the late fourth century and the fifth century, Christianity was no longer a suspect and persecuted movement; now it was the religion of emperors obligated to govern a vast and diffuse population. Under these circumstances, as we have seen, Augustine's theory of human depravity—and, correspondingly, the political means to control it—replaced the previous ideology of human freedom.

Yet the requirements of an authoritarian state alone cannot account for the durability of such teaching throughout the centuries. We can see, too, that such interpretations of suffering as the result of sin are by no means limited to Christianity, much less to Catholicism. Jewish tradition has interpreted personal tragedy similarly, attributing, for example, the sudden death of an infant to the demon Lilith, to whose malevolence the child's parents had made themselves susceptible either through the husband's infidelity or the wife's insubordination. Some rabbis of ancient times would explain, too, to a young widow that she herself caused her husband's sudden heart attack by neglecting ritual regulations concerning the timing of intercourse.[59] Religions far from both Judaism and Christianity often express similar assumptions. A Hopi child is bitten by a poisonous spider while playing near its hole. As the boy hovers between life and death, the medicine man learns that the boy's father has neglected to prepare ritual ornaments for Spider Woman, the tribe's protector, which, he proclaims, has brought on his son's illness.[60]

The British anthropologist Evans-Pritchard tells the story of a sorcery investigation that followed the death of several Azande tribespeople who were resting in the shade of a granary that suddenly collapsed, killing them. The Azande fully recognized what we would call "natural causes": that the wood had begun to rot and crumble, that the nails had given way, that the supports were weakened by weeks of rain. The question was not why the granary collapsed, but why it collapsed at the very moment when these particular people could be trapped and crushed beneath it.[61] The Azande expected to find—and claimed to find—the cause of this disaster in human evil. But Jesus of Nazareth, referring to a remarkably similar disaster, challenged a similar assumption among his fellow Jews by asking, "Those eighteen upon whom the tower in Siloam fell and killed them, do you think that they were worse than any of the people who lived in Jerusalem?" and answering, "I tell you, No . . ."[62] But Jesus' dissent was an anomaly. The overwhelming weight of traditional Jewish and Christian teaching—and perhaps a human tendency to accept personal blame for suffering—implies that suffering and death are the wages of sin.

If Augustinian theology, or that of the rabbis or shamans who have also attributed suffering to sin, served only as a means of social control, why would people accept such sophistry? Why do people *outside* religious communities often ask themselves, as if spontaneously, the same questions, and give similar answers, blaming themselves for events beyond their power as if they had caused—or deserved—their own suffering?

The "social control" explanations assume a manipulative religious elite that *invents* guilt in order to dupe a gullible majority into accepting an otherwise abhorrent discipline. But the human tendency to accept blame for misfortunes is as observable among today's agnostics as among the Hopi or the ancient Jews and Christians, independent of—even prior to—religious belief. For quite apart from political circumstances, many people need to find reasons for their sufferings. Had Augustine's theory not met such a need—were it not that people often *would rather feel guilty than helpless*—I suspect that the idea of original sin would not have survived the fifth century, much less become the basis of Christian doctrine for 1600 years. I am not speaking, now, of cases in which guilt may be appropriate—cases in which people have chosen to take certain risks, or to inflict pain upon themselves or others, with predictable results. Instead I am speaking of those cases in which guilt seems to be an inexplicable, irrational, inappropriate response to suffering. But why would anyone *choose* to feel guilty?

One may know perfectly well the statistical possibilities concerning natural disasters, freak accidents, and life-threatening diseases and regard these—theoretically, at least—as fully natural phenomena. But when such events suddenly threaten (or spare) one's own life, questions occur, so to speak, in the first person. Like the Azande, one asks not what *caused* the earthquake, fire, or disease (for this may be obvious enough) but "Why did this happen now, in this way, to this person?"

What are we to make, I wonder, of this peculiar preference for guilt? Augustine would, I suspect, take it as evidence that human nature itself is "diseased," or, in contemporary terms, neurotic. I would suggest, instead, that such guilt, however painful, offers reassurance that such events do not occur at random but follow specific laws of causation; and that their causes, or a significant part of them, lie in the moral sphere, and so within human control. Augustine, like the Hebrew author of Genesis 2–3, gives religious expression to the conviction that humankind does not suffer and die randomly, but for specific reasons. Asserting one's own guilt for suffering may also encourage one to make specific, perhaps long overdue, changes. Guilt invites the sufferer to review past choices, to amend behavior, redress negligence, and perhaps by such means improve his or her life.

Psychologically simple and compelling, Augustine's view accords with responses that, for many people, arise as if instinctively in the face of suffering: Why has this happened? And why me? Augustine's answer simultaneously acknowledges and denies human helplessness; in this paradox, I suspect, its power lies.

To the sufferer, Augustine says, in effect, "You *personally* are not to blame for what has come upon you; the blame goes back to our father, Adam, and our mother, Eve." Augustine assures the sufferer that pain is unnatural, death an enemy, alien intruders upon normal human existence, and thus he addresses the deep human longing to be free of pain. But he also assures us that suffering is neither without meaning nor without specific cause. Both the cause and the meaning of suffering, as he sees it, lie in the sphere of *moral choice,* not *nature.* If guilt is the price to be paid for the illusion of control over nature—if such control is, as Julian argued, in fact, an illusion—many people have seemed willing to pay it.

By contrast, Julian offers a much reduced sense of power over nature. Our human ancestors no longer are the mythical, semimagic beings celebrated in Jewish legend—for instance, Adam, the ball of whose foot shone more glorious than the sun, whose radiant presence filled the universe with light . . . whose body spanned the continents, and whose shining face filled the angels with envy and awe.[63]

The Protestant Christian painter and engraver Dürer depicted the awesome power of Adam and Eve, as tradition had taught him, in vivid form. While they stand ready to take the fateful bite of that forbidden fruit, a cat waits at their feet, poised to pounce upon the unsuspecting mouse. Her capacity for murderous violence—and that of all living creatures—is about to be unleashed by human sin.[64]

Julian denies that the human will has this power over nature: "All that a person has from nature . . . he has from necessity" . . . since everything in nature depends upon an "immutable order."[65] Free will is not impotent, as Augustine argues, but it enables us "either to *consent* to wrongdoing, or to *refrain* from it." Free will provides the possibility of moral action. Julian might agree with the gnostic or Buddhist precept that "all life is suffering," yet he does not take this as an indictment of human existence, as if ordinary life were an illusion or the result of a "fall," or a form of spiritual death. Instead, Julian stands upon the Jewish and Christian tradition that affirms the essential goodness of the created world: "What is natural cannot be qualified by evil."[66]

Yet if suffering is necessary and normal, misery is optional. Misery, which Augustine equates with suffering, involves, as Julian sees it, human choice: it involves specific—and specifically *sinful*—ways one chooses to deal with natural conditions. One person accepts a serious illness with patience, faith, and love, taking it as the occasion for spiritual growth; another rages against God and nature and weeps with self-pity and terror, turning inevitable suffering into nearly intolerable misery. So, Julian explains, although every one of us will die, "death is not always an evil; since, to the martyrs, for instance, it is for the sake of glory."[67] Julian would agree with the Buddhist teacher who pointedly rejects the usual Christian view of death as, in Paul's words, the "last enemy." For those who are on the path to enlightenment, "death is not . . . an enemy to defeat, but a compassionate friend." But those who choose to indulge in anger, envy, pride, and the consuming fears that suffocate faith, Julian says, experience the physical vulnerabilities common to our species with their pain "greatly increased" through their own fault.

Augustine's holistic, antinaturalistic view of nature—one in which Adam's will directly affected natural events, and in which suffering occurs solely because of human fault—appeals, then, to the human need to imagine ourselves in control, even at the cost of guilt. Julian's alternative, although more consonant with a scientific view of nature, is not in itself scientific but religious—a view that rests upon the ancient affirmation that the world, as originally created, is good, and that each person bears responsibility for moral choice.

Augustine's theology resembles the moralizing views of suffering that arise in many cultures, but with a difference. For unlike all other views, the Augustinian theory of original sin claims that our moral capacity has been so fatally infected that human nature as we know it cannot be trusted. Consequently, Augustine does not urge people to remedy their situation, as the Hopi shaman might, nor, like a rabbi, does he call them to moral reform; for humanity's moral disease is not only universal but also, apart from divine grace, incurable. Throughout western history this extreme version of the doctrine of original sin, when taken as the basis for political structures, has tended to appeal to those who, for whatever reason, suspect human motives and the human capacity for self-government. The counterpoint to the idea of original sin expressed in the hope of humanity's capacity for moral transformation, whether articulated in utopian and romantic versions or in the sober prose of Thomas Jefferson, has appealed, conversely, to more optimistic temperaments.

Yet, as we have seen, Christians during the first centuries would not have imagined that their vision of a society characterized by liberty and justice could be the basis for a political agenda. Instead, most Christians, like many Jews, saw such freedom, and the elevation of the oppressed, as blessings to be anticipated in the Kingdom of God (as Luke says Jesus did). Among the Jews, the Essenes attempted to live out this egalitarian idea in their monastic community as a model of that coming kingdom; and certain Christians, too, like the author of the New Testament book of Acts, projected a similar ideal back onto the early Christian movement during the "golden age" of the apostolic church. Centuries, even millennia, would pass before such visions began to inform actual political aspirations and institutions; and only the most optimistic among us may still hope that such visions will one day achieve political reality.

Meanwhile, we have seen how Christian practices and perceptions concerning sexuality, politics, and human nature changed from the first century through the fourth; how after Jesus had called people to prepare for the coming Kingdom of God, and Paul proclaimed both its imminence and its radical demands, some intensely ascetic Christians in subsequent generations tried to put their teachings into radical practice, while others attempted to accommodate Christian teaching to existing social and political structures.

We have seen, too, that when state persecution pressed Christians to revere the emperors and the gods, the boldest among them, like Perpetua and her companions, defied government officials in the name of liberty and maintained their loyalty to Jesus, crucified for treason against Rome, as their "divine King," and others, like Justin, denounced the emperors and all their gods as the panoply of devils. These embattled Christians forged a vision of what Tertullian called the new "Christian society," which he boasted was marked by freedom from compulsion, voluntary contributions for the welfare of all members, mutual love, and common faith.

As the Christian movement grew, despite persecution, and increasingly developed its own internal organization, its leaders expelled nonconformists from their ranks, including gnostic Christians. They insisted that only orthodox Christians preached the true gospel of Christ—the message of moral freedom, given in creation and restored in baptism.

Some of the most intense Christians, who refused any compromise with "the world," sought to realize that liberty through the ascetic life, rejecting familial, social, and political obligations in order to recover the original glory of humankind, created in the "image and likeness of God." After the persecutions ended, asceticism offered a new path for uncompromising "witness"—a new form of self-chosen martyrdom.

Finally, we have seen how Christian views of freedom changed as Christianity, no longer a persecuted movement, became the religion of the emperors. Augustine not only read into the message of Jesus and Paul his own aversion to "the flesh," but also claimed to find in Genesis his theory of original sin. In his final battle against the Pelagians, Augustine succeeded in persuading many bishops and several Christian emperors to help drive out of the churches as "heretics" those who held to earlier traditions of Christian freedom. From the fifth century on, Augustine's pessimistic views of sexuality, politics, and human nature would become the dominant influence on western Christianity, both Catholic and Protestant, and color all western culture, Christian or not, ever since. Thus Adam, Eve, and the serpent—our ancestral story—would continue, often in some version of its Augustinian form, to affect our lives to the present day.

EPILOGUE

W HAT, THEN, are you saying?" asked a friend of mine, himself a distinguished scholar of early Christianity. "Whose side are you on? Are you saying that the real Christianity is more like John Chrysostom and the Pelagians (God forbid) than like Augustine? Or are you just saying that they all made interesting and different, but all politically and motivationally mixed and a little bit crazy, responses to what they took to be the gospel?"

This question, coming from him, startled me, since he certainly knows from his own experience how historical investigation differs from religious inquiry. Yet his question reminded me that when I was a graduate student at Harvard and dissatisfied with the representatives of Christianity I saw around me, I wanted to find the "real Christianity"—and I assumed that I could find it by going back to the earliest Christians. Later I saw that my search was hardly unique: no doubt most people who have sought out the origins of Christianity have really been looking for the "real Christianity," assuming that when the Christian movement was new, it was also simpler and purer.

What I found was the opposite of what I'd expected, for my professors were exploring the complex history of the construction of the New Testament, and, most surprising of all, they were investigating gnostic gospels and other writings attributed to Jesus' disciples—ancient papyrus texts discovered near Nag Hammadi in Upper Egypt in 1945. Fascinated by these writings, I realized that instead of simplifying the search for the "real Christianity," these texts made it more baffling; they suggested that during the first two centuries the Christian movement may have been even more diversified than it is today. For today, virtually all Christians revere the same canon of Christian writings—the collection of twenty-six books we call the New Testament; most share a common creed; and most celebrate, in various ways, the same rituals (baptism and eucharist). But during the first and second centuries, Christians scattered throughout the world, from Rome to Asia, Africa, Egypt, and Gaul, read and revered quite different traditions, and various groups of Christians perceived Jesus and his message very differently.

In the present book, I set out to see how Christians have interpreted the creation accounts of Genesis. But what intrigued me especially was this question: since the representatives of Christian orthodoxy, from Justin through Irenaeus, Tertullian, Clement, and Origen, had denounced gnostic interpretations of Genesis in the name of moral freedom, how could the majority of Christians in the fifth century be persuaded to give up this primary theme of Christian doctrine—or, at least, to modify it radically—following Augustine's reinterpretation of Adam's sin? This book shows where the question led me.

What I did *not* find in the process of this research was what I had started out to find—a "golden age" of purer and simpler early Christianity. What I discovered instead is that the "real Christianity"—so far as historical investigation can disclose it—was not monolithic, or the province of one party or another, but included a variety of voices, and an extraordinary range of viewpoints, even among the saints (witness Augustine and Chrysostom!), as well as among those denounced as heretics, from Valentinus to Julian, and even, as we have seen, within the New Testament writings themselves. From a strictly historical point of view, then, there is no single "real Christianity."

Yet in saying this I recall how William James, writing his *Varieties of Religious Experience,* distinguishes between his psychological analysis of religious experience and the value judgments—positive or negative—that one can make about such experience; the same distinction applies to historical analysis. James distinguishes two modes of inquiry concerning anything:

> First, what is the nature of it? . . . what is its constitution, origin and history? And second, What is its importance, meaning, or significance now that it is once here? The answer to the one question is given in an *existential judgment* or proposition. The answer to the other is a *proposition of value* . . . what we may, if

we like, denominate a *spiritual judgment.* Neither judgment can be deduced immediately from the other.

As James points out:

> If our theory of revelation-value were to affirm that any book, to possess it, must have been composed automatically . . . or that it must exhibit no scientific and historic errors and express no local or personal passions, the Bible would probably fare ill at our hands. But if, on the other hand, our theory should allow that a book might well be a revelation in spite of errors and passions and deliberate human composition, if only it be a true record of the inner experience of great-souled persons wrestling with the crises of their fate, then the verdict would be much more favorable. You see that the existential facts by themselves are insufficient for determining the value . . . with the same conclusions of fact before them, some take one view, and some another, of the Bible's value as a revelation, according as their spiritual judgment as to the foundation of value differs.

The same proves true of the post-biblical history of Christianity. Some readers of this book, reflecting on the various ways that Christians interpreted Genesis throughout the first four hundred years of Christian history, may conclude that certain theologians—Augustine, or the Pelagians, for example—were opportunistic or mistaken; others will conclude the opposite.

For my own part, I came to realize that using historical means to explore the origins of Christianity most often does not solve religious questions but can offer new perspectives upon these questions. I had long been impressed, for example, with Augustine's perceptive and candid observations of his own experience in his *Confessions,* and with many of the psychological and theological insights he expresses in such works as the *City of God* and *On the Trinity.* Since graduate school I had taken for granted, too, the conventional orthodox view of Pelagius and his followers as superficial rationalists who stubbornly and inexplicably resisted the deeper truths of Augustinian theology. But after investigating Augustine's views in the Pelagian controversy and those of his opponents, I concluded, as this book shows, that even his admirers would do well to reassess and qualify Augustine's singular dominance in much of Western Christian history.

Finally, I came to see that more important, to me, than taking sides on such specific issues—especially since my own position has changed as my perspective and situation changed—is the recognition of a spiritual dimension in human experience. This recognition, after all, is what all participants in Christian tradition, however they disagree, share in common—and share, for that matter, with many people who are involved in Christian tradition only peripherally, or not at all.

NOTES

INTRODUCTION

1. C. Geertz, cited in D. Tracy, *The Anagogical Imagination: Christian Theology and the Culture of Pluralism* (New York, 1981), 7, n. 18.

2. For example, see R.M. Grant, *Early Christianity and Society* (San Francisco, 1977); G. de Ste. Croix, *The Class Struggle in the Ancient Greek World from the Archaic Age to the Arab Conquests* (New York, 1981); R. MacMullen, *Christianizing the Roman Empire (A.D. 100–400)* (New Haven, 1984); W. Meeks, *The First Urban Christians: The Social World of the Apostle Paul* (New Haven, 1983); P. Veyne, articles cited in Chapter 1, also "The Roman Empire," in *A History of Private Life* 1: *From Pagan Rome to Byzantium,* ed. P. Veyne (Cambridge, Mass./London, 1987), 9–233.

3. Tertullian, *Apology* 39.

4. P. Gorday, *Principles of Patristic Exegesis: Romans 9–11 in Origen, John Chrysostom and Augustine* (New York/Toronto, 1983).

CHAPTER ONE

For a more technical and scholarly discussion of this material, see E. Pagels, "Adam and Eve, Christ and the Church: A Survey of Second-Century Controversies Concerning Marriage," in *The New Testament and Gnosis: Essays in Honor of R. McL. Wilson,* ed. A.H.B. Logan and A.J.M. Wedderburn (Edinburgh, 1983), 146–175.

1. For an excellent discussion of the Hellenistic period, see V. Tcherikover, *Hellenistic Civilization and the Jews* (Philadelphia, 1961); on the time of Jesus, see S. Safrai and M. Stern, *The Jewish People in the First Century* (Philadelphia, 1974, vol. 1, and 1976, vol. 2); M. Smith, "The Zealots and the Sicarii," *Harvard Theological Review* 64 (1971), 1–19; J. Gager, *Kingdom and Community: The Social World of Early Christianity* (New Jersey, 1975); A. Segal, "Society in the Time of Jesus," chap. 2 of *Rebecca's Children: Judaism and Christianity in the Roman World* (Cambridge, Mass., 1986).

2. Josephus, the Jewish historian born in 37 C.E., wrote a detailed and polemical history of the Herods and the Jewish war, in which he personally participated: see *The Jewish War*, trans. G.A. Williamson, in the Penguin series (Middlesex, England, 1959, reprinted 1972).

3. Josephus, *The Jewish War* 2,5,2; *Jewish Antiquities* 17,10; M. Hengel, *Crucifixion in the Ancient World and the Folly of the Message of the Cross*, trans. J. Bowden (Philadelphia, 1977), especially chaps. 4 and 7 I am grateful to my colleague Professor Thomas Boslooper for pointing out to me this reference.

4. A. Segal, *Rebecca's Children*, 39.

5. Josephus, *Antiquities* 18,136. According to Jewish custom Herod's marriage to his sister-in-law was of questionable legitimacy

6. See accounts in Mark 1:4–7; Luke 3.1–20.

7. Josephus, *Antiquities* 20,107–112; cf. also *The Jewish War* 2,224. Josephus's figures, like those of other ancient historians, are not necessarily accurate.

8. Cf. A. Segal, "Jesus, the Jewish Revolutionary," chap. 3 in *Rebecca's Children*, 68–95.

9. J. Neusner, *From Politics to Piety. The Emergence of Pharisaic Judaism* (Englewood Cliffs, N.J., 1973), see also E. Rivkin, *A Hidden Revolution: The Pharisees' Search for the Kingdom Within* (Nashville, Tenn., 1978); M. Smith, "Palestinian Judaism in the First Century," in M. Davis, ed., *Israel Its Role in Civilization* (New York, 1986); A. Segal, *Rebecca's Children*, chap. 5: "Origins of the Rabbinic Movement," 117–41.

10 M. Smith, "Palestinian Judaism in the First Century," in *Israel: Its Role in Civilization*, ed. M. Davis (New York, 1956); J Neusner, *From Politics to Piety. The Emergence of Pharisaic Judaism*; Segal, "Origins of the Rabbinic Movement," in *Rebecca's Children*, 117–141.

11. As Peter Brown strikingly states in his forthcoming book, *The Body and Society. Men, Women, and Sexual Renunciation in Early Christianity*.

12. P. Veyne, "La Famille et l'amour sous le Haut-Empire romain," *Annales* 33,1 (1978), 35–63; "L'homosexualité à Rome," *Communications* 35 (1982), 26, summarized in "The Roman Empire," in *A History of Private Life* I: *From Pagan Rome to Byzantium*, ed. P. Veyne (Cambridge, Mass./London, 1987), 9–49 (section on marriage), and 51–69 (on slavery).

13. P. Veyne, "The Roman Empire," 217, in *A History of Private Life*

14. Athenagoras, *Legatio pro Christians* 11.

15. Justin, 1 *Apology* 14–16; 27–29; 2 *Apology*: Tertullian, *Apology* 3.

16. See R. MacMullen, *Christianizing the Roman Empire* (New Haven, 1984), for a different assessment of conversion, especially in Constantinian times.

17. L.M. Epstein, *Marriage Laws in the Bible and the Talmud* (Cambridge, Mass., 1942).

18. Josephus, *Life*, 75; 426–428. Whether Josephus actually was bigamous is not clear from the text.

19. Josephus, *Jewish Antiquities* 17,1,2; 15.

20. *Mishna Yebamot* 6,6.

21. The *Book of Jubilees* 3,8–14.

22. *Ibid.*, 3,26–31.

23. *Mishna Gittin* 9,10.

24. As we shall see, the author of the Gospel of Matthew apparently modified this view; for discussion, pp. 22–23.

25. This passage has engendered much discussion: see, for example, the commentaries on 1 Corinthians by H. Conzelmann, *Der erste Brief an die Korinther* (Göttingen, 1969); R. Scroggs, "Paul and the Eschatological Woman," in *Journal of the American Academy of Religion* 40 (1972), 283–303, and the reply by E. Pagels, "Paul and Women: A Response to Recent Discussion," in *Journal of the American Academy of Religion* 42 (1974), 538–549.

26. G.B. Shaw, "The Monstrous Imposition upon Jesus," reprinted in W. Meeks, ed., *The Writings of Saint Paul* (New York, 1972), 296–302.

27. As Clement of Alexandria attests; *Stromata* 3,74.

28. *Acts of Paul and Thecla,* 7.

29. *Ibid.,* 6.

30. *Ibid.,* 8–9.

31. *Ibid.,* 20.

32. R. Söder, *Die apokryphen Apostelgeschichten und die romanhafte Literatur der Antike* (Stuttgart, 1932); L. Radermacher, *Hippolytus und Thecla: Studien zur Geschichte von Legende und Kultus* (Vienna, 1916); J.D. Kaestli, "Les Principales Orientations de la recherche sur les Actes apocryphes," in *Les Actes apocryphes des Apôtres,* ed. F. Boron (Geneva, 1981).

33. For discussion see D. MacDonald, *The Legend and the Apostle: The Battle for Paul in Story and Canon* (Philadelphia, 1983), 21,90–96.

34. "Mothers of the Church: Ascetic Women in the Late Patristic Age," in *Women of Spirit,* ed. R.R. Ruether and E. McLaughlin (New York, 1979), 74; see also her discussion "Virginal Feminism in the Fathers of the Church," in *Religion and Sexism,* ed. R.R. Ruether (New York, 1974), 150–183; and also the provocative monograph by S. Davies, *The Revolt of the Widows* (Carbondale, Ill., 1980).

35. *Acts of Thomas* 9,83–87.

36. *Ibid.,* 9,88.

37. See, for example, the *Acts of Andrew* 5–7, and discussion in E. Pagels, "Adam and Eve, Christ and the Church," 151–158; also G. Theissen, *The Sociology of Early Palestinian Christianity,* trans. J. Bowden (Philadelphia, 1978).

38. *Epistle to Diognetus* 5,6.

39. *Epistle of Barnabas* 10,1–12; 19,4.

40. Clement of Alexandria, *Stromata* 3,49.

41. The African Christian Tertullian (c. 200) declares that Christians are not "Indian Brahmins or gymnosophists," who live in forests, and exile themselves from ordinary human life." *Apology* 42.

42. For discussion, see H. Koester, *History and Literature of Early Christianity* (Berlin/New York, 1980), vol. 2, 97–146, 261–307; M. Dibelius and H. Conzelmann, *The Pastoral Epistles* (Philadelphia, 1972); D. MacDonald, *The Legend and the Apostle.*

43. Cf. W. Meeks, "Paul: The Domesticated Apostle," in *The Writings of Saint Paul* (New York, 1972).

44. For an excellent and detailed discussion, see D. MacDonald, "The Pastoral Epistles Against 'Old Wives' Tales,' " chap. 3 in *The Legend and the Apostle,* 54–77.

45. Recently, Elizabeth Fiorenza and other scholars have shown how the introduction of such traditional patriarchal attitudes profoundly affected the situation of Christian women, from ancient times to the present. See, for example, *In Memory of Her: A Feminist Theological Reconstruction of Christian Origins* (New York, 1983).

46. For a more detailed discussion of Clement's exegesis, see E. Pagels, "Adam and Eve, Christ and the Church," 153–155. For Clement's own words, see *Stromata*, vol. 3, published in a fine English translation by J. Oulton and H. Chadwick, in *Alexandrian Christianity*, vol. 2, 40–92, in *The Library of Christian Classics* (Philadelphia, 1954).

47. Clement, *Stromata* 3,49.

48. *Ibid.*, 3,49–50.

49. *Ibid.*, 3,53.

50. *Ibid.*, 3,51,85.

51. *Ibid.*, 3,84.

52. *Ibid.* 3,81–82; Irenaeus, *Libris Quinque Adversus Haereses* 3,28,8. Hereafter cited as AH.

53. Clement, *Stromata*, 3,102.

54. *Ibid.*

55. Clement, *Paidagogos* 2,83.

56. Irenaeus, AH 3,22,4.

57. Clement, *Stromata* 3,94; 103.

58. Irenaeus, AH 3,23,5.

59. Such views were by no means unique to Clement; certain Stoic philosophers had propounded similar views, which Clement here sets forth in Christian dress. For discussion see P. Veyne, "La Famille et l'amour sous le Haut-Empire romain," *Annales* 33,1 (1978), 35–63; R.L. Fox, "Living Like Angels," in *Pagans and Christians* (New York, 1987), 336–374.

60. Clement, *Stromata* 3,57–58.

61. Clement, *Paidagogos* 2,95.

62. *Ibid.*, 2,97f.

63. Clement, *Stromata* 6,100.

64. Clement, *Stromata* 7,12.

65. Clement, *Stromata* 7,64.

66. On Paul's ambivalence, see E. Pagels, "Paul and Women: A Response to Recent Discussion," cited in note 25 above.

CHAPTER TWO

For a more technical and scholarly discussion of the material included in Chapter 2, see E. Pagels, "Christian Apologists and the 'Fall of the Angels': An Attack on Roman Imperial Power?" in *Harvard Theological Review* 78,3–4 (1985), 301–325.

1. Tertullian, *Apology* 1.

2. *Ibid.*, 2.

3. As one philosophically minded critic, Celsus, complained; Origen, *Contra Celsum* 3,44.

4. As several distinguished scholars recently have pointed out: see R.M. Grant, *Early Christianity and Society* (San Francisco, 1977); R. MacMullen, *Christianizing the Roman Empire* (New Haven/London, 1984); W. Meeks, *The Moral World of the First*

Christians (Philadelphia, 1986). For a fascinating study of Christian accommodation, see D. Balch, *Let Wives Be Submissive: The Domestic Code in I Peter* (California, 1981).

5. For pagan views of Christians, see the classic study by P. de Labriolle, *La Réaction païenne. Étude sur la polémique antichrétienne du Ier au IVe siècle,* 2nd ed. (Paris, 1948); R. MacMullen, *Paganism in the Roman Empire* (New Haven, 1981); R.L. Wilken, *The Christians as the Romans Saw Them* (New Haven, 1984). Recently the distinguished scholar R.M. Grant has gathered evidence of what he calls "Christian Devotion to the Monarchy," in *Early Christianity and Society,* 13–43.

6. *Passio Sanctarum Perpetuae et Felicitas* 3, trans. H. Musurillo, in *The Acts of the Christian Martyrs* (Oxford, 1972), 106–131. Hereafter cited as *Passio Perpetuae.*

7. For discussion, see W. Meeks, *The Moral World of the First Christians,* 22–28.

8. *Passio Perpetuae* 3.

9. *Passio Perpetuae* 5.

10. *Ibid.,* 6.

11. *Ibid.,* 10.

12. *Ibid.,* 15.

13. *Ibid.,* 16.

14. *Ibid.,* 18.

15. *Ibid.,* 20.

16. *Ibid.,* 21.

17. *The Martyrs of Lyons,* 60, in *The Acts of the Christian Martyrs,* 81.

18. Justin, 2 *Apology* 12.

19. Justin, 1 *Apology* 25. Emphasis added.

20. Justin, *Dialogue with Trypho,* 2.

21. *Ibid.*

22. See G.E.M. de Ste. Croix, "Why Were the Early Christians Persecuted?" in *Past and Present* 26 (1963), 6f., "Aspects of the 'Great' Persecution," *Harvard Theological Review* 47,2 (1954), 75–114.

23. Justin, 2 *Apology* 3.

24. R.M. Grant, *Early Christianity and Society,* "Christian Devotion to the Monarchy," 13–43. Professor Grant acknowledges in the introduction to his book (as I do in the introduction to this one) that he did not intend to write a comprehensive history of the early church, but rather "a venture into the reconstruction of early Christian practicality" (ix), which in many ways he has admirably provided.

25. Justin, 2 *Apology* 2.

26. Clement, *Protreptikos Logos* 10,92.

27. *Ibid,* 11,114.

28. For discussion, see the classical study by L.R. Taylor, *The Divinity of the Roman Emperor* (New York, 1975).

29. Lucian, *Life of Peregrinus* 13.

30. Marcus Aurelius, *Meditations* 2,3–5.

31. For excellent discussions of the political significance of the imperial cult, see J. Beaujeu, *La Religion romaine à l'apogée de l'Empire* (Paris, 1955), and S.R.F. Price, *Rituals and Power* (Cambridge, England, 1984).

32. Beaujeu, *La religion romaine,* 327.

33. S.R.F. Price, *Rituals and Power.*

34. For discussion of pagan views of the imperial cult, see the above; also G.W. Bowersock, "Greek Intellectuals and the Imperial Cult in the Second Century

A.D.," and F. Miller, "The Imperial Cult and the Persecutions," both in W. den Boer, ed., *Le Culte des souverains dans l'empire romain* (Geneva, 1973), 179–211; 145–75.

35. Justin, 2 *Apology* 5.

36. Justin, 1 *Apology* 5.

37. *Ibid.*, 10.

38. *Ibid.*, 5.

39. P. Brown, *The Making of Late Antiquity* (Cambridge, Mass., 1978), 75.

40. Tatian, *Oratione ad Graecis* 22.

41. Athenagoras, *Legatio pro Christianis* 34.

42. Clement, *Protreptikos Logos* 4,60.

43. Suetonius, *The Caesars,* "Tiberius," 44.

44. Clement, *Protreptikos Logos* 2,37.

45. Clement, *Protreptikos Logos* 4,47.

46. Justin, 1 *Apology* 13; cf. R. MacMullen, "The Roman Concept of the Robber-Pretender," *Revue Internationale des Droits de l'Antiquité* 3 (1983), 221–226.

47. Justin, 1 *Apology* 14.

48. Justin, 2 *Apology* 4.

49. Justin, 1 *Apology* 17.

50. *Ibid*, 12.

51. Justin, 2 *Apology* 4.

52. Justin, 1 *Apology* 17.

53. Justin, 1 *Apology* 12.

54. Irenaeus, AH 5,24,2.

55. Athenagoras, *Legatio pro Christianis* 32.

56. *Ibid*, 25.

57. Justin, 1 *Apology* 5.

58. *Ibid*, 9.

59. A. Birley, *Marcus Aurelius* (Boston, 1960), 122.

60. *Acts of the Martyr Justin and His Companions* B,2, in *Acts of the Christian Martyrs,* 49.

61. *Ibid.*, 5,53.

62. Justin, 1 *Apology* 12. As noted above (note 4), see R.M. Grant's argument for Christian patriotism.

63. Tacitus, *The Histories* 5,4.

64. *Ibid.*, 5,5.

65. Tacitus, *Annals* 15,44,3–8.

66. Tertullian, *Apology* 50.

67. *Ibid.*, 39.

68. *Ibid*

69. Clement, *Protreptikos Logos* 10,98.

70. Clement, *Stromata* 4,8. See the excellent discussion by Walter Burghardt, S.J., *The Image of God in Man According to Cyril of Alexandria* (Washington, D.C., 1957), especially chap. 4, "Freedom," and chap. 5, "Dominion," 40–64.

71. Clement, *Paidagogos* 3,3.

72. Justin, 1 *Apology* 27.

73. Minucius Felix, *Octavius* 30.

74. *Ibid.*, 16.

75. Clement, *Stromata* 4,8.

76. Minucius Felix, *Octavius* 38.

77. E. Gibbon, *The History of the Decline and Fall of the Roman Empire* 3 (New York, 1984), 70. Emphasis added.

78. M. Hammond, *The Antonine Monarchy* (Rome, 1959), 211.

79. N. Lewis, *Life in Egypt Under Roman Rule* (Oxford, 1983), 207.

80. *Ibid.*

81. G.E.M. de Ste. Croix, *The Class Struggle in the Ancient Greek World* (Ithaca, N.Y., 1981), 435.

82. *Ibid.,* 439.

83. See, e.g., Tertullian, *Apology* 10; Minucius Felix, *Octavius* 29.

84. Tertullian, *Apology* 25.

85. *Ibid.*

86. Minucius Felix, *Octavius* 25.

87. See the excellent study by R. MacMullen, *Enemies of the Roman Order: Treason, Unrest, and Alienation in the Empire* (Cambridge, Mass., 1966); G.E.M. de Ste. Croix, *The Class Struggle,* 368.

88. Minucius Felix, *Octavius* 37. Emphasis added.

89. See W.H.C. Frend, *Martyrdom and Persecution in the Early Church* (Oxford, 1965).

90. Tertullian, *Apology,* 28,1. Emphasis added.

CHAPTER THREE

For a more scholarly and technical discussion of the sources discussed in this chapter, see E. Pagels, "Exegesis and Exposition of the Genesis Creation Accounts in Selected Texts from Nag Hammadi," in *Nag Hammadi, Gnosticism, and Early Christianity,* ed. C. Hedrick and R. Hodgson (Peabody, Mass., 1986), 257–286.

A more general discussion of the gnostic sources appears in E. Pagels, *The Gnostic Gospels* (New York, 1979). For the convenience of nonspecialists, I have listed the Nag Hammadi texts as they appear in the one-volume English translation, ed. J.M. Robinson, *The Nag Hammadi Library in English* (New York, 1977). Students and scholars will probably wish to consult the technical editions of the texts published by Brill Press in Leiden in the Nag Hammadi series.

1. For the term, see M. Smith, "The History of the term 'Gnostikos,' " in *The Rediscovery of Gnosticism (Proceedings of the International Conference on Gnosticism at Yale),* ed. B. Layton (Leiden, 1981), vol. 2, 796–807.

2. Ignatius, *Letter to the Romans* 5,1.

3. Ignatius, *Letter to the Magnesians* 6,1; *Trallians* 3,1; *Ephesians* 5,3. For discussion, see E. Pagels, "The Demiurge and His Archons: A Gnostic View of the Bishop and Presbyters?" in *Harvard Theological Review* 69,3–4 (1976), 301–324.

4. See, for example, H. von Campenhausen, *Ecclesiastical Authority and Spiritual Power,* trans. J.A. Baker (Stanford, 1969), 96–106.

5. Cf. G. Theissen, *The Sociology of Early Palestinian Christianity,* trans. J. Bowden (Philadelphia, 1978).

6. See especially W. Meeks, *The First Urban Christians* (New Haven, 1983).

7. Galen, *De Platonis Rei Publicae Summariis*, ed. Kraus-Walzer, fragment 1. For discussion of various pagan attitudes toward Christians, see R.L. Wilken, *The Christians as the Romans Saw Them* (New Haven/London, 1984).

8. Justin, 1 *Apology* 14.

9. Theodotus, cited in Clement of Alexandria's *Exerpta ex Theodoto* 78,2.

10. The Greek word here translated "mature" (τέλειος), which gnostic Christians frequently used to describe their adherents, can also mean "complete" or even "initiated."

11. For discussion, see E. Pagels, *The Gnostic Gospels*, xviii–xix.

12. Cf. Irenaeus, AH 4,33,7. Here Irenaeus acknowledges that their purpose is to purify and reform the churches, but he charges that in the attempt they are dividing and damaging the church.

13. AH, *Praefatio.*

14. For discussion, see Morton Smith, "The History of the Term 'Gnostikos,' " note 1 above.

15. Tertullian, *Adversus Valentinianos,* 4.

16. Clement of Alexandria, *Stromata* 7,7. For a reconstruction of Valentinian teaching, see G. Quispel, "The Original Doctrine of Valentine," in *Vigiliae Christianae* 1 (1947), 43–73.

17. For discussion, see E. Pagels, *The Gnostic Gospels*, introduction and passim.

18. Cf. E. Pagels, *The Gnostic Gospels*, xix–xx; 119–141.

19. Justin, 1 *Apology* 61.

20. For a Valentinian view of baptism, see, for example, the *Gospel of Philip* 64,23–40; 74,12–20; E. Pagels, "Valentinian Interpretation of Baptism and Eucharist—and Its Critique of 'Orthodox' Sacramental Theology and Practice," *Harvard Theological Review* 65 (1972), 153–170.

21. Hippolytus, *Refutatio Omnium Haeresium* 6,42.

22. For explication of gnostic exegesis, see E. Pagels, *The Johannine Gospel in Gnostic Exegesis* (Nashville, Tenn., 1973), and *The Gnostic Paul: Gnostic Exegesis of the Pauline Letters* (Philadelphia, 1975); also the fine work of K. Koschorke, *Die Polemik der Gnostiker gegen das kirchliche Christentum* (Leiden, 1978), and one of his more recent articles, "Paulus in den Nag-Hammadi-Texten," in *Zeitschrift für Theologie und Kirche* 78 (1981), 177–185.

23. E. Pagels, *The Johannine Gospel in Gnostic Exegesis*, and *The Gnostic Paul: Gnostic Exegesis of the Pauline Letters.*

24. Tertullian, *De Cultu Feminarum* 1,12. Emphasis added.

25. Tertullian, *De Jejuniis* 3.

26. Tertullian, *De Exhortatione Castitatis* 5.

27. For references and discussion of this type of exegesis see E. Pagels, "Exegesis and Exposition of the Genesis Creation Accounts," cited at the beginning of notes for this chapter.

28. Jerome, *Letter* 22,18.

29. Irenaeus, AH 1,18,1.

30. Irenaeus, AH 3,11,9.

31. Philo, *Opificio Mundi* 66; *Legum Allegoricum* 1,31; 1,90; 3,161.

32. Philo, *Legum Allegoricum* 3,161; 2,2; 2,6.

33. *Philo's Use of the Categories Male and Female* (Leiden, 1970), passim.

34. R.B. Blakney, ed. and trans., *Meister Eckhart* (New York, 1941), 135.

35. *Ibid.,* 14.

36. I owe this formulation to my friend and colleague Professor Theodor H. Gaster, who had in mind, of course, orthodox self-definition. No doubt there were, and are, however, spiritually inclined people from all these traditions who *would* agree with Eckhart on the basis of their own experience and conviction.

37. *Gospel of Philip* 71,35–72,3.

38. *Ibid.*

39. *The Exegesis on the Soul* (or *Interpretation of the Soul*), 133,6–9, in *The Nag Hammadi Library,* ed. J.M. Robinson (New York, 1977), 184.

40. For a further discussion, see the article cited in note 27.

41. *The Hypostasis of the Archons* 89,13–17, published in *The Nag Hammadi Library in English,* 152–160. The same translator, B. Layton, has published the text together with the notes in two articles: "The Hypostasis of the Archons, or the Reality of the Rulers," in *Harvard Theological Review* 67,4 (1974), 351–426; and "Hypostasis of the Archons, Part II," in *Harvard Theological Review* 69,1–2 (1976), 31–102.

42. *The Hypostasis of the Archons* 89,31–90,12.

43. *Thunder: Perfect Mind* 13,16,16,14, in *The Nag Hammadi Library,* 271–277. For discussion of this remarkable text, see G. MacRae, "The Thunder: Perfect Mind," in *The Center for Hermeneutical Studies, Fifth Colloquy* (Berkeley, Calif., 1975), 18, with following discussion by B. Pearson and T. Conley; also the fine and perceptive study by B. Layton, "The Riddle of the Thunder (NHC VI,2): The Function of Paradox in a Gnostic Text from Nag Hammadi," in *Nag Hammadi, Gnosticism, and Early Christianity,* 37–54.

44. *Apocryphon of John* 31,1–6, in *The Nag Hammadi Library,* 98–116.

45. See especially such texts as *The Hypostasis of the Archons, Thunder: Perfect Mind,* and the secondary sources here cited for both. Cf. E. Pagels, *The Gnostic Gospels,* chap. 3, and the articles cited in notes 22, 27, and 43. For more recent studies, see J. Jacobson-Buckley, *Female Fault and Fulfillment in Gnosticism* (Chapel Hill/London, 1986), and the volume forthcoming from the 1985 conference in Claremont, Calif., on "Images of the Feminine in Gnosticism," ed. K. King (Philadelphia, 1988).

46. *Gospel of Philip* 70,10.

47. *Ibid.,* 68,25.

48. Irenaeus, AH 2,27,2.

49. *Testimony of Truth* 45,30–47,10, in *The Nag Hammadi Library,* 406–416.

50. *Ibid.,* 47,15–48,4.

51. *Ibid.,* 33,25.

52. *Ibid.,* 33,21.

53. Irenaeus, AH 1,6,2.

54. *Ibid.*

55. Clement, *Stromata* 3,1.

56. See such passages in the *Gospel of Philip* as 69,1–70,22. For discussion, see R.M. Grant, "The Mystery of Marriage in the Gospel of Philip," in *Vigiliae Christianae* 15 (1961), 129–50; D.H. Tripp, "The 'Sacramental System' of the Gospel of Philip," in *Studia Patristica,* vol. xvii I, ed. E.A. Livingstone (Oxford, 1982), 251–260.

57. G. Quispel, "Birth of the Child," in *Eranos Lectures* 3, *Jewish and Gnostic Man*, (Princeton, 1966), 22–26.

58. M.A. Williams, " 'Gnosis' and 'Askesis,' " in *Aufstieg und Niedergang der Römischen Welt: Geschichte und Kultur Roms im Spiegel der Neueren Forschung* 2,22.

59. *Gospel of Philip* 53,14–19.

60. *Ibid.*, 53,24; for discussion, see K. Koschorke, "Die 'Namen' im Philippusevangelium," in *Zeitschrift für die neutestamentliche Wissenschaft* 64 (1973), 307–322.

61. *Gospel of Philip* 74,5–12.

62. *Ibid.*, 80,23–81,7.

63. *Ibid.*, 77,20–25.

64. *Ibid.*, 77,25–29.

65. *Ibid.*, 83,18–29. Emphasis added.

66. *Ibid.*, 83,29–84,13.

67. Irenaeus, AH 3,2,2; 3,15,2; 1,13,6.

68. Methodius, *Symposium,* passim; for references and discussion, see chap. 4.

69. Gregory of Nyssa, *De Hominis Opificio* 4,1.

70. Irenaeus, AH 4,37,1.

71. This is suggested in the *Acts of Thomas* (82–83) and stated clearly by John Chrysostom (*De Genesi* 4,1; *Homiliae in Epistolam ad Ephesios* 22,2) and Augustine (*City of God* 19,5).

72. See, in New Testament, Philemon; 1 Corinthians 7:20–24. R.L. Fox, *Pagans and Christians* (New York, 1987), 295–299, and R.M. Grant, *Early Christianity and Society* (New York, 1977), 89–95, both categorically state that Paul opposed social mobility, and specifically any concern to free slaves on the basis of Christian teaching.

73. A literal translation of αὐτός and ἐξουσία.

74. For one Valentinian teacher's view of different paths to salvation and redemption, see E. Pagels, *The Johannine Gospel in Gnostic Exegesis,* 83–97.

75. Irenaeus, AH 1,1,1.

76. *Ibid.*, 1,2,2.

77. *Ibid.*, 1,4–5: for a reconstruction of this teaching, see G. Quispel's "Original Doctrine of Valentine," in *Vigiliae Christianiae.*

78. Irenaeus, AH 1,1,1.

79. *Gospel of Truth* 18,30–35.

80. Irenaeus, AH 3,4,1–3.

81. See E. Pagels, *The Gnostic Gospels,* 48–69.

CHAPTER FOUR

Sections of this chapter are forthcoming in more technical form as the article " 'Freedom from Necessity': Philosophical and Psychological Dimensions of Christian Conversion," in *Intrigue in the Garden: Genesis 1–3, A History of Exegesis,* ed. G. Robbins (Lewiston/New York, 1988).

1. Marcus Aurelius, *Meditations,* 8,23; 9,23.

2. *Ibid.*, 8,12.

3. As Gregory of Nyssa said: *De Virginitate* 4. The twentieth-century writer Thomas Merton, who "renounced the world" to become a Cistercian monk, described his decision in similar terms: see his introduction to *The Wisdom of the Desert* (New York, 1960), 3–23.

4. The phrase is Jerome's (*Letter* 22,18). At the end of the fourth century a Roman monk argued against this view, and used the Scriptures, starting from Genesis 1, to defend marriage as being as holy as virginity; but his views were denounced by Ambrose, Jerome, and Augustine, and condemned by Pope Siricius as heresy: see above, pp. 91–96, and the classic study by D. Chitty, *The Desert a City* (New York, 1966), passim; also P. Rousseau, *Ascetics, Authority, and the Church in the Age of Jerome and Cassian* (Oxford, 1978).

5. Gregory of Nyssa, *De Virginitate* 12.

6. P. Brown, *The Body and Society* (forthcoming).

7. Matthew 16:26; also Mark 8:36.

8. As P. Brown shows in *The Body and Society* (forthcoming).

9. Matthew 19:21.

10. Athanasius, *Life of Saint Anthony* 2, published and translated in *Early Christian Biographies,* ed. R.J. Deferrari, in *Fathers of the Church* 15 (Washington, D.C., 1952), 133–224.

11. *Ibid.,* 3.

12. *Ibid.*

13. *Ibid.,* 5.

14. *Ibid.,* 4. As P. Rousseau says of the fourth-century Egyptian monks of Tabennesis, "to enroll oneself in the resurrected economy of Tabennesis . . . was not to abandon society, but to transfer one's allegiance . . . from one rural community to another." *Pachomius: The Making of a Community in Fourth-Century Egypt* (Berkeley/Los Angeles/London, 1985), 13.

15. R. MacMullen, *Christianizing the Roman Empire (A.D. 100–400)* (New Haven/London, 1984), 86.

16. G. Dix and many others depict the monastic movement as a reaction against the increasing worldliness of the churches; *The Shape of the Liturgy* (Glasgow, Scotland, 1945).

17. Gregory of Nyssa, *De Virginitate* 4.

18. *Ibid.,* 3.

19. *Ibid.*

20. *Ibid.,* 4.

21. *Ibid.;* on the recovery of the "image of God" as the goal of the contemplative life, see Gregory of Nyssa, *De Hominis Opificio* 4–9.

22. Gregory of Nyssa, *De Virginitate* 8.

23. For discussion of the significance and dynamics of the story of Clement in the *Clementine Homilies,* especially *Homilies* 4–6, see E. Pagels, " 'Freedom from Necessity': Philosophical and Psychological Dimensions of Christian Conversion," in *Intrigue in the Garden: Genesis 1–3, A History of Exegesis,* ed. G. Robbins (Lewiston/ New York, 1988).

24. Methodius, *Symposium* 1,1–4.

25. *Ibid.,* 2,1.

26. *Ibid.,* 4,1.

27. *Ibid.,* 7,9.

28. *Ibid.*, 8,13.

29. *Ibid.*, 11,2.

30. *Ibid.*

31. R. Ruether, "Mothers of the Church: Ascetic Women in the Late Patristic Age," in *Women of Spirit: Female Leaders in the Jewish and Christian Traditions,* ed. R. Ruether and E. McLaughlin (New York, 1979), 71–98; see also the excellent studies by E. Clark, in *Ascetic Piety and Women's Faith: Essays on Late Ancient Christianity* (Lewiston/Queenston, 1986). Especially valuable on the present point is her essay "Ascetic Renunciation and Feminine Advancement: A Paradox of Late Ancient Christianity," 175–208. See also R. Kraemer, "The Conversion of Women to Ascetic Forms of Christianity," *Signs* 6 (1980/81), 298–307; A. Rousselle, *Porneia: De la Maîtrise du corps à la privation sensorielle, IIe–IVe siècles de l'ère chrétienne* (Paris, 1983). For a very different viewpoint, see E. Castelli's intriguing essay "Virginity and Its Meaning for Women's Sexuality in Early Christianity," in *Journal of Feminist Studies in Religion* 2,1 (1982), 61–88.

32. *Vita Melaniae Junioris* 1, introduced and translated by E. Clark, in *The Life of Melania the Younger* (Lewiston, N.Y., 1984), 1,27–28.

33. *Ibid.*

34. *Ibid.*, 6.

35. *Ibid.*, 10–12.

36. *Ibid.*, 14.

37. E. Clark, "Ascetic Renunciation and Feminine Advancement," as well as her other essays, cited in note 31.

38. Jerome, *Letter* 22, *To Eustochium,* 7.

39. *Ibid.*, 24.

40. *Ibid.*, 16.

41. Jerome, *To Paula,* 6.

42. Jerome, *Adversus Jovinianum* 1,41: for a study of Jovinian, see W. Haller, *Iovinianum: Die Fragmente seiner Schriften, die Quellen zu seiner Geschichte, sein Leben und seine Lehre, Texte und Untersuchungen* 17,2 (Leipzig, 1897). Since Jovinian's writings, condemned by the pope, were destroyed, only fragments of his treatises remain in Jerome's polemics against him.

43. Jerome, *Adversus Jovinianum* 1,1.

44. *Ibid.*, 1,5.

45. *Ibid.*, 1,3. I am grateful to Robert Wilkin for referring me to David Hunter's article in *Theological Studies* 48 (1987), "Resistance to the Virginal Ideal in Late-Fourth-Century Rome: The Case of Jovinian," 45–64. Hunter's argument that Jovinian polemicizes against Manichaeans, not against celibates generally, is intriguing.

46. Jerome, *Adversus Jovinianum* 1,5.

47. *Ibid.*, 1,1,12.

48. *Ibid.*, 1,5.

49. *Ibid.*, 1,4.

50. *Ibid.*, 1,34.

51. *Ibid.*

52. *Ibid.*, 1,16. For a fine discussion of Jerome's exegesis, see E. Clark, "Heresy, Asceticism, Adam, and Eve: Interpretations of Genesis 1–3 in the Later Latin Fathers," in *Ascetic Piety and Women's Faith,* 353–385.

53. Jerome, *Adversus Jovinianum* 1,10; 20.

54. After he joined the Montanist movement, Tertullian's views on marriage became far more rigorist and negative. See, for example, D. Barnes's excellent biography, *Tertullian: A Historical and Literary Study* (Oxford, 1971).

55. Jerome, *Adversus Jovinianum* 1,6.

56. *Ibid.*, 1,7.

57. *Ibid.*, 1,40.

58. *Ibid.*, 2,36.

59. Jerome, *Letter* 48, *To Pammachius*, 2.

60. Yet, as Father William Meninger, Cistercian monk of Saint Benedict's Monastery in Snowmass, Colorado, reminds me, many monastics believe, as he does, that even the most cloistered life of contemplative prayer does, in fact, contribute to the welfare of humankind.

61. T. Merton, *The Wisdom of the Desert* (New York, 1970), 5–6.

CHAPTER FIVE

For a more technical version of this discussion, see E. Pagels, "The Politics of Paradise: Augustine's Exegesis of Genesis 1–3 Versus that of John Chrysostom," in *Harvard Theological Review* 78, 1–2 (1985), 67–95.

1. *Vita Adae et Evae* 22.1–2; *Jubilees* 2:14; see Jacob Jervell, *Imago Dei: Gen. 1,26f. im Spätjudentum, in der Gnosis, und in den paulinischen Briefen* (Göttingen, 1960), 40–41.

2. Gregory of Nyssa, *De Hominis Opificio* 2,1.

3. *Ibid.*, 4,1. The opposite theme—that of the emperor as sole representative of God's sovereignty on earth, a theme often supported with reference to Romans 13:1—does emerge, however, especially among theologians of the Byzantine era, as G.E.M. de Ste. Croix notes: *The Class Struggle in the Ancient Greek World from the Archaic Age to the Arab Conquests* (Ithaca, N.Y., 1981), 397–400.

4. Gregory of Nyssa, *De Hominis Opificio* 4,1.

5. *Ibid.*, 16,11.

6. Both themes, certainly, appear in the works of patristic theologians; for an overview, see Lewis Spitz, "Man of This Isthmus," in Carl S. Meyer, ed., *Luther for an Ecumenical Age: Essays in Commemoration of the 450th Anniversary of the Reformation* (St. Louis, Mo., 1967), 23–66.

7. For citations and discussion, see below.

8. Cf. C. Baur, *John Chrysostom and His Time*, translated from the French original (1907) by M. Gonzaga (London, 1960). J. Quasten, in *Patrology* (Utrecht/Antwerp, 1960), vol. 3, 424, suggests a date between 344 and 354.

9. Chrysostom, *Homiliae de Statuis ad Populum Antiochenum* 7,3. Hereafter cited as *Hom. ad Pop. Ant.*

10. Gregory of Nyssa, 16, *De Hominis Opificio* 16,17. Emphasis added.

11. Chrysostom, *Hom. ad Pop. Ant.* 7,3.

12. *Ibid.*, 6,1–2.

13. Chrysostom, *Homiliae in Epistolam Secundam ad Corinthios* 17,3.

14. Chrysostom, *Homiliae in Epistolam Primam ad Corinthios* 12,9. Hereafter cited as *Hom. in I Cor.*

15. *Ibid.*, 12,10.

16. Chrysostom, *Homiliae in Epistolam Primam ad Thessalonicos* 5,7.

17. Chrysostom, *Hom. in I Cor.* 12,10.

18. Chrysostom, *Hom. ad pop. Ant.* 6,2.

19. Didymus the Blind eloquently describes how baptism restores us to the original state of our creation: "Through the divine insufflation [cf. Genesis 2:7] we had received the image and likeness of God, which the Scripture speaks of, and through sin we had lost it, but now we are found once more such as we were when we were first made: sinless and masters of ourselves" (*De Trinitate* 2,12).

20. Cf., e.g., Tertullian, *Apology* 4,39; Justin, 1 *Apology* 12,42.

21. Chrysostom, *De sacerdotis* 2,3.

22. *Ibid.* Emphasis added.

23. Chrysostom, *Homiliae in Epistolam ad Ephesios* 11,15–16. Hereafter cited as *Hom. in Eph.* Emphasis added.

24. *Ibid.*, 6,7.

25. Chrysostom, *De sacerdotis,* 3,15.

26. Chrysostom, *Hom in Eph.* 11,15–16.

27. Cf. R.L. Wilken's recent book, *John Chrysostom and the Jews: Rhetoric and Reality in the Late Fourth Century* (Berkeley, 1983), 29–33.

28. Augustine, *Confessiones* 2,2. Translations used here are those of William Watts (1631) in *St. Augustine's Confessions* (Cambridge: Harvard University Press, 1977), 69.

29. *Ibid.*, 2,3.

30. *Ibid.*, 6,12.

31. *Ibid.*

32. Ibid., 6,11. For discussion of the relationships of Augustine's theology with Chrysostom, see Pier Franco Beatrice, *Tradux peccati: Alle fonti della dottrina agostiniana del peccato originale* (Studia Patristica Mediolanensia 8, Milan, 1978), chap. 5: "Crisostomo, Agostino e i pelagiani." On Augustine's change of mind, see Paula Fredricksen Landes, *Augustine on Romans* (California, 1982), ix–xii.

33. Augustine, *Confessiones* 2,7.

34. *Ibid.*, 2,6.

35. See P. Gorday, *Principles of Patristic Exegesis: Romans 9–11 in Origen, John Chrysostom, and Augustine* (New York/Toronto, 1983).

36. Augustine, *Confessiones* 7,3.

37. *Ibid.* Emphasis added.

38. *Ibid.*, 8,5.

39. *Ibid.*, 8,10.

40. *Ibid.* Emphasis added.

41. F. Edward Cranz, "The Development of Augustine's Ideas on Society before the Donatist Controversy," *Harvard Theological Review* 47 (1954), 254–316.

42. Augustine, *De Civitate Dei* 14,15. The translation cited generally follows that of Philip Levine in St. Augustine, *The City of God Against the Pagans* (LCL, 1966).

43. *Ibid.*, 13,21: Lignum scientiae boni et mali proprium voluntatis arbitrium. According to the analysis of M. Harl ("Adam et les deux Arbres du Paradis [Gen.

II–III] chez Philon d'Alexandrie," *Recherches de Science Religieuse* 50 [1962], 321–387), Philo, too, saw human autonomy which exercises choice between good and evil as the alternative—and opposite—of true piety. If so, Philo might agree with Augustine that the result of the fall is "personal control over one's own will." Unlike Augustine, however, Philo regards the daily life of a philosophically inclined person as a constant struggle of ethical decision and action (374), and assumes that humanity has a capacity to choose the good (377).

44. Augustine, *De Civitate Dei* 13,13. Emphasis added.

45. *Ibid.,* 14,15.

46. *Ibid.,* 14,12.

47. *Ibid.,* 14,13.

48. *Ibid.,* 14,15.

49. Augustine, *Confessiones* 7,3.

50. Chrysostom, *Hom. in I Cor.* 17,4.

51. Augustine, *De Civitate Dei* 13,3. Emphasis added.

52. *Ibid.,* 13,14. For discussion of the issue of translation, see chap. 6, note 51.

53. *Ibid.*

54. *Ibid.*

55. Which Augustine did not entirely invent; see, for example, Didymus the Blind, *Contra Manichaeos* 8.

56. Cf. Wilhelm Kamlah, *Christentum und Geschichtlichkeit: Untersuchungen zur Entstehung des Christentums und zu Augustins "Bürgerschaft Gottes"* (2nd ed., Stuttgart, 1951), 322: "Wo Augustin über die politische Herrschaft spricht, verweist er immer sogleich auf diese ursprüngliche Herrschafts- und Schöpfungsordnung und auf die Scheinherrschaft derer, die in der Knechtschaft der *libido dominandi* leben."

57. Augustine, *De Civitate Dei* 2,36.

58. *Ibid.,* 14,15.

59. *Ibid.,* 14,3.

60. *Ibid.,* 14,15.

61. *Ibid.,* 13,13.

62. *Ibid.,* 13,24.

63. Augustine, *De Peccatorum Meritis et Remissione* 2,2; cf. Augustine, *De Civitate Dei* 14,17.

64. Augustine, *De Civitate Dei* 14,19–20.

65. *Ibid.,* 14,16.

66. Augustine, *De Peccatorum Meritis et Remissione* 2,22.

67. Augustine, *De Civitate Dei* 14,26.

68. *Ibid.,* 14,17.

69. Augustine, *Confessiones* 8,5.

70. Augustine, *De Civitate Dei* 14,20. Origen, too, associated intercourse with impurity, although, as Henri Crouzel points out, "the impurity inherent in the exercise of sexuality is no more than an intensification of an even more profound uncleanness, that of the bodily condition" ("Marriage and Virginity: Has Christianity Devalued Marriage?" in idem, *Mariage et divorce, célibat et caractère sacerdotaux dans l'église ancienne: Études diverses* [Torino, 1982], 57).

71. Augustine, *De Civitate Dei* 14,19.

72. *Ibid.*, 14,9. For discussion, see Margaret Ruth Miles, *Augustine on the Body* (American Academy of Religion Dissertation Series 31; Missoula, Mont., 1979), especially 1–98.

73. Augustine, *De Civitate Dei* 15,16; 19,13.

74. *Ibid.*, 14,11.

75. See the excellent discussion by Kari Elizabeth Børrensen, *Subordination and Equivalence: The Nature and Role of Women in Augustine and Thomas Aquinas*, trans. Charles H. Talbot (Washington, D.C., 1981), 15–34.

76. Augustine, *De Civitate Dei* 19,15.

77. *Ibid.*

78. *Ibid.*, 15,1.

79. *Ibid.*, 19,15. Emphasis added.

80. *Ibid.* 19,12.

81. Henrik Berkhof, *Kirche und Kaiser: Eine Untersuchung der Entstehung der byzantinischen und der theokratischen Stattsauffassung im vierten Jahrhundert*, trans. Gottfried W. Locher (Zurich, 1947); Wilhelm Kamlah, *Christentum und Geschichtlichkeit.*

82. Augustine, *De Civitate Dei* 19,12; cf. R.A. Markus, *Saeculum: History and Society in the Theology of St. Augustine* (Cambridge, England, 1970), 22–153.

83. Augustine, *De Civitate Dei* 19,12.

84. For discussion of the image and its history, see R. MacMullen, "The Roman Concept Robber-Pretender," *Revue Internationale des Droits de l'Antiquité,* series 3, 10 (1965), 221–225.

85. Justin Martyr, 1 *Apology* 12.

86. Marcus Aurelius, *Meditations* 10,10.

87. Augustine, *De Civitate Dei* 4,4.

88. As R.A. Markus rightly notes; see his discussion in *Saeculum*, 84–86.

89. Irenaeus, AH 5,24,2.

90. Justin, *Apology* 65.

91. Augustine, *De Civitate Dei* 19,16.

92. See P.R.L. Brown, "Saint Augustine's Attitude to Religious Coercion," *Journal of Roman Studies* 54 (1964), 107–116. For a fascinating account of the incorporation of this image into the Roman liturgy, see G.M. Lukken, *Original Sin in the Roman Liturgy: Research into the Theology of Original Sin in the Roman Sacramentaria and the Early Baptismal Liturgy* (Leiden, 1973).

93. We need only recall how in *Confessiones* 8,12 Augustine describes the instrument of his salvation as, first, the child's voice that, he believes, directed him to "take and read" the Scriptures (a Christian version of the *bath kol*), and then the passage in Romans (13:13) to which the "Apostle's book" fell open when he obeyed God's command mediated through that voice.

94. For a detailed discussion, see Markus, *Saeculum.* According to Markus's reconstruction, Augustine from 390, for ten or fifteen years, "appeared to have joined the chorus of his contemporaries in their triumphant jubilation over the victory of Christianity" (31). "For a decade or more, his historical thinking was dominated by this motif" (32). Yet from 410, Augustine became "much less ready to speak of a Christian empire. . . . he became much more reserved" (36).

95. Markus sees Augustine's theory as admirably balanced: "The Empire is not to be seen either in terms of the messianic image of Eusebian tradition, or of the

apocalyptic image, as the Antichrist of the Hippolytan tradition. The Empire has become no more than an historical, empirical society with a chequered career. . . . It is theologically neutral" (*ibid.,* 559). I believe that Markus overstates his case when he goes further and claims that Augustine also sees the church as "theologically neutral."

96. See, e.g., Hans Joachim Diesner's discussion of Ambrose, in "Kirche und Staat im ausgehenden vierten Jahrhundert: Ambrosius von Mailand," in his *Kirche und Staat im Spätromischen Reich: Aufsätze zur Spätantike und zur Geschichte der Alten Kirche* (Berlin, 1963), especially 28–34.

97. Yet, as the British historian G.E.M. de Ste. Croix observes, "In the late Republic there was a totally different kind of *libertas,* and to those who held it the optimate version of *libertas,* that of Cicero & Co., was *servitus* (slavery, political subjection), while their *libertas* was stigmatized by Cicero as mere *licentia* ('license,' lawlessness)—in a word used also by the Roman rhetorician Cornificius as the equivalent of the standard Greek word for freedom of speech, *parrhesia.*" G.E.M. de Ste. Croix, *Class Struggle,* 368.

98. Minucius Felix, *Octavius* 37,1. Emphasis added.

99. *Ibid.,* 38,1.

100. Tertullian, *Apology* 28.

101. Another favorite Christian slogan, *free will,* bore similar connotations. Many of Augustine's contemporaries, hearing Christians advocate free will (*libero arbitrio*), might associate this with those who advocate revolution, or, at least, resistance to Roman rule. See J.N.L. Myres, "Pelagius and the End of Roman Rule in Britain," *Journal of Roman Studies* 50 (1960), 21–36.

102. Augustine, *De Civitate Dei* 13,21.

103. *Ibid.,* 14,15.

104. Claudian, *Stilicho* 3,113–115. For an informative and incisive discussion of Claudian's point of view, see Alan Cameron, *Claudian: Poetry and Propaganda of the Court of Honorius* (Oxford, 1970).

105. I am grateful to Peter Brown for pointing this out, and for referring me to the discussion of *libertas* in Gerd Tellenbach, *Church, State and Christian Society at the Time of the Investiture Contest,* trans. R.F. Bennett, *Studies in Medieval History* 3 (Oxford, 1959), 14–18.

106. On the dating, see note 8 above.

107. Chrysostom, *Hom. ad pop. Ant.* 3,6.

108. *Ibid.,* 6,6.

109. For a detailed and useful analysis, see Florent van Ommeslaeghe, "Jean Chrysostome et le peuple de Constantinople," *AnBoll* 99 (1981), 329–349: "Il est certain qu'une des raisons de l'attachement du peuple de Constantinople à son chef spirituel fut sa bonté, son amour des pauvres, de nos jours on dirait: son sens social" (348). Also see J.H.W.G. Liebeschutz, "Friends and Enemies of John Chrysostom," in Ann Moffatt, ed., *Maistor: Classical, Byzantine and Renaissance Studies for Robert Browning (Byzantina Australiensia* 5, 1984), 85–111.

110. Otto Seeck, *Geschichte des Untergang der antiken Welt* (6 vols. in 8; Berlin, 1897–1920), 5,336–337.

111. Florent van Ommeslaeghe, "Jean Chrysostome en conflit avec l'impératrice Eudoxie: Le dossier et les origines d'une légende," *AnBoll* 97 (1979), 131–159.

112. Chrysostom, *Epistola* 94.

113. Augustine, *Sermo*, 355,2, as cited in Peter Brown, *Augustine of Hippo* (Berkeley, 1969), 138.

114. *Ibid.*, 225.

115. Augustine, *De Moribus Ecclesiae Catholicae et De Moribus Manichaeorum* 1,30,63.

116. See, for example, the account in F. Cayre, *Manual of Patrology and History of Theology* (Rome, 1935), vol. 1, 625–629. For a recent and comprehensive historical study, see W.H.C. Frend, *The Donatist Church: A Movement of Protest in Roman North Africa* (Oxford, 1952).

117. P. Brown, *Augustine*, 235.

118. Augustine, *De Baptismo* 1,15,23–24.

119. P. Brown, *Augustine*, 358. Emphasis added.

CHAPTER SIX

1. H.C. Van Eijk, "Marriage and Virginity, Death and Immortality," in *Mélanges Jean Danielou* (Paris, 1972), 209–235.

2. For a different perspective on John Chrysostom and Augustine in the Pelagian controversy, see F.J. Thonnard, "Saint Jean Chrysostome et Saint Augustin dans la Controverse Pélagienne," in *Mélanges Venance Grumel* (Paris, 1967), 189–218. Thonnard concludes that Augustine's view of original sin "ne manque ni de valeur scientifique ni de vraisemblance historique" (217).

3. For a detailed discussion, see G. de Plinval, *Pélage: Ses Ecrits, Sa Vie, et Sa Réforme* (Lausanne, 1943); also the more recent study of O. Wermelinger, *Rom und Pelagius* (Stuttgart, 1975).

4. Cf. N.Q. King, *The Emperor Theodosius and the Establishment of Christianity* (Philadelphia, 1960). Constantine himself, the first Christian emperor, had deferred to the clergy as to his spiritual superiors; some sixty years later, Augustine's revered teacher Ambrose, the powerful bishop of Milan, literally brought the emperor to his knees. Ambrose had denounced Theodosius the Great for ordering a massacre of people in Thessalonica, and refused to allow the emperor to participate in communion until he had publicly repented.

5. See P. Brown, "Pelagius and His Supporters: Aims and Environment," in *Journal of Theological Studies, New Series*, 19,1 (1968), 93–114; and "The Patrons of Pelagius: The Roman Aristocracy Between East and West," in *Journal of Theological Studies, New Series*, 21,1 (1970), 56–72.

6. For discussion of the social and historical events of Pelagius's condemnation, see the sources cited above, especially the studies of Plinval, Wermelinger, and Brown.

7. See the excellent discussions by G.I. Bonner, "*Libido* and *Concupiscentia* in St. Augustine," in *Studia Patristica* 6 (Berlin, 1962), 303–314, and P. Brown, "Sexuality and Society in the Fifth Century A.D.: Augustine and Julian of Eclanum," in *Tria Corda: Scritti in Onore de Arnaldo Momigliano* (Como, 1983), 49–70; also E. Clark, "Vitiated Seeds and Holy Vessels: Augustine's Manichaean Past," in

E. Clark, *Ascetic Piety and Women's Faith: Essays on Late Ancient Christianity* (New York, 1986), 291–352.

8. Didymus the Blind, *De Trinitate* 2,12.

9. de Plinval, *Pélage*, 344.

10. On Julian, see A. Bruckner, *Julian von Eclanum: Sein Leben und Seine Lehre. Ein Beitrag zur Geschichte des Pelagianismus, Texte und Untersuchungen*, 15,3 (Leipzig, 1897).

11. Augustine, *Opus Imperfectum Contra Julianum*, 4,91. Hereafter cited as *Opus Imperfectum*.

12. *Ibid.* 4,92–93: "Quidquid enim naturale est, voluntarium non esse manifestum est. . . . Istae duae definitiones tam contrariae sibi sunt, quam contrarium est necessitas et voluntas, quarum confirmatio ex mutua negatione generatur. Nam sicut nihil est aliud voluntarium, quam non coactum; ita nihil est aliud coactum, quam non voluntarium." Unlike Bonner, who agrees with de Plinval (*Pélage*, 360) that Julian concerns himself primarily with *libido*, I agree with F. Refoulé, whose excellent article "Julien d'Éclane: Théologien et Philosophe" (in *Recherches de Science Religieuse* 52 [Paris, 1964], 42–74) shows that Julian concerns himself above all with the question of *nature* and *will*. Refoulé states clearly and accurately that "C'est . . . par sa notion de nature que Julien d'Éclane sépare fondamentalement d'Augustin. Toute sa polémique contre l'interprétation d'Augustin du péché originel se fonde sur une distinction rigoureuse entre *nature* et *volunté*, étrangère à Augustin" (67).

13. Augustine, *Opus Imperfectum* 4,40.

14. *Ibid.* 6,30: Non est enim tanti unius meritum, ut universa quae naturaliter sunt instituta perturbet. Emphasis added.

15. *Ibid.* 6,26.

16. *Ibid.* 4,114.

17. *Ibid.* 6,25. Emphasis added.

18. *Ibid.* 6,26.

19. Augustine often returns to this theme, as P. Brown notes in *Augustine of Hippo: A Biography* (Berkeley, 1969), 397; for a few references, see *Contra Julianum* 3,3–6; 9; *Opus Imperfectum* 3,159; 198.

20. Augustine, *Opus Imperfectum* 6,27.

21. *Ibid.*

22. *Ibid.*

23. *Ibid.* 6,30: ". . . potestas vivendi, nec nulla moriendi necessitas."

24. *Ibid.* 6,27.

25. Augustine, *Contra Julianum* 3,3–5.

26. *Ibid.* 3,6.

27. Augustine, *Opus Imperfectum* 6,23,5.

28. Augustine, *Opus Imperfectum* 3,109. For a fine discussion of Augustine's view of divine justice as it relates to original sin, see Y. de Montcheuil, "La Polémique de Saint Augustin contre Julien d'Éclane d'après l'*Opus imperfectum*," in *Recherches de Science Religieuse* 44,2 (Paris, 1956), 193–218.

29. Augustine, *Opus Imperfectum* 5,22.

30. *Ibid.* 1,1–2.

31. *Ibid.* 1,14.

32. *Ibid.* 6,26.

33. *Ibid.*

34. *Ibid.* 6,29.

35. *Ibid.* 6,26; for Julian's reply, 6,26–29.

36. For a fine and nuanced discussion of Chrysostom's position, see E. Clark, "The Virginal *Politeia* and Plato's *Republic:* John Chrysostom on Women and the Sexual Relation," in E. Clark, *Jerome, Chrysostom, and Friends* (New York, 1971), 1–22.

37. Augustine, *Opus Imperfectum* 6,27.

38. *Ibid.*

39. *Ibid.*

40. *Ibid.* 6,40.

41. *Ibid.* 3,82.

42. *Ibid.* 3,154.

43. *Ibid.* 2,33.

44. Augustine, *Contra Julianum* 3,14.

45. *Ibid.* 3,13. Emphasis added.

46. *Ibid.* Emphasis added.

47. *Ibid.* 3,14. Emphasis added.

48. Augustine, *Opus Imperfectum* 3,109.

49. *Ibid.* 4,92. Emphasis added.

50. *Ibid.* 5,45.

51. For some discussion of the exegetical issues, see G. Bonner, "Augustine on Romans 5,12," in *Studia Evangelica* 2 (Berlin, 1968), 242–247; S. Lyonnet, "Le Péché Originel et l'Exégèse de Rom. 5,12–14," in *Recherches de Science Religieuse* 44,1 (Paris, 1956), 63–84; also by Lyonnet, "Le Sens de ἐφ' ᾧ en Rom. 5,12 et l'Exégèse des Pères Grecs," in *Biblica* 36 (Rome, 1955), 427–456; A. d'Alès, "Julien d'Eclane, Exégète," in *Recherches de Science Religieuse* 6 (Paris, 1916), 311–324; H. Wolfson, "Philosophical Implications of the Pelagian Controversy," in *Proceedings of the American Philosophical Society* 103 (Philadelphia, 1959), 554–562; A. Bruckner, *Julian von Eclanum,* 114–123.

52. P. Gorday, *Principles of Patristic Exegesis,* 1–135.

53. A. Bruckner, *Julian von Eclanum,* 100.

54. *Ibid.,* 123–127. Emphasis added.

55. J. Ferguson, *Pelagius: A Historical and Theological Study* (Cambridge, England, 1966).

56. Augustine, *Opus Imperfectum* 6,35. Emphasis added.

57. *Ibid.* 6,30. "Man had it in his power not to die, had he not sinned."

58. *Ibid.* 6,35. Emphasis added.

59. *Midrash Rabbah,* Numbers 9, 4–10.

60. *Sun Chief: The Autobiography of a Hopi Indian,* ed. Leo W. Simmons (New Haven: Yale University Press, 1942), chap. 1.

61. E.E. Evans-Pritchard, "The Notion of Witchcraft Explains Unfortunate Events," in *Witchcraft, Oracles, and Magic Among the Azande* (Oxford, 1976), 18–32.

62. Luke 13:4–5.

63. *Midrash Rabbah,* Genesis 12,6; 21,3; 24,2, *passim*; L. Ginzberg, *Legends of the Jews* (Philadelphia, 1925), I, 49–101; V, 63–142.

64. I am grateful to Dr. Zephirah Gitay for sharing with me her research on Dürer's depictions of the Paradise story.

65. Augustine, *Opus Imperfectum* 5,49; cf. 3,103.

66. *Ibid.* 3,109. For further references and discussion, see Refoulé, "Julien d'Eclane," 66–72.

67. Augustine, *Opus Imperfectum* 6,40.

INDEX

The Origin of Satan

To Sarah and David
with love

ACKNOWLEDGMENTS

This book is based upon research originally presented, for the most part, in scholarly publications (cited at the beginning of each chapter's notes) and revised to make it more generally accessible. During the six years of research and writing, I have consulted with many scholars and friends. First I wish to thank John Gager, Rosemary Reuther, and Krister Stendahl, whose research and teaching have contributed so much to illuminate the issues. I especially thank those colleagues and friends who read the manuscript and offered corrections and criticism: Glen Bowersock, Elizabeth Diggs, Howard Clark Kee, Kent Greenawalt, Wayne Meeks, Sharon Olds, Eugene Schwartz, Alan Segal, Peter Stern, and S. David Sperling; and those who offered comments and criticism on portions of the work as it was in progress, including John Gager, Vernon Robbins, and James Robinson, who read the sections on New Testament sources; Steven Mullaney, who read and commented on the sources presented in chapter 1; John Collins, Louis Feldman, Paul Hanson, Martha Himmelfarb, Helmut Koester, Doron Mendels, and George Nickelsburg, who read and commented on the sources presented in chapter 2; and Peter Brown, who read and commented on the article on which part of chapter 6 is based. No doubt each of these colleagues will disagree with some of my conclusions, for which I must take responsibility.

Research for this book began when I was a visitor at the School of Historical Studies at the Institute for Advanced Study in 1990–91 and resumed there in 1994–95. I am most grateful to the members of that school for their gracious hospitality in making available to me, as to many others, the serene and collegial environment the Institute offers. I owe special thanks to Ruth Simmons, Vice Provost of Princeton University, to Jeffrey Stout, Chair of the Department of Religion, and to Robert Gunning, Dean of the Faculty, for making possible a leave to complete the research and writing in 1994–95, and to the National Endowment for the Humanities for the fellowship that supported me during that year.

I wish to thank my colleagues in the Department of Religion at Princeton University, both for conversations that have contributed much to the process and for their grace and understanding during these years, and also to thank the graduate students who struggled through the Greek texts with me in our seminar: Gideon Bohack, Robert Cro, Nicola Denzey, Obery Hendricks, Anne Merideth, Sharon Hefetz, and Joel Walker.

There are certain people without whose participation I cannot imagine having written this book. I am very fortunate and privileged to have worked with Jason Epstein as editor, and deeply appreciate the insight, wit, and passion for clarity he has brought to this process, along with his enthusiastic support. Helaine Randerson has worked on the manuscript through the entire process, offering incisive comments and editorial criticism along with her astonishingly expert manuscript preparation. John Brockman and Katinka Matson have offered encouragement on the project from the beginning, and have contributed in innumerable ways. I am grateful, too, to Anne Merideth for her collaboration in finding research materials, as well as for her excellent judgment on many issues we discussed. I have appreciated and enjoyed working with Virginia Avery, whose editorial suggestions have improved the text; and also thank Joy de Menil for all that she contributed.

Finally, I am grateful to the many friends whose presence and personal support in ways known to each of them helped see me through these difficult years since my husband's death, and mention in particular Malcolm Diamond, Elizabeth Diggs, Sarah

Duben-Vaughn, Kent Greenawalt, my brother and sister-in-law, Ralph and Jane Hiesey, Kristin Hughes, Elizabeth and Niccola Khuri, Emily McCulley, Sharon and David Olds, Albert Raboteau, Kathy Murtaugh, and Margot Wilkie.

CONTENTS

INTRODUCTION

In 1988, when my husband of twenty years died in a hiking accident, I became aware that, like many people who grieve, I was living in the presence of an invisible being—living, that is, with a vivid sense of someone who had died. During the following years I began to reflect on the ways that various religious traditions give shape to the invisible world, and how our imaginative perceptions of what is invisible relate to the ways we respond to the people around us, to events, and to the natural world. I was reflecting, too, on the various ways that people from Greek, Jewish, and Christian traditions deal with misfortune and loss. Greek writers from Homer to Sophocles attribute such events to gods and goddesses, destiny and fate—elements as capricious and indifferent to human welfare as the "forces of nature" (which is our term for these forces).

In the ancient Western world, of which I am a historian, many—perhaps most—people assumed that the universe was inhabited by invisible beings whose presence impinged upon the visible world and its human inhabitants. Ancient Egyptians, Greeks, and Romans envisioned gods, goddesses, and spirit beings of many kinds, while certain Jews and Christians, ostensibly monotheists, increasingly spoke of angels, heavenly messengers from God, and some spoke of fallen angels and demons. This was especially true from the first century of the common era onward.

Conversion from paganism to Judaism or Christianity, I realized, meant, above all, transforming one's perception of the invisible world. To this day, Christian baptism requires a person to solemnly "renounce the devil and all his works" and to accept exorcism. The pagan convert was baptized only after confessing that all spirit beings previously revered—and dreaded—as divine were actually only "demons"—hostile spirits contending against the One God of goodness and justice, and against his armies of angels. Becoming either a Jew or a Christian polarized a pagan's view of the universe, and moralized it. The Jewish theologian Martin Buber regarded the moralizing of the universe as one of the great achievements of Jewish tradition, later passed down as its legacy to Christians and Muslims.[1] The book of Genesis, for example, insists that volcanoes would not have destroyed the towns of Sodom and Gomorrah unless all the inhabitants of those towns—all the inhabitants who concerned the storyteller, that is, the adult males—had been evil, "young and old, down to the last man" (Gen. 19:4).

When I began this work, I assumed that Jewish and Christian perceptions of invisible beings had to do primarily with moralizing the natural universe, as Buber claimed, and so with encouraging people to interpret events ranging from illness to natural disasters as expressions of "God's will" or divine judgment on human sin. But my research led me in unexpected directions and disclosed a far more complex picture. Such Christians as Justin Martyr (140 C.E.), one of the "fathers of the church," attributes affliction not to "God's will" but to the malevolence of Satan. His student Tatian allows for accident in the natural world, including disasters, for which, he says, God offers solace but seldom miraculous intervention. As I proceeded to investigate Jewish and Christian accounts of angels and fallen angels, I discovered, however, that they were less concerned with the natural world as a whole than with the particular world of human relationships.

Rereading biblical and extra-biblical accounts of angels, I learned first of all what many scholars have pointed out: that while angels often appear in the Hebrew Bible, Satan, along with other fallen angels or demonic beings, is virtually absent. But among certain first-century Jewish groups, prominently including the Essenes (who saw themselves as allied with angels) and the followers of Jesus, the figure variously called Satan, Beelzebub, or Belial also began to take on central importance. While the gospel of Mark, for example, mentions angels only in the opening frame (1:13) and in the final verses of the original manuscript (16:5–7), Mark deviates from mainstream Jewish tradition by introducing "the devil" into the crucial opening scene of the gospel, and goes on to characterize Jesus' ministry as involving continual struggle between God's spirit and the demons, who belong, apparently, to Satan's "kingdom" (see Mark 3:23–27). Such visions have been incorporated into Christian tradition and have served, among other things, to confirm for Christians their own identification with God and to demonize their opponents—first other Jews, then pagans, and later dissident Christians called heretics. This is what this book is about.

To emphasize this element of the New Testament gospels does not mean, of course, that this is their primary theme. "Aren't the gospels about love?" exclaimed one friend as we discussed this work. Certainly they *are* about love, but since the story they have to tell involves betrayal and killing, they also include elements of hostility which evoke demonic images. This book concentrates on this theme.

What fascinates us about Satan is the way he expresses qualities that go beyond what we ordinarily recognize as human. Satan evokes more than the greed, envy, lust, and anger we identify with our own worst impulses, and more than what we call brutality, which imputes to human beings a resemblance to animals ("brutes"). Thousands of years of tradition have characterized Satan instead as a spirit. Originally he was one of God's angels, but a fallen one. Now he stands in open rebellion against God, and in his frustrated rage he mirrors aspects of our own confrontations with otherness. Many people have claimed to see him embodied at certain times in individuals and groups that seem possessed by an intense spiritual passion, one that engages even our better qualities, like strength, intelligence, and devotion, but turns them toward destruction and takes pleasure in inflicting harm. Evil, then, at its worst, seems to involve the supernatural— what we recognize, with a shudder, as the diabolic inverse of Martin Buber's characterization of God as "wholly other." Yet— historically speaking, at any rate—Satan, along with diabolical colleagues like Belial and Mastema (whose Hebrew name means "hatred"), did not materialize out of the air. Instead, as we shall see, such figures emerged from the turmoil of first-century Palestine, the setting in which the Christian movement began to grow.

I do not intend to do here what other scholars already have done well: The literary scholar Neil Forsyth, in his excellent recent book *The Old Enemy,* has investigated much of the literary and cultural background of the figure of Satan;[2] Walter Wink and the psychoanalyst Carl Gustav Jung and some of his followers have studied Satan's theological and psychological implications.[3] Jeffrey Burton Russell and others have attempted to investigate cross-cultural parallels between the figure of Satan and such figures as the Egyptian god Set or the Zoroastrian evil power Ahriman.[4] What interests me instead are specifically *social* implications of the figure of Satan: how he is invoked to express human conflict and to characterize human enemies within our own religious traditions.

In this book, then, I invite you to consider Satan as a reflection of how we perceive ourselves and those we call "others." Satan has, after all, made a kind of profession out of being the "other"; and so Satan defines negatively what we think of as human. The social and cultural practice of defining certain people as "others" in relation to one's own group may be, of course, as old as humanity itself. The anthropologist Robert Redfield has argued that the worldview of many peoples consists essentially of two pairs of binary oppositions: human/nonhuman and we/they.[5] These two are often correlated, as Jonathan Z. Smith observes, so that "we" equals "human" and "they" equals "not human."[6] The distinction between "us" and "them" occurs within our earliest historical evidence, on ancient Sumerian and Akkadian tablets, just as it exists in the language and culture of peoples all over the world. Such distinctions are charged, sometimes with attraction, perhaps more often with repulsion—or both at once. The ancient Egyptian word for Egyptian simply means "human"; the Greek word for non-Greeks, "barbarian," mimics the guttural gibberish of those who do not speak Greek—since they speak unintelligibly, the Greeks call them *barbaroi*.

Yet this virtually universal practice of calling one's own people human and "dehumanizing" others does not necessarily mean that people actually doubt or deny the humanness of others. Much of the time, as William Green points out, those who so label themselves and others are engaging in a kind of caricature that helps define and consolidate their own group identity:

> A society does not simply discover its others, it fabricates them,
> by selecting, isolating, and emphasizing an aspect of another
> people's life, and making it symbolize their difference.[7]

Conflict between groups is, of course, nothing new. What may be new in Western Christian tradition, as we shall see, is how the use of Satan to represent one's enemies lends to conflict a specific kind of moral and religious interpretation, in which "we" are God's people and "they" are God's enemies, and ours as well. Those who adopt this view are encouraged to believe, as Jesus warned his followers, that "whoever kills you will think he is offering a service to God" (John 16:2). Such moral interpretation of conflict has proven extraordinarily effective throughout Western history in consolidating the identity of Christian groups; the same history also shows that it can justify hatred, even mass slaughter.

Research for this book has made me aware of aspects of Christianity I find disturbing. During the past several years, rereading the gospels, I was struck by how their vision of supernatural struggle both expresses conflict and raises it to cosmic dimensions. This research, then, reveals certain fault lines in Christian tradition that have allowed for the demonizing of others throughout Christian history—fault lines that go back nearly two thousand years to the origins of the Christian movement. While writing this book I often recalled a saying of Søren Kierkegaard: "An unconscious relationship is more powerful than a conscious one."

For nearly two thousand years, for example, many Christians have taken for granted that Jews killed Jesus and the Romans were merely their reluctant agents, and that this implicates not only the perpetrators but (as Matthew insists) all their progeny in evil.[8] Throughout the centuries, countless Christians listening to the gospels absorbed, along with the quite contrary sayings of Jesus, the association between the forces of evil and Jesus' Jewish enemies. Whether illiterate or sophisticated, those who heard the gospel stories, or saw them illustrated in their churches, generally assumed both their historical accuracy and their religious validity.

Especially since the nineteenth century, however, increasing numbers of scholars have applied literary and historical analysis to the gospels—the so-called higher criticism. Their critical analysis indicated that the authors of Matthew and Luke used Mark as a source from which to construct their amplified gospels. Many scholars assumed that Mark was the most historically reliable because it was the simplest in style and was written closer to the time of Jesus than the others were. But historical accuracy may not have been the gospel writers' first consideration. Further analysis demonstrated how passages from the prophetic writings and the psalms of the Hebrew Bible were woven into the gospel narratives. Barnabas Lindars and others suggested that Christian writers often expanded biblical passages into whole episodes that "proved," to the satisfaction of many believers, that events predicted by the prophets found their fulfillment in Jesus' coming.[9]

Those who accepted such analysis now realized that the gospel of Mark, as James Robinson shows, is anything but a straightforward historical narrative; rather, it is a theological treatise that assumes the form of historical biography.[10] Recognizing that the authors of Matthew and Luke revised Mark in different ways, scholars have attempted to discriminate between the source materials each accepted from earlier tradition—sayings, anecdotes, and parables—and what each writer added to interpret that material. Some hoped to penetrate the various accounts and to discover the "historical Jesus," recovering his authentic words and deeds from the peripheral material that surrounds them. But others objected to what Albert Schweitzer called the "quest of the historical Jesus,"[11] pointing out that the earliest of the gospels was written more than a generation after Jesus' death, and the others nearly two generations later, and that sorting out "authentic" material in the gospels was virtually impossible in the absence of independent evidence.

Meanwhile, many other scholars introduced historical evidence from the Mishnah, an ancient archive of Jewish tradition, along with other Jewish sources, as well as from Roman history, law, and administrative procedure.[12] One of the primary issues to emerge from these critical studies was the question, What historical basis is there, if any, to the gospels' claim that Jews were responsible for Jesus' death? What makes this question of vital interest is the gospels' claim that this deed was inspired by Satan himself. One group of scholars pointed out discrepancies between Sanhedrin procedure described in the Mishnah and in the gospel accounts of Jesus' "trial before the Sanhedrin," and questioned the accuracy of the accounts in Mark and Matthew. Simon Bernfield declared in 1910 that "the whole trial before the Sanhedrin is nothing but an invention of a later date,"[13] a view that has found recent defenders among Christian literary analysts.[14] Noting that the charge against Jesus and the form of execution are characteristically Roman, many scholars, including Paul Winter in his influential book *On the Trial of Jesus,* published in 1961, argued that it was the Romans who executed Jesus, on political grounds, not religious ones.[15] Others, recently including the Roman historian Fergus Millar, have placed more credence in the accounts of Luke or John, which indicate that the Sanhedrin held only a hearing concerning Jesus, not an actual trial.[16]

Recently, however, one group of scholars has renewed arguments to show that, in Josef Blinzler's words,

> anyone who undertakes to assess the trial of Jesus as a historical and legal event, *reconstructing it from the gospel narratives,*

must come to the same conclusion as the early Christian preachers did themselves, that the main responsibility rests on the Jewish side (emphasis added).[17]

But scholars who take more skeptical views of the historical plausibility of these narratives emphasize Roman responsibility for Jesus' execution, which, they suggest, the gospel writers tended to downplay so as not to provoke the Romans in the aftermath of the unsuccessful Jewish war against Rome.[18]

I agree as a working hypothesis that Jesus' execution was probably imposed by the Romans for activities they considered seditious—possibly for arousing public demonstrations and (so they apparently believed) for claiming to be "king of the Jews." Among his own people, however, Jesus appeared as a radical prophetic figure whose public teaching, although popular with the crowds, angered and alarmed certain Jewish leaders, especially the Temple authorities, who probably facilitated his capture and arrest.

But this book is not primarily an attempt to discover "what really happened"—much less to persuade the reader of this or any other version of "what happened"—since, apart from the scenario briefly sketched above, I find the sources too fragmentary and too susceptible of various interpretations to answer that question definitively. Instead I try to show how the gospels reflect the emergence of the Jesus movement from the postwar factionalism of the late first century. Each author shapes a narrative to respond to particular circumstances, and each uses the story of Jesus to "think with" in an immediate situation, identifying with Jesus and the disciples, and casting those regarded as opponents as Jesus' enemies. To show this, I draw upon a wealth of recent works by historical and literary scholars, many of them discussing (and often disagreeing over) the question of when and how Jesus' followers separated from the rest of the Jewish community.

In this book I add to the discussion something I have not found elsewhere—what I call the social history of Satan; that is, I show how the events told in the gospels about Jesus, his advocates, and his enemies correlate with the supernatural drama the writers use to interpret that story—the struggle between God's spirit and Satan. And because Christians as they read the gospels have characteristically identified themselves with the disciples, for some two thousand years they have also identified their opponents, whether Jews, pagans, or heretics, with forces of evil, and so with Satan.

THE ORIGIN OF SATAN

THE GOSPEL OF MARK AND
THE JEWISH WAR

In 66 C.E., a rebellion against Rome broke out among the Jews of Palestine. Jewish soldiers, recruited at first from the countryside by leaders of the revolt, fought with whatever weapons they could find. But as the revolt spread to towns and cities, the Jewish population divided. Some refused to fight: in Jerusalem, the priestly party and their city-dwelling allies tried to maintain peace with Rome. Among those who joined the revolt, many were convinced that God was on their side: all were passionately intent on ridding their land of foreign domination. Three years into the war, the future emperor Vespasian and his son, the future emperor Titus, marched against Jerusalem with no fewer than sixty thousand well-trained, fully equipped foot soldiers and cavalry and besieged the city.

Some twenty years later, the Jewish historian Joseph ben Matthias, better known by his Romanized name, Flavius Josephus, who had served as governor of Galilee before joining in the fight against Rome, wrote an account of what he calls "not only the greatest war of our own time, but one of the greatest of all recorded wars."[1] Josephus is the only remaining guide to these events. Other accounts of the war have not survived. Although he is a vivid historian, Josephus is also partisan. Born into a wealthy priestly family of royal lineage, Josephus had traveled to Rome when he was about twenty-six—two years before the war—to intervene with the emperor Nero on behalf of several arrested Jewish priests. Rome's wealth and military power impressed the young man, who managed to meet one of Nero's favorite actors—a Jew, as it happened—and, through him, Nero's wife, Poppea. Poppea agreed to help with his mission, and Josephus returned to Palestine. There, he says in his autobiography,

> I found revolutionary movements already begun, and great excitement at the prospect of revolt from Rome. Accordingly, I tried to stop those preaching sedition . . . urging them to place before their eyes those against whom they were fighting; and to remember that they were inferior to the Romans, not only in military skill, but in good fortune. Although earnestly and insistently seeking to dissuade them from their purpose, foreseeing that the results would be disastrous for us, I did not persuade them. The great insanity of those desperate men prevailed.[2]

Wherever he traveled, Josephus says, he found Judea—the Hebrew term for what others called Palestine—in turmoil. Guerrilla leaders such as John of Gischala and his followers dedicated themselves to fight for liberty in the name of God. In the spring of 67, John's fighting men, having routed the Romans from Gischala, their provincial city, burst into Jerusalem. There, urging people to join the revolution, they attracted tens of thousands, Josephus says, and "corrupted a great part of the young men, and stirred them up to war."[3] Others, whom Josephus calls older and wiser, bitterly opposed the revolt. John and other revolutionaries coming into Jerusalem from the countryside escalated the conflict by capturing "the most powerful man in the whole city," the Jewish leader Antipas—the city treasurer—and two other men also connected with the royal dynasty. Accusing their three prisoners of having met with the enemy while plotting to surrender Jerusalem to the Romans, the rebels called them "traitors to our common liberty" and slit their throats.[4]

Josephus says that he himself served at age thirty as governor of Galilee, before joining in the war against Rome under pressure from his countrymen, but doesn't explain why he violated his own principles, though he does say that at first he pretended to agree with the rebels in order not to arouse their suspicion. He describes in detail his own battles against the Romans, and how he barely escaped a Roman massacre at the defeated city of Jotapata. Having managed first to hide and then to survive a suicide pact he made with his fellow refugees, Josephus was captured by the Romans. Brought before Vespasian, the Roman commander, Josephus announced that God had revealed to him that Vespasian would become emperor of Rome. Unimpressed, Vespasian assumed that this was a trick Josephus had contrived to save his life. But after Nero was assassinated, and three other emperors rose and fell within months, Vespasian did become emperor. One of his first acts was to order his soldiers to free Josephus from prison. Henceforth Josephus traveled in Vespasian's entourage as interpreter and mediator. He returned to Jerusalem with Vespasian's son Titus when the young general took over command of the war from his father in order to march against the holy city.

By that time, Josephus says, three factions divided the city: the priestly party working for peace; the revolutionaries from the countryside; and contending against both of these, a second anti-Roman party, led by prominent Jerusalemites, "men of the greatest power," who, according to Josephus, wanted to maintain their power against the radicals from the surrounding countryside. Even before the Roman armies arrived, Josephus says, these "three treacherous factions" were fighting among themselves, while "the people of the city . . . were like a great body torn into pieces."[5] Josephus himself, serving the Roman commander during the siege, stood between two fires: he was bitterly hated by many of his own people as a traitor, and was suspected of treason by the Romans whenever they experienced a setback.

Josephus describes in fine detail the siege of Jerusalem, including the horrors of the famine induced by Roman blockades, in which, he says, "children pulled the very morsels that their fathers were eating out of their mouths, and, what was more pitiable, so did the mothers do to their infants."[6] Even old people and children were tortured for stealing food. Finally, when the Jewish armies could hold out no longer, Roman soldiers entered the city and swarmed over the great Temple. Titus and his staff, apparently curious, entered the Holy of Holies, the sacred room where the ark of the covenant was kept. Roman soldiers looted the treasury, seizing its priceless gold furniture, the golden trumpets, and the massive seven-branched lampstand; then they set the Temple afire and watched it burn.

Later that night they hailed Titus's victory and in triumph desecrated the Temple precincts by sacrificing there to their own gods. Having devastated the Jewish armies, they raped, robbed, and massacred thousands of Jerusalem's inhabitants and left the city in ruins. Josephus, writing from his Roman retirement villa ten to fifteen years later, no doubt hoped not only to express his anguish but also to exonerate himself for collaborating with those who destroyed Jerusalem when he wrote,

> O most wretched city, what misery so great as this did you suffer from the Romans, when they came to purify you from your internecine hatred![7]

Whatever Josephus's motives, his writing conveys a powerful impression of the factions that divided Jerusalem, as well as of the horrifying devastation that the city's inhabitants suffered.

What makes these events important for my purpose in this book is that the first Christian gospel was probably written during the last year of the war, or the year it ended.[8] Where it was written and by whom we do not know; the work is anonymous, although tradition attributes it to Mark, a younger co-worker of the apostle Peter. What we do know is that the author of Mark's gospel was well aware of the war and took sides in the conflicts it aroused, both among Jewish groups and between Jews and Romans.

Mark was writing, after all, about a charismatic Jewish teacher, Jesus of Nazareth, who thirty-five years before had been executed by Pontius Pilate, the Roman governor of Judea, apparently on charges of sedition against Rome. Of all that his followers later claimed to know about him, these charges and his crucifixion are the primary facts on which both Jesus' followers and his enemies agree. None of the surviving accounts of Jesus is contemporaneous with his life, though many people told and retold stories about him and recounted his sayings and parables. Dozens—perhaps even hundreds—of accounts were written about Jesus, including the long-hidden accounts found among the so-called secret gospels discovered at Nag Hammadi in Upper Egypt in 1945.[9] But of these numerous accounts, only four gospels are included in the New Testament. The great majority of those who told and wrote about Jesus did so as his devoted admirers, some even as his worshipers. But others, including Josephus himself, as well as the Roman senator Tacitus, writing c. 115 C.E., mention Jesus and his followers with hostility or contempt.[10] Yet nearly all of these, advocates and adversaries alike, placed Jesus of Nazareth and the movement he started within the context of "the recent troubles in Judea."

According to Mark, Jesus protested at being arrested "like a robber" (Mark 14:48). The author of Luke, writing some ten to twenty years later, says that Jesus was charged, like those crucified along with him, as a robber (Luke 23:40).[11] This Greek term *lēstēs,* literally translated "robber" or "bandit," was in the early first century a catchall term for an undesirable, a troublemaker or criminal. Josephus, however, writing after the Jewish war against Rome, most often uses the term to characterize those Jews who were inciting or participating in anti-Roman activities or in the war against Rome itself.[12] I agree with many other scholars that Jesus himself is unlikely to have been a revolutionary,[13] although each of the four gospels indicates that the Jewish leaders who brought him to Pilate accused him of claiming to be "king of the Jews." According to Mark, Pilate's soldiers, aware of the charge, mocked and abused Jesus as a would-be king of the Jews; apparently the same charge was inscribed over his cross as a warning to others that Rome would similarly dispatch anyone accused of insurrection.

The narratives that we know as the New Testament gospels were written by certain followers of Jesus who lived through the war, and who knew that many of their fellow Jews regarded them as a suspect minority. They wrote their own accounts of some of the momentous events surrounding the war, and the part that Jesus played in events preceding it, hoping to persuade others of their interpretation. We cannot fully understand the New Testament gospels until we recognize that they are, in this sense, wartime literature. As noted before, the gospel we call Mark (although we do not know historically who actually wrote these gospels, I use their traditional attributions) was written either during the war itself, perhaps during a temporary lull in the siege of Jerusalem, or immediately after the defeat, in 70 C.E.[14] Matthew and Luke wrote some ten to twenty years later, each using Mark as his basis and expanding Mark's narrative with further sayings and stories. Most scholars believe that John wrote his gospel, perhaps in Alexandria, about a generation after the war, c. 90–95 C.E.[15]

Only one of Jesus' followers whose writings were later incorporated into the New Testament—Paul of Tarsus—wrote before the war and could, of course, say nothing about Jesus in relation to it. Paul mentions little that concerns Jesus' biography, repeating only a few "sayings of the Lord" (Acts 20:35).[16] What fascinated Paul about Jesus' death was not the crucifixion as an actual event, but what he saw as its profound religious meaning—that, as he says, "Christ died for our sins" (1 Cor. 15:3), that he became an atonement sacrifice, which, Paul believed, transformed the relationship between Israel's God and the whole human race. If he knew the charges made against Jesus—that he was one of many Galileans whom Josephus regards as troublemakers[17] for fomenting rebellion against Rome—Paul apparently regarded these charges as so transparently false or so irrelevant that they needed no rebuttal. Paul died c. 64–65 C.E. in Rome, executed, like Jesus, by order of Roman magistrates.

The catastrophic events of 66–70 permanently changed the world in which Jews lived, not only in Jerusalem, where charred rubble replaced the splendid Temple, but also for Jews throughout the known world. Even those who had never seen Jerusalem knew that the center of their world had been shattered. The hardships and humiliations of defeat exacerbated long-standing divisions within the scattered Jewish communities, some of which had persisted around the eastern Mediterranean for as many as two hundred years, since the time when the armies of the Jewish leader Judas Maccabeus had driven out the Syrian dynasties established by Alexander the Great and had restored the Jewish state. In 65–70 C.E., these divisions were most obvious between those who had advocated war with Rome, and the priestly party, which had worked to keep the fragile peace. In the aftermath of the war against Rome, power relationships among various groups within the Jewish communities scattered around the world from Alexandria and Antioch to Rome shifted to meet the changing situation. In Jerusalem itself, now that the Temple was gone and thousands had been killed or had fled, the priestly class lost much of its influence as other parties jockeyed for position.

The war and its aftermath polarized followers of Jesus, too, in relation to other Jewish communities. Followers of Jesus had refused to fight in the war against the Romans, not because they agreed with Josephus and others that the Romans were invincible, or because they hoped for financial or political advantage. Jesus' followers believed that there was no point in fighting the Romans because the catastrophic events that followed his crucifixion were signs of the end—signs that the whole world was to be shattered and transformed (Mark 13:4–29). Some insisted that what they had seen—the horrors of the war—actually vindicated his call "Repent, for the Kingdom of God is near" (Mark 1:15). Mark shares the conviction, widespread among Jesus' followers, that Jesus himself had predicted these world-shattering events— the destruction of the Temple and its desecration:

> And as he came out of the Temple, one of his disciples said to him, "Look, rabbi, what wonderful stones, and what wonderful buildings!" And Jesus said to him, "Do you see these great buildings? There will not be left here one stone upon another, that will not be thrown down. . . . But when you see the abominable sacrilege set up where it ought not to be (let the

reader understand!), then let those who are in Judea flee to the mountains (Mark 13:1–14).

This was exactly what had now happened. Others believed—and some dared to say—that these very catastrophes occurred as an angry God's punishment upon his own people for the crime of rejecting their divinely sent Messiah.

In any case, Mark insists that Jesus' followers had no quarrel with the Romans but with the Jewish leaders—the council of elders, the Sanhedrin, along with the Jerusalem scribes and priests—who had rejected God's Messiah. Mark says that these leaders now have rejected Mark and his fellow believers, calling them either insane or possessed by demons, the same charges that they directed against Jesus himself.

Mark takes a conciliatory attitude toward the Romans, although it was known that the Roman governor, Pontius Pilate, had sentenced Jesus to death. Nevertheless, the two trial scenes included in this gospel effectively indict the Jewish leaders for Jesus' death, while somewhat exonerating the Romans. Mark virtually invents a new Pilate—a well-meaning weakling solicitous of justice but, as Mark depicts him, intimidated by the chief priests within his own council chamber and by crowds shouting outside, so that he executes a man he suspects may be innocent.

Other first-century writers, Jewish and Roman, describe a very different man. Even Josephus, despite his Roman sympathies, says that the governor displayed contempt for his Jewish subjects, illegally appropriated funds from the Temple treasury, and brutally suppressed unruly crowds.[18] Another contemporary observer, Philo, a respected and influential member of the Alexandrian Jewish community, describes Pilate as a man of "ruthless, stubborn and cruel disposition," famous for, among other things, ordering "frequent executions without trial."[19]

Mark's motives with regard to Pilate are not simple. Insofar as he addresses his narrative to outsiders, Mark is eager to allay Roman suspicions by showing that Jesus' followers are no threat to Roman order, any more than Jesus himself had been. Mark may also have wanted to convert Gentile readers. Yet Mark is primarily interested in conflicts *within* the Jewish community—especially conflicts between his own group and those who reject its claims about Jesus.

Despite the hostility and suspicion he and his movement aroused among both Jews and Gentiles, including, of course, the Romans, Mark wrote to proclaim the "good news of Jesus of Nazareth, Messiah of Israel" (1:1). Yet Mark knows that to justify such claims about Jesus, he has to answer obvious objections. If Jesus had been sent as God's anointed king, how could the movement he initiated have failed so miserably? How could his followers have abandoned him and gone into hiding, while soldiers captured him like a common criminal? Why did virtually all his own people reject the claims about him—not only the townspeople in Galilee but also the crowds he attracted on his travels throughout Judea and in Jerusalem? And wasn't Jesus, after all, a seditionist himself, tainted in retrospect by association with the failed war, having been arrested and crucified as a rebel? Attempting to answer these questions, Mark places the events surrounding Jesus within the context not simply of the struggle against Rome but of the struggle between good and evil in the universe. The stark events of Jesus' life and death cannot be understood, he suggests, apart from the clash of supernatural forces that Mark sees being played out on earth in Jesus' lifetime. Mark intends to tell the story of Jesus in terms of its hidden, deeper dynamics—to tell it, so to speak, from *God's* point of view.

What happened, Mark says, is this: Jesus of Nazareth, after his baptism, was coming out of the water of the Jordan River when "he saw the heavens torn apart and the spirit descending like a dove on him" and heard a voice speaking to him from heaven (1:10–11). God's power anointed Jesus to challenge the forces of evil that now dominate the world, and drove him into direct conflict with those forces.[20] Mark frames his narrative at its beginning and at its climax with episodes in which Satan and his demonic forces retaliate against God by working to destroy Jesus. Mark begins by describing how the spirit of God descended upon Jesus at his baptism, and "immediately drove him into the wilderness, and he was in the wilderness forty days being tempted by Satan, and was with the animals, and the angels ministered to him" (1:12–13). From that moment on, Mark says, even after Jesus left the wilderness and returned to society, the powers of evil challenged and attacked him at every turn, and he attacked them back, and won. Matthew and Luke, writing some ten to twenty years later, adopted and elaborated this opening scenario. Each turns it into a drama of three temptations, that is, three increasingly intense confrontations between Satan and the spirit of God, acting through Jesus. Luke shows that the devil, defeated in these first attempts to overpower Jesus, withdraws "until an opportune time" (Luke 4:13). Luke then says what Mark and Matthew imply—that the devil returned in person in the form of Judas Iscariot to destroy Jesus, initiating the betrayal that led to his arrest and execution (Luke 22:3). All of the New Testament gospels, with considerable variation, depict Jesus' execution as the culmination of the struggle between good and evil—between God and Satan—that began at his baptism.

Satan, although he seldom appears onstage in these gospel accounts, nevertheless plays a central role in the divine drama, for the gospel writers realize that the story they have to tell would make little sense *without* Satan. How, after all, could anyone claim that a man betrayed by one of his own followers, and brutally executed on charges of treason against Rome, not only *was* but still *is* God's appointed Messiah, *unless* his capture and death were, as the gospels insist, not a final defeat but only a preliminary skirmish in a vast cosmic conflict now enveloping the universe? The final battle has not yet been fought, much less won, but it is imminent. As Jesus warns his interrogator at his trial, soon he will be vindicated when the "Son of man" returns in the clouds of heaven (Mark 14:62); here Mark has Jesus recall one of the prophet Daniel's visions, in which "one like a son of man" (that is, a human being), comes "with the clouds of heaven" and is made ruler of God's Kingdom (Dan. 7:13–14). Many of Mark's contemporaries would have read Daniel's prophecy as predicting the coming of a conqueror who would defeat Israel's foreign rulers.

While at first glance the gospel of Mark may look like historical biography, it is not so simple as this, for Mark does not intend to write history, as Josephus had, primarily to persuade people of the accuracy of his account of recent events and make them comprehensible on a human level. Instead Mark wants to show what these events mean for the future of the world, or, in the scholarly jargon, eschatologically. Mark and his colleagues combine a biographical form with themes of supernatural conflict borrowed from Jewish apocalyptic literature to create a new kind of narrative. These gospels carry their writers' powerful conviction that Jesus' execution, which had seemed to signal the victory of the forces of evil, actually heralds their ultimate annihilation and ensures God's final victory.[21]

Many liberal-minded Christians have preferred to ignore the presence of angels and demons in the gospels. Yet Mark intends their presence to address the anguished question that the events of the previous decades had aroused: How could God allow such death and destruction? For Mark and his fellows, the issue of divine justice involves, above all, the issue of human violence. The gospel writers want to locate and identify the specific ways in which the forces of evil act *through certain people* to effect violent destruction, above all, in Matthew's words, "the righteous blood shed on earth, from the blood of innocent Abel to the blood of Zechariah the son of Barachiah" (23:35)—violence epitomized in the execution of Jesus, which Matthew sees as the culmination of all evils. The subject of cosmic war serves primarily to interpret human relationships—especially all-too-human conflict—in supernatural form. The figure of Satan becomes, among other things, a way of characterizing one's actual enemies as the embodiment of transcendent forces. For many readers of the gospels ever since the first century, the thematic opposition between God's spirit and Satan has vindicated Jesus' followers and demonized their enemies.

But how does the figure of Satan characterize the enemy? What is Satan, and how does he appear on earth? The New Testament gospels almost never identify Satan with the Romans, but they consistently associate him with Jesus' Jewish enemies, primarily Judas Iscariot and the chief priests and scribes. By placing the story of Jesus in the context of cosmic war, the gospel writers expressed, in varying ways, their identification with the embattled minority of Jews who believed in Jesus, and their distress at what they saw as the apostasy of the majority of their fellow Jews in Jesus' time, as well as in their own. As we shall see, Jesus' followers did not *invent* the practice of demonizing enemies within their own group, although Christians (and Muslims after them) carried this practice further than their Jewish predecessors had taken it, and with enormous consequences.

Yet who actually *were* Jesus' enemies? What we know historically suggests that they were the Roman governor and his soldiers. The charge against Jesus and his execution were typically Roman. The Roman authorities, ever watchful for any hint of sedition, were ruthless in suppressing it. The historian Mary Smallwood observes that rounding up and killing troublemakers, especially those who ignited public demonstrations, was a routine measure for Roman forces stationed in Judea.[22] During the first century the Romans arrested and crucified thousands of Jews charged with sedition—often, Philo says, without trial. But as the gospels indicate, Jesus also had enemies among his fellow Jews, especially the Jerusalem priests and their influential allies, who were threatened by his activities.

The crucial point is this: *Had Jesus' followers identified themselves with the majority of Jews rather than with a particular minority, they might have told his story very differently—and with considerably more historical plausibility.* They might have told it, for example, in traditional patriotic style, as the story of an inspired Jewish holy man martyred by Israel's traditional enemies, foreign oppressors of one sort or another. The biblical book of Daniel, for example, which tells the story of the prophet Daniel, who, although threatened with a horrible death—being torn apart by lions—nevertheless defies the king of Babylon in the name of God and of the people of Israel (Dan. 6:1–28). The first book of Maccabees tells the story of the priest Mattathias, who defies Syrian soldiers when they order him to worship idols. Mattathias chooses to die rather than betray his devotion to God.[23]

But unlike the authors of Daniel or 1 Maccabees, the gospel writers chose to *dissociate* themselves from the Jewish majority and to focus instead upon intra-Jewish conflict—specifically upon their own quarrel with those who resisted their claims that Jesus was the Messiah. Within the gospels, as we shall see, the figure of Satan tends to express this dramatic shift of blame from "the nations"—*ha goyim,* in Hebrew—onto members of Jesus' own people. The variation in each gospel as it depicts the activity of the demonic opposition—that is, those perceived as enemies—expresses, I believe, a variety of relationships, often deeply ambivalent, between various groups of Jesus' followers and the specific Jewish groups each writer regards as his primary opponents. I want to avoid oversimplification. Nonetheless it is probably fair to say that in every case the decision to place the story of Jesus within the context of God's struggle against Satan tends to minimize the role of the Romans, and to place increasing blame instead upon Jesus' *Jewish* enemies.

This is not to say that the gospel writers simply intended to exonerate the Romans. Mark surely was aware that during his time, and for some thirty years after the war, the Romans remained wary of renewed sedition. Members of a group loyal to a condemned seditionist were at risk, and Mark probably hoped to persuade those outsiders who might read his account that neither Jesus nor his followers offered any threat to Roman order. But within Mark's account, the Romans, even the few portrayed with some sympathy, remain essentially outsiders. Mark tells the story of Jesus in the context that matters to him most—within the Jewish community. And here, as in most human situations, the more intimate the conflict, the more intense and bitter it becomes.

Mark opens his narrative with the account of John's baptizing Jesus and relates that at the moment of baptism the power of God descended upon Jesus, and "a voice spoke from heaven, saying 'This is my beloved son' " (1:11). At that moment, all human beings disappear from Mark's narrative and, as we have seen, the spirit of God drives Jesus into the wilderness to encounter Satan, wild animals, and angels. Recounting this episode, as James Robinson notes, Mark does not depart from events in the human, historical world but signals that he wants to relate these events to the struggle between good and evil in the universe.[24] Mark's account, then, moves directly from Jesus' solitary struggle with Satan in the desert to his first public appearance in the synagogue at Capernaum, where

> immediately on the Sabbath he entered the synagogue and taught. And they were astonished at his teaching, for he taught as one who had authority, and not as the scribes (1:22).

There Jesus encounters a man possessed by an evil spirit who, sensing Jesus' divine power, challenges him: "What have you to do with us, Jesus of Nazareth? Have you come to destroy us?" (1:24). According to Mark, Jesus has come to heal the world and reclaim it for God; in order to accomplish this, he must overcome the evil powers who have usurped authority over the world, and who now oppress human beings. So, Mark says,

> Jesus rebuked him, saying, "Be silent, and come out of him!" And the unclean spirit, convulsing him and crying with a loud voice, came out of him, and they were all amazed, so that they questioned among themselves, saying, "What is this? New teaching! With authority he commands even the unclean spirits, and they obey him." And at once his fame spread everywhere throughout all the surrounding region of Galilee (1:25–28).

Even in this first episode, the astonished crowds recognize that Jesus possesses a special authority, direct access to God's power. Jesus' power manifests itself especially in action, since Mark does not here record what Jesus taught. Even in this first public challenge to the forces of evil, Mark shows how Jesus' power sets him in contrast—and soon into direct conflict—with the scribes commonly revered as religious authorities. Mark's point is to demonstrate that, as he says, Jesus "taught as one who had authority, and not as the scribes" (1:22).

Throughout this opening chapter, Mark emphasizes that Jesus healed "many who were sick with various diseases" and "drove out many demons" (1:34). He traveled throughout Galilee "preaching in the synagogues and casting out demons," for, as he explains to Simon, Andrew, James, and John, who gather around him, "that is what I came to do" (1:38).

During his next public appearance, as Mark tells it, the scribes immediately took offense at what they considered his usurpation of divine authority. In this episode Jesus speaks to a crowd pressed together so tightly that when four men came carrying a paralyzed man,

> they could not get near him because of the crowd; so they removed the roof above him; and when they had made an opening, they let down the pallet on which the paralytic lay. And when Jesus saw their faith, he said to the paralytic, "My son, your sins are forgiven" (2:4–5).

By pronouncing forgiveness, Jesus claims the right to speak for God—a claim that, Mark says, angers the scribes:

> "Why does this man speak this way? It is blasphemy! Who can forgive sins but God alone?" (2:7).

According to Mark, Jesus, aware of the scribes' reaction, immediately performs a healing in order to *prove* his authority to his critics:

> And immediately Jesus, perceiving in his spirit that they thus questioned within themselves, said, "Why do you question thus in your hearts? . . . *But so that you may know that the Son of man has power on earth to forgive sins*"—he said to the paralytic—"I say to you, *rise, take your pallet, and go home.*" And he rose, and immediately picked up his pallet and went out before them all, so that they were all astonished, . . . saying, "We never saw anything like this!" (2:8–12, emphasis added).

When Jesus first appeared proclaiming "Repent: the Kingdom of God is at hand!," he must have sounded to many of his contemporaries like one of the Essenes, who withdrew to the wilderness in protest against ordinary Jewish life. From the desert caves where they lived in monastic seclusion, the Essenes denounced the priestly aristocratic leaders in charge of the Jerusalem Temple—men like Josephus and those he admired—as being hopelessly corrupted by their accommodation to Gentile ways, and by collaboration with the Roman occupiers. The Essenes took the preaching of repentance and God's coming judgment to mean that Jews must separate themselves from such polluting influences and return to strict observance of God's law—especially the Sabbath and kosher laws that marked them off from the Gentiles as God's holy people.[25]

But if Jesus sounded like an Essene, his actions violated the standard of purity that Essenes held sacred. Instead of separating himself from people who polluted themselves by "walking in the ways of the Gentiles" (*Jubilees* 1:9), Jesus chose for one of his disciples a tax collector—a class that other Jews detested as profiteers who collaborated with the hated Romans. Indeed, Mark says, "There were many tax collectors who followed him" (2:15). Instead of fasting, like other devout Jews, Jesus ate and drank freely. And instead of scrupulously observing Sabbath laws, Jesus excused his disciples when they broke them:

> One Sabbath he was going through the grainfields; and as they made their way, his disciples began to pick ears of grain. And the Pharisees said to him, "Look, why are they doing what is not lawful on the Sabbath?" And he said to them, "Have you never read what David did, when he was in need and was hungry, he and those who were with him: how he entered the house of God . . . and ate the sacred bread, . . . and also gave it to those who were with him?" (2:23–26).

Here Jesus dares claim, as precedent for his disciples' apparently casual action, the prerogative of King David himself, who, with his men, broke the sacred food laws during a wartime emergency.

Claiming divine and royal power while simultaneously violating the purity laws, Jesus, at the beginning of his public activity, outrages virtually every party among his contemporaries, from the disciples of John the Baptist to the scribes and Pharisees.

The next time Jesus entered the synagogue on a Sabbath, Mark says,

> a man was there who had a withered hand. And they watched him, to see whether he would heal him on the Sabbath, so that they might accuse him. And he said to the man who had the withered hand, "Come here." And he said to them, "Is it lawful on the Sabbath to do good or to do harm, to save life or to kill?" But they were silent. And he looked around at them with anger, grieved at their hardness of heart, and said to the man, "Stretch out your hand." He stretched it out, and his hand was restored (3:1–5).

Instead of postponing the healing for a day, Jesus had chosen deliberately to defy his critics by performing it on the Sabbath. Seeing this, Mark says:

> The Pharisees went out, and immediately conspired against him with the Herodians [the party of King Herod], how they might kill him (3:6).

For Mark the secret meaning of such conflict is clear. Those who are offended and outraged by Jesus' actions do not know that Jesus is impelled by God's spirit to contend against the forces of evil, whether those forces manifest themselves in the invisible demonic presences who infect and possess people, or in his actual human opponents. When the Pharisees and Herodians conspire to kill Jesus, they themselves, Mark suggests, are acting as agents of evil. As Mark tells the story, Jesus has barely engaged Satan's power before his opponents "conspired . . . how they might kill him" (3:6).

Mark suggests that Jesus recognizes that the leaders who oppose him are energized by unseen forces. Immediately after this powerful coalition has united against him, Jesus retaliates by commissioning a new leadership group, "the twelve," presumably assigning one leader for each of the original twelve tribes of Israel. Jesus orders them to preach and gives them "power to cast out demons" (3:13).

This escalation of spiritual conflict immediately evokes escalating opposition—opposition that begins at home, within Jesus' own family. Mark says that when Jesus "went home . . . his family . . . went out to seize him, for they said, 'He is insane [or: beside himself]' " (3:21).[26] Next "the scribes who came down from Jerusalem" charge that Jesus himself "is possessed by Beelzebub; by the prince of demons he casts out demons" (3:22). Jesus objects:

> "How can Satan cast out Satan? If a kingdom is divided against itself, that kingdom cannot stand. And if a house is divided against itself, that house will not be able to stand. And if Satan has risen up against himself and is divided, he cannot stand, but is coming to an end. But no one can enter a strong man's house and plunder his goods unless he first binds the strong man; then indeed he may plunder his house" (3:23–27).

According to Mark, it is apparently the "house of Israel" that Jesus sees as a divided house, a divided kingdom. Jesus openly contends against Satan, who he believes has overtaken God's own household, which he has come to purify and reclaim: Jesus wants to "bind this enemy" and "plunder his house."

As for the scribes' accusation that Jesus is possessed by the "prince of demons," he throws back upon them the same accusation of demon-possession and warns that in saying this they are sinning so deeply as to seal their own damnation (3:28–30). For, he says, whoever attributes the work of God's spirit to Satan commits the one unforgivable sin:

> "Truly, I say to you, all sins will be forgiven to human beings, and whatever blasphemies they utter; but whoever blasphemes against the holy spirit is never forgiven, but is guilty of an eternal sin"—because they said, "He is possessed by an evil spirit" (3:28–30).

Mark deliberately places these scenes of Jesus' conflict with the scribes between two episodes depicting Jesus' conflict with his own family. Immediately after this, the Greek text of Mark says that members of the family, who had previously declared him insane and had tried to seize him (3:21), now come to the house where he is addressing a large crowd and ask to see him. Jesus repudiates them:

> And his mother and brothers came, and standing outside they sent to him, and called him. And a crowd was sitting about him, and they said to him, "Your mother and your brothers are outside, asking for you." And looking around at those who sat around him, he said, "Here are my mother and brothers! For whoever does the will of God is my brother, and sister, and mother" (3:31–35).

Having formed a new family, and having appointed twelve new leaders for Israel to replace the old ones, Jesus has, Mark suggests, "re-formed God's people." From this point on, Jesus sharply discriminates between those he has chosen, the inner circle, and "those outside." He still draws enormous crowds, but while teaching them, he offers riddling parables, deliberately concealing his full meaning from all but his intimates:

> Again he began to teach beside the sea. And a very large crowd gathered about him . . . and he taught them many things in parables. . . . And when he was alone, those who were around him with the twelve asked him about the parables. And he said to them, "*To you has been given the secret of the Kingdom of God, but for those outside everything is in parables; so that they may indeed see but not perceive; and they may hear but not understand; lest they should turn again, and be forgiven*" (4:1–12, emphasis added).

Although he often criticizes the disciples—in 8:33 he even accuses Peter of playing Satan's role—Jesus shares secrets with them that he hides from outsiders, for the latter, he says, quoting Isaiah, are afflicted with impenetrable spiritual blindness.[27]

Criticized by the Pharisees and the Jerusalem scribes for not living "according to the traditions of the elders" because he and his disciples eat without washing their hands, Jesus, instead of defending his action, attacks his critics as "hypocrites" and charges that they value their own traditions while breaking God's commandments. Then he publicly calls into question the kosher laws themselves—again explaining his meaning to his disciples alone:

> And he called the people to him again, and said to them, "Hear me, all of you, and understand; there is nothing outside a man which by going into him can defile him; but the things which come out of a man are what defile him." And when he had entered the house, and left the people, his disciples asked him about the parable. And he said to them, "Are you, too, without understanding? Do you not see that whatever goes into a man from outside cannot defile him, since it enters not his heart but his stomach, and so passes out of him? What comes out of a man is what defiles him; for from within, from the human heart, come evil thoughts, sexual immorality, theft, murder, . . . envy, pride, foolishness. . . . All these evils come from within" (7:14–23).

Here Mark wants to show that although Jesus discards traditional kosher ("purity") laws, he advocates instead purging the "heart"—that is, impulses, desires, and imagination.

Now that Jesus has alienated not only the scribes, Pharisees, and Herodians, but also his relatives and many of his own townspeople, he travels with his small band of disciples, preaching to the crowds. Anticipating what lies ahead of him in Jerusalem, where he will challenge the priestly party on its own ground, Jesus nevertheless resolutely leads his followers there, walking ahead of them, while "they were astonished, and those who followed were terrified" (10:32). On the way he tells the twelve exactly whom they are to blame for his impending death:

> "The chief priests and scribes . . . will condemn [the Son of man] to death, and hand him over to the nations, and they

will mock him and spit upon him, and scourge him and kill him" (10:33).

Opposition to Jesus intensifies after he enters Jerusalem. Having prepared a formal procession to go into the city, Jesus is openly acclaimed, in defiance of the Romans, as the man who comes to restore Israel's ancient empire: "Blessed is the kingdom of our father David that is coming!" Then, with his followers, he enters the great Temple and makes a shocking public demonstration there:

> He entered the Temple, and began to drive out those who sold and those who bought in the Temple, and he overturned the tables of the money changers and the seats of those who sold pigeons; and he would not allow anyone to carry anything through the Temple (11:15–16).

Now Jesus invokes the words of the prophets Isaiah and Jeremiah, as if to speak for the Lord himself against those who permit financial transactions in the Temple courtyard:

> And he taught, and said to them, "Is it not written, 'My house shall be called a house of prayer for all the nations'? But you have made it a den of robbers." But the chief priests and the scribes heard it, and sought a way to destroy him, for they were afraid of him, because the whole crowd was astonished at his teaching (11:17–18).

When the chief priests and scribes, joined by members of the Jewish council, demand to know by what authority he acts, Jesus refuses to answer. Instead he retells Isaiah's parable of God's wrath against Israel (12:1–12) in a way so transparent that even the chief priests, scribes, and elders recognize that he is telling it "against them" (12:12). The following scenes show Jesus contending first against the Pharisees and Herodians, who fail to trick him into making anti-Roman statements (12:13–15), and then against the scribes (12:35). Finally he warns a great crowd:

Beware of the scribes, who like to go around in long robes, and to have salutations in the marketplaces, and the best seats in the synagogues, and the places of honor at feasts, who devour widows' houses and for a pretense make long prayers. They will receive the greater condemnation (12:38–40).

Then, as Jesus comes out of the Temple, Mark says, he responds to his disciples' awestruck admiration for the sacred precincts by predicting the Temple's destruction: "There will not be left one stone upon another, that will not be thrown down" (13:2). When Peter, James, John, and Andrew privately ask what he means, Jesus sits with them on the Mount of Olives opposite the Temple and explains. He predicts a series of horrifying catastrophes (these are events in which Mark's contemporaries would recognize their own times, especially the events of the war between 66 and 70): "wars and rumors of war," famine, public enthusiasm for false messiahs. Jesus warns in veiled language that when they see "the desolating sacrilege set up where it ought not to be"—the pagan desecration of the Temple—they should flee into the mountains (13:7–14).

Mark intends Jesus' followers, living in terrible times, to take comfort in knowing that their leader had foreseen how they would suffer, out of their loyalty to him ("for my sake"), ostracism and reprisals, hatred and betrayal, even—perhaps especially—from their family members:

"Take heed to yourselves; for they will deliver you up to councils; and you will be beaten in synagogues, and you will stand before governors and rulers for my sake . . . and brother will deliver up brother to death, and the father his child, and children will rise against parents and have their parents put to death; and you will be hated by all for the sake of my name (13:9–13).

What is the believer to do, facing betrayal, isolation, and mortal danger? Mark says that Jesus enjoined his followers to "endure to the end." Now Mark has to tell how Jesus himself "endured to the end," through arrest, trials in both Jewish and Roman courts, torture, and execution, thus giving his endangered followers an example of how to endure. Two days before Passover, Mark says, "the chief priests and the scribes were seeking how to arrest Jesus secretly and kill him, for they said, 'Not during the festival, lest there be a tumult among the people,' " since so far the people remained on Jesus' side. Shortly afterward, Judas Iscariot, obviously aware of the hostility his master had aroused among influential people, "went to the chief priests in order to betray [Jesus] to them, and when they heard it they were glad, and offered him money" (14:1–11).

At night, Mark says, Judas led "a crowd with swords and clubs from the chief priests and the scribes and Temple officers" to Gethsemane, a garden on the Mount of Olives, to capture Jesus. One of his men fought back with a sword, injuring the high priest's slave, and Jesus protested at being treated "like a robber" (the term that Josephus and others commonly use to characterize an "insurrectionist"). But the rest of his followers abandoned him and fled; Jesus was taken. The armed men "brought him to the high priest," apparently to his residence. Although the Sanhedrin traditionally was not allowed to meet at night, Mark tells us that on the night of Jesus' arrest, "all the chief priests and the elders and the scribes were assembled" at the high priest's residence to try his case in a formal proceeding.

Now Mark presents the first of two trial scenes—the "trial before the Sanhedrin," which he follows with the "trial before Pilate." Most scholars assume that even if these events occurred, Jesus' followers could not have witnessed what went on at either his appearance before the Jewish council or his arraignment by the Romans.[28] But Mark is not concerned with reporting history. By introducing these scenes, Mark wants to show above all that the well-known charge against Jesus—sedition—not only was false but was invented by Jesus' *Jewish* enemies; further, Mark says, the Roman governor himself realized this and tried in vain to save Jesus! According to Mark, the Sanhedrin had already prejudged the case. The trial was only a pretense in order "to put him to death" (14:55). After hearing a series of trumped-up charges and lying witnesses, some accusing Jesus of having threatened to destroy the Temple, the chief priest interrogates Jesus, demanding that he answer the charges against him. Jesus, however, remains silent. Finally the chief priest asks, "Are you the Messiah, the son of the Blessed One?" (14:61). Here, for the first time in Mark's gospel, Jesus publicly admits his divine identity to people other than his disciples, and goes on to warn his accusers that they will soon witness his vindication: "I am; and you will see the Son of man sitting at the right hand of power and coming with the clouds of heaven" (14:62). Then, Mark continues, the high priest, tearing his robe, says, " 'You have heard his blasphemy. What is your decision?' And they all condemned him as deserving death" (14:64).

Many scholars have commented on the historical implausibility of this account.[29] Did the Sanhedrin conduct a trial that violated its own legal practices concerning examining witnesses, self-incrimination, courtroom procedure, and sentencing? Although we know little about Sanhedrin procedures during Jesus' time,[30] did this council actually assemble at night, contrary to what seems to have been its precedent? If so, why does Mark go on to add a *second* version of the council meeting to discuss this case—a meeting that takes place the following morning, as if nothing had happened the night before? For after Mark ends his first, more elaborate account, he lets slip what now becomes a redundancy: that "as soon as it was morning the chief priests, with the elders and scribes, and the whole council, held a consultation, and they bound Jesus, and led him away, and delivered him to Pilate" (15:1).

We cannot, of course, know what actually happened, but Mark's second version, which agrees with Luke's, sounds more likely—that the council convened in the morning, and decided that the prisoner should be kept in custody and turned over to Pilate to face charges.[31] The gospel of John, relying upon a source independent of Mark's, offers another reconstructed account that gives a plausible interpretation of these events.[32] According to John, the chief priests, alarmed by the crowds Jesus attracted, feared that his presence in Jerusalem during Passover might ignite public demonstrations, "and the Romans will come and destroy our holy place and our nation" (11:48). The civil strife that preceded the Jewish war, as John and his contemporaries well knew, had verified the accuracy of such concerns about possible Roman reprisals.

Many New Testament scholars who have analyzed the account of Jesus' appearance before the Sanhedrin agree that Mark (or his predecessors) probably wrote the first version to emphasize his primary point: that Pilate merely ratified a previous Jewish verdict, and carried out a death sentence that he himself neither ordered nor approved—but a sentence unanimously pronounced by the entire leadership of the Jewish people.[33]

This does not mean, however, that Mark is motivated by malice toward the Jewish leaders. Indeed, Mark stops far short of the extent to which Matthew, Luke, and John will go to blame the Jewish leaders for the crucifixion, although the tendency to blame them had already begun before Mark's time and had its effect on his narrative. Nevertheless, Mark and his fellow believers, as followers of a convicted criminal, knew that such allegiance would arouse suspicion and invite reprisals. Roman magistrates had already arrested and executed several prominent members of the movement, including Peter and Paul. It is no wonder, then, that, as one historian says, Mark wanted

> to emphasize the culpability of the Jewish nation for the death of Jesus, particularly of its leaders. . . . [Mark's] tendency was defensive rather than aggressive. He was concerned to avoid mentioning anything that would provoke Roman antagonism towards, or even suspicion of, the ideals for which he stood. . . . The evangelist therefore contrived to conceal that Jesus had been condemned and executed on a charge of sedition.[34]

Mark's account also involves an important positive motive. Mark intends the "trial before the Sanhedrin" to mirror the precarious situation in which he and his fellow believers now stand in relation to leaders of the Jewish communities during and after the war.[35] In this account of Jesus' courage before his judges, Mark offers Jesus' followers a model of how to act when they too are put on trial.

Mark weaves into this account a contrapuntal story—the story of Jesus' chief disciple, Peter, who, in terror, denies Jesus, an example of how *not* to act when on trial. For whereas Jesus stands up to the Sanhedrin and confesses his divine mission, boldly risking—and accepting—the death sentence, Peter claims not to have known Jesus. Having surreptitiously followed Jesus to the scene of the trial, Mark says, Peter stood warming his hands by the fire when one of the household servants said to him, "You, too, were with the Nazarene, Jesus" (14:67). But Peter denies this ("I do not know what you mean; . . . I do not know the man") three times, with increasing vehemence, cursing and swearing, and finally escapes. After recognizing what he has done, Peter "broke down and wept" (14:72).

Mark knows that those who publicly confess their conviction that Jesus is "the Messiah, the Son of God" (14:61) may put themselves in danger of abuse, ridicule, even threats to their lives. The terms *Messiah* and *Son of God* would probably have been anachronistic during the time of Jesus; but many of Mark's contemporaries must have recognized them as the way Christians of their own time confessed their faith. In this dramatic scene, then, Mark again confronts his audience with the question that pervades his entire narrative: Who recognizes the spirit in Jesus as divine, and who does not? Who stands on God's side, and who on Satan's? By contrasting Jesus' courageous confession with Peter's denial, Mark draws a dramatic picture of the choice confronting Jesus' followers: they must take sides in a war that allows no neutral ground.

Having tried to show that the whole affair concerning Jesus was essentially an internal Jewish conflict that got out of hand, Mark now offers his version of Jesus' "trial before Pilate." Many scholars think that all Mark actually knew was that Jesus had been crucified as a would-be king of the Jews during Pilate's administration as governor of Judea. While he takes account of this indisputable fact, Mark intends to minimize its significance.

Consider, then, how Mark tells the story. Pilate, apprised that the prisoner was accused of political insurgency, attempts to interrogate him. "Have you no answer to make? See how many charges they make against you" (15:4). Mark says that when Jesus refused to answer his questions, Pilate, instead of demonstrating anger or even impatience, "was amazed" (15:5). Mark goes further. Claiming to know the governor's private assessment of the case, Mark says that Pilate "recognized that it was out of envy that they had handed him over" (15:10). But instead of making a decision and giving orders, Pilate takes no action. Then, hearing shouts from the crowd outside, he goes out to address them, asking what they want: "Do you want me to release for you the king of the Jews?" But the crowd demands instead the release of Barabbas, whom Mark describes as one of the imprisoned insurrectionists, who "had committed murder in the rebellion" (15:7). Pilate seems uncertain, wanting to refuse but afraid to go against the crowd's demand. As if helpless, he again asks the crowd what to do: "What shall I do with the man whom you call the king of the Jews?" (15:12). When the crowd shouts for Jesus' crucifixion, Pilate in effect pleads with his subjects for justice: "Why, what evil has he done?" (15:14). But the shouting continues, and Pilate, "wishing to satisfy the crowd" (15:15), releases Barabbas and, having ordered Jesus to be flogged, acquiesces to their demand that he be crucified. But according to Mark, Pilate never pronounces sentence, and never actually orders the execution. As Mark tells the story, even inside Pilate's own chamber, the chief priests are in charge: it is they who make accusations and it is they who stir up the crowds, whose vehemence forces Jesus' execution upon a reluctant Pilate.

The Pilate who appears in the gospels, as we have noted, has little to do with the historical Pilate—that is, with the man we know from other first-century historical and political sources, both Jewish and Roman, as a brutal governor. As Raymond Brown notes in his meticulous study of the passion narratives, except in Christian tradition, portraits of Pilate range from bitterly hostile to negative.[36] Philo, an educated, influential member of the Jewish community in Alexandria, the capital of Egypt, was

Pilate's contemporary. In one of his writings, his *Embassy to Gaius*, he describes his experiences as a member of an official delegation sent to Rome to represent the interests of the Alexandrian Jewish community to the Roman emperor, Gaius Caligula. In the course of his narrative, Philo, referring to the situation of the Jewish community in Judea, describes governor Pilate as a man of "inflexible, stubborn, and cruel disposition," and lists as typical features of his administration "greed, violence, robbery, assault, abusive behavior, frequent executions without trial, and endless savage ferocity."[37] Philo writes to persuade Roman rulers to uphold the privileges of Jewish communities, as he claims that the emperor Tiberius had done. In this letter, Philo sees Pilate as the image of all that can go wrong with Roman administration of Jewish provinces.

Philo's testimony is partly corroborated in Josephus's history of the same era. As we have seen, Josephus, like Philo, was a man of considerable political experience; as former Jewish governor of Galilee under the Romans, he writes his history under Roman patronage in a tone sympathetic to Roman interests. Yet Josephus records several episodes that show Pilate's contempt for Jewish religious sensibilities. Pilate's predecessors, for example, recognizing that Jews considered images of the emperor to be idolatrous, had instituted the practice of choosing for the Roman garrison in Jerusalem a military unit whose standards did not carry such images. But when Pilate was appointed governor he deliberately violated this precedent. First he ordered the existing garrison to leave; then he led to Jerusalem a replacement unit whose standards displayed imperial images, timing his arrival to coincide with the Jewish high holy days, the Day of Atonement and the Feast of Tabernacles. Pilate apparently knew that he was committing sacrilege in the eyes of his subjects, for he took care to arrive in Jerusalem at night, having ordered the standards to be covered with cloth during the journey.

When the people of Jerusalem heard that Pilate and his troops had introduced images they regarded as idolatrous into the holy city, they gathered in the streets to protest. A great crowd followed Pilate back to Caesarea and stood outside his residence, pleading with him to remove them. Since the standards always accompanied the military unit, this amounted to a demand that Pilate withdraw the garrison. When Pilate refused, the crowds continued to demonstrate. After five days, Pilate, exasperated but adamant, decided to force an end to the demonstrations. Pretending to offer the demonstrators a formal hearing, he summoned them to appear before him in the stadium. There Pilate had amassed soldiers, ordered them to surround the crowd, and threatened to massacre the demonstrators unless they gave in. To Pilate's surprise, the Jews declared that they would rather die than see their law violated. At this point Pilate capitulated and withdrew the unit. As Mary Smallwood comments:

> The Jews had won a decisive victory in the first round against their new governor, but now they knew what sort of man they were up against, and thereafter anything he did was liable to be suspect. . . . But more was to follow.[38]

Roman authorities also respected Jewish sensitivity by banning images considered idolatrous from coins minted in Judea. Only during Pilate's administration was this practice violated: coins depicting pagan cult symbols have been found dated 29–31 C.E. Did Pilate order the change, as the German scholar E. Stauffer believes, "to force [his] subjects to handle representations of pagan culture"?[39] Raymond Brown suggests that Pilate simply "underestimated Jewish sensitivity" on such matters.[40]

Pilate next decided to build an aqueduct in Jerusalem. But to finance the project, he appropriated money from the Temple treasury, an act of sacrilege even from the Roman point of view, since the Temple funds were, by law, regarded as sacrosanct.[41] This direct assault upon the Temple and its treasury aroused vehement opposition. When Pilate next visited Jerusalem, he was met with larger demonstrations than ever; now the angry crowds became abusive and threatening. Anticipating trouble, Pilate had ordered soldiers to dress in plain clothes, conceal their weapons, and mingle with the people. When the crowd refused to disperse, he signaled to the soldiers to break it up with force. Several people were killed, and others were trampled to death in the stampede that followed.[42] Even the gospel of Luke, which gives an astonishingly benign portrait of Pilate in the trial narrative, elsewhere mentions how people told Jesus about certain Galileans "whose blood Pilate mingled with their sacrifices" (13:1).

Late in Pilate's tenure as governor other provocative incidents prompted Jewish leaders to protest to the emperor Tiberius against Pilate's attacks on their religion. In 31 C.E. Pilate angered his subjects by dedicating golden shields in the Herodian palace in Jerusalem. We cannot be certain what occasioned the protest; the scholar B. C. McGinny suggests that the shields were dedicated to the "divine" emperor, a description that would have incensed many Jews.[43] Again Pilate faced popular protest: a crowd assembled, led by four Herodian princes. When Pilate refused to remove the shields, perhaps claiming he was acting only out of respect for the emperor, Josephus says, they replied, "Do not take [the emperor] Tiberius as your pretext for outraging the nation; he does not wish any of our customs to be overthrown."[44] When Pilate proved adamant, the Jewish princes appealed to the emperor, who rebuked Pilate and ordered him to remove the shields from Jerusalem. One recent commentator remarks that

> the bullying of Pilate by his Jewish adversaries in the case of the shields resembles strongly the bullying of Pilate in [the gospel of] John's account of the passion, including the threat of appeal to the emperor.[45]

Yet characterizing these protests as "bullying" seems strange; what recourse did a subject people have to challenge the governor's decision, except to appeal over his head to a higher authority? Five years later, when a Samaritan leader assembled a large multitude, some of them armed, to gather and wait for a sign from God, Pilate immediately sent troops to monitor the situation. The troops blockaded the crowd, killing some and capturing others, while the rest fled. Pilate ordered the ringleaders executed.[46]

Pilate's rule ended abruptly when the legate of Syria finally responded to repeated protests by stripping Pilate of his commission and dispatching a man from his own staff to serve as governor in his place. Pilate was ordered to return to Rome at once to answer charges against him, and disappeared from the historical record. Philo's account coincides with Mark's on one point: that Pilate, aware of the animosity toward him, was concerned lest the chief priests complain about him to the emperor. Yet Mark, as we have seen, presents a Pilate not only as a man too weak to withstand the shouting of a crowd, but also as one solicitous to ensure justice in the case of a Jewish prisoner whom the Jewish leaders want to destroy.

Mark's benign portrait of Pilate increases the culpability of the Jewish leaders and supports Mark's contention that Jews, not Romans, were the primary force behind Jesus' crucifixion. Throughout the following decades, as bitterness between the Jewish majority and Jesus' followers increased, the gospels came to depict Pilate in an increasingly favorable light. As Paul Winter observes,

> the stern Pilate grows more mellow from gospel to gospel [from Mark to Matthew, from Matthew and Luke to John]. . . . The more removed from history, the more sympathetic a character he becomes.[47]

In depicting Jesus' Jewish enemies, the same process works in reverse. Matthew, writing around ten years later, depicts much greater antagonism between Jesus and the Pharisees than Mark suggests. And while Mark says that the leaders restrained their animosity because the crowds favored Jesus, Matthew's account ends with both leaders *and* crowds unanimously shouting for his execution. Furthermore, what Mark merely implies—that Jesus' opponents are energized by Satan—Luke and John will state explicitly. Both Matthew and Luke, writing ten to twenty years after Mark, adapted the earlier gospel and revised it in various ways, updating it to reflect the situation of Jesus' followers in their own times.

Jesus' followers did not invent the practice of demonizing enemies within their own group. In this respect, as in many others, as we shall see, they drew upon traditions they shared with other first-century Jewish sects. The Essenes, for example, had developed and elaborated images of an evil power they called by many names—Satan, Belial, Beelzebub, Mastema ("hatred")—precisely to characterize their own struggle against a Jewish majority whom they, for reasons different from those of Jesus' followers, denounced as apostate. The Essenes never admitted Gentiles to their movement. But the followers of Jesus did—cautiously and provisionally at first, and against the wishes of some members. But as the Christian movement became increasingly Gentile during the second century and later, the identification of Satan primarily with the Jewish enemies of Jesus, borne along in Christian tradition over the centuries, would fuel the fires of anti-Semitism.

The relationship between Jesus' followers and the rest of the Jewish community, however, especially during the first century, is anything but simple. Mark himself, like the Essenes, sees his movement essentially as a conflict within one "house"—as I read it, the house of Israel. Such religious reformers see their primary struggle not with foreigners, however ominously Roman power lurks in the background, but with other Jews who try to define the "people of God."[48] Yet while Mark sees the Jewish leaders as doing Satan's work in trying to destroy Jesus, his own account is by no means anti-Jewish, much less anti-Semitic. After all, virtually everyone who appears in the account is Jewish, including, of course, the Messiah. Mark does not see himself as separate from Israel, but depicts Jesus' followers as what Isaiah calls God's "remnant" *within Israel* (Isaiah 10:22–23). Even the images that Mark invokes to characterize the majority—images of Satan, Beelzebub, and the devil—paradoxically express the *intimacy* of Mark's relationship with the Jewish community as a whole, for, as we shall see, the figure of Satan, as it emerged over the centuries in Jewish tradition, is not a hostile power assailing Israel from without, but the source and representation of conflict *within* the community.

THE SOCIAL HISTORY OF SATAN:
FROM THE HEBREW BIBLE
TO THE GOSPELS

The conflict between Jesus' followers and their fellow Jews is not, of course, the first sectarian movement that divided the Jewish world, a world whose early history we know primarily from the Hebrew Bible, a collection of authoritative law, prophets, psalms, and other writings assembled centuries before the four gospels and other Christian writings were brought together in the New Testament. Who assembled this collection we do not know, but we may infer from its contents that it was compiled to constitute the religious history of the Jewish people, and so to create the basis for a unified society.[1]

Excluded from the Hebrew Bible were writings of Jewish sectarians, apparently because such authors tended to identify with one group of Jews against another, rather than with Israel as a whole. Christians later came to call the writings of such dissidents from the main group the *apocrypha* (literally, "hidden things") and *pseudepigrapha* ("false writings").[2]

But the writings collected to form the Hebrew Bible encourage identification with Israel itself. According to the foundation story recounted in Genesis 12, Israel first received its identity through election, when "the Lord" suddenly revealed himself to Abraham, ordering him to leave his home country, his family, and his ancestral gods, and promising him, in exchange for exclusive loyalty, a new national heritage, with a new identity:

"I will make you a great nation, and I will make your name
great . . . and whoever blesses you I will bless; and whoever
curses you I will curse" (Gen. 12:3).

So when God promises to make Abraham the father of a new,
great, and blessed nation, he simultaneously defines and constitutes its enemies as inferior and potentially accursed.

From the beginning, then, Israelite tradition defines "us" in
ethnic, political, and religious terms as "the people of Israel," or
"the people of God," as against "them"—the (other) nations (in
Hebrew, *ha goyim*), the alien enemies of Israel, often characterized as inferior, morally depraved, even potentially accursed. In
Genesis 16:12, an angel predicts that Ishmael, although he was
Abraham's son, the progenitor of the Arab people, would be a
"wild ass of a man, with his hand against everyone, and everyone's hand against him; and he shall live at odds with all his kin."
The story implies that his descendants, too, are hostile, no better
than animals. Genesis 19:37–38 adds that the Moabite and
Ammonite nations are descended from Lot's daughters, which
means that they are the illegitimate offspring of a drunken and
incestuous union. The people of Sodom, although they are Abraham's allies, not his enemies, are said to be criminally depraved,
"young and old, down to the last man," collectively guilty of
attempting to commit homosexual rape against a party of angels,
seen by the townspeople as defenseless Hebrew travelers (Gen.
19:4). These accounts do not idealize Abraham or his progeny—
in fact, the biblical narrator twice tells how the self-serving lies of
Abraham and Isaac endangered their allies (Gen. 20:1–18;
26:6–10). Nevertheless, God ensures that everything turns out
well for the Israelites and badly for their enemies.

The second great foundation story is that of Moses and the
Exodus, which also confronts "us" (that is, "Israel") with
"them" (that is, "the nations") as Moses urges Pharaoh to let the
Hebrews leave Egypt. Yet the narrator insists that it was God
himself who increasingly hardened Pharaoh's heart, lest he relent
and relieve the suffering of Moses and his own people—and why?
God, speaking through Moses, threatens Pharaoh with devastat-

ing slaughter and concludes by declaring, "but against any of the Israelites, not a dog shall growl—*so that you may know that the Lord makes a distinction between the Egyptians and Israel.*" (Exod. 11:7; my emphasis).

Many anthropologists have pointed out that the worldview of most peoples consists essentially of two pairs of binary oppositions: human/not human and we/they.[3] Apart from anthropology, we know from experience how people dehumanize enemies, especially in wartime.

That Israel's traditions deprecate the nations, then, is no surprise. What is surprising is that there are exceptions. Hebrew tradition sometimes reveals a sense of universalism where one might least expect it. Even God's election of Abraham and his progeny includes the promise of a blessing to extend through them to all people, for that famous passage concludes with the words, "in you all the families of the earth shall be blessed" (Gen. 12:3). Furthermore, when a stranger appears alone, the Israelites typically accord him protection, precisely because they identify with the solitary and defenseless stranger. Biblical law identifies with the solitary alien: "You shall not wrong or oppress a stranger; for you were strangers in the land of Egypt" (Exod. 22:21). One of the earliest creeds of Israel recalls that Abraham himself, obeying God's command, became a solitary alien: "A wandering Aramean was my father . . ." (Deut. 26:5). Moses, too, was the quintessential alien, having been adopted as an infant by Pharaoh's daughter. Although a Hebrew, he was raised as an Egyptian; the family of his future in-laws, in fact, mistook him for an Egyptian when they first met him. He even named his first son Gershom ("a wanderer there"), saying, "I have been a wanderer in a foreign land" (Exod. 2:16–22).

Nevertheless, the Israelites are often aggressively hostile to the nations. The prophet Isaiah, writing in wartime, predicts that the Lord will drive the nations out "like locusts" before the Israelite armies (Isa. 40:22). This hostility to the alien enemy seems to have prevailed relatively unchallenged as long as Israel's empire was expanding and the Israelites were winning their wars against the nations. Psalms 18 and 41, attributed to King David, builder of Israel's greatest empire, declare, "God gave me vengeance and subdued the nations under me" (Ps. 18:47), and "By this I know that God is pleased with me—in that my enemy has not triumphed over me" (Ps. 41:11).

Yet at certain points in Israel's history, especially in times of crisis, war, and danger, a vociferous minority spoke out, not against the alien tribes and foreign armies ranged against Israel, but to blame Israel's misfortunes upon members of its own people. Such critics, sometimes accusing Israel as a whole, and sometimes accusing certain rulers, claimed that Israel's disobedience to God had brought down divine punishment.

The party that called for Israel's allegiance to "the Lord alone," including such prophets as Amos (c. 750 B.C.E.), Isaiah (c. 730 B.C.E.), and Jeremiah (c. 600 B.C.E.), indicted especially those Israelites who adopted foreign ways, particularly the worship of foreign gods.[4] Such prophets, along with their supporters, thought of Israel as a truly separate people, "holy to the Lord." The more radical prophets denounced those Israelites who tended toward assimilation as if they were as bad as the nations; only a remnant, they said, remained faithful to God.

Certain of these prophets, too, had called forth the monsters of Canaanite mythology to symbolize Israel's enemies.[5] Later (sixth century) material now included in the first part of the book of the prophet Isaiah proclaims that "the Lord is coming *to punish the inhabitants of the earth;* and the earth will disclose the blood shed upon her, and will no more cover the slain" (Isa. 26:21; emphasis added). The same author goes on, apparently in parallel imagery, to warn that "in that day, the Lord with his great hand will *punish the Leviathan, the twisting serpent, and he will slay the dragon that is in the sea*" (Isa. 27:1; emphasis added). The author of the second part of Isaiah also celebrates God's triumph over traditional mythological figures—over Rahab, "the dragon," and "the sea"—as he proclaims God's imminent triumph over Israel's enemies. Thereby, as the biblical scholar Jon Levenson observes, "the enemies cease to be merely earthly powers . . . and become, instead or in addition, cosmic forces of the utmost malignancy."[6]

Certain writers of the sixth century B.C.E. took a bold step further. They used mythological imagery to characterize their struggle against some of their fellow Israelites. But when Israelite writers excoriated their fellow Jews in mythological terms, the images they chose were usually not the animalistic or monstrous ones they regularly applied to their foreign enemies. Instead of Rahab, Leviathan, or "the dragon," most often they identified their Jewish enemies with an exalted, if treacherous, member of the divine court whom they called the *satan*. The *satan* is not an animal or monster but one of God's angels, a being of superior intelligence and status; apparently the Israelites saw their intimate enemies not as beasts and monsters but as *superhuman* beings whose superior qualities and insider status could make them more dangerous than the alien enemy.

In the Hebrew Bible, as in mainstream Judaism to this day, Satan never appears as Western Christendom has come to know him, as the leader of an "evil empire," an army of hostile spirits who make war on God and humankind alike.[7] As he first appears in the Hebrew Bible, Satan is not necessarily evil, much less opposed to God. On the contrary, he appears in the book of Numbers and in Job as one of God's obedient servants—a messenger, or *angel*, a word that translates the Hebrew term for messenger (*mal'āk*) into Greek (*angelos*). In Hebrew, the angels were often called "sons of God" (*benē 'elōhīm*), and were envisioned as the hierarchical ranks of a great army, or the staff of a royal court.

In biblical sources the Hebrew term the *satan* describes an adversarial role. It is not the name of a particular character.[8] Although Hebrew storytellers as early as the sixth century B.C.E. occasionally introduced a supernatural character whom they called the *satan*, what they meant was any one of the angels sent by God for the specific purpose of blocking or obstructing human activity. The root *śṭn* means "one who opposes, obstructs, or acts as adversary." (The Greek term *diabolos*, later translated "devil," literally means "one who throws something across one's path.")

The *satan*'s presence in a story could help account for unexpected obstacles or reversals of fortune. Hebrew storytellers often attribute misfortunes to human sin. Some, however, also invoke this supernatural character, the *satan,* who, by God's own order or permission, blocks or opposes human plans and desires. But this messenger is not necessarily malevolent. God sends him, like the angel of death, to perform a specific task, although one that human beings may not appreciate; as the literary scholar Neil Forsyth says of the *satan,* "If the path is bad, an obstruction is good."[9] Thus the *satan* may simply have been sent by the Lord to protect a person from worse harm. The story of Balaam in the biblical book of Numbers, for example, tells of a man who decided to go where God had ordered him not to go. Balaam saddled his ass and set off, "but God's anger was kindled because he went; and the angel of the Lord took his stand in the road as his *satan*" [*le-śāṭān-lō*]—that is, as his adversary, or his obstructor. This supernatural messenger remained invisible to Balaam, but the ass saw him and stopped in her tracks:

> And the ass saw the angel of the Lord standing in the road, with a drawn sword in his hand; and the ass turned aside out of the road, and went into the field; and Balaam struck the ass, to turn her onto the road. Then the angel of the Lord stood in a narrow path between the vineyards, with a wall on each side. And when the ass saw the angel of the Lord, she pushed against the wall, so he struck her again (22:23–25).

The third time the ass saw the obstructing angel, she stopped and lay down under Balaam, "and Balaam's anger was kindled, and he struck the ass with his staff." Then, the story continues,

> the Lord opened the mouth of the ass, and she said to Balaam, "What have I done to you, that you have struck me three times?" And Balaam said to the ass, "Because you have made a fool of me. I wish I had a sword in my hand, for then I would kill you." And the ass said to Balaam, "Am I not your ass, that you have ridden all your life to this very day? Did I ever do such things to you?" And he said, "No" (22:28–30).

Then "the Lord opened the eyes of Balaam, and he saw the angel of the Lord standing in the way, with his drawn sword in his hand, and he bowed his head, and fell on his face." Then the *satan* rebukes Balaam, and speaks for his master, the Lord:

> "Why have you struck your ass three times? Behold, I came here to oppose you, because your way is evil in my eyes; and the ass saw me. . . . If she had not turned away from me, I would surely have killed you right then, and let her live" (22:31–33).

Chastened by this terrifying vision, Balaam agrees to do what God, speaking through his *satan*, commands.

The book of Job, too, describes the *satan* as a supernatural messenger, a member of God's royal court.[10] But while Balaam's *satan* protects him from harm, Job's *satan* takes a more adversarial role. Here the Lord himself admits that the *satan* incited him to act *against* Job (2:3). The story begins when the *satan* appears as an angel, a "son of God" (*ben 'elōhīm*), a term that, in Hebrew idiom, often means "one of the divine beings." Here this angel, the *satan*, comes with the rest of the heavenly host on the day appointed for them to "present themselves before the Lord." When the Lord asks whence he comes, the *satan* answers, "From roaming on the earth, and walking up and down on it." Here the storyteller plays on the similarity between the sound of the Hebrew *satan* and *shût*, the Hebrew word "to roam," suggesting that the *satan*'s special role in the heavenly court is that of a kind of roving intelligence agent, like those whom many Jews of the time would have known—and detested—from the king of Persia's elaborate system of secret police and intelligence officers. Known as "the king's eye" or "the king's ear," these agents roamed the empire looking for signs of disloyalty among the people.[11]

God boasts to the *satan* about one of his most loyal subjects: "Have you considered my servant Job, that there is no one like him on earth, a blessed and upright man, who fears God and turns away from evil?" The *satan* then challenges the Lord to put Job to the test:

"Does Job fear God for nothing? . . . You have blessed the work of his hands, and his possessions have increased. But put forth your hand now, and touch all that he has, and he will curse you to your face" (1:9–11).

The Lord agrees to test Job, authorizing the *satan* to afflict Job with devastating loss, but defining precisely how far he may go: "Behold, all that belongs to him is in your power; only do not touch the man himself." Job withstands the first deadly onslaught, the sudden loss of his sons and daughters in a single accident, the slaughter of his cattle, sheep, and camels, and the loss of all his wealth and property. When the *satan* appears again among the sons of God on the appointed day, the Lord points out that "Job still holds fast to his integrity, although you incited me against him, to harm him without cause." Then the *satan* asks that he increase the pressure:

"Skin for skin. All that a man has he will give for his life. But put forth your hand now, and touch his flesh and his bone, and he will curse you to your face." And the Lord said to the *satan,* "Behold, he is in your power; only spare his life" (2:4–6).

According to the folktale, Job withstands the test, the *satan* retreats, and "the Lord restored the fortunes of Job . . . and he gave him twice as much as he had before" (42:10). Here the *satan* terrifies and harms a person but, like the angel of death, remains an angel, a member of the heavenly court, God's obedient servant.

Around the time Job was written (c. 550 B.C.E.), however, other biblical writers invoked the *satan* to account for division within Israel.[12] One court historian slips the *satan* into an account concerning the origin of census taking, which King David introduced into Israel c. 1000 B.C.E. for the purpose of instituting taxation. David's introduction of taxation aroused vehement and immediate opposition—opposition that began among the very army commanders ordered to carry it out. Joab, David's chief officer, objected, and warned the king that what he was proposing to do was evil. The other army commanders at first refused to obey, nearly precipitating a revolt; but finding the king adamant, the officers finally obeyed and "numbered the people."

Why had David committed what one chronicler who recalls the story regards as an evil, aggressive act "against Israel"? Unable to deny that the offending order came from the king himself, but intent on condemning David's action without condemning the king directly, the author of 1 Chronicles suggests that a supernatural adversary within the divine court had managed to infiltrate the royal house and lead the king himself into sin: "The *satan* stood up against Israel, and incited David to number the people" (1 Chron. 21:1). But although an angelic power incited David to commit this otherwise inexplicable act, the chronicler insists that the king was nevertheless personally responsible—and guilty. "God was displeased with this thing, and he smote Israel." Even after David abased himself and confessed his sin, the angry Lord punished him by sending an avenging angel to destroy seventy thousand Israelites with a plague; and the Lord was barely restrained from destroying the city of Jerusalem itself.

Here the *satan* is invoked to account for the division and destruction that King David's order aroused within Israel.[13] Not long before the chronicler wrote, the prophet Zechariah had depicted the *satan* inciting factions among the people. Zechariah's account reflects conflicts that arose within Israel after thousands of Jews—many of them influential and educated—whom the Babylonians had captured in war (c. 687 B.C.E.) and exiled to Babylon, returned to Palestine from exile. Cyrus, king of Persia, having recently conquered Babylon, not only allowed these Jewish exiles to go home but intended to make them his allies. Thus he offered them funds to reconstruct Jerusalem's defensive city walls, and to rebuild the great Temple, which the Babylonians had destroyed. Those returning were eager to reestablish the worship of "the Lord alone" in their land, and they naturally expected to reestablish themselves as rulers of their people.

They were not warmly welcomed by those whom they had left behind. Many of those who had remained saw the former exiles not only as agents of the Persian king but as determined to retrieve the power and land they had been forced to relinquish when they were deported. Many resented the returnees' plan to take charge of the priestly offices and to "purify" the Lord's worship.

As the biblical scholar Paul Hanson notes, the line that had once divided the Israelites from their enemies had separated them from foreigners. Now the line separated two groups *within Israel*:

> Now, according to the people who remained, their beloved land was controlled by the enemy, and although that enemy in fact comprised fellow Israelites, yet they regarded these brethren as essentially no different from Canaanites.[14]

The prophet Zechariah sides with the returning exiles in this heated conflict and recounts a vision in which the *satan* speaks for the rural inhabitants who accuse the returning high priest of being a worthless candidate:

> The Lord showed me Joshua, the high priest, standing before the angel of the Lord, and the *satan* standing at his right hand to accuse him. The Lord said to the *satan*, "The Lord rebuke you, O *satan*! The Lord who has chosen Jerusalem rebuke you" (Zech. 3:1–2).

Here the *satan* speaks for a disaffected—and unsuccessful—party against another party of fellow Israelites. In Zechariah's account of factions within Israel, the *satan* takes on a sinister quality, as he had done in the story of David's census, and his role begins to change from that of God's agent to that of his opponent. Although these biblical stories reflect divisions within Israel, they are not yet sectarian, for their authors still identify with Israel as a whole.

Some four centuries later in 168 B.C.E., when Jews regained their independence from their Seleucid rulers, descendents of Alexander the Great, internal conflicts became even more acute.[15] For centuries, Jews had been pressured to assimilate to the ways of the foreign nations that successively had ruled their land—the Babylonians, then the Persians, and, after 323 B.C.E., the Hellenistic dynasty established by Alexander. As the first book of Maccabees tells the story, these pressures reached a breaking point in 168 B.C.E., when the Seleucid ruler, the Syrian king Antiochus Epiphanes, suspecting resistance to his rule, decided to eradicate every trace of the Jews' peculiar and "barbaric" culture. First he outlawed circumcision, along with study and observance of Torah. Then he stormed the Jerusalem Temple and desecrated it by rededicating it to the Greek god Olympian Zeus. To enforce submission to his new regime, the king built and garrisoned a massive new fortress overlooking the Jerusalem Temple itself.

Jewish resistance to these harsh decrees soon flared into a widespread revolt, which began, according to tradition, when a company of the king's troops descended upon the village of Modein to force the inhabitants to bow down to foreign gods. The old village priest Mattathias rose up and killed a Jew who was about to obey the Syrian king's command. Then he killed the king's commissioner and fled with his sons to the hills—an act of defiance that precipitated the revolt led by Mattathias's son Judas Maccabeus.[16]

As told in 1 Maccabees, this famous story shows how those Israelites determined to resist the foreign king's orders and retain their ancestral traditions battled on two fronts at once—not only against the foreign occupiers, but against those Jews who inclined toward accommodation with the foreigners, and toward assimilation. Recently the historian Victor Tcherikover and others have told a more complex version of that history. According to Tcherikover, many Jews, especially among the upper classes, actually favored Antiochus's "reform" and wanted to participate fully in the privileges of Hellenistic society available only to Greek citizens.[17] By giving up their tribal ways and gaining for Jerusalem the prerogatives of a Greek city, they would win the right to govern the city themselves, to strike their own coins, and to increase commerce with a worldwide network of other Greek cities. They could participate in such cultural projects as the Olympic games with allied cities and gain the advantages of mutual defense treaties. Many wanted their sons to have a Greek education. Besides reading Greek literature, from the *Iliad* and the *Odyssey* to Sophocles, Plato, and Aristotle, and participating in public athletic competitions, as Greeks did, they could advance themselves in the wider cosmopolitan world.

But many other Jews, perhaps the majority of the population of Jerusalem and the countryside—tradespeople, artisans, and farmers—detested these "Hellenizing Jews" as traitors to God and Israel alike. The revolt ignited by old Mattathias encouraged people to resist Antiochus's orders, even at the risk of death, and oust the foreign rulers. After intense fighting, the Jewish armies finally won a decisive victory. They celebrated by purifying and rededicating the Temple in a ceremony commemorated, ever since, at the annual festival of Hanukkah.

Jews resumed control of the Temple, the priesthood, and the government; but after the foreigners had retreated, internal conflicts remained, especially over who would control these institutions. These divisions now intensified, as the more rigorously separatist party dominated by the Maccabees opposed the Hellenizing party. The former, having won the war, had the upper hand.

Ten to twenty years after the revolt began, the influential Hasmonean family gained control of the high priesthood in what was now essentially a theocratic state. Although originally identified with their Maccabean ancestors, successive generations of the family abandoned the austere habits of their predecessors. Two generations after the Maccabean victory, the party of Pharisees, advocating increased religious rigor, challenged the Hasmoneans. According to Tcherikover's analysis, the Pharisees, backed by tradespeople and farmers, despised the Hasmoneans as having become essentially secular rulers who had abandoned Israel's ancestral ways. The Pharisees demanded that the Hasmoneans relinquish the high priesthood to those who deserved it—people like themselves, who strove to live according to religious law.[18]

During the following decades, other, more radical dissident groups joined the Pharisees in denouncing the great high priestly family and its allies. Such groups were anything but uniform: they were fractious and diverse, and with the passage of time included various groups of Essenes, the monastic community at Kirbet Qûmran, as well as their allies in the towns, and the followers of Jesus of Nazareth. What these groups shared was their opposition to the high priest and his allies and to the Temple, which they controlled.

The majority of Jews, including the Pharisees, still defined themselves in traditional terms, as "Israel against 'the nations.' " But those who joined marginal or more extreme groups like the Essenes, bent on separating Israel radically from foreign influence, came to treat that traditional identification as a matter of secondary importance. What mattered primarily, these rigorists claimed, was not whether one was Jewish—this they took for granted—but rather "which of us [Jews] really are on God's side" and which had "walked in the ways of the nations," that is, adopted foreign cultural and commercial practices. The separatists found ammunition in biblical passages that invoke terrifying curses upon people who violate God's covenant, and in prophetic passages that warn that only a "righteous remnant" in Israel will remain faithful to God.

More radical than their predecessors, these dissidents began increasingly to invoke the *satan* to characterize their Jewish opponents; in the process they turned this rather unpleasant angel into a far grander—and far more malevolent—figure. No longer one of God's faithful servants, he begins to become what he is for Mark and for later Christianity—God's antagonist, his enemy, even his rival.[19] Such sectarians, contending less against "the nations" than against other Jews, denounce their opponents as apostate and accuse them of having been seduced by the power of evil, whom they call by many names—Satan, Beelzebub, Semihazah, Azazel, Belial, Prince of Darkness. These dissidents also borrowed stories, and wrote their own, telling how such angelic powers, swollen with lust or arrogance, fell from heaven into sin. Those who first elaborated such stories, as we shall see, most often used them to characterize what they charged was the "fall into sin" of human beings—which usually meant the dominant majority of their Jewish contemporaries.

As Satan became an increasingly important and personified figure, stories about his origin proliferated. One group tells how one of the angels, himself high in the heavenly hierarchy, proved insubordinate to his commander in chief and so was thrown out of heaven, demoted, and disgraced, an echo of Isaiah's account of the fall of a great prince:

> How are you fallen from heaven, day star, son of the dawn! How are you fallen to earth, conqueror of the nations! You said in your heart, "I will ascend to heaven, above the stars of God; I will set my throne on high . . . I will ascend upon the high clouds. . . ." But you are brought down to darkness [or: the underworld, *sheol*], to the depths of the pit (Isa. 14:12–15).

Nearly two and a half thousand years after Isaiah wrote, this luminous falling star, his name translated into Latin as Lucifer ("light-bearer") was transformed by Milton into the protagonist of *Paradise Lost*.

Far more influential in first-century Jewish and Christian circles, however, was a second group of apocryphal and pseudepigraphic stories, which tell how lust drew the angelic "sons of God" down to earth. These stories derive from a cryptic account in Genesis 6, which says:

> When men began to multiply on the earth, and daughters were born to them, the sons of God saw the daughters of men, that they were fair.

Some of these angels, transgressing the boundaries that the Lord had established between heaven and earth, mated with human women, and produced offspring who were half angel, half human. According to Genesis, these hybrids became "giants in the earth . . . the mighty men of renown" (Gen. 6:4). Other storytellers, probably writing later,[20] as we shall see, say that these monstrous offspring became demons, who took over the earth and polluted it.

Finally, an apocryphal version of the life of Adam and Eve gives a third account of angelic rebellion. In the beginning, God, having created Adam, called the angels together to admire his work and ordered them to bow down to their younger human sibling. Michael obeyed, but Satan refused, saying,

> "Why do you press me? I will not worship one who is younger than I am, and inferior. I am older than he is; he ought to worship me!" (*Vita Adae et Evae* 14:3).

Thus the problem of evil begins in sibling rivalry.[21]

At first glance these stories of Satan may seem to have little in common. Yet they all agree on one thing: that this greatest and most dangerous enemy did not originate, as one might expect, as an outsider, an alien, or a stranger. Satan is not the distant enemy but the intimate enemy—one's trusted colleague, close associate, brother. He is the kind of person on whose loyalty and goodwill the well-being of family and society depend—but one who turns unexpectedly jealous and hostile. Whichever version of his origin one chooses, then, and there are many, all depict Satan as an *intimate* enemy—the attribute that qualifies him so well to express conflict among Jewish groups. Those who asked, "How could God's own angel become his enemy?" were thus asking, in effect, "How could one of *us* become one of *them*?" Stories of Satan and other fallen angels proliferated in these troubled times, especially within those radical groups that had turned against the rest of the Jewish community and, consequently, concluded that others had turned against them—or (as they put it) against *God*.

One anonymous author who collected and elaborated stories about fallen angels during the Maccabean war was troubled by wartime divisions among Jewish communities. He addressed this divisiveness indirectly in the *Book of the Watchers*, one of the apocryphal books that would become famous and influential, especially among Christians, by introducing the idea of a division in heaven. The *Book of the Watchers*, a collection of visionary stories, is set, in turn, into a larger collection called the *First Book of Enoch*. It tells how the "watcher" angels, whom God appointed to supervise ("watch over") the universe, fell from heaven. Starting from the story of Genesis 6, in which the "sons of God" lusted for human women, this author combines two different accounts of how the watchers lost their heavenly glory.[22] The first describes how Semihazah, leader of the watchers, coerced two hundred other angels to join him in a pact to violate divine order by mating with human women. These mismatches produced "a race of bastards, the giants known as the nephilim ["fallen ones"], from whom there were to proceed demonic spirits," who brought violence upon earth and devoured its people. Interwoven with this story is an alternate version, which tells how the archangel Azazel sinned by disclosing to human beings the secrets of metallurgy, a pernicious revelation that inspired men to make weapons and women to adorn themselves with gold, silver, and cosmetics. Thus the fallen angels and their demon offspring incited in both sexes violence, greed, and lust.

Because these stories involve sociopolitical satire laced with religious polemic, some historians have recently asked to what specific historical situations they refer. Are Jews who thus embellish the story of angels that mate with human beings covertly ridiculing the pretensions of their Hellenistic rulers? George Nickelsburg points out that from the time of Alexander the Great, Greek kings had claimed to be descended from gods as well as from human women; the Greeks called such hybrid beings heroes. But their Jewish subjects, with their derisive tale of Semihazah, may have turned such claims of divine descent against the foreign usurpers.[23] The *Book of the Watchers* says pointedly that these greedy monsters "consumed the produce of all the people until the people hated feeding them"; the monsters then turned directly to "devour the people."

Or does the story express instead a pious people's contempt for a specific group of Jewish enemies—namely, certain members of the Jerusalem priesthood? David Suter suggests that the story aims instead at certain priests who, like the "sons of God" in the story, violate their divinely given status and responsibility by allowing lust to draw them into impurity—especially marriages with outsiders, Gentile women.[24]

Either interpretation is possible. As John Collins points out, the author of the *Book of the Watchers,* by choosing to tell the story of the watchers instead of that of the actual Greek rulers or corrupt priests, offers "a paradigm which is not restricted to one historical situation, but which can be applied whenever an analogous situation arises."[25] The same is true of all apocalyptic literature, and accounts for much of its power. Even today, readers puzzle over books that claim the authority of angelic revelation, from the biblical book of Daniel to the New Testament book of Revelation, finding in their own circumstances new applications for these evocative, enigmatic texts.

The primary apocalyptic question is this: Who are God's people?[26] To most readers of the *Book of the Watchers,* the answer would have been obvious—Israel. But the author of *Watchers,* without discarding ethnic identity, insists on moral identity. It is not enough to be a Jew. One must also be a Jew who acts morally. Here we see evidence of a historical shift—one that Christians will adopt and extend and which, ever after, will divide them from other Jewish groups.

The author of the *Book of the Watchers* intended nothing so radical as the followers of Jesus undertook when they finally abandoned Israel to form their own distinct religious tradition. He takes for granted Israel's priority over the rest of the nations, always mentioning Israel first. But this author takes a decisive step by separating ethnic from moral identity and suggesting a contrast between them. He takes his beginning from the opening chapters of Genesis, choosing as his spokesman the holy man Enoch, who far antedates Abraham and Israel's election and, according to Genesis, belongs not to Israel but to the primordial history of the human race. This author omits any mention of the law given to Moses at Sinai, and praises instead the universal law that God wrote into the fabric of the universe and gave to all humankind alike—the law that governs the seas, the earth, and the stars. Addressing his message to "the elect and the righteous" among all humankind, he demonstrates not only, as George Nickelsburg observes, an "unusual openness to the Gentiles," but also an unusually negative view of Israel, or, more precisely, many—perhaps a majority—of Israel's people.[27]

The *Book of the Watchers* tells the stories of Semihazah and Azazel as a moral warning: if even archangels, "sons of heaven," can sin and be cast down, how much more susceptible to sin and damnation are mere human beings, even those who belong to God's chosen people. In the *Book of the Watchers,* when Enoch, moved with compassion for the fallen watchers, tries to intervene with God on their behalf, one of God's angels orders him instead to deliver to them God's judgment: "You used to be holy, spirits possessing eternal life; but now you have defiled yourselves." Such passages suggest that the *Book of the Watchers* articulates the judgment of certain Jews upon others, and specifically upon some who hold positions that ordinarily convey great authority.

In 160 B.C.E., after the Maccabees' victory, a group who regarded themselves as moderates regained control of the Temple priesthood and temporarily ousted the Maccabean party. Recalling this event, one of the Maccabeans adds to the collection called the *First Book of Enoch* another version of the story of the watcher angels, a version aimed against those who had usurped control of the Temple. This author says that the watchers, falling like stars from heaven, themselves spawned Israel's foreign enemies, depicted as bloody predators—lions, leopards, wolves, and snakes intent on destroying Israel, here depicted as a herd of sheep. But, he continues, God's chosen nation is itself divided; some are "blind sheep," and others have their eyes open. When the day of judgment comes, he warns, God will destroy the errant Jews, these "blind sheep," along with Israel's traditional enemies. Furthermore, God will finally gather into his eternal home not only Israel's righteous but also the righteous from the nations (although these will remain forever secondary to Israel).

A third anonymous writer whose work is included in the *First Book of Enoch* is so preoccupied with internal division that he virtually ignores Israel's alien enemies. This author has Enoch predict the rise of "a perverse generation," warning that "all its deeds shall be apostate" (*1 Enoch* 93:9). Castigating many of his contemporaries, this author, as George Nickelsburg points out, like several biblical prophets, speaks for the poor, and denounces the rich and powerful, predicting their destruction.[28] He even insists that slavery, along with other social and economic inequities, is not divinely ordained, as others argue, but "arose from oppression" (*1 Enoch* 98:5b)—that is, human sin.[29]

The story of the watchers, then, in some of its many transformations, suggested a change in the traditional lines separating Jew from Gentile. The latest section of the *First Book of Enoch*, the "Similitudes," written about the time of Jesus, simply contrasts those who are righteous, who stand on the side of the angels, with those, both Jews and Gentiles, seduced by the *satan*s. Accounts like this would open the way for Christians eventually to leave ethnic identity aside, and to redefine the human community instead in terms of the moral quality, or membership in the elect community, of each individual.

Another devout patriot, writing around 160 B.C.E., also siding with the early Maccabean party, wrote an extraordinary apocryphal book called *Jubilees* to urge his people to maintain their separateness from Gentile ways. What troubles this author is this: How can so many Israelites, God's own people, have become apostates? How can so many Jews be "walking in the ways of the Gentiles" (*Jub.* 1:9)? While the author takes for granted the traditional antithesis between the Israelites and "their enemies, the Gentiles" (*Jub.* 1:19), here again this conflict recedes into the background. The author of *Jubilees* is concerned instead with the conflicts over assimilation that divide Jewish communities internally, and he attributes these conflicts to that most intimate of enemies, whom he calls by many names, but most often calls Mastema ("hatred"), Satan, or Belial.

The story of the angels' fall in *Jubilees*, like that in the *First Book of Enoch*, gives a moral warning: if even angels, when they sin, bring God's wrath and destruction upon themselves, how can mere human beings expect to be spared? *Jubilees* insists that every creature, whether angel or human, Israelite or Gentile, shall be judged according to deeds, that is, ethically.

According to *Jubilees,* the angels' fall spawned the giants, who sow violence and evil, and evil spirits, "who are cruel, and created to destroy" (*Jub.* 10:6). Ever since, their presence has dominated this world like a dark shadow, and suggests the moral ambivalence and vulnerability of every human being. Like certain of the prophets, this author warns that election offers no safety, certainly no immunity; Israel's destiny depends not simply on election but on moral action or, failing this, on repentance and divine forgiveness.

Yet Jews and Gentiles do not confront demonic malevolence on equal footing. *Jubilees* says that God assigned to each of the nations a ruling angel or spirit "so that they might lead them astray" (*Jub.* 15:31); hence the nations worship demons (whom *Jubilees* identifies with foreign gods).[30] But God himself rules over Israel, together with a phalanx of angels and spirits assigned to guard and bless them.

What, then, does God's election of his people mean? The author of *Jubilees,* echoing the warnings of Isaiah and other prophets, suggests that belonging to the people of Israel does not guarantee deliverance from evil. It conveys a legacy of moral struggle, but ensures divine help in that struggle.

Jubilees depicts Mastema testing Abraham himself to the breaking point. For according to this revisionist writer, it is Mastema—not the Lord—who commands Abraham to kill his son, Isaac. Later Abraham expresses anxiety lest he be enslaved by evil spirits, "who have dominion over the thoughts of human hearts"; he pleads with God, "Deliver me from the hands of evil spirits, and do not let them lead me astray from my God" (*Jub.* 12:20). Moses, too, knows that he and his people are vulnerable. When he prays that God deliver Israel from their external enemies, "the Gentiles" (*Jub.* 1:19), he also prays that God may deliver them from the intimate enemy that threatens to take over his people internally and destroy them: "Do not let the spirit of Belial rule over them" (*Jub.* 1:20). This sense of ominous and omnipresent danger in *Jubilees* shows the extent to which the author regards his people as corruptible and, to a considerable extent, already corrupted. Like the *Book of the Watchers, Jubilees* warns that those who neglect God's covenant are being seduced by the powers of evil, fallen angels.

Despite these warnings, the majority of Jews, from the second century B.C.E. to the present, reject sectarianism, as well as the universalism that, among most Christians, would finally supersede ethnic distinction. The Jewish majority, including those who sided with the Maccabees against the assimilationists, has always identified with Israel as a whole.

The author of the biblical book of Daniel, for example, who wrote during the crisis surrounding the Maccabean war, also sides with the Maccabees, and wants Jews to shun contamination incurred by eating with Gentiles, marrying them, or worshiping their gods. To encourage Jews to maintain their loyalty to Israel, the book opens with the famous story of the prophet Daniel, sentenced to death by the Babylonian king for faithfully praying to his God. Thrown into a den of lions to be torn apart, Daniel is divinely delivered; "the Lord sent an angel to shut the lions' mouths," so that the courageous prophet emerges unharmed.

Like the authors of *Jubilees* and *Watchers,* the author of Daniel, too, sees moral division within Israel, and warns that some people "violate the covenant; but the people who know their God shall stand firm and take action" (Dan. 11:32). Though concerned with moral issues, he never forgets ethnic identity: what concerns him above all is Israel's moral destiny as a whole. Unlike the writers of the *Book of the Watchers* and *Jubilees,* the author of Daniel envisions no sectarian enemy, either human or divine. Grieved as he is at Israel's sins, he never condemns many, much less the majority, of his people as apostate; consequently, he never speaks of Satan, Semihazah, Azazel, Mastema, Belial, or fallen angels of any kind.

Although there are no devils in Daniel's world, there *are* angels, and there are enemies. The author presents the alien enemies, rulers of the Persian, Medean, and Hellenistic empires, in traditional visionary imagery, as monstrous beasts. In one vision, the first beast is "like a lion with eagles' wings"; the second "like a bear," ferociously devouring its prey; the third like a leopard "with four wings of a bird on its back and four heads"; and "a fourth beast [is] terrible and dreadful and exceedingly strong; and it had great iron teeth: it devoured and broke in pieces, and stamped the residue with its feet." In another vision, Daniel sees a horned ram that the angel Gabriel explains to him "is the king of Greece." Throughout the visions of Daniel, such monstrous animals represent foreign rulers and nations who threaten Israel. When Daniel, trembling with awe and terror, prays for his people, he is rewarded with divine assurance that all Israelites who remain true to God will survive (12:1–3). Thus the book of Daniel powerfully reaffirms the integrity of Israel's moral and ethnic identity. It is for this reason, I suggest, that Daniel, unlike such other apocalyptic books as the *Book of the Watchers* and *Jubilees,* is included in the canonical collection that we call the Hebrew Bible and not relegated to the apocrypha.

The majority of Jews, at any rate those who assembled and drew upon the Hebrew Bible, apparently endorsed Daniel's reaffirmation of Israel's traditional identity, while those who valued such books as *1 Enoch* and *Jubilees* probably included a significant minority more inclined to identify with one group of Jews against another, as Daniel had refused to do. Most of those who *did* take sides within the community stopped far short of proclaiming an all-out civil war between one Jewish group and another, but there were notable exceptions. Starting at the time of the Maccabean war, the more radical sectarian groups we have mentioned—above all, those called Essenes—placed this cosmic battle between angels and demons, God and Satan, at the very center of their cosmology and their politics. In so doing, they expressed the importance to their lives of the conflict between themselves and the majority of their fellow Jews, whom the Essenes consigned to damnation.

Many scholars believe that the Essenes are known to us from such first-century contemporaries as Josephus, Philo, and the Roman geographer and naturalist Pliny the Elder, as well as from the discovery in 1947 of the ruins of their community, including its sacred library, the Dead Sea Scrolls. Josephus, at the age of sixteen, was fascinated by this austere and secretive community: he says that they "practiced great holiness" within an extraordi-

narily close-knit group ("they love one another very much").[31]
Josephus and Philo both note, with some astonishment, that
these sectarians practiced strict celibacy, probably because they
chose to live according to the biblical rules for holy war, which
prohibit sexual intercourse during wartime. But the war in which
they saw themselves engaged was God's war against the power of
evil—a cosmic war that they expected would result in God's vindication of their fidelity. The Essenes also turned over all their
money and property to their leaders in order to live "without
money," as Pliny says, in a monastic community.[32]

These devout and passionate sectarians saw the foreign occupation of Palestine—and the accommodation of the majority of
Jews to that occupation—as evidence that the forces of evil had
taken over the world and—in the form of Satan, Mastema, or the
Prince of Darkness—infiltrated and taken over God's own people, turning most of them into allies of the Evil One.

Arising from controversies over purity and assimilation that
followed the Maccabean war, the Essene movement grew during
the Roman occupation of the first century to include over four
thousand men. Women, never mentioned in the community
rule, apparently were not eligible for admission. Although the
remains of a few women and children have been found among
the hundreds of men buried in the outer cemetery at Qûmran,
they probably were not community members.[33] (Since the whole
cemetery has not yet been excavated, these conclusions remain
inconclusive.) Many adjunct members of the sect, apparently
including many who were married, lived in towns all over Palestine, pursuing ordinary occupations while striving to devote
themselves to God; but the most dedicated withdrew in protest
from ordinary Jewish life to form their own "new Israel," the
monastic community in desert caves overlooking the Dead Sea.[34]
There, following the rigorous community rule, they dressed only
in white and regulated every detail of their lives according to
strict interpretations of the law set forth by their priestly leaders.

In their sacred books, such as the great *Scroll of the War of the
Sons of Light Against the Sons of Darkness*, the brethren could
read how God had given them the Prince of Light as their super-

natural ally to help them contend against Satan, and against his human allies.

> The Prince of Light thou has appointed to come to our support: but Satan, the angel Mastema, thou hast created for the pit; he rules in darkness, and his purpose is to bring about evil and sin (1 QM 19:10–12).

The Essenes called themselves the "sons of light" and indicted the majority as "sons of darkness," the "congregation of traitors," as people who "depart from the way, having transgressed the law, and violated the precept" (CD 1:13–20). The Essenes retell the whole history of Israel in terms of this cosmic war. Even in earliest times, they say, "the Prince of Light raised up Moses" (CD 5:18), but the Evil One, here called Beliar, aroused opposition to Moses among his own people. Ever since then, and especially now, Beliar has set traps in which he intends to "catch Israel," for God himself has "unleashed Beliar against Israel" (CD 4:13). Now the "sons of light" eagerly await the day of judgment, when they expect God will come with all the armies of heaven to annihilate the corrupt majority along with Israel's foreign enemies.

Had Satan not already existed in Jewish tradition, the Essenes would have invented him. In the *Book of the Watchers* fallen angels incite the activities of those who violate God's covenant, but the Essenes go much further and place at the center of their religious understanding the cosmic war between God and his allies, both angelic and human, against Satan, or Beliar, along with his demonic and human allies. The Essenes place themselves at the very center of this battle between heaven and hell. While they detest Israel's traditional enemies, whom they call the *kittim* (probably a coded epithet for the Romans),[35] they struggle far more bitterly against their fellow Israelites, who belong to the "congregation of Beliar." David Sperling, scholar of the ancient Near East, suggests that substitution of Beliar for earlier Belial may be a pun on *belî 'ôr*, "without light."[36] They invoke Satan—or Beliar—to characterize the irreconcilable opposition between themselves and the "sons of darkness" in the war taking place simultaneously in heaven and on earth. They expect that soon God will come in power, with his holy angels, and finally overthrow the forces of evil and inaugurate the Kingdom of God.

The Essenes agree with *Jubilees* that being Jewish is no longer enough to ensure God's blessing. But they are much more radical: the sins of the people have virtually canceled God's covenant with Abraham, on which Israel's election depends. Now, they insist, whoever wants to belong to the true Israel must join in a *new* covenant—the covenant of their own congregation.[37] Whoever applies to enter the desert community must first confess himself guilty of sin—guilty, apparently, of participating in Israel's collective apostasy against God. Then the candidate begins several years of probation, during which he turns over his property to the community leaders and swears to practice sexual abstinence, along with ritual purity in everything he eats, drinks, utters, or touches. During the probationary period he must not touch the pots, plates, or utensils in which the members prepare the community's food. Swearing can earn him instant expulsion, and so can complaining against the group's leaders; spitting or talking out of turn incurs strict penalties.

A candidate who finally does gain admission is required, at his initiation ritual, to join together with the whole community to bless all who belong to the new covenant and ritually curse all who are not initiates, who belong to the "men of Beliar." The leaders now reveal to the initiate the secrets of angelology, and according to Josephus, he must solemnly swear to "keep secret the names of the angels" (*War* 2.8). Through practices of purity, prayer, and worship, the initiate strives to unite himself with the company of the angels. As the historian Carol Newsome has shown, Essene community worship—like the Christian liturgy to this day—reaches its climax as the community on earth joins with angels in singing the hymn of praise that the angels sing in heaven ("Holy, holy, holy, Lord God of hosts; heaven and earth are filled with thy glory").[38] Sacred Essene texts like the *Scroll of the War of the Sons of Light Against the Sons of Darkness* reveal secrets of angelology, which the sectarians regarded as valuable and necessary information, for recognizing and understanding the interrelationship of supernatural forces, both good and evil, is essential for their sense of their own identity—and the way they identify others.[39]

The Essenes, then, offer the closest parallel to Mark's account of Jesus' followers, as they invoke images of cosmic war to divide the universe at large—and the Jewish community in particular—between God's people and Satan's. Yet the two movements differ significantly, especially in relation to outsiders. The Essene covenant, as we have seen, was extremely exclusive, restricted not only to Jews, who must be freeborn and male, but to those devout few who willingly joined the "new covenant." Although Mark and Matthew saw the beginning of Jesus' movement primarily within the context of the Jewish community, its future would increasingly involve the Gentile world outside.

Nonetheless, the Essenes, though rigorously exclusive, were led by their objections to the assimilationist tendencies of their fellow Jews to move, paradoxically, in the universalist direction indicated by the *Book of the Watchers* and *Jubilees*. (The Essenes treasured both of these writings in their monastic library; *Jubilees*, wrote an anonymous Essene, is a book that reveals divine secrets "to which Israel has turned a blind eye" [CD 16.2].) The Essenes outdid their predecessors in setting ethnic identity aside, not as wrong, but as inadequate, and emphasized moral over ethnic identification. When they depict the struggle of the Prince of Light against the Prince of Darkness, they do not identify the Prince of Light with the archangel Michael, the angelic patron of Israel.[40] Instead, they envision the Prince of Light as a universal energy contending against an opposing cosmic force, the Prince of Darkness. For the Essenes these two energies represent not only their own conflicts with their opponents but a conflict within every person, within the human heart itself:

> The spirits of truth and falsehood struggle within the human heart. . . . According to his share in truth and right, thus a man

hates lies; and according to his share in the lot of deceit, thus he hates truth (1 QS 4:12–14).

The Essenes, of course, took their own identification with Israel for granted. Since they required every initiate to their covenant to be Jewish, male, and freeborn, "every person" meant in practice only Jews who met these qualifications. But certain followers of Jesus, especially after 100 C.E., having met with disappointing responses to their message within the Jewish communities, would draw upon such universalist themes as they moved to open their movement to Gentiles.

As we saw in the previous chapter, Jesus' followers, according to Mark, also invoke images of cosmic war to divide the universe at large—and the Jewish community in particular—between God's people and Satan's. Mark, like the Essenes, sees this struggle essentially in terms of intra-Jewish conflict. So does the follower of Jesus we call Matthew, who, as we shall see in the next chapter, took up and revised Mark's gospel some ten to twenty years later. Taking Mark's basic framework, Matthew embellished it and in effect updated it, placing the story of Jesus in a context more relevant to the Jewish world of Matthew's own time, Palestine c. 80–90 C.E. By the time Matthew was writing, Jesus' followers were a marginal group opposed by the ruling party of Pharisees, which had gained ascendancy in Jerusalem in the decades following the Roman war. In the central part of Matthew's version of the gospel, the "intimate enemies" had become primarily Pharisees.

About the same time, another follower of Jesus, whom tradition calls Luke, also took up Mark's account and extended it to fit his own perspective—apparently that of a Gentile convert. Yet Luke, as fervently as any Essene, depicts his own sect as representing Israel at its best; according to Luke, as we shall see, Jesus' followers are virtually the only true Israelites left.

Near the end of the century, c. 90–100 C.E., the writer called John offers a bold interpretation of these events. Many scholars agree that the gospel of John presents the viewpoint of a radically sectarian group alienated from the Jewish community because they have been turned out of their home synagogues for claiming that Jesus is the Messiah. Like the Essenes, John speaks eloquently of the love among those who belong to God (John 10:14); and yet John's fierce polemic against those he sometimes calls simply "the Jews" at times matches in bitterness that of the Essenes.

Let us investigate, then, how each of these New Testament gospel writers reshaped Mark's message as the Christian movement changed throughout the first century.

MATTHEW'S CAMPAIGN AGAINST THE PHARISEES: DEPLOYING THE DEVIL

Jesus' followers succeeded, far more than many of them expected—or perhaps even hoped—in attracting Gentiles (from the Latin term for "nations," *gentes*) but, to their disappointment, largely failed to attract Jews. Between 70 and 100 C.E., this movement, which began, as George Nickelsburg says, as "a relative latecomer among the sects and groups in post-exilic Judaism,"[1] grew rapidly. Although many of Jesus' followers were Jewish, they tended increasingly to separate from other Jews, often meeting for worship in the homes of fellow members, rather than in synagogues. This situation distressed many of them, who insisted that they didn't want to depart from traditional ways but had been forced into it, having been rejected by Jewish leaders, sometimes even expelled from their home synagogues.

As the Jesus movement spread throughout the Roman world, various adherents began to drop distinctively Jewish practices, most notably circumcision, and then also dietary and Sabbath laws. By 100 C.E., in regions that include Greece, Asia Minor, Italy, and Egypt, many Christian churches had become predominantly Gentile. They still insisted, nonetheless, that they alone were the true embodiment of Israel. George Nickelsburg points out the irony of their situation:

A young, upstart group, whose membership had rapidly and radically changed, was asserting that it was more authentic than its parent group; and this attitude of superiority and exclusion was derived, in part, from ideas and attitudes already present in the parent body.[2]

As the historian and New Testament scholar Wayne Meeks notes, the path to separation was by no means simple or uniform.[3] We have already seen that Jewish communities scattered throughout Palestine and the provincial cities of the Roman empire not only were internally diverse but were also undergoing complex postwar changes. The various groups of converts to Christianity were, if anything, even more diverse internally, since they often included Gentiles along with Jews. These groups of Jesus' followers struggled to find a place to stand in relation to the Jewish communities whose Scriptures and traditions they largely appropriated.

Not all Christians abandoned Jewish practices at the same time. In the decades after Jesus' death, many of his followers may not have meant to abandon them at all. The group centered in Jerusalem around Jesus' brother James, for example, remained observant of the law, like James himself (hence his nickname, "James the Just," or "the Righteous"). Other groups, like those who followed teachings associated with Peter, modified observance of dietary and sexual laws. Groups that identified with Paul, the converted Pharisee, largely adopted his conviction that "Christ is the end of the law to everyone who believes," whether Jew or Gentile.[4] Most believers took Paul to mean that practicing circumcision and observing kosher laws and Jewish festivals were antithetical to embracing the gospel, and his preaching attracted many converts among the Gentiles who associated themselves with Jewish synagogue congregations.

When we look at the three other gospels included with Mark in the New Testament, all written between 70 and 100 C.E., we can see three representative communities, each in the process of separating from particular Jewish groups and attempting to forge a new and distinctively Christian pattern of community identity. New Testament scholar Krister Stendahl characterizes Matthew's gospel as a kind of "community rule," considerably more liberal than that of the Essenes.[5] The gospel of Luke, probably written by the only Gentile author in the New Testament for a predominantly Gentile community, insists that his group has inherited Israel's legacy as God's people. The author of John, probably Jewish himself, describes a close-knit group of "Jesus' own"—insiders who follow Jesus' command to "love one another" (15:12) while regarding their Jewish opponents as offspring of Satan.

That such patterns of group identity are found in these gospels—patterns that have shaped Christian churches ever since—is certainly no accident. The four gospels collected in the New Testament were canonized around 200 C.E., apparently by a consensus of churches ranging from those in provincial Gaul to the church in the capital city of Rome; they were chosen not necessarily because they were the earliest or the most accurate accounts of Jesus' life and teaching but precisely because they could form the basis for church communities.

The canonical gospels were not by any means the only accounts of Jesus' life and teaching. During the years following his death, stories about him and his disciples were told and retold, not only in Palestine, but throughout Asia Minor, Greece, Egypt, Africa, Gaul, and Spain. Some twenty years after Jesus' crucifixion, when Paul traveled to synagogues in Antioch, the capital of Syria, and in Greece and Rome to proclaim "the gospel of Jesus Christ," there were as yet no written gospels. According to Paul, "the gospel" consisted of what he preached, which he summarized as follows: "that Christ died for our sins, according to the scriptures; that he was buried; and that he was raised on the third day" (1 Cor. 15:3–4). Although Paul preached in synagogues, he found his audience largely among Gentiles, most often among Gentiles attracted to Jewish congregations. Many were people who had moved from their native towns to sprawling, heterogeneous cities like Syrian Antioch, Asian Ephesus, and Greek Corinth. Proclaiming that Jews and Gentiles, slaves and free people, men and women, could now become "one in Christ" (Gal. 3:28), Paul formed from those he baptized the close-knit groups that Wayne Meeks calls "the first urban Christians"—ethnically diverse communities where tradespeople, slaves, and the groups' wealthy patrons mingled together, now bound to help and support one another as they awaited the time when Christ would return in glory.[6] Writing to various congregations as he traveled, Paul sometimes invoked a "saying of the Lord." Once he invoked Jesus' authority to prohibit divorce (1 Cor. 7:10); another time he explained how Jesus had told his followers to ritually eat bread and drink wine "in order to manifest the Lord's death, until he comes" (1 Cor. 11:26).

Paul had no interest in Jesus' earthly life, however, and none in collecting his sayings. But other Christians did begin to collect Jesus' sayings and write them down.[7] The *Secret Book of James,* one of the many traditions that circulated after Jesus' death, gives a stylized description of this process:

> The twelve disciples were all sitting together at one time and remembering what the savior said to each one of them, whether secretly or openly, and putting it into books (NHC I.27.15).

In fact, many people, not just "the twelve" enshrined in Christian tradition, gathered Jesus' sayings into various collections. Most scholars agree that a collection of Jesus' sayings, translated from the Aramaic he spoke into Greek, circulated widely during the first century, although we do not have an actual copy of that source. If each of the gospel writers had individually translated Jesus' sayings, we would expect to see some variation in the way each presented his words. But gospels as diverse as Matthew and Luke, as well as the suppressed *Gospel of Thomas,* all quote sayings of Jesus in identical translation. This suggests that they relied on the common source, which scholars call Q (for *Quelle,* the German word for "source").[8] To this source we owe many familiar sayings, including the Beatitudes ("Blessed are you poor; for yours is the kingdom of heaven . . .") and what we know from Matthew's gospel as the Sermon on the Mount (which becomes, in Luke's gospel, the Sermon on the Plain). Still other sayings are known to us from scraps of papyrus that have been found preserved in dry climates like that of Upper Egypt. From the late 1800s through this century, archaeologists working in Egypt have found papyrus leaves that contain glimpses of Jesus tradition—for example, a story of Jesus healing a leper, or another of Jesus raising a dead young man to life.[9] Other papyrus fragments yield enigmatic sayings otherwise unknown:

> Jesus said, "I am the light which is above them all. It is I who am the all. From me did all come forth and to me the all extends. Split a piece of wood, and I am there. Lift up the stone, and you will find me there" (NHC II.46.23–38).

As stories, sayings, and anecdotes proliferated, various interpretations of Jesus' life and teaching circulated among diverse Christian groups throughout the Roman world. What Jesus actually taught often became a matter of bitter dispute, as we can see from the *Gospel of Mary Magdalene,* another early source, discovered in 1896 on papyrus fragments in Egypt. This remarkable text, like other noncanonical texts, depicts Mary Magdalene among the disciples—indeed, as one of Jesus' most beloved disciples, to whom he entrusted secret teaching.[10] In the following passage (17:18–18:15), Peter first addresses Mary with a request.

> "Sister, we know that the savior loved you more than the rest of women. Tell us the words of the savior which you remember, which . . . we do not [know] and have not heard."

After Mary answers, revealing to Peter secret teaching on the soul's spiritual journey, Andrew objects:

> "Say what you want about what she has said. I, at least, do not believe that the savior said this. For certainly these teachings are strange ideas."

Peter joins in, challenging Mary's veracity:

> "Did he really speak with a woman without our knowledge, and in secret? Are we all to turn around and listen to her? Did he love her more than us?"

Mary protests:

> "My brother Peter, what do you think? Do you think I made
> this up in my heart? Do you think I am lying about the Lord?"

Then Levi breaks in to mediate the dispute, saying that "the Savior knew her very well, and made her worthy" to receive such
teachings. The *Gospel of Mary* concludes as the disciples agree to
accept what they learn from Mary, and they all prepare to go out
to preach. But most Christian groups, including the one in Rome
identified with Peter, who was often depicted as Mary's antagonist, rejected such claims of revelation given through Mary, since
she was not one of the twelve, and rejected many other widely circulating "gospels" as well. By the late second century, certain
church leaders began to denounce such teachings as heresy.

In 1945, the extraordinary discovery of a hidden library of early
Christian writings at Nag Hammadi greatly extended our understanding of the early Christian movement.[11] This is not the place
to describe that discovery, discussed in my book *The Gnostic
Gospels;* but when we glance at one of the gospels discovered
there, one that most church leaders who knew it rejected, we can
see more clearly their reasons for preferring the gospels of the
New Testament. The *Gospel of Thomas* begins with these words:
"These are the secret words which the Living Jesus spoke, and
which the twin, Judas Thomas, wrote down." Did Jesus have a
twin brother, as this text implies? Could this be an authentic
record of Jesus' sayings? According to its title, the text contained
the gospel according to Thomas. Yet unlike the gospels of the
New Testament, this text identified itself as a *secret* gospel. It contained many sayings that parallel those in the New Testament,
particularly sayings from the Q source; yet others were strikingly
different—sayings as strange and compelling as Zen koans:

> Jesus said, "If you bring forth what is within you, what you
> bring forth will save you. If you do not bring forth what is
> within you, what you do not bring forth will destroy you"
> (NHC II.45.29–33).

Although the complete text of *Thomas*, written in Coptic, probably dates to the third or fourth century C.E., the original probably was written in Greek, perhaps much earlier.[12] New Testament scholar Helmut Koester has argued that the *Gospel of Thomas* contains a collection of sayings that *predates* the gospels of the New Testament.[13] If the earliest of the New Testament gospels, the gospel of Mark, dates from about 70 C.E., the *Gospel of Thomas*, he argues, may date back a generation earlier. Although many scholars dispute Koester's dating of *Thomas*, this gospel, discovered less than fifty years ago, does in some ways resemble the kind of source that the authors of Matthew and Luke used when they composed their own gospels.

Why was this gospel suppressed, along with many others that have remained virtually unknown for nearly two thousand years? Originally part of the sacred library of the oldest monastery in Egypt, these books were buried, apparently, around 370 C.E., after the archbishop of Alexandria ordered Christians all over Egypt to ban such books as heresy and demanded their destruction. Two hundred years earlier, such works had already been attacked by another zealously orthodox bishop, Irenaeus of Lyons. Irenaeus was the first, so far as we know, to identify the four gospels of the New Testament as canonical, and to exclude all the rest. Distressed that dozens of gospels were circulating among Christians throughout the world, including his own Greek-speaking immigrant congregation living in Gaul, Irenaeus denounced as heretics those who "boast that they have more gospels than there really are . . . but really, they have no gospels that are not full of blasphemy."[14] Only the four gospels of the New Testament, Irenaeus insisted, are *authentic*. What was his reasoning? Irenaeus declared that just as there are only four principal winds, and four corners of the universe, and four pillars holding up the sky, so there can be only four gospels. Besides, he added, only the New Testament gospels were written by Jesus' own disciples (Matthew and John) or their followers (Mark, disciple of Peter, and Luke, disciple of Paul).

Few New Testament scholars today agree with Irenaeus. Although the gospels of the New Testament—like those discovered at Nag Hammadi—are *attributed* to Jesus' followers, no one knows who actually wrote any of them; furthermore, what we know about their dating makes the traditional assumptions, in all cases, extremely unlikely. Yet Irenaeus's statements remind us that the collection of books we call the New Testament was formed as late as 180–200 C.E. Before that time, many gospels circulated throughout the Christian communities scattered from Asia Minor to Greece, Rome, Gaul, Spain, and Africa. Yet by the late second century, bishops of the church who called themselves orthodox rejected all but the four canonical gospels, denouncing all the rest, in Irenaeus's words, as "an abyss of madness, and blasphemy against Christ."[15] Irenaeus wanted to consolidate Christian groups threatened by persecution throughout the world. The gospels he endorsed helped institutionalize the Christian movement. Those he denounced as heresy did not serve the purposes of institutionalization. Some, on the contrary, urged people to seek direct access to God, unmediated by church or clergy.

The *Gospel of Thomas*, as noted above, claims to offer secret teaching—teaching quite different from that of Mark, Matthew, Luke, and John. According to Mark, for example, Jesus first appears proclaiming that "the time is at hand; the Kingdom of God is drawing near. Repent, and believe in the gospel" (1:15). According to Mark, the world is about to undergo cataclysmic transformation: Jesus predicts strife, war, conflict, and suffering, followed by a world-shattering event—the coming of the Kingdom of God (13:1–37).

But in the *Gospel of Thomas* the "kingdom of God" is not an event expected to happen in history, nor is it a "place." The author of *Thomas* seems to ridicule such views:

> Jesus said, "If those who lead you say to you, 'Lord, the kingdom is in the sky,' then the birds of the sky will precede you. If they say to you, 'It is in the sea,' then the fish will precede you" (NHC II.32.19–24).

Here the kingdom represents a state of self-discovery:

"Rather, the kingdom is inside of you, and it is outside of you. When you come to know yourselves, then you will become known, and you will realize that it is you who are the sons of the living Father" (NHC II.32.25–33.5).

But the disciples, mistaking that kingdom for a future event, persist in naïve questioning:

"When will . . . the new world come?" Jesus said to them, "What you look forward to has already come, but you do not recognize it" (NHC II.42.10–12).

According to the *Gospel of Thomas,* then, the kingdom of God symbolizes a state of transformed consciousness. One enters that kingdom when one attains self-knowledge. The *Gospel of Thomas* teaches that when one comes to know oneself, at the deepest level, one simultaneously comes to know God as the source of one's being.

If we then ask, "Who is Jesus?," the *Gospel of Thomas* gives an answer different from that in the gospels of the New Testament. Mark, for example, depicts Jesus as an utterly unique being—the Messiah, God's appointed king. According to Mark, it was Peter who discovered the secret of Jesus' identity:

And Jesus went on with his disciples to the villages of Caesarea Philippi; and on the way he asked his disciples, "Who do men say that I am?" And they told him "John the Baptist; and others say, Elijah; and others, one of the prophets." And he asked them, "But who do you say that I am?" Peter answered him, "You are the Messiah" (8:27–29).

But the *Gospel of Thomas* tells the same story differently:

Jesus said to his disciples, "Compare me to someone, and tell me whom I am like." Simon Peter said to him, "You are like a righteous messenger." Matthew said to him, "You are like a wise philosopher." Thomas said to him, "Master, my mouth is wholly incapable of saying whom you are like" (NHC II.34.30–35.3).

The author of *Thomas* here interprets, for Greek-speaking readers, Matthew's claim that Jesus was a rabbinic teacher ("wise philosopher"), and Peter's conviction that Jesus was the Messiah ("righteous messenger"). Jesus does not deny these roles, at least in relation to Matthew and Peter. But according to Thomas, here they—and their answers—represent an inferior level of understanding. Thomas, who recognizes that he himself cannot assign a specific role to Jesus, transcends at that moment the relation of disciple to master. Jesus declares that Thomas has become like himself:

> "I am not your Master, for you have drunk, and become drunk from the bubbling stream I measured out. . . . Whoever drinks from my mouth will become as I am, and I myself will become that person, and things that are hidden will be revealed to him" (NHC II.35.4–7; 50:27–30).

The New Testament gospel of John emphasizes Jesus' uniqueness even more strongly than Mark does. According to John, Jesus is not a mere human being but the divine and eternal Word of God, God's "only begotten son," who descends to earth in human form to rescue the human race from eternal damnation:

> God so loved the world that He gave his only begotten Son, that whosoever believes in him should not perish, but have eternal life. . . . Whoever believes in him is not condemned, but whoever does not believe in him is condemned already because he has not believed in the name of the only begotten Son of God (3:16–18).

But, as we have seen, *Thomas* offers a very different message. Far from regarding himself as the only begotten son of God, Jesus says to his disciples, "When you come to know yourselves" (and discover the divine within you), then "you will recognize that it is *you* who are the sons of the living Father"—just like Jesus. The *Gospel of Philip* makes the same point more succinctly: one is to "become not a Christian, but a Christ." This, I believe, is the symbolic meaning of attributing the *Gospel of Thomas* to Jesus' "twin brother." In effect, "You, the reader, are the twin brother of Christ" when you recognize the divine within you. Then you will see, as Thomas does, that you and Jesus are, so to speak, identical twins.

One who seeks to "become not a Christian, but a Christ" no longer looks only to Jesus—and later to his church and its leaders—as most believers do, as the source of all truth. So, while the Jesus of the gospel of John declares, "I am the door; whoever enters through me shall be saved," the *Teaching of Silvanus* points in a different direction:

> Knock upon yourself as upon a door, and walk upon yourself as on a straight road. For if you walk upon that road, it is impossible for you to go astray. . . . Open the door for yourself, that you may know what is. . . . Whatever you open for yourself, you will open (NHC VII.106.30–35; 117.5–20).

Why did the majority of early Christian churches reject such writings as *Thomas* and accept other, possibly later accounts—for example, Matthew, Luke, and John? *Thomas* appeals to people engaged in spiritual transformation, but it does not answer the practical questions of many potential converts who lived in or near Jewish communities scattered throughout the cities of Palestine and the imperial provinces. Potential converts asked questions like these: Do you want us to fast? How shall we pray? Shall we give alms? What diet should we observe? In short, are believers to follow traditional Jewish practices, or not? According to the *Gospel of Thomas,* when the disciples ask "the living Jesus" these very questions, he refuses to give them specific directions, answering only,

> "Do not tell lies, and do not do what you hate: for all things are manifest in the sight of heaven" (NHC II.33.18–21).

This enigmatic answer leaves each person to his or her own conscience; for who else knows when one is lying, and who else knows what one hates? Profound as such an answer may be, it offers no programmatic guidelines for group instruction, much less for the formation of a religious institution. The gospels included in the New Testament, by contrast, do offer such guidelines. According to Matthew and Luke, for example, Jesus answers each one of these questions authoritatively and specifically:

> "When you pray, say, 'Our Father, who art in heaven . . .'
> When you fast, wash your face. . . . When you give alms, do so
> in secret" (6:2–12).

As for the kosher laws, Mark says that Jesus "proclaimed all foods clean."

Furthermore, while *Thomas* says that finding the kingdom of God requires undergoing a solitary process of self-discovery, the gospels of the New Testament offer a far simpler message: one attains to God not by spiritual self-knowledge, but by believing in Jesus the Messiah. Now that God has sent salvation through Christ, repent; accept baptism and forgiveness of sins; join God's people and receive salvation.

Finally, while *Thomas* blesses "the solitary and the chosen" (*Thomas* 34:29) and addresses the solitary seeker, or at most a select inner circle, Mark and his successors combine many elements of earlier Jesus tradition—miracle stories, teachings, and controversy stories, along with an account of Jesus' passion—to show Jesus and his disciples in a social context, contending at various times with Jewish leaders, with crowds, both friendly and hostile, and with ruling authorities, Jewish and Roman. In the process, Mark and his successors offer social models by which Jesus' followers identify themselves as a group—often a deficient and threatened group, as they describe it, but one that claims to be God's own people, continuing Jesus' work of healing, casting out demons, and proclaiming the coming of God's kingdom.

The author of Mark, then, offers a rudimentary model for Christian community life. The gospels that the majority of Christians adopted in common all follow, to some extent, Mark's example. Successive generations found in the New Testament gospels what they did not find in many other elements of early Jesus tradition—a practical design for Christian communities.

The writer whom tradition calls Matthew updates Mark to address the circumstances he confronts in the immediate postwar decades. Many scholars think that Matthew lived outside of Palestine, perhaps in Antioch, the capital of Syria; he wrote as if he had been part of that thriving Jewish community, which, like all Jewish communities, had experienced intense upheaval following the war.[16]

In Jerusalem the Temple lay in ruins, and Vespasian had stationed a permanent Roman garrison there. Roman troops and civilians had built a settlement that included pagan shrines along with Roman baths, shops, and other amenities of Roman life. Vespasian also penalized Jews throughout the empire for the war by appropriating for the Roman treasury the tax that Jews had previously paid to support their own Temple. With the Temple's destruction the high priest, formerly the chief spokesman for the Jewish people, lost his position, along with all his priestly allies. The Sanhedrin, formerly the supreme Jewish council, also lost its power.

The war permanently changed the nature of Jewish leadership in Jerusalem and in Jewish communities everywhere. Yet even during the war, some Jews and Romans had already begun preparing alternative leadership to replace the priests and the Sanhedrin after the war. When the Romans besieged the Temple in March, 68 C.E., the Jewish teacher Johanan ben Zakkai fled Jerusalem and took refuge in a Roman camp. There, anticipating the Roman victory, he asked Vespasian for permission to found an academy for Jewish teachers in Jamnia, a town the Romans had already recovered. Vespasian and his advisers, apparently expecting that Jews would resume internal self-government after the war, granted permission to Johanan to establish this school as a legitimate Jewish authority. According to the historian Mary Smallwood,

> Rabbi Johanan's escape, technically an act of treachery, was the Jews' spiritual salvation when the rabbinic school which he founded took the place of the Sanhedrin . . . and its president,

the Nasi, or patriarch, replaced the high priest as the Jews' leader and spokesman, both religious and political.[17]

The high-priestly dynasty and its aristocratic allies in the San-hedrin, along with the Sadducean scribes associated with the former Temple, were now swept aside. A growing group of teachers, mostly Pharisees, many of them self-supporting tradesmen (like Paul, a tentmaker, who had been a Pharisee), now took over leadership roles, expanding their authority throughout Judea, and eventually in Jewish communities throughout the world. Thus began the rabbinic movement, which would become increasingly dominant in Jewish commu-nity life.[18]

Matthew, proclaiming the message of Jesus the Messiah c. 80 C.E., found himself in competition primarily with these Pharisaic teachers and rabbis, who were successfully establishing themselves throughout the Jewish world as authoritative inter-preters of the Torah. The Pharisees wanted to place the Torah at the center of Jewish life as a replacement for the ruined Temple. Their aim was to teach a practical interpretation of Jewish law that would preserve Jewish groups throughout the world as a separate and holy people. Matthew saw the Pharisees as the chief rivals to his own teachings about Jesus[19] and decided to present Jesus and his message in terms comprehensible to the Pharisees and their large following—not only as God's Messiah, but also as the one whose teaching embodies and fulfills the true righteous-ness previously taught in "the law and the prophets."

As we shall see, Matthew insists that Jesus offers a universaliz-ing interpretation of Torah ("Love God and your neighbor"; "Do unto others what you would have them do unto you") without giving up "a jot or a tittle" of divine law. But because Matthew's Jesus interprets the Torah so that Gentiles can fulfill it as well as Jews, Matthew in effect encourages people to abandon traditional ethnic identification with Israel. This was a radical position that most Jews found—and declared—anathema. In Matthew, Jesus repeatedly attacks the Pharisees as "hypocrites" obsessed with petty regulations while ignoring "justice and mercy and faith"—attacks that caricature the rabbis' concern to preserve Israel's integrity through observant behavior. Thus Matthew takes part in a bitter controversy central to Jewish—and what will become Christian—identity.[20]

In writing his gospel, Matthew was concerned to refute damaging rumors about Jesus—for example, that his birth was illegitimate, which would disgrace and disqualify him as a suitable candidate for Israel's Messiah. Furthermore, Jesus was known to have come from Nazareth in Galilee, and from a common family—not from the royal, Davidic dynasty established in Bethlehem, as would befit a king of Israel. Even more serious, perhaps, was the charge that Jesus, according to Mark, neglected or even violated observance of Sabbath and kosher laws.

Matthew, like his predecessors in the Christian movement, was troubled by such criticisms. But as he searched through the Scriptures, he was repeatedly struck by biblical passages, especially among the prophets' writings and among the psalms, that he believed illuminated the events surrounding Jesus' life. For example, in opposition to the rumor that Jesus was born illegitimate, Matthew and his predecessors found vindication for their faith in Jesus in Isaiah 7:14. There the Lord promises to give Israel a "sign" of the coming of God's salvation. Apparently Matthew knew the Hebrew Bible in its Greek translation, where he would have read the following:

> "The Lord himself shall give you a sign: Behold, a virgin shall conceive and bear a son; and shall call his name Immanuel— God with us" (Isaiah 7:14).

In the original Hebrew, the passage had read "young woman" (*almah*), apparently describing an ordinary birth. But the translation of *almah* into the Greek *parthenos* ("virgin"), as many of Jesus' followers read the passage, confirmed their conviction that Jesus' birth, which unbelievers derided as sordid, actually was a miraculous "sign."[21] Thus Matthew revises Mark's story by saying that the spirit descended upon Jesus not at his baptism but at the moment of his conception. So, Matthew says, Jesus' mother "was discovered to have a child in her womb through the holy spirit" (1:18); and God's angel explains to Joseph that the child "was conceived through the holy spirit." Jesus' birth was no scandal, Matthew says, but a miracle—one that precisely fulfills Isaiah's ancient prophecy.

To prove that Jesus, despite his humble birth, possessed messianic credentials, Matthew works out a royal genealogy for Jesus, tracing his ancestry back to Abraham by way of King David (Luke does the same, apparently working independently, since Luke's genealogy differs from Matthew's; compare Matthew 1:1–17 with Luke 3:23–38).

Matthew tells an elaborate story to explain why Jesus, the descendant of kings, was thought to belong to an obscure family in the town of Nazareth in Galilee, and not to a royal dynasty based in Bethlehem. Matthew insists that Jesus' miraculous birth shook Jerusalem's ruling powers, both secular and religious. When King Herod, whom the Romans supported as a client king of the Jews, heard that a new star had appeared, which portends a royal birth, Matthew says, "he was troubled, and all Jerusalem with him" (2:3). Frustrated in his first attempt to find and destroy Jesus, Herod "was in a furious rage, and he sent and killed all the male children in Bethlehem, and in all that region who were two years old and under" (2:16). Jesus' father, warned by an angel, took the child and his mother and fled into Egypt. After Herod's death they returned, Matthew says, but Jesus' father, knowing that Herod's son still ruled Judea, chose to protect Jesus by taking his family to live incognito in the village of Nazareth. Thus Matthew explains how Jesus came to be associated with this obscure Galilean town, instead of with Bethlehem, which was his actual birthplace, according to Matthew.

Since no historical record mentions a mass slaughter of infants among Herod's crimes, many New Testament scholars regard the story of the "slaughter of the innocents," like the "flight into Egypt," as reflecting Matthew's programmatic conviction that Jesus' life must recapitulate the whole history of Israel. According to these scholars, Matthew is less concerned to give biographical information than to show a connection between Jesus,

Moses, and Israel's exodus from Egypt. Like Moses, who, as a newborn, escaped the furious wrath of the Egyptian Pharaoh, who had ordered a mass slaughter of Hebrew male infants, so Jesus, Matthew says, escaped the wrath of King Herod. And as God once delivered Israel from Egypt, so now, Matthew claims, he has delivered Jesus. Matthew does here what he does throughout his gospel; he takes words from the prophetic writings (here words from the prophet Hosea), generally understood to apply to the nation of Israel ("Out of Egypt I have called my son"), and applies them to Jesus of Nazareth, whom he sees as the culmination of Israel's history.[22]

Many scholars have noted these parallels between Jesus, Moses, and Israel. But no one, so far as I know, has observed that Matthew *reverses* the traditional roles, casting the Jewish king, Herod, in the villain's role traditionally reserved for Pharaoh. Through this device he turns the alien enemies of Israel's antiquity into the intimate enemies, as Matthew perceives them. Matthew includes among Jesus' enemies the chief priests and scribes as well as all the other inhabitants of Jerusalem, for Matthew says that not only was Herod "troubled" to hear of Jesus' birth, but so was "all Jerusalem with him" (2:3). Matthew intends, no doubt, to contrast Herod, Idumean by background, and so from a suspect dynasty, with Jesus, whose legitimately Davidic (and so royal) lineage Matthew proclaims. Now it is Herod, not Pharaoh, who ruthlessly orders the mass slaughter of Jewish male infants. According to Matthew, no sooner was Jesus born than the "chief priests and the scribes of the people" assembled, apparently united behind Herod's attempt to "search for the child and kill him" (2:13). Matthew's account of Jesus' birth is no Christmas-card idyll, but foreshadows the terrible events of the crucifixion.

While assigning to Herod Pharaoh's traditional role, Matthew simultaneously reverses Israel's symbolic geography. Egypt, traditionally the land of slavery, now becomes a sanctuary for Jesus and his family—a place of refuge and deliverance from the slaughter ordered by the *Jewish* king. This reversal of imagery is nearly as shocking as that in the book of Revelation, which refers to Jerusalem as the place "allegorically called Sodom and Egypt, where our Lord was crucified" (11:8). Later Matthew will have Jesus favorably compare Tyre and Sidon, and even Sodom, with the local towns of Bethsaida, Chorazin, and Capernaum (11:20–24).

Throughout his gospel, Matthew sustains this reversal of alien and intimate enemies. Directly following his Sermon on the Mount, Jesus heals a leper outcast from Israel, and then performs a healing for a Roman centurion who recognizes Jesus' divine power and appeals to him to use it on his behalf. Astonished to hear a Roman officer express faith "greater than any" he has found in Israel, Jesus immediately declares, "I tell you, many shall come from east and west and sit down with Abraham and Isaac and Jacob in the Kingdom of God, while the sons of the kingdom shall be cast out into outer darkness; there people will weep and gnash their teeth" (8:11–12).

From the beginning of his gospel to its end, Matthew indicts Israel's present leaders while he campaigns in favor of Jesus—Israel's Messiah—and those the new King himself appoints. Not only was Herod an Idumean, his family lived in a notoriously Gentile way, despite their religious professions. John the Baptist had been beheaded for proclaiming openly that Herod had married his former sister-in-law and so lived in open violation of Jewish law. Matthew wants to show not only that Jesus was Israel's legitimate king, rather than such unworthy usurpers as Herod, but also that he was God's designated teacher of righteousness, destined, so Matthew claims, to replace the Pharisees, who held that role in the eyes of many of his contemporaries. Matthew, who, along with his fellow Christians, opposes the rival party of Pharisees, casts his gospel primarily as a polemic between Jesus and the Pharisees, in which the two antagonistic parties are not equally matched. The Pharisees are widely respected and honored, accepted by the people as religious authorities; Jesus' followers are a suspect minority, maligned and persecuted.

In Mark, Jesus contests wordlessly against Satan in the wilderness. But Matthew borrows sayings from the Q source and shows Satan appearing three times to "test" Jesus, as Pharisees and other opponents will test him. Here the Q source turns Satan into a caricature of a scribe, a debater skilled in verbal challenge and adept in quoting the Scriptures for diabolic purposes, who repeatedly questions Jesus' divine authority ("If you are the son of God . . ."). Having twice failed to induce Jesus to perform a miracle to prove his divine power and authority, Satan finally offers him "all the kingdoms of this world and their glory," which Satan claims as his own. Thus Matthew, following Mark's lead, implies that political success and power (such as the Pharisees enjoy under Roman patronage) may evince a pact with the devil—and not, as many of Matthew's contemporaries would have assumed, marks of divine favor.

Matthew next assails the Pharisees on the question that concerns them most, the interpretation of Torah. To correct the impression that Jesus simply ignored traditional Jewish concern with righteous obedience to Torah—an impression any reader could get from Mark—Matthew makes Jesus embody all that is best and truest in Jewish tradition. Mark begins his gospel with descriptions of healings and exorcisms, but Matthew begins by showing Jesus proclaiming a new interpretation of divine law. Like Moses, who ascended Mount Sinai to receive and promulgate God's law, Jesus goes up on a mountain, where he proclaims what we know as the Sermon on the Mount. Taking aim at the Pharisees and those impressed by their interpretation of Torah, Matthew insists that Jesus does not reject the Torah. Instead, Matthew says, Jesus proclaims its essential meaning:

"Do not think that I came to abolish the law and the prophets;
I came not to abolish but to fulfill them" (5:17).

Jesus then warns that "unless your righteousness exceeds that of the scribes and the Pharisees, you will never enter the Kingdom of heaven" (5:20). Thus Matthew defends Jesus against charges of laxity in Sabbath and kosher observance by insisting that he practices a *greater* righteousness, not a lesser one. According to Matthew 5 and 6, Jesus demands an enormous *increase* in religious scrupulosity: the traditional Torah is not half strict enough for him! Where Moses' law prohibits murder, Jesus' "new Torah" prohibits anger, insults, and name calling; where Moses' law prohibits adultery, Jesus' prohibits lust. Much of the Mosaic law was couched in negative terms ("You shall not . . ."). Jesus reinterprets it positively:

> "Whatever you would have people do to you, do the same to them; for this is the law and the prophets" (7:12).

Simultaneously Matthew insists that Jesus' critics, "the scribes and the Pharisees," use mere hypocritical "observance" as a cover for violating what Jesus here proclaims to be the Torah's central commands of love for God and neighbor (6:1–18).

As we have seen, Matthew diverges from Mark in making the Pharisees Jesus' primary antagonists.[23] For Mark it was the Jerusalem scribes who were angered by Jesus' powerful effect on the crowd and charged him with demon possession; but Matthew changes the story to say that the Pharisees accused Jesus of "casting out demons by the prince of demons" (12:24). While Mark says that the Pharisees and the Herodians first plotted to kill Jesus, Matthew says that only the Pharisees "went and took counsel, how to destroy him" (12:14). Matthew even has the Pharisees repeat the charge that Jesus is "possessed by Beelzebub" (12:24); Jesus adamantly denies the charge and warns: "If it is by the spirit of God that I cast out demons, then the kingdom of God has come upon you" (12:28). Matthew's Jesus declares that this supernatural conflict has now split God's people into two separate—and opposing—communities: "Whoever is not with me is against me, and whoever does not gather with me scatters" (12:30).

Distressed that the people of Israel are "harassed and helpless, like sheep without a shepherd," lacking true leadership, Jesus now designates the twelve, and gives them "authority over unclean spirits, to cast them out" (10:1). Warning them that the people "will deliver you up to sanhedrins, and beat you in their synagogues" (10:17), Jesus tells them to anticipate murderous hatred within their own households (10:21), as well as from "everyone" (10:22); for, as he says, "if they have called the master of the house Beelzebub, how much more will they malign those members of his household?" (10:25). As the narrative proceeds, the antagonism between Jesus and his enemies becomes—as in the literature of the Essene sectarians—a contest between those whom Matthew's Jesus calls "sons of the kingdom" and the "sons of the evil one" (13:38). Jesus repeats John the Baptist's denunciation of the Pharisees: "You brood of vipers! How can you say good things, when you are evil?" (12:34). Then Jesus predicts that foreigners shall "arise at the judgment of this generation and condemn it" (12:41). Finally, he implicitly accuses those who oppose him of being possessed by demons, telling the parable of a man who, having been exorcised, experiences a new invasion of "seven other spirits more evil" than the first, "so that the last state of that man becomes worse than the first. So shall it be also with this evil generation" (12:45).

Later, Jesus explains privately to his followers that the generation he addresses—except for the elect—*already* has been judged and condemned; his opponents' refusal to receive his preaching, he says, reveals Satan's power over them. In the parable of the sower, Jesus identifies the "evil one" as the enemy who has "snatched away" the seeds he has planted and so prevented his preaching from bearing fruit among his own people (13:19). Immediately thereafter Jesus tells the parable of the weeds, explicitly identifying his opponents as the offspring of Satan: "the weeds are the sons of the evil one, and the enemy who sowed them is the devil" (13:38–39).

Jesus, finally recognized by his disciples as Messiah, tells them that now, by the authority of God's spirit, he is establishing his *own* assembly, which shall triumph over all the forces of evil, as if to say that God has replaced Israel with a new community. Many scholars agree with George Nickelsburg that Matthew's Jesus claims in chapter 16 that what previously was the "congregation of Israel" has become "his church."[24]

Jesus' conflict with the Pharisees reaches a climax in Matthew 23. Throughout this chapter, Matthew takes sayings attributed to Jesus and turns them into stories of conflict that pit Jesus against those he denounces seven times as "scribes and Pharisees, hypocrites," and even "children of hell" (23:15). Matthew has Jesus call down divine wrath upon "this generation" (23:36),

> "that upon you may come all the righteous blood shed on earth, from the blood of the innocent Abel to that of Zechariah, son of Barachiah, whom you murdered between the sanctuary and the altar" (23:35).

Many scholars have noted and commented on the bitter hostility expressed in this chapter.[25] Biblical scholar Luke Johnson shows that philosophic groups in antiquity often attacked their rivals in strong terms.[26] But philosophers did not engage, as Matthew does here, in *demonic* vilification of their opponents. Within the ancient world, so far as I know, it is only Essenes and Christians who actually escalate conflict with their opponents to the level of cosmic war.

Matthew's Jesus acknowledges that the Pharisees say much that is valid ("Practice and observe whatever they tell you, but do not do what they do"), but he charges that they are more concerned with maintaining their authority than anything else. Moreover, he says, they neglect essential moral concerns, preoccupying themselves with legal haggling:

> "Woe to you, scribes and Pharisees, hypocrites! for you tithe mint and dill and cummin, and have neglected the weightier matters of the law, justice and mercy and faith; these you ought to have done, without neglecting the others. You blind guides, straining out a gnat, and swallowing a camel!" (23:23–24)

Scholars know that many Jewish teachers at the time of Jesus—teachers like Hillel and Shammai, Jesus' contemporaries—engaged in moral interpretation of the law. One famous story tells how Hillel answered a student who asked him to teach the whole of the Torah while standing on one foot. Hillel replied, "Whatever you do not want others to do to you, do not do to them. That is the whole of the Torah." Yet even a liberal like Hillel would have opposed a movement that claimed to reinterpret the Torah morally but put aside the ritual precepts that define Jewish identity. Many Jews of the first century saw such tendencies in the Christian movement. Many Pharisees, concerned to keep Israel holy and separate through Torah observance, may well have regarded Jesus' followers as threatening Israel's integrity—even its existence.

Matthew wants to say, as we have seen, that Jesus never deviated from total loyalty to the Torah, but Matthew means by this that Jesus fulfilled the deeper meaning of the law, which, Matthew insists, has nothing essential to do with ethnic identity. In Matthew, Jesus twice summarizes "the law and the prophets," both times in ways that depend solely on moral action. First, what Hillel stated negatively, Jesus states positively: "Whatever you want people to do to you, do the same to them; on this depends the whole of the law and the prophets" (7:12). Second, he summarizes the Torah in the dual command, "Love the Lord your God with all your heart, soul, and mind, and your neighbor as yourself" (22:37). Finally Matthew's Jesus offers a parable depicting the coming of God's judgment. On that day, Jesus says, the divine king will gather *all the nations,* inviting some to enter into God's eternal kingdom, and consigning others to what Jesus calls "the eternal fire prepared for the devil and his angels." What is the criterion of divine judgment? According to Matthew, Jesus says that the king will say to those on his right hand,

> " 'Come, O blessed of my Father, inherit the kingdom prepared for you from the foundation of the world. For I was hungry and you gave me food; I was thirsty and you gave me drink; I was a stranger and you welcomed me; I was sick and you visited me; I was in prison and you came to me.' Then the righteous will answer him, 'Lord, when did we see thee a stranger and welcome thee or naked and clothe thee? And when did we see thee sick or in prison and visit thee?' And the king will answer them, 'Truly, I say to you, as you did it to one of the least of my brethren, you did it to me.' Then he will say to those at his left hand, 'Depart from me, you cursed ones, into

the eternal fire prepared for the devil and his angels; for I was hungry and you gave me no food, I was thirsty and you gave me no drink, I was a stranger and you did not welcome me, naked and you did not clothe me, sick and in prison and you did not visit me.' Then they also will answer, 'Lord, when did we see thee hungry or thirsty or a stranger or sick or in prison, and did not minister to thee?' Then he will answer them, 'Truly I say to you, as you did it not to one of the least of these, you did it not to me.' And they will go away into eternal punishment, but the righteous into eternal life" (25:34–46).

Inclusion in God's kingdom depends, then, not on membership in Israel but on justice combined with generosity and compassion. Ethnicity as a criterion has vanished. Gentiles as well as Jews could embrace this reinterpretation of divine law—and in Matthew's community many did.

According to Matthew, Jesus and the movement he began articulate the true meaning of God's law. Jesus denounces the Pharisees not only as false interpreters but deadly opponents to truth—those who "kill and crucify" God's prophets (23:34). From this final denunciation of the Pharisees, Matthew turns immediately to the story of Jesus' crucifixion. Closely following Mark's account, Matthew describes the involvement of the chief priest, scribes, and elders, but does not mention the Pharisees again until after Jesus' death.

But Matthew does add episodes that highlight the greater guilt of Jesus' Jewish enemies. Only Matthew says that even Judas Iscariot bitterly regretted betraying Jesus, "and throwing down the pieces of silver in the Temple, he departed, and went and hanged himself" (27:3–5). Matthew adds, too, the story of Pilate's wife:

> While Pilate was sitting on the judgment seat, his wife sent word to him, "Have nothing to do with that righteous man, for I have suffered much over him today in a dream" (27:19).

As in Mark, here Pilate offers to release Jesus, and protests to the crowds shouting for Jesus' crucifixion, "Why, what evil has he done?" But Matthew also supplies a pragmatic reason for Pilate's acquiescence to the crowd: Pilate "saw that he was gaining nothing, but rather that a riot was starting" (27:24). At that point, Matthew claims, in a most unlikely scene, Pilate performed a ritual that derives from Jewish law, described in the book of Deuteronomy. He washed his hands to indicate his innocence of bloodshed, and said, "I am innocent of this man's blood; see to it yourselves" (27:24). At that moment, according to Matthew alone, the Jewish leaders as well as "the whole nation" acknowledged collective responsibility and invoked what turned out to be a curse upon themselves and their progeny: "His blood be upon us and upon our children!" (27:25).

Matthew also adds the story that following the crucifixion, "the chief priests and Pharisees" solicited Pilate to secure Jesus' tomb with a guard, lest his followers steal his body to fake a resurrection. To account for the common rumor that Jesus' disciples had stolen his body, Matthew says that the Jewish authorities bribed the Roman soldiers to start this rumor. "So," Matthew concludes, "they took the money and did as they were told; and this story has been spread among the Jews to this day" (28:15).

As the gospel moves toward its conclusion, Matthew dissociates Jesus' followers from those he calls "the Jews," and tries to account for the hostility and disbelief that he and his fellow Christians apparently encounter from the Jewish majority. Matthew takes this to mean that the majority, who reject the gospel, have forfeited their legacy. The former insiders have now become outsiders. According to Matthew, Jesus tells an ominous parable: A great king invited his people to attend his son's wedding. (Here Matthew evokes a prophetic metaphor to imply that the wedding symbolizes the intended union between the Lord himself and Israel, his bride; see Jeremiah 2:1–3:20; Isaiah 50:1; Hosea 1:2–3:5.) But when those who are invited refuse to attend, and even beat, abuse, and kill the king's messengers, Jesus says, the king declares that "the invited guests were not worthy," and proceeds to invite others in their place. Then, Matthew's Jesus continues, "the king was angry, and sent his troops and destroyed those murderers, and burned their city"

(22:7). Thus Matthew goes so far as to suggest that God himself brought on the Roman massacre and destruction of Jerusalem in 70 C.E. to punish the Jews for rejecting "his son."

Most scholars agree that although Matthew's own group probably included both Jewish and Gentile believers, its members were finding more receptive audiences among Gentiles than among Jews. Thus Matthew ends with a scene in which the resurrected Jesus, having received "all authority on heaven and on earth," orders his followers to "go and make disciples of all nations" (28:19). Matthew, himself rooted in the Jewish community, looks at it with enormous ambivalence—ambivalence that will influence Christian communities for centuries, even millennia. Matthew's contemporary and fellow Christian Luke, who also adapts Mark and revises it, takes a different line. This Gentile convert relegates Israel's greatness to the past, and confidently claims its present legacy for his own—predominantly Gentile—community. In both Luke and John, as we see next, Jesus himself identifies his Jewish opponents with Satan.

LUKE AND JOHN CLAIM
ISRAEL'S LEGACY:
THE SPLIT WIDENS

Luke, the only Gentile author among the gospel writers, speaks for those Gentile converts to Christianity who consider themselves the true heirs of Israel. Luke goes beyond Matthew in radically revising Mark's account of Jesus' life. Matthew had said that the Jewish majority had lost their claim on God's covenant by refusing to acknowledge his Messiah; consequently, God had offered his covenant to the Gentiles in their place. Luke goes further, however, and agrees with Paul that God had always intended to offer salvation to everyone. Luke's vision of universal salvation invited Greeks, Asians, Africans, Syrians, and Egyptians to identify themselves, as confidently as any Essene, as members of the "true Israel." Christians everywhere still rely on Luke's message every day in their prayers, hymns, and liturgies. Luke also goes further than Mark and Matthew in making explicit what Mark and Matthew imply—the connection between Jesus' Jewish enemies and the "evil one," the devil. In Luke, Jesus himself, at the moment of his arrest, suggests that the arresting party of "chief priests and scribes and elders" is allied with the evil one, whom Jesus here calls "the power of darkness."

Luke, like Matthew, refutes common allegations against Jesus—that he was illegitimate and lacked the dynastic credentials to be Israel's Messiah. Like Matthew, Luke begins his story before Jesus' conception, to show that God's spirit enacted this miraculous event. According to Luke, it was the spirit, or its agents, the angels, who initiated the marvelous events surrounding Jesus' birth and infancy.

But Luke, unlike Matthew, reports no animosity on the part of Herod or the people of Jerusalem toward the infant Jesus. As in Mark, however, the moment Jesus appears as a grown man, baptized and "full of the holy spirit," the devil immediately challenges him. The devil is thrice defeated, and Luke says that "the devil departed from him *until an opportune time [achri kairou]*" (emphasis added). Frustrated in his initial attempt to overpower Jesus, the devil finds his opportunity only at the end of the story, when the chief priests and scribes "sought to kill Jesus." At that point, Luke says, "Satan entered into Judas Iscariot," who "went and conferred with the chief priest how he might betray him; and they were glad, and agreed to give him money." From that time, Luke says, Judas "sought an opportunity [*eukairan*] to betray him."

After his first engagement with Jesus, Satan did not withdraw from the contest but bided his time; throughout Jesus' public career the devil worked underground—or, more accurately, *on* the ground—through human agents. Immediately after his solitary contest with Satan in the desert, Jesus' first episode of public teaching begins with a favorable reception from the crowd but suddenly turns into a scene of brutal, nearly lethal, violence. Luke says that Jesus, after his baptism, enters the synagogue as usual in his hometown of Nazareth and reads for the congregation a prophetic passage from Isaiah. Then he announces, " 'Today this Scripture has been fulfilled in your hearing.' And they all spoke well of him, and marveled at the gracious words that came from his mouth" (4:21–22). Jesus now predicts that his townspeople will reject him, and declares that God intends to bring salvation to the Gentiles, even at the cost of bypassing Israel, saying:

> "There were many widows in Israel in the days of Elijah . . . and Elijah was sent to none of them, but only to Zarephath, in the land of Sidon, to a woman who was a widow. There were many lepers in Israel in the time of the prophet Elisha and none of them was cleansed, but only Naaman the Syrian" (4:25–27).

Hearing this, Luke continues,

> all those in the synagogue were filled with rage, and they rose
> up to throw him out of the city, and led him to the edge of the
> hill on which the city was built, in order to throw him down
> headlong (4:28–29).

But Jesus quickly departs, and so escapes this first attempt on his life.

Now the "the scribes and the Pharisees" begin to plot against Jesus, eyeing him suspiciously, looking for an opportunity "to make an accusation against him" (6:7). When they see him heal on the Sabbath, they "were filled with fury and discussed with one another what they might do to Jesus" (6:11).

But Luke's Pharisees, unlike Matthew's, are not unanimously hostile to Jesus.[1] Some express interest in him and invite him to dinner, some even warn him of danger, but others willingly play Satan's role, plotting to kill him. Luke sometimes calls the Pharisees "lovers of money" (16:14) and self-righteous (18:9–14), qualities he castigates in others as well; and he shows the special empathy between Jesus and those who are despised—the destitute, the sick, women, and Samaritans. Jesus' followers include many tax collectors and prostitutes; Luke believes that these too are God's people. From the opening scenes in the Temple involving Jesus' infancy and adolescence to the gospel's close, which describes how the disciples "went to Jerusalem, and were continually in the Temple praising God," the followers of Jesus are deeply loyal to the Temple—perhaps the only genuine Israelites left in Jerusalem. Luke certainly intends to show that they are closer to God than the Pharisees or any other Jewish religious leaders.

Spiritual warfare between God and Satan—which is reflected in conflict between Jesus and his followers and the Jewish leaders—intensifies throughout the gospel.[2] As people divide against him, Jesus says,

> "Do not think that I have come to bring peace on earth, no,
> rather division; from now on in one house there shall be five

divided, three against two and two against three; they will be divided, father against son and son against father, mother against daughter and daughter against her mother" (12:51–55).

As the chief priests and their allies harden their opposition, certain Pharisees warn Jesus, in an episode unique to Luke, about the Jewish king: "Herod wants to kill you." Jesus' reply suggests that what angers Herod is that Jesus has challenged Satan, the power that rules this world: "Go and tell that fox, 'Today and tomorrow I cast out demons and heal, and the third day I finish my course' " (13:32). After Jesus sends out seventy apostles to heal and proclaim the message of the kingdom, they return "with joy," astonished and triumphant, saying, "Lord, even the demons are subject to us in your name." Jesus exults, foreseeing Satan's impending defeat:

> "I saw Satan fall like lightning from heaven: Behold, I have given you power to tread on snakes and scorpions, and upon every power of the enemy" (10:18–19).

Immediately before Satan enters into Judas and initiates the betrayal, Jesus warns, in parable, that he himself will return as king to see his enemies annihilated. As soon as he begins his final journey to Jerusalem, where he will enter the city publicly acclaimed as king by his disciples but will be rejected by the majority of Jerusalemites, Jesus tells the story of "a certain nobleman" who travels to a distant land "in order to claim his kingly power and return" (19:12). When the nobleman succeeds and returns in triumph, his first act is to demand that his enemies be killed: "*As for those enemies of mine, who did not want me to rule over them, bring them here and slaughter them before me*" (19:27; emphasis added). Luke makes the parallel unmistakable: "While saying these words, Jesus traveled before [the disciples], going up to Jerusalem." When he arrives, he immediately orders his disciples to prepare for his royal entry into the city (cf. Zech. 9:9). But Luke alone, among the synoptic gospels, i͏͏ ͏e words "the king," taken from Psalm 118, into the ͏n the disciples shouted at Jesus' arrival in Jerusalem:

"Blessed is the one, the king, who comes in the name of the Lord!" (Ps. 118:26; Luke 19:38). When some Pharisees in the crowd, apparently shocked by this open proclamation of Jesus as king, admonished Jesus, "Rabbi, rebuke your disciples," Luke says, he answered, "I tell you, if these were silent, the very stones would cry out."

Then, Luke says, as that fateful Passover drew near, "the chief priests and the scribes were seeking how to put him to death." This was the opportunity for which Satan had been waiting: "Then Satan entered into Judas Iscariot," who immediately conferred with the chief priests and the Temple officers, to arrange the betrayal. But here, as in Mark, Jesus himself declares that neither Satan's role nor God's preordained plan absolves Judas's guilt: "The Son of man goes as it has been determined; but woe to that man by whom he is betrayed" (22:22; cf. Mark 14:21).

John mentions armed Roman soldiers among the arresting party, but Luke mentions only Jews, and omits a saying common to Mark and Matthew, that "the Son of man is betrayed *into the hands of sinners*" (that is, Gentiles). Instead, when the armed party arrives in Gethsemane, Luke's Jesus turns directly to "the chief priests and temple officers and elders who had come out against him," and identifies them as Satan incarnate: "Have you come out as against a robber, with swords and clubs? When I was with you in the temple every day, you did not lay hands upon me. But this is *your* [plural] *hour,* and *the power of darkness*" (22:52–53; emphasis added).

Like Mark, Luke says that the arresting party "seized Jesus and led him away, bringing him to the high priest's house," while Peter followed surreptitiously into the high priest's courtyard. But at this point Luke diverges from Mark, omitting Mark's elaborate scene of a trial before the Sanhedrin in which, as we have seen, the whole Sanhedrin gathered at night to hear a parade of witnesses and to witness the high priest's interrogation of Jesus, which culminated in the unanimously pronounced death sentence for blasphemy. Mark—and Matthew following him—depicts members of the Sanhedrin spitting on Jesus, beating him, and mocking him before the guards join them in beating him (Mark 14:65; Matt. 26:67–68).

Luke tells a starker and simpler story: After his arrest, Jesus is held and guarded all night in the courtyard of the high priest's house to await a morning session of the Sanhedrin. Luke says it is not members of the aristocratic Sanhedrin but "the men holding Jesus" who entertained themselves during the long night by beating and mocking the prisoner (22:63–65). In the morning, the guards lead Jesus to the council chamber near the Temple for interrogation by the assembled Sanhedrin. Instead of a formal trial, this seems to be a kind of court hearing—an interrogation with no witnesses and no formal sentence. Nevertheless, the Sanhedrin decides to take Jesus to Pilate to present formal—and capital—charges against him.

Did Luke have access to independent—perhaps earlier—accounts of what led to the crucifixion? Many scholars, prominently including the British scholar David Catchpole, believe that he did.[3] Luke reconstructs a scene in which the Sanhedrin members interrogate Jesus:

> "If you are the Messiah, tell us." But he said to them, "If I tell you, you will not believe; and if I ask you, you will not answer. But from now on the Son of man will be seated at the right hand of the power of God." And they said to him, "Are you the Son of God, then?" And he said to them, "You say that I am" (22:67–70).

Luke's account, like Matthew's and John's, contradicts Mark's claim that Jesus resoundingly and publicly affirmed his divine appointment at his trial (Mark 14:62). In Luke, Jesus answers only evasively. Given the lack of supporting evidence, no one can say what actually happened, though hundreds of scholars, Jewish and Christian, have attempted an answer. One has only to glance at Catchpole's meticulous monograph *The Trial of Jesus* to see that every act in every episode has become the subject of intense debate.

Despite these uncertainties, everyone who interprets the texts has to sort out the tradition to some extent, and to reconstruct, however provisionally, what may have happened, and correspondingly, what each evangelist added, and for what reasons.

Catchpole himself argues that Luke's account of the Sanhedrin trial is more "historically reliable" than any other.[4] This would mean that the Sanhedrin members accused Jesus of claiming to be Messiah and Son of God. Raymond Brown disagrees, and sides with those who are convinced that the titles Messiah and Son of God emerged later, from Christian communities (in this case, from Luke's community) and not from the Jewish Sanhedrin. In any case, Luke's account suggests that Jesus had received public acclaim as king (19:38) and, as we noted, even when the Pharisees warned him to silence those who were shouting these acclamations, Jesus refused to do so (19:39–40). Whether he made these same claims for himself, as Mark alone insists (14:61), or merely accepted what others said of him, as Matthew, Luke, and John say, apparently mattered less to the Sanhedrin than the effect that such claims could have upon the restless crowds gathered for Passover. Consequently, Luke says, Jesus' enemies decided to bring him to Pilate, accusing him of three charges calculated to arouse the governor's concern: "We found this man guilty of perverting our nation [apparently, of teaching in opposition to the designated religious leaders], forbidding us to pay tribute to Caesar, and saying that he himself is Messiah, a king" (23:2).

Mark and Matthew said that Pilate was skeptical of the charges, but Luke's Pilate pronounces Jesus innocent no less than three times. At first Pilate says, "I find no crime in this man." Then, after the chief priests and the crowds object and insist that Jesus is guilty of disturbing the peace, Pilate tries to rid himself of responsibility by sending Jesus to King Herod. While Mark and Matthew show Pilate's soldiers mocking and beating Jesus, Luke further exonerates Pilate by showing that it was Herod and his officers (like the Jewish officers involved in the arrest) who abused and mocked Jesus as a would-be king (23:11).

Jesus is then returned to Pilate, who formally assembles "the chief priests and the rulers and the people." These three groups, which had previously divided between the leaders, who hated Jesus, and the people, whose presence had protected him, now present a united front against him. To all those assembled before him Pilate declares again:

> "You brought me this man as one who was misleading the people, and after examining him before you, behold, I did not find this man guilty of any of your charges against him; neither did Herod, for he sent him back to us. Behold, nothing deserving death has been done by him; I will therefore chastise him and release him."

But Luke says that the Jewish leaders and people, hearing Pilate's decision, unanimously protested: "They *all* cried out *together,* 'Away with this man' " (23:18; emphasis added). According to Luke, Pilate still refused to give in, and "addressed them once more, desiring to release Jesus, but they shouted out, 'Crucify him, crucify him!' " Luke apparently thinks he cannot emphasize this too much, for he now repeats Pilate's verdict a third time: "What evil has he done? I found in him no crime deserving death; therefore I will chastise him and release him." But the onlookers, Luke says,

> demanded with loud cries that Jesus should be crucified, and their voices prevailed; and Pilate ordered that their demand be granted, and . . . he gave Jesus over *to their will* (emphasis added).

In earlier passages, nevertheless, Luke had followed Mark in saying that Jesus' enemies delivered him "to the Gentiles" (18:32); later, Luke, like Mark, will mention a Roman centurion present at the crucifixion. These clues, along with Luke's acknowledgment that the written accusation was that Jesus had claimed to be "king of the Jews," and the charge was sedition (23:38), indicate that Luke knew that the Romans had actually pronounced sentence and carried out the execution. Yet as Luke tells the story, he allows, and perhaps even wants, the reader—especially one unfamiliar with other accounts—to infer that after Jews had arrested Jesus and a Jewish court had sentenced him to death, it was Jewish soldiers who actually crucified him.

Luke changes many details of the death scene to emphasize Jesus' innocence, and to give a more uplifting account than

Mark's of how God's faithful should die. When Jesus is crucified between two robbers (that is, as we have seen, between two *lēstai*, men perhaps also charged with sedition), he prays for his tormentors: "Father, forgive them; for they do not know what they are doing."[5] Mark had shown the extreme humiliation to which Jesus was subjected, saying that even the other condemned criminals joined in ridiculing Jesus, but Luke offers a different version of the story:

> One of the criminals who were hung there kept mocking him, and saying, "Aren't you the Messiah? Save yourself and us!" But the other rebuked him, saying, "Do you not fear God, since you are under the same sentence? And we are justly condemned, since we are getting what we deserve for what we did. But this man has done nothing wrong." Then he said, "Jesus, remember me when you come into your kingdom." He replied, "Truly, I tell you, today you shall be with me in Paradise."

Thus Luke again emphasizes Jesus' innocence—innocence recognized even by a condemned criminal—and shows that even the dying Jesus has power to forgive, to redeem, and to save the lost. Luke omits Jesus' anguished cry ("My God, my God, why have you forsaken me?" Psalm 22:1), along with Jesus' last, inarticulate scream, and replaces them instead with a prayer of faith taken from Psalm 31:5: "Then Jesus, crying with a loud voice, said, 'Father, into your hands I commit my spirit.' Having said this, he breathed his last." Thus Luke banishes the scene of agony and replaces it with trusting submission to God. Finally, Luke goes so far as to say that many of the bystanders, seeing all this, repented what they had done: "When all the crowds who had gathered there for the spectacle saw what had taken place, they returned home, beating their breasts" (23:48). He also changes Mark's account to say that the Roman centurion who saw Jesus die "praised God," and echoed Pilate's verdict: "Certainly this man was innocent!"

In the early chapters of the Acts of the Apostles Luke again emphasizes the role of the Jews rather than of the Romans in

Jesus' crucifixion. Peter specifically addresses the "men of Israel," charging that they "crucified and killed" the righteous one whom God had sent to Israel. Shortly after, Peter again addresses the "men of Israel," preaching of Jesus,

> "whom you delivered up and denied in the presence of Pilate, when Pilate had decided to release him . . . you denied the holy and righteous one, and you asked instead for a murderer to be granted to you."

Luke provides many details that have contributed to later Christians' perceptions that Pilate was a well-meaning weakling and that the Jewish people—that is, those he regarded as the apostate majority—were responsible for Jesus' death and for the deaths of many of his followers. The well-known French commentator Alfred Loisy says that according to Luke, "The Jews are the authors of all evil."[6] Loisy's comment oversimplifies, yet as we have seen, Luke wants to show that those who reject Jesus accomplish Satan's work on earth.

Writing independently of Luke and probably a decade later, the author of the gospel of John, who most scholars think was a Jewish convert to the movement, speaks with startlingly similar bitterness of the Jewish majority.[7] In one explosive scene, Jesus accuses the Jews of trying to kill him, saying, "You are of your father, the devil!" and "the Jews" retaliate by accusing Jesus of being a Samaritan—that is, not a real Jew—and himself "demon-possessed," or insane.

Most scholars agree that Jesus probably did not make these accusations, but that such strong words reflected bitter conflict between a group of Jesus' followers to which John belonged (c. 90–100 C.E.) and the Jewish majority in their city, especially the synagogue leaders. Writing from within a Jewish community, perhaps in Palestine, John is anguished that after a series of clashes with Jewish leaders, he and his fellow Christians have been forcibly expelled from the synagogues, and denied participation in common worship. We do not know for certain what happened; John says only, "The Jews had already agreed that anyone who confessed Jesus to be the Messiah would be put out of the synagogue"—literally, would become *aposynagoge,* expelled from one's home synagogue. New Testament scholar Louis Martyn has shown that whatever it meant in particular, this traumatic separation defined how John's group saw itself—as a tiny minority of God's people "hated by the world," a group that urged its members to reject in turn the whole social and religious world into which they had been born.[8]

Martyn suggests, too, that the crisis in John's community occurred when a group of Jewish scholars, led by the rabbi Gamalial II (80–115 C.E.), introduced into synagogue worship the so-called *birkat ha-minim* (literally, "benediction of the heretics"), a prayer that invoked a curse upon "heretics," including Christians, here specifically identified as "Nazarenes." This might have enabled synagogue leaders to ask anyone suspected of being a secret "Nazarene" to "stand before the ark" and lead the congregation in the benediction, so that anyone guilty of being a Christian would be calling a curse upon himself and his fellow believers. The historian Reuven Kimelman disagrees, and argues that this ritual curse entered synagogue services considerably later and so could not have precipitated a first-century crisis. The author of John speaks, however, as if synagogue leaders had taken measures more drastic than the *birkat ha-minim,* suggesting that they actually excluded Jesus' followers to prevent them from worshiping alongside other Jews.

Whatever the actual circumstances, John chooses to tell the story of Jesus as a story of cosmic conflict—conflict between divine light and primordial darkness, between the close-knit group of Jesus' followers and the implacable, sinful opposition they encountered from "the world." Ever since the first century, John's version of the gospel has consoled and inspired groups of believers who have found themselves an oppressed minority—but a minority that they believe embodies divine light in the world. Whereas Mark begins his narrative with Jesus' baptism, and Luke and Matthew go beyond Jesus' birth to his conception, John goes back to the very origin of the universe. John begins his gospel with the opening words of Genesis, which tell how "in the beginning" God separated light from darkness. Echoing the grand cosmology of Genesis 1, John's prologue identifies the *logos,* God's energy acting in creation, with life (*zoē*) and light (*phōs*), that is, the "light of human beings." Anticipating the message of his entire gospel, John declares that "the light shines in the darkness, and the darkness has not overcome it." According to John, "the light of humankind" finally came to shine in and through Jesus of Nazareth, who is revealed to be the Son of God.

Thus John takes the primordial elements separated in creation—light and darkness—and casts them in a human drama, interpreting them simultaneously in religious, ethical, and social terms. According to John, this divine "light" not only "became human, and dwelt among us," but also is the spiritual progenitor of those who "become the children of God" (1:12), the "sons of light" (12:35). The crisis of Jesus' appearance reveals others as the "sons of darkness"; thus Jesus explains to the Jewish ruler Nicodemus that

> "this is the judgment [literally, *crisis*]: that the light came into the world and people loved darkness rather than light, because their deeds were evil. . . . But whoever does the truth comes to the light." (3:19–21).

By the end of the gospel, Jesus' epiphany will have accomplished in human society what God accomplished cosmologically in creation: the separation of light from darkness—that is, of the "sons of light" from the offspring of darkness and the devil. Having first placed the story of Jesus within this grand cosmological frame, John then sets it entirely within the dynamics of the world of human interaction, so that "the story of Jesus in the gospel is all played out on earth."[9] The frame, nevertheless, informs the reader that both Jesus' coming and *all* his human relationships are elements played out in a supernatural drama between the forces of good and evil.

Casting the struggle between good and evil as that between light and darkness, John never pictures Satan, as the other gospels do, appearing as a disembodied being. At first glance, then, the image of Satan seems to have receded; the German scholar Gustave Hoennecke goes so far as to claim that "in John, the idea of the devil is completely absent."[10] More accurate, however, is Raymond Brown's observation that John, like the other gospels, tells the whole story of Jesus as a struggle with Satan that culminates in the crucifixion.[11] Although John never depicts Satan as a character on his own, acting independently of human beings, in John's gospel it is *people* who play the tempter's role.

All of the three "temptation scenes" in Luke and Matthew occur in John, but Satan does not appear directly. Instead, as Raymond Brown has shown, Satan's role is taken first by "the people," members of Jesus' audience, and finally by his own brothers.[12] For example, Matthew and Luke show Satan challenging Jesus to claim earthly power (Matt. 4:8–9; Luke 4:5–6); but according to John, this challenge occurs when "the people were about to come and take him by force to make him king" (6:15). Here, as in the other gospels, Jesus resists the temptation, eludes the crowd, and escapes. In another temptation, Matthew and Luke, following Q, relate that the devil challenged Jesus to prove his divine authority by making "these stones into bread." But John says that those who witnessed Jesus' miracles—and in particular his multiplication of five loaves into many—then challenged him to perform *another* miracle as further proof of his messianic identity. Like the devil who quotes the Scriptures in Luke and Matthew, "the people" in John quote them as they urge Jesus to produce bread miraculously:

> So they said to him, "What sign do you do, that we may see and believe you? What work do you perform? Our fathers ate manna in the wilderness; as it is written, 'He gave them bread from heaven to eat' " (6:30–31).

Jesus resists this temptation as well, and just as Matthew's Jesus had answered the devil with a response about spiritual nourishment ("Man does not live by bread alone, but by every word which proceeds from the mouth of God"), so, in John, Jesus speaks of the "true bread from heaven" (6:32). The temptation in which the devil asks Jesus to display his divine powers in public (Matt. 4:5–6; Luke 4:9–12) is echoed in John when Jesus' own brothers, who, John says, did not believe in him, challenge Jesus to "go to Judea," to "show yourself to the world" in Jerusalem where, as he and they are well aware, his enemies want to kill him (7:1–5). This temptation, too, Jesus rejects.

According to John, it is Jesus himself who reveals the identity of the evil one. When Jesus hears Peter declare that "we [disciples] believe that you are the Messiah, the Son of God," he answers brusquely:

> "Have I not chosen you twelve, and one of you is a devil?" He spoke of Judas Iscariot, the son of Simon, for it was he that would betray him, being one of the twelve (6:70–71).

Anticipating his betrayal, Jesus again identifies his betrayer, Judas, along with the accompanying posse of Roman and Jewish soldiers, as his supernatural enemy appearing in human form. According to Matthew, Jesus signals Judas's arrival in Gethsemane with the words, "Rise; let us be going; my betrayer is coming" (26:46); but in John, Jesus announces instead that "the ruler of this world [that is, the "evil one"] is coming. . . . Rise, let us be going" (14:30–31). Shortly before, Jesus had accused "the Jews who had believed in him" of plotting his murder: twice he charged that "you seek to kill me." When they find his words incomprehensible, Jesus proceeds to identify "the Jews" who had previously believed in him as Satan's own: "You are of your father, the devil; and you want to accomplish your father's desires. He was a murderer from the beginning" (8:44). Raymond Brown comments that in these passages,

> for the first time the fact that the devil is Jesus' real antagonist comes to the fore. This motif will grow louder and louder as the "hour" of Jesus['s death] approaches, until the passion is presented as a struggle to the death between Jesus and Satan.[13]

This is true, but Brown is concerned only with theological observations. What do these passages mean in terms of human conflict? Many commentators, along with countless Christian readers, have agreed with the blunt assessment of the influential German New Testament scholar Rudolph Bultmann: "There can be no doubt about the main point of the passage, which is to show that *the Jews' unbelief,* with its hostility to truth and life, *stems from their being children of the devil*" (emphasis added).[14] Bultmann adds that John, like Matthew and Luke, in effect charges the Jews with "intentional murder."[15] (Elsewhere, as we shall see, Bultmann makes statements bearing different implications.) In recent decades these passages from John have elicited a flurry of discussion, often from Christian commentators insisting that these words do not—or morally *cannot*—mean what most Christians for nearly two millennia have taken them to mean.

Many scholars have observed that the term "Jews" occurs much more frequently in John than in the other gospels, and that its usage indicates that John's author and his fellow believers stand even further from the Jewish majority than do the other evangelists. Dozens, even hundreds, of articles propose different solutions to the question of how John uses the Greek term *Ioudaios,* usually translated "Jew."[16] Sometimes, of course, John's usage coincides with general contemporary usage in passages that simply describe people who are Jewish and not Gentile: twice, in John, outsiders, first a Samaritan woman and later the Roman governor, Pontius Pilate, identify Jesus himself as "a Jew" (John 4:9; 18:34). In other passages, the term apparently designates Judeans—that is, people who live in or around Jerusalem—as distinct from Galileans and Samaritans. In still other passages, the term "the Jews" clearly serves as a synonym for the Jewish leaders. But in certain passages that may overlap with these, John uses "the Jews" to designate people alien to Jesus and hostile to him; he repeatedly says, for example, that "the Jews sought to kill [him]," and that Jesus at times avoided travel to Jerusalem "for fear of the Jews."

In chapter 8, when Jesus engages in a hostile dialogue with "the Jews who had believed in him," and finally denounces "the Jews" as Satan's offspring, he is obviously not making a simple ethnic distinction, since, of course, in that scene Jesus and all his disciples are Jews as well as their opponents. Here, just as Jesus embodies the divine light of God's presence, "the Jews" represent "the world" that rejected that light. As John had declared in his prologue:

> The true light that enlightens everyone was coming into the world; he was in the world, and the world was made through him; yet the world did not recognize him. He came unto his own; and his own people did not receive him.

Later, as Bultmann points out, "the Jews" become synonymous with that rejecting, unbelieving "world."[17] The German New Testament scholar Heinrich Schneider expresses a view commonly held by Christian scholars when he says:

> From a general non-acceptance of Jesus by people in the early chapters [of John], the opposition becomes more and more identified with a [specific] group . . . , the Jews. Ultimately the group stands for the forces opposed to Jesus, which are the forces of darkness. *It is obvious that we are not dealing with an ethnic group, but with a dramatic theological symbol. . . . We would miss the full significance of this symbol if we considered the Jew in John only as an historical figure. . . . "The Jews" are an ever-present reality and threat to any worship of God in spirit and in truth* (emphasis added).[18]

Yet other commentators, including Samuel Sandmel, do not find it obvious that "we are not dealing with an ethnic group." Sandmel insists that such interpreters want "to exculpate the gospel from its manifest anti-Semitism." Sandmel points out that John does not charge "humanity" or "the world" in general for actively seeking Jesus's execution, but specifically singles out "the Jews."[19]

Anyone who reads the gospel of John can see that "the Jews" have become for John what Bultmann sees as a symbol of human evil.[20] But those who agree with Rudolph Bultmann and Heinrich Schneider that the use of the term is merely symbolic and thus has no social or political implications seem to be engaging in apologetic evasions. John's decision to make an actual, identifiable group—among Jesus' contemporaries and his own—into a symbol of "all evil" obviously bears religious, social, and political implications. Would anyone doubt this if an influential author today made women, or for that matter Muslims or homosexuals, the "symbol of all evil"? Having cast "the Jews" in that role, John's gospel can arouse and even legitimate hostility toward Judaism, a potential that New Testament scholar Reginald Fuller says "has been abundantly and tragically actualized in the course of Christian history."[21]

It is not my purpose here to describe in detail, as others have done, the complex historical situation that gave rise to the Johannine passion narrative. Let us assume, first, that it is historically likely that certain Jewish leaders may have collaborated with the Roman authorities in Jesus' arrest and execution. Let us assume as valid, too, the point well explicated by Louis Martyn and others, that the author of John reads into his story conflicts he has himself experienced between his own group and those he calls "the Jews," by whom the author probably means primarily the leaders of Jewish communities known to him (c. 90–100 C.E.), together with their followers. My purpose here is not to define precisely John's use of the term "Jew." Instead, it is much simpler: to show how the gospel of John, like the other gospels, associates the mythological figure of Satan with specific human opposition, first implicating Judas Iscariot, then the Jewish authorities, and finally "the Jews" collectively.

From the beginning of the gospel, then, as we have seen, the author of John, like his predecessors at Qûmran, draws the battle lines between the "sons of light" and the "sons of darkness," although in this case the "light" is specifically represented by Jesus. After "the Jews" attempt to stone Jesus for speaking words they take as blasphemy—claiming in effect, the divine name (8:58)—Jesus declares:

> "I must do the work of him who sent me, while it is day; the night is coming, when no one may work. As long as I am in the world, I am the light of the world" (9:4–5).

Moving quickly toward the passion narrative, which here constitutes half of the entire gospel, John, like Luke, makes explicit the charge implicit in Mark and Matthew—that Satan himself initiated Judas' treachery:

> During supper, the devil had already put it into the heart of Judas Iscariot, the son of Simon, to betray him. . . . Then after the morsel, Satan entered into him. Jesus said to him, "What you are going to do, do quickly." . . . So after receiving the morsel, [Judas] immediately went out; and it was night" (13:2, 27–30).

Because John insists that Jesus, fully aware of the future course of events, remains in complete control of them, he writes that Jesus himself gives Judas the morsel that precedes Satan's entry (thus fulfilling the prophecy of Psalm 41:9). Jesus then directs Judas's subsequent action ("What you are going to do, do quickly"). At that fateful moment, which initiates Jesus' betrayal, John, like Luke, depicts the "power of darkness" (cf. Luke 22:53) eclipsing the "light of the world": hence his stark final phrase, *en de nux* (*"it was night"*).

Here the passion narrative is more than a story; in the words of John's Jesus, it is a *judgment,* or *crisis* (to translate literally the Greek term *krisis*). When Jesus predicts his crucifixion, he declares that instead of showing a judgment against *him*, it shows God's judgment against "this world"; instead of destroying Jesus, it will destroy the diabolic "ruler of the world":

> "Now is the judgment [*krisis*] of this world; now the ruler of this world shall be cast out; and I, when I am lifted up from the earth, will draw all people to myself." He said this to show by what death he would die (John 12:31–32; see also 14:30).

John's readers are thus warned that the events he describes—and, for that matter, John's account of them—also serve to judge and condemn as "sons of darkness" those who have participated in Jesus' destruction. John, like Luke, suppresses all traces of Roman initiative in Jesus' execution. In nearly every episode, John displays what one scholar calls "bizarre exaggeration" to insist that the blame for initiating, ordering, and carrying out the crucifixion falls upon Jesus' *intimate* enemies, his fellow Jews.

Apparently using an early source independent of the other gospels, John reports that before Jesus' arrest

> the chief priests and the Pharisees gathered the Sanhedrin together and said, "What shall we do? This man performs many signs. . . . If we let him go on like this, the Romans will come and destroy our holy place and our nation" (11:47–48).

I agree with those, including the British classical scholar Fergus Millar, who regard this part of John's account as perhaps closer to the actual events than the other gospel accounts.[22] Unlike the elaborate trial that Mark and Matthew present, John shows the council members concerned about the disturbances Jesus arouses among the people, a plausible motive for their judgment, for they want to protect their own constituency from the risk of Roman reprisals, even at the risk of a wrongful execution. After "Judas, procuring a band of [presumably Roman] soldiers, and some officers from the chief priests of the Pharisees" (18:8), betrayed Jesus, the arresting party seized and bound him and led him to Annas, "father-in-law of the high priest," who, after interrogating him, "sent him bound to Caiaphas the high priest." Rosemary Reuther observes that John here intends to suppress political charges against Jesus—that he had claimed to be king—in favor of a religious one, that he threatened the Temple.[23]

Although John reports no other trial by a Jewish tribunal, he leaves no doubt that the chief priests want Jesus killed. John depicts the priests as evasive and self-righteous when Pilate inquires about the charge: "If this man were not a malefactor, we would not have brought him to you" (18:30). When Pilate, still having heard no charge, answers, with indifference or contempt, "Take him yourselves and judge him by your own law," the "Jews" answer, "It is not lawful for us to put anyone to death" (18:31).

Some scholars insist that this last statement is wrong. Richard Husband claims that under first-century Roman law the Jewish

Sanhedrin retained its traditional right to execute people for certain crimes defined as religious, such as violating the Temple precincts, transgressing the law, and adultery.[24] Husband and other scholars point out that only about five years after Jesus' death, in 36 C.E., Jews stoned to death his follower Stephen for "speaking against the law." But was this a lynch mob, or a crowd carrying out a Sanhedrin sentence?

Josephus writes that in 62 C.E. the high priest Ananus II assembled the Sanhedrin and condemned Jesus' brother James to death by stoning, along with several others, on charges of transgressing the law. These executions apparently cost Ananus II his position as high priest after some Jerusalemites complained to the Jewish king, Agrippa II, and to the Roman procurator, Albinus, that Ananus had executed James and others without notifying the procurator, much less gaining his permission. Josephus describes a later case—one that suggests that Jewish leaders had become more cautious about executing without Roman permission. A man named Jesus bar Ananias, who had loudly predicted the downfall of Jerusalem and its Temple, was arrested and beaten by prominent Jewish leaders. When they brought him before Albinus, the same Roman prefect, apparently hoping to secure the death penalty,

> Jesus refused to answer the prefect's questions, and so Albinus let him go as a maniac. Thus, despite their anger, the Jewish leaders, who could arrest and flog, did not dare execute this Jesus as they had executed James (*War* 6.2).

By the sixties, then, Roman permission to execute seems to have been a necessary, or at least an expedient, measure. For lack of definitive evidence, intense scholarly investigation and debate have not solved the issue. In the case of Jesus of Nazareth, however, Christian sources seldom suggest that the Jews actually executed Jesus, whether or not this act was ratified by the Romans. Although the gospels do not describe Pilate actually sentencing Jesus to death, the historical evidence and the gospel accounts indicate that the governor must have ordered his soldiers to execute Jesus on grounds of sedition. As for what took place between

Jewish authorities and the governor, our only evidence comes from the gospels themselves and from later Christian and Jewish reinterpretations of these events, charged as they are with mutual accusation and polemic. Whatever the legal situation of the San-hedrin in regard to capital punishment, the point John wants to make is clear enough: that although Romans were known to have carried out Jesus' execution by their own peculiar method (see 19:32), they did so only because "the Jews" forced them to.[25]

When Pilate asks Jesus, "Are you a king?," Jesus parries the question, and Pilate retorts, "*Am I a Jew? Your own nation and the chief priests have handed you over to me:* what have you done?" (18:35; emphasis added). Were his kingdom an earthly one, Jesus says, "my servants would fight so that I might not be handed over to the Jews" (18:36)—an ironic Johannine reversal of the charges in Mark, Luke, and Matthew, which repeatedly describe the Jews "handing Jesus over" to "the nations."

In John as in Luke, Pilate three times proclaims Jesus inno-cent, and proposes three times to release him; but each time the chief priests and those John calls "the Jews" cry out, demanding instead that Pilate "crucify him" (18:38–40; 19:5–7; 19:14–15). John "explains," too, that Pilate allowed his soldiers to scourge and torture Jesus only in order to arouse the crowd's compassion (19:1–4), and so to placate what British scholar Dennis Nineham calls "the insatiable fury of the Jews."[26] John adds that when they protest that Jesus has violated their religious law, and therefore "deserves to die," Pilate is "more terrified" (19:8). Returning to Jesus as if he still hoped to find a way to acquit him, Pilate instead receives from the prisoner relative exoneration of his *own* guilt: speaking as if he were Pilate's judge (as John believes he is), Jesus declares to the governor that "the one who delivered me to you has the greater sin." When the crowd threatens to charge Pilate with treason against Rome (19:12), Pilate makes one more futile attempt to release Jesus—"Shall I crucify your king?"—to which the chief priests answer, "We have no king but Caesar," and at last Pilate gives in to the shouting. At this point, John says, Pilate, having neither sentenced Jesus nor ordered his execution, "handed [Jesus] over to them to be crucified" (19:16). In this scene, as C. H. Dodd has commented, "the priests exert unrelenting pressure, while the governor turns and doubles like a hunted hare."[27] Immediately after Pilate hands Jesus over to the Jews, the narrator goes on to say, "they took Jesus . . . to the place called in Hebrew Golgotha. There they crucified him, and with him two others" (19:17–18).

After John's account of the crucifixion, in which he shows how Jesus' ignominious death fulfills prophecy in every detail, he adds that Joseph of Arimathea, "a disciple of Jesus, though a secret one for fear of the Jews" (19:38), petitions Pilate to allow him to recover Jesus' body and to bury it. The story implies that Jesus' enemies are so vindictive that Joseph and another secret disciple, Nicodemus, are afraid even to offer him a decent burial. Many scholars have discussed John's motives for thus depicting Pilate as wishing to free the innocent Jesus, while presenting the Jews as not only the "villains, but the ultimate in villainy."[28]

Instead of completely exonerating Pilate, however, John's Jesus, playing judge to his judge, as we saw, pronounces Pilate guilty of sin, although "less" sin than the Jews. Nevertheless, as Paul Winter observes:

> The stern Pilate grows more mellow from gospel to gospel [from Mark to Matthew, from Matthew to Luke and then to John]. The more removed from history, the more sympathetic a character he becomes.[29]

With regard to the Jews, Jesus' "intimate enemy," a parallel process occurs, but in reverse; the Jews become increasingly antagonistic. In the opening scene of Mark, Jesus boldly challenges not his fellow Jews but the powers of evil. Then he comes into increasingly intense conflict, first with "the scribes" and then with the Pharisees and Herodians, until crowds of his own people, in a conflict Mark depicts as essentially intra-Jewish, persuade reluctant Roman forces to execute him. Matthew, as we saw, writing some twenty years after Mark, depicts a far more bitter and aggressive antagonism between Jesus and the majority of his Jewish contemporaries, even casting King Herod in the role of the hated tyrant Pharaoh. Indeed, no sooner was Jesus born than Herod and "all Jerusalem with him," specifically including "all the chief priests and scribes of the people," were troubled, and Herod decided to kill him. Matthew describes the Pharisees, religious leaders of his time, as "sons of hell," destined, along with all who reject Jesus' teaching, for eternal punishment in the "fire reserved for the devil and all his angels." Yet I agree with recent analysis by Andrew Overman that even Matthew intends to show, in effect, a battle between rival reform groups of Jews, each insisting upon its own superior righteousness, and each calling the other demon-possessed.[30]

Luke, as we have seen, goes considerably further. No sooner has the devil appeared to tempt and destroy Jesus than all Jesus' townspeople, hearing his first public address in their synagogue, are aroused to fury, and attempt to throw him down a cliff. Only at the climax of Luke's account does Satan return in person, so to speak, to enter into Judas and so to direct the operation that ends with the crucifixion.

Writing c. 100 C.E., John dismisses the device of the devil as an independent supernatural character (if, indeed, he knew of it, as I suspect he did). Instead, as John tells the story, Satan, like God himself, appears incarnate, first in Judas Iscariot, then in the Jewish authorities as they mount opposition to Jesus, and finally in those John calls "the Jews"—a group he sometimes characterizes as Satan's allies, now as separate from Jesus and his followers as darkness is from light, or the forces of hell from the armies of heaven.

The evangelists' various depictions of the devil correlate with the "social history of Satan"—that is, with the history of increasing conflict between groups representing Jesus' followers and their opposition. By presenting Jesus' life and message in these polemical terms, the evangelists no doubt intended to strengthen group solidarity. In the process, they shaped, in ways that were to become incalculably consequential, the self-understanding of Christians in relation to Jews for two millennia.

SATAN'S EARTHLY KINGDOM:
CHRISTIANS AGAINST PAGANS

Between 70 and 100 C.E.—the interval between the writing of the gospel of Mark and of the gospel of John—the Christian movement became largely Gentile. Many converts found that having become Christians placed their lives in danger, and that they were threatened not by Jews but by pagans—Roman officers and city mobs who hated Christians for their "atheism," which pagans feared could bring the wrath of the gods upon whole communities. Only two generations after Mark and Matthew, Gentile converts, many of them former pagans from Roman provinces—Asia Minor, Syria, Egypt, Africa, and Greece—adapted the gospel vocabulary to face a new enemy. As earlier generations of Christians had claimed to see Satan among their fellow Jews, now converts facing Roman persecution claimed to see Satan and his demonic allies at work among *other Gentiles*.

The pressures of state persecution complicated such characterizations of Gentiles as we found in Matthew and Luke; those writers, hoping for a favorable hearing among Gentile audiences, had depicted Romans and other Gentiles in generally favorable ways, as we have seen.[1] So long as Christians remained a minority movement within Jewish communities, they tended to regard other Jews as potential enemies, and Gentiles as potential converts. Although the apostle Paul, writing c. 55 C.E., complained that he had faced danger at every turn—"danger from robbers, danger from my own people, danger from Gentiles, even danger from false brethren" (2 Cor. 11:26)—he mentions actual persecution only from his fellow Jews: "Five times I received at the hands of the Jews forty lashes save one; three times I have been beaten with rods; once I was stoned" (2 Cor. 11:24). According to Luke's account in Acts, Paul regarded Roman magistrates as his protectors against Jewish hostility; and Paul himself, writing to Christians in Rome, orders them to "obey the higher powers; for there is no authority except from God, and the powers that exist are instituted by God," even in their God-given right to "bear the sword" and "execute God's wrath" (Rom. 13:1).

But Paul himself was executed, probably by order of a Roman magistrate; and about ten years later, when many Romans blamed the emperor Nero for starting a fire that devastated much of Rome, the emperor ordered the arrest of a group of Christians, charged them with arson, and had them hung up in his garden and burned alive as human torches.[2]

One follower of Paul, aware of the circumstances of his teacher's death and of the various dangers Christians faced, warned in a letter attributed to Paul, called the Letter to the Ephesians, that Christians are not contending against mere human beings:

> Our contest is not against flesh and blood [human beings] but against powers, against principalities, against the world rulers of this present darkness, against the spiritual forces of evil in heavenly places (6:12).

This Pauline author articulates the sense of spiritual warfare experienced by many Christians, especially by those who face persecution. The author of Revelation, claiming to have suffered exile "on account of the word of God and the testimony of Jesus" (Rev. 1:9), and aware of others suffering imprisonment, torture, and death at the hands of Roman magistrates, describes horrific and ecstatic visions that invoke traditional prophetic images of animals and monsters to characterize the powers of Rome, which he identifies with "the devil and Satan" (20:2; passim). Despite the gospels' generally conciliatory attitude toward the Romans, the crucifixion account nevertheless invites Christians to see demonic forces working through Roman officials as well as through Jewish leaders; Luke goes so far as to suggest that Jesus' crucifixion forged an unholy alliance between Pilate and Herod, so that the Roman and Jewish authorities became friends "that day" (23:12).

Gentile converts who were hated by other Gentiles—often members of their own families, their townspeople, and their city magistrates—believed that worshipers of the pagan gods were driven by Satan to menace God's people. As Christian preachers increasingly appealed to Gentiles, many found that what had offended most Jews about Christianity offended pagans even more: "Christians severed the traditional bonds between religion and a nation or people," and, as the historian Robert Wilken points out, "Ancient people took for granted that religion was indissolubly linked to a particular city, nation or people."[3] Jews identified their religion with the Jewish people as a whole, united by tradition, however dispersed throughout the world; for pagans, *pietas* consisted precisely in respecting ancient customs and honoring traditional mores. The Christian movement, however, encouraged people to abandon ancestral customs and break the sacred bonds of family, society, and nation.

The movement that began as a sect within Judaism and was rejected by the majority of Jews, whom it repudiated in turn, now appealed to people of every nation and tribe to join the new "Christian society" and to break all former bonds of kinship and affiliation. "In Christ," the apostle Paul had declared, "there is no longer Jew nor Greek . . . slave nor free, male nor female" (Gal. 3:28); for those "born again" in baptism (John 3:5–8), the world consists of only two kinds of people—those who belong to God's kingdom, whose citizenship is in heaven (Heb. 12:22–24; 13:14), and those still ruled by the evil one, subjects of Satan.

Despite official Roman censure and popular pagan hostility, the movement grew. The North African convert Tertullian boasts in an appeal to the Roman emperors:

> Those who once hated Christianity . . . now begin to hate
> what they formerly were, and to profess what they formerly
> hated. . . . The outcry is that the State is filled with Chris-
> tians—that they are in the fields, in the cities, in the islands;
> many people lament, as if for some calamity, that both men and
> women, every age and condition, even people of high rank, are
> passing over to professing the Christian faith.[4]

What would impel pagans to "profess what they formerly hated"—
even at the cost of endangering their lives? Tertullian and a few
others—Justin, from the coast of Asia Minor, his student Tatian,
from Syria, and Origen, an Egyptian—have left us some clues.

Justin, a young man who had come to Rome from Asia Minor
about 140 C.E. to pursue his study of philosophy, went one day
with friends to the amphitheater to see the spectacular gladiatorial fights held there to celebrate imperial birthdays. The spectators cheered the men who recklessly courted death, and thrilled
to the moment of the death blow. The crowd would go wild
when a defeated gladiator defiantly thrust out his neck to meet
his antagonist's sword; and they jeered and hooted when a loser
bolted in panic.[5]

Justin was startled to see in the midst of this violent entertainment a group of criminals being led out to be torn apart by wild
beasts. The serene courage with which they met their brutal public execution astonished him, especially when he learned that
these were illiterate people, Christians, whom the Roman senator
Tacitus had called "a class of people hated for their supersti-
tions," whose founder, Christos, had himself "suffered the
extreme penalty under Pontius Pilate" about a hundred years
before.[6] Justin was profoundly shaken, for he saw a group of
uneducated people actually accomplishing what Plato and Zeno
regarded as the greatest achievement of a philosopher—accepting death with equanimity, an accomplishment which the gladiators' bravado merely parodied. As he watched, Justin realized
that he was witnessing something quite beyond nature, a miracle;
somehow these people had tapped into a great, unknown source
of power.

Justin would have been even more startled had he known that these Christians saw themselves not as philosophers but as combatants in a cosmic struggle, God's warriors against Satan.[7] As Justin learned later, their amazing confidence derived from the conviction that their own agony and death actually were hastening God's victory over the forces of evil, forces embodied in the Roman magistrate who had sentenced them, and, for that matter, in spectators like Justin himself.

Sometime later, while taking a solitary walk in a field near the sea, Justin unexpectedly met an old man who turned out to be a member of this group.[8] At first the old man questioned Justin about his pursuit of philosophy; but instead of being impressed, as Justin expected, the old man challenged him and said he could never find illumination in philosophy.

What Justin sought in philosophy was not simply intellectual understanding but self-realization: How shall I live in order to be happy? What are the steps toward transformation?[9] At an earlier stage of his philosophical search, Justin says, he had "surrendered himself" to a Stoic teacher, hoping to transcend his ordinary, "human" point of view. Stoic teachers promised that by studying physics—literally, "nature"—one could learn to place each event, obstacle, or circumstance in one's life within a universal perspective, and to participate in the divine, which is synonymous with nature. Justin says he became frustrated because his teacher seldom spoke about the divine and discouraged questions on the subject; so Justin left, and began to study with a peripatetic philosopher. After a few days, when his new teacher demanded a tuition fee, Justin quit in disgust, deciding that the man "was no philosopher at all." Justin did not give up; next he tried a Pythagorean master, who offered to teach physical and mental discipline to attune the soul to the divine. Told that he would have to master astronomy, mathematics, and music before he could even begin to understand "what makes for a happy life," Justin left this teacher as well.

Defeated and helpless, Justin finally discovered in the teachings of a brilliant expositor of Plato what he believed was the true path. He says he had already made great progress toward enlightenment and expected soon to be able to raise his mind to apprehend the divine. But the old Christian he met walking by the sea challenged his basic philosophic premise: "Is there, then, such a great power in our mind? Will the human mind ever see God through its own capacity?" The old man voiced Justin's worst fear—that he was wasting his time; that the human mind, however one educates and increases its capacity, is intrinsically incapable of reaching that goal; the mind cannot understand God through its own efforts.

When the old man first challenged him, Justin vehemently objected, repeating Platonic clichés. Later, retelling the story, Justin acknowledged the irony of his earlier naïveté: he found himself repeating the phrase "Plato says . . . and I believe him." Feeling increasingly foolish, Justin realized that his objections to the old man's arguments derived simply from his blind acceptance of Plato's authority—not from any conviction or experience of his own.

As Justin and the old man talked, he saw for the first time that he had stumbled into a process much deeper than the intellect could fathom. Justin had assumed that he possessed a mind free to think rationally about everything, including the divine. Now he heard the opposite: that the mind itself is infested with demonic powers that distort and confuse our thinking. Before he—or anyone else—could achieve understanding, the old man said, Justin would have to receive the divine spirit—a power far greater than our comprehension, a power that "illuminates the mind."[10] But first Justin would need to undergo exorcism, a ritual in which the celebrant, himself filled with the divine spirit, would invoke that spirit to drive out the demonic powers inhabiting the candidate's mind and body and holding him, like all the unbaptized, captive to confusion and ignorance.

After heated argument with the old man and considerable internal struggle, Justin became convinced that Christians had discovered access to great power—divine power, which was always there, waiting to break through the clouds, and which was brought to earth by the Christians' powerful rituals, beginning with baptism.[11]

Before the old man left him, Justin says, he admonished the young man to

> "pray that, above all things, the gates of light may be opened to you; for these things cannot be perceived or understood by everyone, but only by the person to whom God and his Christ have given wisdom."[12]

After he left, Justin says,

> immediately a flame was kindled in my soul, and a love . . . of those people who are friends of Christ possessed me; and, while turning his words over and over in my mind, I found this philosophy alone to be safe and profitable.[13]

Seeking out other "friends of Christ," Justin asked to become a candidate for the rite of baptism. He does not tell us the story of his own baptism, but other sources suggest the following: Having fasted and prayed to prepare himself, Justin would await, probably on the night before Easter, the rite that would expel the indwelling demonic powers and charge him with new, divine life. First the celebrant would demand to know whether Justin was willing to "renounce the devil, and all his pomp, and his angels"; Justin would ritually declare three times, "I renounce them." Then Justin would descend naked into a river, immersing himself to signify the death of the old self and the washing away of sins. Once the divine name was pronounced and the celebrant had invoked the spirit to descend on him, he would emerge reborn, to be clothed with new white garments at the shore and offered a mixture of milk and honey—babies' food, suitable for a newborn.[14]

Justin said that he had received in baptism what he had sought in vain in philosophy: "this washing we call illumination; because those who learn these things become illuminated in their understanding."[15] He later explained to other potential converts, "Since at our birth we were born without consciousness or choice, by our parents' intercourse, and were brought up in bad habits and evil customs," we are baptized "so that we may no longer be children of necessity and ignorance, but become the children of choice and knowledge."[16] His ritual rebirth to new parents—God and the holy spirit—enabled Justin to renounce not only his natural family but the "habits and evil customs" they had taught him from childhood—above all, traditional piety toward the gods, whom he now saw as evil spirits. Having entered the stark and polarized Christian world, Justin joined those brave, illiterate Christians whose bloody death he had witnessed in the Roman amphitheater. Now Justin, like them, saw the entire universe as a battleground where cosmic forces clash.

Justin believed that his eyes had suddenly been opened to the truth behind the most apparently innocuous appearances: the marble statues of the goddesses Fortuna and Roma that he saw every day in the marketplace, the image of Hercules that presided over the public baths, and those of Dionysus and Apollo at the theater. Behind those familiar chiseled faces Justin now recognized "spiritual forces of evil in heavenly places." Justin suddenly understood, as Paul had, that the forces that play upon a helpless humanity are neither human nor divine, as pagans imagined, but demonic.

Justin's pagan parents had brought him up in traditional piety, revering the forces of nature as divine. For pious pagans, as the classicist A. H. Armstrong says,

> the old gods have the beauty and goodness of the sun, the sea, the wind, the mountains, great wild animals; splendid, powerful, and dangerous realities that do not come within the sphere of morality, and are in no way concerned about the human race.[17]

Pagan worship mingled awe with terror of the vast forces that threaten our fragile species. The oracle at Delphi warned worshipers, "Know yourself," not as an invitation to lofty contemplation or introspection, but as a blunt reminder that they were mortal, *ephemeral,* literally, "creatures of a day," propelled toward living and dying by the interplay of cosmic forces far beyond their comprehension.

From the sixth century B.C.E. onward, philosophers reflected upon those cosmic forces in various ways. Plato spoke of "necessity," others of the powers of "destiny" or "fate" that govern the universe. Later Stoic philosophers "demythologized" the old myths and reinterpreted the gods themselves—Zeus, Hera, Aphrodite—as representing elements of the natural universe. Some suggested, for example, that Hera represents the air, Zeus the lightning and thunder, Eros and Aphrodite the erotic energies that drive us into copulation, and Ares the aggressive energy that impels us into war.[18] Many classical philosophers agreed that these gods were neither bad nor good in themselves; although the gods might appear to be capricious—sometimes benevolent, sometimes hostile—most pagan thinkers agreed that such judgments had nothing to do with the gods themselves, but only with human reactions to specific events.

For Justin, conversion changed all this. Every god and spirit he had ever known, including Apollo, Aphrodite, and Zeus, whom he had worshiped since childhood, he now perceived as allies of Satan—despite the brilliant panoply of their public processions, their thousands of temples and glittering priesthoods, despite the fact that they were worshiped by the emperor himself, who served in person as their *pontifex maximus* ("greatest priest"). Born again, Justin saw the universe of spiritual energies, which pious pagan philosophers called *daimones*, as, in his words, "*foul daimones*."[19] By the time the Christian movement had swept across the Western world, our language would reflect that reversed perception, and the Greek term *daimones*, "spirit energies," would become, in English, *demons*.[20] So, Justin says,

> we, who out of every race of people, once worshiped Dionysus the son of Semele, and Apollo the son of Leto, who in their passion for human beings did things which it is shameful even to mention; who worshiped Persephone and Aphrodite . . . or Asklepius, or some other of those who are called gods, now, through Jesus Christ, despise them, even at the cost of death. . . . We pity those who believe such things, for which we know that the *daimones* are responsible.[21]

Philosophers who say that "whatever happens, happens according to fatal necessity" are proved wrong, Justin says, by the evidence of those "born again to God"; for in them we see "the same person making transition to opposite things."[22] Justin says that he found that "the words of Christ" have a "terrible power in them that can inspire those who turn away from the right path"[23]; now he and his fellow Christians, once driven, like most others by passion, greed, and hatred,

> stand apart from demons and follow God; ... we, who once took pleasure in fornication, now embrace self-control; we, who ... valued the acquisition of wealth and possessions above everything else, now put what we have into a common fund, and share with everyone in need; we, who hated and killed one another, and would not share our lives with certain people because of their ethnic differences from us, now live intimately with them.[24]

Justin sees in his own life and the lives of Christians all around him evidence of divine power that enables them to live "beyond nature." Just as those Christians he watched die in the amphitheater overcame with their inspired courage the instinct to survive, so, he says, may others have overcome the tyranny of instinctual drives:

> Many among us, both men and women, who have been Christians since childhood, have remained pure at the age of sixty or seventy; and I boast that I could produce such people from every race. . . . and what shall I say of the innumerable multitude who have reformed intemperate habits?[25]

Justin mentions those in whom powerful compulsions—for example, for strong drink—have been broken. Many others, Justin says, "have changed their violent and tyrannical dispositions," overcome by the astonishing forbearance, patience, and unwavering honesty they have found in their Christian neighbors.[26]

Celebrating the new society formed by these "reborn" people,[27] Justin now sees the old society as evil—a society that, for example, abandons infants to die or to be raised by opportunists, who train them as prostitutes and sell them on the slave markets "like herds of goats or sheep."[28] As a privileged philosophy student, Justin might have displayed moral indifference; instead he is indignant about those abandoned children, and castigates moral relativists who pride themselves on their philosophical sophistication: "The worst evil of all is to say that neither good nor evil is anything in itself, but that they are only matters of human opinion."[29]

Justin's life now has a moral direction. He contrasts the natural life he once lived as passive prey to demons, with the spirit-infused life he lives now:

> We have learned to find God . . . and we believe it is impossible for the evil or envious person, or the conspirator, or for the righteous person—to escape God's notice; and every person goes to eternal punishment or salvation according to the value of his works.[30]

In his new life, Justin sees his role in the universe enormously enhanced; the stand he takes and the choices he makes not only decide his eternal destiny but engage him at present as an active combatant in the universal struggle between God's spirit and Satan.[31]

Yet Justin realizes the irony—and the terror—of his new situation: receiving divine illumination has ripped him out of all that was familiar, alienated him from his family and friends, and uprooted him from much of his culture. Most frightening, it has stripped him of all security. His baptismal exorcism placed him in opposition to the gods he had worshiped all his life and in potentially lethal conflict with virtually everyone he had ever known—above all, with governmental authorities. He now belongs to a group that the Roman majority and government magistrates regard with suspicion and contempt, despite all the evangelists' efforts to calm their fears.[32] Those publicly accused of allegiance to Christ are liable to arrest and interrogation, often under torture; to "confess" means immediate condemnation to death, by beheading, if one has the good fortune to be a Roman citizen, or, if not, by prolonged torture and public spectacle, including condemnation *ad bestias*—that is, being torn apart by wild animals in the public sports arena. Justin knows of cases in which believers or their slaves, including women and children, had been tortured until they "admitted" seeing Christians engage in atrocities, including ritual eating of human flesh and drinking blood from freshly slaughtered infants. Only thirty years earlier, even such a sober-minded official as Pliny, governor of Bithynia in Asia Minor, having satisfied himself by torturing Christians that they were not guilty of criminal acts, had decided that they deserved the death penalty, if only for their sheer "obstinacy."[33]

But why does the mere mention of the Christian name arouse such violent, irrational hatred? Reflecting on this question, Justin finds clues in what he calls the apostles' memoirs (which we call the gospels). There Justin reads that after God's spirit descended on Jesus at baptism, Satan and his demonic allies fought back, opposing Jesus, and finally hounded him to his death. So also now, Justin realizes, when the spirit descends on those who are baptized, the same evil forces that fought against Jesus attack his followers. The gospels show Justin how spiritual energies, demonic and divine, can dwell within human beings, often without their knowledge, and drive them toward destruction—or toward God. Now Justin understands the Pauline warning that

> our contest is not against flesh and blood, but against powers, against principalities, against the world-rulers of this present darkness, against spiritual forces of evil in heavenly places (Eph. 6:12).

The conviction that unseen energies impel human beings to action was, of course, nothing new; it was universally accepted throughout the pagan world. A thousand years earlier, Homer had described how such energies played upon human beings— how Athena had inspired Achilles to heroic warfare, and how Aphrodite had seized and possessed Helen of Troy, driving her into the adulterous passion that led her people into war. Recalling the death of Socrates, Justin realizes with a shock that Socrates himself had said the same thing the Christians are saying—that all the gods Homer praises are actually evil energies that corrupt people, "seducing women and sodomizing boys," and terrorizing people into worshiping them as gods.[34] It was for this reason, Justin says, that Socrates denounced traditional religion and was charged with atheism. These same demonic powers, furious with Socrates for threatening to unmask them, drove the Athenian mob to execute him. This universal demonic deception, Justin realizes, accounts for the irrational hatred that the mere presence of Christians arouses among pagans—not merely for the violent passions of the ignorant and unruly mob, but also for the criminalizing of Christians, approved even by the most enlightened emperors who ever ruled Rome.

Justin boldly addresses an open letter of protest to these rulers—the emperor Antoninus Pius and his two sons, the Stoic prince Marcus Aurelius, whom he calls "truest philosopher," and "Lucius the Philosopher"—appealing to them as fellow philosophers, hoping, he says, to open their eyes. Justin declares that he writes on behalf of "those people of every nation who are unjustly hated and slaughtered; I, Justin, son of Priscus and grandson of Bacchius, of Flavia Neapolis, myself being one of them."[35] By publicly identifying himself with those whom the demons seek to kill, Justin initiates a public challenge that will end not with amnesty but, as he admits he fears, with his own arraignment and execution.

Although Justin begins by honorifically addressing the emperor Antoninus Pius and his sons, he soon tells them bluntly that despite their philosophic aspirations, they are not even masters of their own minds. "Even now," Justin warns the rulers of the Roman world, "these demons seek to keep you as their slaves, by preventing you from understanding what we say."[36] Their irrational public hatred of Christians proves, Justin says, that their minds have been captured by the same evil spirits who incited the Athenians to kill Socrates; now, for the same reason, these spirits are driving them to kill Christians.

Not long after Justin wrote to the emperors (and apparently received no answer) he heard of a case involving the arrest of an aristocratic woman convert. Before conversion, Justin says, she had participated with her husband in drunken liaisons with their household slaves and other people; but after baptism, she became sober, refused to participate in such acts, and wanted to divorce him. Her friends persuaded her to stay with him, hoping for a reconciliation, and, Justin says, "she violated her own feeling and remained with him." But when she heard that her husband, on a trip to Alexandria, had behaved worse than ever, she demanded a divorce and left him. Her husband denounced her to the authorities as a Christian, and although she succeeded in delaying her own trial by appealing to the emperor, her husband turned in fury against Porphyry, her teacher in Christianity, and had him and several others summarily arrested and executed.[37]

Alarmed and distressed by this judgment, Justin wrote a second letter of protest, this time addressing himself to the "sacred Senate."[38] Sometime later Justin himself was accused, arrested, and interrogated. Rusticus, prefect of Rome, ordered Justin and those of his students who were arrested with him to "obey the gods and submit to the rulers." When he was offered acquittal from the death penalty if he sacrificed to the gods, Justin defiantly refused: "No person in his right mind turns from piety to impiety." Rusticus again warned the accused of the consequences, and then, finding them adamant, pronounced sentence:

> Let those who have refused to sacrifice to the gods and obey the commands of the emperors be beaten and led away to suffer the punishment of beheading, in accordance to the laws.[39]

Having lost their case in the Roman court, Justin and his companions walked toward the flagellation cell, consoling themselves that they had nonetheless won the decisive battle; they were triumphing over the demons, who wielded terror—fear of pain and death—as their ultimate weapon.

Had the rulers whom Justin addressed actually read his petitions (it is more likely that an imperial secretary deposited them in a government archive), they would have regarded Justin's vision of the spiritual world with contempt.[40] Marcus Aurelius, well known from the writings preserved in his private journal, probably would have detested Justin's "Christian philosophy" as obscenely grandiose—the opposite of what Marcus regarded as the hard-won truths he himself had gained from philosophy.[41] Marcus, revered during his reign as master of the civilized world (c. 161–180), valued more than his imperial wealth and honors the religious philosophy that helped him bear his responsibilities and sustained him through loneliness, disappointment, and grief. In his daily round of duties, Marcus constantly invoked philosophic reflection to remind himself that he, like everyone else, was subject to the forces that rule the universe.

Marcus was raised by his father, the emperor Antoninus Pius, to rule. Reluctantly Marcus gave up philosophy, his first love, to study such practical activities as martial arts, public speaking, riding, and building a character suitable for an emperor. Marcus praises his father as his greatest model of human character, and praises the gods for all the circumstances of his life, especially for his divinely given capacity "to imagine, clearly and often, a life lived according to nature," and for the "reminders—and, almost, the instructions—of the gods," who embody the forces of nature.[42]

Although Marcus often expresses himself in the language of traditional piety, he had adapted for himself the reflections of certain Stoic teachers such as Musonius Rufus, who had reinterpreted the "old gods"—Zeus, Hera, Aphrodite, Apollo—as elements of the natural universe. In the process of demythologizing the ancient myths, Stoic philosophers tended to diminish the uncanny, capricious, and hostile qualities that the ancient poets Homer, Sappho, and Hesiod attributed to the gods.[43] Marcus had come to believe that all gods and *daimones* ("spirit beings"), however chaotic or even conflicting they appear, are actually part of a single cosmic order.[44] Alone, at night, writing in his journal, perhaps in a tent encamped with his soldiers in the alien wilderness along a tributary of the Danube or on the Hungarian plain, Marcus often expresses awe mingled with a clear sense of the vulnerability of our fragile species. Yet he believes that piety consists in willingly submitting to *nature, necessity,* and *destiny,* terms Marcus regards as interchangeable. In his mind there is no question but that we all are subject to these cosmic forces; the only question is whether we can submit ourselves to them with equanimity.

Speaking as a man trying to tame the passions of anger and grief, Marcus continually reminds himself that "death, like birth, is a mystery of nature,"[45] each necessarily complementing the other:

> Everything that happens is as ordinary and predictable as the spring rose or the summer fruit; this is as true of disease, death, slander, and conspiracy as anything else. . . . So, then, if a person has sensitivity and a deeper insight into the things that happen in the universe, virtually everything, even if it be only a by-product of something else, will contribute pleasure, being, in its own way, a harmonious part of the whole.[46]

Recalling gladiatorial fights and shows featuring people being torn to death by wild animals, Marcus reflects that a true philosopher

> will look upon the actual gaping jaws of wild animals with no less pleasure than upon artistic representations of them; and will be able to appreciate, in old people, both men and women, the quality of age, and look with tempered wisdom on the erotic beauty of the young.[47]

Marcus speaks of "the gods" as the vast universal powers through which our own individual lives are woven into the fabric of existence, into which our elements eventually will dissolve:

> The human soul is most arrogant [*hybrystes*] when it becomes, so far as it can, a kind of abscess or tumor in the universe. For to complain at anything that happens is a rebellion against nature.[48]

Acutely aware that catastrophe and good fortune "fall without discrimination on those who are good and those who are evil," Marcus struggles to make sense of this fact. Does the universe simply function chaotically, "with no design and no direction"?[49] Does honesty require us to become atheists? But he rejects the idea that life is meaningless, and says instead,

> It is not a flaw in nature, as if nature were ignorant, or powerless, or making mistakes, that good and evil things fall without discrimination upon those who are good and those who are evil.[50]

On the contrary, this indiscriminateness shows that "living and dying, reputation and disgrace, pain and pleasure, wealth and destitution, actually are neither good nor evil"; instead, all alike are simply part of "nature's work." What *does* involve good and evil, however, is how we *respond* to what nature does:

> The only thing that makes the good man unique is that he loves and welcomes whatever happened, and what has been spun for him by destiny; and . . . does not pollute the divine *daimon* within . . . harmoniously following god.[51]

Intent on transcending his own natural responses to betrayal and loss—anger, self-pity, and grief—Marcus directs his whole moral energy toward the discipline of practicing equilibrium, often returning to what the ancients called "the unbearable grief," the loss of a child. Marcus and his wife, Faustina, like so many of their contemporaries, experienced this repeatedly; eleven of the fourteen children born to them had died in infancy or childhood. During one of these crises Marcus wrote to himself, "I see that my child is ill. I see. But I do not see that he is in danger"[52]—since his philosophy insists that dying is equivalent to living. Marcus chides himself harshly for his impulse to pray, "Let my child be spared"[53]; even to long that his child live and not die, Marcus believes, is to "complain against nature." Marcus consoles himself with the words of Epictetus, one of the great Stoic masters: "When you are kissing your child, whisper under your breath, 'Tomorrow you may be dead.' " "Ominous words," others reproached Epictetus, but he replied, "Not at all, but only indicating an act of nature. Would it be ominous to speak of harvesting ripe corn?"[54] Like Epictetus, Marcus ignores the obvious objection that a child is hardly "ripe" for death's harvesting; he muses only that every one of us will fall, "like grains of incense on an altar, some sooner, some later."[55] So, he continues in his internal dialogue, instead of saying, "How unfortunate I am, that this has happened to me," one should strive to say, "How fortunate I am, that this has happened, and yet I am still unhurt, neither crushed by the present, nor terrified of the future."[56] Reflecting on reverses of fortune—emperors suddenly assassinated, slaves freed—Marcus tells himself:

> Whatever happens to you, this, for you, came from destiny; and the interweaving of causes has woven into one fabric your existence and this event.[57]

Marcus's primary article of faith, then, involves the unity of all being:

> All things are woven into one another, and the bond that unites them is sacred; and hardly anything is alien to any other. For they are ordered in relation to one another, and they join together to order the same universe. For there is one universe, consisting of all things; and one essence, and one law, one divine reason, and one truth; and . . . also one fulfillment of the living creatures that have the same origin, and share the same nature.[58]

Marcus perceives nature and destiny collapsed into one divinely charged reality and strives to accept his own lot as a matter of religious obligation. He expects no less of everyone else—certainly of anyone who aspires to philosophy.

Marcus was unique; few pagans tried to construct such a working synthesis of philosophy, ethics, and piety. Yet virtually all who worshiped the gods would have agreed that these invisible energies preside over every element of life, giving or withholding fertility, fixing at birth each person's life span, allotting health and wealth to some, and to others poverty, disease, and slavery, as well as presiding over each nation's destiny.

Many pagans, perhaps the majority, performed rituals at temple festivals, participated in feasts, and poured out sacred libations, thus revering these supernatural powers as elements of "the divine." By Marcus's time, however, many worshipers would have agreed that all the gods and *daimones,* even those apparently in conflict with one another, must be part of a unified cosmic system, whether they called it the divine, nature, providence, necessity, or fate.

Belief in the universal power of fate, which Marcus struggled to accept, aroused in others a strong impulse to resist its all-pervading power. As Hans Dieter Betz and John Gager have shown, many people visited magicians who claimed to summon certain *daimones* and to bind them, for a fee, to improve one's health, or to guarantee success in love, horse races, or business.[59] Other people sought initiation into foreign cults, hoping to find in such exotic Egyptian gods as Isis and Serapis divine power that surpassed that of all the more familiar gods and could overturn the decrees of destiny. Lucius Apuleius, who may himself have undergone rigorous initiation into the mysteries of Isis, describes his ecstatic discovery that worshiping the Egyptian goddess could break the power of fate:

> Behold, here is Lucius, who rejoices in the providence of powerful Isis. Behold, he is released from the bonds of misery, and is victorious over his fate.[60]

Although many pagans had come to believe that all the powers of the universe are ultimately one, only Jews and Christians worshiped a single god and denounced all others as evil demons. Only Christians divided the supernatural world into two opposing camps, the one true God against swarms of demons; and none but Christians preached—and practiced—division on earth.[61] By refusing to worship the gods, Christians were driving a wedge between themselves and all pagans, between divine sanctions and Roman government—a fact immediately recognized by Rusticus, Marcus's teacher in Stoicism and his personal friend, who, in his public role as prefect of Rome, personally judged and sentenced Justin and his students to death.

After Justin's beheading, his young student Tatian, a zealous young Syrian convert, wrote a blistering "Address to the Greeks," which begins by attacking Greek philosophy and religion, and ends by denouncing Roman government and law. Tatian wants to show "the Greeks"—which Tatian takes to mean "pagans"—their demonically induced delusions. He asks the crucial question:

> For what reason, O pagans, do you wish to set the governmental powers against us, as in a wrestling match?[62]

Then he declares his spiritual independence:

> If I do not wish to comply with some of your customs, why am I hated, as if I were despicable? Does the governor order me to pay taxes? I do so willingly. Does he order me to do service? I acknowledge my servitude. For one must honor human beings in a way appropriate to humans; but one must fear God alone—he who is not visible to human eyes, nor perceptible by any means known to us.[63]

Tatian agrees with Justin that pagans cannot understand the violence of their own response to Christians until they begin to see that all the supernatural powers they worship are evil beings who are holding them captive. All the powers they worship are nothing more than the continuing fallout of a primordial cosmic rebellion. So Tatian, like Justin, begins at the beginning: "God is spirit," he explains, creator of supernatural and human beings alike. Originally, all supernatural beings were free, but, Tatian explains, drawing on Jewish accounts of the angels' fall, "the firstborn of these rebelled against God, and became a demon . . . and those who imitate him . . . and his illusions, become an army of demons."[64] This swarm of demons, enraged when punished for their apostasy, are nevertheless too weak to retaliate against God: "No doubt, if they could, they undoubtedly would pull down the very heavens themselves, together with the rest of creation."[65] Restrained from totally destroying the universe, they turned all their energies toward enslaving humanity. "Inspired by hostile malice toward humankind," they terrify people by images they send in dreams and fantasies. Tatian does not deny that these "gods" actually possess powers; he says they use their power to gain control over human minds. Nor do demons prey only upon the illiterate and superstitious. Philosophical sophisticates like Marcus Aurelius are no less vulnerable than the local shoemaker, for, as Marcus's own philosophy might show, *daimones* can turn philosophy itself into a means of subjugating people to their tyranny. Tatian ridicules the philosophers, calling Aristotle "absurd" for his famous statement that a human being is a mere "rational animal" (*logikon zoon*), part of the natural order.[66] Even elephants and ants, Tatian says, are "rational animals" in the sense that they "participate in the instinctive and rational nature of the universe," but to be human means much more. It means that one participates in *spirit*, having been created in the image of the God who is spirit.[67]

Deriding the philosophers, Tatian adamantly refuses to see himself as merely part of nature. Since baptism, Tatian says, his own sense of self has had virtually nothing to do with nature; "having been born again," he now identifies with the God who stands beyond nature. Tatian perceives his essential being as spirit, ultimately indestructible:

> Even if fire should annihilate my flesh, and the universe disperse its matter, and, although dispersed in rivers and seas, or torn apart by wild animals, I am laid up in the storehouse of a wealthy master . . . and God the king, when he pleases, will restore the matter that is visible to him alone to its primordial order.[68]

The power of destiny is not divine, as Marcus imagines, but merely a demonic conspiracy; for it was *daimones,* Tatian caustically explains, the offspring of fallen angels, who, having shown humans a map of the position of the stars, *invented destiny—an enormous injustice!* For those who judge and those who are judged are made so by destiny; the murderers and their victims, the wealthy and the destitute, are the offspring of the same destiny; and every human birth is regarded as a kind of theatrical entertainment by those beings of whom Homer says, "among the gods arouse unquenchable laughter" (emphasis added).[69]

Like the spectators who flock to the city amphitheater to amuse themselves, making bets while watching some gladiators win and others die in agony, so, Tatian says, the gods entertain themselves with human triumphs and tragedies. But those who revere the gods ignorantly "attribute events and situations to destiny, believing that each person's destiny is formed from birth"; and they "cast horoscopes and pay for oracles and divination" to find out what destiny has in store.

Tatian ridicules such superstitious people for failing to see that disease and other sufferings happen simply because of elements intrinsic to our physical constitution: surprisingly, he *secularizes* disease, accident, and death, removing them from the supernatural. Although everyone is vulnerable to these contingencies, Tatian says, they hold no real power over people who belong to God, since baptism breaks the bonds that once bound us to *destiny* and to *nature*. Now, he says,

> we are superior to destiny, and instead of worshiping planets and *daimones,* we have come to know one Lord. . . . We do not follow the guidance of destiny; rather, we reject those [*daimones*] who established it.[70]

Tatian refuses to acknowledge any subjection to nature and refuses to submit to the demands of the culture and society into which physical birth delivered him:

> I do not want to be a ruler; I am not anxious to be rich; I decline military command; I detest sexual promiscuity; I am

not impelled by any insatiable love of money to go to sea; I do not contend for reputation; I am free from an insane thirst for fame; I despise death; I am superior to every form of disease; grief does not consume my soul. If I am a slave, I endure slavery; if I am free, I do not boast of my fortunate birth. . . . Why are you "destined" so often to grasp for things, and often to die? Die to the world, repudiating the insanity that pervades it. Live to God, and by apprehending God, apprehend your own nature as a spiritual being created in his image.[71]

Tatian rails against nature and culture—polemics that articulate the suspicion of both that will be woven into Christian theology for nearly two thousand years. The kind of attack Tatian launched would eventually transform Western attitudes toward Greek civilization. Classical civilization would become for Western Christendom virtually synonymous with paganism.[72] Like Justin, Tatian protests pagan indifference to human life:

I see people who actually sell themselves to be killed; the destitute sells himself, and the rich man buys someone to kill him; and for this the spectators take their seats, and the fighters meet in single-handed combat for no reason whatever; and no one comes down from the stands to help! . . . Just as you slaughter animals to eat their flesh, so you purchase people to supply a cannibal banquet for the soul, nourishing it with the most impious bloodshed. Robbers commit murder for the sake of loot; but the rich man buys gladiators to watch them being killed![73]

Tatian does not exaggerate here. The French scholar Georges Villes reports that spectators at the Roman amphitheater might watch as many as three hundred and fifty gladiators die before their eyes at a single day's entertainment.[74]

Declaring himself free from all worldly affiliations, Tatian openly defies pagan rulers: "I reject your legislation, along with your entire system of government." Only allegiance to the one true God "can put an end to the slavery that is in the world, and restore us from many rulers, and then from ten thousand tyrants"—freeing the believer from innumerable demonic tyrants and simultaneously from all the thousands of human rulers whom they secretly control.[75]

We know almost nothing about Tatian's life or what this conviction meant for him in practice; but we do know what it meant to the young Egyptian Christian named Origen, who was seventeen years old when he saw his beloved Christian father, Leonides, arrested and summarily executed for refusing to sacrifice to the gods. Thereafter Origen, later nicknamed Adamantius ("the adamant," or "the indomitable"), resolved to be a warrior on God's side against the forces of Satan. From childhood, as we shall see, Origen witnessed bitter conflict—and then the most astounding series of shifts and reverses—in the relationship between Christians and imperial power. He remained wary of those in power all his life. Though he believed that Christians benefited from the peace the Roman empire provided, he became the first Christian to argue publicly that people have an innate moral right to assassinate tyrants.

Born in the year 185 to a Roman father and an Egyptian mother, both baptized Christians, Origen was seven years old when the reigning emperor, Lucius Commodus, the sole surviving son of Marcus Aurelius, was murdered in his bath.[76] Rumor blamed a palace conspiracy involving Commodus's athletic trainer and Marcia, his concubine; but masses of people, hearing that the emperor was dead, poured into the streets to celebrate, for Commodus had rebelled against everything his distinguished father stood for. By the time he was strangled, Commodus was widely despised as a madman and a tyrant; he had shocked his constituents by pretending to be a gladiator, engaging in public combats in the arena, effectively abdicating his imperial responsibilities by playing the role of a slave. He had also neglected to persecute Christians: Marcia apparently favored Christians and had encouraged Commodus to leave them alone.

The battles of succession lasted three years. Septimius Severus emerged as victor, and seven years later, in 202 C.E., initiated new measures to purge his empire of Christians. It was then that Origen saw his father arrested along with others, charged with professing Christianity, and sentenced to beheading; apparently he was protected by Roman citizenship, as Justin had been, from slow torture and public execution.

While Leonides was in prison, Origen impulsively tried to join the group of martyrs and escaped death, it was said, only because his mother hid his clothes so that he could not leave the house. But Origen passionately urged his father not to lose heart out of concern for his wife and their seven children: "Be careful not to change your mind because of us."[77] His father stood firm; but his execution left the family destitute, since the state confiscated his property as that of a condemned criminal. Origen never forgot that imperial forces, however benign they later seemed to many Christians, might at any moment show their demonic origins.

Origen was rescued from destitution by the generosity of a rich Christian, who invited him into her household and supported him for several months while he continued studying literature and philosophy. The following year, already recognized, at the age of eighteen, for his brilliance and learning, Origen began to teach on his own, supporting himself, his mother, and her six younger children. The persecution that had cost Leonides his life continued in Alexandria under several changes of administration; several of Origen's own students were arrested and executed for professing Christianity, and he himself lived under suspicion. More than once, angry crowds threatened his life, especially when he ignored fears for his own safety and publicly embraced a condemned friend, a man named Plutarch, and attended his execution. So far, Origen himself escaped arrest and interrogation, probably because Severus's persecution had targeted upper-class converts, especially Roman citizens, like Origen's father and many of his students. Origen was protected, apparently, by having inherited from his Egyptian mother the low status Roman law accorded to native noncitizens.

When Origen was twenty-six, and still teaching, writing, and interpreting the Scriptures, Septimius Severus died and was succeeded by two sons, one of whom, Caracalla, promptly assassinated his brother Geta but left the Christians alone. For the moment the government seemed almost benign. One day in 215, during Caracalla's reign, soldiers arrived in Alexandria with a letter from the governor of Arabia (present-day Jordan), summoning Origen to appear at the palace. The governor had heard of Origen's brilliance and wanted to meet the young man; and Origen agreed. But after Caracalla had ruled for six years, he was assassinated by Macrinus, who reigned for only a year before he, too, was killed. He was succeeded by Heliogabalus, Caracalla's cousin, a reclusive, fanatical young worshiper of the sun god, a man whom many people regarded as insane.

Four years later, another cousin, Alexander Severus, replaced Heliogabalus on the throne, and now, for the first time in Roman history, members of the imperial house not only tolerated Christians but even favored them. Severus's mother, the empress Julia Mammea, who gathered many distinguished people at her court, sent soldiers to invite Origen to join them; when he arrived, she discussed with him, among other things, the possibility of reconciling Christians to Roman civilization. Christians of the time would have been astonished to hear a rumor circulating in the empire—whether true or not—that the emperor himself had set up statues of Abraham and Jesus along with those of Socrates and other holy men in his private palace sanctuary!

Hopes for a new age of tolerance were shattered, however, when Maximinus, a rough peasant from Thrace, assassinated Severus, took over the throne, and immediately renewed the persecution of the Christians. Origen followed with great concern the threatened arrest of several of his close friends and associates, including Ambrose, his rich and influential patron and friend, and the priest Protoctetus. Origen, who was not arrested, wrote to them in a passionate "exhortation to martyrdom," warning them not to waver, nor to be deceived by apparently genuine pleas to renounce their faith in order to save their lives. To give in, he said, would be to capitulate to Satan; for those arrested for Christ's sake, only death brings victory.[78]

In the struggle for the throne that followed Maximinus' death, the young emperor Gordian III prevailed, and he, too, left Christians alone. Assassinated by his own soldiers after ruling for four years, he was succeeded by his own chief general. The newly acclaimed emperor, Philip, the first Arab to achieve that position, immediately secured his rule by killing Gordian's young son.

Philip the Arabian may have been the first Christian emperor. At least three witnesses attest that he performed public penance for that murder in view of the astonished congregation, during the huge gatherings that attended the Easter vigil the following spring—penance imposed on the emperor by the Christian bishop of Antioch. During Philip's reign, thousands of new converts filled the churches. Now Origen complained in a sermon that conversion had become so common and even fashionable that it was no longer dangerous.

But Origen's suspicions of government power were confirmed when Decius killed Philip, seized power, and initiated a new and more aggressive persecution of Christians. This time, however, Origen, now in his mid-sixties and more renowned than ever, was arrested and brutally tortured; the governor hoped to gain a useful recantation from his most famous prisoner, but the attempt failed.

Origen knew that pagan opposition to Christianity was often based on more than superstition and prejudice. Years before his arrest, Origen had read a tract, "The True Word," which charged that Christian "atheism" masked a rebellion against everything society and government upheld. Only a few years before his arrest, Origen had decided to respond to these charges, for this was one of the most incisive and devastating attacks on Christians ever written.[79]

Celsus, who wrote the tract around 180 C.E., was a religiously inclined Platonic philosopher. He begins by charging that "the cult of Christians is a secret society, whose members hide together in corners for fear of being brought to trial and punishment." Citing their refusal of the magistrates' orders to sacrifice to the gods, Celsus says that if everyone adopted the Christians' attitude, there would be no rule of law.[80] Celsus lived at a time when the Christian movement was growing rapidly, especially among the illiterate. He writes that the Christians' refusal to obey certain laws and to cooperate with local or imperial officials threatens to "destroy legitimate authority, and return the world to chaos and barbarians"—even to "bring down the empire, and the emperor with it."

Origen's defiant reply opens by challenging the moral legitimacy of imperial rule:

> It is not irrational to form associations contrary to the existing laws, if it is done for the sake of the truth. For just as those people would do well who enter a secret association in order to kill a tyrant who had seized the liberties of a state, so Christians also, when tyrannized . . . by the devil, form associations contrary to the devil's laws, against his power, to protect those whom they succeed in persuading to revolt against a government which is barbaric and despotic.[81]

Origen stops short of identifying imperial law directly with the devil, and elsewhere he even praises the pax Romana for having providentially kept the peace during Jesus' lifetime. Nevertheless Origen characterizes as demon-inspired all laws and persons hostile to Christians. Christians, however, will triumph over their enemies; Jesus died, he explains, "to destroy a great *daimon*—in fact, the ruler of *daimones,* who held in subjection the souls of humanity."[82] Whoever considers empirical evidence will have to admit, he says, that the spread of Christianity, although unanimously opposed by human authorities, governmental and military, proves that some enormous, previously unknown power is now at work in the world:

> Anyone who examines the matter will see that Jesus attempted and successfully accomplished works beyond the range of human capacity. For everything opposed the spread of his teaching in the world—including the rulers in each period, and their chief military leaders and generals, everyone—everyone, to speak generally—who possessed even the slightest influence,

and in addition to these, the rulers of all the various cities, and the armies, and the people.[83]

Origen admits that the astounding success of the Christian movement has occurred principally among the poor and illiterate, but only because "the illiterate necessarily outnumber the educated." Yet "some persons of intelligence and education"— he might have mentioned Justin, Tatian, even himself—have committed their lives to the Christian faith. So, against all odds, Origen continues,

> our Jesus, despised for being born in a rural village—not even a Greek [that is, civilized] one, nor belonging to any nation widely respected; and being despised as the son of a poor laboring woman, [nevertheless] has been able to shake the whole civilized world.[84]

Jesus' impact surpasses that of "even Pythagoras or Plato, let alone that of any ruler or military leader in the world."

Astonishing turns of events in world history offer empirical proof that God's spirit, acting in Jesus, is conquering Satan. Origen agrees with Matthew and Luke that

> one fact which proves that Jesus is something divine and sacred is this: that the Jews have suffered because of him for a very long time such terrible catastrophes. . . . For what nation is exiled from its own capital city, and from the place sacred to the worship of its ancestors, except the Jews alone? . . . It was fitting, then, that the city where Jesus underwent sufferings should utterly perish, and the Jewish nation be overthrown. . . . And we can say with confidence it never will be restored to its former condition.[85]

If the suffering of the Jews proves that God is punishing them, what does that say about the suffering of Christians? And what about those innocent people who suffer disease, catastrophe, or human brutality? Here Origen chooses to be inconsistent. Such difficult problems, he says, are insoluble, "matters of deepest and most inexplicable insight into the whole administration of the universe."[86] Unlike many later Christians, Origen refuses to attribute the sufferings of the innocent simply to "God's will," for, he says, "not everything that happens happens according to God's will, or according to divine providence." Some things, he says, are "accidental by-products" of the works of providence; others occur when human beings—and, for that matter, supernatural beings as well—violate the divinely ordered administration of the universe and intentionally inflict harm. Many instances of human evil, as well as certain seemingly gratuitous natural catastrophes, like floods, volcanoes, and earthquakes, are instigated by "evil *daimones* and evil angels."[87]

Celsus would have found such suggestions profoundly disturbing, for as a Platonist philosopher he claims to revere "the one god who rules over all." Here the pagan Celsus argues for monotheism against what he sees—quite accurately—as the Christians' practical dualism:

> If one accepts that all of nature, and everything in the universe, operates according to the will of God, and that nothing works contrary to his purposes, then one must also accept that the angels and *daimones,* heroes—all things in the universe—are subject to the will of the one God who rules over all.[88]

Celsus urges Christians, too, to worship the one God and to revere everything that providence brings as manifestations of his goodness.

In advocating such monotheism, Celsus agrees not only with other philosophically minded intellectuals like Marcus Aurelius, but also with millions of people all over the empire—the vast majority of them illiterate—who worshiped the gods. The hymns that they heard intoned at the temples of Isis, the liturgies celebrated at the great altars of Serapis, the incantations chanted during processions honoring Helios or Zeus, and the prayers intoned at the festivals of Hecateten often identified the particular deity they had come to worship with the whole of the divine being. By the time of Marcus Aurelius, the classicist Ramsay MacMullen says, many took for granted the unity of all the gods and *daimones* in one divine source.[89]

What divided pagans from Christians, then, was not so much monotheism, since many pagans also tended toward monotheism, as the pagans' essential conservatism. Pagan worship binds one to one's place in the world, and asks the worshiper to fulfill whatever obligations destiny, fate, or "the gods" have decreed. As we have seen, Marcus continually reminds himself that piety means taking a reverent attitude toward his familial, social, and national responsibilities. Musing on whether the gods concern themselves with individual destiny, Marcus declares:

> If the gods took counsel together about me, then their counsel was good . . . and even if they have no special thought for me, at least they took thought for the universe; and I ought to welcome and accept everything that happens as a result. And even if the gods care nothing for human concerns, my own nature is a rational and political one; I have a city, and I have a country; as Marcus I have Rome, and as a human being I have the universe; consequently, whatever benefits these communities is the only good I recognize.[90]

We have seen how hard Marcus struggled to accept his obligations, aware as he was of his privileges and responsibilities, but many of his contemporaries found less incentive to do so. As the empire continued to expand and pressures of inflation and war increased, the advantages Roman citizenship had offered to millions of people diminished; furthermore, an increasing number of people found themselves excluded from its benefits while being enormously burdened by taxes and conscription. Emperor Caracalla, in 213, issued an edict that extended citizenship to all inhabitants of the empire, but what actual effect this had is difficult to determine.

The Christian movement offered a radical alternative—perhaps the only genuine alternative besides Judaism in the Roman empire. What the Roman senator Tacitus complained of in the Jews was doubly true of these breakaway sectarians:

> The first thing they do when they get hold of people is to teach them to despise their gods, neglect their cities, and hate their families; everything that we know as piety they neglect.[91]

We have seen that Christians did teach converts not only that the bonds of family, society, and nation are not sacred, but that they are diabolic encumbrances designed to enslave people to "Roman customs," that is, to demons.

What makes the Christians' message dangerous, Celsus writes, is not that they believe in one God, but that they deviate from monotheism by their "blasphemous" belief in the devil. For all the "impious errors" the Christians commit, Celsus says, they show their greatest ignorance in "making up a being opposed to God, and calling him 'devil,' or, in the Hebrew language, 'Satan.' " All such ideas, Celsus declares, are nothing but human inventions, sacrilegious even to repeat: "it is blasphemy . . . to say that the greatest God . . . has an adversary who constrains his capacity to do good." Celsus is outraged that the Christians, who claim to worship one God, "impiously divide the kingdom of God, creating a rebellion in it, as if there were opposing factions within the divine, including one that is hostile to God!"[92]

Celsus accuses Christians of "inventing a rebellion" (*stasis*, meaning "sedition") in heaven to justify rebellion here on earth. He accuses them of making a "statement of rebellion" by refusing to worship the gods—but, he says, such rebellion is to be expected "of those who have cut themselves off from the rest of civilization. For in saying this, they are really projecting their own feelings onto God."[93] Celsus ridicules Paul's warning that Christians must not eat food offered to the gods, lest they "participate in communion with *daimones*" (1 Cor. 10:20–22). Since *daimones* are the forces that energize all natural processes, Celsus argues, Christians really cannot eat anything at all—or even survive—without participating in communion with *daimones*. Celsus declares that

> whenever they eat bread, or drink wine, or touch fruit, do they not receive these things—as well as the water they drink and the air they breathe—from certain various elements of nature?[94]

Therefore, he adds,

> we must either not live, and indeed, not come into this life at
> all, or we must do so on condition that we give thanks and
> offerings and prayers to *daimones* who have been set over the
> administration of the universe; and we must do so as long as we
> live, so that they may be well disposed toward us.[95]

Celsus warns Christians that just as human administrators,
whether Roman or Persian, take action against subjects who
despise their rule, so these ruling *daimones* will surely punish
those who prove insubordinate. Celsus ironically agrees, then,
with Christians who complain that the *daimones* instigate persecution; he argues that they have good reason to do so:

> Don't you see, my excellent sir, that anyone who "witnesses"
> to your [Jesus] not only blasphemes him, and banishes him
> from every city, but that you yourself, who are, as it were, an
> image dedicated to him, are arrested and led to punishment,
> and bound to a stake, while he whom you call "Son of God"
> takes no vengeance at all upon the evildoer?[96]

Origen admits that this is true and concedes that at such
moments one might imagine that the evil powers have won. "It
is true," he says, "that the souls of those who condemn Christians, and those who betray them and enjoy persecuting them,
are filled with evil," being driven on by *daimones*.[97] Yet for martyrs, suffering and death are not the catastrophic defeat they
seem. On the contrary,

> when the souls of those who die for the Christian faith depart
> from the body with great glory, they destroy the power of the
> demons, and frustrate their conspiracy against humankind.[98]

The demons themselves, perceiving this, sometimes retreat,
afraid to kill Christians, lest they thereby ensure their own
destruction. It is for this reason, Origen says, that persecution

occurs only intermittently. But when the *daimones* recover their boldness and rage again at Christians, "then again the souls of the pious will destroy the army of the evil one." The *daimones*' awareness that Christians win by dying manifests itself, Origen declares, in the attitudes and actions of human judges

> who are distressed by those who endure the outrages and tortures, but glad when a Christian is overcome [and yields]. And it is not from any philanthropic impulse that this occurs.[99]

Origen had experienced this firsthand when he was arrested at Caesarea during Decius's persecution in 251. When he refused the judge's demands to renounce his faith, Origen endured repeated torture. He was chained in a dark cell. His torturers first wrenched his limbs apart and chained him into stocks; at other times they burned him and threatened him with terrible forms of execution. One of his grieved companions, moved by the old man's courage, writes that Origen's ordeal ended only after "the judge had tried him every way at all costs to avoid sentencing him to death,"[100] not out of compassion, but hoping to get him to publicly recant his faith. Failing this, the judge released him; but the torture and exposure Origen suffered in prison hastened his death.

Celsus warns that the "insanity" that impels Christians to "refuse their religious obligations, and rush headlong to offend the emperor and governors,"[101] actually may ruin the empire, eclipse the rule of law, and plunge the world into anarchy. Celsus demands that Christians do instead what all pious and patriotic citizens should,

> namely, help the emperor in his effort to provide for the common good, and cooperate with him in what is right, and fight for him, if it becomes necessary.[102]

Origen dismisses such suggestions with contempt. He answers that Christians *do* help the emperor through their prayers, which "conquer all *daimones* who stir up war and . . . disturb the peace . . . so, although we do not believe in being fellow soldiers with him, we do fight on behalf of the emperor."[103] (Tertullian, writing in North Africa, declares that many Christians *do* serve in the army; such practices varied, apparently, from one circumstance to another.)[104] As for taking public office, Origen says, "we recognize in every land the existence of another national organization"—God's church. Origen knows that he is fighting over souls to help diminish the power of Satan; and he ends his polemic against Celsus by saluting his patron Ambrose, who ten years earlier had stood trial and endured prison and torture.

Persecuted Christians like Origen forged a radical tradition that undermined religious sanction for the state, claiming it instead for the religious conscience—a tradition that would enormously influence subsequent Western government and politics. Baptism opened access to vast new dimensions of reality—to the Kingdom of God, where God's people find their true home, and to the dominion of Satan, perceived as the ultimate moral reality underlying "this present evil age." Although unbelievers like Celsus ridiculed Christians for believing absurd and childish fantasies, many converts found in their vision of God's kingdom a place to stand, and new perspectives on the world into which they had been born.

This does not mean that Christians were the seditious conspirators that Celsus imagined. Justin and others staunchly insisted that most Christians were good citizens, most of whom, no doubt, wanted to avoid confrontation with the authorities, and attempted to follow the precepts expressed in New Testament letters like First Peter, which translates into Christian terms ancient conventions of civic virtue:

> For the sake of the Lord, accept the authority of every human institution, whether of the emperor, as supreme, or of governors, as those sent by him to punish those who do wrong and praise those who do not. . . . As slaves of God, live as free people. . . . Honor all people. Love the brotherhood. Fear God. Honor the emperor (1 Pet. 2:13–16).

What *was* revolutionary, however, was that Christians professed primary allegiance to God. Such allegiance could divide one's loyalties; it challenged each believer to do something most pagans had never considered doing—decide for oneself which family and civic obligations to accept, and which to reject.

Tertullian, for example, who lived in a world where what we call freedom of religion was alien or unknown, nevertheless claims such liberty for himself and censures the emperors for "taking away religious liberty [*libertatem religionis*] so that I may no longer worship according to my inclination, but am compelled to worship against it."[105] Origen, as we have noted, defending Christians against charges of illegality, dares argue that people constrained by an evil government are right not only to disobey its laws but even to revolt and to assassinate tyrannical rulers:

> It is not irrational to form associations contrary to the existing laws, if it is done for the sake of the truth. For just as those people would do well who enter a secret association in order to kill a tyrant who had seized the liberties of a state, so Christians also, when tyrannized . . . by the devil, form associations contrary to the devil's laws, against his power, to protect those whom they succeed in persuading to revolt against a government which is barbaric and despotic.[106]

Such convictions did not arise from a sense of the "rights of the individual," a conception that emerged only fifteen hundred years later with the Enlightenment. Instead they are rooted in the sense of being God's people, enrolled by baptism as "citizens in heaven," no longer subject merely to "the rulers of this present evil age," the human authorities and the demonic forces that often control them.

A hundred years after the gospels were written, then, Christians adapted to the circumstances of pagan persecution the political and religious model they found in those gospels—God's people against Satan's people—and identified themselves as allies of God, acting against Roman magistrates and pagan mobs, whom they see as agents of Satan. At the same time, as we shall see in the next chapter, church leaders troubled by dissidents *within* the Christian movement discerned the presence of Satan infiltrating among the most intimate enemies of all—other Christians, or, as they called them, heretics.

THE ENEMY WITHIN:
DEMONIZING THE HERETICS

During the second century Christianity's success in attracting converts raised new questions about what "being a Christian" required. Within provincial cities throughout the empire, Christian groups gained many thousands of new converts. Especially in the cities, conversion aroused conflict within households. When heads of wealthy households converted, they often required their families and slaves to accept baptism. More often, however, conversions occurred among the women of the household, as well as among merchants, traders, soldiers, and the hundreds of thousands of slaves serving in every capacity in Roman apartments, great houses, and palaces. Conversions may even have happened within the emperor's household. Tertullian, writing in the city of Carthage in North Africa (c. 180) boasts to his pagan contemporaries that "we are only of yesterday, and we have filled every place among you: city, islands, fortresses, towns, market places, the army camp, tribes, palace, senate, and forum."[1]

All converts understood, of course, that baptism washes away sins and expels evil spirits, and conveys to the recipient the spirit of God, the spirit that transforms a sinner into an ally of Christ and his angels. But then what? What does a Christian have to do to stand "on the side of the angels" in this world? What precisely is required if, for example, the baptized Christian is married to a pagan, or is a soldier, who has sworn allegiance to the emperor, or is a slave? Most pagans regarded the baptism of a family member or a slave as a calamity portending disruption within the household. Tertullian himself describes how pagans ostracized converts:

> The husband casts the wife out of his house; the father disinherits the son; the master, once gentle, now commands the slave out of his sight; it is a huge offense for anyone to be called by that detested name [Christian].[2]

Among themselves, Christians debated whether converts should maintain ordinary social and familial relationships or break them, as Jesus in the gospels required when he said, "Whoever does not hate his father and mother, wife and children, brothers and sisters, yes, even life itself, cannot be my disciple" (Luke 14:26). Such questions evoked many different answers as the movement increased in size and diversity throughout the empire. Sometimes in one city there were several groups, each interpreting "the gospel" somewhat differently and often contending against one another with all the vehemence ordinarily reserved for family quarrels. The apostle Paul himself, confronted two generations earlier by rival teachers, tried to prevent them from speaking, calling them Satan's servants,

> false apostles, deceptive workers, disguising themselves as apostles of Christ. And no wonder! Even Satan himself disguises himself as an angel of light. So it is not strange if his servants disguise themselves as servants of righteousness (2 Cor. 11:13–15).

"But," Paul adds ominously, "in the end they will get what they deserve." Christians dreaded Satan's attacks from outside—that is, from hostile pagans—but many of them believed that even more dangerous were Satan's forays among the most intimate enemies of all—other Christians, or, as most said of those with whom they disagreed, among heretics.

Within the movement, some people began to develop systems of organization to unify Christian groups internally, and to connect them with other Christian groups throughout the Roman world. The authority all Christians acknowledged, besides that of Jesus himself, was that of the apostles Peter, traditionally revered as the first leader of Christians in Rome, and Paul, founder of churches ranging from Greece to Asia Minor. Some Christians, two or three generations after Paul, wrote letters attributed to Peter and Paul, including First Peter and the letters of Paul to Timothy. These letters, later included in the New Testament and widely believed to have been written by the apostles themselves, attempted to construct a bridge between the apostles and Christians of later generations by claiming, for example, that Paul had "laid hands" on his young convert Timothy to ordain him as "overseer" or "bishop" of the congregation as Paul's successor. These letters are meant to show that, like Timothy, bishops legitimately exercise "apostolic" authority over their congregations.

Those who wrote First Peter and First Timothy were also concerned to deflect pagan hostility to Christians by modifying some of the more strident demands the gospels attribute to Jesus. Needing codes of conduct that offered moral guidance to those who were married and engaged in ordinary society and were not prepared to reject these commitments as, according to Luke, Jesus admonishes, these authors borrowed from pagan catalogues of civic virtue to construct new, "Christian" moral codes. As New Testament scholar David Balch has shown, these letters cast Peter and Paul in the unlikely role of urging believers to emulate conventional Roman behavior.[3] So, in First Peter, "Peter" urges believers, "For the sake of the Lord, accept the authority of every human institution" (2:13), specifically that of the emperor and his government. "Peter" also insists that believers carry out essential household responsibilities; wives must "accept the authority of your husbands, even if some of them do not obey the Word" (3:1); and husbands should "honor the woman, as the weaker vessel" (3:7). Slaves are to serve their masters as if serving the Lord himself, and masters, in turn, are not to mistreat their slaves; children are to show their parents appropriate deference and obedience (2:18–22; 5:5). In First Timothy, likewise, "Paul" offers Timothy similar moral advice, which he tells the young bishop, in turn, to enjoin upon his congregation.

But not everyone accepted these codes of conduct or the leaders determined to enforce them. Around 90 C.E., a famous letter attributed to Clement, a man regarded by many as the second or third bishop of Rome, after the apostle Peter, and written to Christians in the Greek city of Corinth, the site of a church originally founded by Paul himself, shows that the community was in an uproar over a matter of leadership.[4] In this letter, Bishop Clement expresses distress that those he calls "a few rash and self-willed people"[5] are refusing to accept the superior authority of the priests who he insists are their proper leaders. Such dissidents have initiated what Clement calls a "horrible and unholy rebellion"[6] within the church. They have rejected several priests set over them; apparently they also object that distinctions between "clergy" and "laity"—between those who claim to hold positions of authority and those they now call "the people" (in Greek, *laos*)—are not only unprecedented but unacceptable among Christians.

Denying the dissidents' charge that clerical ranks are an innovation, Clement, like the author of First Timothy, insists that the apostles themselves "appointed their first converts . . . to be bishops and deacons." Clement invokes the authority of the prophet Isaiah, making a farfetched claim that in ancient times Isaiah had already endorsed the "offices" of bishop and deacon. Clement cites Isaiah 60:17 ("I will make your *overseers* peace, and your *taskmasters* righteousness"), and interprets the key terms ("bishops" and "deacons," respectively), translated into Greek, to suit his argument.

Clement also appeals to the letters of Paul to Timothy to argue that "the apostles themselves appointed their first converts as 'bishops' and 'deacons.' " Although Clement writes at about the same time as the authors of Matthew and Luke, who depict the Jewish high priests as Jesus' enemies, Clement encourages Christians to imitate the Jewish priesthood. Among Christians, as formerly among Jews, Clement says, the high priests and the subordinate priests are divinely ordained for special duties, while "the layperson is bound by the order for laypeople."[7] Clement even urges his fellow Christians to emulate the Roman army:

> Let us then serve in our army, brethren. . . . Let us consider
> those who serve as our generals. . . . Not all are prefects, nor
> tribunes, nor centurions, nor commanders, or the like, but
> each carries out in his own rank the commands of the emperor
> and of the generals.[8]

Later, Christians actually did adapt from Roman army administration the practice of organizing into districts (dioceses), each administered by a central overseer (bishop), an organizational strategy that persists to this day.

As bishop, Clement describes the dissidents' position as having arisen from arrogance and jealousy. "Even the apostles," he says, "knew that there would be strife over the title of bishop" (*1 Clement* 14:1). The remedy, Clement continues, is for everyone to "submit to the priests," accepting the penance that the priest will impose for their disobedience, "bending the knees of your hearts, and bowing to [the priests'] superiority" (*1 Clement* 17:1). Perhaps hoping that those who had refused to obey would now submit, Clement avoids associating them with Satan, as later leaders would do with more entrenched dissidents.

We do not know the outcome of this dispute; none of the opponents' responses survive. But during the second century, as such controversies plagued churches throughout the empire, church leaders who identified themselves with the proper "apostolic succession" widely copied Clement's letter and circulated it throughout the Roman world, along with several other writings they included in a collection called "the apostolic fathers of the church." We know little about the process from which this collection emerged; but we can see that the writings it includes all tend to emphasize the growing authority of the clergy and enjoin adherence to detailed and practical moral codes.

Most Christians apparently accepted, along with the emerging "canon" of the Scriptures, this second "canon" of church tradition. Several writings included in the "apostolic fathers" sought to revise and, in effect, domesticate for the new influx of converts such radical sayings of Jesus as these: "You cannot serve God and money" (Matt. 6:24); "Give to whoever asks you" (Matt. 5:42);

"Sell all that you have and give . . . the money to the poor; then come, and follow me" (Luke 18:22). Included in the "apostolic fathers," for example, is a famous Christian handbook called the *Teaching of the Twelve Apostles,* which paraphrases Jesus' primary teaching as follows: "Love God and your neighbor; and whatever you do not want done to yourself, do not do to others."[9] Weaving together sayings from the Sermon on the Mount and canny advice, the *Teaching* qualifies Jesus' categorical command "Give to everyone who asks of you" by adding, "Let your money sweat in your hand until you know to whom you are giving it."[10] The *Teaching* adapts and expands some of the Ten Commandments, declaring that "the Second Commandment of the apostles' teaching is this: 'You shall not kill; you shall not commit adultery,' " and specifying that this means in practice that "you [masc.] shall not have intercourse with young boys; you shall not commit fornication; you shall not steal; you shall not procure abortions; you shall not kill newborns."[11]

Another writing included in the "apostolic fathers," the *Letter of Barnabas,* attributes similar moral teaching to Paul's companion and fellow preacher. *Barnabas,* like the *Teaching,* invokes a traditional Jewish teaching of the "two ways"—the "way of light," consisting of a list of actions that are good, and the "way of darkness," consisting of evil actions.[12] *Barnabas* interprets the Ten Commandments for Christians as requiring at least forty specific injunctions, including warnings against "arrogance of power" and "advocating in behalf of the rich" while denying justice to the poor, as well as the same sexual sins denounced in the *Teaching:* "[male] intercourse with boys," "fornication" (which probably means extramarital sexual activity of any kind), adultery, and abortion.[13] Thus *Barnabas* outlines a moral code that would dominate Christian teaching for generations, even millennia, to come.

Barnabas sets these contrasting ways of life in the context of God's spirit contending against Satan during "the present evil time."[14] Reminding Christians that "the spirit of God has been poured out on you from the Lord,"[15] *Barnabas* urges them to exercise moral vigilance, so that "the devil may have no opportunity to enter" the church, even though "the days are evil, and the evildoer is still in power."[16] While encouraging Christians to accept a modified version of Jewish ethical attitudes and practices, *Barnabas* warns Christians not to fall into the ways of the Jews, who, he says, "transgressed because an evil angel was leading them into error."[17] The new people of God are to "shun the way of darkness" and embrace the "way of light," since "over the one is set the light-bearing angels of God, but over the other, angels of Satan."

Although most converts accepted the bishops' instructions about what Christians must—and must not—do, some, probably a minority, questioned the authority of priests and bishops and rejected such practical moralizing. Around 180 C.E., Irenaeus, claiming the authority of apostolic succession as bishop of a congregation in Lyons, wrote a massive five-volume attack on deviant Christians—whom he called heretics—attacking them as secret agents of Satan.[18] In the opening of his enormously influential work, *Against Heresies,* Irenaeus acknowledges that "error is never put forth nakedly," as blatant folly, but only "dressed out in clever and ingenious disguises."[19] There are those, Irenaeus declares, who claim to be Christians, and are taken by all to be such, who actually teach "an abyss of madness and blasphemy against Christ."[20] Such false believers "use the name of Christ Jesus [only] as a kind of lure," in order to teach doctrines inspired by Satan, "infecting the hearers with the bitter and malignant poison of the serpent, the great instigator of apostasy."[21] Irenaeus suggests that those who resist the bishops' moral teaching do so because they themselves are driven by passion; some, he warns, "yield themselves up to the lusts of the flesh with utmost greed."[22]

For nearly two thousand years, most Christians have taken Irenaeus at his word, believing that many of those he called heretics were deceptive, licentious, or both. But after many writings by these so-called heretics were discovered in Upper Egypt in 1945, near the town of Nag Hammadi, those Christians whose works the bishops suppressed could speak for themselves, virtually for the first time in history.[23] When we read their writings, we find in some of them beliefs that sound bizarre; others seem to reflect intense, inquiring minds engaged on a variety of spiritual paths. One of the most extreme is the *Testimony of Truth,* a text that raises the primary question that Christian reformers have asked throughout two millennia, from the second century gnostic teacher Valentinus through Francis of Assisi, Martin Luther, George Fox, founder of the Society of Friends, and Mary Baker Eddy: What *is* "the gospel"? What is the "true testimony" about Christ and his message? Like other would-be reformers, the anonymous author of the *Testimony of Truth* begins by addressing "those who know how to listen, not only with their ears, but with their understanding."[24] Far from endorsing licentiousness, the *Testimony* insists that Christians practice asceticism. This author writes as a guardian of the true gospel; he believes that the great majority of Christians—those who accept the kind of leadership and domesticated morality advocated by the "apostolic fathers"—have fallen into moral error. "Many have sought the truth and have not been able to find it, because they have been taken over by the 'old leaven of the Pharisees and the teachers of the law.' "[25]

Most Christians, this teacher says, unthinkingly accept the Genesis account of creation, according to which the creator "commands one to take a husband or a wife and to beget, to multiply like the sands of the sea" (Gen. 1:28; 13:16).[26] But, this teacher objects, such Christians fail to realize that the gospel stands in diametric opposition to the law: "The Son of man came forth from incorruptibility,"[27] and came into the world to end the old order and initiate the new. He called on those who belong to him to be transformed: "This is the true testimony: when a person comes to know himself and the God who presides over truth, he will be saved."[28] But coming to know God requires that one renounce everything else: "No one knows the God of truth except the one alone who renounces all the things of the world."[29] Renunciation alone enables one to put off the old, false self, riddled with fear, greed, anger, lust, and envy, and to recover one's own true self in God. The true Christian follows a path shunned by most so-called Christians; such a person, this author says, thinks about the power which flowed over the whole universe, which comes upon him . . . and he is a disciple of his mind. . . . He begins to keep silent within himself . . . he rejects for himself argument and disputation . . . he is patient with everyone, makes himself equal with everyone, and he also separates himself from them.[30]

Christians like Justin Martyr, one of the fathers of the church, shared such aspirations for self-mastery. Justin wholeheartedly admired Christians who practiced renunciation and celibacy; he even singled out for special praise a young convert in Alexandria who had petitioned Felix, the governor,

asking that permission might be given to a surgeon to castrate him. For the surgeons had said they were forbidden to do this without the governor's permission. And when Felix absolutely refused to sign such a permission, the young man remained celibate.[31]

Origen, also revered as a father of the church, had been so determined to win his struggle against passion that as a young man he had castrated himself, apparently without asking anyone's permission, least of all the governor's.

The author of the *Testimony* never mentions castration, much less endorses it, but he insists nevertheless that only those who "renounce the whole world," beginning with sexual activity and commercial transactions, ever come to know God. The majority of Christian churches, from the second century to the present, have regarded such renunciation as a counsel of perfection, achieved only by a heroic few—in orthodox churches throughout the world by monastics, and in Roman Catholic churches by all priests and bishops, as well as monks and nuns. The author of the *Testimony* goes much further than Christians like Justin or Origen, however, when he declares that renunciation is not only admirable but essential for any true Christian. He knows, of course, that the great majority of Christians believe that God created male and female and commanded all his creatures, animal and human, to "be fruitful and multiply" (Gen. 1:28). But the author of the *Testimony,* reflecting on his own alienation from the majority of "worldly" Christians, suddenly believes he understands Jesus' warning to his disciples to "beware of the leaven of the scribes and Pharisees" (Mark 8:15). Jesus' words are not to be taken literally, as if they referred only to Jewish teachers; instead, taken symbolically, they warn against *Christian* teachers like the author of *Barnabas* or the *Teaching of the Twelve Apostles,* who invoke the Scriptures to sanction ordinary life.

According to the *Testimony,* the "scribes and Pharisees" and the "blind guides" against whom Jesus warns (Matt. 23) are none other than the majority of Christians—Christians who have been tricked into worshiping not God but supernatural "rulers" who are less than divine. The author of the *Testimony* takes Jesus' warning to mean that believers must shun the influence of the "errant desire of the angels and demons"[32]—the fallen angels who fell into error through their own lust. The *Testimony* even claims that the God whom most Christians worship, the God of the Hebrew Bible, is *himself* one of the fallen angels—indeed, the chief of the fallen angels, from whose tyranny Christ came to set human beings free: for, the *Testimony* declares, "the word of the Son of man . . . separates us from the error of the angels."[33]

What *Barnabas* says of the Jews—that they have been deceived by an "evil angel"—and what the majority of Christians say about pagans—that they unwittingly worship demons spawned by fallen angels—this author says about *other Christians.* This radical teacher does what millions of disaffected Christians have done ever since: regarding the majority of Christians as apostate, he reads them into the gospels as "Pharisees and scribes" (or at least as gullible disciples, susceptible to seduction by these teachers). Fourteen hundred years later, Martin Luther, for example, would come to see his former fellow Christians—Roman Catholics—as the "Pharisees and scribes" against whom Jesus warned his disciples. While most believers see in Christ and his message the power to overcome the forces of evil in the world, some dissenting Christians ever since the second century have claimed that the gospel itself has been co-opted by the forces of evil.

But the author of the *Testimony of Truth* goes far beyond the "protesting" Christians of the Reformation and later times. Convinced that Christ's message is precisely the opposite of "the law"—that is, the Hebrew Bible—this teacher raises radical questions:

> What is the light? And what is the darkness? And who is the one who created the world? And who is God? And who are the angels? . . . And what is the governance (of the world)? And why are some lame, and some blind, and some rich, and some poor?[34]

Approaching the Genesis story with questions like these, this teacher "discovers" that it reveals truth only when one reads it in reverse, recognizing that God is actually the villain, and the serpent the holy one! This teacher points out, for example, that in Genesis 2:17, God commands Adam not to eat from the fruit of the tree in the midst of Paradise, warning that "on the day that you shall eat of it, you shall die." But the serpent tells Eve the opposite: "You will not die, for God knows that when you eat of it your eyes will be opened, and you will be like God, knowing good and evil" (3:4–5). Who, asks the *Testimony,* told the truth? When Adam and Eve obeyed the serpent, "then the eyes of both were opened, and they knew that they were naked" (3:7). They did not die "on that day," as God had warned; instead, their eyes were opened to knowledge, as the serpent had promised. But when God realized what had happened, "he cursed the serpent, and called him 'devil' " (Gen. 3:14–15).[35] Now that Adam had attained godlike knowledge, God decided to evict him from Paradise, "lest he reach out his hand and eat of the tree of life and live forever" (Gen. 3:22), attaining eternal life along with knowledge.

"What kind of god is this god? . . . Surely he has shown himself to be a malicious envier,"[36] says the author of the *Testimony.* Not only is this god jealous of his own creation, he is also ignorant and vindictive. And what of the serpent, whom God cursed and called "devil"? According to the *Testimony of Truth,* the serpent who led Adam and Eve to spiritual enlightenment is actually *Christ,* appearing in this disguise in Paradise to release Adam and Eve from "the error of the angels"[37]—that is, error induced by malevolent supernatural "rulers," who masquerade as God in this world.

Another anonymous Christian teacher whose writing was discovered at Nag Hammadi was asked by one of his students what "the great apostle" Paul meant when he warned that "our contest is not against flesh and blood, but against the rulers of the universe and the spirits of evil" (Eph. 6:12). He replied by writing a secret revelation called the *Reality of the Rulers,* which, he says, "I have sent you since you have asked about the reality of the [cosmic] rulers."[38] The teacher explains that "their chief [the God of the Hebrew Bible] is blind; because of his power and his ignorance and his arrogance, he said, . . . 'It is I who am God, and there is none apart from me.' "[39] This teacher then says:

> When he said this, he sinned against the whole place. And a voice came forth from above the realm of absolute power, saying,
> "You are wrong, Samael," that is, "God of the blind." . . .
> And he said, "If anything else exists before me, let it become visible to me!"
> And immediately Wisdom stretched forth her finger and brought light into matter. . . .
> And he said to his offspring, "It is I who am the god of the whole."
> And Life, daughter of Faith-Wisdom, cried out and said, "You are wrong, Saklas!" (that is, "fool"). She breathed into his face, and her breath became for her a fiery angel; and that angel bound him and cast him down into Tartyros below the abyss.[40]

In the universe depicted by this teacher there is no devil, and no need for one, for "the Lord"—the God of Jews and most Christians alike—himself acts as chief of the fallen angels who seduce and enslave human beings. By declaring himself to be the supreme and unique God of the universe, he "sinned against the whole," refusing to recognize himself as part of a much larger divine reality. His boasts reveal him to be only a lesser, ignorant being whose power has led him into overweening pride (*hybris*) and into destruction.

According to the *Reality of the Rulers,* it is Samael and his fellow "rulers of the darkness" (Eph. 6:12), not the true God, who formed Adam's physical body (Gen. 2:7), set him to work in Paradise "to till it and cultivate it" (Gen. 2:15), then put him to sleep and fashioned his female partner out of his rib (Gen. 2:21–22). These same rulers commanded Adam not to eat from the fruit of the Tree of Knowledge, which could open his eyes to the truth, because they jealously wanted to keep control over him. When Adam and Eve, enlightened by the feminine spiritual principle who appeared to her in the form of the serpent, defied them, the rulers cursed the woman and the snake, and expelled Adam and Eve from Paradise:

> Moreover, they threw humankind into great distraction and into a life of toil, so that humankind might be occupied with worldly affairs, and might not have the opportunity of being devoted to the holy spirit.[41]

According to the authors of such teachings, the human condition, involving work, marriage, and procreation, does not reflect divine blessing, but demonstrates enslavement to cosmic forces that want to blind human beings to their innate capacity for spiritual enlightenment. Such radical Christians believe that most people, including most Christians, have fallen prey to the rulers of darkness and so, like most Jews and pagans, remain entangled in sexual, social, and economic bondage.

There are a few, however, among whom these authors number themselves, whose eyes have been opened, who have awakened to the divine source from which human beings come and to which they belong—a source deeply hidden in ordinary experience. The prototype of the spiritually awakened person is Eve's daughter, Norea. When the "rulers" try to seduce and deceive her, Norea cries out to God and receives divine help; the angel

Eleleth (whose Hebrew name means "understanding") reveals to her how these corrupt and limited powers have come to rule over the world, and assures her that she herself belongs not to them but to the powers above—the Father of the whole, and to his emanation and "daughter," Wisdom, and to divine Life:

> You, together with your offspring, are from above; these souls have come out of the imperishable light. Thus the rulers cannot approach her because of the spirit of truth present within her; and all who know this way live deathless in the midst of dying mankind.[42]

Those who have "the spirit of truth within them" refuse to enter into marriage, business, or any other worldly entanglements, in order to remain an "undominated generation," free "to devote themselves to the holy spirit."[43]

The *Secret Book of John,* another well-known "revelation" discovered at Nag Hammadi, offers another wildly mythological reading of Genesis intended to reveal the ties that bind people to futile and unsatisfying lives. The *Secret Book* explains that after Adam was created, the chief ruler and his allies carried out a series of three assaults intended to overpower and capture the children of Adam. First the chief ruler "seduced [Eve] . . . and begot in her two sons," Cain and Abel; thus from that time "up to the present day, sexual intercourse continued, because of the chief ruler," who "planted sexual desire" in Eve. Yet because certain people still eluded his domination despite the pressures of sexual desire,[44] the chief ruler next "made a plan together with his powers" to subdue even the strongest of human spirits: the rulers "committed adultery with Wisdom, and bitter fate was begotten by them."[45] From that time on, fate proved to be the most inescapable of bonds:

> For from that fate came forth every sin and every injustice and blasphemy and oblivion and ignorance, and every harsh condition, and serious violations, and great terrors. And the whole creation was blinded, so that they might not know God, who is above all of them.[46]

Since even the invention of fate left the rulers uneasy about their control over human beings, they planned a third conspiracy. The chief ruler "sent his angels to the daughters of men"[47] (cf. Gen. 6:2) to mate and procreate with them, and to share with them and to teach them how to mine gold and silver, iron and copper. Thus the *Secret Book* depicts the misery of ordinary human life, enmeshed in labor, driven by instinctive passion, dominated by fate, spent in getting money and trying to amass wealth. By all these devices the rulers kept human beings under their control:

> and they steered the people who followed them into great distraction; the people became old without having joy; they died without having found truth, and without knowing God. . . . And thus the whole creation became enslaved to them, from the foundation of the world until now.[48]

Certain Christians who stood with the majority responded to these extremists. Tertullian, a convert in the North African city of Carthage, and a contemporary of Irenaeus (c. 180 C.E.), agreed with Irenaeus in denouncing all who deviated from the majority consensus as "heretics." Both fathers of the church insist that what characterizes the true church is unanimity—agreement in doctrine, morals, and leadership. Christians, Tertullian says, quoting Paul, should "all speak and think the very same things."[49] Whoever deviates from the consensus is, by definition, a heretic; for, as Tertullian points out, the Greek word translated "heresy" (*hairesis*) literally means "choice"; thus a "heretic" is "one who makes a choice."[50] Tertullian notes that heretics actually pride themselves on the points at which they differ from the majority, regarding these as evidence of their own deeper insight. He says sardonically,

> Wherever they have hit upon any novelty, they immediately call their presumption a "spiritual gift," since they value not unity but diversity. . . . Consequently, most often they are in a divided state themselves, being ready to say—and indeed, quite

sincerely—of certain points in their belief, "This is not so," and "I take this in a different sense," and "I do not accept that."[51]

But Tertullian insists that making choices is evil, since choice destroys group unity. To stamp out heresy, Tertullian says, church leaders must not allow people to ask questions, for it is "questions that make people heretics"[52]—above all, questions like these: Whence comes evil? Why is it permitted? And what is the origin of human beings? Tertullian wants to stop such questions and impose upon all believers the same *regula fidei*, "rule of faith," or creed. Tertullian knows that the "heretics" undoubtedly will object, saying that Jesus himself encouraged questioning, saying, "Ask, and you shall receive; seek, and you shall find; knock, and it shall be opened to you" (Matt. 7:7). But Tertullian has no patience with such people: "Where will the end of seeking be? The point of seeking is to find; the purpose in finding, to believe."[53] Now that the church can provide a direct and simple answer to all questions in its rule of faith, Tertullian says, the only excuse for continuing to seek is sheer obstinacy:

> Away with the one who is always seeking, for he never finds anything; for he is seeking where nothing can be found. Away with the one who is always knocking, for he knocks where there is no one to open; away with the one who is always asking, for he asks of one who does not hear.[54]

The true Christian, Tertullian declares, simply determines to "know nothing . . . at variance with the truth of faith." But when people "insist on our asking about the issues that concern them," Tertullian says, "we have a moral obligation to refute them. . . . They say that we must ask questions in order to discuss," Tertullian continues, "but what is there to discuss?" When the "heretics" object that Christians must discuss what the Scriptures really mean, Tertullian declares that believers must dismiss all argument over scriptural interpretation; such controversy only "has the effect of upsetting the stomach or the brain."[55] Besides, Tertullian says, such debate makes the orthodox position look weak:

If you do discuss with them, the effect on the spectators will be to make them uncertain which side is right . . . the person in doubt . . . will be confused by the fact that he sees you making no progress, while the other side is on an equal basis with you in discussion . . . and *he will go away even more uncertain about which side to find heretical. . . . For, no doubt, they, too, have things to say; they will accuse us of wrong interpretation, since they, no less than we, claim that truth is on their side* (emphasis added).[56]

Instead of admitting heretics into debates over the Scriptures, Tertullian says, "straight thinking" (the literal translation of "orthodox") Christians must simply claim the Scriptures as their own exclusive property:

> Heretics ought not to be allowed to challenge an appeal to the Scriptures, since we . . . prove that they have nothing to do with the Scriptures. For since they are heretics, they cannot be true Christians.[57]

But how do heretics come up with such ingenious and persuasive arguments from Scripture? Their inspiration comes, Tertullian says, from "the devil, of course, to whom belong the wiles that distort the truth."[58] Satan, after all, invented all the arts of spiritual warfare, including false exegesis. Paul's warning against "spiritual forces of evil in heavenly places," which the *Reality of the Rulers* turns against the biblical God and his angels, Tertullian takes in the opposite sense: Here, he says, Paul warns against the devil, who contrives false readings of the Scriptures to lead people into error.[59] In place of choices, questions, and discussions of scriptural interpretation, Tertullian prescribes unanimous acceptance of the rule of faith and, to ensure this, obedience to the proper ecclesiastical "discipline"—that is, to the priests who stand in proper succession from the apostles.[60] Tertullian's "prescriptions," if they had been enforced, might have proven effective against radical teachers like those who wrote the *Testimony of Truth*, the *Reality of the Rulers*, and the *Secret Book of John*. In any case, the groups these texts represented remained marginal among Christians; their appeal was limited to the few who were willing to heed a gospel that required one to break not only with the world but also with the Christian majority.

Others whom Tertullian and Irenaeus recognized as heretics were, however, far less radical—and, precisely for that reason, far more threatening to the emerging clerical authorities and their advocates. Prominent among them were followers of Valentinus, a Christian teacher from Egypt who had emigrated to Rome around the time Justin did, c. 140 C.E. Valentinus had no quarrel with clerical authority; in fact, if we can believe Tertullian on this point, Valentinus "expected to become a bishop himself, because he was an able man, both in genius and eloquence."[61] But Valentinus "broke with the church of the true faith,"[62] Tertullian says, because another man was made bishop instead; Tertullian, like Clement, attributes to those who challenge episcopal authority the motives of envy and frustrated ambition.

Valentinus had been baptized and had accepted the creedal statement of faith and participated in common Christian worship. But after his baptism he received a revelatory dream in which the Logos appeared to him in the form of a newborn child;[63] he took this vision as an impetus to begin his own spiritual explorations. Having heard of a teacher named Theudas who claimed to have received secret teaching from the apostle Paul himself, Valentinus eagerly learned from him all he could. Henceforth he became a teacher himself, amplifying what he had learned from Theudas with his own spiritual explorations, and encouraging his students to develop their inner capacity for spiritual understanding.

Valentinus intended to steer a middle course between two extremes—between those who claimed that the faith of the majority was the only true faith, and those, like the authors of parts of the *Testimony of Truth* and the *Reality of the Rulers,* who rejected it as false and debased. While he took for granted that accepting baptism and professing the common faith in God and Christ were necessary for those making a beginning in the faith, he urged his fellow believers to go beyond what Christian preachers taught and beyond the literal interpretation of the Scriptures to question the gospels' deeper meaning. By so doing, he believed, one could progress beyond faith to understanding, that is, to *gnosis*. This word is often translated "knowledge," but the translation is somewhat misleading, since *gnosis* differs from intellectual knowledge (as in phrases like "they *know* mathematics"), which is characterized in Greek by the word *eidein* (from which we derive the English word *idea*). English is unusual within its language group in having only one verb ("to know") to express different kinds of knowing. Modern European languages use one word to characterize intellectual knowledge and another for the knowledge of personal relationships: French, for example, distinguishes between *savoir* and *connaître,* Spanish between *saber* and *conocer,* Italian between *sapere* and *conoscere,* German between *wissen* and *kennen*. The Greek word *gignōsko,* from which *gnosis* derives, refers to the knowledge of personal relationships (as in "We *know* Christ" or, in the words of the Delphi oracle, "Know thyself"). The term might better be translated "insight," or "wisdom." One gnostic teacher encourages his students to seek *gnosis* within themselves:

> Abandon the search for God, and creation, and similar things of that kind. Instead, take yourself as the starting place. Ask who it is within you who makes everything his own saying, "my mind," "my heart," "my God." Learn the sources of love, joy, hate, and desire. . . . If you carefully examine all these things, you will find [God] in yourself.[64]

Another teacher says that *gnosis* reveals "who we were, and who we have become; where we are going; whence we have come; what birth is, and what is rebirth."[65] What the gnostic Christian finally comes to "know" is that the gospel of Christ can be perceived on a level deeper than the one shared by all Christians. One who takes the path of *gnosis* discovers that the gospel is more than a message about repentance and forgiveness of sins; it becomes a path of spiritual awakening, through which one discovers the divine within. The secret of *gnosis* is that when one comes to know oneself at the deepest level, one comes to know God as the source of one's being.

The author of the *Gospel of Philip,* a follower of Valentinus, describes *gnosis* as a natural progression from faith. Just as a harvest is gathered through the cooperative interaction of the natural elements, water, earth, wind, and light, so, *Philip* says,

> God's farming has four elements—faith, hope, love, and *gnosis.* Faith is our earth, in which we take root. And hope is the water through which we are raised; love is the wind through which we grow. *Gnosis,* then, is the light through which we ripen [or: "become mature"].[66]

Unlike the radical Christians of the *Reality of the Rulers* or the *Secret Book of John,* Valentinus and his followers did not reject the moral injunctions taught by priests and bishops; they did not despise or invert the Hebrew Bible, nor did they openly deny the authority of priests and bishops. Instead they accepted all these, but with a crucial qualification: they accepted the moral, ecclesiastical, and scriptural consensus as binding upon the majority of Christians, but not upon those who had gone beyond mere faith to *gnosis*—those who had become spiritually "mature."

Valentinus and his followers also accepted as necessary for beginners the moral order that the bishops enjoined, prescribing good works and proscribing bad ones. But Valentinus and his followers saw in the churches two different types of Christian.[67] Most Christians they call "ecclesiastic," or "psychic," Christians (that is, those who function on the level of *psyche,* or soul); "and they say," Irenaeus protests indignantly, "that we of the church are such persons."[68] But those who come to accept a second, secret initiation called "redemption" henceforth regard themselves as mature, "spiritual" Christians, who have advanced from mere faith toward spiritual understanding, or *gnosis.*

Because Valentinus and his followers publicly accepted baptism, attended common worship, and pronounced the same creed, most Christians considered them to be completely innocuous fellow believers, and they themselves insisted that this is what they were. But within a generation of Valentinus's teaching in Rome, the movement had won a considerable following throughout the Christian world, especially among the more educated members of the church. Tertullian complains that often it is "the most faithful, the most prudent, and the most experienced" church members "who have gone over to the other side."[69] Irenaeus, to his dismay, found Valentinian teachers active among members of his own congregation in Lyons, inviting believers to attend secret meetings, to raise questions about the faith and discuss its "deeper meaning."[70] In such meetings, unauthorized by the bishop, these Valentinians taught what Irenaeus regarded as blasphemy. They taught, for example, that the creator God described in Genesis is not the only God, as most Christians believe—nor is he the malevolent, degraded chief of the fallen angels, as the radicals imagine. According to Valentinus, he is an anthropomorphic image of the true divine Source underlying all being, the ineffable, indescribable source Valentinus calls "the depth," or "the abyss." When Valentinus does invoke images for that Source, he describes it as essentially dynamic and dyadic, the divine "Father of all" and "Mother of all."[71] Those who attended such meetings might also hear that the bishop—Irenaeus himself—although a good man, was a person of limited understanding who had not progressed beyond faith to *gnosis*.

Irenaeus acknowledges in *Against Heresies* that the followers of Valentinus think of themselves as people who are reforming the church and raising its level of spiritual understanding; but, he says, nothing good they accomplish could possibly compensate for the harm they inflict by "dividing in pieces the great and glorious body of Christ,"[72] the church. As bishop, Irenaeus saw that the very act of committing themselves to spiritual exploration set gnostic Christians apart from the rest, and effectively divided the community. Their presence as an insidious inner group threatened the fragile structures of organizational and moral consensus through which leaders like Irenaeus were attempting to unify Christian groups throughout the world.

While Valentinian Christians agreed that the bishops' moral instruction was necessary for psychic Christians, they tended to regard themselves as exempt, free to make their own decisions about acts that the bishops prohibited. Some Valentinian Christians, Irenaeus says, attend pagan festivals along with their families and friends, convinced that doing so cannot pollute them; others, he charges, go to gladiator shows, and are guilty of what he describes as flagrant sexual transgressions.[73] As an example, Irenaeus cites Marcus, a Valentinian teacher active "in our own district in the Rhone Valley." Irenaeus calls him a seducer who concocts special aphrodisiacs to entice the many women who "have been defiled by him, and were filled with passion for him," including "the wife of one of our deacons . . . a woman of remarkable beauty,"[74] who actually left home to travel with Marcus's group.

But when Irenaeus gets down to describing Marcus's actual techniques of seduction, we can see that he is speaking metaphorically. What concerns the bishop, among other things, is the enormous appeal that Valentinian teaching had for women believers, who were increasingly excluded during the second century from active participation in Irenaeus's church. Marcus, Irenaeus says, "seduces women" by inviting them to participate in celebrating the Eucharist, and by casting the eucharistic prayers in such "seductive words" as prayers to Grace, the divine Mother, along with the divine Father.[75] Worse, Marcus "lays hands" upon women to invoke the holy spirit to come down upon them, and then encourages them to speak in prophecy.[76] When Irenaeus accuses Marcus's followers of adultery, he is invoking a traditional biblical image for participating in "illicit" religious practices. The prophets Hosea, Isaiah, and Jeremiah, for example, often used the metaphors of adultery and prostitution to indict those they accused of being "unfaithful" to God's covenant.[77]

Several Valentinian works discovered at Nag Hammadi, including the *Gospel of Truth* and the *Gospel of Philip,* offer correctives to charges that the Valentinians were immoral. In one of the few remaining fragments of his teachings, Valentinus himself, commenting on Jesus' saying that "God alone is good," says that apart from God's grace, the human heart is a "dwelling place for many demons. But when the Father, who alone is good, looks upon it, he purifies and illuminates it with his light; thus the one who has such a heart is blessed, because he sees God."[78] The *Gospel of Truth*, which may also have been written by Valentinus, offers the following ethical instruction to gnostic Christians:

> Speak of the truth with those who seek for it, and of *gnosis* to those who have committed sins in their error. Secure the feet of those who have stumbled, and stretch out your hands to those who are ill. Feed those who are hungry, and give rest to those who are weary. . . . For you are the understanding which is drawn forth. If strength acts thus, it becomes even stronger. . . . Do not become a dwelling place for the devil, for you have already destroyed him.[79]

The *Gospel of Philip* proposes an alternative to the common Christian perception of good and evil as cosmic opposites.[80] In this gospel, unlike the New Testament gospels, Satan never appears. Instead, the divine Father and the holy spirit, working in harmony with each other, direct all that happens, even the actions of the lower cosmic forces, so that ultimately, in Paul's words, "all things work together for good" (Rom. 8:28). The *Gospel of Philip* offers an original critique of the way all other Christians, orthodox and radical alike, approach morality. Much as they disagree on content, both orthodox and radical Christians assume that morality requires *prescribing* one set of acts, and *proscribing* others. But the author of *Philip* wants to throw away all the lists of good things and bad things—lists that constitute the basis of traditional Christian morality. For, this author suggests, what we identify as opposites—"light and dark, life and death, good and evil"—are in reality pairs of interdependent terms in which each implies the other.[81]

Intending to transpose Christian moral discipline into a new key, the author of *Philip* takes the story of the tree of knowledge of good and evil as a parable that shows the futility of the traditional approach to morality. According to *Philip*, "the law was the tree"; the law, like the tree of knowledge, claims to give "knowledge of good and evil," but it cannot accomplish any moral transformation. Instead, it "created death for those who ate of it. For when it said, 'Eat this, do not eat that,' it became the beginning of death."[82]

To show that one cannot distinguish good from evil in such simple and categorical ways, *Philip* tells another parable, of a householder responsible for an estate that includes children, slaves, dogs, pigs, and cattle. The householder, who feeds each one the diet appropriate to its kind, is an image of the "disciple of God," who "perceives the conditions of [each person's] soul, and speaks to each one" accordingly, recognizing that each has different needs and stands at a different level of spiritual maturity.[83] Thus *Philip* refuses to argue over sexual behavior—whether, for example, Christians should marry or remain celibate. Posed as opposites, these choices, too, present a false dichotomy. This author admonishes, "Do not fear the flesh, nor love it. If you fear it, it will gain mastery over you; if you love it, it will devour and paralyze you."[84] *Philip* intends to follow Paul's insight that for one person marriage may be the appropriate "diet," for another, celibacy.

While rejecting the ordinary dichotomy between good and evil, this author does not neglect ethical questions, much less imply that they are not important. For him the question is not whether a certain act is "good" or "evil" but how to reconcile the freedom *gnosis* conveys with the Christian's responsibility to love others. Here the author has in mind a saying from the gospel of John ("You shall know the truth, and the truth shall make you free") and the apostle Paul's discussion of love and *gnosis* in 1 Corinthians, chapters 8 and 9. There Paul says that he considers himself, because of his own *gnosis*, free to eat and drink whatever he likes, free to travel with a Christian sister as a wife, and free to live as an evangelist at community expense. Yet, Paul says, "since not everyone has this *gnosis*" (1 Cor. 8:7–13), he willingly relinquishes his freedom for the sake of love, in order not to offend potential converts or immature Christians. The author of *Philip* follows Paul's lead, then, when he takes up the central question: How is the Christian to avoid sin? How can one act in harmony with *gnosis*, on the one hand, and with *agape*, or love, on the other?

The central theme of the *Gospel of Philip* is the transforming power of love: that what one becomes depends upon what one loves.[85] Whoever matures in love takes care not to cause distress to others: "Blessed is the one who has not caused grief to anyone."[86] Jesus Christ is the paradigm of the one who does not offend or grieve anyone, but refreshes and blesses everyone he encounters, whether "great or small, believer or unbeliever."[87] The gnostic Christian, then, must always temper the freedom *gnosis* conveys with love for others. The author says, too, that he looks forward to the time when freedom and love will harmonize spontaneously, so that the spiritually mature person will be free to follow his or her own true desires without grieving anyone else. Instead of commanding one to "eat this, do not eat that," as did the former "tree" of the law, the true tree of *gnosis* will convey perfect freedom:

> In the place where I shall eat all things is the tree of knowledge. . . . That garden is the place where they will say to me, "Eat this, or do not eat that, just as you wish."[88]

When *gnosis* harmonizes with love, the Christian will be free to partake or to decline, according to his or her own heart's desire.

The majority of Christians, by contrast, characterized spiritual formation as the Essenes had, as an internal contest between the forces of good and evil. The great Christian ascetic Anthony, who lived in Egypt c. 250–355 C.E. and became a pioneer among the desert fathers, taught his spiritual heirs in monastic tradition to picture Satan as the most intimate enemy of all—the enemy we call our own *self.* The *Life of Anthony,* written in the fourth century by Athanasius, bishop of Alexandria, describes how Satan tempts Anthony by speaking through his inner thoughts and impulses, through imagination and desire. *Philip,* on the other hand, interprets the human inclination to sin without recourse to Satan. But this does not mean, as some orthodox Christians suspected, that Valentinian Christians naïvely believed that they had no need to engage in moral struggle because they were "beyond good and evil," essentially incapable of sin. On the contrary, *Philip* teaches that within each person lies hidden the "root of evil." This is *Philip*'s interpretation of the traditional Jewish teaching of the *yetzer 'hara,* which the rabbis called the "evil impulse." So long as we remain unaware of "the root of evil" within us, *Philip* says, "it is powerful; but when it is recognized, it is destroyed." He continues,

> As for us, let each of us dig down to the root of evil within us, and pull out the root from the heart. It will be plucked out if we recognize it. But if we do not recognize it, it takes root in our hearts and produces its fruits in our hearts. It masters us, and makes us its slaves. It takes us captive, so that "we do what we do not want, and what we do not want to do, we do" [cf. Rom. 7:14–15]. It grows powerful because we have not recognized it.[89]

Essential to *gnosis* is to "know" one's own potential for evil. According to *Philip,* recognizing evil within oneself is necessarily an individual process: no one can dictate to another what is good or evil; instead, each one must strive to recognize his or her own inner state, and so to identify acts that spring from the "root of evil," which consists in such impulses as anger, lust, envy, pride, and greed. This teacher assumes that when one recognizes that a certain act derives from such sources, one loses the conviction needed to sustain the action. In order to do evil—whether to indulge in an angry tirade, commit murder, or declare aggressive war—one seems to require the illusion that one's action is justified, that one is acting for right reasons. This author holds, then, the optimistic conviction that "truth . . . is more powerful than ignorance of error."[90] Knowing the truth in this way involves more than an intellectual process; it involves transformation of one's being, transformation of one's way of living: "If we know the truth, we shall find its fruits within us; if we join ourselves with it, we shall receive our fulfillment."[91]

For the mature Christian, *Philip* suggests, the doctrine and moral strictures of the institutional church have become secondary, if not irrelevant. Yet unlike many later Protestant Christians, Valentinian Christians did not simply reject the ecclesiastical structures. Instead they claimed to build upon them as upon a foundation, just as Christians as a whole claimed to have built upon the foundations of Judaism. The author of *Philip*, in fact, like the author of the *Testimony*, at one point uses the terms "Hebrew" and "Christian" to compare the relationship between those who have received only the *preliminary* revelation, and those who have received the fuller understanding of *gnosis*.

Thus the author of *Philip* criticizes those he calls Hebrews and defines as "apostles and apostolic people," who fail to understand, for example, the meaning of the virgin birth. Many take it literally, as if Jesus' "virgin birth" referred to an actual conception and pregnancy. *Philip* ridicules such belief:

> Some said, "Mary conceived by the holy spirit." They are in error. They do not know what they are saying; for when did a female ever conceive through a female?[92]

As *Philip* sees it, Jesus, born of Mary and Joseph as his human parents, was reborn of the holy spirit, the feminine element of the divine being (since the Hebrew term for spirit, *Ruah*, is feminine) and of the "Father in heaven," whom Jesus urged his disciples to address in prayer ("Our Father, who art in heaven . . ."). Yet, the author adds, the very mention of a feminine spiritual power "is a great anathema to the Hebrews, who are the apostles, and apostolic people."[93]

Such people do see baptism as rebirth through the holy spirit, but they do not understand that they must be reborn from the heavenly Father as well. Thus, says *Philip*,

> when we were Hebrews, we . . . had only our mother; but when we became Christians, we had both father and mother.[94]

Baptism, then, differs for different people. Some, the author says, "go down in the water [of baptism] and come up without receiving anything,"[95] but nonetheless such a person says, "I am a Christian." For such people, according to *Philip*, the name

"Christian" is only a promise of what they may yet receive in the future. For others, however, baptism becomes a moment of transformation: "Thus it is when one experiences a mystery."[96] Whoever is reborn of the heavenly Father and heavenly Mother becomes a whole person again, receiving back a part of the human self that had been lost in the beginning of time—"the spirit, the partner of one's soul." Such a person becomes whole again, and "holy, down to the very body."[97] One can hardly refer to such a person as a Christian, "for this person is no longer a Christian, but a Christ."[98]

What about specific practical questions? This author's attitude recalls that expressed in the *Gospel of Thomas,* where Jesus' disciples ask him for specific directions: "Do you want us to fast? How shall we pray? Shall we give alms? What diet should we observe?" According to Matthew and Luke, Jesus offers specific answers to such questions. But according to the *Gospel of Thomas,* he says only, "Do not tell lies, and do not do what you hate,"[99] an ironic answer, for it turns one back upon one's own resources. Who but oneself can know when one is lying, or what one hates? The *Gospel of Philip,* too, while apparently expressing a preference for asceticism (obviously intended to mirror Paul's own preference for celibacy over marriage expressed in 1 Corinthians 7:1–40), refrains from offering specific instructions about sexual behavior. What matters, apparently, is not so much what one does but the quality of one's intention. Hence the *Gospel of Philip* remains nonprescriptive, but with two important provisos: first, the gnostic Christian must temper with love the freedom *gnosis* conveys; second, the believer must remain continually aware of his or her potential for doing evil, for only such awareness can free the Christian—even the gnostic Christian—from involuntary enslavement to sin.

Although Irenaeus and others charged that Valentinian Christians were dualists, the *Gospel of Philip* indicates the opposite. This author abandons even the modified dualism that characterizes the great majority of Christian teachings, based, as we have seen, on the conviction that God's spirit constantly contends against Satan. Instead of envisioning the power of evil as an alien force that threatens and invades human beings from outside, the author of *Philip* urges each person to recognize the evil within, and consciously eradicate it.

Bishop Irenaeus, determined to check the spread of the gnostic movement within the churches, realized that the measures Tertullian had suggested would not stop the Valentinians. It is not enough, Irenaeus says, to insist that all believers confess the same creed and accept the moral instruction provided by priests and bishops, for the wily "heretics" willingly do these things, at least in public. Nor is it enough simply to insist that Christians accept the authority of all priests and bishops. The Valentinians include within their own number many priests who are, so to speak, on their side; Irenaeus explains, "There are those who many believe are priests, but who . . . conduct themselves with contempt toward orders, . . . doing evil deeds in secret"[100]—like those who are actually initiated into *gnosis*. Rather, Irenaeus declares, believers must accept only *certain* priests—priests who not only are properly ordained but who clearly repudiate secret teaching and refuse to participate in private meetings unauthorized by the bishop. Therefore, Irenaeus concludes, "it is necessary to obey the priests who are in the church—those who, along with apostolic succession, have received the certain gift of truth." At the same time,

> it is also necessary to hold in suspicion other [priests] who depart from the primitive succession, and who assemble themselves in any place whatsoever, regarding these as heretics, or schismatics, or hypocrites . . . who cleave asunder and divide the unity of the church.[101]

These, Irenaeus warns, will receive divine punishment: fire from heaven will consume them.

Finally Irenaeus denounces Valentinian theology as the devious result of Satan's own inspiration. Irenaeus concludes his five-volume work *Against Heresies* by speaking, in God's place, the words of divine judgment:

> Let those persons, therefore, who blaspheme the creator, either by openly expressed disagreement . . . or by distorting

the meaning [of the Scriptures], like the Valentinians and all the falsely called gnostics, be recognized as agents of Satan by all who worship God. Through their agency Satan even now, and not earlier, has been seen to speak against God . . . the same God who has prepared eternal fire for every kind of apostasy.[102]

Just as in the beginning of time Satan led human beings astray by means of the serpent, "so now," Irenaeus declares, "do these people, filled with a Satanic spirit, seduce the people of God." Against "all heretics," Irenaeus helps construct for the Christian churches the structure that has sustained orthodox Christianity ever since, by claiming sole access to "the doctrine of the apostles, and the system of the church throughout the whole world, and the distinct manifestation of the body of Christ (that is, the church) according to the succession of bishops," together with "a very complete system of doctrine."[103]

CONCLUSION

This vision of cosmic struggle, forces of good contending against forces of evil, derived originally from Jewish apocalyptic sources and was developed, as we have seen, by sectarian groups like the Essenes as they struggled against the forces they saw ranged against them. This split cosmology, radically revising earlier monotheism, simultaneously involved a split society, divided between "sons of light," allied with the angels, and "sons of darkness," in league with the power of evil. Followers of Jesus adopted the same pattern. Mark, as we have seen, tells the story of Jesus as the conflict between God's spirit and the power of Satan, manifest in the opposition Jesus encountered from evil spirits and evil people alike. Each of the gospels in its own way invokes this apocalyptic scenario to characterize conflicts between Jesus' followers and the various groups each author perceived as opponents. We have seen, too, that as the movement became increasingly Gentile, converts turned this sectarian vocabulary against other enemies—against pagan magistrates and mobs engaged in bitter struggle with the growing Christian movement, and against various groups of dissident Christians, called heretics—or, in Paul's words, "servants of Satan."

Christians in later generations turned weapons forged in first-century conflict against other enemies. But this does not mean that they simply replaced one enemy with another. Instead, Christian tradition has tended to accumulate them. When pagan converts like Justin Martyr, for example, aimed vocabulary concerning Satan and the demons against Roman persecutors and against heretics, they often took for granted the hostile characterizations of the Jewish majority they found in the gospels. Justin himself praises those he calls Hebrews—that is, the ancient Israelites, revered ancestors of his own faith—but expresses condescension toward those of his contemporaries he calls not Hebrews but Jews for their "blindness" to God's revelation and their "misunderstanding" of their own Scriptures. Justin castigates the Jews in language largely drawn from Matthew's polemic against the Pharisees and often repeats for his Gentile audiences Luke's refrain in Acts that Jesus was "crucified by the Jews." Origen, too, although preoccupied primarily with struggles against Roman persecution and against "heretics"—and despite his own extensive conversations with Jewish teachers, whom he credited with teaching him a great deal about the Hebrew language and scriptural interpretation—nevertheless develops the views expressed in Matthew to characterize the Jewish people as divinely condemned for rejecting their Messiah.

The attitudes Justin and Origen express are not unique to them. They are readily recognized by most Christians from the second century through the twentieth because they draw upon a familiar source, the New Testament gospels. Throughout the centuries, Christians have turned the same polemical vocabulary against a wider range of enemies. In the sixteenth century, for example, Martin Luther, founder of Protestant Christianity, denounced as "agents of Satan" all Christians who remained loyal to the Roman Catholic Church, all Jews who refused to acknowledge Jesus as Messiah, all who challenged the power of the landowning aristocrats by participating in the Peasants' War, and all "protestant" Christians who were not Lutheran.

I am not saying that the gospel accounts are essentially Manichaean in the ordinary sense of the term, that they envision good and evil evenly matched against each other. Christian tradition derives much of its power from the conviction that although the believer may feel besieged by evil forces, Christ has already won the decisive victory. Anthony, one of the pioneers among the desert ascetics, a man famous for wrestling with demons, explains to his followers:

> Since the Lord dwelt among us, the Enemy has fallen, and his powers have been weakened. He does not submit quietly to his fall . . . but keeps on threatening like a tyrant.[1]

Describing how a great, towering figure once appeared to him, Anthony says he asked the intruder, "Who are you?" and was told, "I am Satan." Anthony boldly rebuked the Enemy, reminding him that

> "Christ has come and made you powerless. He has cast you down and stripped you." When he heard the Savior's name, he vanished, for he could not endure its burning heat. . . . If, then, even the devil admits that he is powerless, we ought to despise both him and his demons. . . .
>
> The Enemy with his hounds has only so many stratagems. . . . We should not be disheartened, nor succumb to cowardice of soul, nor invent terrors for ourselves. . . . We should take courage, and always be joyful as people who have been saved. Let us keep in mind that the Lord who defeated and vanquished him is with us.[2]

The faith that Christ has conquered Satan assures Christians that in their own struggles the stakes are eternal, and victory is certain. Those who participate in this cosmic drama cannot lose. Those who die as martyrs win the victory even more gloriously and are assured that they will celebrate victory along with all of God's people and the angels of heaven. Throughout the history of Christianity, this vision has inspired countless people to take a stand against insuperable odds in behalf of what they believe is right and to perform acts that, apart from faith, might seem only futile bravado. This apocalyptic vision has taught even secular-minded people to interpret the history of Western culture as a moral history in which the forces of good contend against the forces of evil in the world.

Philosophically inclined Christians such as Augustine of Hippo have often disparaged such mythological language and declared that, ontologically speaking, evil and Satan do not exist. On this level, orthodox Christianity does not diverge from monotheism. Yet Augustine himself, like many other philosophically sophisticated preachers, often speaks of Satan in sermons and prayers and acknowledges, when he is dealing with people confronted with obstacles, that Christians in this world still struggle against evil in ways that they experience as demonic attack.

So compelling is this vision of cosmic war that it has pervaded the imagination of millions of people for two thousand years. Christians from Roman times through the Crusades, from the Protestant Reformation through the present, have invoked it to interpret opposition and persecution in myriad contexts. To this day, many Christians—Roman Catholic, Protestant, Evangelical, and Orthodox—invoke the figure of Satan against "pagans" (among whom they may include those involved with non-Christian religions throughout the world) and against "heretics" (that is, against other Christians with whom they disagree), as well as against atheists and unbelievers. Millions of Muslims invoke similar apocalyptic visions and switch the sides, so that those who Christians believe are God's people become, for many Muslims, allies of "the great Satan."

Many religious people who no longer believe in Satan, along with countless others who do not identify with any religious tradition, nevertheless are influenced by this cultural legacy whenever they perceive social and political conflict in terms of the forces of good contending against the forces of evil in the world. Although Karl Marx's extreme and resolutely materialist version of this apocalyptic vision is now nearly defunct, a secularized version of it underlies many social and political movements in Western culture, both religious and antireligious.

So long as the Christian movement remained a persecuted, suspect minority within Jewish communities and within the Roman empire, its members, like the Essenes, no doubt found a sense of security and solidarity in believing that their enemies were (as Matthew's Jesus says of the Pharisees) "sons of hell," already, in effect, "sentenced to hell." This vision derives its power not only from the conviction that one stands on God's side, but also from the belief that one's opponents are doomed to fail. The words Matthew places in Jesus' mouth characterize his opponents as people accursed, whom the divine judge has already consigned "into the eternal fire prepared for the devil and his angels."

Yet among first-century Christian sources we also find profoundly different perceptions of opponents. Although Matthew's Jesus attacks the Pharisees and bitterly condemns them, and John at one point characterizes Jesus' opponents as Satan's progeny, the Q source that Matthew uses also suggests different ways of perceiving others, in sayings attributed to Jesus that urge reconciliation with one's opponents:

> If you are offering your gift at the altar, and there remember that your brother has something against you, leave your gift there before the altar and go; first be reconciled to your brother, and then come and offer your gift (5:23–24).

Or Matthew 5:43–44:

> You have heard that it was said, "You shall love your neighbor and hate your enemy." But I say to you, "Love your enemies and pray for those who persecute you, so that you may be children of your father in heaven."

To pray for one's enemies suggests that one believes that whatever harm they have done, they are capable of being reconciled to God and to oneself. Paul, writing about twenty years before the evangelists, holds a still more traditionally Jewish perception that Satan acts as God's agent not to corrupt people but to test them; at one point he suggests that a Christian group "deliver to Satan" one of its errant members, not in order to consign him to hell, but in the hope that he will repent and change (1 Cor. 5:5). Paul also hopes and longs for reconciliation between his "brothers," "fellow Israelites," and Gentile believers (Rom. 9:3–4).

Many Christians, then, from the first century through Francis of Assisi in the thirteenth century and Martin Luther King, Jr., in the twentieth, have believed that they stood on God's side without demonizing their opponents. Their religious vision inspired them to oppose policies and powers they regarded as evil, often risking their well-being and their lives, while praying for the reconciliation—not the damnation—of those who opposed them.

For the most part, however, Christians have taught—and acted upon—the belief that their enemies are evil and beyond redemption. Concluding this book, I hope that this research may illuminate for others, as it has for me, the struggle within Christian tradition between the profoundly human view that "otherness" is evil and the words of Jesus that reconciliation is divine.

NOTES

Introduction

1. Martin Buber, cited in discussion with Malcolm Diamond, professor of religion at Princeton University, May 1994.
2. Neil Forsyth, *The Old Enemy: Satan and the Combat Myth* (Princeton: Princeton University Press, 1987).
3. Walter Wink, *Unmasking the Powers: The Invisible Forces That Determine Human Existence* (Philadelphia: Fortress Press, 1986); C. G. Jung, *Answer to Job*, trans. R. F. C. Hull (London: Routledge and Kegan Paul, 1954).
4. Jeffrey B. Russell, *The Devil: Perceptions of Evil from Antiquity to Primitive Christianity* (Ithaca, N.Y.: Cornell University Press, 1970).
5. Robert Redfield, "Primitive World View," in Redfield, ed., *The Primitive World and Its Transformations* (Ithaca: Cornell University Press, 1953), 92.
6. Jonathan Z. Smith, "What a Difference a Difference Makes," in Jacob Neusner and Ernest S. Frerichs, eds., *To See Ourselves As Others See Us: Christians, Jews, "Others" in Late Antiquity* (Chico, Calif.: Scholars Press, 1985), 3–48.
7. William Scott Green, "Otherness Within: Towards a Theory of Difference in Rabbinic Judaism," in Neusner and Frerichs, eds., *To See Ourselves As Others See Us,* 46–69.
8. Even a well-known passage in the Talmud assumes that Jewish courts condemned and executed Jesus. See b. Sahn. 107b and parallel passages, b. Sotha 47a and j. Hag. 2.2., part of the Gemara on Sanh. 10.2. For discussion, see E. Bammel, "Christian Origins in Tradition," *New Testament Studies* 13 (1967): 317–35; see also David R. Catchpole, *The Trial of Jesus: A Study in the Gospels and Jewish Historiography from 1770 to the Present Day* (Leiden: E. J. Brill, 1971), for a fascinating and detailed discussion of the history of scholarship on this passage.

9. Barnabas Lindars, *New Testament Apologetic: The Doctrinal Significance of the Old Testament Quotations* (London: SCM Press, 1973).

10. James Robinson, *The Problem of History in Mark* (London: SCM Press, 1957; reprinted, Philadelphia: Fortress Press, 1982).

11. Albert Schweitzer, *The Quest of the Historical Jesus: A Critical Study of Its Progress from Reimarus to Wrede* (London: A. and C. Black, 1926).

12. Josef Jacobs, *Jesus as Others Saw Him* (New York: B. G. Richards, 1925); H. Danby, "The Bearing of the Rabbinical Code on the Jewish Trial Narratives in the Gospels," *Journal of Theological Studies* 21 (1920): 26–51; C. G. Montefiori, *The Synoptic Gospels* I, 2nd rev. ed. (London: Macmillan, 1927); Richard W. Husband, *The Prosecution of Jesus: Its Date, History and Legality* (Princeton: Princeton University Press, 1916); Josef Blinzler, *The Trial of Jesus: Jewish and Roman Proceedings Against Jesus Christ*, trans. I. and F. McHugh, 2nd rev. ed. (Westminster, Md.: Newman, 1959).

13. Simon Bernfield, "Zur ältesten Geschichte des Christentums," *Jahrbucher für Jüdische Geschichte und Literatur* 13 (1910): 117.

14. Hans Lietzmann, *Synopsis of the First Three Gospels*, trans. F. L. Cross, 9th rev. ed. (Oxford: Basil Blackwell, 1968); Martin Dibelius, *Die Form-geschichte des Evangeliums* (Tübingen: Mohr, 1919), trans. and reprinted in 1971; Dibelius, *From Tradition to Gospel* (New York: Scribner, 1965), 178–219; John R. Donahue, *Are You the Christ?* (Missoula, Mont.: Society of Biblical Literature, 1973).

15. Paul Winter, *On the Trial of Jesus*, 2nd ed (Berlin: De Gruyter, 1974); see also M. Radin, *The Trial of Jesus of Nazareth* (Chicago: University of Chicago Press, 1931); J. Klausner, *Jesus von Nazareth, Seine Zeit, Sein Leben und Seine Lehre*, 2nd ed. (Berlin: Jüdischer Verlag, 1934); E G. Hirsch, *The Crucifixion from the Jewish Point of View* (Chicago: Bloch Publishing & Printing, 1921).

16. Fergus Millar, "Reflections on the Trial of Jesus," in P. R. Davies and R. White, eds., *A Tribute to Geza Vermes: Essays on Jewish and Christian Literature and History* (Sheffield: JSOT Press, 1990), 355–81.

17. *The Trial of Jesus; the Jewish and Roman Proceedings Against Jesus Christ Described and Assessed from the Oldest Accounts* (Westminster, Md.: Newman, 1959), 290. See, for example, A. N Sherwin-White, *Roman Society and Roman Law in the New Testament* (Oxford: Oxford University Press, 1983); T. A. Burkill, "The Condemnation of Jesus: A Critique of Sherwin-White's Thesis," *Novum Testamentum* 12 (1970):321–42; R. E. Brown, *The Death of the Messiah: From Gethsemane to the Grave* (New York. Doubleday, 1994).

18. See Winter; Lietzmann; Dibelius; G. Volkmar, *Die Evangelien* (Leipzig: Fues' Verlag, 1870), 588–91; J. Norden, "Jesus von Nazareth in der Beurteilung der Juden einst und jetzt," *Jüdische Literarische Zeitung* (June 18, 1930): 25; S. Grayzel, *A History of the Jews* (Philadelphia: Jewish Publication Society of America, 1947), 1337; J. Isaac, *Jésus et Israel* (Paris: A. Michel, 1948), 509; G. Bornkamm, *Jesus von Nazareth* (Stuttgart: Kohlhammer, 1956), 1504; E. P. Sanders, *Jesus and*

Judaism (Philadelphia: Fortress Press, 1985), states that "Jesus was executed by the Romans as would-be 'King of the Jews' " (p. 294) and also that internal conflict among Jews was "the principal cause of Jesus' death" (p. 296; cf. pp. 294–318). See also the important article reviewing recent scholarship by G. S. Sloyan, "Recent Literature on the Trial Narratives of the Four Gospels," in T. J. Ryan, ed., *Critical History and Biblical Faith: New Testament Perspectives* (Villanova: Villanova University Press, 1979), 136–76.

Chapter I

For a more technical discussion of the material in this chapter, see "The Social History of Satan, Part II: Satan in the New Testament Gospels," *Journal of the American Academy of Religions* 52/1 (February 1994): 201–41.

1. Josephus, *The Jewish War* 1.1, Loeb edition, vol. 2, trans. H. St. J. Thackery (London: Heinemann, 1926). For an excellent recent discussion of Josephus's works, see Shaye J. D. Cohen, *Josephus in Galilee and Rome: His Vita and Development as a Historian* (Leiden: E. J. Brill, 1979).

2. Josephus, *Life of Josephus* 4, Loeb edition, vol. 1, trans. H. St. J. Thackery (London: Heinemann, 1926).

3. Josephus, *War* 4.128.

4. *Ibid.*, 4.146.

5. *Ibid.*, 5.5.

6. *Ibid.*, 5.430.

7. *Ibid.*, 5.19.

8. For discussion of the dating of Mark, see Dennis E. Nineham, *The Gospel of Mark* (Baltimore: Penguin, 1963); Vincent Taylor, *The Gospel According to St. Mark*, 2nd ed. (London: Macmillan, 1966).

9. For discussion, see E. Pagels, *The Gnostic Gospels* (New York: Random House, 1979); for a summary edition and translation of the texts, see James M. Robinson, ed., *The Nag Hammadi Library in English* (New York: Harper, 1977); for Coptic texts, translation, and scholarly notes, see the series of over twenty volumes published in Leiden by E. J. Brill as *Nag Hammadi Studies*.

10. Tacitus, *Annals* 15.44, Loeb edition, trans. J. Jackson (Cambridge, Mass.: Harvard University Press, 1931).

11. Cited in the excellent discussion by Brent D. Shaw, "Bandits in the Roman Empire," *Past and Present* 165 (November 1984): 3–52. See also G. Humbert, "Latrocinium," in C. Davemberg and E. Saglio, eds., *Dictionnaire des antiquités greques et romaines* iii, 2 (1904): 991–92; R. MacMullen, "Brigandage," appendix B in *Enemies of the Roman Order: Treason, Unrest, and Alienation in the Empire* (Cambridge, Mass.: Harvard University Press, 1967), 255–68. E. J. Hobsbawm, *Bandits* (London: Penguin, 1969), singles out "social banditry"; Anton Block criticizes his view in "The Peasant and the Brigand: Social Banditry Reconsidered," *Comparative Studies in Society and History* 14 (1972): 494–504. See Richard A. Horsley, *Bandits, Prophets and Messiahs: Popular Movements in the Time of Jesus* (Minneapolis: Winston Press, 1985).

12. For discussion of the term *lēstēs* in Josephus, see Richard A. Horsley, "Josephus and the Bandits," *Journal for the Study of Judaism* 10 (1979): 37–63.

13. Most recently see Raymond E. Brown, *The Death of the Messiah* (New York: Doubleday, 1994).

14. Ched Myers has recently argued for an early date (68 C.E.) in *Binding the Strong Man* (Maryknoll, N.Y.: Orbis Books, 1981), 40–42.

15. The dating of the gospels is still a debated issue among New Testament scholars. I intend to follow the consensus, not to present any original arguments about dating.

16. For an excellent recent discussion of Jesus' sayings in Paul's writings, see H. Koester, *Ancient Christian Gospels: Their History and Development* (London: SCM Press, and Philadelphia: Trinity Press, 1990), 52–55.

17. Josephus, *Jewish Antiquities* 18.63 and 20.200, Loeb edition, vol. 9, trans. L. H. Feldman (Cambridge, Mass.: Harvard University Press, 1965).

18. See below, pp. 30–33.

19. Philo, *Embassy to Gaius,* 301–2, Loeb edition, vol. 10, trans. F. H. Colson (London: Heinemann, 1962).

20. James M. Robinson, *The Problem of History in Mark* (London: SCM Press, 1957).

21. *Ibid.,* p. 80: "The ministry of Jesus . . . consists in proclaiming the new situation (1:15) and in carrying through the struggle against Satan in the power of the spirit."

22. Mary Smallwood, *The Jews Under Roman Rule from Pompey to Diocletian* (Leiden: E. J. Brill, 1981), 164.

23. 1 Maccabees 2.

24. Robinson, *The Problem of History in Mark,* 63.

25. See, for example, G. Vermes, *The Dead Sea Scrolls: Qûmran in Perspective* (London: Collins, 1977), and the recent revisionist views of L. H. Schiffmann, *The Eschatological Community of the Dead Sea Scrolls* (Atlanta: Scholars Press, 1989).

26. The wording of the Greek text of Mark indicates that it was Jesus' family (*hoi perī autoû*) who went to seize him (3:21) and his family who were saying that he was insane (3:22). Many translators, however, apparently finding the obvious reading objectionable, have worded their translation in ways that avoid attributing such acts and beliefs to his family. The Revised Standard Version, for example, adds several words that suggest that his family intended to protect him from the hostile suspicions of outsiders: "When his family heard it, they went out to restrain him, for people were saying, 'He has gone out of his mind.' "

27. E. Best, "The Role of the Disciples in Mark," *New Testament Studies* 23 (1977):377–401; T. J. Weeden, *Mark: Traditions in Conflict* (Philadelphia: Fortress Press, 1971); Elizabeth Struthers Malbon, "Disciples/Crowds/Whoever: Mark on Characters and Readers," *Novum Testamentum* 28, 2 (1986): 104–30.

28. See Georg Bentram, *Die Leidengeschichte Jesu und der Christuskult,* FRLANT N.F. 22 (Göttingen: Vandenhoeck und Ruprecht, 1922), 55–71.

29. Dennis Nineham, on Mark 14:53–72, in *The Gospel of St. Mark* (Baltimore: Penguin, 1967), 398: "The proceedings which were the cause of Jesus' death . . . are shown as the work of the Jews. The Romans, in the person of Pilate, also played their part (15:25ff.) but the aim of this section is to show that the primary initiative and the real responsibility lay with the Jews, who, through their official representatives, solemnly rejected and destroyed the Messiah in full consciousness of what they were doing." Nineham discusses the reasons for doubting the historicity of Mark's trial narrative in 400–12; see also Rudolf Bultmann, *The History of the Synoptic Tradition,* trans. John Marsh, rev. ed. (New York: Harper and Row, 1968), 262–87; Eta Linnemann, *Studien zur Passionsgeschichte,* FRLANT 102 (Göttingen: Vandenhoeck und Ruprecht, 1970); John R. Donahue, S.J., *Are You the Christ? The Trial Narrative in the Gospel of Mark* (Missoula, Mont.: SBL Press, 1973). An opposite viewpoint is taken by David Catchpole in *The Trial of Jesus: A Study in the Gospels and Jewish Historiography from 1770 to the Present Day* (Leiden: E. J. Brill, 1971). Catchpole concludes that Luke's version of the Sanhedrin trial "plays a vital role in the historical reconstruction of the trial of Jesus" (p. 278). See also Raymond E. Brown, *The Death of the Messiah,* vol. 1, *From Gethsemane to the Grave* (New York: Doubleday, 1994), 516–60.

30. We do not know precisely what practices the Sanhedrin followed during the first century, since extant evidence comes from a later time; see David Goodblatt's article "Sanhedrin" in the *Encyclopedia of Religion.* I am also grateful to Professor Louis Feldman for his comments on this in a letter (May 1994), and for showing me a copy of an unpublished article, "Comments on the Physical Death of Jesus."

31. See the analysis in David Catchpole, *The Trial of Jesus,* and Raymond E. Brown, *Death of the Messiah,* vol. 1, 516–60.

32. Fergus Millar, "Reflections on the Trial of Jesus," in P. R. Davies and R. T. White, eds., *A Tribute to Geza Vermes: Essays on Jewish and Christian Literature and History,* JSOT Suppl. Series 100 (Sheffield: Academia, 1990), 355–81.

33. See bibliography in note 29. Typical is Nineham's comment that the trial before Pilate "is by no means an eyewitness report; indeed, it is not a report at all, so much as a series of traditions, each making some apologetic point about the trial" (*The Gospel of St. Mark,* 411).

34. Paul Winter, *On the Trial of Jesus,* 2d ed. (Berlin and New York: Walter de Gruyter, 1974), 33–34.

35. Bentram, *Die Leidengeschichte Jesu, passim;* John R. Donahue, *Are You the Christ?* (Missoula, Mont.: Society of Biblical Literature, 1973), 139–236.

36. Brown, *Death of the Messiah,* 696.

37. Philo, *Embassy to Gaius,* 301–2.

38. Smallwood, *The Jews Under Roman Rule,* 161–62.

39. E. Stauffer, "Zur Münzprägung des Pontius Pilate," *La Nouvelle Clio* 1–2 (1949–50), 495–514.

40. Brown, *Death of the Messiah,* 700.

41. See Smallwood, *The Jews Under Roman Rule,* 162, for discussion and references.

42. Josephus, *War* 2.176–77.

43. B. C. McGinny, "The Governorship of Pontius Pilate: Messiahs and Sources," *Proceedings of the Irish Biblical Association* 10(1986): 64.

44. Josephus, *Antiquities* 2.169–74.

45. Brown, *Death of the Messiah,* 703.

46. Josephus, *Antiquities* 18.85–87.

47. Winter, *On the Trial of Jesus,* 88.

48. See Howard C. Kee, *Who Are the People of God?* Forthcoming from Yale University Press, New Haven.

Chapter II

1. For a more detailed scholarly treatment of the material in this chapter, see E. Pagels, "The Social History of Satan, the 'Intimate Enemy': A Preliminary Sketch," *Harvard Theological Review* 84:2 (1991): 105–28.

2. See M. Hengel, *Judaism and Hellenism* (London, 1974), 209, which argues that apocalyptic writings are the work of a pious minority who segregated themselves from the official cult. See also M. Barker, "Some Reflections on the Enoch Myth," *Journal for the Study of the Old Testament* 15 (1980): 7–29; her article interprets *1 Enoch* as the work of a group protesting against Jerusalem cult practices, and suggests a link between such works as *Enoch* and the later development of Christian tradition.

3. See, in particular, the incisive essays by Jonathan Z. Smith, "What a Difference a Difference Makes," and William S. Green, "Otherness Within: Towards a Theory of Difference in Rabbinic Judaism," in Jacob Neusner and Ernest S. Frerichs, eds., *To See Ourselves as Others See Us: Christians, Jews, "Others" in Late Antiquity* (Chico, Calif.: Scholars Press, 1985), 3–48 and 49–69.

4. See Morton Smith, *Palestinian Parties and Politics That Shaped the Old Testament* (New York: Columbia University Press, 1971), especially 62–146; also Paul Hanson, *The Dawn of Apocalyptic* (Philadelphia: Fortress Press, 1975).

5. Jon D. Levenson, *Creation and the Persistence of Evil: The Jewish Drama of Divine Omnipotence* (San Francisco: Harper and Row, 1988). I am grateful to John Collins for referring me to this work.

6. *Ibid.,* 44.

7. Many scholars have made this observation; for a recent discussion see Neil Forsyth, *The Old Enemy: Satan and the Combat Myth* (Princeton: Princeton University Press, 1987), 107: "In the collection of documents . . . known to Christians as the Old Testament, the word [Satan] never appears . . . as the name of the adversary. . . . rather, when the satan appears in the Old Testament, he is a member of the heavenly court, albeit with unusual tasks." See also the article on *démon,* in *La Dictionnaire de Spiritualité* 3 (Paris: Beauschesne, 1957), 142–46; H. A. Kelly, "Demonology and Diabolical Temptation," *Thought* 46 (1965): 165–70.

8. M. Delcor, "Le Mythe de la chute des anges et l'origine des géants comme explication du mal dans le monde dans l'apocalyptique juive: Histoire des traditions," *Revue de l'histoire des religions* 190:5–12; P. Day, *An Adversary in Heaven: Satan in the Hebrew Bible* (Atlanta, Ga.: Scholars Press, 1988).

9. Forsyth, *The Old Enemy*, 113.

10. See discussion in Day, *An Adversary*, 69–106.

11. Forsyth, *The Old Enemy*, 114.

12. Note that 2 Samuel 24:1–17 tells a different version of the story, in which the Lord himself, not "the *satan*," incites David to take the census. For discussion, see Morton Smith, *Palestinian Parties and Politics That Shaped the Old Testament* (New York: Columbia University Press, 1971), 62–146; Forsyth, *The Old Enemy*, 119–20.

13. Pagels, "The Social History of Satan, the 'Intimate Enemy': A Preliminary Sketch," *Harvard Theological Review* 84:2 (1991): 112–14.

14. Paul D. Hanson, *The Dawn of Apocalyptic* (Philadelphia: Fortress Press, 1975), 125.

15. An excellent account of these events is to be found in Victor Tcherikover's *Hellenistic Civilization and the Jews* (New York: Atheneum, 1970).

16. 1 Maccabees, 2.

17. Tcherikover, *Hellenistic Civilization*, 132–74.

18. *Ibid.*, 253–65.

19. Such scholars as Knut Schäferdick, in his article "Satan in the Post Apostolic Fathers," s.v. "σατανᾶς," *Theological Dictionary of the New Testament* 7 (1971): 163–65, attributes this development to Christians. Others, including Harold Kuhn, "The Angelology of the Non-Canonical Jewish Apocalypses," *Journal of Biblical Literature* 67 (1948): 217; Claude Montefiore, *Lectures on the Origin and Growth of Religion as Illustrated by the Religion of the Ancient Hebrews* (London: Williams and Norgate, 1892), 429; and George Foote Moore, *Judaism in the First Centuries of the Christian Era*, vol. 1, *The Age of the Tannaim* (Cambridge, Mass.: Harvard University Press, 1927), rightly locate the development of angelology and demonology in pre-Christian Jewish sources, and offer different interpretations of this, as noted in Pagels, "The Social History of Satan, the 'Intimate Enemy,' " 107.

20. Which account is earlier—that in Genesis 6 or in *1 Enoch* 6–11—remains a debatable issue. See, for example, J. T. Milik, *The Books of Enoch: Aramaic Fragments of Qûmran Caves* (Oxford: Clarendon, 1976); George W. E. Nickelsburg, "Apocalyptic and Myth in *1 Enoch* 6–11," *Journal of Biblical Literature* 96 (1977): 383–405; Margaret Barker, "Some Reflections on the Enoch Myth," *JSOT* 15 (1980): 7–29; Philip S. Alexander, "The Targumim and Early Exegesis of the 'Sons of God' in Genesis 6," *Journal of Jewish Studies* 23 (1972): 60–71.

21. For a survey of this theme of rivalry between angels and humans, see Peter Schäfer's fine work *Rivalität Zwischen Engeln und Menschen: Untersuchungen zur rabbinischen Engelvorstellung* (Berlin and New York: de Gruyter, 1975). For a discussion of one strand of Muslim tra-

dition, see Peter Awn, *Satan's Tragedy and Redemption: Iblīs in Sufi Psychology* (Leiden: E. J. Brill, 1983).

22. Note scholarly debate cited in note 20 concerning the priority of Genesis 6. I am following those scholars who see *1 Enoch* 6–11 as amplifications of Gen. 6:1–4, including Philip S. Alexander and Paul Hanson, "Rebellion in Heaven, Azazel, and Euhemenistic Heroes in *1 Enoch* 6–11," *Journal of Biblical Literature* 96 (1977): 195–233.

23. George W. E. Nickelsburg, "Apocalyptic and Myth in *1 Enoch* 6–11," *Journal of Biblical Literature* 96 (1977): 383–405.

24. David Suter, "Fallen Angel, Fallen Priest: The Problem of Family Purity in *1 Enoch* 6–16," *Hebrew Union College Annual* 50 (1979): 115–35. Cf. George W. E. Nickelsburg, "The Book of Enoch in Recent Research," *Religious Studies Review* 7 (1981): 210–17.

25. John Collins, *The Apocalyptic Imagination: An Introduction to the Jewish Matrix of Christianity* (New York: Crossroad, 1984), 127.

26. This question dominated the concerns of many others as well; for discussion, see the forthcoming book by Howard C. Kee, *Who Are the People of God?*

27. George W. E. Nickelsburg, "Revealed Wisdom as a Criterion for Inclusion and Exclusion," in Neusner and Frerichs, eds., *To See Ourselves As Others See Us*, 76.

28. See the article by George W. E. Nickelsburg, "Riches, the Rich, and God's Judgment in *1 Enoch* 92–105 and the Gospel According to Luke," *New Testament Studies* 25 (1979), 324–49.

29. On the basis of the Watcher story in *1 Enoch* 6–16, Forsyth (*The Old Enemy*, 167–70) comments that it implies "a radically different theology" from that of the Genesis primordial history, in that "in Enoch we have heard nothing about a wicked humanity. Instead, all human suffering is attributed to the angelic revolt and the sins of their giant brood." Yet as I read the Enoch literature, its authors demonstrate awareness of the tension between—and correlation of—human and angelic guilt, or at least of the possibility of contradiction. The passage may be included as a corrective to any who exempt humans from responsibility by blaming the angels' transgressions. For a discussion, see Martha Himmelfarb, *Tours of Hell: An Apocalyptic Form in Jewish and Christian Literature* (Philadelphia: University of Pennsylvania Press, 1983).

30. This identification occurs commonly in later Jewish sources, often traced to the Septuagint translation of 1 Chronicles 16:26: οἱ τῶν ἐθνῶν θεοί δαίμωνες ἐίσιν.

31. Josephus, *Life*, 10.

32. Pliny the Elder, *Natural History*, Loeb edition, vol. 2, 5.15, 73. For discussion of Pliny's description of the Essenes, see J. P. Audet, "Qûmran et la notice de Pline sur les Esséniers," *Revue Biblique* 68 (1961): 346–87; D. F. Graf, "Pagan Witness to the Essenes," *Biblical Archaeologist* 40 (1977): 125–29.

33. L. H. Schiffman, *Archaeology and History in the Dead Sea Scrolls* (Sheffield: JSOT Press, 1989).

34. G. Vermes, *The Dead Sea Scrolls: Qûmran in Perspective* (Atlanta, Ga.: Scholars Press, 1989).

35. See F. F. Bruce, "The Romans Through Jewish Eyes," in M. Simon, ed., *Paganisme, Judaïsme, Christianisme* (Paris: E. de Boccard, 1978), 3–12; G. Vermes, *Post Biblical Jewish Studies* (Leiden: E. J. Brill, 1975), 215–24.

36. S. David Sperling, "Belial," forthcoming in Karel van der Toorn, *Dictionary of Deities and Demons* (Leiden: E. J. Brill).

37. See, for example, Matthew Black, *The Scrolls and Christian Origins* (New York: Scribner, 1961), 91–117.

38. Carol Newsome, *Songs of Sabbath Sacrifice: A Critical Edition* (Atlanta, Ga.: Scholars Press, 1985).

39. Yigael Yadin, who edited the *War Scroll,* commented that this text, like others from Qûmran, "considerably extends our knowledge of Jewish angelology—a subject of utmost importance in the Judaism of that time" (*Scroll,* 229). But Yadin did not tell us what constitutes its importance: Discernment of spirits, the capacity to recognize and understand the interrelationship of supernatural forces, both good and evil, is essential to the Essenes' sense of their own identity and the way they identify others. Having set aside, not so much as wrong but as inadequate, more traditional forms of Jewish identity, the Essenes articulate, through their accounts of the battle between angelic and demonic forces, on which side of the cosmic battle each person and each group of Jews stands.

40. Yigael Yadin assumes that the Prince of Light "is Michael, Prince of Israel": *The Scroll of the War of the Sons of Light Against the Sons of Darkness* (Oxford: Oxford University Press, 1962), 236. But this identification ignores the sectarianism that dominates the Qûmran texts. Instead, as John Collins observes, "In 1 QM Michael is no longer simply the Prince of Israel but leader of the Sons of Light. This designation may have been correlated in practice with members of the congregation, but in principle it was open to broader interpretations and freed from ethnic associations. Belial, too, is no longer the prince of a specific nation. . . . Rather, he represents evil at large, like Satan or Mastema in the book of *Jubilees.* . . . The adoption of this terminology in preference to the traditional, national, and social affiliations opens up considerably the range of application of the eschatological language. Specifically, it invites the correlation of the eschatological drama with the . . . moral conflict of good and evil within every individual" (*The Apocalyptic Imagination,* 128–31).

Chapter III

1. George W. E. Nickelsburg, "Revealed Wisdom as a Criterion for Inclusion and Exclusion: From Jewish Sectarianism to Early Christianity," in Jacob Neusner and Ernest S. Frerichs, eds., *To See Ourselves As Others See Us: Christians, Jews, "Others" in Late Antiquity* (Chico, Calif.: Scholars Press, 1985), 73.

2. *Ibid.*

3. Wayne A. Meeks, "Breaking Away: Three New Testament Pictures of Christianity's Separation from the Jewish Communities," in Neusner and Frerichs, eds., *To See Ourselves*, 94–115.

4. For a different perspective in Paul's view of Jews and Judaism, see John Gager, *The Origins of Anti-Semitism: Attitudes Toward Judaism in Pagan and Christian Antiquity* (Oxford: Oxford University Press, 1983), 193–264; Lloyd Gaston, "Paul and the Torah," in A. Davies, ed., *Anti-Semitism and the Foundation of Christianity* (New York: Paulist Press, 1979), 48–71.

5. K. Stendahl, *The School of St. Matthew* (Uppsala: C. W. K. Gleerup, 1954).

6. Wayne A. Meeks, *The First Urban Christians: The Social World of the Apostle Paul* (New Haven: Yale University Press, 1983).

7. For a discussion of this process, see H. Koester, *Ancient Christian Gospels: Their History and Development* (London: SCM Press, and Philadelphia: Trinity Press, 1990), 42–162.

8. See J. Kloppenborg, *The Formation of Q* (Philadelphia: Fortress Press, 1987), for a recent, revisionist view of the development of the Q source.

9. G. R. S. Mead, *Fragments of a Faith Forgotten* (reprint, New York: University Books, 1960), summarized what was known of such fragments at the turn of the century; see Morton Smith, *Clement of Alexandria and a Secret Gospel of Mark* (Cambridge: Harvard University Press, 1973).

10. For discussion of passages concerning women in gnostic sources, see Elaine Pagels, *The Gnostic Gospels* (New York: Random House, 1979), 48–69; Karen King, ed., *Images of the Feminine in Gnosticism* (Chapel Hill: University of North Carolina Press, 1986); Jorunn Jacobsen Buckley, *Female Fault and Fulfillment in Gnosticism* (Chapel Hill, University of North Carolina Press, 1986).

11. For a fuller discussion of some of the implications of this discovery, see Pagels, *Gnostic Gospels*.

12. For a discussion of the original language, see Bentley Layton, "Introduction to the Gospel of Thomas, NHC II.2," in B. Layton, ed., *Nag Hammadi Codex II. 2–7, together with Brit. Lib. Or. 4926 (1) and P. Oxy. 1, 654, 655* (Leiden: E. J. Brill, 1989), vol. 1, Nag Hammadi Series 20.

13. Koester, *Ancient Christian Gospels*, 49–172.

14. Irenaeus, *Libros Quinque Adversus Haereses*, ed. W. W. Harvey (Cambridge: Typis Academicis, 1857), vol. 1, 3.11.9. Hereafter cited as *Against Heresies*.

15. *Ibid.*, preface.

16. For assessment of Matthew's provenance, see the summary in Wayne A. Meeks, "Breaking Away," 108–14; Alan F. Segal, "Matthew's Jewish Voice," in David L. Balch, ed., *Social History of the Matthean Community* (Minneapolis: Fortress Press, 1991), 3–37; also, in the same volume: Anthony J. Saldarini, "The Gospel of Matthew and Jewish-Christian Conflict," 38–62; Robert H. Gundrey, "A Responsive Evaluation of the Social History of the Matthean Community in Roman Syria," 62–67; William R. Schoedel, "Ignatius and the Reception of the Gospel of

Matthew in Antioch," 129–77; Rodney Stark, "Antioch as the Social Situation for Matthew's Gospel," 189–210; also J. Andrew Overman, *Matthew's Gospel and Formative Judaism: The Social World of the Matthean Community* (Philadelphia: Fortress Press, 1990); Amy-Jill Levine, *The Social and Ethnic Dimensions of Matthean Salvation History:* "Go Nowhere Among the Gentiles" (Matt. 10:56) (Lewiston, N.Y.: Edwin Mellen, 1988).

17. Mary Smallwood, *The Jews Under Roman Rule from Pompey to Diocletian* (Leiden: E. J. Brill, 1981), 349.

18. Jacob Neusner's pioneering work has opened an understanding of this process; see, for example, *Formative Judaism: Religious, Historical, and Literary Studies,* Brown Judaic Studies, no. 91 (Chico, Calif.: Scholars Press, 1983).

19. See the incisive comments of Alan F. Segal, "Matthew's Jewish Voice," and J. Andrew Overman, *Matthew's Gospel and Formative Judaism.*

20. Alan F. Segal, *Rebecca's Children: Judaism and Christianity in the Roman World* (Cambridge: Harvard University Press, 1986); idem, "Matthew's Jewish Voice."

21. For discussion, see Raymond E. Brown, *The Birth of the Messiah: A Commentary on the Infancy Narratives in Matthew and Luke* (New York: Doubleday, 1977).

22. *Ibid.*

23. When Matthew retells the passion narrative, however, he drops his otherwise frequent references to the Pharisees. There, following Mark, he depicts the chief priests, scribes, and elders as Jesus' primary opponents.

24. George W. E. Nickelsburg, "The Genre and Function of Mark's Passion Narrative," *Harvard Theological Review* 73 (1980): 174.

25. For discussion, see, for example, Michael J. Cook, "Jesus and the Pharisees—The Problem As It Stands Today," *The Journal of Ecumenical Studies* 15 (1978): 441–60; D. Garland, *The Intention of Matthew 23* (Leiden: E. J. Brill, 1979); J. Andrew Overman, *Matthew's Gospel and Formative Judaism;* Klaus Pantle-Schieber, "Anmerkungen zur Auseinandersetzung von *ekklesia* und Judentum im Matthäusevangelium" *Zeitschrift für Neutestamentliche Wissenschaft* 80 (1989), 145–62.

26. Luke T. Johnson, "The New Testament: Anti-Jewish Slander and the Conventions of Ancient Polemic," *Journal of Biblical Literature* 108 (1989): 419–41.

Chapter IV

1. David B. Gowler, *Host, Guest, Enemy, and Friend: Portraits of the Pharisees in Luke and Acts* (New York: Lang, 1991); David A. Neale, *None But the Sinners: Religious Categories in the Gospel of Luke* (Sheffield: JSOT Press, 1991); Robert L. Brawley, "The Pharisees in Luke-Acts: Luke's Address to Jews and His Irenic Purpose," Ph.D. dissertation, Princeton Theological Seminary, 1978; Jack T. Sanders, *The Jews in Luke-Acts* (Philadelphia: Fortress Press, 1987); Joseph R. Tyson, *Images of Judaism in Luke-Acts* (Columbia: University of South Carolina Press, 1992).

2. See Susan Garrett, *The Demise of the Devil: Magic and the Demonic in Luke's Writings* (Minneapolis: Fortress Press, 1989).

3. David R. Catchpole, *The Trial of Jesus: A Study in the Gospels and Jewish Historiography from 1770 to the Present Day* (Leiden: E. J. Brill, 1971); Richard W. Husband, *The Prosecution of Jesus: Its Date, History and Legality* (Princeton: Princeton University Press, 1916); G. S. Sloyan, *Jesus on Trial: The Development of the Passion Narratives and Their Historical and Ecumenical Implications* (Philadelphia: Fortress Press, 1973); R. E. Brown, *The Death of the Messiah: From Gethsemane to the Grave* (New York: Doubleday, 1994).

4. Catchpole, *The Trial of Jesus*, 203.

5. Richard A. Horsley, "Josephus and the Bandits," *Journal for the Study of Judaism* 10 (1979): 37–63.

6. Alfred F. Loisy, *Les Évangiles Synoptiques* (Ceffons près Montieren Der: Chez l'Auteur, 1907–08), 787.

7. On the gospel of John, see J. Louis Martyn, *History and Theology in the Fourth Gospel*, 2nd ed. (Nashville: Abingdon, 1978); Norman R. Petersen, *The Fourth Gospel* (Valley Forge, Pa.: Trinity Press, 1993); C. H. Dodd, *The Interpretation of the Fourth Gospel* (Cambridge: Cambridge University Press, 1953).

8. Martyn, *History and Theology in the Fourth Gospel*; see also William Horbury, "The Benediction of the Minim and Early Jewish-Christian Controversy," *Journal of Theological Studies* 33 (1982): 19–61; T. C. G. Thornton, "Christian Understandings of the Birkath ha-Minim in the Eastern Roman Empire," *Journal of Theological Studies* 38 (1987), 419–31; Asher Finkel, "Yavneh's Liturgy and Early Christianity," *Journal of Ecumenical Studies* 18:2 (1981): 231–50; Alan F. Segal, "Ruler of This World: Attitudes About Mediator Figures and the Importance of Sociology for Self-Definition," in E. P. Sanders, ed., *Jewish and Christian Self-Definition*, vol. 2 (Philadelphia: Fortress Press, 1980), 245–68.

9. Wayne A. Meeks, "The Man from Heaven in Johannine Sectarianism," *Journal of Biblical Literature* 91 (1972): 50.

10. Gustave Hoennecke, "Die Teufelsidee in den Evangelien," *Neutestamentliche Studien: Für Georg Heinrici zu seinem 70* (Leipzig: J. C. Heinrichs, 1912), 208.

11. Raymond Brown, *The Gospel According to John*, Anchor Bible Commentary, vols. 29/29a (Garden City, N.Y.: Anchor Bible, 1966), 364–76.

12. *Ibid.*

13. Raymond Brown, "Incidents That Are Units in the Synoptic Gospels But Dispersed in St. John," *Catholic Biblical Quarterly* 23 (1961).

14. Rudolph Bultmann, *Das Evangelium Johannis* (Göttingen: Vandenhoeck und Ruprecht, 1941), trans. G. R. Beasley-Murray, *The Gospel of John: A Commentary* (Oxford: Basil Blackwell, 1971), 319.

15. *Ibid.*, 321.

16. See, for example, Robert Brachter, "The 'Jews' in the Gospel of John," *Practical Papers for the Bible Translator* 26/4 (1975): 365–409; R. Alan Culpepper, "The Gospel of John and the Jews," *Expository Times* 84 (1987): 273–88; C. J. Cuming, "The Jews in the Fourth Gospel," *Expos-*

itory Times 60 (1948–49): 290–92; Reginald Fuller, "The 'Jews' in the Fourth Gospel," *Dialog* 16 (1971): 37; Malcolm Lowe, "Who Were the 'Ioudaioi'?" *Novum Testamentum* 18/2 (1976):101–30; Massey Shepherd, "The Jews in the Gospel of John: Another Level of Meaning," *Anglican Theological Review Supplementary Series* 3 (1974): 96; John Townsend, "The Gospel of John and the Jews: The Story of a Religious Divorce," in Alan Davies, ed., *Anti-Semitism and the Foundations of Christianity* (New York: Paulist Press, 1979), 72–97; Urban C. von Wahlde, "The Johannine 'Jews': A Critical Survey," *New Testament Studies* 28 (1982): 33–60.

17. Rudolph Bultmann, 59.
18. Heinrich Schneider, "The Word Was Made Flesh: An Analysis of Revelation in the Fourth Gospel," 347–51.
19. Samuel Sandmel, *Anti-Semitism in the New Testament* (Philadelphia: Fortress Press, 1978), 115–17.
20. Rudolph Bultmann, 85–94, *passim*.
21. Fuller, "The 'Jews' in the Fourth Gospel," 20.
22. Fergus Millar, "Reflections on the Trial of Jesus," in P. R. Davies and R. White, eds., *A Tribute to Geza Vermes: Essays on Jewish and Christian Literature and History* (Sheffield: JSOT Press, 1990), 355–81.
23. Rosemary Reuther, *Faith and Fratricide: The Theological Roots of Anti-Semitism* (Minneapolis: Seabury Press, 1974).
24. Husband, *The Prosecution of Jesus,* 173–81.
25. Sandmel, *Anti-Semitism in the New Testament,* 115.
26. Dennis Nineham, *The Gospel of St. Mark* (Baltimore: Penguin Books, 1967), 412.
27. Dodd, *The Interpretation of the Fourth Gospel,* 97.
28. See, for example, Paul Winter, *On the Trial of Jesus,* 2nd ed. (Berlin: De Gruyter, 1974).
29. *Ibid.,* 88–89.
30. J. Andrew Overman, *Matthew's Gospel and Formative Judaism* (Minneapolis: Fortress Press, 1990).

Chapter V

1. See W. H. C. Frend, *Martyrdom and Persecution in the Early Church* (Oxford: Blackwell, 1965), on the persecution of Christians from 50 to 313 C.E.
2. Tacitus, *Annals* 15.44.
3. Robert L. Wilken, "Pagan Criticism of Christianity: Greek Religion and Christian Faith," in W. Schoedel, ed., *Early Christian Literature and the Classical Intellectual Tradition* (Paris: Éditions Beauchesne, 1979), 117–34. For an excellent discussion, see Wilken, *The Christians As the Romans Saw Them* (New Haven: Yale University Press, 1984).
4. Tertullian, *Apology* 1.
5. Georges Villes, *La Gladiature en Occident des origines à la mort de Domitien* (Rome: École française de Rome, 1981); Carlin Barton, *The Sorrows of the Ancient Romans: The Gladiator and the Monster* (Princeton: Princeton University Press, 1992).

6. Tacitus, *Annals* 15.44.
7. See *The Acts of the Christian Martyrs*, ed. and trans. H. A. Musurillo (Oxford: Oxford University Press, 1972).
8. See Justin Martyr, *Dialogue with Trypho*, chaps. 1–6, for Justin's own account of these events; see also L. Barnard, *Justin Martyr: His Life and Thought* (London: Cambridge University Press, 1967).
9. P. Hadot, *Exercices Spirituels et Philosophie Critique* (Paris: Études augustiniennes, 1981), 13–58.
10. Justin Martyr, *First Apology* 61.
11. See Ramsay MacMullen, *Christianizing the Roman Empire: A.D. 100–400* (New Haven: Yale University Press, 1984), 27–31, for a discussion of Justin Martyr's conversion to Christianity. This statement paraphrases and borrows from MacMullen's incisive discussion.
12. Justin Martyr, *Dialogue with Trypho* 7.
13. *Ibid.*, 8.
14. On baptism in early Christianity, see Peter Cramer, *Baptism and Change in the Early Middle Ages, c. 200–1150* (New York: Cambridge University Press, 1993).
15. Justin Martyr, *First Apology* 61.
16. *Ibid.*
17. A. H. Armstrong, "The Ancient and Continuing Pieties of the Greek World," in A. H. Armstrong, ed., *Classical Mediterranean Spirituality* (London: SCM Press, 1989), 66–101.
18. Felix Buffiere, *Les Mythes d'Homère et la pensée grecque* (Paris: Société d'édition, 1956), chap. 5, 136–54; for a fascinating discussion of later reinterpretation of Homer, see Robert Lamberton, *Homer the Theologian* (Berkeley: University of California Press, 1989).
19. Justin Martyr, *First Apology* 5, *passim*.
20. For an excellent discussion of Justin and the other apologists, see H. Wey, *Die Funktionen der bösen Geisten bei den griechischen Apologeten des zweiten Jahrhunderts nach Christus* (Wintermur: Keller, 1957), 3–32 (on Justin).
21. Justin Martyr, *First Apology* 25.
22. *Ibid.*, 43.
23. Justin Martyr, *Dialogue with Trypho* 8.
24. Justin Martyr, *First Apology* 14.
25. *Ibid.*
26. *Ibid.*, 16.
27. *Ibid.*, 61.
28. *Ibid.*, 27.
29. *Ibid.*, 28.
30. *Ibid.*, 12.
31. Elaine Pagels, "Christian Apologists and the 'Fall of the Angels': An Attack on Roman Imperial Power?," *Harvard Theological Review* 78 (1985): 301–25.
32. See P. de Labriolle, *La Réaction païenne: Étude sur la polémique antichrétienne du I⁰ au IV⁰ siècle*, 2nd ed. (Paris, 1948); Ramsay MacMullen,

Enemies of the Roman Order (Cambridge, Mass.: Harvard University Press, 1966).

33. Pliny, *Epistle* 10.96. For discussion of Pliny's letter, see Wilken, *The Christians As the Romans Saw Them*, 15–17; A. N. Sherwin-White, *The Letters of Pliny: A Historical and Social Commentary* (Oxford: Oxford University Press, 1966).

34. Justin Martyr, *First Apology* 5.

35. *Ibid.*, 1.

36. *Ibid.*, 14.

37. Justin Martyr, *Second Apology* 2.

38. Justin Martyr, *Second Apology* 1.

39. Musurillo, *Acts of the Christian Martyrs*, chap. 5, "Martyrdom of Justin and His Companions."

40. Fergus Millar, *The Emperor in the Roman World, 31 B.C.–337 A.D.* (Ithaca: Cornell University Press, 1977).

41. P. A. Brunt, "Marcus Aurelius and the Christians." See also Brunt, "Marcus Aurelius and His Meditations," *Journal of Roman Studies* 64 (1974): 1–20, and Wilken, *The Christians As the Romans Saw Them*, 48–67.

42. Marcus Aurelius, *Meditations* 1.17.5; on Marcus Aurelius in general, see the biography by A. Birley, *Marcus Aurelius* (Boston: Little, Brown, 1966).

43. See note 18.

44. André-Jean Voelke, *L'Idée de Volonté dans le Stoïcisme* (Paris: Presses Universitaires de France, 1973), 109–12.

45. Marcus Aurelius, *Meditations* 4.5.

46. *Ibid.*, 4.44.

47. *Ibid.*, 3.2.

48. *Ibid.*, 2.16.

49. *Ibid.*, 12.14.

50. *Ibid.*, 2.11.

51. *Ibid.*, 3.16.

52. *Ibid.*, 8.49.

53. *Ibid.*, 9.40.

54. *Ibid.*, 9.34.

55. *Ibid.*, 4.15.

56. *Ibid.*, 4.49.

57. *Ibid.*, 10.5; see also 5.1.

58. *Ibid.*, 7.9.

59. Hans Dieter Betz, *The Greek Magical Papyri* (Chicago: University of Chicago Press, 1986); John G. Gager, *Curse Tablets and Binding Spells* (New York: Oxford University Press, 1992).

60. Marcus Aurelius, *Meditations* 11.15.

61. See Wayne Meeks, *The Moral World of the First Christians* (Philadelphia: Westminster Press, 1986).

62. Tatian, *Address to the Greeks* 4.

63. *Ibid.*

64. *Ibid.*, 7.

65. *Ibid.*, 16.
66. *Ibid.*, 15.
67. *Ibid.*
68. *Ibid.*, 6.
69. *Ibid.*, 8.
70. *Ibid.*, 9.
71. *Ibid.*, 11.
72. For a discussion of changing perceptions of Hellenism in the Eastern Empire, see Glen W. Bowersock, *Hellenism in Late Antiquity* (Ann Arbor: University of Michigan Press, 1990).
73. Tatian, *Address to the Greeks* 23.
74. Georges Villes, *La Gladiature en Occident des origines à la mort de Domitien*, 395–97; Alan Cameron, *Circus Factions: The Blues and the Greens at Rome and Byzantium* (Oxford: Clarendon Press, 1976); Carlin Barton, *The Sorrows of the Ancient Romans: The Gladiator and the Monster.*
75. Tatian, *Address to the Greeks* 28.
76. See Henri Crouzel, *Origen: The Life and Thought of the First Great Theologian,* trans. A. S. Worrall (San Francisco: Harper and Row, 1989); see also the discussion of Origen in Peter Brown, *The Body and Society: Men, Women, and Sexual Renunciation in Early Christianity* (New York: Columbia University Press, 1988), 160–77.
77. Quoted by Eusebius, *Historia Ecclesiae* 6.26, possibly from a letter. For discussion see Henri Crouzel, *Origen,* 6.
78. Origen, *Exhortation to Martyrdom.*
79. See Origen, *Contra Celsum.*
80. *Ibid.*, 8.68.
81. *Ibid.*, 1.1.
82. *Ibid.*, 1.31.
83. *Ibid.*, 1.27.
84. *Ibid.*, 1.29.
85. *Ibid.*, 4.22.
86. *Ibid.*, 7.68.
87. *Ibid.*; see also 8.31–32.
88. *Ibid.*, 7 68.
89. Ramsay MacMullen, *Christianizing the Roman Empire,* 21.
90. Marcus Aurelius, *Meditations* 6.44.
91. Tacitus, *Histories* 5.5.
92. Origen, *Contra Celsum* 6.42.
93. *Ibid.*, 7.2.
94. *Ibid.*, 8.28.
95. *Ibid.*, 8.33.
96. *Ibid.*, 8.39.
97. *Ibid.*, 1.43.
98. *Ibid.*, 1.44.
99. *Ibid.*, 8.44.
100. Eusebius, *Historia Ecclesiae* 6.34.
101. Origen, *Contra Celsum* 8.65.
102. *Ibid.*, 8.73.

103. *Ibid.*
104. Tertullian, *Apology* 42.
105. *Ibid.*, 24. See also *Apology* 28 and *To Scapula* 2.
106. Origen, *Contra Celsum* 1.1.

Chapter VI

1. Tertullian, *Apology*, chap. 37.
2. *Ibid.*, chap. 3.
3. David L. Balch, *Let Wives Be Submissive: The Domestic Code in 1 Peter* (Chico, Calif.: Scholars Press, 1981). See also John H. Elliott, *A Home for the Homeless: A Sociological Exegesis of 1 Peter, Its Situation and Strategy* (Philadelphia: Fortress Press, 1981). For a fascinating discussion of the various depictions of Paul, see Dennis Ronald MacDonald, *The Legend and the Apostle: The Battle for Paul in Story and Canon* (Philadelphia: Westminster Press, 1983).
4. For discussion, see Karlmann Beyschlag, *Clemens Romanus und der Frühkatholizismus* (Tübingen: Mohr, 1966); on 2 Clement, Karl Paul Donfried, *The Setting of Second Clement in Early Christianity* (Leiden: E. J. Brill, 1974).
5. *1 Clement*, chap. 1.
6. *Ibid.*
7. *Ibid.*, chap. 40.
8. *Ibid.*, chap. 37.
9. *Teaching of the Twelve Apostles* 1.2.
10. *Ibid.*, 1.6.
11. *Ibid.*, 2.2.
12. *Letter of Barnabas*, chap. 18.
13. *Ibid.*, chap. 22.1–2; 19.
14. *Ibid.*, 18.2; cf. 2.1; 4.9.
15. *Ibid.*, chap. 2.
16. *Ibid.*
17. *Ibid.*, chap. 9.9.
18. *Ibid.*, chap. 18.
19. Irenaeus, *Against Heresies*, ed. W. W. Harvey (Cambridge: Typis Academicis, 1857), vol. 1, preface.
20. *Ibid.*
21. *Ibid.*, 1.27.4.
22. *Ibid.*, 1.6.3.
23. For discussion, see Elaine Pagels, *The Gnostic Gospels* (New York: Random House, 1979).
24. *Testimony of Truth* (NHC IX, 3) 3.29.6.
25. *Ibid.*, 29.9–10.
26. *Ibid.*, 30.2–4.
27. *Ibid.*, 30.18–19.
28. *Ibid.*, 44.30–45.4.
29. *Ibid.*, 41.4–7.
30. *Ibid.*, 43.29–44.16.
31. Justin, *First Apology* 29.

32. *Testimony of Truth* (NHC IX, 3) 29.15–17.
33. *Ibid.,* 41.3–4.
34. *Ibid.,* 41.28–42.14.
35. *Ibid.,* 47.5–6.
36. *Ibid.,* 47.14–30.
37. *Ibid.,* 41.4.
38. *Hypostasis of the Archons* (NHC II,4) 86.26–27.
39. *Ibid.,* 86.27–31.
40. *Ibid.,* 86.31–87.4; 94.22–95.13.
41. *Ibid.,* 91.7–11.
42. *Ibid.,* 96.17–27.
43. On the "undominated generation," see Michael Williams, *The Immoveable Race: A Gnostic Designation and the Theme of Stability in Late Antiquity* (Leiden: E. J. Brill, 1985).
44. *Apocryphon of John* (NHC II, 1) 24.15–27.
45. *Ibid.,* 28.11–14.
46. *Ibid.,* 28.21–29.
47. *Ibid.,* 29.17–20.
48. *Ibid.,* 29.32–30.7.
49. Tertullian, *Prescription Against Heretics,* chap. 5.
50. *Ibid.,* chap. 6.
51. Tertullian, *Against the Valentinians,* chap. 4.
52. Tertullian, *Prescription,* chap. 7.
53. *Ibid.,* chap. 8.
54. *Ibid.,* chap. 11.
55. *Ibid.,* chap. 16.
56. *Ibid.,* chap. 18.
57. *Ibid.,* chap. 37.
58. *Ibid.,* chap. 40.
59. *Ibid.,* chap. 18.
60. *Ibid.,* chap. 39.
61. Tertullian, *Against the Valentinians,* chap. 4.
62. *Ibid.*
63. Walther Völker, ed., *Quellen zur Geschichte der Christlichen Gnosis* (Tübingen: J. C. B. Mohr, 1932), "Die Fragmente Valentins," Fragment 7, p. 59.
64. Hippolytus, *Refutation of All Heresies* 8.15.1–2.
65. Theodotus, cited by Clement of Alexandria, *Excerpts from Theodotus* 78.2.
66. *Gospel of Philip* (NHC II, 3) 79.22–31.
67. For discussion, see Pagels, *The Johannine Gospel in Gnostic Exegesis* (Nashville, Tenn.: Abingdon Press, 1993), 83–97.
68. Irenaeus, *Against Heresies* 1.6.2.
69. Tertullian, *Prescription,* chap. 3.
70. Irenaeus, *Against Heresies* 3.15.2.
71. *Ibid.,* 1.11.1; I.21.3.
72. *Ibid.,* 4.33.7.
73. *Ibid.,* 1.6.2–3.

74. *Ibid.*, 1.13.7, 1.13.5.
75. *Ibid.*, 1.13.3.
76. *Ibid.*, 1.13.3.
77. See, for example, Jeremiah 2:1–3:5; Hosea 2:1–4:19; Isaiah 60:1.
78. Völker, *Quellen,* Fragment 2, p. 58.
79. *Gospel of Truth* (NHC I, 3)32.35–33.21.
80. For a fuller discussion, see Pagels, "The Mystery of Marriage in the Gospel of Philip, Revisited," in Birger A. Pearson, ed., *The Future of Early Christianity: Essays in Honor of Helmut Koester* (Minneapolis: Fortress Press, 1991).
81. For an excellent discussion, see Klaus Koschorke, "Die 'Namen' in Philippusevangelium: Beobachtungen zur Auseinandersetzung zwischen gnostischem und kirchlichlem Christentum," *Zeitschrift für Neutestamentliche Wissenschaft* 64 (1973): 307–22.
82. *Gospel of Philip* (NHC II, 3) 74.5–12.
83. *Ibid.*, 80.23–81.14.
84. *Ibid.*, 66.5 5–7.
85. *Ibid.*, 78.24–79.14.
86. *Ibid.*, 79.34–35.
87. *Ibid.*, 80.10.
88. *Ibid.*, 73.33–74.2.
89. *Ibid.*, 83.13–30.
90. *Ibid.*, 84.1–6.
91. *Ibid.*, 84.11–14.
92. *Ibid.*, 55.23–26.
93. *Ibid.*, 55.26–30.
94. *Ibid.*, 52.21–25.
95. *Ibid.*, 64.22–24.
96. *Ibid.*, 64.29–30.
97. *Ibid.*, 77.2–3.
98. *Ibid.*, 67.26.
99. *Gospel of Thomas* (NHC II, 2) 33.19–20.
100. Irenaeus, *Against Heresies* 4.26.3.
101. *Ibid.*, 4.26.2.
102. *Ibid.*, 5.26.2.
103. *Ibid.*, 4.33.8.

Conclusion

1. Athanasius, *Life of Anthony* 28.
2. *Ibid.*, 41.

I discovered John Dominick Crossan's incisive book *Who Killed Jesus? Exposing the Roots of Anti-Semitism in the Gospel Story of the Death of Jesus* (San Francisco: HarperCollins, 1995) only after I had completed my work on this book and so was not able to refer to it in the text.

INDEX